Treasury of the True Dharma Eye
Dōgen's *Shōbōgenzō*

Treasury of the True Dharma Eye
Dōgen's *Shōbōgenzō*

Volume III

The Seventy-five-Chapter Compilation
Part 3
Chapters 31–45

An annotated translation
by the Sōtō Zen Text Project

Sōtōshū Shūmuchō
Tokyo

University of Hawai'i Press
Honolulu

© 2023 by Sōtōshū Shūmuchō
The Administrative Headquarters of Sōtō Zen Buddhism
All rights reserved.
Printed in China

Treasury of the True Dharma Eye: Dōgen's *Shōbōgenzō*
Volume III: The Seventy-five-Chapter Compilation, Part 3, Chapters 31–45

Published in Japan by Sōtōshū Shūmuchō, Tokyo
ISBN: 978-4-911061-00-8

Published for the rest of the world by University of Hawai'i Press, Honolulu

Library of Congress Cataloging-in-Publication Data

Names: Dōgen, 1200–1253, author. | Sōtō Zen Text Project, translator.

Title: Treasury of the true dharma eye : Dōgen's Shōbōgenzō / an
annotated translation by the Sōtō Zen Text Project.

Other titles: Shōbō genzō. English

Description: Honolulu : University of Hawai'i Press, [2024] | Published in
Japan by Sōtōshū Shūmuchō, 2023. | Includes bibliographical
references and index. | Contents: v. 3. The seventy-five-chapter
compilation, part 3, chapters 31–45

Identifiers: LCCN 2024004760 (print) | LCCN 2024004761 (ebook) | ISBN
9780824899172 (v. 1 ; paperback) | ISBN 9780824899189 (v. 2 ; paperback)
| ISBN 9780824899196 (v. 3 ; paperback) | ISBN 9780824899202 (v. 4 ;
paperback) | ISBN 9780824899219 (v. 5 ; paperback) | ISBN 9780824899226
(v. 6 ; paperback) | ISBN 9780824899233 (v. 7 ; paperback) | ISBN
9780824899240 (v. 8 ; paperback) | ISBN 9780824899257 (paperback) | ISBN
9798880700264 (v. 1 ; pdf) | ISBN 9798880700271 (v. 2 ; pdf) | ISBN
9798880700288 (v. 3 ; pdf) | ISBN 9798880700295 (v. 4 ; pdf) | ISBN
9798880700301 (v. 5 ; pdf) | ISBN 9798880700318 (v. 6 ; pdf) | ISBN
9798880700325 (v. 7 ; pdf) | ISBN 9798880700332 (v. 8 ; pdf)

Subjects: LCSH: Sōtōshū—Doctrines—Early works to 1800.

Classification: LCC BQ9449.D653 E5 2024 (print) | LCC BQ9449.D653 (ebook)
| DDC 294.3/85—dc23/eng/20240318

LC record available at https://lccn.loc.gov/2024004760
LC ebook record available at https://lccn.loc.gov/2024004761

Cover art: Eihei Dōgen Zenji Gyōjōzu scroll, courtesy of Rev. Ōtani Tetsuo
Cover design by Urs App

University of Hawai'i Press books are printed on acid-free paper and meet the
guidelines for permanence and durability of the Council on Library Resources.
Printer-ready copy has been provided by Sōtōshū Shūmuchō

CONTENTS

VOLUME III

THE SEVENTY-FIVE-CHAPTER COMPILATION

PART 3

Conventions iii

Abbreviations v

31. Do No Evil *Shoaku makusa* 諸惡莫作 1

32. Transmitting the Robe *Den'e* 傳衣 25

33. Sayings *Dōtoku* 道得 69

34. The Teachings of the Buddhas *Bukkyō* 佛教 83

35. Spiritual Powers *Jinzū* 神通 109

36. The Arhat *Arakan* 阿羅漢 141

37. Spring and Autumn *Shunjū* 春秋 155

38. Tangled Vines *Kattō* 葛藤 171

39. The Inheritance Certificate *Shisho* 嗣書 189

40. The Cypress Tree *Hakujushi* 柏樹子 221

41. The Three Realms Are Only Mind *Sangai yui shin* 三界唯心 241

42. Talking of the Mind, Talking of the Nature *Sesshin sesshō*
    説心説性 259

43. The Real Marks of the Dharmas *Shohō jissō* 諸法實相 283

44. The Way of the Buddhas *Butsudō* 佛道 315

45. Secret Words *Mitsugo* 密語 353

Conventions

This publication is an annotated translation, in seven volumes, of one hundred three texts of Dōgen's Japanese *Shōbōgenzō,* plus an additional volume containing an introduction, supplementary notes, appendices, and list of works cited. The translation is based on the edition of the *Shōbōgenzō* published in Kawamura Kōdō 河村孝道, ed., *Dōgen zenji zenshū* 道元禅師全集, vols. 1-2 (Tokyo: Shunjūsha, 1991, 1993), cited herein as DZZ.1 and DZZ.2; volume and page numbers of this edition are noted in braces at the corresponding locations in the translation.

The Japanese text accompanying the translation here follows the punctuation and *kanazukai* of the Kawamura edition; for ease of reference to premodern sources, Kawamura's modern Japanese kanji have been replaced with traditional forms. Also, for ease of reference, the sections into which the texts of the Kawamura edition are divided have been assigned numbers in square brackets by the translators. The translation of Kawamura's longer sections is sometimes broken into separate paragraphs, and transitions to new topics between sections are sometimes marked by a string of asterisks.

Though primarily written in Japanese, the *Shōbōgenzō* includes many passages of Chinese, ranging from long quotations of texts to short phrases inserted into the Japanese sentences. Since this inclusion of Chinese is a prominent linguistic feature of the original texts, the translation seeks to indicate such passages by the use of oblique font. The reader is warned that, given the ubiquity in the Japanese language of expressions adopted from Chinese, the identification of the shorter phrases as Chinese, rather than Japanese, is often rather arbitrary.

Much of the *Shōbōgenzō* is devoted to comment on material in other texts. The translation uses quotation marks to indicate terms and passages on which Dōgen is commenting. Here, again, the reader is warned that the distinction between use and mention can often be difficult to draw.

Sanskrit, Chinese, and Japanese terms appearing in the *Oxford English Dictionary* (3rd edition) are considered to have been adopted into English; other such terms are treated as foreign words and rendered in italics. Romanization of all such terms, whether treated as foreign or English, is given with diacritics.

iv DŌGEN'S *SHŌBŌGENZŌ* VOLUME II

With some exceptions, Chinese transliterations of Sanskrit terms are rendered as romanized Sanskrit. Indic proper nouns, whether transliterated or translated in the Chinese, are rendered as their presumed originals where possible; the reader is warned that some such reconstructions are unattested and speculative.

The proper noun "Zen" is used in reference to (a) the tradition that Dōgen calls the "buddhas and ancestors," and (b) the Japanese instantiation of that tradition; the Chinese name "Chan" is used in reference to the Chinese instantiation of the tradition.

Romanized readings of the Japanese text given in the notes follow wherever possible the ruby in Kawamura's text; readings not provided by Kawamura are based on *Zengaku daijiten* 禅学大辞典 (1978) and/or Katō Shūkō 加藤宗厚, *Shōbōgenzō yōgo sakuin* 正法眼藏用語索引 (1962).

Citations of T (*Taishō shinshū daizōkyō* 大正新脩大藏經) are from the *SAT Daizōkyō Text Database* (https://21dzk.l.u-tokyo.ac.jp/SAT). Citations of ZZ (*Dainihon zokuzōkyō* 大日本続藏經) are from the *CBETA Hanwen dazangjing* 漢文大藏經 (http://tripitaka.cbeta.org). Citations of KR are from *Kanripo* 漢リポ *Kanseki Repository* (https://www.kanripo.org).

The Kawamura edition provides colophons from several sources, some following the relevant chapter, some in the head notes of the chapter, some in the collation notes (*honbun kōi* 本文校異) for that chapter in the end matter of DZZ.1 and DZZ.2. For the convenience of the reader, this translation collects these colophons (and occasionally others omitted by Kawamura) at the end of each chapter. Colophons without attribution are assumed to have been written by Dōgen.

ABBREVIATIONS

C   Chinese language

DZZ   *Dōgen zenji zenshū* 道元禅師全集, Kagamishima Genryū 鏡島
        元隆 et al., compilers. 7 vols. Tokyo: Shunjūsha, 1988–1993.

ESST   *Eihei Shōbōgenzō shūsho taisei* 永平正法眼蔵蒐書大成,
        Kawamura Kōdō 河村孝道, ed. 27 vols. Tokyo: Taishūkan
        Shoten, 1974-1982.

J   Japanese language

KR   Kanseki Repository (Kanseki Ripo 漢籍リポ). Online: https://
        www.kanripo.org

M   *Dai kanwa jiten* 大漢和辞典, Morohashi Tetsuji 諸橋轍次, ed. 13
        vols. (plus 2-vol. supplement). Tokyo: Taishūkan Shoten, 1955-
        1960.

S   Sanskrit

SCZ   *Shōbōgenzō chūkai zensho* 正法眼藏註解全書, Jinbo Nyoten 神
        保如天 and Andō Bun'ei 安藤文英, eds. 11 vols. Reprint Tokyo:
        Nihon Bussho Kankōkai, 1956-1957.

SZ   *Sōtōshū zensho* 曹洞宗全書. 20 vols. Tokyo: Kōmeisha, 1929-
        1938.

T   *Taishō shinshū daizōkyō* 大正新脩大藏經, Takakusu Junjirō 高
        楠順次郎 and Watanabe Kaikyoku 渡邊海旭, eds. 100 vols.
        Tokyo: Daizōkyōkai, 1924–1935.

ZT   *Zengaku taikei* 禪學大系. 8 vols. Tokyo: Kokusho Kankōkai,
        1952 (orig. publ. 1910-11).

ZTS   *Zengaku tenseki sōkan* 禅学典籍叢刊, Yanagida Seizan 柳田
        聖山 and Shiina Kōyū 椎名宏雄, eds. 12 vols. Kyoto: Rinsen
        Shoten, 1999-2001.

ZZ   *Dainihon zokuzōkyō* 大日本続蔵經. 150 vols. Kyoto: Bussho
        Kankōkai, 1905-1912.

Treasury of the True Dharma Eye

Number 31

Do No Evil
Shoaku makusa

諸悪莫作

Do No Evil

Shoaku makusa

INTRODUCTION

This work represents one of the earlier texts of the *Shōbōgenzō*. It was composed in 1240, while Dōgen was living at Kōshōji. The chapter occurs as number 10 in the Honzan edition of the *Shōbōgenzō* and as number 31 in the sixty- and seventy-five-chapter compilations.

The title comes from the famous verse that Dōgen quotes at the start of the work. This verse, sometimes referred to as "the precepts of the seven buddhas," probably represents one of the earliest and most often quoted sayings of the Buddha preserved in the Buddhist canon. It appears in the very earliest layers of Buddhist scriptures as well as in the later Mahāyāna texts.

The verse was widely cited by Buddhists in China and Japan and was no less important in the Zen tradition. It is quoted in the recorded sayings of numerous Chinese teachers and forms the opening lines of the *Shukke taikō* 出家大綱 (*Essentials for Monastics*), written by Dōgen's older contemporary Eisai 榮西 (1141-1215) for his new Zen community at Kenninji 建仁寺. Eisai's essay might very well have been the first textbook that Dōgen studied when he entered Kenninji in 1217. Elsewhere Dōgen also quotes this verse in the "Gabyō" 畫餅 chapter of the *Shōbōgenzō* and in the *Eihei kōroku* 永平廣錄.

Dōgen comments at length here on each line of the verse, often on each word in each line. He then takes up the popular story of Niaoke Daolin's 鳥窠道林 teaching to the famous Tang poet and official Bai Juyi 白居易 that, while a child of three might be able to recite the verse, an elder of eighty can't put it into practice.

正法眼藏第三十一
Treasury of the True Dharma Eye
Number 31

諸惡莫作
Do No Evil

[31:1] {1:343}

古佛云、諸惡莫作、衆善奉行、自淨其意、是諸佛教。

The old buddhas say,
To do no evil,
Practice the good,
And purify one's own mind:
This is the teaching of the buddhas.[1]

[31:2]

これ七佛祖宗の通戒として、前佛より後佛に正傳す、後佛は前佛に相嗣せり。ただ七佛のみにあらず、是諸佛教なり。この道理を功夫參究すべし。いはゆる、七佛の法道、かならず七佛の法道のごとし。相傳相嗣、なほ箇裏の通消息なり。すでに是諸佛教なり、百千萬佛の教・行・證なり。

As the common precept of our ancestors, the seven buddhas, this is directly transmitted from prior buddhas to later buddhas; the later buddhas have inherited it from the prior buddhas.[2] It is not just of the seven buddhas: "this is the teaching of the buddhas." We should investigate this truth with concentrated effort. That is, the dharma words of the seven buddhas must be like the dharma words of the seven buddhas.[3] Trans-

---

1 **old buddhas** (*kobutsu* 古佛): The so-called "Gāthā of the Common Precepts of the Seven Buddhas" (*shichi butsu tsūkai ge* 七佛通戒偈), this verse is found widely throughout Buddhist literature; see Supplementary Notes, s.v. "Old buddha" and "Seven buddhas."

evil (*shoaku* 諸惡); **good** (*shūzen* 衆善): The translation here takes a certain liberty with the verse, which has these terms as plurals: i.e., "evil deeds" and "good deeds." The plural forms will be used below where more appropriate to the context.

2 **common precept** (*tsūkai* 通戒): I.e. "the precept shared among." Some MS witnesses read "the common admonishment" (*tsūkai* 通誡).

seven buddhas (*shichi butsu* 七佛): The traditional story of the Zen lineage often begins with the ancient Buddhist legend of a series of seven buddhas of the past, through Buddha Śākyamuni; see Supplementary Notes, s.v. "Seven buddhas."

3 **the dharma words of the seven buddhas must be like the dharma words of the**

4 DŌGEN'S *SHŌBŌGENZŌ* VOLUME III

mitted and inherited, it is still the common circumstances in here.[4] Since it is "this is the teaching of the buddhas," it is the teaching, practice, and verification of hundreds of thousands of myriads of buddhas.

[31:3]

いまいふところの諸惡は、善性・惡性・無記性のなかに惡性あり。その性、これ無生なり。善性・無記性等もまた無生なり、無漏なり、實相なりといふとも、この三性の裏箇に、許多般の法あり。諸惡は、此界の惡と他界の惡と同・不同あり、先時と後時と同・不同あり、天上の惡と人間の惡と同・不同なり。いはんや佛道と世間と、道惡・道善・道無記、はるかに殊異あり。善惡は時なり、時は善惡にあらず。善惡は法なり、法は善惡にあらず。法等・惡等なり、法等・善等なり。

The "evils" mentioned here belong to the evil nature listed among the good nature, evil nature, and indeterminate nature.[5] This nature is unborn. The good nature and indeterminate nature are also unborn, are uncontaminated, are the real mark; yet there are many kinds of dharmas here within these three natures.[6] Among the "evils," there are similarities and dissimilarities between the evil of this world and the evil of other worlds; similarities and dissimilarities between prior and later times; similarities and dissimilarities between the evil of the devas and the evil of humans. Even greater still is the divergence between what is called

---

seven buddhas (*shichi butsu no hōdō, kanarazu shichi butsu no hōdō no gotoshi* 七佛の法道、かならず七佛の法道のごとし): I.e., the seven buddhas all have the same teachings.

4 **it is still the common circumstances in here** (*nao kori no tsū shōsoku nari* なほ箇裏の通消息なり): The location of "in here" (*kori* 箇裏) is unclear but suggests "within the individual." The translation "common circumstances" for the expression *tsū shōsoku* 通消息 assumes that Dōgen is playing on the description of the verse as the "common precept" (*tsūkai* 通戒) of the seven buddhas; while this expression does not occur elsewhere in the *Shōbōgenzō*, it is common enough in Zen literature in the sense "communicating information."

5 **good nature, evil nature, and indeterminate nature** (*zenshō akushō mukishō* 善性・惡性・無記性): I.e., the three moral qualities of karma (S. *kuśala, akuśala, avyākṛta*, respectively); the last refers to karma that is neither good nor evil.

6 **are also unborn, are uncontaminated, are the real mark** (*mushō nari, muro nari, jissō nari* 無生なり、無漏なり、實相なり): Characteristics commonly attributed to dharmas (phenomena) in Mahāyāna literature. "Unborn" (*mushō* 無生) (or "unarisen"; S. *anutpatti*) is regularly used to express the doctrine that phenomena are "empty" and, therefore, do not really occur. "Uncontaminated" (*muro* 無漏) expresses the doctrine that all states of mind are ultimately pure (or "untainted"; S. *anāsrava*). "The real mark" (or "marked by reality"; *jissō* 實相) is a technical term, used especially in the Tiantai 天台 literature, for the ultimate reality of the dharmas.

here within these three natures (*kono sanshō no riko ni* この三性の裏箇に): The translation follows most MS witnesses in reading the familiar *kori* 箇裏 ("in here"), rather than the unusual *riko* 裏箇. If we were to render the latter, we might get something like, "in 'the here' [i.e., actual working in the world?] of these three natures."

31. Do No Evil *Shoaku makusa* 諸惡莫作   5

"evil," what is called "good," and what is called "indeterminate" in the way of the buddhas and the secular world. Good and evil are temporal, but time is neither good nor evil. Good and evil are dharmas, but dharmas are neither good nor evil. It is the dharmas are equal, the evils are equal; it is the dharmas are equal, the goods are equal.[7]

[31:4] {1:344}

しかあるに、阿耨多羅三藐三菩提を學するに、聞教し、修行し、證果するに、深なり、遠なり、妙なり。この無上菩提を或從知識してきき、或從經卷してきく。はじめは、諸惡莫作ときこゆるなり。諸惡莫作ときこへざるは、佛正法にあらず、魔説なるべし。

Thus, when we study *anuttara-samyak-saṃbodhi*, when we hear the teachings, cultivate the practice and realize the fruit, it is deep, it is distant, it is wondrous.[8] This unsurpassed bodhi, we hear *whether from a wise friend*, we hear *whether from a sūtra scroll*.[9] In the very beginning, we hear *"do no evil."* If we do not hear *"do no evil,"* it is not the true dharma of the buddhas; it is the talk of Māra.[10]

---

7 **It is the dharmas are equal, the evils are equal; it is the dharmas are equal, the goods are equal** (*hōtō akutō nari, hōtō zentō nari* 法等・惡等なり、法等・善等なり): A common rhetorical pattern, seen, for example, in the saying of Mazu Daoyi 馬祖道一 (709-788) (e.g., at *Jingde chuandeng lu* 景德傳燈錄, T.2076.51:440a12-13):

名等義等一切諸法皆等、純一無雜。

The names are equal, the meanings are equal, and all the dharmas are equal, pure and unadulterated.

Dōgen quotes this line in his *Fushukuhanpō* 赴粥飯法 (DZZ.6:46) and uses a variant of the pattern in his "Shōbōgenzō shinjin gakudō" 正法眼藏身心學道 (DZZ.1: 49):

語等なり、心等なり、法等なり。

The words are equal, the minds are equal, the dharmas are equal.

See also "Shōbōgenzō gabyō" 正法眼藏畫餅 (DZZ.1:270):

畫等餅等法等

The paintings are equal, the cakes are equal, the dharmas are equal.

8 **it is deep, it is distant, it is wondrous** (*jin nari, on nari, myō nari* 深なり、遠なり、妙なり): From the expression "deep, distant, and wondrous" (*jin on myō* 深遠妙), typically used in reference to the voice.

9 **whether from a wise friend** (*waku jū chishiki* 或從知識); **whether from a sūtra scroll** (*waku jū kyōkan* 或從經卷): I.e., whether from a teacher or from a text. Fixed expressions occurring together several times in the *Shōbōgenzō*; see Supplementary Notes, s.v. "Whether from a wise friend, whether from a sūtra scroll."

10 **talk of Māra** (*masetsu* 魔説): Or "demonic preachings." I.e., false teachings by the god Māra, who seeks to prevent the spread of the dharma.

6 DŌGEN'S *SHŌBŌGENZŌ* VOLUME III

[31:5]

しるべし、諸悪莫作ときこゆる、これ佛正法なり。　この、諸悪つくるこ
となかれ、といふ、凡夫のはじめて造作してかくのごとくあらしむるにあ
らず、菩提の説となれるを聞教するに、しかのごとくきこゆるなり。しか
のごとくきこゆるは、無上菩提のことばにてある道著なり。すでに菩提語
なり、ゆえに語菩提なり。無上菩提の説著となりて聞著せらるるに轉ぜら
れて、諸悪莫作とねがひ、諸悪莫作とおこなひもてゆく。諸悪すでにつく
られずなりゆくところに、修行力たちまちに現成す。この現成は、盡地・
盡界・盡時・盡法を量として現成するなり。その量は、莫作を量とせり。

We should realize that hearing "*do no evil*" is the true dharma of the
buddhas. This [phrase], "do not do evil," is not something first created
and made to be like this by the common person; we hear it like this when
we hear the teaching that is bodhi become talk.[11] What we hear like this
is speech that is unsurpassed bodhi in words. Since it is the words of
bodhi, it is the bodhi of words. Being turned by what is heard when
unsurpassed bodhi becomes talk, we aspire to "*do no evil*" and continue
practicing "*do no evil*." And where evils are no longer done, the power of practice suddenly appears. This appearance appears taking as its
measure all the earth, all the worlds, all time, all dharmas. This measure
takes "do no" as its measure.

[31:6]

正當恁麼時の正當恁麼人は、諸悪つくりぬべきところに住し、往來し、諸
悪つくりぬべき縁に對し、諸悪つくる友にまじわるににたりといへども、
諸悪さらにつくられざるなり、莫作の力量現成するゆえに。諸悪みづから
諸悪と道著せず、諸悪にさだまれる調度なきなり。一拈一放の道理あり。
正當恁麼時、すなはち悪の、人ををかさざる道理しられ、人の、悪をやぶ
らざる道理あきらめらる。

Just such a person at just such a time, though staying or traveling in
places where evil might be done, or encountering situations in which
evil might be done, or mixing with friends who do evil, can no longer do
evil; for there appears the power of "do no."[12] "Evils" do not themselves
speak of "evils," and there are no fixtures fixed as "evils."[13] There is the

---

11　**This [phrase], "do not do evils"** (*kono, shoaku tsukuru koto nakare to iu* この、諸
悪つくることなかれといふ): Dōgen here translates the Chinese phrase into a Japanese
imperative form.

bodhi become talk (*bodai no setsu to nareru* 菩提の説となれる): I.e., the awakening of
the buddhas expressed in words.

12　**for there appears the power of "do no"** (*makusa no rikiryō genjō suru yue ni* 莫作
の力量現成するゆえに): The translation follows Kawamura's punctuation. This phrase
is sometimes read with the following sentence, yielding, ". . . can no longer do evil.
Because there appears the power of 'do no,' 'evils' do not speak of 'evils,' and there are
no fixtures fixed as 'evils.'"

13　**"Evils" do not themselves speak of "evils," and there are no fixtures fixed as**

31. Do No Evil *Shoaku makusa* 諸惡莫作 7

principle of one taken up and one let go.[14] At just such a time, the principle that evil does not violate the person is known, and the principle that the person does not destroy evil is clarified.[15]

[31:7] {1:345}
みづからが心を擧して修行せしむ、身を擧して修行せしむるに、機先の八九成あり、腦後の莫作あり。なんぢが身心を拈來して修行し、たれの身心を拈來して修行するに、四大五蘊にて修行するちから、驀地に見成するに、四大五蘊の自己を染汚せず、今日の四大五蘊までも修行せられもてゆく。如今の修行なる四大五蘊のちから、上項の四大五蘊を修行ならしむるなり。山河大地・日月星辰にても修行せしむるに、山河大地・日月星辰、かへりてわれらを修行せしむるなり。一時の眼睛にあらず、諸時の活眼なり。眼睛・活眼にてある諸時なるがゆえに、諸佛諸祖をして修行せしむ、聞教せしむ、證果せしむ。諸佛諸祖、かつて教・行・證を染汚せしむることなきがゆえに、教・行・證いまだ諸佛諸祖を罣礙することなし。このゆえに、佛祖をして修行せしむるに、過・現・當の機先・機後に廻避する諸佛諸祖なし。衆生、作佛・作祖の時節、ひごろ所有の佛祖を罣礙せずといへども、作佛祖する道理を、十二時中の行・住・坐・臥に、つらつら思量すべきなり。作佛祖するに衆生をやぶらず、うばはず、うしなふにあらず。しかあれども、脱落しきたれるなり。

When we ourselves take up our minds and put them into practice, take up our bodies and put them into practice, there are eight or nine tenths complete before the function, there is "do no" behind the head.[16] As you bring your body and mind to practice, as you bring anyone's body and mind to practice, as the power of practicing with the four elements and

---

"evils" (*shoaku mizukara shoaku to dōjaku sezu, shoaku ni sadamareru chōdo naki nari* 諸惡みづから諸惡と道著せず、諸惡にさだまれる調度なきなり): I.e., nothing "announces itself" as evil; our world is not "furnished" with evils.

14 **There is the principle of one taken up and one let go** (*ichinen ippō no dōri ari* 一拈一放の道理あり): The phrase *ichinen ippō* 一拈一放 is not in fact a common idiom, though one does sometimes encounter the similar *nen'ichi hōichi* 拈一放一 ("take one up and let one go"). The sense may be that we define some things as evil ("take them up") but do not take the definitions as fixed properties ("let them go").

15 **the principle that evil does not violate the person** (*aku no, hito o okasazaru dōri* 惡の、人ををかさざる道理); **the principle that the person does not destroy evil** (*hito no, aku o yaburazaru dōri* 人の、惡をやぶらざる道理): This would seem to reverse the order of the previous sentence: one "takes up" evil and does not "destroy" it; one "lets go" of evil and is not "violated" by it.

16 **there are eight or nine tenths complete before the function, there is "do no" behind the head** (*kisen no hakku jō ari, nōgo no makusa ari* 機先の八九成あり、腦後の莫作あり): Perhaps to be understood, "the deed is almost done before we start, while the 'not doing' of it remains long after." Dōgen is playing here with the "before" and "after" of *kisen* 機先, used in the sense, "before anything happens," and *nōgo* 腦後 (literally, "the back of the head [or brain]"), likely used here in the sense "beyond memory," "long forgotten." For the expression *hakku jō* 八九成, see Supplementary Notes, s.v. "Eight or nine tenths complete."

8 　　　　DŌGEN'S *SHŌBŌGENZŌ* VOLUME III

five aggregates instantly appears, it does not defile the self of the four elements and five aggregates, and even today's four elements and five aggregates are made to carry on the practice.[17] The power of today's four elements and five aggregates as practice makes practice of our old four elements and five aggregates. It also causes the mountains, rivers, and the whole earth, the sun, moon, and stars to practice; and then the mountains, rivers, and the whole earth, the sun, moon, and stars in turn cause us to practice. It is not the eye of one time; it is the living eye of all times.[18] Because they are times that are the eye, the living eye, they cause the buddhas and the ancestors to practice, to hear the teachings, to verify the fruit. Because the buddhas and the ancestors have never defiled the teachings, practice, and verification, the teaching, practice, and verification do not obstruct the buddhas and the ancestors.[19] Therefore, as they make the buddhas and ancestors practice, there are no buddhas or ancestors who have avoided them, whether before the function or after the function in past, present or future. When living beings become buddhas and become ancestors, it does not obstruct the buddha and ancestor they have long possessed; yet the principle of becoming a buddha and ancestor, we should think on deeply throughout the standing, walking, sitting, and reclining of the twelve times.[20] When we become a buddha and ancestor, we do not destroy or rob or lose the living being; nevertheless, we have sloughed it off.[21]

---

17 **it does not defile the self of the four elements and five aggregates** (*shidai goun no jiko o zenna sezu* 四大五蘊の自己を染汚せず): This rendering takes the *no* の here as genitive ("of"), with the grammatical subject being *chikara* ちから ("power"). It is also possible to take *no* の as marking the agent — a reading that would yield, "the four major elements and five aggregates do not defile the self." "The four elements [earth, water, fire, and wind] and the five aggregates [form, sensation, perception, formations, and consciousness]" is a combination used often by Dōgen for the individual as psychophysical organism; roughly synonymous with the more familiar "body and mind" (*shinjin* 身心). See Supplementary Notes, s.v. "Four elements and five aggregates."

18 **It is not the eye of one time; it is the living eye of all times** (*ichiji no ganzei ni arazu, shoji no katsugan nari* 一時の眼睛にあらず、諸時の活眼なり): Perhaps meaning, "this is not a one-time experience; it is the way we always see things (or, perhaps, ought to see things)." For the meanings of "eye" (*ganzei* 眼睛) in Zen texts, see Supplementary Notes, s.v. "Eye."

19 **the buddhas and the ancestors have never defiled the teachings, practice, and verification** (*shobutsu shoso, katsute kyō gyō shō o zenna seshimuru koto naki* 諸佛諸祖、かつて教・行・證を染汚せしむることなき): A turn on one of Dōgen's most famous teachings, that practice and verification are "not defiling" (*fuzenna* 不染汚) for the buddhas and ancestors; see Supplemental Notes, s.v. "Practice and verification" and "Not defiled."

20 **the twelve times** (*jūni ji* 十二時): I.e., the twenty-four hours of the day figured traditionally in two-hour divisions.

21 **we have sloughed it off** (*datsuraku shikitareru nari* 脱落しきたれるなり): Remi-

31. Do No Evil *Shoaku makusa* 諸惡莫作

[31:8]

善惡・因果をして修行せしむ。いはゆる、因果を動ずるにあらず、造作するにあらず。因果、あるときはわれらをして修行せしむるなり。この因果の本來面目、すでに分明なる、これ莫作なり、無生なり、無常なり、不昧なり、不落なり、脱落なるがゆえに。かくのごとく參究するに、諸惡は、一條にかつて莫作なりけると現成するなり。この現成に助發せられて、諸惡莫作なりと見得徹し、坐得斷するなり。

We cause good and evil, cause and effect, to practice. This is not moving, is not creating, cause and effect. Cause and effect at times cause us to practice. That the original face of cause and effect is already clearly discerned — this is "do no," is unborn, is impermanent, is "not in the dark," is "not fallen"; for it is sloughed off.[22] When we investigate them like this, [the truth that] the "evils," in one strip, have always been "do no" appears to us. Aided by this appearance, we can see through, can sit and cut off, [the truth that] the "evils" are "do no."[23]

[31:9] {1:346}

正當恁麼のとき、初中後、諸惡莫作にて現成するに、諸惡は因緣生にあらず、ただ莫作なるのみなり。諸惡は因緣滅にあらず、ただ莫作なるのみなり。諸惡もし等なれば、諸法も等なり。諸惡は因緣生としりて、この因緣の、おのれと莫作なるをみざるは、あはれむべきともがらなり。佛種從緣起なれば、緣從佛種起なり。

At this very moment, when they appear as "do no evil" in the beginning, middle, and end, the "evils" are not born of causes and conditions; they are just "do no." "Evils" are not extinguished by causes and

---

niscent of the expression "body and mind sloughed off" (*shinjin datsuraku* 身心脱落), that, in several places, Dōgen attributes to his teacher, Tiantong Rujing 天童如淨 (1162-1227); see Supplementary Notes, s.v. "Slough off" and "Body and mind sloughed off."

22 **is unborn, is impermanent, is not in the dark, is "not fallen"** (*mushō nari, mujō nari, fumai nari, furaku nari* 無生なり、無常なり、不昧なり、不落なり): Two sets of contrasting approaches to cause and effect. The second set recalls the famous tale of Baizhang Huaihai 百丈懷海 (749-814) and the teacher who was reborn as a fox for saying that the person of great practice "does not fall into cause and effect" (*furaku inga* 不落因果); Baizhang released him from his fox body by teaching that the person "is not in the dark about (or does not ignore) cause and effect" (*fumai inga* 不昧因果). (See, e.g., *Liandeng huiyao* 聯燈會要, ZZ.136:495a9-b2; *shinji Shōbōgenzō* 眞字正法眼藏, DZZ.5:178, case 102.)

23 **we can see through, can sit and cut off, [the truth that] the "evils" are "do no"** (*shoaku makusa nari to kentokutetsu shi, zatokudan suru* 諸惡莫作なりと見得徹し、坐得斷する): I.e., we can clearly discern and transcend the view that "do no evil" means that evils are doing nothing. Dōgen has here read the imperative *makusa* 莫作 ("do not do") as a predicate nominative. "Can sit and cut off" represents one interpretation of the expression *zatokudan* 坐得斷, from the more common *zadan* 坐斷, a term used in Zen texts in the sense "to break completely," "to reject totally" (where *za* 坐 is taken as *za* 挫), but often interpreted in Sōtō literature as "sitting completely" or "just sitting."

10 DŌGEN'S *SHŌBŌGENZŌ* VOLUME III

conditions; they are just "do no." If the "evils" are equal, the dharmas are equal.[24] Those that know "evils" as born of causes and conditions, not seeing that these causes and conditions are themselves "do no," are a pitiful lot. Since *the seeds of buddhahood sprout from conditions,*" *conditions sprout from the seeds of buddhahood.*[25]

[31:10]
諸悪なきにあらず、莫作なるのみなり。諸悪あるにあらず、莫作なるのみなり。諸悪は、空にあらず、莫作なり。諸悪は、色にあらず、莫作なり。諸悪は、莫作にあらず、莫作なるのみなり。たとへば、春松は、無にあらず、有にあらず、つくらざるなり。秋菊は、有にあらず、無にあらず、つくらざるなり。諸佛は、有にあらず、無にあらず、莫作なり。露柱燈籠・拂子拄杖等、あるにあらず、なきにあらず、莫作なり。自己は、有にあらず、無にあらず、莫作なり。

It is not that "evils" do not exist; it is just that they are "do no." It is not that "evils" do exist; it is just that they are "do no." "Evils" are not emptiness; they are "do no." "Evils are not form; they are "do no."[26] "Evils" are not "do no"; it is just that they are "do no." For example, the spring pine is not non-existent and is not existent; "it does not do."[27] The autumn chrysanthemum is not existent and is not non-existent; "it does not do." The buddhas are not existent and are not non-existent; they are "do no." The pillars and lanterns, the whisk and staff, neither exist nor do not exist; they are "do no."[28] The self is not existent and is not non-existent; it is "do no."

---

24 **If the evils are equal, the dharmas are equal** (*shoaku moshi tō nareba, shohō mo tō nari* 諸悪もし等なれば、諸法も等なり): See above, Note 7.

25 **"the seeds of buddhahood sprout from conditions"** (*busshu jū en gi* 佛種從緣起): From the *Lotus Sūtra* (*Miaofa lianhua jing* 妙法蓮華經, T.262.9:9b8-9):

諸佛兩足尊、知法常無性、佛種從緣起、是故説一乘。

The buddhas, honored among the two-legged,
Know that the dharmas are always without natures,
And that the seeds of buddhahood sprout from conditions;
Therefore, they preach the one vehicle.

26 **not emptiness** (*kū ni arazu* 空にあらず); **not form** (*shiki ni arazu* 色にあらず): Reminiscent of the famous formula of the *Heart Sūtra*; see Supplementary Notes, s.v. "Form is itself emptiness; emptiness is itself form."

27 **"it does not do"** (*tsukurazaru nari* つくらざるなり): Dōgen here and in the following sentence translates the term *makusa* 莫作 ("not doing") into the negative of the Japanese verb *tsukuru* ("to do," "to make").

28 **The pillars and lanterns, the whisk and staff** (*rochū tōrō hossu shujō tō* 露柱燈籠・拂子拄杖等): Examples drawn from the monastic setting regularly used in Zen texts for the inanimate objects of the world around us; see Supplementary Notes, s.v. "Pillars and lanterns," "Whisk," and "Staff."

31. Do No Evil *Shoaku makusa* 諸惡莫作   11

[31:11]
恁麼の參學は、見成せる公案なり、公案の見成なり。主より功夫し、賓よ
り功夫す。すでに恁麼なるに、つくられざりけるをつくりけるとくやしむ
も、のがれず、さらにこれ莫作の功夫力なり。

This kind of study is the kōan realized, is the realization of the kōan.[29]
We work at it from the host, and we work at it from the guest.[30] Since it
is like this, we cannot escape regretting that we have done what was not
done, and this too is the power of our working at "do no."[31]

[31:12]
しかあれば、莫作にあらばつくらまし、と趣向するは、あゆみをきたにし
て越にいたらんとまたんがごとし。諸惡莫作は、井の驢をみるのみにあら
ず、井の井をみるなり。驢の驢をみるなり、人の人をみるなり、山の山を
みるなり。説箇の應底道理あるゆゑに、諸惡莫作なり。佛眞法身、猶若虚
空、應物現形、如水中月なり。應物の莫作なるゆゑに、現形の莫作あり。
猶若虚空、左拍右拍なり。如水中月、被水月礙なり。これらの莫作、さら
にうたがふべからざる現成なり。

Thus, to proceed with the view that, if it's "do no," then let us do it,
would be like walking north expecting to get to Yue.[32] "*Do no evil*" is
not only "the well looking at the donkey": it is the well looking at the
well; it is the donkey looking at the donkey; it is the person looking at
the person; it is the mountain looking at the mountain.[33] Because there is
"explaining the principle of this response," it is "*do no evil.*" It is:

---

29   **the kōan realized** (*genjō seru kōan* 見成せる公案); **the realization of the kōan**
(*kōan no genjō* 公案の見成): Terms appearing throughout Dōgen's writing, from the
famous saying, "It's a settled case, but I spare you the thirty blows." See Supplementary
Notes, s.v. "Realized kōan."

30   **We work at it from the host, and we work at it from the guest** (*shu yori kufū shi,
hin yori kufū su* 主より功夫し、賓より功夫す): Probably meaning, "we consider 'not
doing evils' in terms of 'not doing' and in terms of 'evils.'" "Host" (*shu* 主) and "guest"
(*hin* 賓) are typically used in reference respectively to "subject" and "object," though here
they may well refer respectively to "the kōan realized" and "the realization of the kōan."

31   **we cannot escape regretting that we have done what was not done** (*tsukura-
rezarikeru o tsukurikeru to kuyashimu mo, nogarezu* つくられざりけるをつくりけると
くやしむも、のがれず): Seemingly an ironic response to the fact that we do in fact the
"evils" that are said to be "not doing."

32   **like walking north expecting to get to Yue** (*ayumi o kita ni shite etsu ni itaran to
matan ga gotoshi* あゆみをきたにして越にいたらんとまたんがごとし): I.e., heading
in exactly the wrong direction ("Yue" 越 here referring to the territory south of China);
from the Chinese idiom *bei yuan shi yue* 北轅適楚 ("pointing your cart thills north to get
to Yue"), a simile Dōgen uses more than once in the *Shōbōgenzō*.

33   **"the well looking at the donkey"** (*i no ro o miru* 井の驢をみる): From a dialogue,
featuring Caoshan Benzhi 曹山本寂 (840-901) and the Senior Seat De 德上座 (dates unknown), recorded in Dōgen's *shinji Shōbōgenzō* 眞字正法眼藏 (DZZ.5:194, case 125);
see Supplementary Notes, s.v. "Like the well looking at the donkey."

12   DŌGEN'S *SHŌBŌGENZŌ* VOLUME III

> The true dharma body of the buddha
> Is just like empty space.
> It manifests its shape in response to beings,
> Like the moon in the water.[34]

Because "in response to beings" is "do no," there is the "do no" of "it manifests its shape." "*Just like empty space*" *is clapping on the left, clapping on the right.*[35] "*Like the moon in the water*" *is the moon obstructed by the water.*[36] These [examples of] "do no" are phenomena not to be further doubted.

* * * * *

[31:13] {1:347}

衆善奉行。この衆善は、三性のなかの善性なり。善性のなかに衆善ありといへども、さきより現成して行人をまつ衆善いまだあらず。作善の正當恁麼時、きたらざる衆善なし。萬善は無象なりといへども、作善のところに計會すること、磁鐵よりも速疾なり。そのちから、毘嵐風よりもつよきなり。大地山河・世界國土・業增上力、なほ善の計會を罣礙することあたはざるなり。

"*Practice the good.*" These "good deeds" are the good nature among the three natures.[37] Although there may be "good deeds" within the good nature, there are no "good deeds" that appear in advance and await a person to practice them: there are no "good deeds" that do not come about at the very moment that the good is done. Although the myriad goods may be formless, in doing good they accumulate faster than iron to a magnet. Their power exceeds that of the *vairambha* wind.[38] The mountains and rivers of the whole earth, the countries of the world, the generative power of karma, cannot obstruct the accumulation of good.

---

34   **The true dharma body of the buddha** (*butsu shin hosshin* 佛眞法身): Quoting the *Jin guangming jing* 金光明經, T.663.16:344b3-4. Dōgen also quotes these lines at the opening of his "Shōbōgenzō tsuki" 正法眼藏都機.

35   **clapping on the left, clapping on the right** (*sa haku u haku* 左拍右拍): An unusual expression, perhaps suggesting unimpeded action.

36   **"Like the moon in the water" is the moon obstructed by the water** (*nyo suichū getsu, hi sui getsu ge nari* 如水中月、被水月礙なり): This could also be parsed, "'Like the moon in the water' is being obstructed by the water moon."

37   **the good nature among the three natures** (*sanshō no naka no zenshō* 三性のなかの善性): See above, section 3.

38   *vairambha* **wind** (*biranpū* 毘嵐風): The great destructive wind that blows at the beginning and end of a kalpa.

31. Do No Evil *Shoaku makusa* 諸惡莫作

[31:14]

しかあるに、世界によりて善を認ずることおなじからざる道理、おなじ認
得を善とせるがゆえに。如三世諸佛説法之儀式。おなじ、といふは、在世
説法、ただ時なり。壽命・身量、またときに一任しきたれるがゆえに、説
無分別法なり。

Be that as it may, the principle that the recognition of good differs
according to each world is because it is the same recognition that determines the good — "*in the manner that the buddhas of the three times
preach the dharma.*"[39] "The same" means that their preaching the dharma while in the world is just [a matter of] the time. Because their lifespan and physical size are also left up to the time, they "*preach a dharma
without distinctions.*"

[31:15]

しかあればすなはち、信行の機の善と、法行の機の善と、はるかにことな
り、別法にあらざるがごとし。たとへば、聲聞の持戒は菩薩の破戒なるが
ごとし。

Therefore, it is like the case of the good of those with the capacity
for practice through faith and the good of those with the capacity for
practice through dharma — they are very different but are not separate
dharmas.[40] It is like the case in which the *śrāvaka*'s keeping the precepts

---

39 **the principle that the recognition of good differs according to each world is
because it is the same recognition that determines the good** (*sekai ni yorite zen o
ninzuru koto onajikarazaru dōri, onaji nintoku o zen to seru ga yue ni* 世界によりて善を
認ずることおなじからざる道理、おなじ認得を善とせるがゆえに): The translation
follows the punctuation of Kawamura's edition, though the resulting construction, "the
principle is because" hardly seems satisfactory. Others would read the passage, "Because
it is the same recognition that determines the good, the principle that the recognition of
good differs according to each world is 'in the manner that the buddhas of the three times
preach the dharma.'" In either reading, the passage is difficult to interpret but seems to
claim that, while what is recognized as good may vary from world to world, the good is
always what is recognized as such.

"in the manner that the buddhas of the three times preach the dharma" (*nyo sanze
shobutsu seppō shi gishiki* 如三世諸佛説法之儀式): I.e., the buddhas of past, present,
and future. Quoting Buddha Śākyamuni in the *Lotus Sūtra* (*Miaofa lianhua jing* 妙法蓮
華經, T.262.9:10a22-23):

如三世諸佛、説法之儀式、我今亦如是、説無分別法。

In the manner that the buddhas of the three times
Preach the dharma,
I now also in this way
Preach a dharma without distinctions.

40 **those with the capacity for practice through faith** (*shingyō no ki* 信行の機); **those
with the capacity for practice through dharma** (*hōgyō no ki* 法行の機): I.e., those
of lower spiritual capacity, who practice Buddhism through faith in the teachings, and

14 DŌGEN'S *SHŌBŌGENZŌ* VOLUME III

is the bodhisattva's breaking the precepts.[41]

[31:16] {1:346}

衆善、これ因縁生・因縁滅にあらず。衆善は諸法なりといふとも、諸法は
衆善にあらず。因縁と生滅と衆善と、おなじく頭正あれば尾正あり。衆善
は奉行なりといへども、自にあらず、自にしられず、他にあらず、他にし
られず。自・他の知見は、知に自あり、他あり、見の自あり、他あるがゆ
えに、各各の活眼睛、それ日にもあり、月にもあり、これ奉行なり。奉行
の正當恁麼時に、現成の公案ありとも、公案の始成にあらず、公案の久住
にあらず、さらにこれを本行といはんや。

"Good deeds" are not born of causes and conditions and do not cease
by causes and conditions. "Good deeds" may be dharmas, but the dharmas are not "good deeds." Cause and condition, arising and ceasing, and
"good deeds" are the same in that, when the head is right, the tail is right.
We may say "good deeds" are "to practice," but it is not self and is not
known by the self; it is not other and is not known by the other. Because,
in the knowing and seeing of self and other, there is self and other in
knowing and self and other in seeing, the living eye of each is in the sun
and in the moon.[42] This is "to practice." Precisely at the moment of "to
practice," although there is the realized kōan, it is not that the kōan is
initially realized, nor that the kōan long abides; can we further call this
"original practice"?[43]

---

those of higher capacity, who practice based on personal understanding of the teachings;
a standard distinction in Buddhist literature.

41   **the *śrāvaka*'s keeping the precepts is the bodhisattva's breaking the precepts**
(*shōmon no jikai wa bosatsu no hakai naru* 聲聞の持戒は菩薩の破戒なる): I.e., what
is "good" for those of the Small Vehicle is not necessarily good for the bodhisattva. A
view appearing also in the "Sanjūshichi hon bodai bunpō" chapter, where it is attributed
to the Buddha.

42   **the living eye of each is in the sun and in the moon** (*kakukaku no katsu ganzei,
sore hi ni mo ari, tsuki ni mo ari* 各各の活眼睛、それ日にもあり、月にもあり): Per-
haps meaning that the perceptions of the subjective "self" are everywhere present in
the objective "other." An alternative form of the "living eye" (*katsu ganzei* 活眼睛) has
appeared above, section 7. See Supplementary Notes, s.v. "Eye."

43   **can we further call this "original practice"?** (*sara ni kore o hongyō to iwanya* さ
らにこれを本行といはんや): Some MS witnesses read *bugyō* 奉行 ("to practice"; "to
practice reverently") for *hongyō* 本行 ("original practice"). The latter, a term occurring
several times in the *Shōbōgenzō*, evokes a famous passage in the *Lotus Sūtra* (*Miaofa
lianhua jing* 妙法蓮華經, T.262.9:42c22-23):

諸善男子、我本行菩薩道所成壽命、今猶未盡、復倍上數。

Good sons, the lifespan attained by my original practice of the bodhisattva path is
even now still not exhausted; it is twice the above number.

31. Do No Evil *Shoaku makusa* 諸惡莫作

[31:17]

作善の、奉行なるといへども、測度すべきにはあらざるなり。いまの奉行、これ活眼睛なりといへども、測度にはあらず、法を測度せんために現成せるにあらず。活眼睛の測度は、餘法の測度とおなじかるべからず。

Doing good may be "to practice," but it is not to be calculated. "To practice" here may be the living eye, but it is not calculating. It has not appeared in order to calculate dharmas. The calculation of the living eye cannot be the same as the calculation of other dharmas.[44]

[31:18]

衆善、有・無・色・空等にあらず、ただ奉行なるのみなり。いづれのところの現成、いづれの時の現成も、かならず奉行なり。この奉行に、かならず衆善の現成あり。奉行の現成、これ公案なりといふとも、生滅にあらず、因縁にあらず。

"Good deeds" are not existent or non-existent, form or emptiness, or the like; they are just "to practice." Wherever they appear, whenever they appear, they are always "to practice." In this "to practice," there will always be the realization of "good deeds." The realization of "to practice" may be a kōan, but it is not arising and ceasing, it is not causes and conditions.

[31:19]

奉行の入・住・出等も、又かくのごとし。衆善のなかの一善、すでに奉行するところに、盡法・全身・眞實地等、ともに奉行せらるるなり。

The entering, abiding, and exiting of "to practice" is also like this. Where we "practice" a single good among the "good deeds," all dharmas, the whole body, the true land, and the like, are all "practiced."[45]

[31:20]

この善の因果、おなじく奉行の現成公案なり。因はさき、果はのちなるにあらざれども、因圓滿し、果圓滿す。因等法等、果等法等なり。因にまたれて果感ずといへども、前・後にあらず前後等の道あるがゆえに。

The cause and effect of this good is similarly the realized kōan of "to practice." It is not that the cause is before and the effect after, but the cause is perfectly complete, and the effect is perfectly complete. It is *the causes are equal, the dharmas are equal; the effects are equal, the dharmas are equal.*[46] While the response of effects may be expected by

---

44 **the calculation of other dharmas** (*yohō no shikitaku* 餘法の測度): Probably meaning "the calculation done by other methods (or other things)."

45 **the true land** (*shinjitsu chi* 眞實地): I.e., the realm of reality; a term not occurring elsewhere in the *Shōbōgenzō*.

46 **The causes are equal, the dharmas are equal** (*in tō hō tō* 因等法等): For this usage, see above, Note 7.

16 DŌGEN'S *SHŌBŌGENZŌ* VOLUME III

causes, they are not before and after; for it is said that before and after are equal.[47]

* * * * *

[31:21] {1:349}
自淨其意といふは、莫作の自なり、莫作の淨なり。自の其なり、自の意なり。莫作の其なり、莫作の意なり。奉行の意なり、奉行の淨なり、奉行の其なり、奉行の自なり。かるがゆえに、是諸佛教といふなり。

To "purify one's own mind" is the "one's" of "do no," is the "purify" of "do no"; it is the "own" of "one's," the "mind" of "one's"; it is the "own" of "do," is the "mind" of "do no"; it is the "mind" of "to practice," is the "purify" of "to practice," is the "own" of "to practice," is the "one's" of "to practice."[48] Therefore, it is said, *"This is the teaching of the buddhas."*

[31:22]
いはゆる諸佛、あるひは自在天のごとし。自在天に同・不同なりといへども、一切の自在天は諸佛にあらず。あるひは轉輪王のごとくなり。しかあれども、一切の轉輪聖王の、諸佛なるにあらず。かくのごとくの道理、功夫參學すべし。諸佛はいかなるべしとも學せず、いたづらに苦辛するに相似せりといへども、さらに受苦の衆生にして、行佛道にあらざるなり。莫作をよび奉行は、驢事未去、馬事到來なり。

"The buddhas" may be like *īśvaras*.[49] While there may be similarities and dissimilarities to *īśvaras*, all *īśvaras* are not *"the buddhas."* Or they may be like the *cakravartins*. However, all *cakravartins* are not *"the buddhas."*[50] We should make concentrated effort and study such truths. Without studying what *"the buddhas"* must be, while we may have seemed to be toiling in vain, we are nothing but living beings enduring pain and not practicing on the way of the buddhas.[51] *"Do no"* and *"to*

---

47 **for it is said that before and after are equal** (*zengo tō no dō aru* 前後等の道ある): A tentative translation; an alternative might read, "they have a way on which before and after are equal."

48 **"To purify one's own mind" is the "one's" of "do no," is the "purify" of "do no"** (*ji jō go i to iu wa, makusa no ji nari, makusa no jō nari* 自淨其意といふは、莫作の自なり、莫作の淨なり): Here and below in this section, the grotesque translation tries to mirror in English Dōgen's play with each glyph of the Chinese phrase.

49 **īśvaras** (*jizai ten* 自在天): A term, meaning "sovereign," used for the devas of the *akaniṣṭha* heaven (*shiki kukyō ten* 色究竟天), highest of the heavens in the realm of form in Buddhist cosmology. Though clearly used in the plural here, the term often denotes Maheśvara ("the great lord"), chief of the devas in this heaven and often identified with the Hindu deity Śiva.

50 **cakravartins** (*tenrin'ō* 轉輪王): Literally, "wheel-turning kings"; a standard reference to great benevolent rulers.

51 **while we may have seemed to be toiling in vain** (*itazura ni kushin suru ni sōji seri*

31. Do No Evil *Shoaku makusa* 諸惡莫作   17

practice" are "*the donkey business isn't gone yet, and the horse business has already arrived.*"[52]

* * * * *

[31:23]

唐の白居易は、佛光如滿禪師の俗弟子なり。江西大寂禪師の孫子なり。杭州の刺史にてありしとき、鳥窠の道林禪師に参じき。ちなみに居易とふ、如何是佛法大意。道林いはく、諸惡莫作、衆善奉行。　居易いはく、もし恁麼にてあらんは、三歳の孩兒も道得ならん。道林いはく、三歳孩兒縦道得、八十老翁行不得なり。　恁麼いふに、居易すなはち拜謝してさる。

Bai Juyi of the Tang was the lay disciple of Chan Master Fokuang Ruman.[53] He was the grandchild of Chan Master Daji of Jiangxi. While governor of Hangzhou, he visited Chan Master "Bird Nest" Daolin.[54] There, Juyi asked, "*What is the great meaning of the buddha dharma?*"

Daolin said, "*Do no evil, practice the good.*"

Juyi said, "If it were that, even a child of three could say it."

Daolin said, "A *child of three might be able say it, but an elder of eighty can't practice it.*"

That being said, Juyi bowed and departed.

---

to iedomo いたづらに苦辛するに相似せりといへども): Presumably, a comment on the monks' practice.

52   **"The donkey business isn't gone yet, and the horse business has already arrived"** (*roji miko baji tōrai* 驢事未去馬事到來): Although normally carrying a sense akin to English "one damned thing after another," here no doubt suggesting that "do no" and "to practice" overlap or are continuous. The saying, attributed to Lingyun Zhiqun 靈雲志勤 (dates unknown), appears in several Zen sources (see, e.g., *Jingde chuandeng lu* 景德傳燈錄, T.2076.51:285b12-13; and Dōgen's *shinji Shōbōgenzō* 眞字正法眼藏, DZZ.5:206, case 156):

師問、如何是佛法大意。雲云、驢事未去、馬事到來。

The Master [Changqing Huileng (854-932)] asked, "What is the great meaning of the buddha dharma?"

Yun said, "The donkey business isn't gone yet, and the horse business has already arrived."

53   **Bai Juyi** (*Haku Kyoi* 白居易): Famous Tang-dynasty poet and administrator (772-846), lay follower of Fokuang Ruman 佛光如滿 (dates unknown), who was a disciple of Chan Master Daji of Jiangxi 江西大寂禪師 (i.e., Mazu Daoyi 馬祖道一 [709-788]).

54   **While governor of Hangzhou** (*Kōshū no shishi nite arishi toki* 杭州の刺史にてありしとき): Bai served as governor of Hangzhou 822-824.

Chan Master "Bird Nest" Daolin (*Chōka no Dōrin zenji* 鳥窠の道林禪師): I.e., Niaoke Daolin 鳥窠道林 (741-824), posthumously known as Chan Master Yuanxiu 圓修禪師. His sobriquet "Bird Nest" (*Niaoke* 鳥窠) derived from the legend that he lived in a tree house. The famous story here of his conversation with Bai Juyi can be found at *Jingde chuandeng lu* 景德傳燈錄, T.2076.51:230b24-27.

[31:24]

まことに居易は、白將軍がのちなりといへども、奇代の詩仙なり。人つた
ふらくは、二十四生の文學なり。あるひは文殊の號あり、あるひは彌勒の
號あり。風情のきこえざるなし、筆海の朝せざるなかるべし。しかあれど
も、佛道には初心なり、晩進なり。いはんやこの諸惡莫作、衆善奉行は、
その宗旨、ゆめにもいまだみざるがごとし。

Truly, Juyi, though he may have been a descendant of General Bai, was a poet immortal, rare for ages.[55] It was said of him that he was a literatus of twenty-four lives.[56] He was called Mañjuśrī; he was called Maitreya. There is no one who has not heard of his taste; there is no one in the literary world who does not attend upon him.[57] Nevertheless, on the way of the buddhas, he was a beginner, he was a latecomer. Needless to say, when it comes to this "*do no evil, practice the good*," it was as if he had never seen its meaning even in his dreams.

[31:25] {1:350}

居易おもはくは、道林ひとへに有心の趣向を認じて、諸惡をつくることなか
れ、衆善奉行すべし、といふならんとおもひて、佛道に千古萬古の諸惡莫
作、衆善奉行の亙古亙今なる道理、しらず、きかずして、佛法のところをふ
まず、佛法のちからなきがゆえに、しかのごとくいふなり。たとひ造作の諸
惡をいましめ、たとひ造作の衆善をすすむとも、現成の莫作なるべし。

Juyi thought that Daolin, recognizing only conscious intention, was saying, "do not do evil deeds; you should *practice the good*"; the principle of "*do no evil, practice the good*" that has been on the way of the buddhas for a thousand, for a myriad ages past, that spans the past and spans the present — of this, he knows nothing, has heard nothing. And because he has not set foot in the place of the buddha dharma and lacks the power of the buddha dharma, he talks like this. Even to warn against "evils" intentionally committed, even to encourage "the good" intentionally committed, must be "do no" realized.

[31:26]

おほよそ佛法は、知識のほとりにしてはじめてきくと、究竟の果上もひと
しきなり。これを頭正尾正といふ。妙因妙果といひ、佛因佛果といふ。佛
道の因果は、異熟・等流等の論にあらざれば、佛因にあらず、佛果を感得
すべからず。道林、この道理を道取するゆえに、佛法あるなり。

---

55 **General Bai** (白將軍): I.e., Bai Qi 白起 (d. 257 BCE), famed general of the state of Qin during the Warring States period (475–221 BCE).

56 **a literatus of twenty-four lives** (*nijūshi shō no bungaku* 二十四生の文學): I.e., a literatus over twenty-four lifetimes.

57 **there is no one in the literary world who does not attend upon him** (*hikkai no chōsezaru nakaru beshi* 筆海の朝せざるなかるべし): More literally, "no one of the ocean of the brush who does not flow [to him]." The image is drawn from courtiers attending the morning session of the court, likened to rivers flowing to the ocean.

31. Do No Evil *Shoaku makusa* 諸惡莫作   19

In sum, in the buddha dharma, what one first hears in the company of a wise friend and the ultimate fruit are the same. This is called "*right at the head, right at the tail*"; it is called "*marvelous cause, marvelous effect*"; it is called "*buddha cause, buddha effect.*" Since the cause and effect on the way of the buddhas are not such theories as differentiated maturation or continuity, if it is not a buddha cause, we cannot experience a buddha effect.[58] Because Daolin expressed this principle, he had the buddha dharma.

[31:27]

諸惡、たとひいくかさなりの盡界に彌綸し、いくかさなりの盡法を呑却せりとも、これ莫作の解脱なり。衆善、すでに初・中・後、善にてあれば、奉行の性・相・體・力等を如是せるなり。居易、かつてこの蹤跡をふまざるによりて、三歳の孩兒も道得ならんとはいふなり。道得をまさしく道得するちからなくて、かくのごとくいふなり。

Even if "evils" have filled to the brim all the worlds of however many layers, and swallowed up all the dharmas of however many layers, this is the liberation of "do no." And since "good deeds" are "good at the beginning, middle, and end," it makes "such" the nature, marks, substance, power, and so on, of "to practice."[59] Juyi, because he has never set foot in these traces, says that even a three-year-old child could say it. Lacking the power himself really to make a statement, he says this.

[31:28]

あはれむべし、居易、なんぢ道甚麼なるぞ、佛風いまだきかざるがゆえに。三歳の孩兒をしれりやいなや、孩兒才生せる道理をしれりやいなや。もし三歳の孩兒をしらんものは、三世諸佛をもしるべし。いまだ三世諸佛をしらざらんもの、いかでか三歳の孩兒をしらん。對面せるはしれり、とおもふことなかれ、對面せざればしらざる、とおもふことなかれ。一塵をしれるものは盡界をしり、一法を通ずるものは萬法を通ず。萬法に通ぜざるもの、一法に通ぜず。通を學せるもの通徹のとき、萬法をもみる、一法

---

58 **differentiated maturation or continuity** (*ijuku tōru* 異熟・等流): Technical terms in Buddhist theories of cause and effect. The former expression (elsewhere rendered simply "ripened"), is used to render Sanskrit *vipāka* ("ripen"), in reference to karma as effect, distinct from the karma that is its cause; the latter, used for Sanskrit *niṣyanda* ("streaming"), refers to what cause and effect have in common. Dōgen's point is that such distinctions do not apply to "buddha cause" and "buddha effect."

59 **"good in the beginning, middle, and end"** (*sho chū go, zen* 初・中・後、善): Standard praise of a buddha's teachings; see Supplementary Notes, s.v. "Good in the beginning, middle, and end."

it makes "such" the nature, marks, substance, power, and so on, of "to practice" (*bugyō no shō sō tai riki tō o nyoze seru nari* 奉行の性・相・體・力等を如是せるなり): After a famous passage on "the ten suchnesses" (*jū nyoze* 十如是) in Kumārajīva's translation of the *Lotus Sūtra*; see Supplementary Notes, s.v. "Only buddhas with buddhas can exhaustively investigate the real marks of the dharmas."

20 DŌGEN'S *SHŌBŌGENZŌ* VOLUME III

をもみるがゆえに、一塵を學するもの、のがれず盡界を學するなり。三歳
の孩兒は佛法をいふべからず、とおもひ、三歳の孩兒のいはんことは容易
ならん、とおもふは、至愚なり。そのゆえは、生をあきらめ、死をあきら
むるは、佛家一大事の因縁なり。

How pitiful. Juyi, what are you saying? It is because you have not
heard of the style of the buddhas.[60] Do you know the "child of three"?
Do you know the principle of the child just born? Those who know the
"child of three" must know the buddhas of the three times; those who do
not yet know the buddhas of the three times, how could they know the
"child of three"?

Do not think that facing something is knowing it; do not think that, if
you do not face it, you do not know it. One who knows a single dust mote
knows all the worlds; one who penetrates a single dust mote penetrates
all the worlds. One who has not penetrated the myriad dharmas has not
penetrated a single dharma. Because when those who study penetration
fully penetrate it, they see the myriad dharmas and see the single dharma,
those who study a single dust mote study all the worlds without remainder.

It is the utmost stupidity to think that the "child of three" could not
speak the buddha dharma, or that what the "child of three" would say is
easy. Therefore, to clarify birth and to clarify death are the "cause of *the
one great matter" in the house of the buddhas.*[61]

[31:29] {1:351}

古德いはく、なんぢがはじめて生下せりしとき、すなはち師子吼の分あ
り。師子吼の分とは、如來轉法輪の功德なり、轉法輪なり。

An ancient worthy said, "When you were first born, you had the allotment of the lion's roar."[62] "The allotment of the lion's roar" means the
virtue of the tathāgatas' turning the dharma wheel, means turning the
dharma wheel.

---

60 **It is because you have not heard of the style of the buddhas** (*buppū imada kikaza-
ru ga yue ni* 佛風いまだきかざるがゆえに): The punctuation here follows Kawamura's
edition; others would read this clause with the sentence following: "Because you have
never heard of the style of the buddhas, do you know the three-year-old child?"

61 **"the cause of the one great matter" in the house of the buddhas** (*bukke ichi daiji
no innen* 佛家一大事の因縁): I.e., the single reason that Buddhism exists. From a passage in the *Lotus Sūtra*, in which Śākyamuni announces that the purpose of Buddhism is
to lead beings to buddhahood. See Supplementary Notes, s.v. "Buddhas, the world-honored ones, appear in the world for the reason of one great matter alone."

62 **An ancient worthy** (*kotoku* 古德): The source of this quotation is unidentified.

"allotment of the lion's roar" (*shishi ku no bun* 師子吼の分): I.e., the inherent abilities
of a buddha. "The lion's roar" refers to a buddha's preaching of the dharma; here, no
doubt, the famous first words of a buddha, often identified as his "lion's roar," proclaimed
immediately upon his birth; see Supplementary Notes, s.v. "I alone am honored."

31. Do No Evil *Shoaku makusa* 諸惡莫作

[31:30]
又、古德いはく、生死去來、眞實人體なり。

Again, an ancient worthy said, "*Birth and death, coming and going, are the true human body.*"[63]

[31:31]
しかあれば、眞實體をあきらめ、師子吼の功德あらん、まことに一大事なるべし、たやすかるべからず。かるがゆえに、三歳孩兒の因緣行履、あきらめんとするに、さらに大因緣なり。それ三世諸佛の行履因緣と、同・不同あるがゆえに。

Thus, to clarify "the true body," to have the virtue of "the lion's roar" — this is surely the "one great matter"; this is surely not easy. Therefore, when we would clarify the cause and the conduct of the "child of three," this is even more the great cause; for it has similarities and dissimilarities with the conduct and the cause of the buddhas of the three times.

[31:32]
居易おろかにして、三歳の孩兒の道得をかつてきかざれば、あるらんとだにも疑著せずして、恁麼道取するなり。道林の道聲の、雷よりも顯赫なるをきかず。道不得をいはんとしては、三歳孩兒還道得、といふ。これ、孩兒の師子吼をもきかず、禪師の轉法輪をも蹉過するなり。

Foolishly, Juyi, never having heard what a child of three could say, without even suspecting that it had anything [to say], spoke like this. He did not hear Daolin's voice, more obvious than thunder. As if to say, "You couldn't say anything," he said, "*Even a child of three could say it.*" This does not hear the child's "lion's roar"; it totally misses the Chan master's "turning the dharma wheel."

[31:33] {1:352}
禪師、あはれみをやむるにあたはず、かさねていふしなり、三歳の孩兒はたとひ道得なりとも、八十老翁は行不得ならん、と。

The Chan master, unable to restrain his pity, spoke again, "A child of three might be able say it, but an elder of eighty can't practice it."

[31:34]
いふこころは、三歳の孩兒に道得のことばあり、これをよくよく參究すべし。八十の老翁に行不得の道あり、よくよく功夫すべし。孩兒の道得は、なんぢに一任す、しかあれども孩兒に一任せず、老翁の行不得は、なんぢに一任す、しかあれども、老翁に一任せず、といひしなり。

What he is saying is this. The "child of three" has words "able to say it"; you should investigate this well. The eighty-year old elder has words

---

63 **an ancient worthy** (*kotoku* 古德): Likely a reference to Yuanwu Keqin 圓悟克勤 (1063-1135); see Supplementary Notes, s.v. "True human body."

22   DŌGEN'S *SHŌBŌGENZŌ* VOLUME III

that "can't practice it"; you should work at them well.[64] What the child is "able to say" is entirely left up to you; nevertheless, it is not entirely left up to the child.[65] What the elder cannot practice is entirely left up to you; nevertheless, it is not entirely left up to the elder. This is what he said.

[31:35]

佛法は、かくのごとく辨取し、宗取するを、道理とせり。

The buddha dharma takes as its principle distinguishing and revering the meaning like this.[66]

正法眼藏諸惡莫作第三十一

Treasury of the True Dharma Eye

Do No Evil

Number 31

[Ryūmonji MS:]

爾時延應庚子月夕、在雍州宇治縣觀音導利興聖寶林寺示衆

Presented to the assembly at Kannon Dōri Kōshō Hōrin Monastery, Uji District, in the domain of Yōshū; on the evening of the harvest moon of the senior metal year of the rat, in En'ō [2 September 1240][67]

---

64 **has words that "can't practice it"** (*gyōfutoku no dō ari* 行不得の道あり): Ambiguous; perhaps "has words that cannot be practiced"; or "has words that he (or you?) cannot practice." Perhaps reflecting the words of Dongshan Liangjie 洞山良价 (807-869) (see, e.g., *shinji Shōbōgenzō* 眞字正法眼藏, DZZ.5:164, case 77):

説取行不得底、行取説不得底。

He talks of what can't be practiced and practices what can't be talked of.

65 **entirely left up to you** (*nanji ni ichinin su* なんぢに一任す); **not entirely left up to the child** (*gaiji ni ichinin sezu* 孩兒に一任せず): Here and in the following sentence, the meaning is unclear; perhaps "you decide what the child can say and the elder can't practice, but they are not what the child and the old man think."

66 **distinguishing and revering the meaning like this** (*kaku no gotoku benshu shi, shūshu suru* かくのごとく辨取し、宗取する): Some MS witnesses read "distinguishing, explicating, and revering the meaning like this" (*kaku no gotoku benshu shi sesshu shi shūshu suru* かくのごとく辨取し説取し宗取する). The term *shūshu* 宗取 is an unusual expression not appearing elsewhere in Dōgen's writing. The translation takes the glyph *shu* 取 as a verbal affix, in parallel with *benshu* 辨取 and *sesshu* 説取.

67 The Tōunji 洞雲寺 MS shares an identical colophon.

evening of the harvest moon (*gesseki* 月夕): I.e., the fifteenth of the eighth lunar month.

31. Do No Evil *Shoaku makusa* 諸惡莫作

[Tōunji MS:]

寛元元年癸卯三月下旬七日、於侍司寮書寫之。懷奘

Copied at the acolyte's quarters; seventh day, last third of the third month of the junior water year of the rabbit, the first year of Kangen [17 April 1243]. Ejō

于時永正七年庚午七月五日、於阿陽路桂林寺丈室下、用兼七十三歲書
寫焉

Copied in the abbot's quarters of Keirin Monastery, Katsuura District, Ayō; fifth day, seventh month, senior metal year of the horse, the seventh year of Eishō [9 August 1510], by Yōken, in his seventy third year[68]

---

68 **Ayō** 阿陽: I.e., Awa 阿波, present-day Tokushima Prefecture.
Yōken 用兼: I.e., Kinkō Yōken 金岡用兼 (1437–1513?).

Treasury of the True Dharma Eye

Number 32

Transmitting the Robe
Den'e

傳衣

Transmitting the Robe

Den'e

INTRODUCTION

The colophon of this work states that it was composed at Kōshōji, on October 17, 1240, the same date given for the "Uji" 有時 chapter of the *Shōbōgenzō*, as well as for the "Kesa kudoku" 袈裟功徳, a text of the twelve-chapter *Shōbōgenzō*. The "Den'e" represents number 32 of the seventy-five-chapter *Shōbōgenzō* and number 13 of the Honzan edition; it does not occur in the sixty-chapter compilation but appears in the twenty-eight-text *Shōbōgenzō* collection as number 1 of fascicle 2.

The title theme of this lengthy essay derives especially from the tradition with which Dōgen opens the piece: that the robe of Bodhidharma was handed down, together with his dharma, through the first generations of Chinese Chan ancestors till it reached the Sixth Ancestor, Huineng 慧能. Dōgen expands on this tradition to make the broader claim that, while Bodhidharma's robe itself may have been preserved at the Sixth Ancestor's monastery at Caoxi 曹溪, the formal vestment (*kāṣāya*) worn by Zen monks uniquely represents, or embodies, the orthodox type of robe transmitted by all the buddhas and ancestors.

Unlike most of the representative essays in the *Shōbōgenzō*, the "Den'e" is not a collection of comments on Zen sayings. Rather, it draws on various sources to offer Dōgen's personal vision of the history, characteristics, and spiritual significance of the Buddhist robe. The religious emotion behind that vision is palpable in a remarkable passage toward the end of the essay, in which the author recalls the tears of joy that moistened his gown when, as a young pilgrim to China, he first witnessed the veneration of the robe by the monks in the saṃgha hall at Mount Tiantong 天童山 and vowed to carry the practice back to his native land. The practice he carried back is still followed by Sōtō monks in Japan today.

正法眼藏第三十二
Treasury of the True Dharma Eye
Number 32
傳衣
Transmitting the Robe

[32:1] {1:353}

佛佛正傳の衣法、まさに震旦に正傳することは、少林の高祖のみなり。高祖は、すなはち釋迦牟尼佛より第二十八代の祖師なり。西天二十八代、嫡嫡あひつたはれ、震旦に六代、まのあたり正傳す。西天・東地、都盧三十三代なり。

The direct transmission to Cīnasthāna of the robe and dharma directly transmitted by buddha after buddha was truly done only by the Eminent Ancestor of Shaolin.[1] The Eminent Ancestor is the ancestral master in the twenty-eighth generation after Buddha Śākyamuni. Passed down from successor to successor through twenty-eight generations in Sindh in the West, they were directly transmitted in person through six generations in Cīnasthāna. In Sindh in the West and the Land of the East, it is thirty-three generations in all.[2]

[32:2]

第三十三代の祖、大鑑禪師、この衣法を黄梅の夜半に正傳し、生前護持しきたる。いまなほ曹溪寶林寺に安置せり。諸代の帝王、あひつぎて内裏に請入して供養す。神物護持せるものなり。

The Ancestor in the thirty-third generation, Chan Master Dajian, received the direct transmission of this robe and dharma in the middle of

---

1 **Cīnasthāna** (*Shintan* 震旦): Dōgen uses here the Chinese transliteration of a Sanskrit term for China meaning "Land of the Qin."

the robe and dharma (*e hō* 衣法): From the tradition, dating from the eighth century, that the early ancestors of Chan in China handed down the *kāṣāya* of Bodhidharma as a token of the inheritance of his dharma.

the Eminent Ancestor of Shaolin (*Shōrin no kōso* 少林の高祖): I.e., the First Ancestor in China, Bodhidharma, said to have resided at the Shaolin Monastery 少林寺.

2 **In Sindh in the West and the Land of the East, it is thirty-three generations in all** (*Saiten Tōchi, toro sanjūsan dai nari* 西天・東地、都盧三十三代なり): The total of thirty-three generations results from the standard practice of counting Bodhidharma as both the twenty-eighth Indian and first Chinese ancestor.

28   DŌGEN'S *SHŌBŌGENZŌ* VOLUME III

the night from Huangmei and guarded them throughout his life.[3] Even now, it is preserved in the Baolin Monastery at Caoxi.[4] Generations of emperors in succession welcomed it into the imperial palace and made offerings to it. It is something guarded by spiritual beings.

[32:3]

唐朝の中宗・肅宗・代宗、しきりに歸内供養しき。請するにも、おくるにも、勅使をつかはし、詔をたまふ。すなはちこれ、おもくする儀なり。代宗皇帝、あるとき佛衣を曹溪山におくる詔にいはく、今遣鎮國大將軍劉崇景頂戴而送。朕爲之國寶。卿可於本寺安置、令僧衆親承宗旨者、嚴加守護勿令遺墜。

The Tang-dynasty emperors Zhongzong, Suzong, and Daizong repeatedly recalled it to court and made offerings to it.[5] When requesting it and when returning it, they dispatched an imperial envoy and handed down an imperial edict. This is a rite showing how seriously they regarded it. When, on one occasion, the Emperor Daizong sent the buddha robe back to Caoxi, his imperial edict said:[6]

We now dispatch Liu Chongjing, Great Defender-General of the State, reverently to receive and escort [the robe]. We regard it as a national treasure. Our liege [Liu Chongjing] is to place it for safekeeping in its original monastery and have those of the monks who have personally received the essential import strictly protect it and not allow it to be lost.

---

3   **Chan Master Dajian** (*Daikan zenji* 大鑑禪師): I.e., the Sixth Ancestor, Huineng 慧能.

in the middle of the night from Huangmei (*Ōbai no yahan ni* 黄梅の夜半に): From the legend that the Fifth Ancestor, Hongren 弘忍 (602-675), whose monastery was on Mount Huangmei 黄梅山 (in present-day Hubei), transmitted the robe and dharma to Huineng secretly, in the middle of the night.

4   **it is preserved in the Baolin Monastery at Caoxi** (*Sōkei Hōrinji ni anchi seri* 曹溪寶林寺に安置せり): I.e., Huineng's monastery in present-day Guangdong. The grammatical subject here, though unexpressed, must be "the robe" (rather than "the robe and dharma"). This claim reflects a common tradition in Zen literature.

5   **The Tang-dynasty emperors Zhongzong, Suzong, and Daizong** (*Tōchō no Chūsō Shukusō Daisō* 唐朝の中宗・肅宗・代宗): Based on a tradition, found in the *Jingde chuandeng lu* 景德傳燈錄 (T.2076.51:236c25-237a2), that, in the year 760, the Emperor Suzong 肅宗 (r. 756-763) requested that Huineng's robe and begging bowl be installed in the palace and given offerings. In 765, the Emperor Daizong 代宗 (r. 763-780), after a dream in which Huineng requested the return of his robe and bowl, sent them back to Caoxi, with the edict quoted here. The Emperor Zhongzong 中宗, though he is said to have honored Huineng, was assassinated in 710, three years before Huineng's death.

6   **the buddha robe** (*butsue* 佛衣): A term normally meaning "Buddhist robe," used synonymously with *kāṣāya*; it can also have the sense "the robe of the buddhas (or of Buddha Śākyamuni)." See Supplementary Notes, s.v. "Robe of the Tathāgata."

32. Transmitting the Robe *Den'e* 傳衣

[32:4] {1:354}

しかあればすなはち、數代の帝者、ともに、くにの重寶とせり。まことに
無量恒河沙の三千大千世界を統領せんよりも、この佛衣、くににたもてる
は、ことにすぐれたる大寶なり。卞璧に準ずべからざるものなり。たとひ
傳國璽となるとも、いかでか傳佛の奇寶とならん。大唐よりこのかた、瞻
禮せる緇白、かならず信法の大機なり。宿善のたすくるにあらずよりは、
いかでかこの身をもちて、まのあたり佛佛正傳の佛衣を瞻禮することあら
ん。信受する皮肉骨髓は、よろこぶべし、信受することあたはざらんは、
みづからなりといふとも、うらむべし、佛種子にあらざることを。

Thus, each of several generations of emperors regarded it as a major
treasure of the state. Truly the preservation of this buddha robe in one's
land is a great treasure far surpassing even the rule over trichiliocosms
equal to the incalculable sands of the Ganges.[7] It is not to be compared
to Bian's jade disc: even if the latter is taken as the signet of the transmission of the state, how could it be regarded as the rare treasure of
the transmission of the buddhas.[8] From the time of the Great Tang, the
black- and the white-robed who have venerated it have always been
those of great capacities for faith or dharma.[9] Without the help of good
karma from previous lifetimes, how could one, with this body, venerate
the buddha robe directly transmitted in person by buddha after buddha?
The skin, flesh, bones, and marrow who believe will surely rejoice; those

---

7   **trichiliocosms** (*sanzen daisen sekai* 三千大千世界): A term used to render the Sanskrit *trisāhasra-mahāsāhasra-lokadhātu* ("three-thousandfold great thousandfold world
system"), equaling one billion Mount Sumeru world systems; a standard measure of the
domain of a buddha.

8   **Bian's jade disc** (*Benpeki* 卞璧): Reference to the legend of a jade annulus, discov-
ered by a certain Bian He 卞和, of the ancient kingdom of Chu 楚, and presented to King
Wen of Zhou 周文王. The disc, better known as the "jade disk of He" (*He shi bi* 和氏璧),
was supposed to have been used by Qin Shihuang 秦始皇, founder of the Qin dyanasty,
to create the signet of imperial succession that was the token of the "mandate of heaven"
for emperors down through the Tang. See Supplementary Notes, s.v. "Bian's jade disc."

the rare treasure of the transmission of the buddhas (*denbutsu no kihō* 傳佛の奇寶):
Or "of the transmission of buddhahood." Dōgen here draws an analogy between "the
signet of the transmission of the state" (*denkoku ji* 傳國璽) as token of political authority
and the buddha robe as marker of Buddhist legitimacy; on this analogy, just as the holder
of the signet in each generation is the reigning monarch, so the owner of the robe is a
buddha.

9   **the black- and the white-robed** (*shihaku* 緇白): I.e., clerics and Buddhist laity, respectively.

those of great capacities for faith or dharma (*shinpō no daiki* 信法の大機): The expression *shinpō* 信法 can refer either to "faith in the dharma" or to two types of Buddhists: "those who advance by faith" (*zuishingyō* 隨信行; S. *śraddhānusārin*) and "those
who advance by [study of] dharma" (*zuihōgyō* 隨法行; S. *dharmānusārin*); given that
Dōgen will introduce the two types below (section 11), the latter reading seems prefer-
able here.

30　　　DŌGEN'S *SHŌBŌGENZŌ* VOLUME III

who cannot believe, though it is of their own doing, should regret their failing to be seeds of buddhahood.[10]

[32:5]

俗なほいはく、その人の行李をみるは、すなはちその人をみるなり。いま佛衣を瞻禮せんは、すなはち佛をみたてまつるなり。百千萬の塔を起立して、この佛衣に供養すべし。天上・海中にも、こころあらんはおもくすべし。人間にも、轉輪聖王等のまことをしり、すぐれたるをしらんは、おもくすべきなり。

Even in the secular world, it is said, "To see the person's belongings is to see the person."[11] Now, to venerate the buddha robe is to see the buddha. We should erect hundreds of thousands of myriads of stūpas and offer them to the buddha robe. Even in the heavens above or the depths of the sea, any being with a heart must surely value it. Among humans as well, the wheel-turning sage kings, who would know what is true and know what is excellent, must surely value it.[12]

[32:6]

あはれむべし、よよに國主となれるやから、わがくにに重寶のあるをしらざること。ままに道士の教にまどはされて、佛法を廢せるおほし。そのとき、袈裟をかけず、圓頂に葉巾をいただく。講ずるところは、延壽長年の方なり。唐朝にもあり、宋朝にもあり。これらのたぐひは、國主なりといへども、國民よりもいやしかるべきなり。

How sad that, over the generations, those who became monarchs have not known that there is a major treasure in their own land. Periodically seduced by the teachings of the Daoists, many abolished the buddha dharma.[13] At those times, instead of wearing the *kāṣāya*, they wore caps on their round heads; and the lectures were on methods for extending the

---

10　**skin, flesh, bones, and marrow** (*hi niku kotsu zui* 皮肉骨髓): Allusion to the four disciples of Bodhidharma, of whom he famously said they had got, in turn, his "skin, flesh, bones, and marrow" (see Supplementary Notes). Here, perhaps, referring to anyone who has got even a part of Bodhidharma's teachings.

seeds of buddhahood (*butsu shūji* 佛種子): I.e., those with potential to become a buddha.

11　**"To see the person's belongings"** (*sono hito no anri o miru wa* その人の行李をみるは): "Belongings" renders *anri* 行李 (also written 行履 and read *kōri*), a term often used in Chan texts for "conduct" or "observance." Given the context, the sense is more likely the common meaning of "parcel" or "luggage" — here, perhaps to be understood more broadly as "accoutrements" or "gear."

12　**wheel-turning sage kings** (*tenrin jōō* 轉輪聖王): The *cakravartin*, the ideal Buddhist monarch. Here, no doubt, in contrast to the benighted emperors of China criticized in the next section.

13　**many abolished the buddha dharma** (*buppō o hai seru ooshi* 佛法を廢せるおほし): A bit of an exaggeration: there were several persecutions of Buddhism in China, the most serious in the years following the death of Huineng and supposed enshrinement of his robe occurring in 845, under the Tang Emperor Wuzong 武宗 (r. 840-846).

32. Transmitting the Robe *Den'e* 傳衣   31

life span and lengthening the years.[14] They were in the Tang dynasty and in the Song dynasty. These types, though they may have been monarchs, were surely more vulgar than their own people.

[32:7] {1:355}

しづかに觀察しつべし、わがくにに佛衣とどまりて現在せり。衣佛國土なるべきか、とも思惟すべきなり。舍利等よりもすぐれたるべし。舍利は、輪王にもあり、師子にもあり、人にもあり、乃至辟支佛等にもあり。しかあれども、輪王には袈裟なし、師子に袈裟なし、人に袈裟なし。ひとり諸佛のみに袈裟あり、ふかく信受すべし。

They should have quietly reflected that the buddha robe had come to rest and still existed in their own land. They should even have considered whether theirs might be the robe buddha land.[15] It is surely more excellent than relics or the like. With relics, wheel-turning kings have them, lions have them, humans have them, and so on down to *pratyeka-buddhas*, and the like, have them.[16] However, wheel-turning kings do not have the *kāṣāya*, lions do not have the *kāṣāya*, humans do not have the *kāṣāya*: only the buddhas have the *kāṣāya*.[17] This we should firmly believe.

---

14 **instead of wearing the *kāṣāya*, they wore caps on their round heads** (*kesa o kakezu, enchō ni yōkin o itadaku* 袈裟をかけず、圓頂に葉巾をいただく): The grammatical subject is unexpressed; possibly, the "monarchs" themselves; more likely, the religious serving at the imperial court. The headgear in question is generally assumed to be a Daoist cap; the "round head" suggests a shaved head.

extending the life span and lengthening the years (*enju chōnen* 延壽長年): Favorite topics of the Daoists. Ironically, it is thought that the Emperor Wuzong 武宗 shortened his life by ingesting Daoist elixirs of immortality.

15 **the robe buddha land** (*e butsu kokudo* 衣佛國土): A novel expression apparently coined by Dōgen; probably to be understood as "a buddha land of the robe," though it might also be parsed "the land of the robe buddha."

16 **With relics, wheel-turning kings have them, lions have them** (*shari wa, rinnō ni mo ari, shishi ni mo ari* 舍利は、輪王にもあり、師子にもあり): It is possible that "lion" (*shishi* 師子) here refers not (or not only) to the animal but to great teachers. Elsewhere, in his "Shōbōgenzō nyorai zenshin," Dōgen gives a longer list of beings that produce relics:

古佛舍利あり、今佛舍利あり、辟支佛舍利あり、轉輪王舍利あり、師子舍利あり、あるいは木佛舍利あり、繪佛舍利あり、あるいは人舍利あり。

There are relics of old buddhas, there are relics of present buddhas, there are relics of *pratyeka-buddhas*, there are relics of wheel-turning kings, there are relics of lions; or there are relics of wooden buddhas, and there are relics of painted buddhas; or there are relics of humans.

17 **only the buddhas have the *kāṣāya*** (*hitori shobutsu nomi ni kesa ari* ひとり諸佛のみに袈裟あり): Presumably, by *kāṣāya* here, Dōgen is still referring to what he calls above the "buddha robe" — i.e., the robe handed down from the buddhas to Huineng. As he continues below, however, Dōgen's use of this term becomes more ambiguous, seeming to expand to cover the *kāṣāya* worn by the clerics in the Zen lineage as a token of (or avatar of?) the robe of the buddha.

32 DŌGEN'S *SHŌBŌGENZŌ* VOLUME III

[32:8]

いまの愚人、おほく舍利はおもくすといへども、袈裟をしらず、護持すべきとしれるもまれなり。これすなはち、先來より袈裟のおもき、これをきけるものまれなり、佛法正傳いまだきかざるがゆえに、しかあるなり。

Stupid people today, while they may often value relics, do not know about the *kāṣāya*; those who recognize that it is to be preserved are also rare. This is so because, to begin with, those who have heard of the importance of the *kāṣāya* are rare; for they have yet to hear of the direct transmission of the buddha dharma.

[32:9]

つらつら釋尊在世をおもひやれば、わづかに二千餘年なり。國寶神器のいまにつたはれるも、これよりもすぎてふるくなれるもおほし。この佛法・佛衣は、ちかくあらたなり。若田・若里に展轉せんこと、たとひ五十轉轉なれりとも、その益、これ妙なるべし。かれ、なほ功德あらたなり、この佛衣、かれとおなじかるべし。かれは正嫡より正傳せず、これは正嫡より正傳せり。

When we carefully reflect on the time when Śākya, the Honored One, was in the world, it is a mere two thousand plus years ago.[18] Many national treasures and imperial regalia handed down to the present are older than this. This buddha dharma and buddha robe are recent and new.[19] Their successive handing on, "*whether in fields or in villages*," even when passed on fifty times, has a benefit sure to be marvelous.[20] Even they have a merit that is phenomenal; and this buddha robe is surely like them.[21] Yet they are not directly transmitted from a direct heir, while this has been directly transmitted from a direct heir.

---

18 **two thousand plus years ago** (*nisen yo nen* 二千餘年): Dōgen is calculating here from 949 BCE, the date traditionally used in East Asia for the *parinirvāṇa* of Buddha Śākyamuni.

19 **recent and new** (*chikaku arata* ちかくあらた): The advantage of being "recent and new" (as is suggested in the *Lotus Sūtra* passage alluded to in the next sentence) derives from a principle that, the closer to the original source, the greater the merit.

20 **"whether in fields or in villages"** (*nyaku den nyaku ri* 若田・若里): Allusion to an oft-cited passage in the *Lotus Sūtra*, in which Buddha Śākyamuni exhorts his followers to go forth and preach what they have heard from him; see Supplementary Notes.

21 **Even they have a merit that is phenomenal** (*kare, nao kudoku arata nari* かれ、なほ功德あらたなり): Taking the antecedent of "they" (*kare* かれ) here and in the next sentence as "national treasures and imperial regalia," in contrast to "this" (*kore* これ) buddha robe.

32. Transmitting the Robe *Den'e* 傳衣

[32:10]

しるべし、四句偈をきくに得道す、一句子をきくに得道す。四句偈および
一句子、なにとしてか恁麼の靈驗ある。いはゆる、佛法なるによりてな
り。いま一頂衣・九品衣、まさしく佛法より正傳せり。四句偈よりも劣な
るべからず、一句法よりも驗なかるべからず。

We should realize that we may gain the way upon hearing a four-line
gāthā or gain the way upon hearing a single line.[22] How could the four-
line gāthā or the single line have such spiritual efficacy? It is because
they are the buddha dharma. The one robe, or robe of nine grades, here
has certainly been transmitted directly from the buddha dharma.[23] It
could not be inferior to the four-line gāthā; it could not be less effica-
cious than the dharma of a single line.

[32:11] {1:356}

このゆえに、二千餘年よりこのかた、信行・法行の諸機、ともに隨佛學
者、みな袈裟を護持して身心とせるものなり。諸佛の正法にくらきたぐひ
は、袈裟を崇重せざるなり。いま釋提桓因、および阿那跋達多龍王等、と
もに在家の天主なりといへども、龍王なりといへども、袈裟を護持せり。

Therefore, for over two thousand years, those who study as followers
of the buddha, those of the capacities both that proceed by faith and
proceed by dharma, have all preserved the *kāṣāya* and regarded it as the
body and mind.[24] The types that are ignorant of the true dharma of the

---

22　**four-line gāthā** (*shiku ge* 四句偈): Likely a reference to the famous *Verse of Impermanence* (*Mujō ge* 無常偈) from the story in the *Nirvāṇa Sūtra* (*Da banniepan jing* 大
般涅槃經, T.374.12:449b8ff), to which Dōgen will allude again below (section 61), in
which Buddha Śākyamuni in a previous life received a four-line verse from a *rākṣasa*
("hungry demon"):

諸行無常、是生滅法、生滅滅已、寂滅爲樂。

All things are impermanent:
This is the law of arising and ceasing.
When the arising and ceasing have ceased,
Their cessation is ease.

See Supplementary Notes, s.v. "Whether on trees or on rocks."

a single line (*ikkusu* 一句子): In Chan texts, regularly used in reference especially to any
spiritually insightful utterance.

23　**the one robe, or robe of nine grades, here** (*ima itchō e kubon e* いま一頂衣・九
品衣): I.e., the buddha robe under discussion here. The glyph *chō* 頂 is used as a numer-
ical classifier for robes; "nine grades" (*kubon* 九品) refers to nine levels of the formal
kāṣāya, or *saṃghāti* (*sōgyari* 僧伽梨) robe, according to the number of panels, from
nine to twenty-five, from which it is assembled (see below, section 21). Dōgen is using
the numbers one and nine here in parallel with the "four" and "one" in the sentences just
preceding.

24　**the capacities both that proceed by faith and proceed by dharma** (*shingyō hōgyō
no shoki* 信行・法行の諸機): See above, Note 9.

34　　DŌGEN'S *SHŌBŌGENZŌ* VOLUME III

buddhas do not respect the *kāṣāya*. Now, beings like Śakra-devānām-indra and the dragon king Anavatapta, though householder lord of devas and dragon king both may be, still preserve the *kāṣāya*.[25]

[32:12]

しかるに、剃頭のたぐひ、佛子と稱するともがら、袈裟におきては、受持すべきものとしらず。いはんや體・色・量をしらんや、いはんや著用の法をしらんや、いはんやその威儀、ゆめにもいまだみざるところなり。

Yet the types who shave their heads, those who call themselves "children of the Buddha," when it comes to the *kāṣāya*, do not know that it is something to receive and keep.[26] How much less do they know its material, color, or dimensions; how much less do they know how to put it on; how much less have they seen, even in their dreams, the proper deportment [when wearing it].

[32:13]

袈裟をば、ふるくよりいはく、除熱惱服となづく、解脱服となづく。おほよそ功德、はかるべからざるなり。龍鱗の三熱、よく袈裟の功德より解脱するなり。諸佛成道のとき、かならずこの衣をもちひるなり。まことに、邊地にむまれ、末法にあふといへども、相傳あると、相傳なきと、たくらぶることあらば、相傳の正嫡なるを信受護持すべし。

The *kāṣāya* has long been called "the vestment that removes the torments," or called "the vestment of liberation."[27] Put more generally, its

---

regarded it as the body and mind (*shinjin to seru* 身心とせる): Probably, to be understood as "their own body and mind," though it might also be read as "the buddha's body and mind." See Supplementary Notes, s.v. "Body and mind."

25　**Śakra-devānāṃ-indra and the dragon king Anavatapta** (*Shakudaikan'in, oyobi Anabadatta ryūō* 釋提桓因、および阿那跋達多龍王): I.e., the deva Indra, or Śakra, and the dragon king who lives in Lake Anavatapta, imagined to be north of the Himalayas.

though householder lord of devas and dragon king both may be (*zaike no tenshu nari to iedomo, ryūō nari to iedomo* 在家の天主なりといへども、龍王なりといへども): The force of the modifier "householder" (*zaike no* 在家の) here is probably that (in contrast to the monks in the following section), even though they are not themselves clerics, the gods and dragons preserve the clerical robe.

26　**when it comes to the *kāṣāya*, do not know that it is something to receive and keep** (*kesa ni okite wa, juji su beki mono to shirazu* 袈裟におきては、受持すべきものとしらず): The robe in question here could be the buddha robe preserved at Caoxi; but it seems more likely that Dōgen is here criticizing his fellow monks for their indifference toward and ignorance of their own robes. The verb *juji* 受持 ("receive and keep"), while it may refer simply to the acts of receiving and wearing the robe, is here more likely the attitude of accepting and bearing in mind the robe's significance as symbol of the buddha.

27　**"the vestment that removes the torments"** (*jo netsunō fuku* 除熱惱服); **"the vestment of liberation"** (*gedappuku* 解脱服): The first expression has not been found in extant sources and is likely meant simply to introduce the following "three torments

32. Transmitting the Robe *Den'e* 傳衣

merits are incalculable. It is the merit of the *kāṣāya* that brings about liberation from the three torments of the dragon.[28] When the buddhas attain the way, they always make use of this robe. Truly, though we may be born in a marginal land and are encountering the end of the dharma, if we compare what has the transmission and what lacks the transmission, we should believe and preserve that which is the legitimate successor of the transmission.[29]

[32:14]
いづれの家門にか、わが正傳のごとく、まさしく釋尊の衣法ともに正傳せる。ひとり佛道のみにあり。この衣法にあはんとき、たれか恭敬供養をゆるくせん。たとひ一日に無量恒河沙の身命をすてて供養すべし、生生世世値遇頂戴をも發願すべし。われら、佛生國をへだつること十萬餘里の山海のほかにむまれて、邊邦の愚蒙なりといへども、この正法をきき、この袈裟を一日一夜なりといへども受持し、一句一偈なりといへども參究する、これただ一佛二佛を供養せる福德のみにはあるべからず、無量百千億のほとけを供養・奉覲せる福德なるべし。たとひ自己なりといへども、たうとぶべし、愛すべし、おもくすべし。

In what other houses have both the robe and dharma of Śākya, the Honored One, truly been directly transmitted, as they have in our direct transmission? Only in the way of the buddhas alone.[30] Upon encountering this robe and dharma, who would be casual in venerating and making

---

of the dragon." The second expression is well known from the four-line verse still recited by monks when donning the *kāṣāya*; see Supplementary Notes, s.v. "Robe of the Tathāgata."

28   **the three torments of the dragon** (*ryūrin no sannetsu* 龍鱗の三熱): From the well-known tradition that dragons are subject to three afflictions: hot winds and sands that burn them, evil winds that expose them, and garuḍas (giant mythical birds) that eat them. The claim (repeated in "Shōbōgenzō kesa kudoku" 正法眼藏袈裟功德) that the dragons are liberated from these torments by the *kāṣāya* doubtless reflects the tradition that a thread from the Tathāgata's robe will protect dragons from the garuḍa (see, e.g., *Sāgara-nāga-rāja-paripṛcchā-sūtra; Fo shuo hailongwang jing* 佛説海龍王經, T.598.15:151a6-16). The term *ryūrin* 龍鱗 ("dragon scales") normally refers to the pattern of the dragon's scales, rather than to the dragon itself; but elsewhere Dōgen uses it as synecdoche for "dragon," by analogy with *kinrin* 金鱗 ("gold scales") for "golden fish" (see *Eihei kōroku* 永平廣録, DZZ.3:86, no. 139):

清淨海中釣得龍鱗金鱗
In the clear ocean, we can catch a dragon and a golden fish.

29   **we should believe and preserve that which is the legitimate successor of the transmission** (*sōden no shōteki naru o shinju goji su beshi* 相傳の正嫡なるを信受護持すべし): Dōgen treats the robe here in anthropomorphic terms, as a legitimate heir (*shōchaku* 正嫡) in the lineage of the buddhas and ancestors.

30   **Only in the way of the buddhas alone** (*hitori butsudō nomi ni ari* ひとり佛道のみにあり): As is often the case in his writing, Dōgen here identifies "the way of the buddhas" (*butsudō* 佛道) with the tradition of the buddhas and ancestors of his Bodhidharma lineage. See Supplementary Notes, s.v. "Buddhas and ancestors."

36 DŌGEN'S *SHŌBŌGENZŌ* VOLUME III

offerings to them? Even for one day, casting aside lives numerous as the incalculable sands of the Ganges, we should make offerings to them; we should make a vow to encounter and receive them in life after life, through age after age. Though we may be simpletons from a marginal land, born beyond the mountains and seas, more than a hundred thousand miles from the land of the Buddha's birth, to hear this true dharma, to receive and keep this *kāṣāya* even for a single day and night, to investigate even one line or one *gāthā* — these are surely not the merit of offerings made to one buddha or two buddhas; they are surely the merit of having made offerings to and paying respects before incalculable hundreds of thousands of *koṭis* of buddhas. Though it may be of our own doing, we should honor it; we should love it; we should value it.[31]

[32:15] {1:357}

祖師傳法の大恩、ねんごろに報謝すべし。畜類なほ恩を報ず、人類いかでか恩をしらざらん。もし恩をしらずば、畜類よりも劣なるべし、畜類よりも愚なるべし。

We should sincerely repay the great beneficence of the transmission of the dharma by the ancestral masters.[32] Even animals repay beneficence; how could humans fail to recognize beneficence?[33] If we fail to recognize beneficence, we must be inferior to animals; we must be stupider than animals.

[32:16]

この佛衣の功德、その傳佛正法の祖師にあらざる餘人は、ゆめにもいまだしらざるなり。いはんや體・色・量をあきらむるにおよばんや。諸佛のあとをしたふべくは、まさにこれをしたふべし。たとひ百千萬代ののちも、この正傳を正傳せん、まさに佛法なるべし。證驗これあらたなり。

The merit of this buddha robe, those other than these ancestral masters who transmit the true dharma of the buddhas have never seen even in their dreams. How much less could they achieve an understanding of its material, color, and dimensions. Should we yearn for the traces of the buddhas, truly we should yearn for this. Even a hundred thousand myriads of generations later, to transmit directly this direct transmission

---

31 **Though it may be of our own doing** (*tatoi jiko nari to iedomo* たとひ自己なりといへども): The antecedent of "it" here is likely the "merit" (*fukutoku* 福德) of accepting the robe and studying the dharma.

32 **the transmission of the dharma by the ancestral masters** (*soshi denbō* 祖師傳法): The term *soshi* 祖師 ("ancestral master") may refer here specifically to Bodhidharma.

33 **Even animals repay beneficence** (*chikurui nao on o hōzu* 畜類なほ恩を報ず): In "Shōbōgenzō gyōji" 正法眼藏行持, part 2, Dōgen refers to two famous Chinese stories, in which a sparrow and a tortoise express their gratitude for help given them by humans.

32. Transmitting the Robe Den'e 傳衣

would still truly be the buddha dharma. The evidence for this is obvious.[34]

[32:17]

俗なほいはく、先王の服にあらざれば服せず、先王の法にあらざればおこなはず。佛道もまたしかあるなり、先佛の法服にあらざれば、もちいるべからず。もし先佛の法服にあらざらんほかは、なにを服してか佛道を修行せん、諸佛に奉覲せん。これを服せざらんは、佛會にいりがたかるべし。

Even in the secular world it is said, "If they are not the raiment of the prior kings, they do not wear them; if they are not the laws of the prior kings, they do not promulgate them."[35] The way of the buddhas is also like this: if it is not the dharma garment of the prior buddhas, we should not use it. If it is something other than the dharma garment of the prior buddhas, what could we wear to practice the way of the buddhas, to pay our respects to the buddhas? Those who do not wear this, will surely find it difficult to enter a buddha assembly.

[32:18]

後漢の孝明皇帝永平年中よりこのかた、西天より東地に來到する僧侶、くびすをつぎてたえず。震旦より印度におもむく僧侶、ままにきこゆれども、たれ人にあひて佛法を面授せりけるといはず。ただいたづらに、論師および三藏の學者に習學せる名相のみなり、佛法の正嫡をきかず。このゆえに、佛衣正傳すべきといひつたへるにもおよばず、佛衣正傳せりける人にあひあふといはず、傳衣の人を見聞すとかたらず。はかりしりぬ、佛家の闈奥にいらざりけるといふことを。これらのたぐひは、ひとへに衣服とのみ認じて、佛法の尊重なりとしらず、まことにあはれむべし。

Since the Yongping era of the Emperor Xiao Ming of the Later Han, monks arriving in the Land of the East from Sindh in the West have ceaselessly followed on each other's heels.[36] We sometimes hear of monks who headed to Sindhu from Cīnasthāna, but who they met there that might have given them a face-to-face conferral of the buddha dharma is not reported.[37] They did not hear of any direct descendants of the

---

34 **The evidence for this is obvious** (shōken kore arata nari 證驗これあらたなり): Likely intended to introduce the following discussion of historical examples.

35 **Even in the secular world it is said** (zoku nao iwaku 俗なほいはく): A loose Japanese paraphrase of a teaching of the Xiaojing 孝經 (Qing dafu 卿大夫, KR.1f0001.004.1a):

非先王之法服不敢服、非先王之法言不敢道、非先王之德行不敢行。

They [i.e., the lords and ministers] dare not wear what are not the robes prescribed by the prior kings; they dare not speak what are not the words prescribed by the prior kings; they dare not engage in what is not the virtuous conduct of the prior kings.

36 **the Yongping era of the Emperor Xiao Ming of the Later Han** (Gokan no Kōmei kōtei Eihei nenjū 後漢の孝明皇帝永平年中): I.e., 58-75 CE, the era in the tenth year of which it is traditionally said that Buddhism was introduced to China.

37 **monks who headed to Sindhu from Cīnasthāna** (Shintan yori Indo ni omomuku

38   DŌGEN'S *SHŌBŌGENZŌ* VOLUME III

buddha dharma, but only of names and appearances learned from treatise masters or scholars of the tripiṭaka. As a result, they do not even report that the buddha robe should be directly transmitted; they do not say that they met with anyone who had directly received transmission of the buddha robe; they do not state that they saw or heard of anyone transmitting the robe. It is clear that they did not enter the inner sanctum of the house of the buddhas. These types recognize [the robe] solely as clothing and do not know it as something esteemed by the buddha dharma. Truly pitiful.

[32:19] {1:358}
佛法藏相傳の正嫡に、佛衣も相傳相承するなり。法藏正傳の祖師は、佛衣を見聞せざるなきむねは、人中・天上あまねくしれるところなり。しかあればすなはち、佛袈裟の體・色・量を正傳しきたり、正見聞しきたり、佛袈裟の大功德を正傳し、佛袈裟の心身骨髓を正傳せること、ただまさに正傳の家業のみにあり。もろもろの阿笈摩教の家風には、しらざるところなり。おのおの今案に自立せるは、正傳にあらず、正嫡にあらず。

Among the direct descendants of the transmission of the treasury of the buddha dharma, the buddha robe is also transmitted and inherited. The point that there are no ancestral masters of the direct transmission of the treasury of the dharma that have not seen and heard of the buddha robe is something widely known among humans and in the heavens. This being the case, truly it is only in the family business of the direct transmission that the material, color, and dimensions of the buddha *kāṣāya* have been directly transmitted and correctly seen and heard; that the great merit of the buddha *kāṣāya* was transmitted; that the mind and body, bones and marrow of the buddha *kāṣāya* were directly transmitted — these are not something known in the various house styles of the teachings of the *āgamas*.[38] What they set up by themselves, from their own ideas, is not the direct transmission, is not a direct descendant.[39]

---

sōryo 震旦より印度におもむく僧侶): Using Chinese transliterations of Sanskrit terms for India and China. The "Shōbōgenzō gyōji" 正法眼藏行持, part 2, also has a dismissal of Chinese pilgrims to India for failing to encounter any authentic masters and merely studying doctrine.

38 **the family business of the direct transmission** (*shōden no kagō* 正傳の家業): I.e., the tradition of those in the direct line of transmission.

the mind and body, bones and marrow of the buddha *kāṣāya* (*butsu kesa no shinjin kotsuzui* 佛袈裟の心身骨髓): Probably meaning something like "the true meaning of the buddha *kāṣāya*."

the various house styles of the teachings of the *āgamas* (*moromoro no agōma kyō no kafū* もろもろの阿笈摩教の家風): I.e., in the traditions of those who follow the Small Vehicle teachings of the *āgama* texts.

39 **What they set up by themselves, from their own ideas** (*onoono kon'an ni jiryū seru wa* おのおの今案に自立せるは): Or, perhaps, "that they set up something by them-

32. Transmitting the Robe *Den'e* 傳衣

[32:20]

わが大師釋迦牟尼如來、正法眼藏無上菩提を摩訶迦葉に附授するに、佛衣
ともに傳附せりしより、嫡嫡相承して、曹溪山大鑑禪師にいたるに、三十
三代なり。その體・色・量を親見・親傳せること、家門、ひさしくつた
はれて、受持、いまにあらたなり。すなはち五宗の高祖、おのおの受持
せる、それ正傳なり。あるいは五十餘代、あるひは四十餘代、おのおの師
資みだることなく、先佛の法によりて搭し、先佛の法によりて製すること
も、唯佛與佛の相傳し證契して、代代をふるに、おなじくあらたなり。

When our Great Master, Tathāgata Śākyamuni, bequeathed the trea-sury of the true dharma eye, the unsurpassed bodhi, to Mahākāśyapa, he passed it on together with the buddha robe; and thereafter, it was inher-ited by successor after successor, until it reached Chan Master Dajian of Mount Caoxi, in the thirty-third generation. The personal experience and personal transmission of its material, color, and dimensions have long been handed down in our house, and the receiving and keeping of them are apparent even now. That is, what each of the eminent ancestors of the five lineages received and kept is the direct transmission.[40] Whether for fifty-odd generations or forty-odd generations, without disruption, the masters and disciples donned it in accordance with the dharma of the prior buddhas and tailored it in accordance with the dharma of the prior buddhas; and this, too, transmitted and verified by "only buddhas with buddhas," remains apparent through generation after generation.[41]

[32:21]

嫡嫡正傳する佛訓にいはくは、

九條衣　三長一短
九條衣　四長一短
十一條衣　　三長一短 或四長一短
十三條衣　　三長一短 或四長一短

---

selves, from their own ideas " or "those who set up something by themselves, from their own ideas."

40　**the eminent ancestors of the five lineages** (*goshū no kōso* 五宗の高祖): I.e., the ancestral masters of the five houses (*goke* 五家) into which the Song-dynasty historians organized the Chan tradition: Weiyang 潙仰, Linji 臨濟, Caodong 曹洞, Yunmen 雲門, and Fayan 法眼. The term *kōso* 高祖 is used most often in reference to a founding ances-tor, but Dōgen uses it also as a term of respect for other eminent monks. The point here seems to be that, while of course the members of the five houses did not transmit the original robe of the buddha, what they did "receive and keep" was "the direct transmis-sion" of that robe — either in the sense that their robes replicate it or that their teachings preserve its tradition.

41　**"only buddhas with buddhas"** (*yui butsu yo butsu* 唯佛與佛): From a line in Kumārajīva's translation of the *Lotus Sūtra*, often cited by Dōgen; see Supplementary Notes, s.v. "Only buddhas with buddhas can exhaustively investigate the real marks of the dharmas."

40 DŌGEN'S *SHŌBŌGENZŌ* VOLUME III

十五條衣　四長一短
十七條衣　四長一短
十九條衣　四長一短
二十一條衣　四長一短
二十三條衣　四長一短
二十五條衣　四長一短
二百五十條衣　四長一短
八萬四千條衣　八長一短

In the instructions of the buddha directly transmitted by successor after successor, it is said,

nine-panel robe: three long, one short
nine-panel robe: four long, one short
eleven-panel robe: three long, one short, or four long, one short
thirteen-panel robe: three long, one short, or four long, one short
fifteen-panel robe: four long, one short
seventeen-panel robe: four long, one short
nineteen-panel robe: four long, one short
twenty-one-panel robe: four long, one short
twenty-three-panel robe: four long, one short
twenty-five-panel robe: four long, one short
two-hundred-fifty-panel robe: four long, one short
eighty-four-thousand-panel robe: eight long, one short[42]

42　**In the instructions of the buddha directly transmitted by successor after successor** (*tekiteki shōden suru bukkun ni* 嫡嫡正傳する佛訓に): The source of the list that follows is unknown, and its content differs from standard descriptions of the nine levels of robe, which typically describe the 9-, 11-, and 13-panel robes as composed of two long strips and one short strip of cloth in each panel, with 15-, 17-, and 19-panel robes having three long and one short, and 21-, 23-, and 25-panel robes having four long and one short. Such is the description, quoted from the *Yiqie you bu baiyi jiemo* 一切有部百一羯磨, that Dōgen provides in his "Shōbōgenzō kesa kudoku" 正法眼藏袈裟功德. The Chan monks' practice of wearing a nine-panel *kāṣāya* of three or four long sections is criticized by the Song-dynasty vinaya scholar Yuanzhao 元照 (1048-1116) at *Fozhi biqiu liuwu tu* 佛制比丘六物圖 (T.1900.45:899a2-4).

two-hundred-fifty-panel robe: four long, one short (*nihyakugojū jō e shichō ittan* 二百五十條衣四長一短); **eighty-four-thousand-panel robe: eight long, one short** (*hachiman shisen jō e hatchō ittan* 八萬四千條衣八長一短): Dōgen here playfully extends his list to include what is doubtless meant to suggest a robe composed of the two hundred fifty precepts of the Buddhist monk and a robe of the eighty-four thousand teachings of the Buddha (or, perhaps, simply "countless things").

32. Transmitting the Robe *Den'e* 傳衣 41

[32:22] {1:359}

いま略して舉するなり。このほか、諸般の袈裟あるなり、ともにこれ僧伽
梨衣なるべし。

I give here an abbreviated summary. There are, in addition to these, various kinds of *kāṣāya*, all of which should be considered *saṃghāti* robes.

[32:23]

あるひは在家にしても受持し、あるひは出家にしても受持す。受持すると
いふは、著用するなり。いたづらに、たたみもちたらんずるにあらざるな
り。たとひ、かみ・ひげをそれども、袈裟を受持せず、袈裟をにくみいと
ひ、袈裟をおそるるは、天魔外道なり。

Some receive and keep [the robe] as householders; some receive and keep it as renunciants. To "receive and keep it" means to wear it; it does not mean merely keeping it folded up to no avail. Even if they shave off their hair and beards, those who do not receive and keep the *kāṣāya*, who abhor and reject the *kāṣāya*, who fear the *kāṣāya*, are Deva Māras and followers of other paths.

[32:24] {1:360}

百丈大智禪師いはく、宿殖の善種なきものは、袈裟をいむなり、袈裟をい
とふなり、正法をおそれいとふなり。

Chan Master Dazhi of Baizhang said, "Those without good seeds planted in former lives shun the *kāṣāya*, reject the *kāṣāya*, fear and hate the *kāṣāya*.[43]

[32:25]

佛言、若有衆生、入我法中、或犯重罪、或墮邪見、於一念中、敬心尊重僧
伽梨衣、諸佛及我、必於三乘、授記此人當得作佛。若天・若龍・若人・若
鬼、若能恭敬此人袈裟少分功德、即得三乘不退不轉。若有鬼神及諸衆生、
能得袈裟乃至四寸、飮食充足。若有衆生、共相違反、欲墮邪見、念袈裟
力、依袈裟力、尋生悲心、還得清淨。若有人在兵陣、持此袈裟少分、恭敬
尊重、當得解脱。

---

43 **Chan Master Dazhi of Baizhang** (*Hyakujō Daichi zenji* 百丈大智禪師): I.e., Baizhang Huaihai 百丈懷海 (749-814). The source of this saying, given in Japanese, is unknown.

DŌGEN'S *SHŌBŌGENZŌ* VOLUME III

The Buddha said,[44]

If there is a living being who, having entered my dharma, either commits grave offenses or sinks into false views, but who for even a single thought reverently respects the saṃghāti robe, then all the other buddhas and I, [for those] in the three vehicles, will certainly confer a prediction that this person will become a buddha. Whether devas, dragons, humans, or demons, if they can venerate the merit of even a small part of this person's kāṣāya, they will attain non-regression in the three vehicles.[45] If there are demons and spirits or other living beings who can obtain even so much as four inches of the kāṣāya, they will have plenty to eat and drink. If there are living beings opposing one another, about to fall into false views, if they think on the power of the kāṣāya and rely on the power of the kāṣāya, they will quickly give rise to the thought of compassion and gain purity. If there people in the military, if they keep even a small part of this kāṣāya, respecting and valuing it, they will attain liberation.

[32:26]

しかあればしりぬ、袈裟の功徳、それ無上不可思議なり。これを信受護持するところに、かならず得授記あるべし、得不退あるべし。ただ釋迦牟尼佛のみにあらず、一切諸佛、またかくのごとく宣説しましますなり。

---

44 **The Buddha said** (*Butsu gon* 佛言): Abbreviated version of a vow, found in the *Karuṇā-puṇḍarīka-sūtra* (*Peihua jing* 悲華經, T.157.3:220a10-b6), that Dōgen also quotes in his "Shōbōgenzō kesa kudoku" 正法眼藏袈裟功徳. The version here, given in Chinese, is akin to (though not identical with) summaries of the sūtra passage found in the *Shishi yaolan* 釋氏要覽, by Daocheng 道誠 (T.2127.54:269c21-28), and the *Lüzong xinxue mingju* 律宗新學名句, by Weixian 惟顯 (ZZ.105:638b8-13); the latter reads:

袈裟五種功徳(悲華經)。一入我法中、或犯重邪見、於一念中、敬心尊重、必於三乘授記。二天龍人鬼、若能恭敬此人袈裟少分、即得三乘不退。三若有鬼神諸人、得袈裟乃至四寸、飲食充足。四若衆生共相違反、念袈裟力、尋生悲心。五若在兵陣、持此少分恭敬尊重、當得解脱。

The five kinds of merit of the *kāṣāya* (from the *Peihua jing*): (1) If there are those who, having entered my dharma, have a grave offense or false view, but who for even a single thought reverently respect it, then [for those] in the three vehicles, I will certainly confer a prediction. (2) If there are devas, dragons, humans, or demons who can venerate even a small part of this person's *kāṣāya*, then they will attain non-regression in the three vehicles. (3) If there are demons, spirits, or humans who obtain even so much as four inches of the *kāṣāya*, they will have plenty to eat and drink. (4) If there are living beings opposing one another who think on the power of the *kāṣāya*, they will quickly give rise to the thought of compassion. (5) If there are those in the military who keep even a small part of it, respecting and valuing it, they will attain liberation.

45 **non-regression in the three vehicles** (*sanjō futai futen* 三乘不退不轉): I.e., will not backslide on the spiritual paths of *śrāvaka*, *pratyeka-buddha*, and bodhisattva; see Supplementary Notes, s.v. "Three vehicles."

32. Transmitting the Robe *Den'e* 傳衣

Thus, we know that the merit of the *kāṣāya* is unsurpassed, is inconceivable. Where we believe and preserve it, we shall surely get a prediction, surely attain non-regression. Not only Buddha Śākyamuni but all the buddhas explain it like this.

[32:27] {1:361}

しるべし、ただ諸佛の體相、すなはち袈裟なり。かるがゆえに、佛言、當
堕惡道者、厭惡僧伽梨。

We should recognize that the substance and characteristics of the buddhas are just this *kāṣāya*. That is why the Buddha said, "*Those who will fall into the evil paths, hate the saṃghāti.*"[46]

[32:28]

しかあればすなはち、袈裟を見聞せんところに、厭惡の念おこらんには、
當堕惡道のわがみなるべし、と悲心を生ずべきなり、慚愧懺悔すべきな
り。

Thus, when hateful thoughts arise upon our seeing or hearing of the *kāṣāya*, we should produce the thought of remorse that we "*will fall into the evil paths*" and should feel ashamed and repent.

[32:29]

いはんや釋迦牟尼佛、はじめて王宮をいでて、山にいらんとせし時、樹
神、ちなみに僧伽梨衣一條を擧して、釋迦牟尼佛にまうす、この衣を頂戴
すれば、もろもろの魔嬈をまぬかるるなり。ときに釋迦牟尼佛、この衣を
うけて、頂戴して十二年をふるに、しばらくもおかずといふ。これ阿含經
等の説なり。

Not to mention Buddha Śākyamuni. It is said that, on the occasion when he first left the royal palace and was entering the mountains, a tree spirit held up a *saṃghāti* robe and said to Buddha Śākyamuni, "By placing this robe on your head, you will avoid every sort of confusion caused by Māra." Whereupon, Buddha Śākyamuni received the robe, placed it on his head, and spent twelve years without ever setting it aside even for a moment. This is an account in the *āgama* sūtras.[47]

---

46   **The Buddha said** (*butsu gon* 佛言): The source is unknown. The "evil paths" (*akudō* 惡道) refers to the three lower realms of rebirth: animal, hungry ghost, and hell-being; see Supplementary Notes, s.v. "Six paths."

47   **This is an account in the *āgama* sūtras** (*kore agon gyō tō no setsu nari* こ
れ阿含經等の説なり): Just what sūtra Dōgen may have had in mind here is uncertain. His account, given in Japanese, is likely based on a passage in the seventh-century encyclopedia *Fayuan zhulin* 法苑珠林 (T.2122.53:560a26ff). The reference to "twelve years" reflects the tradition, found, e.g., in the *Jingde chuandeng lu* 景德傳燈
錄 (T.2076.51:205b12-24), that Prince Siddhārtha spent six years in ascetic practice and another six in meditation; the *Fayuan zhulin* version gives the standard "six years of ascetic practice" (*rokunen kugyō* 六年苦行).

[32:30]

あるいはいふ、袈裟はこれ吉祥服なり。これを服用するもの、かならず勝位にいたる。おほよそ世界に、この僧伽梨衣の現前せざる時節なきなり。一時の現前は、長劫中事なり、長劫中事は、一時來なり。袈裟を得するは、佛標幟を得するなり。このゆえに、諸佛如來の、袈裟を受持せざる、いまだあらず。袈裟を受持せしともがらの、作佛せざる、あらざるなり。

It is also said that the *kāṣāya* is a "vestment of felicity"; those who wear it invariably reach high position.[48] More generally, there is never a time when this *saṃghāti* robe does not appear in the world. Its appearance at one time is an event of long kalpas; the event of long kalpas comes at one time.[49] To obtain a *kāṣāya* is to obtain the banner of the buddhas. Therefore, there has never been a case in which the buddhas, the tathāgatas, failed to receive and keep the *kāṣāya*; and there are none among those who have received and kept the *kāṣāya* who do not become buddhas.

[32:31]

搭袈裟法

偏袒右肩は常途の法なり。通兩肩搭の法もあり。兩端ともに左の臂肩にかさねかくるに、前頭を表面にかさね、 前頭を裏面にかさね、後頭を表面にかさね、 後頭を裏面にかさぬること、佛威儀の一時あり。この儀は、諸聲聞衆の見聞し、相傳するところにあらず、諸阿笈摩教の經典に、もらしとくにあらず。おほよそ佛道に袈裟を搭する威儀は、現前せる傳正法の祖師、かならず受持せるところなり。受持、かならずこの祖師に受持すべし。

Procedure for donning the *kāṣāya*:

Baring the right shoulder is the usual procedure.[50] There is also a procedure for wearing it over both shoulders. When doubling it up, so that the two ends are both over the left arm and shoulder, the front edge is folded over the front surface; or the front edge is folded over the back surface; or the back edge is folded over the front surface; or the back edge is folded over the back surface — depending on the occasion, this is the deportment of a buddha. These forms are not seen or heard of, are not something transmitted by, communities of *śrāvakas*; they are omitted and not explained in the scriptures that contain the teachings of the *āgamas*. More generally, the deportment for donning the *kāṣāya* in the

---

48 **"vestment of felicity"** (*kichijō fuku* 吉祥服): Or "auspicious vestment"; the expression does not, in fact, seem to be a common one, and Dōgen's source for it is unclear.

49 **an event of long kalpas** (*chōgōchū ji* 長劫中事): An unusual expression, here probably meaning "a thing that lasts forever" (rather than "a thing extremely rare").

50 **Baring the right shoulder** (*hendan uken* 偏袒右肩): A fixed expression for the standard practice of draping the *kāṣāya* over the left shoulder only.

32. Transmitting the Robe *Den'e* 傳衣

45

way of the buddhas is something always received and kept by the ancestral masters, right before us, who transmit the true dharma. In receiving and keeping it, we should always receive and keep it with these ancestral masters.[51]

[32:32] {1:362}

佛祖正傳の袈裟は、これすなはち佛佛正傳みだりにあらず。先佛後佛の袈裟なり、古佛新佛の袈裟なり。道を化し、佛を化す。過去を化し、現在を化し、未來を化するに、過去より現在に正傳し、現在より未來に正傳し、現在より過去に正傳し、過去より過去に正傳し、現在より現在に正傳し、未來より未來に正傳し、未來より現在に正傳し、未來より過去に正傳して、唯佛與佛の正傳なり。

The *kāṣāya* directly transmitted by the buddhas and ancestors — this is directly transmitted by buddha after buddha without disruption. It is the *kāṣāya* of prior buddhas and later buddhas; it is the *kāṣāya* of old buddhas and new buddhas. It converts the way; it converts the buddhas.[52] In converting the past, converting the present, and converting the future, it is the direct transmission of *"only buddhas with buddhas"* that is directly transmitted from past to present, directly transmitted from present to future, directly transmitted from present to past, directly transmitted from past to past, directly transmitted from present to present, directly transmitted from future to future, directly transmitted from future to present, directly transmitted from future to past.

[32:33]

このゆえに、祖師西來よりこのかた、大唐より大宋にいたる數百歳のあひだ、講經の達者、おのれが業を見徹せるものおほく、教家・律教等のともがら、佛法にいるとき、從來舊巢の弊衣なる袈裟を抛却して、佛道正傳の袈裟を正受するなり。かの因縁、すなはち傳・廣・續・普燈等の錄につらなれり。教・律局量の小見を解脱して、佛祖正傳の大道をたふとみし、みな佛祖となれり。いまの人も、むかしの祖師をまなぶべし。

For this reason, from the time that the Ancestral Master came from the west, for several hundred years from the Great Tang to the Great Song, there were many adepts in lecturing on the sūtras who saw into their own deeds, those of the teaching houses and vinaya teachings who, when

---

51 **we should always receive and keep it with these ancestral masters** (*juji, kanarazu kono soshi ni juji su beshi* 受持、かならずこの祖師に受持すべし): The exact sense is uncertain. The antecedent of "it" here could be either the *kāṣāya* or the "deportment" of the previous sentence, while the particle *ni* に, translated "with" here, might also be rendered "from," "by," "in accordance with," etc.

52 **It converts the way; it converts the buddhas** (*dō o keshi, butsu o kesu* 道を化し、佛を化す): The verb *ke* 化 ("to change," "to transform," etc.) is usually understood here as *kyōke* 教化 ("to teach," "to guide," "to convert," etc.); hence, the claim seems to be that the robe teaches the dharma to Buddhism and to the buddhas.

46 DŌGEN'S *SHŌBŌGENZŌ* VOLUME III

they entered the buddha dharma, abandoned the *kāṣāya* of the tattered robe of their previous old nest and properly received the *kāṣāya* directly transmitted in the way of the buddhas.[53] Their cases appear one after another in the records of the *Chuan, Guang, Xu, Pudeng,* and the like.[54] Liberating themselves from the small views confined to the teachings and vinaya, they esteemed the great way directly transmitted by the buddhas and ancestors, and all became buddhas and ancestors. People now as well should learn from the ancestral masters of old.

[32:34]
袈裟を受持すべくは、正傳の袈裟を正傳すべし、信受すべし。僞作の袈裟を受持すべからず。その正傳の袈裟といふは、いま少林・曹溪より正傳せるは、これ如來より嫡嫡相承すること、一代も虧闕せざるところなり。このゆえに、道業まさしく稟受し、佛衣したしく手にいれるによりてなり。

If we are to receive and keep the *kāṣāya*, we should directly transmit and believe in the directly transmitted *kāṣāya*; we should not receive and keep a counterfeit *kāṣāya*. The "directly transmitted *kāṣāya*" means the present one that was directly transmitted from Shaolin and Caoxi, the inheritance of which by successor after successor from the Tathāgata has not lapsed for even a single generation.[55] For this reason, it depends on our truly accepting the work of the way and personally laying hands on the buddha robe.

---

53 **the Ancestral Master came from the west** (*soshi seirai* 祖師西來): I.e., Bodhidharma arrived in China. See Supplementary Notes, s.v. "Coming from the west."

the teaching houses and vinaya teachings (*kyōke ritsukyō* 教家・律教): In Dōgen's day, elite, state-supported Buddhist monasteries in China were commonly divided into three types, according to the lineages of their abbots: Teachings (*jiao* 教), Vinaya (*lü* 律), and Zen (*chan* 禪).

the tattered robe of their previous old nest (*jūrai kyūsō no heie* 從來舊巣の弊衣): I.e., the ragged or improper (*hei* 弊) robes of their previous Buddhist commitments. "Old nest" (*kyūsō* 舊巣) is likely a synonym for the more common "old den" (*kyūka* 舊窠), regularly used for old or habitual ways of thinking; here, perhaps, "former sectarian affiliations."

54 **records of the *Chuan, Guang, Xu, Pudeng,* and the like** (*Den Kō Zoku Futō tō no roku* 傳・廣・續・普燈等の錄): I.e., the major collections of Chan hagiography: the *Jingde chuandeng lu* 景德傳燈錄 (compiled in 1004), *Tiansheng guangdeng lu* 天聖廣燈錄 (1036), *Jianzhong Jingguo xudeng lu* 建中靖國續燈錄 (1101), and *Jiatai pudeng lu* 嘉泰普燈錄 (1204).

55 **directly transmitted from Shaolin and Caoxi** (*Shōrin Sōkei yori shōden seru* 少林・曹溪より正傳せる): I.e., passed down in the lineage descended from Bodhidharma and the Sixth Ancestor, Huineng 慧能.

32. Transmitting the Robe *Den'e* 傳衣

[32:35] {1:363}

佛道は佛道に正傳す、閑人の傳得に一任せざるなり。俗諺にいはく、千聞
は一見にしかず、千見は一經にしかず。これをもてかへりみれば、千見萬
聞たとひありとも、一得にしかず、佛衣正傳せるにしくべからざるなり。
正傳あるをうたがふべくは、正傳をゆめにもみざらんは、いよいようたが
ふべし。佛經を傳聞せんよりは、佛衣正傳せらんはしたしかるべし。千經
萬得ありとも、一證にしかじ。佛祖は證契なり、教・律の凡流にならふべ
からず。

The way of the buddhas is directly transmitted in the way of the buddhas; it is not left to dissemination by the idle. A secular adage says,
"Hearing it a thousand times is not like seeing it once; seeing it once
is not like experiencing it once."[56] If we consider this, even seeing it a
thousand times and hearing it ten thousand times are not like getting it
once; they could not be like having received the direct transmission of
the buddha robe. If one is to doubt that there is a direct transmission,
those who do not see the direct transmission even in their dreams will
surely be even more doubtful. Those who directly transmit the buddha
robe are surely more familiar with it than those who would spread ru-
mors about the sūtras of the buddhas. Even experiencing it a thousand
times and getting it ten thousand times are not like verifying it once. The
buddhas and ancestors are the verification and accordance; we should
not learn from the common followers of the teachings and precepts.

[32:36]

おほよそ祖門の袈裟の功德は、正傳まさしく相承せり、本樣まのあたりつ
たはれり。受持、あひ嗣法して、いまにたえず。正受せる人、みなこれ證
契傳法の祖師なり、十聖三賢にもすぐる。奉覲恭敬し、禮拜頂戴すべし。

In sum, regarding the merit of the *kāṣāya* of the ancestral tradition, its
direct transmission has truly been inherited, and its original appearance
has been handed down right before us. The receiving and keeping of it
are [passed down in] inheritance of the dharma and are not cut off even
now. The people who have directly received it are all ancestral masters
who verify the accord and transmit the dharma; they surpass even the
ten sages and three worthies.[57] We should attend and venerate them, pay
obeisance to them and hold them aloft.

---

56 **A secular adage says** (*zokugen ni iwaku* 俗諺にいはく): The usual form of the
Chinese proverb is simply "Hearing a thousand times is not like seeing once" (*qianwen
buru yijian* 千聞不如一見).

57 **ten sages and three worthies** (*jisshō sanken* 十聖三賢): Advanced bodhisattvas on
the ten stages (S. *bhūmi*) of the path and the three *bhadra* levels preceding them.

48 DŌGEN'S *SHŌBŌGENZŌ* VOLUME III

[32:37]

ひとたびこの佛衣正傳の道理、この身心に信受せられん、すなはち値佛の
兆なり、學佛の道なり。不堪受是法ならん、悲生なるべし。この袈裟を、
ひとたび身體におほはん、決定成菩提の護身符子なりと深肯すべし。一句
一偈を信心にそめつれば、長劫の光明にして、虧闕せずといふ。一法を身
心にそめん、亦復如是なるべし。

To believe even once, with this body and mind, the truth of the direct
transmission of the buddha robe is itself a sign of meeting the buddhas,
is the way of studying the buddhas. To be "*incapable of receiving this
dharma*" is surely to have a pitiful life.[58] We should deeply affirm that
this *kāṣāya*, once draped over our body, is a protective talisman that
makes one *certain to achieve bodhi*.[59] It is said that, if one line or one
gāthā is dyed into the believing mind, it stays bright for long kalpas
without dimming. To dye the body and mind with one dharma is surely
also like this.

[32:38]

かの心念も無所住なり。我有にかかはれずといへども、その功德、すでに
しかあり。身體も無所住なりといへども、しかあり。袈裟、無所從來な
り、亦無所去なり。我有にあらず、他有にあらずといへども、所持のとこ
ろに現住し、受持の人に加す。所得功德も、またかくのごとくなるべし。

That thought is without abode.[60] Although it has nothing to do with
the self's possessions, its merit is like this.[61] Although the body, too, is
without abode, it is like this. The *kāṣāya* is "*without any place whence
it comes*," and is "*without any place where it goes*."[62] Although it is not

---

58 **"incapable of receiving this dharma"** (*fukan ju ze hō* 不堪受是法): From the *Lotus
Sūtra* (*Miaofa lianhua jing* 妙法蓮華經, T.262.9:7c17), said by Buddha Śākyamuni of
the five thousand followers who withdrew from his assembly before he preached the
sūtra:

斯人尟福德、不堪受是法。

These people are lacking in merit and incapable of receiving this dharma.

59   **certain to achieve bodhi** (*ketsujō jō bodai* 決定成菩提): A fixed phrase for the
bodhisattva assured of attaining buddhahood.

60   **That thought is without abode** (*kano shinnen mo mushojū nari* かの心念も無所
住なり): The antecedent of "that thought" is uncertain. Given its juxtaposition with the
following "body" (*shintai* 身體), it likely refers to the "believing mind" of the "body and
mind." "Without abode" is a standard term in Buddhist literature for the "emptiness" of
the referents of our conceptual thought.

61   **Although it has nothing to do with the self's possessions** (*gau ni kakawarezu to
iedomo* 我有にかかはれずといへども): The unexpressed grammatical subject is likely
"that thought": i.e., while our belief in the *kāṣāya* may not belong to us, the merit of such
belief is as described above.

62   **"without any place whence it comes," and is "without any place where it goes"**
(*mu sho jūrai nari, yaku mu sho ko nari* 無所從來なり、亦無所去なり): A fixed phrase

32. Transmitting the Robe *Den'e* 傳衣 49

the possession of the self, and not the possession of the other, it presently abides where it is maintained and empowers the person who receives and keeps it.[63] The merit obtained from it must also be like this.

[32:39] {1:364}

作袈裟の作は、凡聖等の作にあらず。その宗旨、十聖三賢の究盡するとこ
ろにあらず。宿殖の道種なきものは、一生二生、乃至無量生を經歴すとい
へども、袈裟をみず、袈裟をきかず、袈裟をしらず。いかにいはんや受持
することあらんや。ひとたび身體にふるる功德も、うるものあり、えざる
ものあるなり。すでにうるは、よろこぶべし、いまだえざらんは、ねがふ
べし、うべからざらんは、かなしむべし。

The "making" involved in making the *kāṣāya* is not the "making" of common people or sages.[64] Its essential point is not something exhaustively investigated by the ten sages and three worthies. Those without seeds of the way planted in former lives, though they pass through one lifetime or two lifetimes or even incalculable lifetimes, will not see the *kāṣāya*, will not hear of the *kāṣāya*, will not know of the *kāṣāya*. How much less could they receive and keep it? The merit of having it once touch one's body, some get and others do not. Those who have already got it should rejoice; those who have not yet got it should hope for it; those who cannot get it should grieve.

[32:40]

大千界の内外に、ただ佛祖の門下のみに佛衣つたはれること、人天ともに
見聞普知せり。佛衣の様子をあきらむることも、ただ祖門のみなり、餘門
にはしらず。これをしらざらんもの、自己をうらみざらんは愚人なり。た
とひ八萬四千の三昧陀羅尼をしれりとも、佛祖の衣法を正傳せず、袈裟の
正傳をあきらめざらんは、諸佛の正嫡なるべからず。

Inside and out of the great chiliocosm, that the buddha robe is passed down only in the tradition of the buddhas and ancestors is seen, heard,

---

in Mahāyāna literature, best known, perhaps, from the *Diamond Sūtra* (*Jingang bore boluomi jing* 金剛般若波羅蜜經, T.235.8:752b3-5), where it is used in a play on the term *tathāgata*:

> 須菩提、若有人言如來若來若去若坐若臥、是人不解我所説義。何以故。如來者
> 無所從來亦無所去、故名如來。

> Subhūti, if there were a person who said, "The tathāgata ['thus-come one'] may come or may go, may sit or may recline," that person would not understand the meaning of what I have preached. Why? Because the tathāgata has no place whence he comes and has no place where he goes; therefore, he is called the "thus-come one."

63　**empowers the person who receives and keeps it** (*juji no hito ni ka su* 受持の人
に加す): Taking *ka* 加 as *kabi* 加被 ("to empower," "to protect").

64　**common people or sages** (*bonshō* 凡聖): The two categories of Buddhists: ordinary people (*bonbu* 凡夫; S. *pṛthagjana*) and the advanced "nobles" (*shōja* 聖者; S. *ārya*).

50   DŌGEN'S *SHŌBŌGENZŌ* VOLUME III

and widely known by humans and devas alike.[65] The understanding of the design of the buddha robe, too, is limited to the tradition of the ancestors and is not known in other traditions. Those who do not know it and yet do not regret their state are fools. Even though they know eighty-four thousand samādhi and *dhāraṇī*, those who do not directly transmit the robe and dharma of the buddhas and ancestors, and are not clear about the direct transmission of the *kāṣāya*, are surely not direct descendants of the buddhas.[66]

[32:41]
他界の衆生は、いくばくかねがふらん、震旦國に正傳せるがごとく、佛衣まさしく正傳せんことを。おのれがくにに正傳せざること、はづるおもひあるらん、かなしむこころふかかるらん。

How the living beings of other realms must wish that the buddha robe had truly been directly transmitted to them, as it has been directly transmitted to the Land of Cīnasthāna. They must have feelings of shame and a deep sense of sorrow that it has not been directly transmitted to their land.

[32:42]
まことに如來世尊の衣法正傳せる法に値遇する、宿殖般若の大功德種子によるなり。いま末法惡時世は、おのれが正傳なきことをはぢず、正傳をそねむ魔儻おほし。おのれが所有・所住は、眞實のおのれにあらざるなり。ただ正傳を正傳せん、これ學佛の直道なり。

Truly, to encounter the dharma in which the robe and dharma of the Tathāgata, the World-Honored One, has been directly transmitted depends on seeds of great merit from the prajñā of former lives. In the present evil age at the end of the dharma, there are many minions of Māra who detest the direct transmission and feel no shame that they lack the direct transmission. Their possessions and abode are not their true self.[67] Only to transmit directly the direct transmission — this the direct path to the study of Buddhism.

---

65   **the great chiliocosm** (*dai sen kai* 大千界): A buddha's realm, consisting of one billion worlds.

66   **eighty-four thousand samādhi and *dhāraṇī*** (*hachiman shisen no zanmai darani* 八萬四千の三昧陀羅尼): The expression *zanmai darani* 三昧陀羅尼 occurs with some frequency in Buddhist literature as a pair; some readers take it here (and in the "Shōbōgenzō darani" 正法眼藏陀羅尼) as a tatpurusha referring to a particular type of *dhāraṇī*.

67   **Their possessions and abode are not their true self** (*onore ga sho'u shojū wa, shinjitsu no onore ni arazaru nari* おのれが所有・所住は、眞實のおのれにあらざるなり): Presumably, harking back to the "possessions" (*sho'u* 所有) and "abode" (*shojū* 所住) introduced in section 38, above. The translation takes this as a reference to the "minions of Māra," but it could also be read as a general statement.

32. Transmitting the Robe *Den'e* 傳衣

[32:43] {1:365}

おほよそしるべし、袈裟はこれ佛身なり、佛心なり。また解脱服と稱し、
福田衣と稱す。忍辱衣と稱し、無相衣と稱し、慈悲衣と稱し、如來衣と稱
し、阿耨多羅三藐三菩提衣と稱するなり。まさにかくのごとく受持すべ
し。

In sum, we should realize that the *kāṣāya* is the buddha body, is the buddha mind. It is also called the "vestment of liberation," called the "robe that is a field of merit."[68] It is called the "robe of forbearance," called the "formless robe," called the "robe of compassion," called the "robe of the Tathāgata," called the "robe of *anuttara-samyak-saṃbodhi*."[69] We should receive and keep it in this way.

[32:44]

いま現在大宋國の律學と名稱するともがら、聲聞酒に醉狂するによりて、
おのれが家門に、しらぬいえを傳來することを慚愧せず、うらみず、覺知
せず。西天より傳來せる袈裟、ひさしく漢唐につたはれることをあらため
て、小量にしたがふる、これ小見によりてしかあり、小見のはづべきな
り。もしいまなんぢが小量の衣をもちいるがごときは、佛威儀おほく虧闕
することあらん。佛儀を學傳せることのあまねからざるによりて、かくの
ごとくあり。

Today, in the present Land of the Great Song, those who call themselves "vinaya scholars," drunk on the wine of the *śrāvaka*, are not ashamed, do not regret, do not perceive, that, in their house, they have transmitted an ignorant tradition.[70] They revise the fact that the *kāṣāya* transmitted from Sindh in the West has long been handed down in the Han and Tang, and adopt a small size; this is due to their small view, and

---

68 **"vestment of liberation"** (*gedappuku* 解脱服); **"robe that is a field of merit"** (*fukuden e* 福田衣): Expressions found in the "Verse for Donning the *Kāṣāya*" (see above, Note 27).

69 **"robe of forbearance"** (*ninniku e* 忍辱衣): Likely reflecting a verse in the *Lotus Sūtra*; see Supplementary Notes, s.v. "Robe of the Tathāgata."

"formless robe" (*musō e* 無相衣): Again, likely drawn from the "Verse for Donning the *Kāṣāya*" (see above, Note 27).

"robe of compassion" (*jihi e* 慈悲衣): Included in a list of names for the *kāṣāya* given in the *Fozhi biqiu liuwu tu* 佛制比丘六物圖 (T.1900.45:899c21).

"robe of the Tathāgata" (*nyorai e* 如來衣): Probably reflecting the *Lotus Sūtra* verse cited above.

"robe of *anuttara-samyak-saṃbodhi*" (*anokutara sanmyaku sanbodai e* 阿耨多羅三藐三菩提衣): An expression seemingly of Dōgen's own invention.

70 **drunk on the wine of the *śrāvaka*** (*shōmon shu ni suikyō suru* 聲聞酒に醉狂する): I.e., under the influence of the Small Vehicle, a pejorative appearing elsewhere in the *Shōbōgenzō*. The particular "vinaya scholars" (*ritsugaku* 律學) in question here have not been identified.

52 DŌGEN'S *SHŌBŌGENZŌ* VOLUME III

they should be ashamed of this small view.[71] You who use small robes must have many deficiencies in the deportment of the buddhas. Things are like this because the study and transmission of the observances of the buddhas are not widespread.

[32:45]

如來の身心、ただ祖門に正傳して、かれらが家業に流散せざること、あきらかなり。もし萬一も佛儀をしらば、佛衣をやぶるべからず。文なほあきらめず、宗いまだきくべからず。

It is clear that the body and mind of the Tathāgata are directly transmitted only in the tradition of the ancestors and have not been disseminated in their family enterprise. If they knew even one among the myriad observances of the buddhas, they would not destroy the buddha robe. Unclear even of the words, they could not have heard their meaning.

[32:46]

又、ひとへに麤布を衣財にさだむ、ふかく佛法にそむく。ことに佛衣をやぶれり、佛弟子きるべきにあらず。ゆえはいかん。布見を擧して、袈裟をやぶれり。あはれむべし、小乘聲聞の見、まさに迂曲かなしむべきことを。なんぢが布見やぶれてのち、佛衣見成すべきなり。いふところの絹・布の用は、一佛二佛の道にあらず、諸佛の大法として、糞掃を上品清淨の衣財とせるなり。そのなかに、しばらく十種の糞掃をつらぬるに、絹類あり、布類あり、餘帛の類もあり。絹類の糞掃をとるべからざるか。もしかくのごとくならば、佛道に相違す。絹すでにきらはば、布またきらふべし。絹・布きらふべき、そのゆえなににかある。絹絲は殺生より生ぜるときらふ、おほきにわらふべきなり、布は生物の緣にあらざるか。情非情の情、いまだ凡情の情を解脱せず、いかでか佛袈裟をしらん。

Again, to stipulate only coarse plant fiber as the robe material seriously violates the buddha dharma. This has been particularly destructive of the buddha robe and is not something that disciples of the Buddha should wear. Why? By taking up views about plant fiber, they have destroyed the *kāṣāya*.[72] How pitiful, that the views of the *srāvaka* of the Small Vehicle are truly twisted. After your views on plant fiber are refuted, the buddha robe will appear. The use of silk or plant fiber I am speaking of

---

71 **the *kāṣāya* transmitted from Sindh in the West** (*Saiten yori denrai seru kesa* 西天より傳來せる袈裟): Since he claims that this robe was already handed down in the Han dynasty, when Buddhism was first introduced to China, Dōgen seems to be thinking here simply of an Indian-style *kāṣāya*, rather than the robe associated with the lineage of Bodhidharma.

adopt a small size (*shōryō ni shitagauru* 小量にしたがふる): Presumably, a criticism of the use of an abbreviated *kāṣāya* (*kara* 掛絡).

72 **views about plant fiber** (*fuken* 布見): Or "views about cloth." The term *fu* 布 can refer to cloth in general or, as in this discussion, to cloth made of plant fiber, as opposed to silk (or wool); the cloth in question can include cotton, linen, hemp, ramie, etc.

32. Transmitting the Robe *Den'e* 傳衣   53

is not a saying of one buddha or two buddhas: as the great dharma of
all the buddhas, discarded rags have been taken as high quality, pure
robe material.[73] Among them, if for the moment we list the ten types of
discarded rags, there are those of silk, there are those of plant fiber, there
are those of other fibers.[74] Should we not take the discarded rags of silk?
In that case, we contradict the words of the Buddha. If we were to hate
silk, we should also hate plant fiber. What reason do we have to hate
silk and plant fiber? To hate silk thread because it has been produced by
taking life is hugely laughable: is not plant fiber connected with living
things?[75] The sentience of sentient and insentient is still not liberated
from the sentiment of the commoner's sentiment.[76] How could it know
the buddha *kāṣāya*?

[32:47] {1:366}

又、化絲の説をきたして亂道することあり、又わらふべし。いづれか化に
あらざる。なんぢ、化をきくみみを信ずといへども、化をみる目をうたが
ふ。目にみみなし、耳に目なきがごとし。いまの耳目、いづれのところ
にかある。しばらくしるべし、糞掃をひろふなかに、絹ににたるあり、
布のごとくなるあらん。これをもちいんには、絹となづくべからず、布と
稱すべからず、まさに糞掃と稱すべし。糞掃なるがゆえに、糞掃にして絹

---

73   **discarded rags** (*funzō* 糞掃): Loose rendering of a term, meaning something like
"soiled sweepings," used for the Sanskrit *pāṃsukūla* ("dung heap"), to designate soiled
cloth taken from refuse and used to make the Buddhist robe.

74   **ten types of discarded rags** (*jisshu no funzō* 十種の糞掃): A list, found in the *Sifen
lü* 四分律, provided near the end of this chapter, section 66.

those of silk (*kenrui* 絹類); **those of plant fiber** (*furui* 布類); **those of other fibers** (*yo-
haku no rui* 餘帛の類): The list of ten types of rags does not, in fact, mention the fabrics
from which they are made. It is not clear what "other fibers" Dōgen may have in mind
here. The term *haku* 帛 (rendered "fiber" here) can refer both to fabrics in general and to
silk in particular; hence, it may here indicate various types of silk.

75   **To hate silk thread because it has been produced by taking life** (*kenshi wa
sesshō yori shōzeru to kirau* 絹絲は殺生より生ぜるときらふ): A standard Buddhist argument against the practice of wearing robes made from silk, the production of which
requires the stifling of the pupae of the silkworms inside their cocoons.

is not plant fiber connected with living things? (*fu wa shōbutsu no en ni arazaru ka* 布
は生物の縁にあらざるか): A tentative translation; the meaning of *en* 縁 ("connection,"
"condition," "occasion," etc.) here is unclear. Buddhists have no prohibition against
killing plants; so, it may be that Dōgen means simply that the agricultural process of
producing plant fiber involves the taking of life (for which reason, it is said, monks are
prohibited from farming).

76   **The sentience of sentient and insentient is still not liberated from the sentiment of the commoner's sentiment** (*jō hijō no jō, imada bonjō no jō o gedatsu sezu* 情
非情の情、いまだ凡情の情を解脱せず): A play on the term *jō* 情 ("feeling") used for
both "sentient" and "insentient" beings, and for the "sentiment," or "emotions," of the
ordinary person. Elsewhere in the *Shōbōgenzō*, Dōgen questions the distinction between
sentient and insentient beings.

にあらず、布にあらざるなり。たとひ人天の、糞掃と生長せるありとも、有情といふべからず、糞掃なるべし。たとひ松・菊の、糞掃となれるありとも、非情といふべからず、糞掃なるべし。糞掃の、絹・布にあらず、珠玉をはなれたる道理をしるとき、糞掃衣は現成するなり、糞掃衣にはむまれあふなり。絹・布の見、いまだ零落せざるは、いまだ糞掃を夢也未見なり。たとひ氎布を袈裟として一生受持すとも、布見をおぼえらんは、佛衣正傳にあらざるなり。

Again, there is the confused talk that introduces a theory of transformation thread; this is also laughable.[77] What is not a transformation? Although you trust the ears that hear of transformation, you doubt the eyes that see the transformation. It seems your eyes lack ears and your ears lack eyes. Where are your eyes and ears now?

Now, for a moment, let us recognize that, among the discarded rags that are picked up, there may be those that resemble silk and those that resemble plant fiber; [yet] when we use them, we should not call them "silk," nor should we call them "plant fiber": we should call them "discarded rags." Because they are discarded rags, they are discarded rags and neither silk nor plant fiber. If there were humans or devas that had grown into discarded rags, we would not say [the rags] were sentient: they would just be discarded rags; if there were pines or chrysanthemums that had become discarded rags, we would not say [the rags] were insentient: they would just be discarded rags. When we understand the principle that discarded rags are not silk or plant fiber and are beyond pearls and jade, then the robe of discarded rags appears and is born with the robe of discarded rags.[78] When views of silk or plant fiber have not yet dropped off, we have not seen the discarded rags even in our dreams. Even if we were to receive and keep coarse plant fiber as our *kāṣāya* for an entire lifetime, as long as we retain views about the cloth, it is not the direct transmission of the buddha robe.

---

77 **transformation thread** (*keshi* 化絲): Likely a reference to the notion that the silk thread of the Buddha's *kāṣāya* does not involve injury because it does not come from the mouth of the silkworm, but rather emerges as a "transformation," or "manifestation" (*ke* 化), or from the mouths of "transformation girls" (*kenyo* 化女; presumably, females born spontaneously, rather than from the womb) on another continent. (See *Fayuan zhulin* 法苑珠林, T.2122.53:561a16-23; b22-c8.)

78 **beyond pearls and jade** (*shugyoku o hanaretaru* 珠玉をはなれたる): Perhaps in the sense, not subject to our distinctions.

the robe of discarded rags appears and is born with the robe of discarded rags (*funzō e wa genjō suru nari, funzō e ni wa mumareau nari* 糞掃衣は現成するなり、糞掃衣にはむまれあふなり): A tentative translation, taking the sense to be that the robe appears and is born as a robe of discarded rags; others would read the grammatical subject of the second predicate to be an unexpressed "we" (who have understood the principle).

32. Transmitting the Robe *Den'e* 傳衣

[32:48] {1:367}

又、數般の袈裟のなかに、布袈裟あり、絹袈裟あり、皮袈裟あり。ともに諸佛のもちいるところ、佛衣佛功德なり。正傳せる宗旨あり、いまだ斷絕せず。しかるを、凡情いまだ解脱せざるともがら、佛法をかろくし、佛語を信ぜず、凡情に隨他去せんと擬する、附佛法の外道といふつべし、壞正法のたぐひなり。

Again, among the various types of *kāṣāya*, there are plant fiber *kāṣāya*, there are silk *kāṣāya*, there are skin *kāṣāya*.[79] They are all used by the buddhas and are buddha robes with the merits of the buddhas. They have an essential point that has been directly transmitted and even now is not cut off. Nevertheless, those who are not yet liberated from the sentiments of commoners, who make light of the buddha dharma, do not believe the word of the Buddha, and think to follow the sentiment of commoners, may surely be called followers of other paths attached to the buddha dharma, types who despoil the true dharma.

[32:49]

あるひはいふ、天人のおしへによりて佛衣をあらたむ、と。しかあらば、天佛をねがふべし、又天の流類となれるか。佛弟子は、佛法を天人のために宣説すべし、道を天人にとふべからず。あはれむべし、佛法の正傳なきは、かくのごとくなり。

Or they say that the buddha robe was altered according to the instructions of the devas.[80] If that were the case, they should seek deva buddhahood.[81] Or have they become followers of the devas? Disciples of the Buddha should expound the buddha dharma for the devas; they should not ask the devas about the way. How pitiful that those who lack the direct transmission of the buddha dharma are like this.

[32:50]

天衆の見と佛子の見と、大小はるかにことなることあれども、天くだりて法を佛子にとぶらふ。そのゆえは、佛見と天見と、はるかにことなるがゆえなり。律家聲聞の小見、すててまなぶことなかれ、小乘なりとしるべし。

Although the view of the devas and the view of the children of the Buddha are vastly different in scope, the devas descend and ask the children of the Buddha about the dharma. The reason is that the view of the

---

79 **skin *kāṣāya*** (*hi gesa* 皮袈裟): The term *hi* 皮 ("skin") may refer to hide, bark, etc.

80 **according to the instructions of the devas** (*tennin no oshie ni yorite* 天人のおしへによりて): Perhaps alluding to the tradition (found in the *Lüxiang gantong zhuan* 律相感通傳, T.1898) that the vinaya master Daoxuan 道宣 (596-667) was aided in his writings on the robe by heavenly beings.

81 **deva buddhahood** (*ten butsu* 天佛): A sarcastic neologism, presumably meaning a buddha who is a god (or, perhaps, a god who is a buddha).

56 DŌGEN'S *SHŌBŌGENZŌ* VOLUME III

buddhas and the view of the devas are vastly different. Throw away the small views of the *śrāvaka* vinaya masters and do not study them. We should realize that they are the Small Vehicle.

[32:51]

佛言、殺父殺母は懺悔しつべし、謗法は懺悔すべからず。

The Buddha said, "Patricide and matricide can be repented; denigrating the dharma cannot be repented."[82]

[32:52]

おほよそ、小見狐疑の道は、佛本意にあらず。佛法の大道は、小乘、およぶところなきなり。諸佛の、大戒を正傳すること、付法藏の祖道のほかには、ありとしれるものなし。

In sum, the words of "*small views and vulpine suspicions*" are not the original intention of the Buddha.[83] The great way of the buddha dharma is not something the Small Vehicle can reach. No one has ever known of a direct transmission of the great precepts of the buddhas apart from the way of the ancestors who bequeath the treasury of the dharma.

[32:53]

むかし黄梅の夜半に、佛の衣法、すでに六祖の頂上に正傳す。まことにこれ、傳法傳衣の正傳なり、五祖の、人をしるによりてなり。四果・三賢のやから、および十聖等のたぐひ、教家の論師・經師等のたぐひは、神秀にさづくべし、六祖に正傳すべからず。しかあれども、佛祖の佛祖を選する、凡聖路を超越するがゆえに、六祖すでに六祖となれるなり。しるべし、佛祖嫡嫡の知人・知己の道理、なほざりに測量すべきところにあらざるなり。

Long ago, in the middle of the night on Huangmei, the robe and dharma of the Buddha were directly transmitted atop the head of the Sixth Ancestor. Truly, this was the direct transmission of the transmission of the dharma and transmission of the robe; it depended on the Fifth Ancestor's knowing the person. Those of the four fruits or the three worthies, as well as types like the ten sages, types like the treatise masters and sūtra masters of the teaching houses, and the like — they would

---

82 **The Buddha said** (*butsu gon* 佛言): The source of this saying, given here in Japanese, is uncertain.

83 **the words of "small views and vulpine suspicions"** (*shōken kogi no dō* 小見狐疑の道): From a line in the *Xinxin ming* 信心銘, attributed to the Third Ancestor, Sengcan 僧璨 (d. 606) (T.2010.48:376c11-12):

大道體寛、無易無難。小見狐疑、轉急轉遲。

The great way, its substance vast,
With nothing easy, nothing hard;
Small views and vulpine suspicions,
Ever faster, ever slower.

32. Transmitting the Robe *Den'e* 傳衣　57

have conferred them on Shenxiu and would not have directly transmitted them to the Sixth Ancestor.[84] However, because the selection of the buddhas and ancestors by the buddhas and ancestors transcends the paths of the common person and the sage, the Sixth Ancestor did become the Sixth Ancestor. We should realize that the principle that successor after successor of buddhas and ancestors knows the person and knows the self is not something to be casually measured.

[32:54]

のちに、ある僧、すなはち六祖にとふ、黄梅の夜半の傳衣、これ布なりとやせん、絹なりとやせん、帛なりとやせん、畢竟じてこれなにものとかせん。六祖いはく、これ布にあらず、これ絹にあらず、これ帛にあらず。

Later, a monk asked the Sixth Ancestor, "The robe transmitted in the middle of the night on Huangmei — do we take it as plant fiber, or take it as thick silk, or take it as fine silk?[85] After all, what do we take it as?"

The Sixth Ancestor said, "It wasn't plant fiber; it wasn't thick silk; it wasn't fine silk."

[32:55]

曹溪高祖の道、かくのごとし。しるべし、佛衣は絹にあらず、布にあらず、屈眴にあらざるなり。しかあるを、いたづらに絹と認じ、布と認じ、屈眴と認ずるは、謗佛法のたぐひなり、いかにして佛裟裟をしらん。いはんや善來得戒の機縁あり、かれらが所得の裟裟、さらに絹・布の論にあらざるは、佛道の佛訓なり。

Such were the words of the Eminent Ancestor of Caoxi. We should realize that the buddha robe is not thick silk, not plant fiber, not fine cotton.[86] Those who nevertheless regard it as thick silk, regard it as plant fiber, or regard it as fine cotton, are types who slander the buddha dharma; how could they know the buddha *kāṣāya*? Not to mention those with the opportunity *to obtain the precepts with the welcome*; that the *kāṣāya* they receive is not a matter of silk or plant fiber is the buddha instruction on the way of the buddhas.[87]

84　**four fruits** (*shika* 四果); **three worthies** (*sanken* 三賢); **ten sages** (*jisshō* 十聖): I.e., those still on the Buddhist path. The "four fruits" refers to the four stages on the path of the *śrāvaka*; the "three worthies and ten sages" refer to the stages of the bodhisatttva path.

they would have conferred them on Shenxiu (*Jinshū ni sazuku beshi* 神秀にさづくべし): I.e, they would have chosen Hongren's accomplished disciple Shenxiu 神秀 (d. 706) to inherit the robe and dharma.

85　**a monk** (*aru sō* ある僧): The source of this conversation, given in Japanese, is unknown.

86　**fine cotton** (*kutsujun* 屈眴): Reference to the tradition that the robe transmitted by Bodhidharma was made of a fabric called *qushun* 屈眴, said to be made from Indian cotton. (See, e.g., *Jingde chuandeng lu* 景德傳燈録, T.2076.51:236c13.)

87　**those with the opportunity to obtain the precepts with the welcome** (*zenrai tok-*

58 DŌGEN'S *SHŌBŌGENZŌ* VOLUME III

[32:56]

また商那和修が衣は、在家の時は俗服なり、出家すれば袈裟となる。この道理、しづかに思量功夫すべし。見聞せざるがごとくしてさしをくべきにあらず。いはんや佛佛祖祖正傳しきたれる宗旨あり。文字かぞふるたぐひ、覺知すべからず、測量すべからず。まことに佛道の千變萬化、いかでか庸流の境界ならん。三昧あり、陀羅尼あり。算砂のともがら、衣裏の寶珠をみるべからず。

Again, the robe of Śaṇavāsa was a secular garment when he was a householder and became a *kāṣāya* when he left home.[88] We should quietly make concentrated effort to think about the truth behind this. We should not set it aside as if we had never seen or heard of it. How much more [the fact that] there is an essential point that has been directly transmitted by buddha after buddha and ancestor after ancestor. The types who count words and letters could not perceive it, could not take its measure. Indeed, how could the thousand changes and a myriad transformations of the way of the buddhas be within the realm of the mediocre. They have samādhi, and they have *dhāraṇī*; but the bunch that counts sand cannot be expected to see the precious jewel in their robes.[89]

---

kai no kien 善來得戒の機緣): The expression "obtain the precepts with the welcome" refers to the tradition that, at the time of Buddha Śākyamuni, disciples were considered to have been inducted into the order by the Buddha's act of welcoming them. The term *kien* 機緣, taken here to mean "karmic circumstances," or "opportunity," is interpreted by some readers as "records," or "episodes." There is a common trope in the early Buddhist literature that reads,

佛言、善來比丘、鬚髮自落、袈裟著身。

When the Buddha said, "Welcome, bhikṣu," his beard and hair fell off by themselves, and a *kāṣāya* cloaked his body.

In his "Shōbōgenzō senmen" 正法眼藏洗面 and "Shukke" 出家 chapters, Dōgen cites this trope in the case of Mahākāśyapa (from *Jingde chuandeng lu* 景德傳燈錄, T.2076.51:206a2-3).

88 **the robe of Śaṇavāsa** (*Shōnawashu ga e* 商那和修が衣): Reference to the legend, recorded in Xuanzang's 玄奘 *Datang xiyu ji* 大唐西域記 (T.2087.51:873b28-c5), that the Third Ancestor, Ānanda's disciple Śaṇavāsa, was born wearing a miraculous robe, which enlarged as he grew, became a monk's habit when he left home, and a nine-panel *saṃghāṭī* robe when he took the full precepts.

89 **They have samādhi, and they have *dhāraṇī*** (*zanmai ari, darani ari* 三昧あり、陀羅尼あり): Taking these as concessive: "[the mediocre] may have their samādhi and their *dhāraṇī*." It is also possible to read this, "there are samādhis and there are *dhāraṇīs* [beyond the realm of the mediocre]."

the precious jewel in their robes (*eri no hōjū* 衣裏の寶珠): Play with the famous parable in the *Lotus Sūtra* of the man who is unaware that his friend had sewn a priceless jewel into the lining of his robe; see Supplementary Notes, s.v. "Jewel in the robe." In the sūtra, the robe in question is not a monk's habit, and the jewel represents the man's unrecognized potential for buddhahood, not the unappreciated significance of the *kāṣāya*.

bunch that counts sand (*sansha no tomogara* 算砂のともがら): I.e., those obsessed

32. Transmitting the Robe *Den'e* 傳衣

[32:57]

いま佛祖正傳せる袈裟の體・色・量を、諸佛の袈裟の正本とすべし。その例、すでに西天東地、古往今來ひさしきなり。正邪を分別せし人、すでに超證しき。祖道のほかに袈裟を稱するありとも、いまだ枝葉とゆるす本祖あらず。いかでか善根の種子をきざささん、いはんや果實あらんや。

The material, color, and dimensions of the present *kāṣāya* directly transmitted by the buddhas and ancestors should be considered the true original for the *kāṣāya* of the buddhas. Their precedent is age-old, from ancient times to the present, in Sindh in the West and the Land of the East. People who discriminated the true and false fully realized this.[90] While there may be those outside of the way of the ancestors who claim the *kāṣāya*, there has never been an original ancestor who acknowledged them as branches and leaves.[91] How could any seeds of good roots ever sprout from them, let alone ever bear fruit?

[32:58] {1:369}

われらいま、曠劫以來、いまだあはざる佛法を見聞するのみにあらず、佛衣を見聞し、佛衣を學習し、佛衣を受持することえたり。すなはちこれ、まさしく佛を見たてまつるなり。佛音聲をきく、佛光明をはなつ、佛受用を受用す、佛心を單傳するなり、得佛髓なり。

Now, not only have we seen and heard the buddha dharma that we had yet to meet for vast kalpas, but we have been able to see and hear about the buddha robe, to study the buddha robe, to receive and keep the buddha robe. This is precisely to look upon the Buddha; it is to hear the voice of the Buddha, to emit the radiance of the Buddha, to enjoy what the Buddha enjoys; it is uniquely to transmit the buddha mind; it is to get the buddha marrow.

傳衣
Transmitting the Robe[92]

---

with the details, what we might call "spiritual bean counters"; see Supplementary Notes, s.v. "Counting sand."

90 **People who discriminated the true and false fully realized this** (*shōja o funbetsu seshi hito, sude ni chōshō shiki* 正邪を分別せし人、すでに超證しき): Probably meaning that those who knew right from wrong recognized this claim. The expression *chōshō* 超證 is often read as a verb-object compound, "to transcend verification"; but here, it would seem more likely to have the sense "abruptly verify," or "immediately realize."

91 **an original ancestor who acknowledged them as branches and leaves** (*shiyō to yurusu honso* 枝葉とゆるす本祖): I.e., accepted that they might be offshoots of the "true original" (*shōhon* 正本). The English "true original" for *shōhon* 正本 and "original ancestor" for *honso* 本祖 lose Dōgen's play here with the botanical terms "root" (*hon* 本) and "branches and leaves" — a play that continues in the next sentence, with "seeds," "roots," and "fruit."

92 **Transmitting the Robe** (*den'e* 傳衣): This repetition of the title would normally occur at the end of the chapter. Its occurrence here suggests that some version of the

60 DŌGEN'S *SHŌBŌGENZŌ* VOLUME III

[32:59]

予、在宋のそのかみ、長連牀に功夫せしとき、齊肩の隣單をみるに、毎曉
の開靜のとき、袈裟をささげて頂上に安置し、合掌恭敬しき。一偈を默誦
す。ときに予、未曾見のおもひをなし、歡喜、みにあまり、感涙、ひそか
におちて襟をうるほす。阿含經を披閲せしとき、頂戴袈裟文をみるといへ
ども、不分曉なり。いまは、まのあたりみる。ちなみにおもはく、あはれ
むべし、郷土にありしには、おしふる師匠なし、かたる善友にあはず、い
くばくかいたづらにすぐる光陰をおしまざる、かなしまざらめやは。い
ま、これを見聞す、宿善よろこぶべし。もしいたづらに本國の諸寺に交肩
せば、いかでか、まさしく佛衣を著せる僧寶と、隣肩なることをえん。悲
喜、ひとかたにあらず、感涙千萬行。

When I was in the Song, making concentrated effort on the long platform, I observed that, every morning at the breaking of silence, my
neighbors seated shoulder to shoulder on the platform would take up the
kāṣāya, place it on their heads, and join their palms in veneration.[93] They
would silently recite a gāthā. At the time, realizing this was something
I had never seen before, I was overcome with joy, and tears of gratitude
secretly fell, moistening my lapels. Although, when I had previously pe-
rused the *āgama* sūtras, I had seen the text on placing the *kāṣāya* on the
head, it had not been clear to me.[94] Now, I saw it right before my very
eyes. Whereupon, I thought, "What a pity, that when I was in my native
land, I had no master to teach me this and met no wise friend to tell me
about it. How could I not regret, not lament, so many years and months
spent in vain? Now I have seen and heard it and should be happy for the
good karma of former lives. Had I been futilely rubbing shoulders with
those in the monasteries of my original land, how could I ever have been
able to be shoulder to shoulder with the saṃgha treasure that truly wore

---

text may originally have ended with section 58, the content of which does indeed seem
to represent a conclusion. The Honzan edition omits this title and proceeds directly to
our section 64, shifting our sections 59-63 to the end of the chapter, just preceding the
colophon (where similar material is to be found in the "Kesa kudoku" 袈裟功德 chapter).

93 **When I was in the Song** (*yo, zaisō no sono kami* 予、在宋のそのかみ): Dōgen was
in Song-dynasty China 1223-1227.

long platform (*chōrenjō* 長連牀): The extended daises in the saṃgha hall (*sōdō* 僧堂)
on which monks of the great assembly (*daishu* 大衆) sat in meditation, chanted sūtras in
prayer services, took their meals, and slept at night. Reference to the author's training at
the Jingde Monastery on Mount Tiantong 天童山景德寺.

breaking of silence (*kaijō* 開靜): In this case, the wake-up signal in the saṃgha hall. The
term can also refer to the signal for the end of a meditation session.

94 **text on placing the *kāṣāya* on the head** (*chōdai kesa mon* 頂戴袈裟文): What passage Dōgen is referring to here is unclear; the instructions given at the end of this chapter
on placing the robe on the head and reciting a verse do not seem to occur in the *āgama*
literature.

32. Transmitting the Robe *Den'e* 傳衣

the buddha robe?"[95] My sadness and joy were extraordinary, and my tears of gratitude flowed by the thousands and tens of thousands.

[32:60] {1:370}
ときにひそかに發願す、いかにしてかわれ不肖なりといふとも、佛法の正嫡を正傳して、郷土の衆生をあはれむに、佛佛正傳の衣法を見聞せしめん。

At that time, I privately made a vow that, however inadequate I might be, I would somehow directly transmit the true succession of the buddha dharma and, out of pity for the living beings in my native land, would let them see and hear of the robe and dharma directly transmitted by buddha after buddha.

[32:61]
かのときの正信、ひそかに相資することあらば、心願むなしかるべからず。いま受持袈裟の佛子、かならず日夜に頂戴する勤修をはげむべし、實功德なるべし。一句一偈を見聞することは、若樹・若石の因緣もあるべし。袈裟正傳の功德は、十方に難遇ならん。

My true belief at the time was that, if there were some secret assistance, my vow would not be in vain.[96] Now, children of the Buddha who receive and keep the *kāṣāya* should without fail exert themselves day and night in the practice of placing it on their heads; this is surely real merit. In seeing and hearing one line or one *gāthā*, there is surely a case of "whether on trees or on rocks"; the merit of the direct transmission of the *kāṣāya* is hard to encounter anywhere in the ten directions.[97]

[32:62]
大宋嘉定十七年癸未冬十月中、三韓の僧二人ありて、慶元府にきたれり。一人はいはく智玄、一人は景雲。この二人、ともにしきりに佛經の義をいひ、あまさへ文學の士なり。しかあれども、袈裟なし、鉢盂なし、俗人のごとし。あはれむべし、比丘形なりといへども、比丘法なきこと、小國邊地のゆえなるべし。我朝の比丘形のともがら、他國にゆかんとき、ただかの二僧のごとくならん。

---

95 **to be shoulder to shoulder with the saṃgha treasure** (*sōbō to, rinken naru* 僧寶 と、隣肩なる): I.e., sit next to members of the saṃgha, who represent one of the three treasures. Dōgen is playing in this sentence with "shoulder" (*ken* 肩).

96 **if there were some secret assistance** (*hisoka ni sōshi suru koto araba* ひそかに相資することあらば): Presumably meaning some help from the buddhas and ancestors or, perhaps, from other spiritual forces.

97 **a case of "whether on trees or on rocks"** (*nyaku ju nyaku seki no innen* 若樹・若石の因緣): Allusion to a well-known story, found in the *Nirvāṇa Sūtra*, of the "boy of the Himalayas" (Śākyamuni in a previous life) who wrote a Buddhist teaching on trees and rocks; see Supplementary Notes, s.v. "Whether on trees or on rocks." Dōgen's point here seems to be that, whereas one can encounter the Buddhist teachings everywhere, the merit of transmitting the robe is exceedingly rare.

62   DŌGEN'S *SHŌBŌGENZŌ* VOLUME III

In the winter of the junior water year of the sheep, the seventeenth year of the Jiading era of the Great Song, during the tenth month, there were two monks from the three Korean states who came to the Qingyuan Prefecture.[98] One was called Jihyeon; the other was Gyeongun. These two both spoke constantly of the doctrines of the sūtras of the buddhas and were gentlemen of letters as well. Nevertheless, they had no *kāṣāya* and no bowls, like lay people. How pitiful, the fact that they had the appearance of the bhikṣu without the dharma of the bhikṣu must be due their small country in a peripheral land. When those with the appearance of the bhikṣu in our own domain venture to another land, they will be just like those two monks.

[32:63]

釋迦牟尼佛、すでに十二年中頂戴して、さしおきましまさざるなり。その遠孫として、これを學すべし。いたづらに名利のために天を拜し、神を拜し、王を拜し、臣を拜する頂門を、いま佛衣頂戴に廻向せん、よろこぶべき大慶なり。

Buddha Śākyamuni kept [the *kāṣāya*] on his head for twelve years, without setting it aside; as his distant descendants, we should learn from this. To turn this head that, for the sake of fame and profit, has bowed to devas, bowed to gods, bowed to kings, and bowed to ministers, toward now accepting the buddha robe on the head is a great felicity in which we should take delight.

[Ryūmonji MS:]

ときに仁治元年庚子開冬日、記于觀音導利興聖寶林寺
入宋傳法沙門道元

Recorded at Kannon Dōri Kōshō Hōrin Monastery; on the first day of winter, in the senior metal year of the rat, the first year of Ninji [17 October 1240].

The Śramaṇa Dōgen, who entered the Song and transmitted the dharma[99]

---

98 **winter of the junior water year of the sheep, the seventeenth year of the Jiading era of the Great Song** (*Daisō Katei jūshichi nen kimi tō* 大宋嘉定十七年癸未冬): I.e., the winter of 1223-1224 on the Gregorian calendar.

The cyclical calendar year of the "tenth stem, eighth branch" (*kimi* 癸未) corresponds to the sixteenth year of Jiading 嘉定, which ended 21 January 1224.

three Korean states (*sankan* 三韓): I.e., the three ancient kingdoms on the southern Korean peninsula: Silla 新羅, Baekje 百濟, and Goryeo 高麗.

Qingyuan Prefecture (*Keigen fu* 慶元府): In present-day Zhejiang, location of Mount Tiantong 天童山.

99 In the Honzan edition, this colophon (preceded by the title but without a chapter number), occurs at the end of the chapter, just preceding the final instructions on donning the robe (sections 70-72, below).

the first day of winter (*kaitōbi* 開冬日): I.e., the first day of the tenth lunar month.

32. Transmitting the Robe *Den'e* 傳衣

[32:64] {1:371}

袈裟をつくる衣財、かならず清淨なるをもちいる。清淨といふは、淨信檀
那の供養するところの衣財、あるいは市にて買得するもの、あるいは天衆
のおくるところ、あるいは龍神の淨施、あるいは鬼神の淨施、かくのごと
く衣財、もちいる。あるいは國王・大臣の淨施、あるいは淨皮、これら、
もちいるべし。

For the robe material for making a *kāṣāya*, we always use that which
is pure. By "pure" we mean robe material offered by a *dānapati* of pure
faith, or something purchased at a market, or something sent by the
devas, or the pure offering of dragons and spirits, or the pure offering
of demons and spirits — we use such robe material. Or we may use the
pure offering of a ruler or great minister, or pure skin.

[32:65]

また十種糞掃衣を清淨なりとす。いはゆる

十種の糞掃衣

一者牛嚼衣 二者鼠噛衣 三者火燒衣 四者月水衣 五者産婦衣 六者神廟
衣 七者塚間衣 八者求願衣 九者王職衣 十者往還衣

Also, the ten kinds of discarded rag robes are considered pure. Namely,
The ten kinds of discarded rag robes:

> 1. *Cow-chewed robe*
> 2. *Mouse-chewed robe*
> 3. *Fire-singed robe*
> 4. *Menstrual fluid robe*
> 5. *Childbirth robe*
> 6. *God shrine robe*
> 7. *Burial ground robe*
> 8. *Prayer robe*
> 9. *Royal office robe*
> 10. *Gone and returned robe*[100]

---

100   **The ten kinds of discarded rag robes** (*jisshu no funzō e* 十種の糞掃衣): A list
found in the *Sifen lü* 四分律 (T.1428.22:850a21-28; 1011b25-28). The ten types, all considered polluted in ancient India, are defined as follows:

1. Cow-chewed robe (*goshaku e* 牛嚼衣): *Kāṣāya* made from cloth damaged by being
chewed by cattle.

2. Mouse-gnawed robe (*soshi e* 鼠噛衣): *Kāṣāya* made from cloth damaged by being
gnawed by mice.

3. Fire-singed robe (*kashō e* 火燒衣): *Kāṣāya* made from cloth damaged by being partially burned.

4. Menstrual fluid robe (*gessui e* 月水衣): *Kāṣāya* made from cloth stained by a wom-
an's menstrual flow.

64   DŌGEN'S *SHŌBŌGENZŌ* VOLUME III

[32:66]

この十種を、ことに清淨の衣財とせるなり。世俗には抛捨す、佛道には
もちいる。世間と佛道と、その家業、はかりしるべし。しかあればすな
はち、清淨をもとめんときは、この十種をもとむべし。これをえて、淨を
しり、不淨を辨肯すべし。心をしり、身を辨肯すべし。この十種をえて、
たとひ絹類なりとも、たとひ布類なりとも、その淨不・淨を商量すべきな
り。

These ten kinds are considered especially pure robe materials. They
are cast away in the secular world but used in the way of the buddhas.
The respective house enterprises of the worldly and the way of the buddhas should be gauged from this. Thus, when we seek what is pure, we
should seek these ten types. Having obtained them, we should recognize
purity and confirm impurity; we should recognize the mind and confirm
the body. Having obtained these ten types, whether they are of silk or of
plant fiber, we should consider their impurity and purity.

[32:67]

この糞掃衣をもちいることは、いたづらに弊衣にやつれたらんがため、と
學するは至愚なるべし。莊嚴奇麗ならんがために、佛道に用著しきたれる
ところなり。佛道に、やつれたる衣服とならはんことは、錦繡綾羅・金銀
珍珠等の衣服の、不淨よりきたれるを、やつれたるとはいふなり。おほよ
そ此土他界の佛道に、清淨奇麗をもちいるには、この十種それなるべし。
これ淨・不淨の邊際を超越せるのみにあらず、漏・無漏の境界にあらず。
色・心を論ずることなかれ、得・失にかかはれざるなり。ただ正傳受持す
るは、これ佛祖なり、佛祖たるとき、正傳稟受するがゆえに、佛祖として
これを受持するは、身の現・不現によらず、心の擧・不擧によらず、正傳
せられゆくなり。

With regard to the use of discarded rag robes, to consider that it is for
the sake of meaninglessly looking shabby in tattered robes is surely the
height of stupidity. It is because they are splendid and elegant that they
have been worn in the way of the buddhas. In the way of the buddhas,
what we regard as shabby clothes are clothes of brocade, embroidery,

---

5. Childbirth robe (*sanpu e* 産婦衣): *Kāṣāya* made from cloth stained by blood during
childbirth.

6. God shrine robe (*shinbyō e* 神廟衣): *Kāṣāya* made from cloth left at a shrine as an
offering to a deity.

7. Burial mound robe (*chōken e* 塚間衣): *Kāṣāya* made from cloth found in a cemetery,
having been used to shroud a corpse.

8. Prayer robe (*gugan e* 求願衣): *Kāṣāya* made from cloth left outdoors on a mountain
or in a forest as an offering to a deity, in support of prayers.

9. Royal office robe (*ōshoku e* 王職衣): *Kāṣāya* made from clothing donated by kings or
ministers who, upon leaving office, no longer need their regal wear or uniforms.

10. Gone and returned robe (*ōgen e* 往還衣): *Kāṣāya* made from cloth used to carry a
corpse to a cemetery and brought back after the body was deposited.

32. Transmitting the Robe *Den'e* 傳衣   65

damask, and gauze, with gold, silver, rare gems, and the like, that come from impurity — these, we call "shabby." In sum, in the way of the buddhas of this land and other worlds, when we use what is pure and elegant, these ten types are it.[101] Not only have they transcended the boundaries of pure and impure; they are not in the realm of the contaminated or uncontaminated. Do not discuss them as form or mind; they have nothing to do with gain or loss. It is just that those who receive and keep the direct transmission are the buddhas and ancestors.[102] When one is a buddha or ancestor, because one accepts the direct transmission, the receiving and keeping of it as a buddha and ancestor, without depending on the appearance or non-appearance of the body and without depending on the presentation or non-presentation of the mind, goes on being directly transmitted.

[32:68] {1:372}

ただまさにこの日本國には、近來の僧尼、ひさしく袈裟を著せざりつるこ
とをかなしむべし、いま受持せんことをよろこぶべし。在家の男女、なほ
佛戒を受得せんは、五條・七條・九條の袈裟を著すべし。いはんや出家
人、いかでか著せざらん。はじめ梵王・六天より、婬男・婬女・奴婢にい
たるまでも、佛戒をうくべし、袈裟を著すべしといふ、比丘・比丘尼、こ
れを著せざらんや。畜生なほ佛戒をうくべし、袈裟をかくべしといふ、佛
子、なにとしてか佛衣を著せざらん。

However, in truth, it is lamentable that, in this Land of Japan, monks and nuns of recent times, have long neglected wearing the *kāṣāya*; we should rejoice that now we receive and keep it. Even among male and female householders, those who receive the buddha precepts should wear *kāṣāya* of five, seven, or nine panels. How much more, then, those who have gone forth from the household: how could they fail to wear one? It is said that, beginning with King Brahmā and denizens of the six heavens, and extending down to licentious men, licentious women, and male and female slaves — all should receive the buddha precepts and wear the *kāṣāya*; are bhikṣus and *bhikṣunīs* not to wear it?[103] It is said that even

---

101   **the way of the buddhas of this land and other worlds** (*shido takai no butsudō* 此
土他界の佛道): I.e., Buddhism everywhere.

102   **those who receive and keep the direct transmission** (*shōden juji suru wa* 正傳受
持するは): The unexpressed object of the transmission here and below is probably "the
buddha robe" (rather than "the ten types").

103   **King Brahmā and denizens of the six heavens** (*bonnō rokuten* 梵王・六天): I.e.,
the deva who rules the heavens of the first dhyāna in the realm of form (*shikikai* 色界;
S. *rūpa-loka*); and the devas in the heavens of the realm of desire (*yokukai* 欲界; S. *kāma-loka*). These and the other members of Dōgen's list here, and the "beasts" in the next
sentence, probably reflect a passage in the *Fanwang jing* 梵網經 (T.1484.24:1004b7-10)
listing those who should receive the precepts:

國王王子百官宰相、比丘比丘尼、十八梵天六欲天子、庶民黃門婬男婬女奴婢。

66 DŌGEN'S *SHŌBŌGENZŌ* VOLUME III

beasts should receive the buddha precepts and drape themselves in the *kāṣāya*; how could the children of the Buddha fail to wear the buddha robe?

[32:69]

しかあれば、佛子とならんは、天上・人間・國王・百官をとはず、在家・出家・奴婢・畜生を論ぜず、佛戒を受得し、袈裟を正傳すべし。まさに佛位に正入する直道なり。

Thus, those who would be children of the Buddha — without asking whether they are in the heavens or humans, kings of nations or the hundred officials, without discussing whether they are householders or renunciants, slaves or beasts — should receive the buddha precepts and directly transmit the *kāṣāya*. Truly, this is the direct path for proper entry into the buddha stage.

[*Himitsu* MS:]

正法眼藏第三十二
Treasury of the True Dharma Eye
Number 32[104]

[32:70]

袈裟浣濯之時、須用衆末香花和水。灑乾之後、畳収安置高處、以香花而供養之三拜。然後踞跪、頂戴合掌、致信唱此偈、

When washing the kāṣāya, one should use water in which are mixed powdered scents and flowers.[105] *After washing and drying, fold it and set it on a high place. Make an offering of incense and flowers, and, after making three prostrations, half kneel, place it on the head, join the palms, and intone this gāthā in faith:*[106]

[32:71]

大哉解脱服、無相福田衣、披奉如來教、廣度諸衆生。

八部鬼神金剛神畜生乃至變化人。

Kings, princes, the hundred officials, the prime minister; bhikṣu and *bhikṣunī*; devas of the eighteen heavens of Brahmā and six heavens of the desire realm; commoners, eunuchs, licentious males and females, slaves; the eight classes of demons and spirits, vajra spirits, beasts, and magically transformed beings.

104 Amending Kawamura's text, which gives here:

正法眼藏傳衣第三十二
Treasury of the True Dharma Eye
Transmission of the Robe
Number 32

105 **When washing the kāṣāya** (*kesa kantaku shi ji* 袈裟浣濯之時): The source of these instructions, given in Chinese, is unidentified.

106 **half kneel** (*koki* 踞跪): Literally, "squat and kneel," a posture of respect, in which one kneels on the right knee, with the left knee raised; also written *koki* 胡跪.

32. Transmitting the Robe *Den'e* 傳衣

How great the vestment of liberation,
Robe that is a signless field of merit.[107]
Wrapped in the teaching of the Tathāgata,
We deliver living beings everywhere.

[32:72]

三唱而後、立地如披奉。

After reciting this three times, immediately enrobe.[108]

---

107 **How great the vestment of liberation** (*dai sai gedappuku* 大哉解脱服): See above, Note 27. This is the verse still chanted by Sōtō monks before donning the robe for morning zazen.

108 The seventy-five-chapter *Shōbōgenzō* version of this chapter adds here an appendix quoting the *Da biqiu sanqian weiyi* 大比丘三千威儀 (at T.1470.24:915b10-19) on ten rules for the treatment of the *kāṣāya*.

TREASURY OF THE TRUE DHARMA EYE

NUMBER 33

Sayings
Dōtoku

道得

Sayings

Dōtoku

Introduction

This essay was written at Kōshōji in the autumn of 1242. It appears as number 33 in the seventy-five- and sixty-chapter compilations of the *Shōbōgenzō* and as number 39 in the Honzan edition.

The title theme, *dōtoku* 道得, refers both to the act of saying something and to the saying itself. For Dōgen, to have something to say is a defining characteristic of the Zen masters; as he says in his opening line here, "The buddhas and the ancestors are their sayings." Indeed, elsewhere, Dōgen is often dismissive of those figures in Zen literature who have nothing significant to say for themselves. Yet, here, he reminds us to take a broad view of what it means to say something.

In the first section of the essay, Dōgen makes clear that not saying anything can also be the expression of a saying; and, in the subsequent section, he explores a saying by the famous Tang-dynasty monk Zhaozhou Congshen 趙州從諗 that recommends "sitting fixedly without saying anything." Then, he ends his brief essay with the example of a hermit whose saying consisted in having his head shaved.

正法眼藏第三十三
Treasury of the True Dharma Eye
Number 33
道得
Sayings

[33:1] {1:374}

諸佛諸祖は道得なり。このゆえに、佛祖の佛祖を選するには、かならず道得也未と問取するなり。この問取、こころにても問取す、身にても問取す、拄杖・拂子にても問取す、露柱・燈籠にても問取するなり。佛祖にあらざれば問取なし、道得なし、そのところなきがゆえに。

The buddhas and the ancestors are their sayings.[1] Therefore, when the buddhas and ancestors select buddhas and ancestors, they invariably ask whether or not they can say something. This question, they ask with their minds, they ask with their bodies, they ask with their staffs and whisks, they ask with the pillars and lanterns.[2] If they are not buddhas and ancestors, they have no question, they have no saying; for they have no place for them.

[33:2]

その道得は、他人にしたがひてうるにあらず、わがちからの能にあらず、ただまさに佛祖の究辨あれば、佛祖の道得あるなり。かの道得のなかに、むかしも修行し證究す、いまも功夫し辨道す。佛祖の佛祖を功夫して、佛祖の道得を辨肯するとき、この道得、おのづから三年、八年、三十年、四十年の功夫となりて、盡力道得するなり。

These sayings are not something got from another, not something expressing their own abilities; it is just that, when they truly have the thorough investigation of the buddhas and ancestors, the buddhas and ancestors have sayings. Amidst those sayings, they practice and fully verify in the past, they concentrate and pursue the way in the present. When

---

1 **The buddhas and the ancestors are their sayings** (*shobutsu shoso wa dōtoku nari* 諸佛諸祖は道得なり): Or, "the buddhas and ancestors are those who can say something." Depending on context, the term *dōtoku* 道得 can mean "to say," "to be able to say," or "a saying." Often, as no doubt here, Dōgen uses the term in the sense "to say something worth saying," "a significant statement," etc.

2 **staffs and whisks** (*shujō hossu* 拄杖・拂子); **pillars and lanterns** (*rochū tōrō* 露柱・燈籠): I.e., the regalia of the Zen master's office and the free-standing columns and lanterns of the monastic buildings, items occurring regularly in Zen discourse; see Supplementary Notes, s.v. "Pillars and lanterns," "Whisk," and "Staff."

72 DŌGEN'S *SHŌBŌGENZŌ* VOLUME III

the buddhas and ancestors, concentrating on the buddhas and ancestors, confirm a saying of the buddhas and ancestors, this saying, naturally becoming three years, eight years, thirty years, or forty years of concentrated effort, is said with all their might.[3]

[33:3]
このときは、その何十年の間も、道得の間隙なかりけるなり。しかあれば
すなはち、證究のときの見得、それまことなるべし。かのときの見得をま
こととするがゆえに、いまの道得なることは、不疑なり。ゆえに、いまの
道得、かのときの見得をそなへたるなり、かのときの見得、いまの道得を
そなへたり。このゆえに、いま道得あり、いま見得あり。いまの道得と、
かのときの見得と、一條なり、萬里なり。いまの功夫、すなはち道得と見
得とに功夫せられゆくなり。

During this time, even over a period of some decades, there will have been no break in the saying.[4] This being the case, what they see when they fully verify will be its truth. Since what they see at that time is its truth, they have no doubt that it is the present saying. Therefore, the present saying is endowed with the seeing at that time; and the seeing at that time is endowed with the present saying. Therefore, there is the saying now; there is the seeing now. The present saying and the seeing at that time are one strip, are ten thousand miles.[5] The present concentration continues to be concentrated by the saying and the seeing.[6]

[33:4] {1:375}
この功夫の把定の、月ふかく、年おほくかさなりて、さらに従來の年月の
功夫を脱落するなり。脱落せんとするとき、皮肉骨髓おなじく脱落を辨肯
す、國土山河ともに脱落を辨肯するなり。このとき、脱落を究竟の寶所と

---

3 **said with all their might** (*jinriki dōtoku* 盡力道得): The agent is unspecified; presumably, the one who is concentrating on the saying.

The manuscripts include at this point in the text the following note:

裡書云、三十年、二十年は、みな道得のなれる年月なり。この年月、ちからを
あはせて道得せしむるなり。

A note on the reverse says, "Thirty years or twenty years is the time it takes for the saying to be formed; these years combine to enable him to say it."

4 **there will have been no break in the saying** (*dōtoku no kenkyaku nakarikeru nari* 道得の間隙なかりけるなり): I.e., the saying will always have been present in the person's practice.

5 **are one strip, are ten thousand miles** (*ichijō nari, banri nari* 一條なり、萬里な り): From the phrase, "one strip of iron for ten thousand miles" (*banri ichijō tetsu* 萬里 一條鐵), a common Zen expression for the ultimate unity of the myriad phenomena; see Supplementary Notes, s.v. "One strip of iron."

6 **The present concentration continues to be concentrated by the saying and the seeing** (*ima no kufū, sunawachi dōtoku to kentoku to ni kufū serareyuku nari* いまの功 夫、すなはち道得と見得とに功夫せられゆくなり): I.e., the spiritual effort to engage the saying is informed by both the saying and the insight into it.

33. *Sayings Dōtoku* 道得   73

して、いたらんと擬しゆくところに、この擬到はすなはち現出にてあるゆ
えに、正當脱落のとき、またざるに現成する道得あり。心のちからにあら
ず、身のちからにあらずといへども、おのづから道得あり。すでに道得せ
らるるに、めづらしく、あやしくおぼえざるなり。

Having accumulated long months and many years of holding fast to
this concentrated effort, one goes on to slough off the efforts of the past
months and years. When one is to slough them off, skin, flesh, bones,
and marrow all confirm the sloughing off; the land, and the mountains
and rivers all confirm the sloughing off. At this point, where we think to
reach the sloughing off as the ultimate treasure trove, since this thinking
to reach it is actually realized, just at the point of the sloughing off, there
is a saying that occurs unexpectedly.[7] Though it is not by the power of
the mind and not by the power of the body, of its own accord there is a
saying. Once it has been said, it does not seem unusual or strange.

[33:5]
しかあれども、この道得を道得するとき、不道得を不道するなり。道得す
ると認得せるも、いまだ不道得底を不道得底と證せざるは、なほ佛祖の面
目にあらず、佛祖の骨髄にあらず。しかあれば、三拜依位而立の道得底、
いかにしてか皮肉骨髄のやからの道得底とひとしからん。皮肉骨髄のやか
らの道得底、さらに三拜依位而立の道得に接するにあらず、そなはれるに
あらず。いまわれと他と、異類中行と相見するは、いまかれと他と、異類
中行と相見するなり。われに道得底あり、不道得底あり、かれに道得底あ
り、不道得底あり、道底に自他あり、不道底に自他あり。

Nevertheless, when one says this saying, one does not say what is not
said. Though one has recognized it as a saying, if one has not yet verified
not saying as not saying, it is not the face of the buddhas and ancestors,
it is not the bones and marrow of the buddhas and ancestors.[8] This being the case, how could the saying of "*making three bows and standing
in place*" be on the same level as the sayings of the skin, flesh, bones,
and marrow bunch?[9] The sayings of the skin, flesh, bones, and marrow

---

7   **the ultimate treasure trove** (*kukyō no hōsho* 究竟の寶所): The metaphor of the
"treasure trove" (*hōsho* 寶所) as the true goal of Buddhism comes from a famous parable
in the *Lotus Sūtra*, in which the buddha is depicted as a caravan leader taking people to
a treasure (*Miaofa lianhua jing* 妙法蓮華經, T.262.9:25c26ff).

8   **Though one has recognized it as a saying** (*dōtoku suru to nintoku seru mo* 道得す
ると認得せるも): Some MS witnesses read here *dōtoku ni dōtoku suru to nintoku seru
mo* 道得に道得すると認得せるも ("Though in saying one has recognized it as saying").

not saying (*fudōtokutei* 不道得底): Generally taken here to mean to leave unsaid what
cannot be said. The term *fudōtoku* 不道得 is also regularly used in the sense "cannot say
[what needs to be said]."

9   **"making three bows and standing in place"** (*sanpai e i ni ryū* 三拜依位而立):
Allusion to the famous story of Bodhidharma's testing of his four disciples, in which the
first three gave answers but Huike 慧可 simply bowed and stood in place. Bodhidharma

74   DŌGEN'S *SHŌBŌGENZŌ* VOLUME III

bunch do not entertain, are not endowed with, the saying of "*making three bows and standing in place.*" The meeting here of self and other as "*moving among different types*" is the meeting of other and other as "*moving among different types.*"[10] The self has saying and has not saying; the other has saying and has not saying. Saying has self and other; not saying has self and other.

* * * * *

[33:6] {1:376}

趙州眞際大師、示衆云、儞若一生不離叢林、兀坐不道十年五載、無人喚作儞啞漢。已後諸佛也不及儞哉。

Great Master Zhenji of Zhaozhou addressed the assembly, saying, "*If for a lifetime you don't leave the grove, sitting fixedly without saying anything for ten years or five years, no one will call you a mute; after that, even the buddhas won't reach you.*"[11]

---

said of each in turn that he (or, in one case, she) had "got his skin, flesh, bones, and marrow." See Supplementary Notes, s.v. "Skin, flesh, bones, and marrow."

the skin, flesh, bones, and marrow bunch (*hi niku kotsu zui no yakara* 皮肉骨髓のやから): One would expect here a reference to the first three disciples to answer Bodhidharma, but the interpretation is complicated by the fact that Huike 慧可 was said to have received the marrow.

10   **The meeting here of self and other as "moving among different types"** (*ima ware to ta to, irui chū gyō to shōken suru* いまわれと他と、異類中行と相見する): The expression "moving among different types" (*irui chū gyō* 異類中行) is generally taken to indicate the salvific activities of the buddhas and bodhisattvas among the various forms of living beings. It is associated especially with a comment by Nanchuan Puyuan 南泉普願 (748-835) about the monk Zongzhi 宗智, a saying widely repeated in Zen sources and quoted in Dōgen's *shinji Shōbōgenzō* 眞字正法眼藏 (DZZ.5:154, case 57); see Supplementary Notes, s.v. "Move among different types." The antecedents of the pronouns translated here as "self" (*ware* われ) and "other" (*ta* 他) are subject to various interpretations. Perhaps the most plausible takes Huike 慧可 as "self" and the other three disciples as "other." Hence, the point becomes Huike's not speaking and the others' speaking are equally instances of "moving among different types."

11   **Great Master Zhenji of Zhaozhou** (*Jōshū Shinsai daishi* 趙州眞際大師): I.e., Zhaozhou Congshen 趙州從諗 (778-897). Dōgen's version of Zhaozhou's words here (repeated with slight variation in his *Eihei kōroku* 永平廣錄) has no known source. For the saying on which it is likely based (quoted accurately in "Shōbōgenzō gyōji" 正法眼藏行持), see Supplementary Notes, s.v. "For a lifetime not leaving the grove."

"the grove" (*sōrin* 叢林): A common idiom for the monastery or the monastic institution.

"a mute" (*akan* 啞漢): Used in Chan conversations for one unable to respond.

33. *Sayings* Dōtoku 道得　　75

[33:7]

しかあれば、十年五載の在叢林、しばしば霜華を經歴するに、一生不離叢林の功夫辦道をおもふに、坐斷せし兀坐は、いくばくの道得なり。不離叢林の經行坐臥、そこばくの無人喚作儞啞漢なるべし。一生は所從來をしらずといへども、不離叢林ならしむれば、不離叢林なり。一生と叢林の、いかなる通霄路かある。ただ兀坐を辦肯すべし、不道をいふことなかれ。不道は道得の頭正尾正なり。

Thus, as we reside in "the grove" for "ten years or five years," passing through frosts and flowers time and again, when we reflect on the concentrated effort to pursue the way *without leaving the grove for a lifetime*," the "fixed sitting" that has completely sat is so many sayings.[12] Walking about, sitting, and reclining "without leaving the grove" must be numerous instances of "*no one will call you a mute*." Though we may not know whence "a lifetime" comes, once we have made it "not leaving the grove," it is "not leaving the grove." What kind of path through the clouds is there between "a lifetime" and "the grove"?[13] We should just confirm "fixed sitting"; do not say "without saying anything."[14] "Without saying anything" is a saying true from head to tail.

[33:8]

兀坐は一生・二生なり、一時・二時にはあらず。兀坐して不道なる十年五載あれば、諸佛も、なんぢをないがしろにせんことあるべからず。まことにこの兀坐不道は、佛眼也覷不見なり、佛力也牽不及なり。諸佛也不奈儞何なるがゆえに。

"Fixed sitting" is for "a lifetime" or two lifetimes; it is not for one time or two times. When you have "ten years or five years" of "fixed sitting" "without saying anything," even the buddhas will not ignore you. Truly,

---

12　**frosts and flowers** (*sōke* 霜華): I.e, autumns and springs; the years.

the "fixed sitting" that has completely sat (*zadan seshi gotsuza* 坐斷せし兀坐): For the meaning of the term *gotsuza* 兀坐, translated here as "fixed sitting," see Supplementary Notes, s.v. "Sit fixedly." The term *zadan* 坐斷, rendered here somewhat awkwardly as "completely sat," ordinarily means "to occupy," "to control," also "to press down," "to oppress," "to break," "to reject" (*zadan* 挫斷), in which the element *dan* 斷 ("to cut off") functions as a verbal suffix with the sense "completely." Dōgen uses the term several times in the *Shōbōgenzō*, and commentators typically read it as "sitting completely" or, when used as a transitive verb, as it will be below, "sitting and cutting off."

13　**path through the clouds** (*tsūshōro* 通霄路): Or "road to the firmament." A fixed expression, found in Song-dynasty Chan texts, indicating a "higher" way, beyond the standard understandings of Buddhist practice. The term *shō* 霄, translated here as "clouds," can also refer to, and is probably more often interpreted as, the "heavens," as well as the "night."

14　**do not say "without saying anything"** (*fudō o iu koto nakare* 不道をいふことなかれ): Taking the term *fudō* 不道 to refer to Zhaozhou's phrase, "sitting fixedly without saying anything" (*gotsuza fudō* 兀坐不道). Some versions of the text read *fudō o itou koto nakare* 不道をいとふことなかれ ("do not worry about 'without saying anything'").

76 DŌGEN'S *SHŌBŌGENZŌ* VOLUME III

this "fixed sitting without saying anything" is *even the eye of a buddha cannot see it*, is *even the strength of a buddha cannot rein it in*; for "*even the buddhas won't know what to make of you.*"[15]

[33:9]

趙州のいふところは、兀坐不道の道取は、諸佛も、これを啞漢といふにお
よばず、不啞漢といふにおよばず。しかあれば、一生不離叢林は、一生不
離道得なり。兀坐不道十年五載は、道得十年五載なり。一生不離不道得な
り、道不得十年五載なり、坐斷百千諸佛なり、百千諸佛坐斷儞なり。

What Zhaozhou says is that the saying, "sitting fixedly without saying anything" — even the buddhas "won't reach" calling this "a mute,"
"won't reach" calling it "not a mute."[16] Hence, "*not leaving the grove
for a lifetime*" is "*not leaving the saying for a lifetime*"; "*sitting fixedly
without saying anything for ten years or five years*" is "*saying something
for ten years or five years.*" It is "*not leaving not saying for a lifetime*";
it is "*not saying for ten years or five years*"; it is *sitting and cutting off
hundreds of thousands of buddhas*; it is *hundreds and thousands of buddhas sitting and cutting off you.*[17]

[33:10] {1:377}

しかあればすなはち、佛祖の道得底は、一生不離叢林なり。たとひ啞漢な
りとも、道得底あるべし、啞漢は道得なかるべし、と學することなかれ。
道得あるもの、かならずしも啞漢にあらざるにあらず、啞漢また道得ある
なり。啞聲きこゆべし、啞語きくべし。啞にあらずば、いかでか啞と相見
せん、いかでか啞と相談せん。すでにこれ啞漢なり、作麼生相見、作麼生
相談。かくのごとく參學して、啞漢を辨究すべし。

---

15 **even the eye of a buddha cannot see it** (*butsugen ya chofuken* 佛眼也覷不見);
even the strength of a buddha cannot rein it in (*butsuriki ya ken fugyū* 佛力也牽不
及); **"even the buddhas won't know what to make of you"** (*shobutsu ya fu na ni ka*
諸佛也不奈儞何): Three phrases in Chinese. The first is a fixed expression found in Zen
literature, referring to the "buddha eye" (*butsugen* 佛眼; S. *buddha-cakṣus*), the eye of
omniscience; see Supplementary Notes, s.v. "Eye.". The second phrase, which seems to
be Dōgen's own variation on the linguistic pattern, is more literally, "even the strength
of a buddha would try to rein it in without reaching it," perhaps referring back to the
final line of his quotation of Zhaozhou: "After that, even the buddhas won't reach you."
Curiously enough, the third phrase here is a quotation of Zhaozhou's words in the extant
versions of his saying (rather than Dōgen's version in section 6, above).

16 **"won't reach" calling this "a mute," "won't reach" calling it "not a mute"** (*kore
o akan to iu ni oyobazu, fuakan to iu ni oyobazu* これを啞漢といふにおよばず、不啞漢
といふにおよばず): The awkward form "won't reach" here tries to preserve what seems
to be a reference to the last line of Dōgen's quotation of Zhaozhou: "After that, even the
buddhas won't reach you." The sense is simply that "the saying" cannot be described as
either "a mute" or "not a mute."

17 **sitting and cutting off** (*zadan* 坐斷): See above, Note 12.

33. *Sayings Dōtoku* 道得

This being the case, the sayings of the buddhas and ancestors are "*not leaving the grove for a lifetime.*" Even if they are "mutes," they should have sayings; do not study that a "mute" has no saying. It is not the case that someone with a saying is necessarily not a "mute": "mutes" also have sayings. We should hear their mute voices; we should listen to their mute words. Since they are "mutes," how does one meet with them? How does one talk with them? Studying in this way, we should thoroughly investigate the "mute."

* * * * *

[33:11]
雪峰の眞覺大師の會に一僧ありて、山のほとりにゆきて、草をむすびて庵を卓す。とし、つもりぬれど、かみをそらざりけり。庵裏の活計、たれかしらん、山中の消息、悄然なり。みづから一柄の木杓をつくりて、溪のほとりにゆきて、水をくみてのむ。まことに、これ飲溪のたぐひなるべし。かくて日往月來するほどに、家風ひそかに漏泄せりけるによりて、あるとき、僧きたりて庵主にとふ、いかにあらんかこれ祖師西來意。庵主云、溪深杓柄長。とふ僧、おくことあらず、禮拜せず、請益せず。山にのぼりて雪峰に擧似す。雪峰ちなみに擧をききていはく、也甚奇怪、雖然如是、老僧自去勘過始得。

In the community of Great Master Zhenzhue of Xuefeng, there was a monk who built a thatched hermitage in the vicinity of the mountain.[18] The years passed, but he never shaved his head. Who knows his life in the hermitage — so lonely was his situation in the mountains? He made himself a wooden ladle and scooped up water to drink at a nearby stream. Truly, he was the type who drinks from the stream.[19] In this way, as the days passed and the months came, his style of life secretly leaked out, and consequently one day a monk visited and asked the hermit, "What is the intention of the Ancestral Master coming from the west?"

The hermit said, "The stream is deep, the ladle handle long."

---

18 **Great Master Zhenzhue of Xuefeng** (*Seppō no Shinkaku daishi* 雪峰の眞覺大師): I.e., Xuefeng Yicun 雪峰義存 (822-908). A version of this story is recorded in Dōgen's *shinji Shōbōgenzō* 眞字正法眼藏 (DZZ.5:218, case 183), most likely taken from Dahui Zonggao's 大慧宗杲 *Zhengfayanzang* 正法眼藏 (ZZ.118:7b12-17). Dōgen tells the story here in Japanese, with only some of the speech of the characters in Chinese.

in the vicinity of the mountain (*yama no hotori ni* 山のほとりに): I.e., near Yicun's monastery on Xuefeng 雪峰, located in Fuzhou 福州 (modern Fujian).

19 **the type who drinks from the stream** (*inkei no tagui* 飲溪のたぐい): I.e., lives the simple life of the sage; more commonly described as "drinking from the river" (*inka* 飲河).

The monk who asked, unable to handle it, did not bow, and did not seek instruction.[20] He climbed the mountain and reported it to Xuefeng. Xuefeng listened to the report and said, "*Very strange. Even so, this old monk had better go himself and investigate.*"

[33:12]

雪峰のいふこころは、よさは、すなはちあやしきまでによし、しかあれども、老僧みづからゆきてかんがへみるべし、となり。かくてあるに、ある日、雪峰たちまちに侍者に剃刀をもたせて率しゆく。直に庵にいたりぬ。わづかに庵主をみるに、すなはちとふ、道得ならば、なんぢが頭をそらじ。

What Xuefeng meant was that it sounded too good to be true; nevertheless, the old monk himself should go and investigate it.[21] Thus, one day, Xuefeng suddenly went to him with his acolyte carrying a razor. When they arrived at the hermitage, as soon as they saw the hermit, he questioned him, "If you can say something, I won't shave your head."

[33:13] {1:378}

この問、こころうべし。道得不剃汝頭とは、不剃頭は道得なりときこゆ、いかん。この道得、もし道得ならんには、畢竟じて不剃ならん。この道得、きくちからありてきくべし。きくちからあるもののために開演すべし。

We should understand this questioning. "*If you can say something, I won't shave your head*" sounds like "not shaving your head" is "saying something."[22] How about it? If this saying is a saying, in the end, he will not shave him. We should hear this saying with the power to hear it; we should expound it for the sake of those with the power to hear it.

---

20   **unable to handle it** (*oku koto arazu* おくことあらず): A tentative translation of a Japanese expression not appearing in the Chinese sources; taking *oku* おく as *so* 措 ("to deal with"). Other readers take it as "to be unconvinced," "to be startled," "to be unable to respond."

21   **the old monk himself should go and investigate it** (*rōsō mizukara yukite kangaemiru beshi* 老僧みづからゆきてかんがへみるべし): Dōgen is here merely translating Xuefeng's Chinese.

22   **"If you can say something, I won't shave your head" sounds like "not shaving your head" is "saying something"** (*dōtoku futei nyo tō to wa, futei tō wa dōtoku nari to kikoyu* 道得不剃汝頭とは、不剃頭は道得なりときこゆ): Dōgen here gives Xuefeng's words in Chinese syntax, which could be parsed, "My saying is 'I won't shave your head'"; hence, the following, "not shaving your head is a saying." Dōgen seems here to be making the following sort of playful argument: (1) If there is a saying, he won't shave his head; (2) "Not shaving your head" is a saying; (3) Therefore, he won't shave his head.

33. *Sayings Dōtoku* 道得

[33:14]

ときに庵主、かしらをあらひて、雪峰のまへにきたれり。これも、道得に
てきたれるか、不道得にてきたれるか。雪峰、すなはち菴主のかみをそ
る。

Thereupon, the hermit washed his head and came to Xuefeng. Did he
come as [an act of] "saying something"? Or did he come as "not saying
something"? Xuefeng immediately shaved the hermit's head.

[33:15]

この一段の因縁、まことに優曇の一現のごとし。あひがたきのみにあら
ず、ききがたかるべし。七聖・十聖の境界にあらず、三賢・七賢の覤見
にあらず。經師・論師のやから、神通變化のやから、いかにもはかるべか
らざるなり。佛出世にあふといふは、かくのごとくの因縁をきくをいふな
り。

This single episode is truly like the singular appearance of the *udumbara*.[23] It is not only difficult to encounter; it is difficult to hear of. It is not
in the realm of the seven sages or ten sages; it is not in the ken of the
three worthies or seven worthies.[24] The sūtra master and treatise master types, the types who practice spiritual powers and transformations,
have no way of fathoming it. Meeting a buddha who has appeared in the
world means hearing a story like this.

[33:16]

しばらく雪峰のいふ道得不剃汝頭、いかにあるべきぞ。未道得の人、これ
をききて、ちからあらんは驚疑すべし、ちからあらざらんは茫然ならん。
佛と問著せず、道といはず、三昧と問著せず、陀羅尼といはず。かくのご
とく問著する、問に相似なりといへども、道に相似なり。審細に參學すべ
きなり。

For now, [let us consider,] what is this "*If you can say something, I
won't shave your head*"? People who cannot yet say something, upon
hearing this, if they have ability will be startled, and if they lack ability

---

23 **the singular appearance of the *udumbara*** (*udon no ichigen* 優曇の一現): I.e., the
rare blossoming of a legendary plant, sometimes said in Buddhist texts to occur only
once every three thousand years; a standard symbol of the rare good fortune of encountering the dharma.

24 **the seven sages or ten sages** (*shichishō jisshō* 七聖・十聖); **the three worthies or
seven worthies** (*sanken shichiken* 三賢・七賢): I.e., those on the various stages of the
Buddhist path. Practitioners are typically divided into two basic stages: the "worthy"
(*ken* 賢; S. *bhadra*), who are still "commoners" (*bonbu* 凡夫; S. *pṛthagjana*); and the
"sages" (*shō* 聖; S. ārya), who have reached the more advanced stages of the "nobles."
The "three worthies" refers to three stages of development; the "seven worthies" refers
to seven types of practitioners on these stages. The "seven sages" refers to the types of
realization achieved by the seven types of practitioner; the "ten sages" refers to those on
the ten stages (*ji* 地; S. *bhūmi*) of the bodhisattva path.

80　DŌGEN'S *SHŌBŌGENZŌ* VOLUME III

will be at a loss. He does not ask about the buddha; he does not speak of the way; he does not ask about samādhi; he does not speak of *dhāraṇī.* Posing this kind of question, though it may resemble a question, resembles a statement.[25] We should study it in detail.

[33:17]

しかあるに、庵主、まことあるによりて、道得に助發せらるるに、茫然ならざるなり。家風かくれず、洗頭してきたる。これ佛自智慧、不得其邊の法度なり。現身なるべし、説法なるべし、度生なるべし、洗頭來なるべし。

However, since the hermit was authentic, he was encouraged by the saying and not at a loss. Without obscuring the traditional style, he washed his head and came to him. This is a rule *"the limits of which cannot be reached by the buddha's own wisdom."*[26] He must be manifesting his body; he must be preaching the dharma; he must be delivering beings; he must be "washing his head and coming to him."[27]

[33:18] {1:379}

ときに雪峰、もしその人にあらずば、剃刀を放下して呵呵大笑せん。しかあれども、雪峰、そのちからあり、その人なるによりて、すなはち庵主のかみをそる。まことにこれ雪峰と庵主と、唯佛與佛にあらずよりは、かくのごとくならじ、一佛・二佛にあらずよりは、かくのごとくならじ、龍と龍とにあらずよりは、かくのごとくならじ。驪珠は驪龍のをしむこころ慳倦なしといへども、おのづから解收の人の手にいるなり。

25　**though it may resemble a question, resembles a statement** (*mon ni sōji nari to iedomo, dō ni sōji nari* 問に相似なりといへども、道に相似なり): I.e., it might seem that Xuefeng is interrogating the hermit, but it appears rather that he is giving a teaching to the hermit. (Grammatically speaking, of course, Xuefeng's words are a declarative sentence.)

26　**"the limits of which cannot be reached by the buddha's own wisdom"** (*butsu ji chie, futoku go hen* 佛自智慧、不得其邊): Likely after a passage in the *Lotus Sūtra* (*Miaofa lianhua jing* 妙法蓮華經, T.262.9:54b19-21):

若人得聞此法華經、若自書、若使人書、所得功德、以佛智慧籌量多少不得其邊。

If one hears this *Lotus Sūtra*, if one copies it, if one has it copied, the limits of the merit acquired cannot be reached if the amount were to be calculated by the wisdom of a buddha.

27　**manifesting his body** (*genshin* 現身); **preaching the dharma** (*seppō* 説法); **delivering beings** (*doshō* 度生): Recalling the famous description of the thirty-three manifestations of Bodhisattva Avalokiteśvara (*Kannon* 觀音); see Supplementary Notes, s.v. "Manifesting a body to preach the dharma."

33. *Sayings Dōtoku* 道得

At this point, had Xuefeng not been that person, he would have thrown down the razor and given a great laugh, "ha, ha!"[28] However, since Xuefeng had the power, was that person, he immediately shaved the hermit's head. Truly, were Xuefeng and the hermit not "only a buddha with a buddha," it probably would not have been like this; were they not one buddha and two buddhas, it probably would not have been like this; were they not a dragon and a dragon, it probably would not have been like this.[29] The black dragon's pearl, though the black dragon never flags in its determination to keep it, falls naturally into the hand of the one who can take it.[30]

[33:19]
しるべし、雪峰は庵主を勘過す、庵主は雪峰をみる。道得不道得、かみを
そられ、かみをそる。しかあればすなはち、道得の良友は、期せざるにと
ぶらふみちあり。道不得のとも、またざれども知己のところありき。知己
の參學あれば、道得の現成あるなり。

We should realize that Xuefeng investigated the hermit, and the hermit saw Xuefeng; one said something, and one did not say anything; one had his head shaved, one shaved his head. In this way, there is a path on which a good friend who can say something pays an unexpected visit. Although the friend who did not say anything was not expecting it, he had a chance to know himself. When there is the study of knowing oneself, there is the realization of a saying.

正法眼藏道得第三十三
Treasury of the True Dharma Eye
Number 33
Sayings

---

28 **had Xuefeng not been that person** (*Seppō, moshi sono hito ni arazu ba* 雪峰、もし
その人にあらずば): "That person" (*sono hito* そのひと) is a fixed expression, appearing frequently in the *Shōbōgenzō*, for an authentic Zen practitioner.

29 **"only a buddha with a buddha"** (*yui butsu yo butsu* 唯佛與佛): From a line in Kumārajīva's translation of the *Lotus Sūtra*; see Supplementary Notes, s.v. "Only buddhas with buddhas can exhaustively investigate the real marks of the dharmas."

30 **the black dragon's pearl** (*rijū* 驪珠): Reference to the precious pearl held under the chin of the black dragon; a symbol of a most precious treasure, best known from the miscellaneous chapters of the *Zhuangzi* 莊子 (Lie Yukou 列御寇, KR.5c0126.032.9a).

DŌGEN'S *SHŌBŌGENZŌ* VOLUME III

[Ryūmonji MS:]

仁治三年壬寅十月五日、書于觀音導利興聖寶林寺。沙門敦撰 校了

Written at Kannon Dōri Kōshō Hōrin Monastery; fifth day of the tenth month of the senior water year of the tiger, the third year of Ninji [30 October 1242].

Carefully composed by the Śramaṇa.

Proofed[31]

[Tōunji MS:]

同三年壬寅十一月二日、書寫之。懷奘

Copied this the second day of the eleventh month of the senior water year of the tiger, third year of the same [era] [November 25, 1242]. Ejō

---

31   The Tōunji 洞雲寺 MS shares an almost identical colophon.

Carefully composed by the Śramaṇa. Proofed (*shamon tonsen, kyōryō* 沙門敦撰、校了): Presumably, Dōgen's own colophon, though the final "proofed" here (lacking in the Tōunji 洞雲寺 MS) is likely by another, unknown copyist.

TREASURY OF THE TRUE DHARMA EYE

NUMBER 34

The Teachings of the Buddhas
Bukkyō

佛教

The Teachings of the Buddhas

Bukkyō

INTRODUCTION

This chapter occurs as number 34 in the seventy-five-chapter compilation of the *Shōbōgenzō* and as number 24 in the Honzan edition. The former version is undated, while the latter bears a colophon giving its composition as December 17, 1241, at Kōshōji. The work also appears as number 2 in fascicle 2 of the twenty-eight-text *Himitsu* collection of the *Shōbōgenzō*, with a colophon giving the date November 30, 1242, at the same monastery.

The content of the essay is a somewhat odd combination of elements. It begins with a critique of the claim, common in the Chinese Chan literature of Dōgen's day, that Bodhidharma's tradition is "a separate transmission outside the teachings." Ultimately, Dōgen argues, the buddhas' teachings and Bodhidharma's tradition are not two. He then comments on two Chan sayings on the teachings. The occurrence, in the second of these teachings, of the stock phrase, "the three vehicles and twelvefold teachings," leads to an extended excursus on the content of the *śrāvaka*, *pratyeka-buddha*, and bodhisattva vehicles, and the traditional division of the Buddhist canon into twelve (or nine) genres. The essay ends with comments on a passage in the *Lotus Sūtra* that mentions the ninefold teachings.

正法眼藏第三十四
Treasury of the True Dharma Eye
Number 34
佛教
The Teachings of the Buddhas

[34:1] {1:380}

諸佛の道現成、これ佛教なり。これ佛祖の佛祖のためにするゆえに、教の教のために正傳するなり、これ轉法輪なり。この法輪の眼睛裏に、諸佛祖を現成せしめ、諸佛祖を般涅槃せしむ。その諸佛祖、かならず一塵の出現あり、一塵の涅槃あり、盡界の出現あり、盡界の涅槃あり、一須臾の出現あり、多劫海の出現あり。しかあれども、一塵・一須臾の出現、さらに不具足の功德なし、盡界・多劫海の出現、さらに補虧闕の經營にあらず。このゆえに、朝に成道して夕に涅槃する諸佛、いまだ功德かけたり、といはず。もし、一日は功德すくなし、といはば、人間の八十年、ひさしきにあらず。人間の八十年をもて、十劫・二十劫に比せんとき、一日と八十年とのごとくならむ。此佛・彼佛の功德、わきまへがたからん。長劫壽量の所有の功德と八十年の功德とを、擧して比量せんとき、疑著するにもおよばざらん。このゆえに、佛教はすなはち教佛なり、佛祖究盡の功德なり。諸佛は高廣にして、法教は狹少なるにあらず。まさにしるべし、佛、大なるは、教、大なり、佛、小なるは、教、小なり。このゆえにしるべし、佛および教は、大小の量にあらず、善・惡・無記等の性にあらず、自教・教他のためにあらず。

The realization of the sayings of the buddhas — these are the teachings of the buddhas.[1] Since the buddhas and ancestors do this for the sake of the buddhas and ancestors, their teachings directly transmit them for the sake of the teachings. This is turning the dharma wheel. Within the eye of this dharma wheel, it causes the buddhas and ancestors to appear; it causes the buddhas and ancestors to enter *parinirvāṇa*. The buddhas and ancestors always make their appearance in a single dust mote and enter nirvāṇa in a single dust mote, make their appearance throughout all the worlds and enter nirvāṇa throughout all the worlds; make their appearance in a single moment and make their appearance throughout many

---

1 **The realization of the sayings of the buddhas — these are the teachings of the buddhas** (*shobutsu no dō genjō, kore bukkyō nari* 諸佛の道現成、これ佛教なり): The common term *bukkyō* 佛教, translated throughout here as "the teachings of the buddhas," could as well be (and doubtless more often is) rendered "the teaching of the Buddha" (i.e., the teaching of Buddha Śākyamuni); but, as the next sentence here makes clear, Dōgen is using the term in reference to teachings of the "buddhas and ancestors" of his tradition. See Supplementary Notes, s.v. "Buddhas and ancestors."

86 DŌGEN'S *SHŌBŌGENZŌ* VOLUME III

oceans of kalpas.[2] However, their appearance in a single dust mote or single moment is quite without any lack of virtues, and their appearance in all the worlds and many oceans of kalpas is not at all an undertaking that compensates for deficiencies. Therefore, the buddhas who attain the way in the morning and enter nirvāṇa in the evening have never been said to lack any virtues.[3] If we say the virtues in one day are few, the eighty years of a human is not long; and when we compare the eighty years of a human with ten kalpas or twenty kalpas, one day is like eighty years.[4] It is hard to distinguish between the virtues of this buddha and that buddha: when we try to compare the virtues possessed by a lifespan of long kalpas and the virtues of eighty years, we cannot even conceive of it. Therefore, the teachings of the buddhas are the teaching buddhas, are the virtues exhaustively investigated by the buddhas and ancestors.[5] It is not that the buddhas are tall and broad, while their dharma teachings are narrow and scant: we should realize that where the buddha is great, his teachings are great; where the buddha is small, his teachings are small. Therefore, we should realize that a buddha and his teachings are not a quantity great or small, are not a nature good, evil, or neutral, are not for the sake of one's own teaching or teaching others.[6]

---

2 **a single moment** (*ichi shuyu* 一須臾): The term *shuyu* 須臾 is used for Sanskrit *muhūrta*, a very short period of time, sometimes reckoned as 216,000 *kṣāna*, or one thirtieth part of a day.

3 **the buddhas who attain the way in the morning and enter nirvāṇa in the evening** (*ashita ni jōdō shite yūbe ni nehan suru shobutsu* 朝に成道して夕に涅槃する諸佛): Reminiscent of the famous words of Confucius (*Lunyu* 論語, Li Ren 里仁, KR.1h0005.002.13a):

朝聞道、夕死可矣。
If one hears the way in the morning, one can die in the evening.

4 **eighty years of a human** (*ningen no hachijū nen* 人間の八十年): I.e., the lifespan of Buddha Śākyamuni.

5 **the teachings of the buddhas are the teaching buddhas** (*bukkyō wa sunawachi kyōbutsu nari* 佛教はすなはち教佛なり): The unusual expression *kyōbutsu* 教佛 here can be taken either as "the buddha that teaches" or as "the buddha that is the teachings."

6 **a quantity great or small** (*dai shō no ryō* 大小の量): Possibly a reference to the Great and Small Vehicles (*daijō shōjō* 大乘小乘).

a nature good, evil, or neutral (*zen aku muki tō no shō* 善・惡・無記等の性): I.e., the three types of karma.

for the sake of one's own teaching or teaching others (*ji kyō kyō ta no tame* 自教・教他のため): The unusual phrase "one's own teaching or teaching others" (*ji kyō kyō ta* 自教教他) suggests a common division of the Buddhist path into "one's own benefit and benefiting others" (*ji ri ri ta* 自利利他), a distinction that can be applied either to two aspects of the bodhisattva's training or to a difference between the aspiration of the *śrāvaka* and the bodhisattva respectively.

34. The Teachings of the Buddhas *Bukkyō* 佛教   87

[34:2] {1:381}

ある漢いはく、釋迦老漢、かつて一代の教典を宣説するほかに、さらに上
乗一心の法を摩訶迦葉に正傳す、嫡嫡相承しきたれり。しかあれば、教は
赴機の戲論なり、心は理性の眞實なり。この正傳せる一心を、教外別傳と
いふ。三乘十二分教の所談にひとしかるべきにあらず。一心上乘なるゆえ
に、直指人心、見性成佛なり、といふ。

Some fellows say that old man Śākya, besides preaching the scriptures
throughout his lifetime, also directly transmitted to Mahākāśyapa the
dharma of the one mind of the higher vehicle, which has been inherited
by successor after successor.[7] Therefore, the teachings are frivolous discourse directed at capacities, while the mind is the true reality of the essential nature.[8] They call this one mind directly transmitted "*a separate
transmission outside the teachings.*"[9] It should not be equated with what
is talked about in the three vehicles and twelvefold teachings.[10] Because
it is the higher vehicle of the one mind, they say it is "*pointing directly at
the person's mind, seeing the nature and attaining buddhahood.*"[11]

---

7   **the dharma of the one mind of the higher vehicle** (*jōjō isshin no hō* 上乘一心の
法): I.e., the teaching of the one Buddha mind, as understood in the highest form of Buddhism. Often associated with a description of Bodhidharma's Buddhism by Mazu Daoyi
馬祖道一 (709-788); see, e.g., *Jingde chuandeng lu* 景德傳燈錄 (T.2076.51:246a5-6):

> 達磨大師、從南天竺國來、躬至中華、傳上乘一心之法。

Great Master Dharma came from a kingdom in the south of Sindhu, arriving in China
and transmitting the dharma of the one mind of the higher vehicle.

8   **frivolous discourse directed at capacities** (*fuki no keron* 赴機の戲論): I.e., *upāya*,
teachings accommodated to the spiritual needs and abilities of the audience but not ultimately true.

9   **"a separate transmission outside the teachings"** (*kyōge betsuden* 教外別傳): A
common slogan of the Zen tradition, often combined with the phrases quoted below
here, in the famous four-line "creed" traditionally (though spuriously) attributed to
Bodhidharma:

> 教外別傳、不立文字、直指人心、見性成佛。

> A separate transmission outside the teachings,
> No dependence on words and letters,
> Direct pointing at the person's mind,
> Seeing the nature and attaining buddhahood.

See Supplementary Notes, s.v. "A separate transmission outside the teachings."

10   **the three vehicles and twelvefold teachings** (*sanjō jūnibun kyō* 三乘十二分教):
I.e., the Buddhism of the Buddhist canon, as opposed to the "mind dharma" (*shinbō* 心
法) said to be transmitted by the Zen lineage; see Supplementary Notes, s.v. "Three vehicles and twelvefold teachings." Dōgen will treat this topic below, beginning in section
14.

11   **"pointing directly at the person's mind, seeing the nature and attaining buddhahood"** (*jikishi ninshin, kenshō jōbutsu* 直指人心、見性成佛): A famous Zen dictum;
traditionally attributed to Bodhidharma; see Supplementary Notes.

88 DŌGEN'S *SHŌBŌGENZŌ* VOLUME III

[34:3]

この道取、いまだ佛法の家業にあらず、出身の活路なし、通身の威儀にあらず。かくのごとくの漢、たとひ數百千年のさきに先達と稱すとも、恁麼の説話あらば、佛法・佛道はあきらめず、通せざりける、としるべし。ゆえはいかん。佛をしらず、教をしらず、心をしらず、内をしらず、外をしらざるがゆえに。そのしらざる道理は、かつて佛法をきかざるによりてなり。いま諸佛という本末、いかなるとしらず。去來の邊際すべて學せざるは、佛弟子と稱するにたらず。ただ一心を正傳して佛教を正傳せず、といふは、佛法をしらざるなり。佛教の一心、をしらず、一心の佛教、をきかず。一心のほかに佛教あり、といふなんぢが一心、いまだ一心ならず、佛教のほかに一心あり、といふなんぢが佛教、いまだ佛教ならざらん。たとひ教外別傳の謬説を相傳すといふとも、なんぢいまだ内外をしらざれば、言理の符合あはざるなり。

These words are not in the family occupation of the buddha dharma; they lack the survival route for leaving the body; they are not the deportment of the body throughout.[12] We should realize that fellows like this, if they have such talk, have not clarified, have not penetrated, the buddha dharma or the way of the buddhas, even though they were calling themselves guides hundreds or thousands of years ago. Why? Because they do not know the "buddha," they do not know the "teachings," they do not know the "mind," they do not know the "inside," they do not know the "outside." The reason that they do not know is that they have never heard the buddha dharma. They do not know what the roots and branches are of "the buddhas" spoken of here.[13]

Those who have studied nothing of the boundaries of their coming and going do not deserve to be called disciples of the buddhas. To say that only the one mind is directly transmitted, but the teachings of the buddhas are not directly transmitted, is not to know the buddha dharma.

---

12 **the family occupation of the buddha dharma** (*buppō no kagō* 佛法の家業): I.e., the spiritual practice in the "house" of the buddhas and ancestors.

the survival route for leaving the body (*shusshin no katsuro* 出身の活路): The term *katsuro* 活路 has the sense "escape route" — i.e., the way out of a dangerous situation; the term *shusshin* 出身, while having the colloquial sense "to advance one's status," is regularly used in Zen texts for "liberation."

the deportment of the body throughout (*tsūshin no iigi* 通身の威儀): The term *tsūshin* 通身 occurs frequently in the *Shōbōgenzō*; it is most familiar from the saying, discussed in the "Shōbōgenzō Kannon" 正法眼藏觀音, that Bodhisattva Avalokiteśvara's "body throughout is hands and eyes" (*tsūshin ze shugen* 通身是手眼). See Supplementary Notes, s.v. "His body throughout is hands and eyes."

13 **They do not know what the roots and branches are of "the buddhas" spoken of here** (*ima shobutsu to iu honmatsu, ikanaru to shirazu* いま諸佛という本末、いかなるとしらず): Perhaps referring back to Dōgen's discussion of "the buddhas" in section 1. "Roots and branches" (*honmatsu* 本末) is a standard expression for the "beginning and end," or "nature and characteristics," of something.

34. The Teachings of the Buddhas *Bukkyō* 佛教　　　89

They do not know the one mind that is the teachings of the buddhas; they have not heard the teachings of the buddhas that are the one mind. Your one mind, of which you say there are teachings of the buddhas outside the one mind, is not yet the one mind; your teachings of the buddhas, of which you say there is one mind outside the teachings of the buddhas, is not yet the teachings of the buddhas. Though the erroneous talk of a *"separate transmission outside the teachings"* may have been transmitted to you, since you do not yet understand "inside" and "outside," your words do not accord with reason.[14]

[34:4] {1:382}

佛正法眼藏を單傳する佛祖、いかでか佛教を單傳せざらん。いはんや釋迦老漢、なにとしてか、佛家の家業にあるべからざらん教法を、施設することあらん。釋迦老漢、すでに單傳の教法をあらしめん、いづれの佛祖かならしめん。このゆえに、上乘一心といふは、三乘十二分教、これなり、大藏・小藏、これなり。

How could the buddhas and ancestors, who uniquely transmit the treasury of the true dharma eye of the buddha, not uniquely transmit the teachings of the buddhas? Not to mention why old man Śākya would have provided teachings that are not supposed to be the family occupation of the house of the buddhas? Since old man Śākya brought into being the teachings uniquely transmitted, which buddha or ancestor would nullify them? Therefore, "the one mind of the higher vehicle" is the three vehicles and twelvefold teachings, is the great treasury and small treasury.[15]

[34:5]

しるべし、佛心といふは、佛の眼睛なり、破木杓なり、諸法なり、三界なるがゆえに、山海國土・日月星辰なり。佛教といふは、萬像森羅なり。外といふは、這裏なり、這裏來なり。正傳は、自己より自己に正傳するがゆえに、正傳のなかに自己あるなり、一心より一心に正傳するなり、正傳に一心あるべし。上乘一心は、土石砂礫なり、土石砂礫は、一心なるがゆえに、土石砂礫は、土石砂礫なり。もし上乘一心の正傳といはば、かくのごとくあるべし。

We should realize that, because the buddha mind is the eye of the buddha, is a broken wooden dipper, is the dharmas, is the three realms, it is the mountains, oceans, and lands, the sun, moon, and stars.[16] The teach-

---

14　**your words do not accord with reason** (*gonri no fugō awazaru nari* 言理の符合あはざるなり): Taking the somewhat unusual compound *gonri* 言理 (also appearing in "Shōbōgenzō busshō" 正法眼藏佛性) as "words and reason."

15　**the great treasury and small treasury** (*daizō shōzō* 大藏・小藏): I.e., the scriptural canons of the Great and Small Vehicles.

16　**a broken wooden dipper** (*ha mokushaku* 破木杓): A common expression in Zen texts for something worthless; often used (as surely here) in an ironic positive sense.

90 DŌGEN'S *SHŌBŌGENZŌ* VOLUME III

ings of the buddhas are the thicket of myriad images.[17] "Outside" is in here, is what comes in here.[18] Because direct transmission directly transmits from self to self, the self is within direct transmission; it directly transmits from one mind to one mind, so there must be the one mind in direct transmission. "The one mind of the higher vehicle" is earth, stones, sand, and pebbles; because earth, stones, sand, and pebbles are the one mind, earth, stones, sand, and pebbles are earth, stones, sand, and pebbles. If we talk of the direct transmission of "the one mind of the higher vehicle," it should be like this.

[34:6]
しかあれども、教外別傳を道取する漢、いまだこの意旨をしらず。かるがゆえに教外別傳の謬説を信じて、佛教をあやまることなかれ。もしなんぢがいふがごとくならば、教をば心外別傳といふべきか。もし心外別傳といはば、一句半偈つたはるべからざるなり、もし心外別傳といはずば、教外別傳といふべからざるなり。

Nevertheless, the fellows who say "*a separate transmission outside the teachings*" do not know its meaning. Therefore, do not misunderstand the teachings of the buddhas by believing in the erroneous talk of "a separate transmission outside the teachings." If it were as you say, would you call the teachings "*a separate transmission outside the mind*"? If you say "*a separate transmission outside the mind*," then not a single line or half a gāthā would have been transmitted; if you do not say "*a separate transmission outside the mind*," you should not say "*a separate transmission outside the teachings.*"

[34:7]
摩訶迦葉、すでに釋尊の嫡子として法藏の教主たり、正法眼藏を正傳して佛道の住持なり。しかありとも、佛教は正傳すべからずといふは、　學道の偏局なるべし。しるべし、一句を正傳すれば、一法の正傳せらるるなり、一句を正傳すれば、山傳・水傳あり。不能離却這裏なり。

Mahākāśyapa, since he was master of the teachings of the dharma treasury as the legitimate heir of Śākya, the Honored One, was maintainer of the way of the buddhas by directly transmitting the treasury of the true dharma eye.[19] In spite of this, to maintain that he would not have directly

---

17　**the thicket of myriad images** (*banzō shinra* 萬像森羅): A fixed expression (often written *shinra banzō* 森羅萬像) for the myriad things of the universe, based on the image of a dense growth of trees. See Supplementary Notes, s.v. "Myriad forms."

18　**"Outside" is in here, is what comes in here** (*ge to iu wa, shari nari, shari rai nari* 外といふは、這裏なり、這裏來なり): The sense of "outside" here is unclear; the most obvious sense would seem to be "outside of the teachings," though some take it as "outside the mind." Similarly, "in here" and "what comes [from?] in here" are subject to interpretation.

19　**master of the teachings of the dharma treasury** (*hōzō no kyōshū* 法藏の教主):

34. The Teachings of the Buddhas *Bukkyō* 佛教   91

transmitted the teachings of the buddhas, is a narrow, one-sided view in the study of the way. We should realize that, when we directly transmit one line, one dharma is directly transmitted; when we transmit one line, there are the transmission of mountains and the transmission of waters.[20] It is, *we can't get free from here.*[21]

[34:8] {1:383}

釋尊の正法眼藏無上菩提は、ただ摩訶迦葉に正傳せしなり、餘子に正傳せず、正傳はかならず摩訶迦葉なり。このゆえに、古今に佛法の眞實を學する箇箇、ともにみな從來の教學を決擇するには、かならず佛祖に參究するなり、決を餘輩にとぶらはず。もし佛祖の正決をゑざるは、いまだ正決にあらず。依教の正不を決せんとおもはんは、佛祖に決すべきなり。そのゆえは、盡法輪の本主は、佛祖なるがゆえに。道有・道無、道空・道色、ただ佛祖のみこれをあきらめ、正傳しきたりて、古佛・今佛なり。

The unsurpassed bodhi of the treasury of the true dharma eye of Śākya, the Honored One, was directly transmitted only to Mahākāśyapa and was not directly transmitted to anyone else; the direct transmission was without doubt to Mahākāśyapa. For this reason, in past and present, all who study the truth of the buddha dharma always investigate it with the buddhas and ancestors in order to determine the teachings that have been handed down; they do not seek the determination from others. If they

---

Likely a reference to the tradition that Mahākāśyapa was responsible for the compilation of the sūtras following the death of the Śākyamuni.

20   **one dharma is directly transmitted** (*ippō no shōden seraruru* 一法の正傳せらる る): Or "the one dharma [in its entirety] is directly transmitted."

21   **We can't get free from here** (*funō rikyaku shari* 不能離却這裏): Perhaps expressing the thought that the transmission is going on in the landscape all around us. This phrase in Chinese has no known source but may reflect an address recorded in the *Dahui Pujue chanshi yulu* 大慧普覺禪師語錄 (T.1998A.47:825b4-9):

上堂舉、鏡清問玄沙、學人乍入叢林。乞師指箇入路。沙云、還聞偃谿水聲麼。清云聞。沙云、從這裏入。鏡清於此得箇入處。五祖師翁云、果是得入、一任四方八面。若也未然、輒不得離却這裏。師云、若要眞箇得入、直須離却這裏。下座。

Ascending the hall, [Dahui] raised [the following]:
Jingqing asked Xuansha, "I'm just entering the grove. I beg the Master point out the entrance road."
Sha said, "Do you hear Yanxi's sound of water?"
Qing said, "I hear it."
Sha said, "You enter from here."
At this, Jinqing gained the entrance.
My master's teacher, Wuzu, said, "If he really gained the entrance, it was entirely due to the four quarters and eight directions. If it wasn't, he couldn't get free from here."
The Master [Dahui] said, "If you really want to gain the entrance, just get free from here."
He got down from the seat.

92 DŌGEN'S *SHŌBŌGENZŌ* VOLUME III

have not received the correct determination of the buddhas and ancestors, it is not a correct determination. If we wish to determine what is correct or not according to the teachings we rely on, we should determine it with the buddhas and ancestors. The reason is that the original masters of the entire dharma wheel are the buddhas and ancestors. Whether speaking of existence, speaking of nonexistence, speaking of emptiness, speaking of form, only the buddhas and ancestors are the past buddhas and present buddhas who have clarified and directly transmitted them.

* * * * *

[34:9]
巴陵、因僧問、祖意・教意、是同是別。師云、鶏寒上樹、鴨寒入水。

Baling was once asked by a monk, "The intention of the ancestors and the intention of the teachings — are they the same or different?"[22]

The Master said, "When the chicken's cold, it goes up a tree; when the duck's cold, it goes into the water."

[34:10]
この道取を參學して、佛道の祖宗を相見し、佛道の教法を見聞すべきなり。いま祖意・教意と問取するは、祖意は祖意と是同・是別と問取するなり。いま鶏寒上樹、鴨寒入水といふは、同・別を道取すといへども、同・別を見取するともがらの見聞に、一任する同・別にあらざるべし。しかあればすなはち、同・別の論にあらざるがゆえに、同・別と道取しつべきなり。このゆえに、同・別と問取すべからず、といふがごとし。

Studying these words, we should meet with the ancestors of the way of the buddhas and experience the teachings of the way of the buddhas. To ask here about "the intention of the ancestors" and "the intention of the teachings" is to ask, "the intention of the ancestors and the intention of the ancestors — are they the same or are they different?" To say here, *"when the chicken's cold, it goes up in a tree; when the duck's cold, it goes into the water,"* may be speaking of sameness and difference; but it should not be a sameness and difference left entirely up to the experience of those who perceive sameness and difference. This being the case, since it is not a question of sameness or difference, he must have said, "same or different."[23] Therefore, it is as if he said, "you should not ask about same or different."

---

22 **Baling** (*Haryō* 巴陵): I.e., Baling Haojian 巴陵顥鑑 (dates unknown), a disciple of Yunmen Wenyan 雲門文偃 (864-949). This conversation is recorded at *Jingde chuandeng lu* 景德傳燈録, T.2076.51:386a24-26.

23 **he must have said, "same or different"** (*dō betsu to dōshu shitsu beki nari* 同・別と道取しつべきなり): Or perhaps "He could have said, 'same and different.'"

34. The Teachings of the Buddhas *Bukkyō* 佛教   93

* * * * *

[34:11] {1:384}

玄沙、因僧問、三乘十二分教即不要、如何是祖師西來意。師云、三乘十二分教總不要。

Xuansha was once asked by a monk, "The three vehicles and twelve-fold teachings are unnecessary, but what is the intention of the Ancestral Master's coming from the west?"[24]

The Master said, "The three vehicles and twelvefold teachings are wholly unnecessary."

[34:12]

いはゆる僧問の三乘十二分教即不要、如何是祖師西來意、といふ、よのつねにおもふがごとく、三乘十二分教は、條條の岐路なり、そのほか祖師西來意あるべし、と問するなり。三乘十二分教これ祖師西來意なり、と認ずるにあらず、いはんや、八萬四千法門蘊すなはち祖師西來意、としらんや。しばらく參究すべし、三乘十二分教、なにとしてか即不要なる。もし要せんときは、いかなる規矩かある。三乘十二分教を不要なるところに、祖師西來意の參學を現成するか。いたづらにこの問の出現するにあらざらん。

As it is commonly thought, the monk's question, "T*he three vehicles and twelvefold teachings are unnecessary, but what is the intention of the Ancestral Master's coming from the west?*" is saying that "the three vehicles and twelvefold teachings" are so many branch roads, but there must be some other "*intention of the Ancestral Master's coming from the west.*" It does not recognize that the "the three vehicles and twelve-fold teachings" are "*the intention of the Ancestral Master's coming from the west,*" much less realize that the aggregate of eighty-four thousand dharma gates is "*the intention of the Ancestral Master's coming from*

---

24 **Xuansha** (*Gensha* 玄沙): I.e., Xuansha Shibei 玄沙師備 (835-908). This conversation is recorded in Dōgen's *shinji Shōbōgenzō* 眞字正法眼藏 (DZZ.5:150, case 45); the text found in the *Jingde chuandeng lu* 景德傳燈錄 (T.2076.51:416c9-11) has a slightly different version of the exchange: the monk said,

三乘十二分教即不問。如何是祖師西來意。玄沙曰、三乘十二分教不要。

"I'm not asking about the three vehicles and the twelvefold teachings, but what is the intention of the Ancestral Master's coming from the west?"

Xuansha said, "The three vehicles and twelvefold teachings are unnecessary."

See Supplementary Notes, s.v. "Three vehicles and twelvefold teachings."

the intention of the Ancestral Master's coming from the west (*soshi seirai i* 祖師西來意): I.e., "the reason Bodhidharma came to China"; a common topic of Zen conversation and title theme of Dōgen's "Shōbōgenzō soshi seirai i" 正法眼藏祖師西來意. See Supplementary Notes, s.v. "Intention of the Ancestral Master's coming from the west."

94 DŌGEN'S *SHŌBŌGENZŌ* VOLUME III

the west."[25] We should investigate for a bit why "the three vehicles and twelvefold teachings" are "unnecessary." When they are necessary, what standard is there?[26] Does the study of "the intention of the Ancestral Master's coming from the west" occur where "the three vehicles and twelvefold teachings" are "unnecessary"? He probably did not produce this question idly.

[34:13]

玄沙いはく、三乗十二分教総不要。この道取は、法輪なり。この法輪の轉ずるところ、佛教の、佛教に處在することを參究すべきなり。その宗旨は、三乗十二分教は佛祖の法輪なり、有佛祖の時處にも轉ず、無佛祖の時處にも轉ず、祖前・祖後おなじく轉ずるなり、さらに佛祖を轉ずる功德あり。祖師西來意の正當恁麼時は、この法輪を総不要なり。総不要といふは、もちいざるにあらず、やぶるにあらず。この法輪、このとき、総不要輪の轉ずるのみなり。三乗十二分教なしといはず、総不要の時節を覰見すべきなり。総不要なるがゆえに、三乗十二分教なり、三乗十二分教なるがゆえに、三乗十二分教にあらず、このゆえに、三乗十二分教総不要と道取するなり。

Xuansha said, "*The three vehicles and twelvefold teachings are wholly unnecessary.*" These words are the dharma wheel. We should investigate the fact that, where this dharma wheel turns, the teachings of the buddhas are located in the teachings of the buddhas.[27] The essential point is that "the three vehicles and twelvefold teachings" are the dharma wheel of the buddhas and ancestors, which turns in times and places where there are buddhas and ancestors, and turns in times and places where there are no buddhas and ancestors; it turns similarly before the ancestors and after the ancestors; and further, it has the virtue of turning the buddhas and ancestors. At the very time of *"the intention of the Ancestral Master coming from the west,"* this dharma wheel is "wholly unnecessary." "Wholly unnecessary" does not mean "not used" or "broken." It is just that this dharma wheel at this time turns the wheel of "wholly unnecessary."[28] It

---

25 **aggregate of eighty-four-thousand dharma gates** (*hachiman shisen hōmon'un* 八萬四千法門蘊): I.e., the entirety of the Buddhist teachings. Usually, *hachiman shisen hō'un* 八萬四千法蘊 or *hachiman shisen hōmon* 八萬四千法門; the combination *hōmon'un* 法門蘊 is unusual.

26 **what standard is there?** (*ikanaru kiku ka aru* いかなる規矩かある): Presumably, what is the criterion on the basis of which "the three vehicles and twelvefold teachings" would be necessary?

27 **the teachings of the buddhas are located in the teachings of the buddhas** (*bukkyō no, bukkyō ni shozai suru* 佛教の、佛教に處在する): Perhaps, meaning something like, "Xuansha's saying is a teaching of a buddha that belongs to the teachings of the buddhas."

28 **It is just that this dharma wheel at this time turns the wheel of "wholly unnecessary"** (*kono hōrin, kono toki, sō fuyō rin no tenzuru nomi nari* この法輪、このとき、総不要輪の轉ずるのみなり): I.e., the dharma wheel being turned here by Xuansha is just

34. The Teachings of the Buddhas *Bukkyō* 佛教

does not say "the three vehicles and twelvefold teachings" do not exist; we should see the time when they are "wholly unnecessary." Because it is "wholly unnecessary, it is "the three vehicles and twelvefold teachings"; because it is "the three vehicles and twelvefold teachings," it is not "the three vehicles and twelvefold teachings."[29] Therefore, he says, *"The three vehicles and twelvefold teachings are wholly unnecessary."*

[34:14] {1:385}
その三乗十二分教、そこばくあるなかの一隅をあぐるには、すなはちこれなり。三乗

Giving one corner of the several [versions of the] "three vehicles and twelvefold teachings," they are as follows. "The three vehicles":

[34:15]
一者聲聞乗

First, the śrāvaka vehicle.

[34:16]
四諦によりて得道す。四諦といふは、苦諦・集諦・滅諦・道諦なり。これをきき、これを修行するに、生老病死を度脱し、般涅槃を究竟す。この四諦を修行するに、苦・集は俗なり、滅・道は第一義なりといふは、論師の見解なり。もし佛法によりて修行するがごときは、四諦ともに唯佛與佛なり、四諦ともに法住法位なり、四諦ともに實相なり、四諦ともに佛性なり。このゆえに、さらに無生・無作等の論におよばず、四諦ともに総不要なるゆえに。

One gains the way on the basis of the four truths. "The four truths" means the truth of suffering, the truth of its cause, the truth of its extinction, and the truth of the path. By hearing these and putting them into practice, one is delivered from birth, old age, sickness, and death, and completes *parinirvāna*. The claim that, in practicing these four dharmas, suffering and cause are conventional, while extinction and the path are ultimate truths, is the view of the treatise masters.[30] For those who

---

the teaching of "wholly unnecessary."

29 **because it is "the three vehicles and twelvefold teachings," it is not "the three vehicles and twelvefold teachings"** (*sanjō jūni bun kyō naru ga yue ni, sanjō jūni bun kyō ni arazu* 三乗十二分教なるがゆえに、三乗十二分教にあらず): Perhaps meaning something like, "when we understand the texts of the Buddhist canon as "wholly unnecessary," we realize that the canon is something quite different from what we usually think it to be.

30 **suffering and cause are conventional, while extinction and the path are ultimate truths** (*ku shū wa zoku nari, metsu dō wa daiichi gi nari* 苦・集は俗なり、滅・道は第一義なり): Dōgen invokes here a standard Buddhist distinction between two levels of discourse: conventional truth (*zokutai* 俗諦; S. *saṃvṛti-satya*) and ultimate truth (*shintai* 眞諦; S. *paramārtha-satya*); but the use of this distinction in treatments of the four truths

96 DŌGEN'S *SHŌBŌGENZŌ* VOLUME III

practice according to the buddha dharma, the four truths are all "*only buddhas with buddhas*"; the four truths are all "*dharmas abiding in their dharma positions*"; the four truths are all "the real marks"; the four truths are all the buddha nature.[31] Therefore, there is no question of their being unborn or unproduced, and the like; for the four truths are all "wholly unnecessary."[32]

[34:17]
二者縁覺乗

Second, the *pratyeka-buddha* vehicle.

[34:18]
十二因縁によりて般涅槃す。十二因縁といふは、一者無明、二者行、三者識、四者名色、五者六入、六者觸、七者受、八者愛、九者取、十者有、十一者生、十二者老死。

One attains *parinirvāṇa* on the basis of the twelve causes and conditions.[33] The "twelve causes" means (1) ignorance, (2) formations, (3) consciousness, (4) name and form, (5) the six senses, (6) contact, (7) sensation, (8) craving, (9) grasping, (10) becoming, (11) birth, (12) old age and death.

[34:19]
この十二因縁を修行するに、過去・現在・未来に因縁せしめて、能觀・所觀を論ずといへども、一一の因縁を擧して參究するに、すなはち總不要輪轉なり、總不要因縁なり。しるべし、無明これ一心なれば、行・識等も一心な

---

is not in fact so typical of the Buddhist treatises — which speak more often of the first two truths as "mundane" (*seken* 世間; S. *laukika*), or "defiled" (*uro* 有漏; S. *sāsrava*) and the last two as "transmundane" (*shusseken*), or "undefiled" (*muro* 無漏; S. *anāsrava*).

31 **"only buddhas with buddhas"** (*yui butsu yo butsu* 唯佛與佛); **"dharmas abiding in their dharma positions"** (*hō jū hō i* 法住法位); **"the real marks"** (*jissō* 實相): I.e., the ultimate truth of the dharmas known only to the buddhas; from two passages in the *Lotus Sūtra* often cited by Dōgen; see Supplementary Notes, s.v. "Only buddhas with buddhas can exhaustively investigate the real marks of the dharmas," and "Dharmas abide in their dharma positions."

32 **unborn or unproduced** (*mushō musa* 無生・無作): Likely a reference to the classification, popular in Tiantai scholarship, of the four truths into four ways of understanding them: (1) as "arising and ceasing" (*shōmetsu* 生滅), (2) as not arising and ceasing (*mushōmetsu* 無生滅; i.e., "empty"), (3) as "incalculable" (*muryō* 無量; or both [1] and [2]), and (4) as "unproduced" (*musa* 無作; or neither [1] nor [2]).

33 **One attains *parinirvāṇa* on the basis of the twelve causes and conditions** (*jūni innen ni yorite hatsunehan su* 十二因縁によりて般涅槃す): A common claim in East Asian Buddhism, arising from the interpretation of the term *pratyeka* as derived from *pratyaya* ("condition"). "The twelve causes and conditions" (*jūni innen* 十二因縁) refers to the ancient Buddhist formula of the "twelvefold dependent origination" (*jūni engi* 十二緣起; S. *dvadaśāṅga-pratītya-samutpāda*), the members of which Dōgen lists here.

34. The Teachings of the Buddhas *Bukkyō* 佛教

り。無明これ滅なれば、行・識等も滅なり。無明これ涅槃なれば、行・識
等も涅槃なり。生も滅なるがゆえに恁麼いふなり。無明も道著の一句なり、
識・名色等もまたかくのごとし。しるべし、無明・行等は、吾有箇斧子與汝
住山なり。無明・行・識等は、發時蒙和尚許斧子、便請取なり。

In the practice of the twelve causes and conditions, while one may assign the causes and conditions to past, present, and future, and discuss the agent of contemplation and the object of contemplation, when we take up each of the causes and conditions and investigate them, they are the turning of the wheel of the "wholly unnecessary," the "wholly unnecessary" causes and conditions.[34] We should realize that, since "ignorance" is the one mind, "formations, consciousness," and the rest, are also the one mind. Since "ignorance" is "cessation," "formations, consciousness," and the rest, are also "cessation."[35] Since "ignorance" is nirvāṇa, "formations, consciousness," and the rest, are also nirvāṇa. Because "birth" is also "cessation," we can say this.[36] "Ignorance" is also the single line of a saying; and "consciousness, name, and form," and the rest, are also like this.[37] We should realize that "ignorance, formations," and the rest, are, "*I have an ax; I'll give it to you, and you can live on this mountain.*" "Ignorance, formations," and the rest, are, "*When I left, the Reverend honored me with the offer of an ax, which I now beg to take.*"[38]

---

34 **assign the causes and conditions to past, present, and future** (*kako genzai mirai ni innen seshimete* 過去現在未來に因緣せしめて): Reference to a standard analysis of the twelve links that assigns the first two members to the past life, the next eight to the present life, and the last two to the future life.

35 **Since "ignorance" is "cessation"** (*mumyō kore metsu nareba* 無明これ滅なれば): Presumably, "cessation" (*metsu* 滅) here refers to the third truth, the cessation (S. *nirodha*) of suffering — i.e., nirvāṇa.

36 **"birth" is also "cessation"** (*shō mo metsu naru* 生も滅なる): "Birth" (*shō* 生) here likely refers to the penultimate member of the twelvefold chain; it is unclear whether "cessation" (*metsu* 滅) here refers to nirvāṇa or to the final member of the chain, "old age and death."

37 **"Ignorance" is also the single line of a saying** (*mumyō mo dōjaku no ikku nari* 無明も道著の一句なり): Probably meaning that we can also treat "ignorance" and the other members of the twelvefold chain as the words of the buddhas and ancestors — as in the following example.

38 **"I have an ax; I'll give it to you, and you can live on this mountain"** (*go u ko fusu yo nyo jūzan* 吾有箇斧子與汝住山); **"When I left, the Reverend honored me with the offer of an ax, which I now beg to take"** (*hotsuji mō oshō ko fusu ben shō shu* 發時蒙和尚許斧子便請取): Lines from an exchange between Qingyuan Xingsi 青原行思 (d. 740) and his follower Shitou Xiqian 石頭希遷 (700-790). The former line is Qingyuan's words to Shitou as the latter was leaving Qingyuan to visit Nanyue Huairang 南嶽懷讓 (677-744); the latter is Shitou's request upon his return from the visit, in response to which Qingyuan let one leg hang down (an act to which Dōgen will refer below, section 29). The story can be found at *Jingde chuandeng lu* 景德傳燈錄 (T.2076.51:240b18-27). The two statements may be intended as an example of the cause and effect relationships among the members of the twelvefold chain.

98　DŌGEN'S *SHŌBŌGENZŌ* VOLUME III

[34:20] {1:386}

三者菩薩乗

Third, the bodhisattva vehicle.

[34:21]

六波羅蜜の教行證によりて、阿耨多羅三藐三菩提を成就す。その成就とい
ふは、造作にあらず、無作にあらず、始起にあらず、新成にあらず、久成
にあらず、本行にあらず、無爲にあらず。ただ成就阿耨多羅三藐三菩提な
り。

On the basis of the teaching, practice, and verification of the six
pāramitās, one achieves *anuttara-samyak-saṃbodhi*. That "achieve-
ment" is not constructed; it is not unconstructed; it is not initially arisen;
it is not newly attained; it is not attained long ago; it is not originally
practiced; it is not unconditioned: it is just *anuttara-samyak-saṃbodhi*
achieved.[39]

[34:22]

六波羅蜜といふは、檀波羅蜜・尸羅波羅蜜・羼提波羅蜜・毘梨耶波羅蜜・
禪那波羅蜜・般若波羅蜜なり。これは、ともに無上菩提なり。無生・無作
の論にあらず。かならずしも檀をはじめとし、般若をおはりとせず。

The six *pāramitās* are *dāna-pāramitā*, *śīla-pāramitā*, *kṣānti-pāramitā*,
vīrya-pāramitā, *dhyāna-pāramitā*, and prajñā-pāramitā.[40] These are all
unsurpassed bodhi; it is not a question of their being unborn or uncreat-
ed. *Dāna* is not necessarily made the first and prajñā the last.

39　**it is not attained long ago; it is not originally practiced** (*kujō ni arazu, hongyō ni
arazu* 久成にあらず、本行にあらず): Perhaps reflecting a famous passage in the *Lotus
Sūtra* (*Miaofa lianhua jing* 妙法蓮華經, T.262.9:42c19-23):

> 如是我成佛已來甚大久遠。壽命無量阿僧祇劫、常住不滅。諸善男子。我本行菩
> 薩道所成壽命、今猶未盡、復倍上數。

> In this way, since I attained buddhahood, it has been a very long time. My lifespan is
> incalculable *asaṃkhyeya kalpas*, constantly abiding without extinction. Good sons,
> the lifespan attained by my original practice of the bodhisattva path is even now still
> not exhausted; it is twice the above number.

it is just *anuttara-samyak-saṃbodhi* achieved (*tada jōju anokutara sanmyaku sanbodai nari* ただ成就阿耨多羅三藐三菩提なり): Or "it is just achieving *anuttara-samyak-
saṃbodhi*."

40　**The six *pāramitās*** (*roku haramitsu* 六波羅蜜): Dōgen gives here the transliteration
of the Sanskrit terms for the six perfections of the bodhisattva: *dāna-pāramitā* (*dan
haramitsu* 檀波羅蜜; the perfection of giving), *śīla-pāramitā* (*shira haramitsu* 尸羅波
羅蜜; the perfection of morality), *kṣānti-pāramitā* (*sendai haramitsu* 羼提波羅蜜; the
perfection of patience), *vīrya-pāramitā* (*biriya haramitsu* 毘梨耶波羅蜜; the perfection
of vigor), *dhyāna-pāramitā* (*zenna haramitsu* 禪那波羅蜜; the perfection of meditation),
and prajñā-pāramitā (*hannya haramitsu* 般若波羅蜜; the perfection of wisdom).

34. The Teachings of the Buddhas *Bukkyō* 佛教

[34:23]

經云、利根菩薩、般若爲初、檀爲終。鈍根菩薩、檀爲初、般若爲終。

It is said in a sūtra, "Bodhisattvas of keen faculties make prajñā first and dāna last; bodhisattvas of dull faculties make dāna first and prajñā last."[41]

[34:24]

しかあれども、羼提もはじめなるべし、禪那もはじめなるべし。三十六波羅蜜の現成あるべし。籮籠より籮籠をうるなり。

However, *kṣānti* could be first, or *dhyāna* could be first. There could be the appearance of thirty-six *pāramitās*.[42] It is getting nets and cages from nets and cages.[43]

[34:25] {1:387}

波羅蜜といふは、彼岸到なり。彼岸は去來の相貌蹤跡にあらざれども、到は現成するなり、到は公案なり。修行の、彼岸へいたるべしとおもふことなかれ。これ彼岸に修行あるがゆえに、修行すれば彼岸到なり。この修行、かならず徧界現成の力量を具足せるがゆえに。

十二分教
一者素咀纜 此云契經。
二者祇夜 此云重頌。
三者和伽羅那 此云授記。
四者伽陀 此云諷誦。
五者憂陀那 此云無問自説。
六者尼陀那 此云因緣。
七者波陀那 此云譬喻。
八者伊帝目多伽 此云本事。
九者闍陀伽 此云本生。
十者毘佛略 此云方廣。
十一者阿浮陀達磨 此云未曽有。
十二者優婆提舍 此云論議。

"*Pāramitā*" means "arrived at the other shore." Although "the other shore" is not the features and traces of coming and going, the "arrival" is "realized," the "arrival" is "the kōan."[44] Do not think that practice will

---

41 **a sūtra** (*kyō* 經): The source is unknown.

42 **thirty-six *pāramitās*** (*sanjūroku haramitsu* 三十六波羅蜜): Usually taken to mean that each of the six perfections contains the others; hence, six times six.

43 **It is getting nets and cages from nets and cages** (*rarō yori rarō o uru nari* 籮籠 より籮籠をうるなり): The idiom "nets and cages" (*rarō* 籮籠) is used very commonly in Zen, and in Dōgen's writings, for spiritual or cognitive "traps," or "snares"; see Supplementary Notes, s.v. "Nets and cages." Here, probably used ironically, for going from one perfection to another.

44 **Although "the other shore" is not the features and traces of coming and going**

100 DŌGEN'S *SHŌBŌGENZŌ* VOLUME III

arrive at "the other shore"; since there is practice on "the other shore," when we practice, it is "the other shore." For this practice is invariably endowed with the power to appear in the realms everywhere.

The twelvefold teachings:[45]

    1. Sūtra. Here, called "tally texts."[46]

    2. Geya. Here, called "repeated verse."[47]

    3. Vyākaraṇa. Here, called "prediction."[48]

    4. Gāthā. Here, called "chant."[49]

    5. Udāna. Here, called "voluntary preaching without a question."[50]

(*higan wa korai no sōbō shōseki ni arazaredomo* 彼岸は去來の相貌蹤跡にあらざれど も): I.e., although "the other shore" is not a place where one can arrive and depart. Some versions of the text read here "long ago" (*korai* 古來) for "coming and going" (*korai* 去 來).

the "arrival" is "realized," the "arrival" is "the kōan" (*tō wa genjō suru nari, tō wa kōan nari* 到は現成するなり、到は公案なり): I.e., the "arrival" actually occurs as the "realized kōan" (or "settled case"; *genjō kōan* 現成公案). See Supplementary Notes, s.v. "Realized kōan."

45 **The twelvefold teachings** (*jūni bun kyō* 十二分教): The following list draws on a passage from the *Miaofa lianhua jing xuanyi* 妙法蓮華經玄義, by Zhiyi 智顗 (538-597) (T.1716.33:752c27-753a6). Some manuscript traditions include notes, also reflecting the *Xuanyi*, for some members of the list, possibly by the fifteenth-century monk Bonsei 梵 清 (d. 1427), who was responsible for the 84-chapter Bonsei text of the *Shōbōgenzō*. Though they appear in the body of the Kawamura edition, they are relegated here to the annotation. The first such note occurs just following this heading but clearly belongs after the first member of the list:

修多羅、亦云線經、此云法本、亦云契經。

Sūtra. Also called "threaded text"; here, called "dharma source"; also called "tally text."

The expression, "here, called" (*shi un* 此云) in the following list and notes refers to the Chinese terms used to interpret the Sanskrit names for the twelve genres.

46 **Sūtra** (*sotaran* 素咀纜): Prose passage of a scripture.

47 **Geya** (*giya* 祇夜): Verse rephrasing the prose of a sūtra. The note here reads:

以偈頌修多羅也

Sūtra expressed in verse.

48 **Vyākaraṇa** (*wakarana* 和伽羅那): Prophetic statement on the future spiritual attainments, especially the buddhahood, of individuals.

49 **Gāthā** (*kada* 伽陀): Verse. The note here reads:

此云不重頌、如此間詩頌。

Here, called "non-repeated verse"; like the poem and verse of praise here.

50 **Udāna** (*udana* 憂陀那): Unprompted teaching, not in response to the audience. The note here reads:

無問自説經者、聖人説法、皆待請問、然爲衆生、作不請之師、故無問自説、 又佛法難知、名無能人間、若不自説、衆則不知爲説不説、又復不知爲説、何法 故、無問自説、乃所以彰所説甚深唯證、是以寄無問自説、以彰所顯也〉

34. The Teachings of the Buddhas *Bukkyō* 佛教

6. Nidāna. Here, called "causes and conditions."[51]
7. Avadāna. Here, called "parable."[52]
8. Itivṛttaka. Here, called "former matter."[53]
9. Jātaka. Here, called "former birth."[54]
10. Vaipulya. Here, called "expanded."[55]
11. Abhūta-dharma. Here, called "unprecedented."[56]
12. Upadeśa. Here, called "disquisitions."[57]

[34:26] {1:388}

如來則爲直說陰界入等假實之法、是名修多羅。或四五六七八九言偈、重頌

A sūtra voluntarily preached without a question: when the sages preach the dharma, they normally wait to be asked a question; however, for the sake of living beings, they may act as a teacher without a request — hence, "voluntary preaching without a question." Again, the buddha dharma is so difficult to know, it can be called "without anyone able to ask." If [the sages] do not preach voluntarily, the beings would not know what he would preach for them that he did not preach, and they would never know what dharma he would preach to them — hence, "voluntary preaching without a question." It is in order to make clear the extremely profound unique verification they preach that they rely on "voluntary preaching without a question" to make clear what is to be shown.

51 **Nidāna** (*innen* 因緣): An historical narrative, as in accounts of the circumstances leading to the formulation of a monastic rule. The note here reads:

因緣經者、欲明戒法、必因犯彰過、過相彰現、方得立制、此亦託因緣、以明所顯也

Scriptures of causes and conditions seek to explain the precepts, clarifying the error on the basis of the violation. Once the error is clearly shown, one can establish the regulation. This also makes use of "causes and conditions" to clarify what is to be shown.

52 **Avadāna** (*badana* 波陀那): Parable, allegory, and the like. The note here simply gives the full transliteration of the Sanskrit:

阿波陀那

Avadāna.

53 **Itivṛttaka** (*iteimokutaka* 伊帝目多伽): "So it is said"; account of a past life or lives. The note here reads:

此云如是語、亦云本事

Here, it is called "thus is it said"; also called "former matter."

54 **Jātaka** (*jataka* 闍陀伽): Account of a prior life of Buddha Śākyamuni. The note here reads:

本生事者、謂說前生菩薩行事。本事事者、謂說前世諸相應事

The material in a "former life" describes events in a previous life of the Bodhisattva; the material in a "former matter" describes various relevant events in former lives.

55 **Vaipulya** (*biburyaku* 毘佛略): "Extended," or "extensive," text; often used in reference to Mahāyāna (or certain Mahāyāna) scriptures.

56 **Abhūta-dharma** (*abudadaruma* 阿浮陀達磨): Something that "has never been"; an account of miracles.

57 **Upadeśa** (*ubadaisha* 優婆提舍): Doctrinal discussion.

102 DŌGEN'S *SHŌBŌGENZŌ* VOLUME III

世界陰入等事、是名祇夜。或直記衆生未來事、乃至記鴿雀成佛等、是名和
伽羅那。或孤起偈記世界陰入等事、是名伽陀。或無人問、自説世界事、是
名優陀那。或約世界不善事、而結禁戒、是名尼陀那。或以譬喩説世界事、
是名阿波陀那。或説本昔世界事、是名伊帝目多伽。或説本昔受生事、是名
闍陀伽。或説世界廣大事、是名毘佛略。或説世界未曽有事、是名阿浮達
磨。或問難世界事、是名優婆提舎。此是世界悉檀、爲悦衆生故、起十二部
經。

When the Tathāgata speaks directly of the provisional and real dharmas, such as the aggregates, constituents, and spheres, this is called
"sūtra."[58] Or, when, in gāthās of four, five, six, seven, eight, or nine
words, he restates in verse things such as the aggregates and bases of
the world, this is called "geya." Or, when he directly records the future
events of living beings, extending even to recording such things as the
buddhahood of pigeons and sparrows, this is called "vyākaraṇa." Or,
when, in independent verses, he records such things as the aggregates
and bases of the world, this is called "gāthā." Or, when, without anyone asking, he voluntarily preaches on the things of the world, this is
called "udāna." Or, when he explains the unwholesome matters of the
world and then establishes a prohibitive precept, this is called "nidāna."
Or, when he speaks of the things of the world through parables, this is
called "avadāna." Or, when he speaks of past things of the world, this
is called "itivṛttaka." Or, when he speaks of his past births, this is called
"jātaka." Or, when he speaks of the vast things of the world, this is called
"vaipulya." Or, when he speaks of unprecedented things of the world,
this is called "abhūta-dharma." Or, when he disputes the things of the
world, this is called "upadeśa." This is his worldly siddhānta: in order to
please living beings, he created the twelvefold scripture.[59]

[34:27] {1:389}

十二部經の名、きくことまれなり。佛法よのなかにひろまれるとき、これ
をきく。佛法すでに滅するときはきかず、佛法いまだひろまらざるとき、
またきかず。ひさしく善根をうゑてほとけをみたてまつるべきもの、これ
をきく。すでにきくものは、ひさしからずして阿耨多羅三藐三菩提をうべ
きなり。

---

58 **When the Tathāgata speaks directly** (*nyorai soku i jiki setsu* 如來則爲直説): This
entire passage is quoted directly from the *Miaofa lianhua jing xuanyi* 妙法蓮華經玄義
(T.1716.33:688b5-b20), which uses transliterations of the Sanskrit for the twelve terms.

aggregates, constituents, and spheres (*on kai nyū* 陰界入): Examples of basic Buddhist
teachings. The five heaps (S. *skandhas*) into which the psychophysical organism can be
analyzed; the eighteen factors (S. *dhātu*) involved in cognition: the six sense objects,
six sense organs, and six sense consciousnesses; and the twelve bases (S. *āyatana*) of
cognition: the six sense objects and the six sense organs.

59 **This is his worldly** *siddhānta* (*shi ze sekai shiddan* 此是世界悉檀): I.e., teachings
based on worldly understandings.

34. The Teachings of the Buddhas *Bukkyō* 佛教　　103

It is rare to hear the names of the twelvefold scripture. One hears them when the buddha dharma is spread throughout the world. One does not hear them when the buddha dharma has ceased; one does not hear them when the buddha dharma has not yet spread. Those who, having long since planted good roots, will be able to see the buddha, hear them. Those who have heard them will before long attain *anuttara-samyak-saṃbodhi.*

[34:28]

この十二、おのおの經と稱す、十二分教ともいひ、十二部經ともいふなり。十二分教おのおの十二分教を具足せるゆえに、一百四十四分教なり。十二分教おのおの十二分教を兼含せるゆえに、ただ一分教なり。しかあれども、億前億後の數量にあらず、これみな佛祖の眼睛なり、佛祖の骨髓なり、佛祖の家業なり、佛祖の光明なり、佛祖の莊嚴なり、佛祖の國土なり。十二分教をみるは、佛祖をみるなり、佛祖を道取するは、十二分教を道取するなり。

Each of these twelve is called a "scripture"; they are also called "the twelvefold teachings," or called "the twelvefold scripture." Because each of the twelvefold teachings is endowed with the twelvefold teachings, it is a one hundred forty-fourfold teaching. Because each of the twelvefold teachings combines the twelvefold teachings, it is just a one-fold teaching. However, it is not a matter of numbers, more or less than a hundred thousand: they are all the eyes of the buddhas and ancestors; they are the bones and marrow of the buddhas and ancestors; they are the family business of the buddhas and ancestors; they are the radiance of the buddhas and ancestors; they are the adornments of the buddhas and ancestors; they are the land of the buddhas and ancestors. To see the twelvefold teachings is to see the buddhas and ancestors; to say "the buddhas and ancestors" is to say "the twelvefold teachings."

[34:29]

しかあればすなはち、青原の垂一足、すなはち三乘十二分教なり。南嶽の説似一物即不中、すなはち三乘十二分教なり。いま玄沙の道取するは、總不要の意趣、それかくのごとし。この宗旨、擧拈するときは、ただ佛祖のみなり。さらに半人なし、一物なし、一事未起なり。正當恁麼時如何。いふべし、總不要。

Thus, Qingyuan's *"letting one leg hang down"* is the three vehicles and twelvefold teachings; Nanyue's *"to say it's like any thing wouldn't hit it"* is the three vehicles and twelvefold teachings.[60] The intent of

---

60　**Qingyuan's "letting one leg hang down"** (*Seigen no sui issoku* 青原の垂一足): Reference to the story of Qingyuan and Shitou cited above; see Note 38.

Nanyue's "to say it's like any thing wouldn't hit it" (*Nangaku no setsu ji ichimotsu soku fuchū* 南嶽の説似一物即不中): Reference to the words of Nanyue Huairang 南嶽懷讓 when asked by the Sixth Ancestor, Huineng 慧能, "What thing is it that comes like

104 DŌGEN'S *SHŌBŌGENZŌ* VOLUME III

Xuansha's saying here "wholly unnecessary" is like this. When we take up its essential point, it is just the buddhas and ancestors. Beyond this, there is not half a person, not a single thing; nothing is happening. *At this very time, what about it?* We should say, "wholly unnecessary."

[34:30]

あるひは九部といふあり、九分教といふべきなり。

九部
一者修多羅
二者伽陀
三者本事
四者本生
五者未曽有
六者因縁
七者譬喩
八者祇夜
九者優婆提舎

There are also nine divisions, which should be called the ninefold teachings.[61]

The nine divisions:

1. Sūtra
2. Gāthā
3. Former matter
4. Former birth
5. Unprecedented
6. Causes and conditions
7. Parable
8. Geya
9. Upadeśa

---

this?" A conversation included in the *shinji Shōbōgenzō* 眞字正法眼藏 (DZZ.5:178, case 101) and appearing often in Dōgen's writing; see Supplementary Notes, s.v. "What thing is it that comes like this?"

61 **the ninefold teachings** (*kubu kyō* 九部經): An early list of the types of the Buddha's discourse, containing the twelvefold teachings (see above, section 25), except for *vyākaraṇa*, *udāna*, and *vaipulya*. Given the quotation below (section 32), probably taken here from the *Lotus Sūtra* (*Miaofa lianhua jing* 妙法蓮華經, T.262.9:7c25-27).

34. The Teachings of the Buddhas *Bukkyō* 佛教　　　105

[34:31] {1:390}

この九部、おのおの九部を具足するがゆえに、八十一部なり。九部おのお
の一部を具足するゆえに、九部なり。歸一部の功徳あらずば、九部なるべ
からず。歸一部の功徳あるがゆえに、一部歸一部なり。このゆえに八十一
部なり、此部なり、我部なり、拂子部なり、　拄杖部なり、正法眼藏部な
り。

Because each of these nine divisions is endowed with the nine divisions, it is eighty-one divisions; because each of the nine divisions is endowed with the one division, it is nine divisions.[62] If they did not have the virtue of reducing to one division, they would not be nine divisions. Because they have the virtue of reducing to one division, it is one division reducing to one division. Therefore, it is the eighty-one divisions; it is "this" division; it is "I" division; it is the whisk division; it is the staff division; it is the treasury of the true dharma eye division.[63]

[34:32]

釋迦牟尼佛言、我此九部法、隨順衆生説。入大乘爲本、以故説是經。

> *Buddha Śākyamuni said,*
>
> *I this ninefold dharma,*
> *In accordance with the living beings, preach,*
> *As the basis for entering the Great Vehicle;*
> *For this reason, I preach this sūtra.*[64]

[34:33]

しるべし、我此は如來なり、面目身心あらはれきたる。この我此、すで
に九部法なり、九部法、すなはち我此なるべし。いまの一句一偈は、九部
法なり、我此なるがゆえに隨順衆生説なり。しかあればすなはち、一切衆
生の生從這裏生、すなはち説是經なり、死從這裏死は、すなはち説是經な
り、乃至、造次動容、すなはち説是經なり、化一切衆生、皆令入佛道、す
なはち説是經なり。この衆生は、我此九部法の隨順なり。この隨順は、隨
他去なり、隨自去なり、隨衆去なり、隨生去なり、隨我去なり、隨此去な
り。その衆生、かならず我此なるがゆえに、九部法の條條なり。

62　**because each of the nine divisions is endowed with one division, it is nine divisions** (*kubu onoono ichibu o gusoku suru yue ni, kubu nari* 九部おのおの一部を具足するゆえに、九部なり): Generally, interpreted to mean that the nine divisions are parts of a single whole; it could also be read to mean that each of the nine divisions is a single division.

63　**it is "this" division; it is "I" division** (*shi bu nari, ga bu nari* 此部なり、我部なり): From the lines, quoted just below, section 32: "I this ninefold dharma, in accordance with the living beings, preach."

64　**Buddha Śākyamuni** (*Shakamuni butsu* 釋迦牟尼佛): From a verse in the *Lotus Sūtra* (*Miaofa lianhua jing* 妙法蓮華經, T.262.9:8a6-7). Rendered awkwardly here according to the Chinese syntax, in deference to Dōgen's play with the text below.

106 DŌGEN'S *SHŌBŌGENZŌ* VOLUME III

We should realize that "I this" is the Tathāgata, whose face, and body and mind have been revealed.[65] Since this "I this" is the "ninefold dharma," the ninefold dharma must be "I this." Because the single line, the single gāthā, here is the ninefold dharma, is "I this," it is "*in accordance with the living beings, preach.*" Thus, that *the living of all living beings lives from here* is "*I preach this sūtra*"; that *their dying dies from here* is "*I preach this sūtra;*" *and so on, to their hasty acts and demeanor* are "*I preach this sūtra,*" and "*I have converted all the living beings, causing them all to enter the way of the buddhas*" is "*I preach this sūtra.*"[66] These "living beings" are "in accordance with" "*I this ninefold dharma.*" This "in accordance with" is "*to go along with it,*" is "*to go along with oneself,*" is "*to go along with 'beings,'*" is "*to go along with 'living,'*" is "*to go along with 'I,'*" is "*to go along with 'this.'*"[67] Because those "living beings" are invariably "I this," they are passages of the ninefold dharma.

[34:34] {1:391}

入大乘爲本、といふは、證大乘といひ、行大乘といひ、聞大乘といひ、説大乘といふ。しかあれば、衆生は天然として得道せり、といふにあらず、その一端なり。入は、本なり、本は、頭正尾正なり。ほとけ、法をとく、法、ほとけをとく。法、ほとけにとかる、ほとけ、法にとかる。火熖、ほとけをとき、法をとく。ほとけ、火熖をとき、法、火熖をとく。

To say, "*the basis for entering the Great Vehicle*" means "to verify the Great Vehicle," means "to practice the Great Vehicle," means "to hear the Great Vehicle," means "to preach the Great Vehicle." Therefore, it is

---

65 **"I this" is the Tathāgata** (*ga shi wa nyorai nari* 我此は如來なり): Dōgen here makes a compound term from the first two words of the sūtra sentence, "I this ninefold dharma . . . preach," that expresses his claim that the Buddha and his dharma are one.

66 **the living of all living beings lives from here** (*issai shujō no shō jū shari shō* 一切衆生の生從這裏生); **their dying dies from here** (*shi jū shari shi* 死從這裏死): I.e., the living beings that are the audience of the preaching have their life and death in the preaching. The translation of the phrase *shō jū shari shō* 生從這裏生 as "the living lives from here" seeks to preserve Dōgen's play with the word *shō* 生 in "living beings" (*shujō* 衆生); alternatively, the phrase could be rendered, "the 'living' [in 'living beings'] is born from here." The phrase is put in Chinese, as if a fixed saying, though no precedent for it has been identified.

"I have converted all the living beings, causing them all to enter the way of the buddhas" (*ke issai shujō, kai ryō nyū butsudō* 化一切衆生、皆令入佛道): From the *Lotus Sūtra* (*Miaofa lianhua jing* 妙法蓮華經, T.262.9:8b7).

67 **"to go along with it"** (*zui ta ko* 隨他去): From a saying of Dasui Fazhen 大隋法眞 (834-919), recorded in the *shinji Shōbōgenzō* 眞字正法眼藏 (DZZ.5:138, case 24), that "this" (*shako* 這箇) "goes along with it" when the chiliocosm is destroyed at the end of the kalpa; see Supplementary Notes.

"to go along with 'beings'" (*zui shu ko* 隨衆去); **"to go along with 'living'"** (*zui shō ko* 隨生去): An attempt to retain in English something of Dōgen's play here with the two elements of the term "living beings" (*shujō* 衆生).

34. The Teachings of the Buddhas *Bukkyō* 佛教

not the case that "the living beings" have spontaneously gained the way; it is one edge.[68] "Entering" is "the basis"; "the basis" is right from head to tail. The Buddha preaches the dharma; the dharma preaches the Buddha.[69] The dharma is preached by the Buddha; the Buddha is preached by the dharma. The flames preach the Buddha and preach the dharma; the Buddha preaches the flames; the dharma preaches the flames.

[34:35]

是經、すでに説故の良以あり、故説の良以あり。是經、とかざらんと擬するに、不可なり。このゆえに、以故説是經といふ。故説は亙天なり、亙天は故説なり。此佛・彼佛ともに是經と一稱し、自界・他界、ともに是經と故説す。このゆえに説是經なり、是經これ佛教なり。しるべし、恆沙の佛教は竹篦・拂子なり、佛教の恆沙は、拄杖・拳頭なり。

For "this sūtra," there is surely good cause to preach its reason, there is good cause for [the Buddha to say] "for this reason I preach." Even if he considered not preaching "this sūtra," that would not be possible. Therefore, he says, "*for this reason, I preach this sūtra.*" "For this reason, I preach" is "across the heavens"; "across the heavens" is "for this reason, I preach."[70] Both this buddha and that buddha praise "this sūtra"; both in our world and other worlds, "this sūtra" is "for this reason, I preach."[71] Therefore, it is "I preach this sūtra." "This sūtra" is the teachings of the buddhas. We should realize the teachings of the buddhas, as the sands of the Ganges, are a bamboo stick and a whisk; that the sands of the Ganges, as the teachings of the buddhas, are a staff and a fist.[72]

---

68 **it is one edge** (*sono ittan nari* その一端なり): Or, perhaps, "one tip." The grammatical subject is unexpressed and uncertain. A common interpretation is that the "living beings" are but one part of "attaining the way." Alternatively, one could read the phrase to mean that those who "attain the way" are but one part of "living beings," or that "attaining the way" is but one part of what is meant by "entering the great vehicle."

69 **The Buddha preaches the dharma; the dharma preaches the Buddha** (*hotoke, hō o toku, hō, hotoke o toku* ほとけ、法をとく、法、ほとけをとく): This and the concluding sentences of this section seem to reflect lines from a verse by Yuanwu Keqin 圜悟克勤 (1063-1135) (see *Yuanwu Foguo chanshi yulu* 圓悟佛果禪師語錄, T.1997.47:802b26-c2) that Dōgen discusses in "Shōbōgenzō gyōbutsu iigi" 正法眼藏行佛威儀:

烈焰亙天佛説法。亙天烈焰法説佛。

Blazing flames across the heavens; the Buddha preaches the dharma.
Across the heavens blazing flames; the dharma preaches the Buddha.

70 **"For this reason, I preach" is "across the heavens"; "across the heavens" is "for this reason, I preach"** (*ko setsu wa gōten nari, gōten wa ko setsu nari* 故説は亙天なり、亙天は故説なり): "Across the heavens" (*gōten* 亙天) alludes again to the verse by Yuanwu used in the preceding section; see above, Note 69.

71 **our world and other worlds** (*jikai takai* 自界・他界): Or "this world and the other world." Terms of ambiguous reference but here probably meaning simply "everywhere."

72 **the teachings of the buddhas, as the sands of the Ganges** (*Gōsha no bukkyō* 恆

[34:36]

おほよそしるべし、三乘十二分教等は、佛祖の眼睛なり。これを開眼せざらんもの、いかでか佛祖の兒孫ならん。これを拈來せざらんもの、いかでか佛祖の正眼を單傳せん。正法眼藏を體達せざるは、七佛の法嗣にあらざるなり。

In sum, we should realize that the three vehicles and twelvefold teachings are the eyes of the buddhas and ancestors. How could those who have not opened their eyes to this be the descendants of the buddhas and ancestors? How could those who have not taken this up uniquely transmit the true eye of the buddhas and ancestors? Those who have not personally realized the treasury of the true dharma eye are not the dharma heirs of the seven buddhas.

正法眼藏佛教第三十四
The Treasury of the True Dharma Eye
The Teachings of the Buddhas
Number 34

[Honzan edition:]

于時仁治二年辛丑十一月十四日、在雍州興聖寺精舍示衆

Presented to the assembly at the Kōshōji Vihāra, Yōshū; on the fourteenth day, eleventh month of the junior metal year of the ox, the second year of Ninji [17 December 1241][73]

[*Himitsu* MS:]

于時仁治三年壬寅十一月七日、在雍州興聖精舍示衆

Presented to the assembly at the Kōshō Vihāra, Yōshū; on the seventh day, eleventh month of the senior water year of the tiger, third year of Ninji [30 November 1242]

沙の佛教): I.e., Buddhist teachings as numerous as the sands of the Ganges; a standard expression that Dōgen reverses in the next clause. The bamboo stick, whisk, staff, and fist are all attributes of the Zen master; see Supplementary Notes, s.v. "Whisk," "Staff," and "Fist."

73   The seventy-five-chapter *Shōbōgenzō* lacks a colophon for this chapter.

TREASURY OF THE TRUE DHARMA EYE

NUMBER 35

Spiritual Powers
Jinzū

神通

Spiritual Powers

Jinzū

INTRODUCTION

This work was composed in the winter of 1241, at Kōshōji. It appears as number 35 in both the seventy-five- and sixty-chapter compilations of the *Shōbōgenzō* and as number 25 in the Honzan edition.

As its title indicates, the theme of the work is the Buddhist teaching of the paranormal powers ascribed to the buddhas, bodhisattvas, and other adepts of the religion. This teaching was widespread throughout both the technical and popular literature of Buddhism and represented one of the common assumptions of the Buddhist community. Discussion of the powers also occurs with some frequency in the texts of the Chinese Chan masters, who often tended in one way or another to redefine, dismiss, or make light of the traditional understandings of the teaching.

Dōgen's text takes up several of the passages on the powers from the Chinese Chan literature, using them to develop his own vision of the higher meaning of what he calls "the great powers" and "the powers of the buddha." In this vision, the powers become the welling up of the world itself, the fundamental activity through which all things emerge and in celebration of which the Chan masters act out their own eccentric powers. Throughout the text, Dōgen has harsh words for those Buddhists who lack this vision and remain limited to what he calls "the small powers" of the thaumaturgical tradition.

正法眼藏第三十五

Treasury of the True Dharma Eye
Number 35

神通

Spiritual Powers

[35:1] {1:392}

かくのごとくなる神通は、佛家の茶飯なり、諸佛いまに懈倦せざるなり。
これに六神通あり、一神通あり、無神通あり、最上神通あり。朝打三千な
り、暮打八百なるを爲體とせり。與佛同生せりといへども、ほとけにしら
れず、與佛同滅すといへども、ほとけをやぶらず。上天に同條なり、下天
にも同條なり、修行・取證みな同條なり、同雪山なり、如木石なり。過去
の諸佛は、釋迦牟尼佛の弟子なり、袈裟をささげてきたり、塔をささげて
きたる。このとき釋迦牟尼佛いはく、諸佛神通不可思議なり。しかあれば
しりぬ、現在・末來も亦復如是なり。

Such spiritual powers are the tea and rice in the house of the buddhas.[1]
The buddhas even now do not neglect them. Among them, there are the
six spiritual powers; there is the one spiritual power; there is no spiritual power; there is the supreme spiritual power.[2] They have taken the

---

1   **Such spiritual powers** (*kaku no gotoku naru jinzū* かくのごとくなる神通): The
use of the adjective *kaku no gotoku naru* かくのごとくなる ("such") in the opening line
here is odd, given that there is of course no antecedent. Presumably, Dōgen is indicating
the sort of powers of which he will be speaking below, but Sōtō commentators have also
given the phrase a more metaphysical reading: "the spiritual powers that are such" (i.e.,
are just as they are), or "the spiritual powers of suchness" (*nyoze no jinzū* 如是の神通).

"Spiritual powers" is a loose translation for the standard term (*jinzū* 神通) in East Asian
Buddhist usage for Sanskrit *abhijñā*, or "higher knowledges" (also sometimes Sanskrit
ṛddhi, or "powers," etc.); it may refer to a variety of paranormal powers held to be ac-
cessible to advanced spiritual adepts, several of which appear in the text below. The term
jinzū has the connotation of "penetration" or "mastery" of matters of the "spirit" (or the
"spirits"). See Supplementary Notes, s.v. "Spiritual powers."

tea and rice in the house of the buddhas (*bukke no sahan* 佛家の茶飯): I.e., the "everyday fare" in the "family" of the buddhas; see Supplementary Notes, s.v. "Everyday
tea and rice."

2   **six spiritual powers** (*roku jinzū* 六神通): A standard list of paranormal powers
found throughout Buddhist literature; see Supplementary Notes, s.v. "Spiritual powers."

the one spiritual power (*ichi jinzū* 一神通): Dōgen may here have in mind "that one
power" (*na ittsū* 那一通) discussed in the story of the Buddha and the seer that he will
cite below, section 16.

no spiritual power (*mu jinzū* 無神通): No doubt a reference to the saying of Baizhang

112   DŌGEN'S *SHŌBŌGENZŌ* VOLUME III

form of *morning blows, three thousand; evening blows, eight hundred.*[3] Though they were *born together with the buddha*, they are not known by the buddha; though *extinguished together with the buddha*, they do not destroy the buddha.[4] In ascending to the heavens, they do so together; in descending from the heavens, they do so together; cultivating the practice and getting the verification, they do so together.[5] They are the same as the Snowy Mountains, like trees and rocks.[6] The buddhas of the

---

Huaihai 百丈懷海 quoted below, section 23.

the supreme spiritual power (*saijō jinzū* 最上神通): Though the reference is uncertain, Dōgen may have in mind the "one 'surpassing' spiritual power" (*ichijō no jinzū* 一上の神通) mentioned in the story of Weishan Lingyu 溈山靈祐 and Yangshan Huiji 仰山慧寂 introduced in the following sections and described there by Dōgen as "unsurpassed" (*mujō* 無上).

3 **morning blows, three thousand; evening blows, eight hundred** (*chō da sanzen nari, bo da happyaku naru* 朝打三千なり、暮打八百なる): A fixed expression in Zen literature; generally taken as an indication of strict training. Some readers prefer to take *da* 打 ("to beat") here simply as a particle: "Mornings, three thousand; evenings, eight hundred."

4 **born together with the buddha** (*yo butsu dō shō* 與佛同生); **extinguished together with the buddha** (*yo butsu dō metsu* 與佛同滅): Usually interpreted to mean that the buddha and his powers are indistinguishable.

5 **ascending to the heavens** (*jōten* 上天); **descending from the heavens** (*geten* 下天); **cultivating the practice and getting the verification** (*shugyō shushō* 修行・取證): Dōgen seems here to be tracing the Buddha's career, from his penultimate birth as a bodhisattva in Tuṣita heaven and his subsequent descent into this Sahā world, to his six years of ascetic practice and his awakening under the bodhi tree.

they do so together (*dōjō* 同條): I.e., the buddhas and the powers "do so together." The translation follows the adverbial use of *dōjō* encountered in Chan expressions like, "born together, die together" (*dōjō shō dōjō shi* 同條生同條死). See, for example, *Biyan lu* 碧巖錄, T.2003.48:197a14:

同條生同條死。朝三千暮八百。

Born together, die together. Morning, three thousand; evening, eight hundred.

6 **They are the same as the Snowy Mountains, like trees and rocks** (*dō Sessen nari, nyo bokuseki nari* 同雪山なり、如木石なり): The exact sense here is uncertain or, perhaps, multivalent. The juxtaposition of "Snowy Mountains" (*Sessen* 雪山) with "trees and rocks" (*bokuseki* 木石) suggests an allusion to the famous story, invoked elsewhere in the *Shōbōgenzō*, of the prior life of Śākyamuni as the so-called "boy of the Snowy Mountains [i.e., Himalayas]" (*Sessen dōji* 雪山童子), who wrote the *Verse of Impermanence* (*Mujō ge* 無常偈) on trees and rocks (*nyaku ju nyaku seki* 若樹若石). See Supplementary Note, s.v. "Whether on trees or on rocks." At the same time, the phrase "like trees and rocks" (*nyo bokuseki* 如木石) seems to pick up the well-known expression, "a mind like trees and rocks" (*shin nyo bokuseki* 心如木石), as in the saying of Huangbo Xiyun 黃檗希運 (dates unknown) (*Guzunsu yulu* 古尊宿語錄, ZZ.118:188a9):

心如木石始有學道分。

Only when your mind is like trees and rocks do you have the status to study the way.

35. Spiritual Powers *Jinzū* 神通 113

past are the disciples of Buddha Śākyamuni.[7] They present him with a *kāṣāya*; they present him with a stūpa.[8] At this time, the Buddha said, "*The spiritual powers of the buddhas are inconceivable.*"[9] So, we know that the present and future are also such.[10]

* * * * *

---

7 **The buddhas of the past are the disciples of Buddha Śākyamuni** (*kako no shobutsu wa, Shakamuni butsu no deshi nari* 過去の諸佛は、釋迦牟尼佛の弟子なり): Likely reflecting a tradition found in the *Zongmen tongyao ji* 宗門統要集 (ZTS.1:10c7-10):

世尊嘗與阿難行次、見一古佛塔。世尊便作禮。阿難云、此是什麼人塔。世尊云、此是過去諸佛塔。阿難云、過去諸佛是什麼人弟子。世尊云、是吾弟子。阿難云、應當如是。

Once, when the World-Honored One was traveling with Ānanda, they saw an old Buddhist stūpa. The World-Honored One bowed to it. Ānanda said, "Whose stūpa is this?"
The World-Honored One said, "This is a stūpa of the buddhas of the past."
Ānanda, said, "Whose disciples were the buddhas of the past?"
The World-Honored One said, "They were my disciples."
Ānanda said, "So it must be."

Dōgen quotes a version of this exchange in his "Shōbōgenzō shisho" 正法眼藏嗣書 (DZZ.1:425). It also occurs at case number 245 in the Eishōin 永晶院 text of Dōgen's *shinji Shōbōgenzō* 眞字正法眼藏 (see DZZ.5:254, case 245n).

8 **They present him with a *kāṣāya*; they present him with a stūpa** (*kesa o sasagete kitari, tō o sasagete kitaru* 袈裟をささげてきたり、塔をささげてきたる): It is not clear whether the gifts are singular or plural. Commentators have so far been unable to establish a likely source for this claim. The adverbial phrase immediately following, "at this time" (*kono toki*), suggests that the presentations took place on the occasion when the Buddha spoke the words subsequently quoted. Unfortunately, the quotation (see below) seems to be from the chapter on spiritual powers in the *Lotus Sūtra*, which, while it describes many gifts presented to Śākyamuni, does not include among them robes or stūpas.

9 **"The spiritual powers of the buddhas are inconceivable"** (*shobutsu jinzū fukashigi* 諸佛神通不可思議): Probably after a passage in Chapter 21 of the *Lotus Sūtra*, "The Spiritual Powers of the Tathāgata" (*Julai shenli* 如來神力) (*Miaofa lianhua jing* 妙法蓮華經, T.262.9:52a14-15), in which the Buddhas Śākyamuni and Prabhūtaratna, and their entourage, demonstrate their spiritual powers, and Śākyamuni then declares:

諸佛神力如是無量無邊不可思議。

The spiritual powers of the buddhas are thus incalculable, limitless, inconceivable.

10 **such** (*nyoze* 如是): Generally interpreted to mean that the powers of present and future buddhas are also inconceivable. The Chinese version of the term "such" (*kaku no gotoku*) with which Dōgen began this text (see Note 1, above).

114   DŌGEN'S *SHŌBŌGENZŌ* VOLUME III

[35:2]

大潙禪師は、釋迦如來より直下三十七世の祖なり、百丈大智の嗣法なり。
いまの佛祖、おほく十方に出興せる、　　大潙の遠孫にあらざる、すなはち
大潙の遠孫なり。

Chan Master Dawei was an ancestor in the thirty-seventh generation
in direct descent from the Tathāgata Śākya; he was the dharma heir of
Baizhang Dazhi.[11] The present buddhas and ancestors who have arisen
throughout the ten directions, not the distant descendants of Dawei, are
the distant descendants of Dawei.[12]

[35:3]

大潙、あるとき臥せるに、仰山來參す。大潙すなはち轉面向壁臥す。仰山
いはく、慧寂、これ和尚の弟子なり、形迹もちいざれ。大潙、おくる勢を
なす。仰山すなはちいづるに、大潙召して、寂子、とめす。仰山かへる。
大潙いはく、老僧、ゆめをとかん、きくべし。仰山、かうべをたれて聽勢
をなす。大潙いはく、わがために原夢せよ、みん。仰山、一盆の水、一條
の手巾をとりてきたる。大潙、つひに洗面す。洗面しをはりて、わづかに
坐するに、香嚴きたる。大潙いはく、われ適來、寂子と一上の神通をな
す、不同小小なり。香嚴いはく、智閑、下面にありて、了了に得知す。大
潙いはく、子、こころみに道取すべし。香嚴すなはち一椀の茶を點來す。
大潙ほめていはく、二子の神通智慧、はるかに鶖子・目連よりもすぐれた
り。

On one occasion, when Dawei was lying down, Yangshan came to
visit him.[13] Dawei turned and lay facing the wall.

11　**Chan master Dawei** (*Daii zenji* 大潙禪師): I.e., Weishan Lingyu 潙山靈祐 (771-
853).

Baizhang Dazhi (*Hyakujō Daichi* 百丈大智): I.e., Baizhang Huaihai 百丈懷海 (749-
814), disciple of Mazu Daoyi 馬祖道一 (709-788).

12　**the ten directions** (*jippō* 十方): I.e., everywhere (throughout China). The term "ten
directions" designates the cardinal and ordinal compass points, plus the zenith and the
nadir; but it is regularly used in a less cosmic sense to mean something like "the entire
realm" — as, for example, in the expression, "monastery of the ten directions" (*jippō
setsu* 十方刹; i.e., monastery the abbacy of which is open to everyone regardless of
lineage).

not the distant descendants of Dawei (*daii no onson ni arazaru* 大潙の遠孫にあら
ざる): Presumably, this means those who are not themselves in Dawei's lineage. Some
versions of the text read here *arazaru nashi* あらざるなし, which would yield something like, "Among the present buddhas and ancestors who have arisen throughout the
ten directions, there are none who are not the distant descendants of Dawei; they are the
distant descendants of Dawei."

13　**On one occasion, when Dawei was lying down** (*Daii, aru toki gaseru ni* 大潙、
あるとき臥せるに): Dōgen's Japanese rendering of a story, versions of which appear
in *Zongmen tongyao ji* 宗門統要集 (ZTS.1:86a), *Jingde chuandeng lu* 景德傳燈錄
(T.2076.51:265c16-21), *Liandeng huiyao* 聯燈會要 (ZZ.136:543b13-a1), etc. It is case
number 61 in the *shinji Shōbōgenzō* 眞字正法眼藏 (DZZ.5:158).

35. Spiritual Powers *Jinzū* 神通   115

Yangshan said, "Huiji is the Reverend's disciple; no need for appearances."

Dawei went to get up. As Yangshan was about to leave, Dawei stopped him, calling, "Master Hui."

Yangshan came back. Dawei said, "Listen while this old monk tells you his dream."

Yangshan lowered his head as if to listen. Dawei said, "Try interpreting it for me."

Yangshan brought him a basin of water and a hand towel. Dawei washed his face. Just as he had finished washing his face and sat down, Xiangyan came in.[14]

Dawei said, "Master Ji and I just did a higher spiritual power.[15] It wasn't like the little stuff."[16]

Xiangyan said, "Zhixian was down there; I know all about it."[17]

Dawei said, "Try saying something."

Xiangyan went and made a bowl of tea.

Dawei praised them, saying, "The spiritual power and wisdom of these two masters far exceeds that of Śāriputra and Maudgalyāyana."[18]

Yangshan (Kyōzan 仰山): I.e., Weishan's disciple Yangshan Huiji 仰山慧寂.

14 **Xiangyan** (Kōgen 香嚴): I.e., Xiangyan Zhixian 香嚴智閑 (d. 898).

15 **"just did a higher spiritual power"** (*ichijō no jinzū o nasu* 一上の神通をなす): The term *ichijō* 一上 (literally, "one up," or "one higher") may well be simply an idiom in the Chinese here for "one time" or "once" (like the colloquial *yixia* 一下); but Dōgen will play with the literal sense in his commentary below; hence, the English "higher" here.

16 **"It wasn't like the little stuff"** (*fudō shōshō* 不同小小): The expression *shōshō* (literally, "small small") here probably just indicates something trivial; but Dōgen will associate it below with the Small Vehicle and make a sharp distinction between "great" and "small" powers.

17 **"Zhixian was down there; I know all about it"** (*Chikan, amen ni arite, ryōryō ni tokuchi su* 智閑、下面にありて、了了に得知す): Xiangyan is of course referring to himself as "Zhixian" here. The term *amen* 下面, translated here as "down there," may be taken as "nearby" or "next door." It is not clear whether we are supposed to understand that Zhixian simply overheard the conversation or he used spiritual powers to know about it.

18 **"Śāriputra and Maudgalyāyana"** (*Shūshi Mokuren* 鷲子・目連): Two disciples of the Buddha, known respectively for their wisdom and spiritual powers.

116 DŌGEN'S *SHŌBŌGENZŌ* VOLUME III

[35:4] {1:393}

佛家の神通をしらんとおもはば、大潙の道取を参學すべし。不同小小のゆ
えに、作是學者、名爲佛學、不是學者、不名佛學なるべし。嫡嫡相傳せる
神通智慧なり。さらに西天竺國の外道・二乗の神通、および論師等の所學
を、學することなかれ。

If we wish to understand the spiritual powers of the house of the buddhas, we should study Dawei's saying. Because it "wasn't like the little
stuff," *to engage in its study is called Buddhist study; not to study it is
not called Buddhist study.*[19] It is the spiritual power and wisdom transmitted from heir to heir.[20] We are not to go on to study what is studied by
such as the treatise masters or the spiritual powers of the other paths and
the two vehicles in the Land of Sindhu in the West.[21]

[35:5]

いま大潙の神通を學するに、無上なりといへども、一上の見聞あり。いは
ゆる臥次よりこのかた、轉面向壁臥あり、起勢あり、召寂子あり、説箇夢
あり、洗面了纔坐あり、仰山又低頭聽あり、盆水來・手巾來あり。

Now, in studying Dawei's spiritual powers, though they may be unsurpassed, there are "higher" experiences: that is, beginning with *"when he
was lying down,"* we have *"he turned and lay facing the wall"*; we have
"he went to get up"; we have *"he called, 'Master Ji'"*; we have *"let me
tell you of my dream"*; we have *"he had finished washing his face and sat
down"*; we have *"Yangshan bent down to listen"*; we have *"he brought a
basin of water and a wash cloth."*[22]

---

19 **to engage in its study is called Buddhist study; not to study it is not called Buddhist study** (*sa ze gaku sha, myō i butsugaku, fu ze gaku sha, fu myō butsugaku* 作是
學者、名為佛學、不是學者、不名佛學): Or "One who engages in this study is called
a student of Buddhism; one who does not study it is not called a student of Buddhism."
For some reason, Dōgen here shifts to Chinese, as if this were a quotation. No one seems
yet to have found precedent for it in the literature.

20 **It is the spiritual power and wisdom transmitted from heir to heir** (*chakuchaku
sōden seru jinzū chie nari* 嫡嫡相傳せる神通智慧なり): The grammatical subject here
is unstated; presumably, "Dawei's saying."

21 **treatise masters** (*ronshi* 論師): I.e., those who specialize in the Buddhist scholastic
literature of the śāstras. A common target of Zen masters' criticism.

the other paths and the two vehicles (*gedō nijō* 外道二乘): I.e., those who follow
non-Buddhist religions (S. *tīrthika*) and the two "lesser" Buddhist vehicles of the *śrāvaka* and *pratyeka-buddha* (as opposed to the Mahāyāna); see Supplementary Notes, s.v.
"Three vehicles."

Land of Sindhu in the West (*Sai Tenjiku koku* 西天竺國): I.e., the Indian subcontinent,
the Chinese *tianzhu* 天竺 representing a transliteration of the Sanskrit *sindhu*.

22 **though they may be unsurpassed, there are "higher" experiences** (*mujō nari to iedomo, ichijō no kenmon ari* 無上なりといへども、一上の見聞あり): Dōgen plays here
with the terms *mujō* ("unsurpassed") and *ichijō* 一上 (literally, "one higher") taken from

35. Spiritual Powers *Jinzū* 神通   117

[35:6]

しかあるを、大潙いはく、われ適來、寂子と一上の神通をなす、と。この
神通を學すべし。佛法正傳の祖師、かくのごとくいふ。説夢洗面といはざ
ることなかれ、一上の神通なりと決定すべし。すでに不同小小といふ、小
乘・小量・小見におなじかるべからず、十聖三賢等に同ずべきにあらず。
かれらみな小神通をならひ、小身量のみをえたり、佛祖の大神通におよば
ず。これ佛祖通なり、佛向上神通なり。この神通をならはん人は、魔外に
うごかさるべからざるなり。經師・論師いまだきかざるところ、きくとも
信受しがたきなり。二乘・外道、經師・論師等は、小神通をならふ、大神
通をならはず。諸佛は大神通を住特す、大神通を相傳す、これ佛神通な
り。佛神通にあらざれば、盆水來・手巾來せず、轉面向壁臥なし、洗而了
纔坐なし。

Of such [acts], Dawei says, "Master Ji and I just did a higher spiritual
power." We should study this spiritual power. The ancestral masters who
correctly transmit the buddha dharma speak like this. Do not fail to say
that [Weishan] was "telling his dream and washing his face"; we should
be certain that this is "a higher spiritual power." Since he says, "it wasn't
like the little stuff," it must not be the same as the Small Vehicle, a small
measure, a small view. It must not be the same as the ten sages and three
worthies, and the like.[23] They all learn the small spiritual powers and
only acquire small stature; they do not reach the great spiritual powers of the buddhas and ancestors. These are the spiritual powers of the
buddhas and ancestors, the spiritual powers beyond the buddha.[24] Those
who would learn these spiritual powers should not be moved by Māra or
the other paths.[25] What the sūtra masters and treatise masters have never
heard is hard [for them] to believe even when they do hear it. The two
vehicles, the other paths, the sūtra masters and treatise masters, and the
like, learn the small spiritual powers; they do not learn the great spiritual

---

Dawei's line, "Master Ji and I just did 'a higher' (*ichijō no* 一上の) spiritual power."

23　**the ten sages and three worthies** (*jisshō sanken* 十聖三賢): The ten ārya stages
and three *bhadra* levels on the bodhisattva path. Notice that here Dōgen has extended
Dawei's reference to "the little stuff" from the "small vehicle" to the bodhisattvas of the
"great vehicle." Thus, the distinction Dōgen draws here between the "great" and "small"
spiritual powers is not between Mahāyāna and Hīnayāna but between both of these and
the "buddhas and ancestors."

24　**spiritual powers of the buddhas and ancestors** (*busso tsū* 佛祖通); **spiritual powers beyond the buddha** (*butsu kōjō jinzū* 佛向上神通): The first expression picks up the
Lotus Sūtra passage on a buddha's powers quoted above (Note 9) and also points ahead
to the saying of Linji Yixuan 臨濟義玄 (d. 866) quoted below. The second expression is
likely an allusion to the saying of Baizhang Huaihai 百丈懷海 that Dōgen will also quote
below. For the contrast drawn in Chan texts between "what is within the confines of the
buddha" (*buppen ji* 佛邊事) and "what lies beyond the buddha" (*butsu kōjōji* 佛向上事),
see Supplementary Notes, s.v. "Beyond the buddha."

25　**Māra or the other paths** (*mage* 魔外): Taken as an abbreviation for *tenma* 天魔 (S.
deva-māra) and *gedō* 外道 (S. *tīrthika*).

118   DŌGEN'S *SHŌBŌGENZŌ* VOLUME III

powers. The buddhas maintain the great spiritual powers; they transmit the great spiritual powers. These are the spiritual powers of a buddha. If they were not the spiritual powers of a buddha, [Yangshan] would not "*bring a basin of water and a hand towel*"; there would be no "*he turned and lay facing the wall*"; there would be no "*after he had finished washing his face and sat down.*"

[35:7] {1:394}

この大神通のちからにおほはれて、小神通等もあるなり。大神通は小神通を接す、小神通は大神通をしらず。小神通といふは、いはゆる毛呑巨海、芥納須彌なり。又身上出水、身下出火等なり。また五通・六通、みな小神通なり。これらのやから、佛神通は夢也未見聞在なり。五通・六通を小神通といふことは、五通・六通は修證に染汚せられ、際斷を時處にうるなり。在生にありて身後に現ぜず、自己にありて他人にあらず。此土に現ずといへども他土に現ぜず、不現に現ずといへども、現時に現ずることをえず。

Covered by the power of these great spiritual powers, there are also the small spiritual powers. The great spiritual powers take in the small spiritual powers; the small spiritual powers do not know the great spiritual powers. By "small spiritual powers," we mean "*a hair follicle swallowing the vast ocean, a mustard seed containing Sumeru.*"[26] Or "*emitting water from the upper body, emitting fire from the lower body,*" and the like.[27] Further, the five powers or six powers are all small spiritual pow-

---

26   "**a hair follicle swallowing the vast ocean, a mustard seed containing Sumeru**" (*mō don kokai, ke nō Shumi* 毛呑巨海、芥納須彌): From a famous story about Linji Yixuan 臨濟義玄 and the notoriously wild monk Puhua 普化 (dates unknown) (see, e.g., *Linji lu* 臨濟錄, T.1985.47:503b3-9), recorded in Dōgen's *shinji Shōbōgenzō* 眞字正法眼藏 (DZZ.5:174, case 96):

普化與臨濟、在施主家齋。濟問、毛呑巨海芥納須彌、爲復是神通妙用、爲復是法爾如然。師遂趯倒飯牀。

Puhua and Linji were at a meal at a donor's home. Ji asked, "A hair follicle swallowing the vast ocean, a mustard seed containing Sumeru. Are these the spiritual powers and marvelous functions, or are they the dharma itself just as it is?"

The Master [Puhua] kicked over the table.

Linji's question derives from a description in the *Vimalakīrti Sūtra* of the remarkable powers possessed by the bodhisattva who dwells in the liberation called "inconceivable" (*Weimo jing* 維摩經, T.475.14:546b25-c1):

若菩薩住是解脱者、以須彌之高廣内芥子中無所增減 . . . . 又以四大海水入一毛孔、不嬈魚鼈黿鼉水性之屬。

Bodhisattvas abiding in this liberation can put Sumeru, so high and broad, into a mustard seed, without increasing [the seed] or decreasing [the mountain]. . . . Again, they can put the four great oceans into a single hair follicle, without injuring the fish, tortoises, sea turtles, crocodiles, and other forms of water life.

27   "**emitting water from the upper body, emitting fire from the lower body**" (*shinjō shussui, shinge shukka* 身上出水、身下出火): The ability to fly into the air and emit water and fire from the sides of the body is one of the earliest examples of Buddhist powers

35. Spiritual Powers *Jinzū* 神通   119

ers.[28] These types have never experienced the spiritual powers of a buddha even in their dreams.[29] To say that the five powers or six powers are small spiritual powers is [to say that] the five powers and six powers are defiled by practice and verification; they are cut off in time and place.[30] While one has them in life, one does not show them after the body. They belong to the self and not to others. Though they may appear in this land, they do not appear in other lands.[31] Though they may appear when we do

---

in the literature, a feat said to have been demonstrated by Gautama himself in the famous "twin miracle" (S. *yamakaprātihārya*) at Śrāvastī. It became a standard motif in accounts of the *ṛddhi-pāda*, the first of the six *abhijñā*. (See Note 2, above.) Commentators have singled out a passage in the *Lotus Sūtra* as a particularly likely source for Dōgen's phrase here. It occurs in Chapter 27, on the king Śubhavyūha (*Miao Zhuangyan Wang* 妙莊嚴王), whose two sons convert their father to the buddha dharma by impressing him with their powers (*Miaofa lianhua jing* 妙法蓮華經, T.262.9:60a5-7):

踊在虛空高七多羅樹。現種種神變。於虛空中行住坐臥。身上出水身下出火。身下出水身上出火。

They leap into empty space to the height of seven *tāla* trees and show various spiritual transformations. They walk, stand, sit, and recline in empty space. They emit water from their upper bodies; they emit fire from their lower bodies. They emit water from their lower bodies; they emit fire from their upper bodies.

28   **the five powers or six powers are all small spiritual powers** (*gotsū rokutsū mina shōjinzū nari* 五通・六通みな小神通なり): The five powers are the first five of the six powers; see Supplementary Notes, s.v. "Spiritual powers."

29   **These types** (*korera no yakara* これらのやから): A dismissive expression, the referent of which here is not entirely clear; from the context, presumably, those who cultivate the five or six spiritual powers.

30   **defiled by practice and verification** (*shushō ni zenna serare* 修證に染汚せられ): Likely reflecting the words of Nanyue Huairang 南嶽懷讓 (677-744) often quoted by Dōgen (see Supplementary Notes, s.v. "Not defiled"): When asked by the Sixth Ancestor, "What thing is it that comes like this?" Nanyue replies,

説似一物即不中。祖曰、還假修證否。師曰、修證即不無、染汚即不得。

"To say it's like any thing wouldn't hit it."
The Ancestor said, "Then does it depend on practice and verification?"
The Master [Nanyue] answered, "It's not that it lacks practice and verification, but it can't be defiled by them."

they are cut off in time and place (*saidan o jisho ni uru* 際斷を時處にうる): A rough translation of an odd locution, generally interpreted to mean "they are temporally and spatially limited." The compound expression *saidan* 際斷 occurs several times in the *Shōbōgenzō*, most often in the fixed Buddhist expression *zengo saidan* 前後際斷 ("before and after cut off"); see Supplementary Notes, s.v. "Before and after cut off."

31   **Though they may appear in this land, they do not appear in other lands** (*shido ni gen zu to iedomo tado ni gen zezu* 此土に現ずといへども他土に現ぜず): The exact nature of this claim is unclear. If, as is commonly done, we take Dōgen's point here to be that expressions of spiritual powers in our Sahā world system (*shido*) do not extend to other systems (*tado*), it would seem to fly in the face of the many Mahāyāna sūtra accounts of miraculous acts that reach across countless world systems.

DŌGEN'S *SHŌBŌGENZŌ* VOLUME III

not show them, they fail to appear when it is time to show them.[32]

[35:8]

この大神通は、しかあらず。諸佛の教・行・證、おなじく神通に現成せしむるなり。ただ諸佛の邊に現成するのみにあらず、佛向上にも現成するなり。神通佛の化儀、まことに不可思議なるなり。有身よりさきに現ず、現の三際にかかはれぬあり。佛神通にあらざれば、諸佛の發心・修行・菩提・涅槃いまだあらざるなり。いまの無盡法界海の常不變なる、みなこれ佛神通なり。毛呑巨海のみにあらず、毛保任巨海なり、毛現巨海なり、毛吐巨海なり、毛使巨海なり。一毛に盡法界を呑却し吐却するとき、ただ一盡法界かくのごとくなれば、さらに盡法界あるべからず、と學することなかれ。芥納須彌等もまたかくのごとし。芥吐須彌および芥現法界無盡藏海にてもあるなり。毛吐巨海、芥吐巨海するに、一念にも吐却す、萬劫にも吐却するなり。萬劫・一念、おなじく毛・芥より吐却せるがゆえに。毛・芥は、さらになによりか得せる、すなはちこれ神通より得せるなり。この得、すなはち神通なるがゆえに、ただまさに神通の、神通を出生するのみなり。さらに三世の存没あらずと學すべきなり。諸佛は、この神通のみに遊戯するなり。

These great spiritual powers are not like this. The teaching, practice, and verification of the buddhas are equally brought to realization in the spiritual powers. They are not realized only in the vicinity of the buddhas; they are also realized beyond the buddhas. The manner of converting [beings] of the buddha of the spiritual powers is truly inconceivable.[33] It appears before he has a body; its appearance has nothing to

---

32 **Though they may appear when we do not show them, they fail to appear when it is time to show them** (*fugen ni gen zu to iedomo, genji ni gen zuru koto o ezu* 不現に現ずといへども、現時に現ずることをえず): A tentative translation of an obscure sentence, on which there is considerable difference of opinion. Some commentators take the *gen* 現 of *fugen* 不現 and *genji* 現時 to mean something like "the constant present"; hence, the small powers appear only occasionally (*fugen ni*) but cannot appear throughout all time (*genji*). Others have taken this *gen* as "real"; hence, the small powers seem to appear but do not really. Still others suggest the small powers appear when they are not expected to but not when they ought to. The present translation takes the verb *gen* 現 as both intransitive and transitive, as found in such Zen challenges as, "why not show your spiritual powers?" (*ka fugen jinzū* 何不現神通), or "try to show your spiritual powers" (*shiki gen jinzū kan* 試現神通看). Hence, on this reading, the small powers may appear even when one does not try to show them, but they may also fail to appear when one ought to show them. Whether Dōgen had examples of such failings in mind here is unclear.

33 **The manner of converting [beings]** (*kegi* 化儀): I.e., teaching methods; especially in the Tendai literature, used in contrast to *kehō* 化法, "the dharma for converting [beings] (i.e., the doctrines taught)."

the buddha of the spiritual powers (*jinzū butsu* 神通佛): Dōgen has here reversed the syntax of the expected "spiritual powers of the buddha" (*butsu jinzū* 佛神通), no doubt to reinforce his identification of the two terms.

35. Spiritual Powers *Jinzū* 神通　　　121

do with the three junctures.[34] If it were not for the spiritual powers of a buddha, there would never be the bringing forth of the mind [of bodhi], the practice, the bodhi, or the nirvāṇa of the buddhas.[35]

The ocean of this inexhaustible dharma realm, constant and unchanging, is all the spiritual powers of a buddha. It is not only that "*a hair follicle swallows the vast ocean*": *a hair follicle maintains the vast ocean, a hair follicle manifests the vast ocean, a hair follicle vomits the vast ocean, a hair follicle employs the vast ocean.* When the entire dharma realm has been swallowed into and vomited forth by one hair follicle, we are not to learn that, since the one entire dharma realm has become like this, there must be no more dharma realm.[36] "*A mustard seed containing Sumeru*" is the same: *a mustard seed vomiting Sumeru* and *a mustard seed expressing the dharma realm* are also the ocean of the inexhaustible treasury.[37]

When *a hair follicle vomits forth the vast ocean* or *a mustard seed vomits forth the vast ocean,* they vomit it forth in a single moment; they vomit it forth in ten thousand kalpas. Since the ten thousand kalpas and the single moment have both been vomited forth from the hair follicle and the mustard seed, how are the hair follicle and mustard seed themselves obtained? They have been obtained from the spiritual powers. Since this obtaining is itself the spiritual powers, this is just the spiritual powers giving rise to the spiritual powers. We should learn that the three

---

34　**It appears before he has a body** (*ushin yori saki ni genzu* 有身よりさきに現ず): Or "it appears before there is a body." Dōgen may be alluding here to the line in Fu Dashi's poem he will quote below (section 21): "Having a body is not the substance of his awakening."

three junctures (*sansai* 三際): I.e., "the three times" (*sansei* 三世), or periods, of past, present, and future.

35　**bringing forth of the mind** (*hosshin* 發心): S. *cittotpāda,* the generation of the aspiration to achieve unsurpassed, perfect bodhi, which marks the start of the bodhisattva's career; see Supplementary Notes, s.v. "Bring forth the mind."

36　**there must be no more dharma realm** (*sara ni jinhokkai aru bekarazu* さらに盡法界あるべからず): I.e., we should not think that the dharma realm disappears into the hair follicle.

37　**a mustard seed vomiting Sumeru and a mustard seed expressing the dharma realm are also the ocean of the inexhaustible treasury** (*ke to Shumi oyobi ke gen hokkai mujinzō kai nite mo aru nari* 芥吐須彌および芥現法界無盡藏海にてもあるなり): The "inexhaustible treasury" (*mujinzō* 無盡藏) is a common metaphor for the dharma realm, seen as the source of all things. The translation here takes *nite mo aru* as a copula ("are also"); it might also be read as a locative ("are also in"). Some interpreters take the term *mujinzō kai* 無盡藏海 ("ocean of the inexhaustible treasury") in apposition to *hokkai* 法界 ("dharma realm"); hence, they would read the sentence, "A mustard seed also vomits Sumeru, and a mustard seed also expresses the dharma realm, the ocean of the inexhaustible treasury."

122   DŌGEN'S *SHŌBŌGENZŌ* VOLUME III

times have no other persistence or perishing. The buddhas disport themselves only in these spiritual powers.[38]

* * * * *

[35:9] {1:395}
龐居士蘊公は、祖席の偉人なり。江西・石頭の兩席に參學せるのみにあらず、有道の宗師におほく相見し、相逢しきたる。あるときいはく、神通竝妙用、運水及搬柴。この道理、よくよく參究すべし。

Layman Pang, the Honorable Yun, was an extraordinary person of the ancestral seat.[39] He not only studied at the two seats of Jiangxi and Shitou, he met and encountered many masters possessed of the way.[40] Once he said, "*The spiritual powers and the wondrous functions: bearing water and carrying firewood.*"[41] We should investigate well the rationale [of this saying].

---

38 **The buddhas disport themselves only in these spiritual powers** (*shobutsu wa kono jinzū nomi ni yuge suru nari* 諸佛はこの神通のみに遊戲するなり): Dōgen is here recalling the common expression *yuge jinzū* 遊戲神通 (or *jinzū yuge* 神通遊戲), meaning "to play in, or enjoy, the spiritual powers;" also "to wander freely in, or by means of, the spiritual powers."

39 **Layman Pang, the Honorable Yun** (*Ho koji On kō* 龐居士蘊公): I.e., Pang Yun 龐蘊 (740?-808), famous Tang-dynasty lay Buddhist, usually treated as a disciple of Mazu Daoyi 馬祖道一.

ancestral seat (*soseki* 祖席): I.e., the Zen school, seen as the tradition of the Zen ancestors. The "two seats" (*ryōseki* 兩席) in the next sentence invokes the traditions descended from the Sixth Ancestor through his two major disciples, Nanyue Huairang 南嶽懷讓 and Qingyuan Xingsi 青原行思 (d. 740).

40 **Jiangxi and Shitou** (*Kōzei Sekitō* 江西・石頭): The two leading eighth-century masters of the Nanyue 南嶽 and Qingyuan 青原 traditions respectively: Mazu Daoyi 馬祖道一, disciple of Nanyue, and Shitou Xiqian 石頭希遷 (700-790), disciple of Qingyuan.

masters possessed of the way (*udō no shūshi* 有道の宗師): I.e., accomplished Chan masters. The term *udō* ("having the way") is usually understood as mastery of Buddhist training. The term *shūshi* 宗師, translated here simply as "master," apart from its ordinary sense of an eminent teacher, can have the connotation, "master of the essential meaning" or "master of the essential gate" (*shūmon* 宗門; i.e., the Zen school), and be used in contrast to the terms *ronshi* 論師 ("treatise master") or *kyōshi* 經師 ("sūtra master") dismissed by Dōgen above.

41 **"The spiritual powers and the wondrous functions: bearing water and carrying firewood"** (*jinzū hei myōyū, unsui gyū hansai* 神通竝妙用、運水及搬柴): Famous lines from the poem addressed by Pang to Shitou 石頭; occurs at *Jingde chuandeng lu* 景德傳燈錄 (T.2076.51:263b12). The term *myōyū* ("wondrous functions") is a common designation for paranormal abilities or acts, especially of a buddha. The saying recalls a famous story in the *Lotus Sūtra* of the prior career of Buddha Śākyamuni, in which he "drew water and gathered firewood" (*kyūsui shūshin* 汲水拾薪) for his teacher, the future Devadatta (*Miaofa lianhua jing* 妙法蓮華經, T.262.9:34c6).

35. Spiritual Powers *Jinzū* 神通   123

[35:10]

いはゆる運水とは、水を運載しきたるなり。自作自爲あり、他作教他あり
て水を運載せしむ。これすなはち神通佛なり。しることは有時なりといへ
ども、神通はこれ神通なり。人のしらざるには、その法の廢するにあら
ず、その法の滅するにあらず。人はしらざれども、法は法爾なり。運水の
神通なりとしらざれども、神通の運水なるは不退なり。

"*Yunshui*" means to transport water.[42] *Doing it oneself by oneself,
another doing it by another*, water is transported.[43] This is the buddha of
spiritual powers. Although our knowledge of them may be at a certain
time, the spiritual powers are the spiritual powers.[44] It is not that, when
people do not know them, their dharma is destroyed, or their dharma
is extinguished. Even though people do not know it, the dharma is the
dharma as it is.[45] Even if we do not know that bearing water is the spiritual powers, that the spiritual powers are bearing water is irreversible.[46]

---

42 **"*Yunshui*" means to transport water** (*iwayuru unsui to wa, mizu o unsai shikitaru
nari* いはゆる運水とは、水を運載しきたるなり): Dōgen is here merely defining the
Chinese expression for his Japanese reader.

43 **Doing it oneself by oneself, another doing it by another, water is transported**
(*jisa jii ari, tasa kyōta arite mizu o unsai seshimu* 自作自為あり、他作教他ありて水を
運載せしむ): A somewhat loose translation of a somewhat odd and ambiguous sentence.
It is generally taken to mean that one carries water of one's own accord or at the initiative
of another. The identity of the agent of these actions is unclear: it could be anyone; it
could be the "buddha of spiritual powers" in the next line; it could conceivably be the
"water" itself.

44 **Although our knowledge of them may be at a certain time, the spiritual powers
are the spiritual powers** (*shiru koto wa uji nari to iedomo, jinzū wa kore jinzū nari* しる
ことは有時なりといへども、神通はこれ神通なり): I.e., the powers remain what they
are whether we happen to experience (or recognize) them or not.

45 **the dharma is the dharma as it is** (*hō wa hōni nari* 法は法爾なり): The expression *hōni* 法爾, translated here as "the dharma as it is," is a common Buddhist term for
"the dharma itself," "the natural state of, or nature of, the dharma," etc. The claim here
could be taken as a general one about the dharma (i.e., the Buddhist truth), a general one
about dharmas (i.e., phenomena), or a specific one about the dharma (i.e., nature) of the
spiritual powers.

46 **irreversible** (*futai* 不退): I.e., is permanently established; a term regularly used for
the "irreversible" (or "non-regressing"; S. *avaivartika*) bodhisattva of the seventh stage
(S. *bhūmi*), who can no longer fall back from the Mahāyāna.

124 DŌGEN'S *SHŌBŌGENZŌ* VOLUME III

[35:11] {1:396}

搬柴とは、たき木をはこぶなり。たとへば、六祖のむかしのごとし。朝打
三千にも神通としらず、暮打八百にも神通とおぼえざれども、神通の見成
なり。

"*Banchai*" means to carry firewood, as the Sixth Ancestor once did.[47]
Although we may not recognize *morning blows, three thousand* as the
spiritual powers, although we may not think of *evening blows, eight
hundred* as the spiritual powers, they are the realization of the spiritual
powers.[48]

[35:12]

まことに諸佛如來の神通妙用を見聞するは、かならず得道すべし。このゆえ
に、一切諸佛の得道、かならずこの神通力に成就せるなり。しかあれば、い
ま小乘の出水、たとひ小神通なりといふとも、運水の大神通なることを學す
べし、運水運柴はいまだすたれざるところ、人さしおかず。ゆえに、むかし
よりいまにおよぶ、これよりかれにつたはれり。須臾も退轉せざるは、神通
妙用なり。これは大神通なり、小小とおなじかるべきにあらず。

Indeed, one who perceives the "spiritual powers and wondrous functions" of the buddhas, the tathāgatas, will inevitably gain the way; therefore, the gaining of the way of all the buddhas has always been achieved
through these spiritual powers.[49] This being the case, while the emitting
of water in the Small Vehicle may be a spiritual power, we should study
the fact that the bearing of water is a great spiritual power. "*Bearing
water and carrying firewood*" have never been discarded, nor have people neglected them. That they have, therefore, from ancient times to the
present, been handed down from this one to that, without ever revert-
ing for a moment, is the "spiritual powers and wondrous functions."
They are the great spiritual powers; they cannot be the same as "the little
stuff."

* * * * *

47　"*Banchai*" **means to carry firewood, as the Sixth Ancestor once did** (*hansai to
wa, takigi o hakobu nari, tatoeba, rokuso no mukashi no gotoshi* 搬柴とは、たきぎをは
こぶなり、たとへば、六祖のむかしのごとし): Again, Dōgen is defining the Chinese
term. The reference to the Sixth Ancestor invokes the story that, as a youth, he sold firewood to support his mother. The story appears already in the Dunhuang manuscript of
the *Platform Sūtra* (*Liuzu tan jing* 六祖壇經, T.2007.48:337a16) and is repeated throughout the later literature (see, e.g., *Jingde chuandeng lu* 景德傳燈錄, T.2076.51:235b13).

48　**morning blows, three thousand** (*chō da sanzen* 朝打三千); **evening blows, eight
hundred** (*bo da happyaku* 暮打八百): See above, Note 3.

49　**achieved through these spiritual powers** (*kono jinzūriki ni jōju seru* この神通力
に成就せる): Or "through the strength of these spiritual powers." The term *jinzūriki* 神
通力 is a common alternative for *jinzū* 神通. The logic here is, of course, technically
invalid.

35. Spiritual Powers *Jinzū* 神通　　　125

[35:13]

洞山悟本大師、そのかみ雲巖に侍せしとき、雲巖とふ、いかなるかこれ价子神通妙用。ときに洞山、又手近前而立。また雲巖とふ、いかならんか神通妙用。洞山、ときに珍重而出。

Once, when Great Master Dongshan Wuben was attending Yunyan, Yunyan asked him, "What are Master Jie's spiritual powers and wondrous functions?"[50]

Dongshan joined his hands, stepped forward, and stood.[51]

Yunyan asked again, "What about the spiritual powers and wondrous functions?"

Dongshan paid his respects and left.[52]

[35:14]

この因縁、まことに神通の承言會宗なるあり、神通の事存函蓋合なるあり。まさにしるべし、神通妙用は、まさに兒孫あるべし、不退なるものなり。まさに高祖あるべし、不進なるものなり。いたづらに外道・二乘にひとしかるべきとおもはざれ。

Truly, in this episode, there is "*receiving the words, understanding their sense*" of the spiritual powers; there is "*things exist, box and lid matching*" of the spiritual powers.[53] We should realize that the "spiritual powers and wondrous functions" must have their children and grandchildren, those who do not regress; they must have their eminent ancestors, those who do not advance.[54] Do not foolishly think that they should be the same as the other paths and the two vehicles.

50　**Great Master Dongshan Wuben** (*Tōzan Gohon daishi* 洞山悟本大師): I.e., Dongshan Liangjie 洞山良价 (807-869), founder of the Caodong lineage, disciple of Yunyan Tansheng 雲巖曇晟 (782-841). Dōgen retells in Japanese here an encounter recorded in the *Dongshan yulu* 洞山語錄 (T.1986A.47:508b2-4).

"Master Jie's" (*Kaisu* 价子): I.e., "your"; diminutive for "Liangjie."

51　**joined his hands** (*shashū* 又手): I.e., the traditional polite Chinese gesture of placing one hand over the other at the breast.

52　**paid his respects** (*chinchō* 珍重; also read *shinjū*): A loose translation of the common Chinese polite farewell; akin to English, "Take good care of yourself."

53　**"receiving the words, understanding their sense"** (*shō gon e shū* 承言會宗); **"things exist, box and lid matching"** (*ji son kangai gō* 事存函蓋合): After lines from the famous poem *Cantong qi* 參同契, by Shitou Xiqian 石頭希遷 (*Jingde chuandeng lu* 景德傳燈錄, T.2076.51:459b18-19):

事存函蓋合。理應箭鋒拄。承言須會宗。勿自立規矩。

Things exist, box and lid matching;
Principle responds, arrow heads meeting.
Receiving the words, understand their sense;
Don't set up standards of your own.

54　**children and grandchildren** (*jison* 兒孫); **eminent ancestors** (*kōso* 高祖): I.e., the

126 DŌGEN'S *SHŌBŌGENZŌ* VOLUME III

[35:15]

佛道に身上・身下の神變神通あり。いま盡十方界は、沙門一隻の眞實體
なり。九山八海、乃至性海、薩婆若海水、しかしながら身上・身下・身
中の出水なり。又非身上・非身下・非身中の出水なり。乃至、出火もまた
かくのごとし。ただ水・火・風等のみにあらず、身上出佛なり、身下出佛
なり、身上出祖なり、身下出祖なり、身上出無量阿僧祇劫なり、身下出無
量阿僧祇劫なり、身上出法界海なり、身上入法界海なるのみにあらず、さ
らに世界・國土を吐却七八箇し、呑却兩三箇せんことも、またかくのごと
し。いま四大・五大・六大・諸大・無量大、おなじく出なり、没なる神通
なり、呑なり、吐なる神通なり。いまの大地・虚空の面面なる、呑却な
り、吐却なり。芥に轉ぜらるるを力量とせり、毛にかかれるを力量とせ
り。識知のおよばざるより同生して、識知のおよばざるを住特し、識知の
およばざるに實歸す。まことに短長にかかはれざる佛神通の變相、ひとへ
に測量を擧して擬するのみならんや。

On the way of the buddhas, there are the spiritual transformations
and spiritual powers of the upper body and the lower body.[55] This entire
world of the ten directions is "the one true body of the śramaṇa."[56] The
[waters of] *the nine mountains and eight oceans, down to the ocean of
the nature and the waters of the ocean of sarvajña*, are all water emitted
from the upper body, lower body, and mid-body.[57] Again, they are the

---

powers and functions have a family lineage, a posterity with its founding figures. Commentators take these two terms to refer to the disciple Dongshan and Master Yunyan,
respectively.

those who do not regress (*futai naru mono* 不退なるもの); **those who do not advance**
(*fushin naru mono* 不進なるもの): Dōgen is here continuing his play with the term *futai*
("not regress") that he introduced in his discussion of Layman Pang's saying. The exact
sense of the predicates here is uncertain, but they suggest that both the "children and
grandchildren" and the "eminent ancestors" are advanced adepts: the former are "irreversible" in their practice, the latter need no further "progress" in their practice. Some
commentators take this passage to mean that, in the lineage of the "spiritual powers and
wondrous functions," the disciple (Dongshan) is not inferior and master (Yunyan) superior; master and disciple are on the same perfected plane.

55 **spiritual transformations and spiritual powers of the upper body and the lower body** (*shinjō shinge no jinpen jinzū* 身上・身下の神變神通): These terms come, of
course, from the "small powers" of emitting water and fire from the body discussed
above (section 7). Presumably, Dōgen is here associating Dongshan's physical acts in the
story with the tradition of these Buddhist paranormal physical transformations, which he
will now go on to explore.

56 **"the one true body of the *śramaṇa*"** (*shamon isseki no shinjitsu tai* 沙門一隻の眞
實體): Here, Dōgen is likely playing with one of his favorite sayings, attributed to the
Tang-dynasty monk Changsha Jingcen 長沙景岑 (dates unknown); see Supplementary
Notes, s.v. "All the worlds in the ten directions are the single eye of the *śramaṇa*."

57 **the nine mountains and eight oceans** (*kusen* [or *kyūsen, kyūzan*] *hakkai* 九山八海):
A reference to the topography surrounding Mount Sumeru in Buddhist cosmology. The
central mountain is ringed by a series of eight mountains separated by seas.

down to the ocean of the nature (*naishi shōkai* 乃至性海): The term *naishi* 乃至

35. Spiritual Powers *Jinzū* 神通 127

water emitted from the non-upper body, the non-lower body, the non-mid-body; and so on, down to the fire emitted [from the body, which] is also like this.[58]

This is not only [true of] water, fire, wind, and so on: not only are buddhas emitted from the upper body, and buddhas emitted from the lower body, and ancestors emitted from the upper body, and ancestors emitted from the lower body, and incalculable *asaṃkhyeya-kalpas* emitted from the upper body, and incalculable *asaṃkhyeya-kalpas* emitted from the lower body, and the ocean of the dharma realm emitted from the upper body, and the ocean of the dharma realm absorbed in the upper body; but also the vomiting out of seven or eight lands of this world and the swallowing up of two or three, are also like this.[59]

("down to") here suggests that Dōgen is abbreviating a list of items ending in "the ocean of the nature," though it is not clear what such a list would be. "The ocean of the nature" (*shōkai* 性海) is a common term in East Asian Buddhist texts, perhaps especially popular in Huayan literature, for the ultimate realm of suchness.

the ocean of *sarvajña* (*sabanya kai* 薩婆若海): *Sabanya* transliterates the Sanskrit *sarvajña*, "all knowing," or "omniscience." Though not a common image in Chan texts, the "ocean of all knowing" occurs regularly in the Chinese Buddhist literature with a sense close to that of the "ocean of the nature" above — as is seen in passages, for example, such as, "thought after thought is quiescent and flows naturally into the ocean of *sarvajña*" (*shinshin jakumetsu jinen runyū sabanya kai* 心心寂滅自然流入薩婆若海). (*Fahua xuanyi* 法華玄義, T.1716.33:734b-3.)

58　**the non-upper body, the non-lower body, the non-mid-body** (*hishinjō hishinge hishinchū* 非身上・非身下・非身中): It is also possible to read these playful expressions as "the upper non-body," etc.

down to the fire emitted (*naishi shukka* [also read *suika*] 乃至出火): Again, the list implied by the term *naishi* ("down to") is unclear; perhaps Dōgen is signaling that the "fire emitted" from the body is also "like this" (*kaku no gotoshi*) in the sense that it can also be treated in all the ways he has just treated "water."

59　**water, fire, wind, and so on** (*sui ka fū tō* 水・火・風等): Dōgen is here introducing the Buddhist list of physical "elements" he will discuss below.

buddhas emitted from the upper body (*shinjō shutsu butsu* 身上出佛): The term "buddha" (*butsu* 佛) could be read in the singular, but its pairing with "ancestor" (*so* 祖) in the next phrase suggests Dōgen's common expression "buddhas and ancestors" (*busso* 佛祖).

incalculable *asaṃkhyeya-kalpas* (*muryō asōgikō* 無量阿僧祇劫): A kalpa is an (almost) infinitely long period of time; *asaṃkhyeya-kalpas* are kalpas of "countless" number. Some texts define *asaṃkhyeya* as the specific number 10^{59}.

ocean of the dharma realm (*hokkai kai* 法界海): The realm of all dharmas (S. *dharma-dhātu*) seen as an ocean; very similar in connotation to the "ocean of the nature" and the "ocean of *sarvajña*" seen above.

lands of this world (*sekai kokudo* 世界國土): Without an obvious technical Buddhist usage, this expression suggests merely the various countries of the world. It may be that Dōgen introduces it here to emphasize that the spiritual powers govern the activity not only of a sacred Buddhist realm but of the ordinary world.

128 DŌGEN'S *SHŌBŌGENZŌ* VOLUME III

The four elements, the five elements, the six elements, the various elements, the incalculable elements — all are the spiritual powers emitted and submerged, the spiritual powers swallowed and vomited forth.[60] The present whole earth and empty space, in every direction, are swallowed up and vomited forth.[61] Their strength is their being turned by the mustard seed; their strength is their being connected to the hair follicle.[62] Born together where knowledge does not reach; they abide where knowledge does not reach; they return where knowledge does not reach.[63] The marks of the transformations of the spiritual powers of the buddhas, which surely have nothing to do with short or long — how could we merely consider them in terms of [their] measurement?[64]

* * * * *

[35:16] {1:397}

むかし五通仙人、ほとけに事奉せしとき、仙人とふ、佛有六通、我有五通、如何是那一通。ほとけ、ときに仙人を召していふ、五通仙人。仙人應諾す。佛言、那一通、爾問我。

Long ago, when a seer with the five powers was serving the Buddha, the seer asked, *"The Buddha has six powers; I have five powers. What is that one power?"*[65]

60 **The four elements, the five elements, the six elements** (*shidai godai rokudai* 四大・五大・六大): The nested lists of Buddhist "elements" (S. *mahābhūta*) comprising the natural world. The four are earth, water, fire, and wind; the five add space; the six add consciousness. See Supplementary Notes, s.v. "Four elements and five aggregates."

61 **The present whole earth and empty space, in every direction** (*ima no daichi kokū no menmen naru* いまの大地虚空の面面なる): Taking *menmen* here as referring to *hōmen* 方面 ("direction"); some would take it as "in every instance" or "in every aspect."

62 **Their strength is their being turned by the mustard seed; their strength is their being connected to the hair follicle** (*ke ni tenzeraruru o rikiryō to seri, mō ni kakareru o rikiryō to seri* 芥に轉ぜらるるを力量とせり、毛にかかれるを力量とせり): The subject here and in the following sentence is unexpressed; presumably, we are to understand the "great earth and empty space" of the preceding sentence.

63 **Born together where knowledge does not reach** (*shikichi no oyobazaru yori dōshō shite* 識知のおよばざるより同生して): The term *dōshō* 同生 ("born together") recalls the discussion above of the powers "born together" with the buddha; here, however, it seems to suggest only that "the great earth and empty space" are "born together."

64 **how could we merely consider them in terms of [their] measurement?** (*hitoe ni shikiryō o ko shite gi suru nomi naran ya* ひとへに測量を擧して擬するのみならんや): Although Dōgen often uses the term *shikiryō* ("measurement") in a somewhat loose sense of intellectual "calculation," its association here with "short and long" suggests he wants to retain its stricter sense of "to fathom," "to survey." Presumably his point here is that, when taken as "the spiritual powers of the buddha," there is more to "the great earth and empty space" than spatial extension.

65 **Long ago** (*mukashi* むかし): A Japanese version of a story appearing in the *Mingjue*

35. Spiritual Powers *Jinzū* 神通 129

The Buddha called the seer, saying, "Seer with the five powers."
The seer responded. The Buddha said, "*That one power, ask me about it.*"[66]

[35:17]

この因縁、よくよく参究すべし。仙人、いかでか佛有六通としる。佛有無
量神通智慧なり、ただ六通のみにあらず。たとひ六通のみをみるといふと
も、六通もきはむべきにあらず、いはんやその餘の神通におきて、いかで
かゆめにもみん。

We should study this episode very well. How could the seer know
that the Buddha has six powers? *The Buddha has incalculable spiritual
powers and wisdom, not just six powers.* Even if one looks only at his
six powers, the six powers cannot be exhausted. Not to mention, when it
comes to the rest of the [Buddha's] spiritual powers, how could [he] see
them even in his dreams?[67]

[35:18]

しばらくとふ、仙人たとひ釋迦老子をみるといふとも、見佛すやいまだ
しや、といふべし。たとひ見佛すといふとも、釋迦老子をみるやいまだ
しや。たとひ釋迦老子をみることをえ、たとひ見佛すといふとも、五通仙
人をみるやいまだしや、と問著すべきなり。この問處に、用葛藤を學すべ
し、葛藤斷を學すべし。いはんや佛有六通、しばらく隣珍を算數するにお
よばざるか。

Now, let us ask something. We should ask, even if the seer may have
seen Old Master Śākya, has he seen the Buddha or not?[68] Even if he has

---

chanshi yulu 明覺禪師語録 (T.1996.47:671a15-17) and elsewhere. Dōgen also cites this
story in his *Eihei kōroku* 永平廣録 (DZZ 3:264, no. 394).

seer with the five powers (*gotsū sennin* 五通仙人): The term *sennin* 仙人, translated
here as "seer," has the connotations in Chinese texts of a mysterious, transcendent being,
of a solitary hermit with miraculous powers, a Daoist "immortal," etc. In Buddhist texts,
the term is often used to render Sanskrit terms like *ṛṣi* (often translated "seer") or *muni*
(often rendered "sage" or "ascetic").

"that one power" (*na ittsū* 那一通): For a list of the six powers, see above, Note 2. In
traditional discussions of this list, the first five are considered available to any advanced
yogi, Buddhist or otherwise; in contrast, the sixth power, the knowledge that one has
eliminated the defilements, can only be accomplished by a realized Buddhist adept.

66　**"That one power, ask me about it"** (*na ittsū ni mon ga* 那一通爾問我): The sense
is uncertain and the commentaries varied here. Most follow some version of Dōgen's
view, expressed below, that the seer has not understood the meaning of "that one power"
he has asked about. Some would see the exchange itself as demonstrations of "that one
power," in which case, we would want to read the last clause not as an imperative but as
a declarative: "that one power [is] your asking me."

67　**how could [he] see them even in his dreams?** (*ikade ka ya yume ni mo min* いかで
かやゆめにもみん): Taking the unexpressed subject to be "the seer of the five powers."

68　**Old Master Śākya** (*Shaka rōshi* 釋迦老子): Dōgen is here using a common Zen term of
endearment for the Buddha, treating him as just one of the venerable teachers of the community.

130 DŌGEN'S *SHŌBŌGENZŌ* VOLUME III

seen the Buddha, has he seen Old Master Śākya or not? We should ask, even if he has seen Old Master Śākya, even if he has seen the Buddha, has he seen the seer with the five powers or not? In this questioning, one should study using entanglements; one should study entanglements cut off.[69] How much less does [the question of] the Buddha having six powers reach [the level of] counting the neighbor's valuables?[70]

[35:19] {1:398}

いま釋迦老子道の那一通爾問我のこころ、いかん。仙人に那一通あり、と
いはず、仙人になし、といはず。那一通の通塞はたとひとくとも、仙人い
かでか那一通を通ぜん。いかんとなれば、仙人に五通あれど、佛有六通の
なかの五通にあらず。仙人通は、たとひ佛通の所通に通破となるとも、仙
通いかでか佛通を通ずることをえん。もし仙人、佛の一通をも通ずること
あらば、この通より佛を通ずべきなり。仙人をみるに、佛通に相似せるあ
り、佛儀をみるに、仙通に相似せることあるは、佛儀なりといへども、佛
神通にあらずとしるべきなり。通ぜざれば、五通みな佛と同じからざるな
り。

What about the point of the Old Master Śākya's saying here, "*That one power, ask me about it*"? He does not say the seer has "that one power"; he does not say the seer lacks it. Even if he explains the passage and blockage of "that one power," how can the seer penetrate "that one power"?[71] For, though the seer has the five powers, they are not the five

---

seen the Buddha (*kenbutsu* 見佛): The exact distinction between "Old Master Śākya" and "the Buddha" here is not clear but suggests a difference between the buddha as historical figure and the buddha of more cosmic proportions that Dōgen is describing — in scholastic terms, between the buddha's "transformation body" (*ōjin* 應身; S. *nirmāṇa-kāya*) and "dharma body" (*hosshin* 法身; S. *dharma-kāya*).

69 **one should study using entanglements; one should study entanglements cut off** (*yō kattō o gaku su beshi, kattō dan o gaku su beshi* 用葛藤を學すべし、葛藤斷を學す べし): The subject here is unexpressed; it could be interpreted either as "we" or as "he" (i.e., the "seer" in the story). For the term *kattō* 葛藤, here translated "entanglements," see Supplementary Notes, s.v. "Tangled vines." Dōgen's own language here is rather tangled and subject to somewhat varied interpretation.

70 **counting the neighbor's valuables** (*rinchin o sansū suru* 隣珍を算數する): I.e., the "seer's" concern with the six powers of the buddha is less productive than calculating another's property.

71 **Even if he explains the passage and blockage of "that one power"** (*na ittsū no tsūsoku wa tatoi toku tomo* 那一通の通塞はたとひとくとも): The unexpressed subject here is probably "Old Master Śākya." "Passage and blockage" here translates *tsūsoku* 通塞, an expression that has the idiomatic sense of "things going well or not" (what we might call "the ups and downs" of life); but Dōgen is here beginning an extended play with the word *tsū* 通, the first element of *tsūsoku* and the second element of the term *jinzū* 神通, the translation of which by "spiritual powers" misses the connotation of "passage" (also "thorough understanding," "mastery") in its second element. Hence, some of Dōgen's play in this passage with that connotation is masked by the translation.

35. Spiritual Powers *Jinzū* 神通

131

powers in "*the Buddha has six powers.*"[72] Even if the powers of the seer get utterly penetrated in what the powers of the buddha penetrate, how could the powers of the seer penetrate the powers of the Buddha?[73] If the seer could penetrate even one power of the Buddha, by this penetration he should penetrate the Buddha.

When we look at the seer, he has something resembling the powers of the Buddha; when we look at the deportment of the Buddha, it has something resembling the powers of the seer.[74] Though this may be [true of] the deportment of the Buddha, we should realize that [such deportment] is not the spiritual powers of the Buddha. Since they do not penetrate [the Buddha], none of the five powers is the same as [those of] the Buddha.

[35:20]

たちまちに那一通をとふ、なにの用かある、となり。釋迦老子のこころ
は、一通をもとふべし、となり。那一通をとひ、那一通をとふべし、一通
も仙人はおよぶところなしとなり。しかあれば、佛神通と餘者通とは、神
通の名字おなじといへども、神通の名字はるかに殊異なり。ここをもて、

What is the use of his suddenly asking about "that one power"? The Old Master Śākya's point is that he should be asking about even one of the powers. He should be asking about "that one power" and asking about "that one power."[75] Even one of the powers is not something the sage could reach. This being the case, [when we speak of] "the spiritual powers of the Buddha" and the spiritual powers of others, while the term

---

72 **they are not the five powers in "the Buddha has six powers"** (*butsu u rokutsū no naka no gotsū ni arazu* 佛有六通のなかの五通にあらず): Or, "they are not the five powers among the six powers that the Buddha has."

73 **get utterly penetrated in what the powers of the Buddha penetrate** (*buttsū no shotsū ni tsūha to naru* 佛通の所通に通破となる): An odd locution, presumably meaning simply "are fully penetrated by the powers of the Buddha." The element *ha* 破 ("to break") in the term *tsūha* 通破 should probably be taken as an emphatic; hence, "utterly."

74 **deportment of the Buddha** (*butsugi* 佛儀): The glyph *gi* 儀 usually connotes formal or ritual action; here, it can probably be understand simply as the Buddha's "manner," or "way of behaving." The point would seem to be that, while in their behavior, the Buddha and the seer may sometimes act alike in displaying powers, such displays are not the real powers of the Buddha.

75 **he should be asking about even one of the powers. He should be asking about "that one power" and asking about "that one power"** (*ittsū o mo tou beshi, to nari. na ittsū o toi, na ittsū o tou beshi* 一通をもとふべし、となり。那一通をとひ、那一通をとふべし): A confusing passage, generally interpreted to mean that, instead of asking about "that one power" distinctive of the Buddha, the seer should be asking again and again about any one of the powers. On this reading, Dōgen is using "that one power" (*na ittsū* 那一通) here to mean, not the sixth power, but whichever power the seer may ask about.

132   DŌGEN'S *SHŌBŌGENZŌ* VOLUME III

"spiritual powers" may be the same, the term "spiritual powers" is very different.[76]

In regard to this [we have the following]:

* * * * *

[35:21]

臨濟院慧照大師云、古人云、如來擧身相、爲順世間情。恐人生斷見、權且立虛名。假言三十二、八十也空聲。有身非覺體、無相乃眞形。儞道、佛有六通、是不可思議。一切諸天・神仙・阿修羅・大力鬼、亦有神通、應是佛否。道流莫錯、祇如阿修羅與天帝釋戰、戰敗領八萬四千眷属、入藕孔中藏、莫是聖否。如山僧所擧、皆是業通・依通。夫如佛六通者不然。入色界不被色惑、入聲界不被聲惑、入香界不被香惑、入味界不被味惑、入觸界不被觸惑、入法界不被法惑。所以達六種色聲香味觸法皆是空相、不能繫縛此無依道人。雖是五蘊漏質、便是地行神通。道流、眞佛無形、眞法無相。儞祇麼幻化上頭、作模作樣。設求得者、皆是野狐精魅。竝不是眞佛、是外道見解。

Great Master Huizhao of Linji Cloister said,[77]

An ancient has said,
The Tathāgata's presentation of the bodily marks
Is done to accord with the sentiments of the worldly.[78]
Lest people produce annihilationist views,

---

76 **while the term "spiritual powers" may be the same, the term "spiritual powers" is very different** (*jinzū no myōji onaji to iedomo, jinzū no myōji haruka ni shui nari* 神通の名字おなじといへども、神通の名字はるかに殊異なり): Presumably to be understood, "though the term may be the same, its meaning in each case is very different."

77 **Great Master Huizhao of Linji Cloister** (*Rinzai in Eshō daishi* 臨濟院慧照大師): I.e., Linji Yixuan 臨濟義玄. This entire section is a quotation in Chinese of a passage from the *Linji lu* 臨濟錄, T.1985.47:49c29-50a14.

78 **An ancient** (*kojin* 古人): Linji is quoting here the *Liang zhao Fu dashi song Jingang bore jing* 梁朝傅大師頌金剛般若經 (T.2732.85:2b23-26; Stein 1846), preserved among the Dunhuang documents. Though traditionally attributed to the semi-legendary sixth-century figure Fu Dashi 傅大師, or Great Master Fu (497-569), it is thought to have been composed in the Tang. The verse quoted by Linji here is commenting on the *Diamond Sūtra*'s famous discussion of the "marks" (*xiang* 相; S. *lakṣana*) of a buddha. It is introduced in the original Fu Dashi text by two passages (T.2732.85:2b18-21) from Kumārajīva's translation of the *Diamond Sūtra* (*Jingang bore boluomi jing* 金剛般若波羅蜜經, T.235.8:750a20-23; T.235:8.749a23-25):

須菩提、於意云何、可以三十二相見如來不。不也世尊、不可以三十二相得見如來。何以故。如來説三十二相即是非相。是名三十二相。

"Subhūti, what do you think? Can one see the Tathāgata by his thirty-two marks?" "No, World-Honored One, one cannot see the Tathāgata by his thirty-two marks. Why is this? The thirty-two marks spoken of by the Tathāgata are no-marks. These are called 'the thirty-two marks.'"

佛告須菩提、凡所有相皆是虛妄。若見諸相非相、則見如來。

35. Spiritual Powers *Jinzū* 神通

133

He expediently sets up vacuous names.[79]
He provisionally speaks of the thirty-two
And the eighty, just empty sounds.[80]
Having a body is not the substance of his awakening;
Having no marks is his true shape.[81]

You say that the buddha has six powers, and that they are inconceivable. All the devas, transcendent seers, *asuras*, and powerful spirits have spiritual powers.[82] Does this make them buddhas? Followers of the way, don't be mistaken. The *asuras* battled with Deva Lord Śakra; defeated in battle, they led their eighty-four thousand followers to hide inside a lotus root.[83] Are they not sages?

What this mountain monk has brought up are all karmic powers or dependent powers; they are not like the six powers of the buddha.[84]

The Buddha admonished Subhūti, "Whatever marks there are, they are all vain delusion. If one sees the marks as no-marks, that is seeing the Tathāgata."

bodily marks (*shinsō* 身相): I.e., the extraordinary physical "marks" (S. *lakṣana*) held to adorn the body of a buddha (and a *cakravartin*, or "wheel-turning" monarch).

79 **annihilationist views** (*danken* 斷見): S. *uccheda-dṛṣṭi*, the false view that denies the reality of karma and rebirth.

80 **the thirty-two and the eighty** (*sanjūni, hachijū* 三十二、八十): I.e., the traditional lists of thirty-two "marks" (*sō* 相; S. *lakṣana*;) and eighty "auspicious signs" (*kō* 好; S. *anuvyañjana*) that scripture attributes to a buddha's body.

81 **Having a body** (*ushin* 有身); **Having no marks** (*musō* 無相): Or, perhaps, "his existing (i.e., physical) body"; "his nonexisting marks."

82 **All the devas, transcendent seers, *asuras*, and powerful spirits** (*issai shoten, shinsen, ashura, dairikiki* 一切諸天、神仙、阿修羅、大力鬼): "devas" (*shoten* 諸天): i.e, the "gods" of the various buddhist "heavens." "Transcendent seers" (*shinsen* 神仙): i.e., spiritual adepts like the "seer" who interviewed the Buddha in the story above; in Chinese context, often translated as "immortals." "*Asura*" (*ashura* 阿修羅): sometimes translated "titans"; powerful beings of Indian mythology, sometimes pictured as warring with the devas. "Powerful spirits" (*dairikiki* 大力鬼): could refer to a variety of demonic beings; sometimes interpreted as powerful demons in the realm of the "hungry ghosts" (*gaki* 餓鬼; S. *preta*).

83 **The *asuras* battled with Deva Lord Śakra** (*ashura yo Ten Taishaku sen* 阿修羅與天帝釋戰): "Deva Lord Śakra" (*Ten Taishaku* 天帝釋) refers to the powerful Vedic god Indra, sometimes said to be the king of the devas. The example of the *asura* king hiding his troops in the lotus root can be seen at *Huayan jing* 華嚴經, T.279.10:220a25.

84 **What this mountain monk has brought up** (*nyo sansō shokyo* 如山僧所舉): I.e., "the powers I have just discussed."

karmic powers or dependent powers (*gōtsū etsū* 業通依通): "Karmic powers" (*gōtsū* 業通) likely correspond to what are elsewhere called "recompensive powers" (*hōtsū* 報通) — i.e., powers derived from the karma of one's birth as a dragon, demon, etc. "Dependent powers" (*etsū* 依通) refer to paranormal events in the environment, such as "miraculous" cures, etc. For these definitions, see *Baozang lun* 寶藏論 (T.1857.45:127b1-9), and *Zongjing lu* 宗鏡錄 (T.2016.48:494b18ff).

134 DŌGEN'S *SHŌBŌGENZŌ* VOLUME III

He enters the realm of form without being deluded by form, enters the realm of sound without being deluded by sound, enters the realm of smell without being deluded by smell, enters the realm of taste without being deluded by taste, enters the realm of touch without being deluded by touch, enters the realm of dharma without being deluded by dharma.[85]

Therefore, when he realizes that the six types — form, sound, smell, taste, touch, and dharma — are all empty marks, they cannot bind this person of the way who depends on nothing.[86] *Though his is the defiled quality of the five aggregates, it is yet the spiritual power of walking the earth.*[87]

Followers of the way, the true buddha is without a shape; the true dharma is without marks. You are just making models and making patterns on top of phantom transformations. Even supposing you get something through your seeking, it will all be fox spirits.[88] *None of it is the true buddha; it is the view of other paths.*

[35:22] {1:400}

しかあれば、諸佛の六神通は、一切諸天・鬼神、および二乘等のおよぶべきにあらず、はかるべきにあらざるなり。佛道の六通は、佛道の佛弟子のみ單傳せり、餘人の相傳せざるところなり。佛六通は、佛道に單傳す、單傳せざるは、佛六通をしるべからざるなり。佛六通を單傳せざらんは、佛道人なるべからず、と參學すべし。

Thus, the six spiritual powers of the buddhas are not something that could be reached by, not something that could be reckoned by, any of the devas or demonic spirits, or by the two vehicles and the like. The

---

85 **He enters the realm of form without being deluded by form** (*nyū shikikai fuhi shiki waku* 入色界不被色惑): Linji is giving here the venerable list of the six "entrances" (*nyū* 入; S. *āyatana*, "sense field"). The "realm of dharma" here refers to the objects of the sixth sensory organ, the mind (*i* 意; S. *manas*). Though the association of the six sense fields with the six spiritual powers became common in Chan texts, there does not seem to have been any serious attempt actually to match the members of the two lists. "Deluded" (*waku* 惑) translates a term regularly used as a synonym for the "defilements" (*bonnō* 煩惱; S. *kleśa*).

86 **empty marks** (*kūsō* 空相): Or, "marked by emptiness"; in ordinary parlance, "an empty form."

87 **the defiled quality of the five aggregates** (*goun ro shitsu* 五蘊漏質): I.e., the ordinary state of a human being. See Supplementary Notes, s.v. "Four elements and five aggregates."

the spiritual power of walking the earth (*jigyō jinzū* 地行神通): No doubt a play with the sense, "grounded," in the term *jigyō* 地行 ("walking the earth"), as in the "grounded seer" (*jigyō sen* 地行仙), who has not yet mastered the art of flying.

88 **fox spirits** (*yako seimi* 野狐精魅): A common Zen dismissal of paranormal powers as no better than the bewitchments of fox spirit possession; more often in the abbreviated form *yako zei* 野狐精.

35. Spiritual Powers *Jinzū* 神通   135

six powers of the way of the buddhas have been uniquely transmitted only by the disciples of the buddha on the way of the buddhas; they are not something transmitted by others.[89] The six powers of the buddha are uniquely transmitted on the way of the buddhas; those that do not uniquely transmit them cannot be expected to know them. We should study that those who have not uniquely transmitted the six powers of the buddha are not people of the way of the buddhas.

* * * * *

[35:23]

百丈大智禪師云、眼耳鼻舌、各各不貪染一切有無諸法、是名受持四句偈、亦名四果。六入無迹、亦名六神通。祇如今但不被一切有無諸法礙、亦無不依住知解、是名神通。不守此神通、是名無神通。如云無神通菩薩、蹤跡不可得尋。是佛向上人、最不可思議人、是自己天。

Chan Master Baizhang Dazhi said,[90]

The eyes, ears, nose, and tongue are each without the stain of craving for any of the dharmas, whether being or non-being — this is called "receiving and keeping the four-line gāthā"; it is also called "the four fruits."[91] *The six entrances without traces are also called "the six spiritual powers."*[92] *To be unobstructed by all the dharmas, whether being*

---

89 **uniquely transmitted** (*tanden* 單傳): A term commonly used in Zen to describe the transmission of the dharma from master to disciple. Though the term suggests (and in some cases is used to indicate) a lineage in which there is only one legitimate representative, or "ancestor," in each generation, it regularly appears in contexts where the element *tan* 單 is better understood as "unique," "pure," or "simple."

90 **Chan Master Baizhang Dazhi** (*Hyakujō Daichi zenji* 百丈大智禪師): I.e., Baizhang Huaihai 百丈懷海. The quotation here is from a passage appearing in the *Tiansheng guangdong lu* 天聖廣燈錄, ZZ.135:681a17-b3. A portion of the passage is also quoted in the "Shōbōgenzō arakan" 正法眼藏阿羅漢 chapter.

91 **"the four-line gāthā"** (*shiku ge* 四句偈): Here, probably referring to the verse found throughout the Buddhist literature; see, e.g., the *Nirvāṇa Sūtra* (*Da banniepan jing* 大般涅槃經, T.7.1:204c23-24):

諸行無常、是生滅法、生滅滅已、寂滅爲樂。

All things are impermanent:
This is the law of arising and ceasing.
When the arising and ceasing have ceased,
Their cessation is ease.

See Supplementary Notes, s.v. "Whether on trees or on rocks."

"the four fruits" (*shika* 四果): The four stages on the path of the *śrāvaka*: "stream entry" (*yoru* 預流; S. *srotāpanna*), "once-returning" (*ichirai* 一來; S. *sakṛdāgami*), "non-returning" (*fugen* 不還; S. *anāgami*), and "worthy" (*arakan* 阿羅漢; S. *arhat*).

92 **six entrances** (*rokunyū* 六入): The six sense spheres (S. *āyatana*) of eye, ear, nose, tongue, body, and mind.

136   DŌGEN'S *SHŌBŌGENZŌ* VOLUME III

*or non-being, and not to rely on the understanding — this is called
"spiritual power." Not to guard this spiritual power — this is called
"no spiritual power." Such is the bodhisattva of no spiritual powers,
whose traces cannot be found. He is a person beyond the buddha, the
most inconceivable person; he is himself a deva.*[93]

[35:24]

いま佛佛祖祖相傳せる神通、かくのごとし。諸佛神通は、佛向上人なり、
最不可思議人なり、是自己天なり、無神通菩薩なり、知解不依住なり、神
通不守此なり、一切諸法不被礙なり。いま佛道に六神通あり、諸佛の傳持
しきたれることひさし。一佛も傳持せざるなし、傳持せざれば諸佛にあら
ず。その六神通は、六入を無迹にあきらむるなり。

The spiritual powers transmitted here by buddha after buddha and ancestor after ancestor are like this. The spiritual powers of the buddhas
are "*the person beyond the buddha*," are "*the most inconceivable person*," are "*he is himself a deva*," are "*the bodhisattva of no spiritual
powers*," are *the understanding not relying*, are *the spiritual powers not
guarding this*, are *all the dharmas not being obstructed*.[94] On the way of
the buddhas, there are the six spiritual powers here. The buddhas have
transmitted and kept them for a long time. Not a single buddha has failed
to transmit and keep them. Those who do not transmit and keep them
are not buddhas. Those six spiritual powers clarify "the six entrances"
"without traces."[95]

[35:25] {1:401}

無迹といふは、古人のいはく、六般神用空不空、一顆圓光非内外。

   "Without traces," [means what] an ancient has said:

---

93 **person beyond the buddha** (*butsu kōjō nin* 佛向上人): Or "human beyond the buddha," in contrast to "deva." The expression became a popular one in the Zen literature;
see Supplementary Notes, s.v. "Beyond the buddha."

he is himself a deva (*ze jiko ten* 是自己天): A tentative translation of an unusual locution; alternatively, it might be read "he is our own deva," after *jiko nin* 自己人 ("our own
people"). The interpretation is rendered more difficult by the fact that Dōgen has broken
off the quotation in mid-sentence: the original (ZZ.135:681b2-3) reads,

   是佛向上人、最不可思議。人是自己、天是智照。

   He is a person beyond the buddha, the most inconceivable. The person is the self; the
   devas are the illumination of his wisdom.

94 **the understanding not relying** (*chige fu ejū* 知解不依住); **the spiritual powers
not guarding this** (*jinzū fushu shi* 神通不守此); **all the dharmas not being obstructed**
(*issai shohō fuhige* 一切諸法不被礙): Dōgen is here simply playing with the syntax of
Baizhang's Chinese.

95 **clarify "the six entrances" "without traces"** (*rokunyū o mushaku ni akiramuru* 六
入を無迹にあきらむる): I.e., "clarify the six senses without leaving any traces"; again
Dōgen is playing here with Baizhang's expression "six entrances without traces."

35. Spiritual Powers *Jinzū* 神通

137

The six spiritual functions, empty and not empty;
The one circular light, neither inside nor out.[96]

[35:26]

非内外は、無迹なるべし。無迹に修行し、參學し、證入するに、六入を動
著せざるなり。動著せずといふは、動著するもの三十棒分あるなり。

"Neither inside nor outside" must be "without traces." When, "without traces," we practice, study, and enter verification, we do not move "the six entrances." To say, "we do not move," means, the one who moves deserves thirty blows.[97]

[35:27]

しかあればすなはち、六神通かくのごとく參究すべきなり。佛家の嫡嗣
にあらざらん、たれかこのことわりあるべしともきかん。いたづらに向
外の馳走を、歸家の行履とあやまれるのみなり。又、四果は、佛道の調度
なりといへども、正傳せる三藏なし。算沙のやから、跉跰のたぐひ、いか
でかこの果實をうることあらん。得小爲足の類、いまだ參究の達せるにあ
らず。ただまさに佛佛相承せるのみなり。いはゆる四果は、受持四句偈な
り。受持四句偈といふは、一切有無諸法におきて、眼・耳・鼻・舌各各不
貪染なるなり。不貪染は不染汚なり。不染汚といふは、平常心なり、吾常
於此切なり。

So, we should study the six spiritual powers in this way. Those who are not legitimate heirs of the house of the buddhas — which of them has even heard of this principle? They just mistake vainly chasing about outside for the conduct of coming home.[98] Further, while the "four fruits" may be implements on the way of the buddhas, there is no Tripiṭaka [master] who has correctly transmitted them. How could those who count sand, the types who wander abroad, get these fruits?[99] The types

---

96 **an ancient** (*kojin* 古人): Variant of the poem *Zhengdao ge* 證道歌, by Yungjia Xuan-jue 永嘉玄覺 (d. 713) (T.2014.48:395c22-23). The second line of the original reads, "The one circular light, form and not form" (*ikka enkō shiki hi shiki* 一顆圓光色非色).

The one circular light (*ikka enkō* 一顆圓光): A reference to the halo about the head of a buddha or bodhisattva.

97 **the one who moves deserves thirty blows** (*dōjaku suru mono sanjū bō bun* 動著するもの三十棒分): Echoing the stock Zen phrase, "If you move, thirty blows" (*dōjaku sanjū bō* 動著三十棒).

98 **They just mistake vainly chasing about outside for the conduct of coming home** (*itazura ni kōge no chisō o, kika no anri to ayamareru nomi nari* いたづらに向外の馳走を、歸家の行履とあやまれるのみなり): "Chasing about" (*chisō* 馳走) and "coming home" (*kika* or *kike* 歸家) are terms often used in Zen in a psychological sense, for seeking the goals of Buddhism "outside" and "within" the self, respectively. The term *anri* 行履 ("conduct") is a common expression for Buddhist religious activities.

99 **those who count sand** (*sansha no yakara* 算沙のやから); **the types who wander abroad** (*reihei no tagui* 跉跰のたぐひ): "Counting sand" (*sansha* 算沙) is a common pejorative for those who merely study the details of doctrine; see Supplementary Notes,

138 DŌGEN'S *SHŌBŌGENZŌ* VOLUME III

who get a little and consider it enough — their investigations have not mastered it; it is something only buddha after buddha inherits.[100]

The "four fruits" are "*to receive and keep the four-line gāthā*." "*To receive and keep the four-line gāthā*" means, in regard to "*all dharmas, whether being or non-being*," "*the eyes, ears, nose, and tongue are each without the stain of craving*." "*Without the stain of craving*" is "undefiled." "Undefiled" means the ordinary mind, means "*I'm always close to this*."[101]

---

s.v. "Counting sand." "Wander abroad" renders *reihei* (or *ryōbyō*) 跉跰, a term occurring elsewhere in the *Shōbōgenzō* in allusion to the wanderings of the rich man's son in Chapter 4 of the *Lotus Sūtra*; likely a variant for the compound term *lingping* 伶俜 appearing at *Miaofa lianhua jing* 妙法蓮華經, T.262.9:17b11.

100 **The types who get a little and consider it enough** (*toku shō i soku no rui* 得小爲足の類): Doubtless an allusion to the parable in Chapter 8 of the *Lotus Sūtra*, in which a man, not realizing that he has a precious jewel sewn in his robe, wanders in poverty satisfied with whatever he can get; see Supplementary Notes, s.v. "Jewel in the robe." So too those on the *śrāvaka* path, not realizing that they could attain the complete knowledge of a tathāgata, "take little knowledge as enough" (*i shōchi i soku* 以小智爲足). (*Miaofa lianhua jing* 妙法蓮華經, T.262.9:29a5.)

101 **the ordinary mind** (*byōjō shin* 平常心): A popular Zen expression, seen especially in the common phrase, "The ordinary mind is the way" (*byōjō shin ze dō* 平常心是道); see Supplementary Notes.

"I'm always close to this" (*go jō o shi setsu* 吾常於此切): A phrase also cited in the "Henzan" 遍參 and (in the variant *go jō o ze setsu* 吾常於是切) the "Gabyō" 画餅 chapters of the *Shōbōgenzō*. The sense of the glyph *setsu* 切 here is subject to interpretation: the translation takes it as *sekkin* 切近 ("to be familiar with," "to be intimate with"), but it could also be, and has been, understood as *shinsetsu* 深切 ("to be ardent," "to care deeply," etc.). From a remark attributed to Dongshan Liangjie 洞山良价, in answer to a question about the three bodies of a buddha. The *Dongshan yulu* 洞山語錄 (T.1986A.47:510b24-25) gives the question as:

問、三身之中、阿那身不墮衆數。

[A monk] asked, "Among the three bodies [of the buddha], which body doesn't fall among the numbered?"

Dōgen's *shinji Shōbōgenzō* 眞字正法眼藏 (DZZ.5:152, case 55) has a variant version:

洞山因僧問、三身中那身説法。師曰、吾常於此切。僧後問曹山、洞山道吾常於此切、意旨云何。山云、要頭斫將去。僧又問雪峰。峯以拄杖劈口打曰、我也曾到洞山來。

Dongshan was asked by a monk, "Among the three bodies, which preaches the dharma?"

The Master said, "I'm always close to this."

The monk later asked Caoshan [i.e., Caoshan Benzhi 曹山本寂, 840-901], "Dongshan said, 'I'm always close to this.' What does that mean?"

Shan said, "If you want my head, cut it off and take it."

The monk again asked Xuefeng [i.e., Xuefeng Yicun 雪峰義存 (822-908)]. Feng struck him in the mouth with his staff and said, "I've been to Dongshan."

35. Spiritual Powers *Jinzū* 神通

[35:28]

六通・四果を佛道に正傳せる、かくのごとし。相違あらんは、佛法にあらざらんとしるべきなり。しかあれば、佛道はかならず神通より達するなり。その達する、涓滴の、巨海を吞吐する、微塵の、高嶽を拈放する、たれか疑著することをえん。これすなはち神通なるのみなり。

The correct transmission of the six powers and four fruits in the way of the buddhas is like this. We should realize that what differs from this is not the buddha dharma. This being the case, the way of the buddhas is always mastered from the spiritual powers. Who could doubt that, in this mastery, the smallest drop of water swallows and vomits the vast ocean, an infinitesimal dust mote takes up and lets go of a tall peak? This is just the spiritual powers.

正法眼藏神通第三十五

Treasury of the True Dharma Eye

Spiritual Powers

Number 35

[Ryūmonji MS:]

爾時仁治二年辛丑十一月十六日、在於觀音導利興聖寶林寺示衆

Presented to the assembly at Kannon Dōri Kōshō Hōrin Monastery; sixteenth day, eleventh month of the junior metal year of the ox, the second year of Ninji [19 December 1241]

[Tōunji MS:]

寬元甲辰中春初一日書寫之、在於越州吉峰侍者寮。懷奘

Copied this in the acolyte's quarters, Kippō, Esshū; first day of mid-spring, senior wood year of the dragon, Kangen [11 March 1244].

Ejō[102]

---

102 **mid-spring** (*chūshun* 中春): I.e., the second lunar month.

TREASURY OF THE TRUE DHARMA EYE

NUMBER 36

The Arhat
Arakan

阿羅漢

The Arhat

Arakan

INTRODUCTION

This work was composed in the summer of 1242, at Kōshōji. According to the colophon, it was copied out over thirty years later by Dōgen's disciple Ejō. The work, one of the shorter pieces in the *Shōbōgenzō*, appears as number 36 in both the seventy-five- and sixty-chapter versions of the collection and as number 34 in the Honzan edition.

As its title indicates, the text is a discussion of the arhat, or "worthy" one, who has eliminated all his or her spiritual defilements (*kleśa*) and achieved nirvāṇa. In much Buddhist literature, the term "arhat" was used to refer to any fully realized Buddhist (and, indeed, was applied to Buddha Śākyamuni himself); but, with the rise of the bodhisattva ideal, the word came to refer specifically to the goal of the *śrāvaka-yāna*, or "vehicle of the hearers," those held to aspire only to nirvāṇa and not to the *anuttara-samyak-saṃbodhi* ("unsurpassed, perfect awakening") of a buddha.

Dogen's discussion of the term dismisses the distinction between the arhat and the buddha. As in most of the chapters of the *Shōbōgenzō*, the discussion proceeds by way of comments on passages drawn from earlier literature — in this case, from the *Lotus Sūtra* and the sayings of several Chinese Chan masters. Expanding on the famous *Lotus Sūtra* doctrine that all Buddhism is ultimately intended to guide beings to buddhahood, Dōgen argues that the true arhat is a fully awakened buddha. Reiterating a theme found in much of his writing, he argues that true awakening is to be found in the spiritual practice of the Zen masters.

143

正法眼藏第三十六
Treasury of the True Dharma Eye
Number 36
阿羅漢
The Arhat

[36:1] {1:403}

諸漏已盡、無復煩惱、逮得己利、盡諸有結、心得自在。

Their contaminants having been exhausted, without further afflictions, having attained their own benefits, having eliminated the bonds of existence, their minds set free.[1]

[36:2]

これ大阿羅漢なり、學佛者の極果なり。第四果となづく、佛阿羅漢あり。

This is the great arhat; it is the ultimate fruit for students of Buddhism. It is called the "fourth fruit."[2] There is a buddha arhat.[3]

---

1 **Their contaminants having been exhausted** (*shorō* [or *shoro*] *i jin* 諸漏已盡): Quoting the *Lotus Sūtra* (*Miaofa lianhua jing* 妙法蓮華經, T.262.9:1c17-19). A description of the twelve thousand monks, all of whom were arhats, present at the preaching of the sūtra.

2 **"fourth fruit"** (*daishi ka* 第四果): I.e., last of the "four fruits" (*shi ka* 四果), or stages on the *śrāvaka* path to nirvāṇa: (1) "stream-enterer" (*yoru* 預流; S. *srotāpanna*); (2) "once-returner" (*ichirai* 一來; S. *sakṛdāgāmin*); (3) "nonreturner" (*fugen* 不還; S. *anāgāmin*); and (4) "worthy" (*arakan* 阿羅漢; S. *arhat*).

3 **There is a buddha arhat** (*butsu arakan ari* 佛阿羅漢あり): Some versions give *nari* なり here for *ari* あり, which could be read either "it [i.e., the fourth fruit?] is a buddha arhat," or "a buddha is an arhat." While the term "arhat" is a common epithet for buddhas, the unusual expression "buddha arhat" (*butsu arakan* 佛阿羅漢) is not used in reference to arhats in general but only in the sense, "an arhat who is a buddha." So, e.g., the *Guoqu xianzai yinguo jing* 過去現在因果經 (T.189.3:645a11-13), describing the conversion of Buddha Śākyamuni's first five disciples:

於是世間、始有六阿羅漢。佛阿羅漢、是爲佛寶。四諦法輪、是爲法寶。五阿羅漢。是爲僧寶、如是世間三寶具足。

There were for the first time in the world six arhats. The buddha arhat represented the buddha treasure; the four truths represented the dharma treasure; the five arhats represented the saṃgha treasure. Thus, the world was provided with the three treasures.

144　　DŌGEN'S *SHŌBŌGENZŌ* VOLUME III

[36:3]

諸漏は、没柄破木杓なり。用來すでに多時なりといふとも、已盡は木杓の渾身跳出なり。逮得已利は、頂顛に出入するなり。盡諸有結は、盡十方界不曾藏なり。心得自在の形段、これを高處自高平、低處自低平と參究す。このゆえに、牆壁瓦礫あり。自在といふは、心也全機現なり。無復煩惱は、未生煩惱なり、煩惱被煩惱碍をいふ。

"The contaminants" are broken wooden dippers missing their handles.[4] Though they may have been used for a long time, their "having been exhausted" is the whole body of the wooden dipper springing forth.[5] "*Having attained their own benefits*" is going in and out of the crown of the head. "*Having eliminated the bonds of existence*" is *in the realms everywhere in the ten directions, it has never been hidden.*[6] The shape of "*their minds set free,*" we should investigate as *the high places are naturally high and level; the low places are naturally low and level.*[7] Therefore, there are "fences, walls, tiles, and pebbles."[8] "Free"

4　**"The contaminants" are broken wooden dippers missing their handles** (*shorō wa, motsu bei ha mokushaku* 諸漏は、没柄破木杓): "Contaminant" (*rō* [or *ro*] 漏) translates the Buddhist technical term *āsrava*, used in reference to the impurity that characterizes the "contaminated" (*uro* 有漏; S. *sāsrava*) states of mind of the spiritual "commoner" (*bonbu* 凡夫; S. *pṛthagjana*), as opposed to the "uncontaminated" (*muro* 無漏; S. *anāsrava*) states of the spiritual "noble" (*shō* 聖; S. *ārya*). "Broken wooden dipper" (*ha mokushaku* 破木杓) is a common expression in Zen texts for something worthless, sometimes used in an ironic positive sense; the "missing handles" here seems a novel addition.

5　**their "having been exhausted" is the whole body of the wooden dipper springing forth** (*i jin wa mokushaku no konjin chōshutsu nari* 已盡は木杓の渾身跳出なり): Perhaps meaning that the exhaustion of the contaminants is their complete liberation. While both "whole body" (*konjin* 渾身) and "springing forth" (*chōshutsu* 跳出) occur regularly, this combination is unusual, being found only here and in the "Henzan" 遍參 chapter.

6　**in the realms everywhere in the ten directions, it has never been hidden** (*jin jippō kai fuzōzō* 盡十方界不曾藏): I.e., everywhere obvious; variation on the popular saying, "in the realms everywhere, it has never been hidden" (*henkai fuzōzō* 徧界不曾藏), attributed to Chan Master Shishuang Qingzhu 石霜慶諸 (807-888). Recorded in the *shinji Shōbōgenzō* 眞字正法眼藏 (DZZ.5:157-158, case 58); see Supplementary Notes, s.v. "In the realms everywhere, it has never been hidden."

7　**the high places are naturally high and level; the low places are naturally low and level** (*kōsho ji kōhei, teisho ji teihei* 高處自高平、低處自低平): Variation on a well-known saying by Yangshan Huiji 仰山慧寂 (803-887), recorded in the *shinji Shōbōgenzō* 眞字正法眼藏 (DZZ.5:138, case 23); see Supplementary Notes, s.v. "High places are high and level, low places are low and level."

8　**"fences, walls, tiles, and pebbles"** (*shō heki ga ryaku* 牆壁瓦礫): A well-known definition of the buddha mind, first attributed to Nanyang Huizhong 南陽慧忠 (d. 775). See Supplementary Notes, s.v. "Fences, walls, tiles, and pebbles."

36. The Arhat *Arakan* 阿羅漢

means, *mind, "the manifestation of the full function."*[9] "*Without further afflictions*" is the afflictions not yet arisen; it means the afflictions are obstructed by the afflictions.

[36:4]

阿羅漢の神通・智慧・禪定・説法・化導・放光等、さらに外道・天魔等にひとしかるべからず。見百佛世界等の論、かならず凡夫の見解に準ずべからず。將謂胡鬚赤、更有赤鬚胡の道理なり。入涅槃は、阿羅漢の入拳頭裏の行業なり。このゆえに、涅槃妙心なり、無廻避處なり。入鼻孔の阿羅漢を、眞阿羅漢とす、いまだ鼻孔に出入せざるは、阿羅漢にあらず。

The spiritual powers, wisdom, meditation, preaching, guidance, and radiance of the arhat cannot be compared with those of the other paths or the Deva Māra.[10] Discussions of *seeing a hundred buddha worlds*, and the like, we should never judge on the basis of the views of common people.[11] It is the principle of "*I always thought the foreigner's beard is red, but now here's a red-bearded foreigner.*"[12] Their entering nirvāṇa is the action of the arhat's entering the fist; therefore, it is the wondrous mind of nirvāṇa, the place of no escape. The arhat who enters the nostrils is considered the true arhat; those who do not yet go in and out of the nostrils are not arhats.

---

9   **mind, "the manifestation of the full function"** (*shin ya zenki gen* 心也全機現): Variation on the words of a verse, quoted elsewhere by Dōgen, by Yuanwu Keqin 圜悟克勤 (1063–1135) (*Yuanwu Foguo chanshi yulu* 圓悟佛果禪師語錄, T.1997.47:793c6). When Daowu Yuanzhi 道吾圓智 was asked at a funeral whether what was in the coffin was alive or dead, he said, "Alive, I don't say; dead, I don't say." On this, Yuanwu commented,

> 生也全機現、死也全機現。
> Alive, the manifestation of the full function;
> Dead, the manifestation of the full function.

For the conversation and Yuanwu's entire verse, see Supplementary Notes, s.v. "Manifestation of the full function."

10   **other paths or the Deva Māra** (*gedō tenma* 外道・天魔): I.e., followers of non-Buddhist religions and the deity Māra, who seeks to obstruct Buddhism.

11   **Discussions of seeing a hundred buddha worlds** (*ken hyaku butsu sekai tō no ron* 見百佛世界等の論): I.e., discussions of the strength of the "deva eye" (*tengen* 天眼) of the arhat relative to that of the common person, the *pratyeka-buddha*, and the bodhisatta or buddha. It is sometimes said that the arhat's eye can see one lesser chiliocosm (*shōsen sekai* 小千世界) — i.e., one thousand world systems. The source of Dōgen's "hundred buddha worlds" is unclear.

12   **"I always thought the foreigner's beard is red, but now here's a red-bearded foreigner"** (*shō i koshu shaku, kō u shakushu ko* 將爲胡鬚赤、更有赤鬚胡): "The red-bearded foreigner" and "the foreigner's beard is red" are used as we might say "six of one, a half-dozen of the other" — i.e., a distinction without a difference. From the saying of Baizhang Huaihai 百丈懷海 (749-814) to his disciple Huangbo Xiyun 黃檗希運 (dates unknown) (see, e.g., *Zongmen tongyao ji* 宗門統要集, ZTS.1:58c4-5; *shinji Shōbōgenzō* 眞字正法眼藏, DZZ.5:178, case 102).

146 DŌGEN'S *SHŌBŌGENZŌ* VOLUME III

* * * * *

[36:5] {1:404}

古云、我等今日、眞阿羅漢、以佛道聲、令一切聞。

Of old, it was said,
Today, we are
Truly arhats,
Who cause all to hear
The voice of the way of the buddhas.[13]

[36:6]

いま令一切聞といふ宗旨は、令一切諸法佛聲なり。あにただ諸佛及弟子の
みを擧拈せんや。有識有知、有皮有肉、有骨有髓のやから、みなきかしむ
るを、令一切といふ。有識有知といふは、國土草木・牆壁瓦礫なり。揺落
盛衰、生死去來、みな聞著なり。以佛道聲、令一切聞の由來は、渾界を耳
根と參學するのみにあらず。

The essential point here of "*cause all to hear*" is to *cause all dharmas
[to be] the voice of the buddha*.[14] How could it be taking up only the buddhas and their disciples? Beings with *consciousness and with knowing,
with skin and with flesh, with bones and with marrow* — letting all of
them hear is called "cause all." "*With consciousness and with knowing*"
means *the land and the plants,* "*fences, walls, tiles, and pebbles.*" *Shak-
ing and falling, flourishing and declining, being born and dying, coming
and going* — all are "*hearing.*" The origin of "*causing all to hear the
voice of the way of the buddha*" is not only studying that the entire world
is the ear faculty.[15]

---

13 **Of old, it was said** (*dō un* 古云): Variation on a verse in the *Lotus Sūtra* (*Miaofa
lianhua jing* 妙法蓮華經, T.262.9:18c20-21), which in the original is punning on the
word *śrāvaka* ("hearer") as one who causes others to hear the dharma:

我等今者、眞是聲聞、以佛道聲、令一切聞。

Now, we are truly *śrāvakas*,
Who cause all to hear the voice of the way of the buddhas.

14 **cause all dharmas [to be] the voice of the buddha** (*ryō issai shohō busshō* 令一切諸
法佛聲): Both the grammar and the context would lead one to expect here the predicate
"cause to hear" (*mon* 聞), but apparently this reading is not attested.

15 **not only studying that the entire world is the ear faculty** (*konkai o nikon to sangaku suru nomi ni arazu* 渾界を耳根と參學するのみにあらず): Probably meaning that
"causing all to hear" is not limited to the ordinary sense of hearing with the ear.

36. The Arhat *Arakan* 阿羅漢　　　147

[36:7]

釋迦牟尼佛言、若我弟子、自謂阿羅漢・辟支佛者、不聞不知諸佛如來但教化菩薩事、此非佛弟子、非阿羅漢、非辟支佛。

Buddha Śākyamuni said,[16]

If my disciples themselves say that they are arhats or pratyeka-buddhas and have not heard and do not know the fact that the buddhas, the tathāgatas, only teach bodhisattvas, these are not disciples of the buddha, are not arhats, are not pratyeka-buddhas.

[36:8]

佛言の但教化菩薩事は、我及十方佛、乃能知是事なり、唯佛與佛、乃能究盡、諸法實相なり、阿耨多羅三藐三菩提なり。しかあれば、菩薩・諸佛の自謂も、自謂阿羅漢・辟支佛者に一齊なるべし。そのゆえはいかん。自謂、すなはち聞知諸佛如來、但教化菩薩事なり。

The Buddha's words, "only teaching bodhisattvas," is "*I and the buddhas of the ten directions can know these matters,*" is "*only buddhas with buddhas can exhaustively investigate the real marks of the dharmas,*" is *anuttara-samyak-saṃbodhi*.[17] Therefore, the bodhisattvas and buddhas "themselves saying" must be equivalent to "*themselves saying that they are arhats or pratyeka-buddhas.*" Why? "Themselves saying" is precisely *hearing and knowing* "*the fact that the buddhas, the tathāgatas, only teach bodhisattvas.*"

* * * * *

[36:9] {1:405}

古云、聲聞經中、稱阿羅漢、名爲佛地。

Of old, it was said, "In the *śrāvaka* scriptures, what is called the arhat is termed 'the buddha stage.'"[18]

16　**Buddha Śākyamuni** (*Shakamuni butsu* 釋迦牟尼佛): From the *Lotus Sūtra* (*Miaofa lianhua jing* 妙法蓮華經, T.262.9:7b27-29).

17　"**I and the buddhas of the ten directions can know these matters**" (*ga gyū jippō butsu, nai nō chi ze ji* 我及十方佛、乃能知是事); "**only buddhas with buddhas can exhaustively investigate the real marks of the dharmas**" (*yui butsu yo butsu, nai nō gūjin, shohō jissō* 唯佛與佛、乃能究盡、諸法實相): Two quotations from the *Lotus Sūtra* (*Miaofa lianhua jing* 妙法蓮華經, T.262.9:5c24 and 5c11-13, respectively); for the latter, see Supplementary Notes, s.v. "Only buddhas with buddhas can exhaustively investigate the real marks of the dharmas."

18　**Of old** (*ko un* 古云): Quoting the *Mohe zhiguan* 摩訶止觀 (T.1911.46:33c24-6):

阿羅漢辟支佛佛如醍醐。大論云、聲聞經中稱阿羅漢名爲佛地。故三人同是醍醐。

The arhat, *pratyeka-buddha*, and buddha are like ghee [the best of the five forms of milk]. The *Dazhidu lun* says that, in the *śrāvaka* scriptures, what is called the arhat is termed "the buddha stage." Therefore, all three are equally ghee.

148　　DŌGEN'S *SHŌBŌGENZŌ* VOLUME III

[36:10]

いまの道著、これ佛道の證明なり。論師、胸臆の説のみにあらず、佛道の
通軌あり。阿羅漢を稱して佛地とする道理をも參學すべし、佛地を稱して
阿羅漢とする道理をも參學すべきなり。阿羅漢果のほかに、一塵・一法
の剰法あらず、いはんや三藐三菩提あらんや。阿耨多羅三藐三菩提のほ
かに、さらに一塵・一法の剰法あらず、いはんや四向四果あらんや。阿羅
漢擔來諸法の正當恁麼時、この諸法、まことに八兩にあらず、半斤にあら
ず。不是心、不是佛、不是物なり、佛眼也覰不見なり。八萬劫の前後を論
ずべからず、抉出眼睛の力量を參學すべし。剰法は渾法剰なり。

The saying here is attested on the way of the buddhas; it is not merely
an explanation from the bosom of a treatise master; it has the universal
standard of the way of the buddhas.[19] We should study the principle that
the arhat is called "the buddha stage"; we should study the principle that
the buddha stage is called "the arhat." Apart from the fruit of the arhat,
there is not a single dust mote or a single dharma of remaining dharmas,
much less *samyak-sambodhi*; apart from *anuttara-samyak-sambodhi*,
there is not a single dust mote or a single dharma of remaining dharmas,
much less the four approaches and four fruits.[20] At the very moment that
the arhat comes bearing the dharmas, truly these dharmas are not eight
tael, are not half a catty.[21] *"They are not the mind, not the buddha, not
a thing"; even the buddha eye cannot see them.*[22] Without discussing
whether it is before or after eighty thousand kalpas, we should study the

---

19　**attested on the way of the buddhas** (*butsudō no shōmyō* 佛道の證明): Or "attested
in the word of the Buddha." The "treatise master" (*ronshi* 論師) in the next clause may
be a reference to Tiantai Zhiyi 天台智顗 (538-597), author of the *Mohe zhiguan* 摩訶止
觀, from which Dōgen has just quoted.

20　**the four approaches and four fruits** (*shikō shika* 四向四果): I.e., the four stages of
the *śrāvaka* path to nirvāṇa, divided into the "access" (*kō* 向; S. *pratipanna*) and "fruit"
(*ka* 果; S. *phala*).

21　**the arhat comes bearing the dharmas** (*arakan tanrai shohō* 阿羅漢擔來諸法):
Probably a reference to the Buddhist spiritual life undertaken by the arhat, perhaps reflecting a saying of Dōgen's teacher Rujing 如淨 (1162-1227); see Supplementary Notes
s.v. "Bearing the load coming, bearing the load going, bearing the load coming again."

eight tael (*hachi ryō* 八兩); **half a catty** (*han kin* 半斤): A tael (*ryō* 兩) is a Chinese unit
of weight, varying throughout history, equal to 1/16th catty (*kin* 斤); hence the expression "eight tael, half a catty" (*hachi ryō han kin* 八兩半斤) is akin to English "six of one,
half dozen of the other." Here, perhaps, meaning that the weight of the dharmas borne by
the arhat is beyond measure.

22　**"They are not the mind, not the buddha, not a thing"** (*fu ze shin, fu ze butsu,
fu ze motsu* 不是心、不是佛、不是物): Words attributed to Nanquan Puyuan 南泉普願
(748-835) (*Jingde chuandeng lu* 景德傳燈錄, T.2076.51:257c14).

even the buddha eye cannot see them (*butsugen ya chōfuken* 佛眼也覰不見): A fixed
expression found in Zen literature, referring to the all-seeing eye of a buddha (*butsugen*
佛眼; S. *buddha-cakṣus*), or a buddha's omniscience.

36. The Arhat *Arakan* 阿羅漢 149

power that gouges out the eye.[23] Remaining dharmas are the whole of the dharma remaining.[24]

* * * * *

[36:11]

釋迦牟尼佛言、是諸比丘・比丘尼、自謂已得阿羅漢、是最後身、究竟涅槃、便不復志求阿耨多羅三藐三菩提。當知、此輩皆是增上慢人。所以者何、若有比丘實得阿羅漢、若不信此法、無有是處。

Buddha Śākyamuni said,[25]

Bhikṣus and bhikṣunīs who say they have already attained arhatship, that this is their last body, that they are in final nirvāṇa, and do not aspire further to seek anuttara-samyak-saṃbodhi — this bunch, you should realize, are all arrogant people. Why is this? Because it is never the case that a bhikṣu who has really attained arhatship does not believe in this dharma.

[36:12] {1:406}

いはゆる阿耨多羅三藐三菩提を能信するを、阿羅漢と證す。必信此法は、附屬此法なり、單傳此法なり、修證此法なり。實得阿羅漢は、是最後身、究竟涅槃にあらず、阿耨多羅三藐三菩提を志求するがゆえに。志求阿耨多羅三藐三菩提は、弄眼睛なり、壁面打坐なり、面壁開眼なり。徧界なりといへども、神出鬼没なり。互時なりといへども、互換投機なり。かくのごとくなるを、志求阿耨多羅三藐三菩提といふ。このゆえに、志求阿羅漢なり、志求阿羅漢は、粥足飯足なり。

This verifies that one who believes in "*anuttara-samyak-saṃbodhi*" is an arhat. To believe fully in "this dharma" is to bequeath "this dharma," is uniquely to transmit "this dharma," is to practice and verify "this dharma." Those who "have really attained arhatship" are not "in their last body," in "final nirvāṇa"; for they "aspire to seek *anuttara-samyak-*

---

23 **before or after eighty thousand kalpas** (*hachiman kō no zengo* 八萬劫の前後): From the tradition that one who has attained the first fruit (*yoru ka* 預流果; S. *śrotāpanna*) of the *śrāvaka* path can attain buddhahood (or produce the aspiration to attain buddhahood) only after 84,000 kalpas.

the power that gouges out the eye (*kesshutsu ganzei no rikiryō* 抉出眼睛の力量): The expression "gouge out the eye" (*kesshutsu ganzei* 抉出眼睛, or *ganzei kesshutsu* 眼睛抉出), is used, like the more common "poke out the eye" (*tosshutsu ganzei* 突出眼睛), for getting the point of Zen. See Supplementary Notes, s.v. "Eye" and "Gouge out Bodhidharma's eye."

24 **Remaining dharmas are the whole of the dharma remaining** (*jōhō wa konpō jō nari* 剩法は渾法剩なり): I.e., to suggest that there are dharmas beyond what the arhat practices is to say the entire dharma is beyond.

25 **Buddha Śākyamuni** (*Shakamuni butsu* 釋迦牟尼佛): A continuation of the *Lotus Sūtra* passage quoted in section 7 (*Miaofa lianhua jing* 妙法蓮華經, T.262.9:7b29-c5).

150   DŌGEN'S *SHŌBŌGENZŌ* VOLUME III

saṃbodhi." "Aspiring to seek *anuttara-samyak-saṃbodhi*" is playing with the eye, is sitting facing the wall, is facing the wall and opening the eye.[26] Though it may be in the realms everywhere, "*the spirit appears, and the demon vanishes*"; though it may span time, "they have an exchange and a meeting of minds."[27] To be like this is called "*aspiring to seek anuttara-samyak-saṃbodhi*." Therefore, it is *aspiring to seek arhatship; aspiring to seek arhatship is the gruel is enough, the rice is enough.*[28]

* * * * *

[36:13]

夾山圜悟禪師云、古人得旨之後、向深山・茆茨・石室、折脚鐺子煮飯喫十年二十年、大忘人世、永謝塵寰。今時不敢望如此、但只韜名晦迹守本分、作箇骨律錐老衲、以自契所證、隨己力量受用。消遣舊業、融通宿習。或有餘力、推以及人、結般若緣、練磨自己脚跟純熟。正如荒草裏撥剔一箇半箇。同知有、共脱生死、轉益未來、以報佛祖深恩。抑不得已、霜露果熟、推將出世、應緣順適、開托人天、終不操心於有求。何況依倚貴勢、作流俗阿師、擧止欺凡罔聖、苟利圖名、作無間業。縱無機緣、只恁度世、亦無業果、眞出塵羅漢耶。

Chan Master Yuanwu of Jiashan said,[29]

The ancients, after getting the point, headed to the deep mountains, to a thatched hut or a cave; for ten or twenty years, they ate rice boiled in

---

26   **sitting facing the wall** (*hekimen taza* 壁面打坐): Presumably, "sitting in meditation facing a wall," on the model of Bodhidharma's nine years "facing a wall" (*menpeki* 面壁) at the Shaolin Monastery.

27   **"the spirit appears, and the demon vanishes"** (*shin shutsu ki botsu* 神出鬼没); **"they have an exchange and a meeting of minds"** (*gokan tōki* 互換投機): The former phrase is an idiomatic expression for "one thing after another," but here the two phrases allude to a verse by Yuanwu Keqin 圜悟克勤 commenting on the words of two Chan masters (*Yuanwu Foguo chanshi yulu* 圜悟佛果禪師語錄, T.1997.47:802b29):

將謂猴白、更有猴黑。互換投機、神出鬼没。

Here we thought it was the Marquise White,
But then there's also the Marquis Black.
They have an exchange and a meeting of minds;
The spirit appears, and the demon vanishes.

Dōgen discusses the verse in "Shōbōgenzō gyōbutsu iigi" 正法眼藏行佛威儀). The use of Yuanwu's phrases here seems to suggest that, while the aspiration to attain buddhahood may reach "throughout the world" and "across time," it is expressed in the actual interactions of Zen practitioners.

28   **the gruel is enough, the rice is enough** (*shuku soku han soku* 粥足飯足): A common Zen expression meaning that the monk's meals are sufficient and suggesting, by metaphorical extension, that the monk is spiritually replete.

29   **Chan Master Yuanwu of Jiashan** (*Kassan Engo zenji* 夾山圜悟禪師): I.e., Yuanwu Keqin 圜悟克勤. His words here can be found in the *Yuanwu Foguo chanshi yulu* 圜悟佛果禪師語錄, T.1997.47:777c23-778a4.

36. The Arhat *Arakan* 阿羅漢   151

a pot with a broken leg, totally forgetting the human world and forever abandoning the dusty realm. Nowadays, we dare not hope for such a thing. Just concealing our name, covering our tracks, and guarding our original lot, we make ourselves into this old patch-robe with bones like awls, conforming ourselves to what we have realized, and using it according to our capacities. We erase our old karma and melt away past practices; and, if we have any remaining energy, we reach out to others and establish a bond of prajñā, polishing our own heels and becoming proficient.[30] This is just like digging up one or a half in the wilds.[31] Together, we know existence; together, we shed birth and death; turning the benefits over to the future, we repay the deep kindness of the buddhas and ancestors.[32] And, inevitably, as the fruit ripens under frost and dew, we exert ourselves and appear in the world; accommodating ourselves to circumstances, we present [the teachings] to humans and devas, without ever harboring thoughts of seeking anything. Still less do we generate the karma of *avīci* hell by relying on the aristocratic powers, becoming worldly teachers, cheating the common folk and deceiving the sages, coveting profit and scheming for fame. Even if we lack disciples, if we just pass our lives like this and avoid karmic consequences, we are a true arhat beyond the dust.

[36:14] {1:407}

しかあればすなはち、而今の本色の衲僧、これ眞出塵阿羅漢なり。阿羅漢をしらんことは、かくのごとくしるべし。西天の論師等のことばを、妄計することなかれ。東地の圜悟禪師は、正傳の嫡嗣ある佛祖なり。

Thus, the present patch-robed monk of true colors is "*a true arhat beyond the dust.*" If we wish to know about arhats, we should know they are like this. Do not misjudge them from the words of the treatise masters of Sindh in the West; Chan Master Yuanwu of the Land of the East is a buddha and ancestor with legitimate inheritance of the correct transmission.[33]

* * * * *

---

30 **We erase our old karma and melt away past practices** (*shōken kugō, yūzū shukujū* 消遣舊業、融通宿習): In the context, taking *yūzū* 融通 here as something like "cause to flow" (rather than the more common "run together" or "integrate").

polishing our own heels and becoming proficient (*renma jiko kyakkon junjūku* 練磨自己脚跟純熟): The reference is to spiritual training together with others.

31 **This is just like digging up one or a half in the wilds** (*shō nyo kōsōri hatteki ikko hanko* 正如荒草裏撥剔一箇半箇): I.e., finding a few authentic fellow practitioners.

32 **turning the benefits over to the future** (*ten'eki mirai* 轉益未來): I.e., to people in the future.

33 **the words of the treatise masters of Sindh in the West** (*Saiten no ronji tō no kotoba* 西天の論師等のことば): I.e., the technical definitions of the arhat in the treatises of Indian authors.

152 DŌGEN'S *SHŌBŌGENZŌ* VOLUME III

[36:15]

洪州百丈山大智禪師云、眼耳鼻舌身意、各各不貪染一切有無諸法、是名受持四句偈、亦名四果。

Chan Master Dazhi of Mount Baizhang in Hongzhou said,[34]

The eyes, ears, nose, and tongue are each without the stain of craving for any of the dharmas, whether being or non-being — this is called "receiving and keeping the four-line gāthā"; it is also called "the fourth fruit."[35]

[36:16]

而今の自他にかかはれざる眼耳鼻舌身意、その頭正尾正、はかりきはむべからず。このゆえに、渾身おのづから不貪染なり、渾一切有無諸法に不貪染なり。受持四句偈おのづからの渾渾を、不貪染といふ、これをまた四果となづく。四果は阿羅漢なり。

The eye, ear, nose, tongue, body, and mind of the present, regardless of self or other — their rightness from head to tail is beyond measure. Therefore, the whole body, of itself, is "without the stain of craving," is "*without the stain of craving for the whole of* "*any of the dharmas, whether being or non-being.*" The natural wholeness of "*receiving and keeping the four-line gāthā*" is called "without the stain of craving"; it is also called the "the fourth fruit." "The fourth fruit" is the arhat.

[36:17] {1:408}

しかあれば、而今現成の眼・耳・鼻・舌・身・意、すなはち阿羅漢なり。構本宗末、おのづから透脱なるべし。始到牢關なるは、受持四句偈なり、すなはち四果なり。透頂透底全體現成、さらに糸毫の遺漏あらざるなり。畢竟して道取せん、作麼生道。いはゆる、

Thus, the eye, ear, nose, tongue, body, and mind appearing in the present are the arhat. From beginning to end, they are naturally liberated.[36]

---

34 **Chan Master Dazhi of Mount Baizhang in Hongzhou** (*Kōshū Hyakujōzan Daichi zenji* 洪州百丈山大智禪師): I.e., Baizhang Huaihai 百丈懷海; from a passage appearing in the *Tiansheng guangdong lu* 天聖廣燈錄, ZZ.135:681a17, also quoted in "Shōbōgenzō jinzū" 正法眼藏神通.

35 **"four-line gāthā"** (*shiku ge* 四句偈): Here, probably referring to the verse on impermanence found throughout the Buddhist canon:

諸行無常、是生滅法、生滅滅已、寂滅爲樂。

Compounded things are impermanent:
This is the dharma of arising and ceasing.
When arising and ceasing have ceased,
Their calm cessation is bliss.

36 **From beginning to end** (*kōhon shūmatsu* 構本宗末): A loose, tentative translation of an obscure phrase, not occurring elsewhere in the *Shōbōgenzō*, perhaps meaning something like, "arrange the roots and assemble the branches"; taken here as referring to the list of the six sense organs.

36. The Arhat *Arakan* 阿羅漢

"First reaching the solid barrier" is *"receiving and keeping the four-line gāthā,"* is *"the fourth fruit."*[37] *From top to bottom, the entire body appears,* without a hair omitted. In the end, *what shall we say?* Let us say,[38]

[36:18]

羅漢在凡、諸法教他罣礙。羅漢在聖、諸法教他解脱。須知、羅漢與諸法同參也。既證阿羅漢、被阿羅漢碍也。所以空王已前老拳頭也。

When the arhat is a commoner, the dharmas obstruct him; when the arhat is a sage, the dharmas liberate him. We should realize that the arhat and the dharmas study together. Since they have verified arhatship, they are obstructed by arhatship. Therefore, they are an old fist from before King of Emptiness.[39]

正法眼藏阿羅漢第三十六
Treasury of the True Dharma Eye
The Arhat
Number 36

[Ryūmonji MS:]

爾時仁治三年壬寅夏五月十五日、住于雍州宇治郡觀音導利興聖寶林寺示衆

Presented to the assembly while residing at the Kannon Dōri Kōshō Hōrin Monastery, Uji District, Yōshū; fifteenth day, fifth month, summer of the senior water year of the tiger, the third year of Ninji [14 June 1242]

[Tōunji MS:]

建治元年六月十六日書寫之。懷奘

Copied this sixteenth day, sixth month, first year of Kenji [10 July 1275]. Ejō

---

37 **"First reaching the solid barrier"** (*shi tō rōkan* 始到牢關): From the saying, "once the final line is said, you first reach the solid barrier" (*matsugo ikku shitō rōkan* 末後一句始到牢關); here, perhaps, playing on the first clause, "once the final line is said."

38 **Let us say** (*iwayuru* いわゆる): What follows in the next section is Dōgen's conclusion, composed in Chinese.

39 **an old fist from before King of Emptiness** (*Kūō izen rō kentō* 空王已前老拳頭): Perhaps meaning something like, "a master before all differentiation." "Old fist" (*rō kentō* 老拳頭) is regularly used in Zen texts, and in Dōgen's writings, as a synecdoche for the Zen master. The expression "before King of Emptiness" (*Kūō izen* 空王已前) seems to be Dōgen's own creation; see Supplementary Notes, s.v. "Before King of Emptiness," "Fist."

Treasury of the True Dharma Eye

Number 37

Spring and Autumn

Shunjū

春秋

Spring and Autumn

Shunjū

INTRODUCTION

According to its colophon, this chapter dates from 1244, at a time when its author was staying at Kippōji, in Echizen (modern Fukui prefecture); it is said to have been "re-presented to the assembly" at that time, indicating that there must have been an earlier version that has not survived. The text occurs as number 37 in the seventy-five-chapter compilation of the *Shōbōgenzō* and number 66 in the Honzan edition; it is not included in the sixty-chapter compilation.

A note in the colophon associates the essay with the Chinese classic *Spring and Autumn Annals* (*Chunqiu* 春秋) that is evoked by its title. Despite this evocation, Dōgen's text is not about ancient Chinese history and only indirectly about the seasons. Rather, it focuses on a single saying by the Tang-dynasty master Dongshan Liangjie 洞山良价 (807-869), founder of the Caodong tradition of Chan that Dōgen introduced to Japan. When a monk asked Dongshan how one might avoid cold and heat, the Master replied, "Why not go where there is no cold and heat?" When asked where such a place might be, Dongshan said, "When it's cold, the cold kills you; when it's hot, the heat kills you."

Dōgen holds up this conversation as a case necessarily studied by the buddhas and ancestors; and, indeed, Dongshan's words were well known in Chan circles and attracted many comments — including those in the famous *Blue Cliff Records* (*Biyan lu* 碧巖錄). In our text, Dōgen collects eight of these comments, to which he offers his own reactions, sometimes fairly extended, sometimes no more than a single line.

Most noteworthy in these reactions are Dōgen's dismissals of those comments that interpret the conversation through the rubric of the "five ranks (*wu wei* 五位) of Dongshan" — an heuristic device employing the terms "upright" (*zheng* 正) and "inclined" (*pian* 偏) to discuss the relationships between the absolute and relative truths. Such passages in our text are often held up by later readers as evidence that Dōgen's own version of Sōtō Zen had no use for this venerable schema widely associated with Dongshan and his lineage in both China and medieval Japan. While several of Dōgen's reactions seem at least grudgingly appreciative of previous comments, in his conclusion, he appears to reject them all, calling them "pitiful," ignorant of the cold and heat of the buddhas and ancestors, and evidence of the decline of the way of the ancestral masters.

158

正法眼藏第三十七
Treasury of the True Dharma Eye
Number 37

春秋

Spring and Autumn

[37:1] {1:409}

洞山悟本大師、因僧問、寒暑到來、如何廻避。師云、何不向無寒暑處去。
僧云、如何是無寒暑處。師云、寒時寒殺闍梨、熱時熱殺闍梨。

Great Master Wuben of Dongshan was once asked by a monk, "When cold and heat come, how can we escape them?"[1]

The Master said, "Why not go where there is no cold and heat?"

The monk said, "Where is there no cold and heat?"

The Master said, "When it's cold, the cold kills the Ācārya; when it's hot, the heat kills the Ācārya."[2]

[37:2]

この因緣、かつておほく商量しきたれり、而今おほく功夫すべし。佛祖か
ならず參來せり、參來せるは佛祖なり。西天東地古今の佛祖、おほくこの
因緣を現成の面目とせり。この因緣の面目現成は佛祖公案なり。

This episode has been discussed by many in the past and should be worked on by many in the present. The buddhas and ancestors have invariably studied it, and those who have studied it are buddhas and ancestors. Many of the buddhas and ancestors of past and present, in Sindh in the West and the Land of the East, have taken this episode as the face of their realization.[3] The realization of the face of this episode is the kōan of the buddhas and ancestors.

---

1   **Great Master Wuben of Dongshan** (*Tōzan Gohon daishi* 洞山悟本大師): I.e., Dongshan Liangjie 洞山良价 (807-869), founder of the Caodong 曹洞 tradition of Chan. The conversation here appears in the *Dongshan yulu* 洞山語錄 (T.1986A.47:509c8-10, and 1986B.47:523c8-10), as well as several other Chan collections; it is treated as case 43 in the *Biyan lu* 碧巖錄 (T.2003.48:180a16ff). Dōgen cites a slightly variant version in his *shinji Shōbōgenzō* 眞字正法眼藏 (DZZ.5:244, case 225).

2   **"the cold kills the Ācārya"** (*kan satsu jari* 寒殺闍梨): The phrase could be taken to mean, "when it's cold, you freeze to death." Dongshan uses *ācārya* ("teacher," "preceptor") in reference to his interlocutor.

3   **buddhas and ancestors of past and present, in Sindh in the West and the Land of the East** (*Saiten Tōchi kokon no busso* 西天東地古今の佛祖): It is not clear in what

37. Spring and Autumn *Shunjū* 春秋   159

[37:3]

しかあるに、僧問の寒暑到來、如何廻避、くはしくすべし。いはく、正當
寒到來時、正當熱到來時の參詳看なり。この寒暑、渾寒渾暑ともに寒暑づ
からなり。寒暑づからなるゆゑに、到來時は寒暑づからの頂顁より到來す
るなり、寒暑づからの眼睛より現前するなり。この頂顁上、これ無寒暑の
ところなり。この眼睛裏、これ無寒暑のところなり。高祖道の寒時寒殺闍
梨、熱時熱殺闍梨は、正當到時の消息なり。いはゆる寒時たとひ道寒殺な
りとも、熱時かならずしも熱殺道なるべからす。寒也徹蒂寒なり、熱也
徹蒂熱なり。たとひ萬億の廻避を參得すとも、なほこれ以頭換尾なり。寒
は、これ祖宗の活眼睛なり、暑は、これ先師の煖皮肉なり。

Given this, we should become familiar with the monk's question,
"*When cold and heat come, how can we escape them?*" This is to say
that we should try considering in detail the very time when cold comes,
the very time when heat comes. In this cold and heat, the entire cold and
the entire heat are both cold and heat itself. Because they are cold and
heat itself, when they come, they come from the head of cold and heat
itself, they appear from the eye of cold and heat itself. On this head is
where there is no cold and heat; in this eye is where there is no cold and
heat. The Eminent Ancestor's saying, "*When it's cold, the cold kills the
Ācārya; when it's hot, the heat kills the Ācārya*," is the circumstances at
the very time they come. Though "when it's cold" may say that "the cold
kills," "when it's hot" is not necessarily a saying that "the heat kills."
"Cold" is cold through and through; "heat" is heat through and through.
Though we had learned myriad *koṭis* of means of "escape," this would
still be exchanging head for tail.[4] "Cold" is the living eye of the ancestors; "heat" is the warm skin and flesh of the former masters.[5]

* * * * *

---

sense we are to take the curious claim here that Dongshan's dialogue was studied in
India.

the face of their realization (*genjō no menmoku* 現成の面目): Or "their realized face."
Here, and in the following sentence, Dōgen plays with the expression "realized kōan"
(*genjō kōan* 現成公案); see Supplementary Notes, s.v. "Realized kōan."

4   **exchanging head for tail** (*i tō kan bi* 以頭換尾): A Chinese colloquialism meaning
"to get something backwards."

5   **the warm skin and flesh of the former masters** (*senshi no dan piniku* 先師の煖
皮肉): The translation takes *senshi* 先師 ("former master"), like the parallel *soshū* 祖宗
("ancestors"), as a general reference to earlier Chan masters; it could also refer specifically here to Dongshan or (though less likely) to Dōgen's own former master, Rujing.

[37:4] {1:410}

淨因枯木禪師、　嗣芙蓉和尚、諱法成和尚。云、衆中商量道、這僧問既落偏。洞山答歸正位。其僧言中知音、却入正來、洞山却從偏去。如此商量、不唯謗瀆先聖、亦乃屈沈自己。不見道、聞衆生解、意下丹青、目前雖美、久蘊成病。大凡行脚高士、欲窮此事、先須識取上祖正法眼藏。其餘佛祖言教、是什麼熱椀鳴聲。雖然如是、敢問諸人、畢竟作麼生是無寒暑處、還會麼。玉樓巢翡翠、金殿鎖鴛鴦。

Chan Master Jingyin Kumu succeeded Reverend Furong; he is known as Reverend Facheng.[6] He said,

Some among the assembly who discuss this say, "The question of this monk has fallen into the inclined; Dongshan's answer returns to the rank of the upright.[7] The monk, knowing the music in his words, enters the upright; Dongshan then goes off from the inclined."[8] [Those who] discuss it like this not only blaspheme the prior sages, they humiliate themselves. Have they not seen the saying?[9]

Producing opinions from what we hear,
The mind turns scarlet and blue.
While beautiful to behold,
When long accumulated, they make you ill.

Generally speaking, eminent gentlemen who tread [the way], if you wish to exhaust this matter, you should first recognize the treasury of the true dharma eye of the Ancient Ancestor.[10] The other teachings of the buddhas and ancestors are but the sounds of a heated bowl.[11]

---

6 **Chan Master Jingyin Kumu** (*Jōin Koboku zenji* 淨因枯木禪師): I.e., Kumu Facheng 枯木法成 (1071-1128), disciple of the important Caotong master Furong Daokai 芙蓉道楷 (1043-1118). The name Jingyin derives from the Jingyin Chan Cloister 淨因禪院, in Dongjing 東京 (in modern Henan), where Daokai was abbot. The quotation is from a passage appearing in the *Jiatai pudeng lu* 嘉泰普燈錄, ZZ.137:186-187.

7 **the inclined** (*hen* 偏); **the upright** (*shō* 正): Terms of art in Zen associated especially with the schema of the "five ranks" (*go i* 五位) attributed to Dongshan; "the inclined" (or "the partial") is used in reference to the relative truth, or the phenomenal world; "the upright," to the absolute truth. The two glyphs connote respectively both (a) "slanted" and "vertical," and (b) "side" and "center" (or "main"). See Supplementary Notes, s.v. "Upright or inclined."

8 **knowing the music** (*chi in* 知音): A Chinese idiom indicating "to know a person's mind" (from hearing him or her playing music); see Supplementary Notes, s.v. "Know the music."

9 **Have they not seen the saying?** (*fu ken dō* 不見道): The following saying is attributed to Jiashan Shanhui 夾山善會 (805-881); see, e.g., the (slightly variant) version at *Congrong lu* 從容錄, T.2004.48:260b10-11.

10 **Ancient Ancestor** (*jōso* 上祖): I.e., Dongshan.

11 **The other teachings of the buddhas and ancestors** (*ki yo busso gongyō* 其餘佛祖言教): The phrase could also be read, "the teachings of other buddhas and ancestors."

37. Spring and Autumn *Shunjū* 春秋   161

Nevertheless, I dare to ask you people, after all, where is there no cold or heat? Do you understand?

> *The jeweled tower is nest to the kingfisher;*
> *The golden pavilion locks in the duck.*

[37:5] {1:411}

師は、これ洞山の遠孫なり、祖席の英豪なり。しかあるに、箇箇おほくあやまりて、偏正の窟宅にして高祖洞山大師を禮拜せんとすることを烱誠するなり。佛法もし偏正の局量より相傳せば、いかでか今日にいたらん。あるひは野猫兒、あるひは田庫奴、いまだ洞山の堂奥を參究せず。かつて佛法の道闈を行李せざるともがら、あやまりて洞山に偏正等の五位ありて人を接す、といふ。これは胡説亂説なり、見聞すべからず。ただまさに上祖の正法眼藏あることを參究すべし。

The Master is a distant descendant of Dongshan, a hero of the ancestral seat. As such, he clearly admonishes the many mistaken ones who would pay obeisance to the Eminent Ancestor, Great Master Dongshan, within the cave of the inclined and upright. If the buddha dharma were transmitted based on the confines of the inclined and upright, how could it have reached the present? Wild kittens, field hands, those who have not yet investigated the interior of the hall of Dongshan, who have never practiced at the threshold of the way of the buddha dharma, mistakenly say that Dongshan had the five ranks of the inclined and upright with which he dealt with people. This is barbaric talk, wild talk; we should not see or hear it. We should just investigate the fact that the Ancient Ancestor did indeed have the treasury of the true dharma eye.

* * * * *

[37:6]

慶元府天童山宏智禪師、嗣丹霞和尚、諱正覺和尚。云、若論此事、如兩家著碁相似。儞不應我著、我即瞞汝去也。若恁麼體得、始會洞山意。天童不免下箇注脚。裏頭看勿暑寒、直下滄溟瀝得乾、我道巨鼇能俯拾、笑君沙際弄釣竿。

Chan Master Hongzhi of Mount Tiantong in the Prefecture of Qingyuan succeeded Reverend Danxia; he was known as Reverend Zhengjue.[12] *He said,*

---

the sounds of a heated bowl (*netsu wan myōshō* 熱椀鳴聲): An idiomatic expression for talk meaningless as the sounds of a bowl expanding.

12 **Chan Master Hongzhi of Mount Tiantong** (*Tendōzan Wanshi zenji* 天童山宏智禪師): I.e., Hongzhi Zhengjue 宏智正覺 (1091-1157).

Reverend Danxia (*Tanka oshō* 丹霞和尚): I.e., Danxia Zixia 丹霞子淳 (1064-1117). The saying occurs in a lecture (*shangtang* 上堂) on Dongshan's case, above, in the *Hongzhi chanshi yulu* 宏智禪師語錄, T.2001.48:46c25-29.

162 DŌGEN'S *SHŌBŌGENZŌ* VOLUME III

If we discuss this matter, it is like two people playing chess: if you don't respond to my move, I will trick you. Only when we experience it like this, do we understand Dongshan's intention. Tiantong cannot resist giving a comment:

> *Seen from inside, it's neither hot nor cold.*
> *The blue depths are drained dry.*
> *In my way, you could stoop down and pick up a giant tortoise.*
> *It's laughable to fiddle in the sand with your fishing rod.*

[37:7] {1:412}

しばらく著碁はなきにあらず、作麼生是兩家。もし兩家著碁といはば、八目なるべし。もし八目ならん、著碁にあらず、いかん。いふべくは、かくのごとくいふべし、著碁一家敵手相逢なり。しかありといふとも、いま宏智道の儞不應我著、こころをおきて功夫すべし、身をめぐらして參究すべし。儞不應我著といふは、なんぢ、われなるべからず、といふなり。我即瞞汝去也、すごすことなかれ。泥裏有泥なり、踏者あしをあらひ、また纓をあらふ。珠裏有珠なり、光明するに、かれをてらし、自をてらすなり。

It is not that there is no chess game, but for the moment, *how about the two people?* If we say that two people are playing chess, we should be eight moves ahead; if we are eight moves ahead, it is not a chess game.[13] How about it? If we are to say something, we should say this: *a chess game is one person encountering an opponent.* Though we say this, we should fix in our minds and concentrate on, we should circulate in our bodies and investigate, these words of Hongzhi: "if you don't respond to my move." "*If you don't respond to my move*" means "you cannot be I." Do not pass over "*I will trick you.*" There is mud within mud, and those who step in it wash their feet or wash their chin strap; *there is a pearl within a pearl*, and when it shines, it illumines the other and illumines the self.[14]

* * * * *

---

13 **eight moves ahead** (*hachi moku* 八目): From the saying, "the onlooker [in a chess game] is eight moves ahead" (*okame hachimoku* 傍目八目).

14 **wash their feet or wash their chin strap** (*ashi o arai, mata ei o arau* あしをあらひ、また纓をあらふ): I.e., take it as dirty or take it as clean. From the song of the "Fisherman" (*Yufu* 漁父) in the Chinese classic *Chuci* 楚辞 (KR.4a0001.007-2a):

滄浪之水清兮、可以濯吾纓。滄浪之水濁兮、可以濯吾足。

When the waters of the Canglang are clear,
I'll wash my chin strap in them;
When the waters of the Canglang are dirty,
I'll wash my feet in them.

[37:8]
夾山圜悟禪師、嗣五祖法演禪師、諱克勤和尚。云、盤走珠、珠走盤。偏中正、正中偏。羚羊掛角無蹤跡、獵狗遶林空踧躇。

Chan Master Yuanwu of Jiashan succeeded Chan Master Fayan of Wuzu; he was known as Reverend Keqin.[15] *He said,*

The bowl rolls in the pearl; the pearl rolls in the bowl.[16]
The upright within the inclined; the inclined within the upright.[17]
The antelope hangs up its horns, leaving no traces;
The hunting dogs circle the wood, stalking in vain.[18]

[37:9]
いま盤走珠の道、これ光前絕後、古今罕聞なり。古來はただいはく、盤にはしる珠の、住著なきがごとし。羚羊、いまは空に掛角せり、林、いま獵狗をめぐる。

This saying, "*the bowl rolls in the pearl,*" is *bright before and extinct after, is hardly heard in past or present.*[19] Up till now, it seems it was said simply that the pearl rolling in the bowl is without rest.[20] Here, the antelope has hung up its horns in the sky; here, the wood circles the hunting dogs.[21]

* * * * *

---

15 **Chan Master Yuanwu of Jiashan** (*Kassan Engo zenji* 夾山圜悟禪師): I.e., Yuanwu Keqin 圜悟克勤 (1063-1135), important master in the Linji 臨濟 lineage; disciple of Wuzu Fayan 五祖法演 (d. 1104). Yuanwu's poem appears among his "praises to the ancients" (*songgu* 頌古) in the *Yuanwu yulu* 圜悟語錄 (T.1997.47:804a29-b1).

16 **The bowl rolls in the pearl; the pearl rolls in the bowl** (*ban sō shu, shu sō ban* 盤走珠、珠走盤): The pearl rolling in a bowl is a fairly common image in Zen for the freedom of the spiritual life.

17 **The upright within the inclined; the inclined within the upright** (*hen chū shō, shō chū hen* 偏中正、正中偏): The first two of the "five ranks" (see above, Note 7).

18 **The antelope hangs up its horns** (*reiyō kai kaku* 羚羊掛角): Said to derive from the habit of the antelope to sleep with its horns hanging from branches.

19 **bright before and extinct after, is hardly heard in past or present** (*kō zen zetsu go, kokon kan mon* 光前絕後、古今罕聞): I.e., is virtually unique; an expression occurring in several Chan texts (see, e.g., *Jingde chuandeng lu* 景德傳燈錄, T.2076.51:275b14).

20 **it seems it was said simply that the pearl rolling in the bowl is without rest** (*tada iwaku, ban ni hashiru tama no, jūjaku naki ga gotoshi* ただいはく、盤にはしる珠の、住著なきがごとし): Or "it was said simply that it seems the pearl rolling in the bowl is without rest."

21 **the antelope has hung up its horns in the sky** (*reiyō, ima wa kū ni kakaku seri* 羚羊、いまは空に掛角せり): The graph for "sky" (*sora, kū* 空), being that used for the term "emptiness" (S. *śūnyatā*), the passage could be read, "the antelope has hung up its horns in emptiness."

164 DŌGEN'S *SHŌBŌGENZŌ* VOLUME III

[37:10]

慶元府雪竇山資聖寺明覺禪師、嗣北塔祚和尚、諱重顯和尚。云、垂手還同萬仞崖、正偏何必在安排。瑠璃古殿照明月、忍俊韓獹空上階。

Chan Master Mingjue, of Zisheng Monastery at Mount Xuedou in the Prefecture of Qingyuan, succeeded Reverend Zuo of Beita; he was known as Reverend Zhongxian.[22] He said,

Extending a hand is the same as a cliff of a myriad fathoms.[23]
Why must the upright and the inclined be set in order?
The old *vaiḍūrya* palace reflects the bright moon;
The resolute hound of Han climbs the stair in vain.[24]

[37:11] {1:413}

雪竇は、雲門三世の法孫なり。參飽の皮袋といひぬべし。いま垂手還同萬仞崖といひて、奇絕の標格をあらはすといへども、かならずしもしかあるべからず。いま僧問山示の因緣、あながちに垂手・不垂手にあらず、出世・不出世にあらず。いはんや偏正の道をもちいんや。偏正の眼をもちいざれば、此因緣に下手のところなきがごとし。參請の巴鼻なきがごとくなるは、高祖の邊域にいたらず、佛法の大家を覷見せざるによれり。さらに草鞋を拈來して參請すべし。みだりに、高祖の佛法は正偏等の五位なるべし、といふことやみね。

Xuedou was a dharma descendant in the third generation after Yunmen. He can be called a skin bag who has studied his fill. In his saying, "*extending a hand is the same as a cliff of a myriad fathoms,*" though we may say he is displaying a rare standard, this is not necessarily the case. This episode of the monk asking and Shan showing is not necessarily "*extending a hand or not extending a hand,*" is not "*appearing in the*

---

22 **Chan Master Mingjue, of Zisheng Monastery at Mount Xuedou in the Prefecture of Qingyuan** (*Keigen fu Setchōzan Shishō ji Myōkaku zenji* 慶元府雪竇山資聖寺明覺禪師): I.e., Xuedou Zhongxian 雪竇重顯 (980-1052), disciple of Zhimen Guangzuo 智門光祚 (dates unknown), in the lineage of Yunmen 雲門; served as abbot of the Zishengsi 資聖寺 (in modern Zhejiang province). Xuedou's poem occurs as his comment on Dongshan's dialogue in the *Biyan lu* 碧巖錄 (T.2003.48:180b26-29).

23 **a cliff of a myriad fathoms** (*banjin gai* 萬仞崖): "Fathom" translates *ren* 仞, an ancient measure said to equal the arm span of an adult male.

24 *vaiḍūrya* (*ruri* 瑠璃): Also written *ruri* 琉璃; a Sanskrit term used for beryl, crystal, and other minerals; one of the seven precious substances.

The resolute hound of Han (*ninshun Kan ro* 忍俊韓獹): "Resolute" is a tentative translation. The colloquial Chinese sense of the term *renjun* 忍俊 as "smiling" seems unlikely here, but opinion is divided on the alternatives: some would take it as two adjectives meaning "cruel and great"; others (following the *Shōbōgenzō monge* 正法眼藏聞解, SCZ.7:604) read it as a verb-object compound, "to hide one's excellence." The "hound of Han" refers to the black hunting dogs raised in the ancient state of Han 韓 during the Warring States period. Since the beast was famous for catching rabbits, it may be that here it stupidly seeks the rabbit in the moon reflected on the jewelled palace.

37. Spring and Autumn *Shunjū* 春秋 165

world or not appearing in the world."[25] How much less does it employ talk of the inclined and the upright. Without using the eye of the inclined and the upright, it seems that he has no place to lay his hand on this episode; that he seems to have no nose grip with which to inquire about it is because he has not gone to the borderlands of the Eminent Ancestor, he has not seen the great house of the buddha dharma.[26] He should take up his sandals again and inquire about it.[27] Stop saying that the buddha dharma of the Eminent Ancestor is the five ranks of the upright and the inclined.

* * * * *

[37:12]

東京天寧長靈禪師守卓和尚云、偏中有正正中偏、流落人間千百年、幾度欲歸歸未得、門前依舊草芊芊。

Reverend Shouzhou, Chan Master Changling of Tianning in Dongjing, said,[28]

In the inclined there is the upright; in the upright, the inclined.
Drifting along among humans for a thousand centuries;
How often have I longed to return yet could never return.
Before the gate, as of old, the weeds are thick.

---

25 **"extending a hand or not extending a hand"** (*suishu fu suishu* 垂手・不垂手); **"appearing in the world or not appearing in the world"** (*shusse fu shusse* 出世・不出世): To "extend (literally, 'let down') a hand" is to offer a teaching; to "appear in the world" is to undertake a career as a teacher. Dōgen is doubtless alluding here to a comment immediately following Xuedou's poem also found in the *Biyan lu* 碧巖錄 (T.2003.48:180c1):

曹洞下有出世不出世、有垂手不垂手。

In Caodong, there is appearing in the world and not appearing in the world; there is extending a hand and not extending a hand.

26 **the great house of the buddha dharma** (*buppō no taike* 佛法の大家): The term *taike*, translated here as "great house," can also refer to a "great one" (i.e., an accomplished person, or master). This passage could also be parsed somewhat differently:

The fact that, without using the eye of "the inclined and the upright," he seems to have no place to lay his hand on this incident, seems to have no nose grip with which to inquire about it, is because he has not reached the borderlands of the Eminent Ancestor and has not seen the great house of the buddha dharma.

27 **take up his sandals again** (*sara ni sōai o nenrai shite* さらに草鞋を拈來して): I.e., should continue his pilgrimage.

28 **Reverend Shouzhou, Chan Master Changling of Tianning in Dongjing** (*Tonkin Tennei Chōrei zenji Shutaku oshō* 東京天寧長靈禪師守卓和尚): I.e., Changling Shouzhou 長靈守卓 (1065-1123), abbot of Tianning Monastery 天寧寺 in Dongjing 東京 (in modern Henan). Shouzhou's poem occurs in the *Zhangling Shouzhou chanshi yulu* 長靈守卓禪師語錄, ZZ.120:325b17-18.

166 DŌGEN'S *SHŌBŌGENZŌ* VOLUME III

[37:13]

これもあながちに偏正と道取すといへども、しかも拈來せり。拈來はなき
にあらず、いかならんかこれ偏中有。

Although here he too forces himself to talk about the inclined and the
upright, he has still taken it up. It is not that he has not taken it up, but
what is "being in the inclined"?[29]

* * * * *

[37:14]

潭州大潙佛性和尚、嗣圜悟、諱法泰。云、無寒暑處爲君通、枯木生華又一
重、堪笑刻舟求劍者、至今猶在冷灰中。

*Reverend Foxing of Dawei in Tanzhou succeeded Yuanwu; he was
known as Fatai.*[30] *He said,*

Where there is no cold or heat, he's communicated for you.
The dried-up tree blooms one more time.
The laughable ones who notch the boat to find the sword
Remain still now in the cold ashes.[31]

[37:15] {1:414}

この道取、いささか公案踏著・戴著の力量あり。

This saying has just enough power for him to step on the kōan and to
put it on his head.

* * * * *

[37:16]

泐潭湛堂文準禪師云、熱時熱殺寒時寒、寒暑由來總不干、行盡天涯諳世
事、老君頭戴猪皮冠。

---

29 **what is "being in the inclined"** (*ikanaran ka kore hen chū u* いかならんかこれ偏
中有): The translation obscures Dōgen's play with the first phrase of Shouzhou's poem,
"in the inclined there is the upright" (*hen chū u shō* 偏中有正), in which he here takes
the predicate "there is" as if it were the nominal "being."

30 **Reverend Foxing of Dawei in Tanzhou** (*Tanshū Daii Busshō oshō* 潭州大潙佛性和
尚): I.e., Dawei Fatai 大潙法泰 (also known as Foxing Fatai 佛性法泰; dates unknown),
disciple of Yuanwu Keqin 圜悟克勤. The verse can be found in the *Chanzong songgu
lianzhu tongji* 禪宗頌古聯珠通集, ZZ.115:295a8-9.

31 **dried-up tree** (*koboku* 枯木); **cold ashes** (*reikai* 冷灰): The expression "dried-up
trees and dead ashes" (*koboku shikai* 枯木死灰) is regularly used in Zen texts for states
of mental concentration, or trance; see Supplementary Notes, s.v. "Dried-up tree."

notch the boat to find the sword (*kokushū kyūken* 刻舟求劍): From the story, found in
the *Lüshi Chunqiu* 呂氏春秋 ("Master Lü's Spring and Autumn Annals"; KR.3j0009.015-
22a-b), of the stupid man of Chu 楚 who dropped his sword from a boat and marked the
spot by notching the side of the boat.

37. Spring and Autumn *Shunjū* 春秋   167

Chan Master Zhantang Wenzhun of Letan said,[32]
When it's hot, the heat kills; when it's cold, the cold.
The origins of cold and heat are of no concern.
Going all the way to heaven's shore, while memorizing worldly matters.
On the old master's head, place a crown of boar skin.

[37:17]
しばらくとふべし、作麼生ならんかこれ不干底道理、速道速道。

Now, we must ask, "What is the principle of 'no concern'? Speak! Speak!"

* * * * *

[37:18]
湖州何山佛燈禪師、嗣太平佛鑑慧懃禪師、諱守珣和尚。云、無寒暑處洞山道、多少禪人迷處所、寒時向火熱乘涼、一生免得避寒暑。

Chan Master Heshan Fodeng of Huzhou succeeded Chan Master Fojian Huiqin of Taiping; he was known as Reverend Shouxun.[33] *He said,*
Where there's no cold or heat, as Dongshan says —
How many Chan people have got lost in that place?
When it's cold, I turn to the fire; in heat, I keep cool in the shade.
Avoiding them my whole life, I've escaped cold and heat.

[37:19]
この珣師は、五祖法演禪師の法孫といへども、小兒子の言語のごとし。しかあれども、一生免得避寒暑、のちに老大の成風ありぬべし。いはく、一生とは、盡生なり、避寒暑は、脱落身心なり。

This Master Qin is a dharma descendant of Chan Master Wuzu Fayan, but his words are like a little child's.[34] Nevertheless, "*avoiding them my whole life, I've escaped cold and heat,*" must later have had the sound

---

32   **Chan Master Zhantang Wenzhun of Letan** (*Rokutan Tandō Bunjun* [also read *Monjun*] *zenji* 泐潭湛堂文準禪師): I.e., Zhantang Wenzhun 湛堂文準 (1061-1115), disciple of Zhenjing Kewen 眞淨克文, in the Linji 臨濟 lineage. Letan 泐潭 is in modern Jiangxi Prefecture. Wenzhun's verse occurs at *Chanzong songgu lianzhu tongji* 禪宗頌古聯珠通集, ZZ.115:295a2-3.

33   **Chan Master Heshan Fodeng of Huzhou** (*Koshū Kazan Buttō zenji* 湖州何山佛燈禪師): I.e., Fodeng Shouxun 佛燈守珣 (or Heshan Shouxun 何山守珣; 1079-1134), disciple of Taihei Huiqin 太平慧懃 (1059-1117) in the Linji 臨濟 lineage. Mount He 何山 is in modern Zhejiang Prefecture. Shouxun's verse can be found at *Chanzong songgu lianzhu tongji* 禪宗頌古聯珠通集, ZZ.115:295a6-7.

34   **a dharma descendant of Chan Master Wuzu Fayan** (*Goso Hōen zenji no hōson* 五祖法演禪師の法孫): Shouxun's master, Huiqin 慧懃, was a disciple of Wuzu Fayan 五祖法演 (d. 1104).

168   DŌGEN'S *SHŌBŌGENZŌ* VOLUME III

of a great elder. That is, "my whole life" means exhausting life; "*I've escaped cold and heat*" is "*sloughing off body and mind.*"[35]

* * * * *

[37:20] {1:415}

おほよそ諸方の諸代、かくのごとく鼓兩片皮をこととして、頌古を供達すといへども、いまだ高祖洞山の邊事を覰見せず。いかんとならば、佛祖の家常には、寒暑いかなるべし、ともしらざるによりて、いたづらに乘涼向火とらいふ。ことにあはれむべし、なんぢ老尊宿のほとりにして、なにを寒暑といふ、とか聞取せし。かなしむべし、祖師道廢せることを。この寒暑の形段をしり、寒暑の時節を經歷し、寒暑を使得しきたりて、さらに高祖爲示の道を頌古すべし、拈古すべし。いまだしかあらざらんは、知非にはしかじ。俗なほ、日月をしり、萬物を保任するに、聖人・賢者のしなじなあり、君子と愚夫とのしなじなあり。佛道の寒暑、なほ愚夫の寒暑とひとしかるべし、と錯會することなかれ。直須勤學すべし。

In sum, then, though the various generations from all quarters, taking it upon themselves to *flap their lips* like this, have offered praises to the ancients, they have not seen the marginal matters of the Eminent Ancestor Dongshan.[36] The reason is that, because they do not know what cold and heat are in the daily life of the buddhas and ancestors, they talk in vain of "availing oneself of the cool" or "turning to the fire." It is particularly pitiful for you in the vicinity of the old Venerable: did you hear what he called cold and hot?[37] What a pity that the way of the ancestral masters has declined. After having known the shape of cold and heat, passing through the moments of cold and heat, and making use of cold and heat, we should go on to praise the ancients, to take up the ancients, on the words with which the Eminent Ancestor has instructed us.[38] Those who are not yet like this, fail to recognize their error. Even among the secular, in knowing the days and months, in maintaining the ten thousand things, there are differences between sages and worthies, differences between lords and foolish commoners.[39] Do not mistakenly think that the cold

---

35 **"sloughing off body and mind"** (*datsuraku shinjin* 脱落身心): A fixed phrase that Dōgen attributes to his master, Tiantong Rujing 天童如淨 (1162–1227); occurs several times in the *Shōbōgenzō*, also in reverse order: *shinjin datsuraku* 身心脱落. See Supplementary Notes, s.v. "Body and mind sloughed off."

36 **flap their lips** (*ku ryō henpi* 鼓兩片皮): An idiomatic expression for useless talk.

37 **vicinity of the old Venerable** (*rō sonshuku no hotori* 老尊宿のほとり): I.e., near Dongshan.

38 **praise the ancients** (*juko* 頌古); **take up the ancients** (*nenko* 拈古): I.e. to compose verse appreciations and comments on the words of the prior masters.

39 **sages and worthies** (*shōnin kenja* 聖人・賢者): In technical Buddhist parlance, higher and lower ranks respectively on the spiritual path; given the "secular" context here, perhaps we should understand them in a more generic sense common in Chinese usage.

37. Spring and Autumn *Shunjū* 春秋   169

and heat of the way of the buddhas must be the same as the cold and heat of the foolish commoners. We should *study this with diligence.*[40]

正法眼藏春秋第三十七
Treasury of the True Dharma Eye
Spring and Autumn
Number 37

[Ryūmonji MS:]
爾時寛元二年甲辰、在越宇山奧再示衆
Re-presented to the assembly in the mountains of Etsuu; senior wood year of the dragon, the second year of Kangen [1244][41]

逢佛時而轉佛麟經。祖師道、衆角雖多一麟足矣
On encountering the Buddha, turning the Buddha's Lin Classic. The Ancestral Master said, "However many the horns, a single lin will suffice."[42]

---

40 **We should study this with diligence** (*jikishu gongaku su beshi* 直須勤學すべし): A set phrase appearing regularly in Zen texts and occasionally in the *Shōbōgenzō*. Here and elsewhere, the translation makes no attempt to reproduce the odd doubling of the imperative forms, *jikishu . . . su beshi* 直須 . . .すべし, resulting from the combination of Chinese and Japanese.

41 **Re-presented to the assembly** (*saijishū* 再示衆): Indicating a revised version; no earlier is known to have survived.

in the mountains of Etsuu (*Etsu u san oku* 越宇山奧): I.e., in the province of Echizen (modern Fukui); "in the mountains" is thought to be a reference to Kippōji 吉峰寺, the monastery where Dōgen taught after his arrival in Echizen and before the completion there of his Daibutsuji 大佛寺.

42 **turning the Buddha's *Lin Classic*** (*ten butsu rin kyō* 轉佛麟經): Associates Dōgen's "spring and autumn" text with the Chinese classic *Chunqiu* 春秋 ("Spring and Autumn Annals"; KR.1e0001), which was known as the *Lin Classic* (*Lin jing* 麟經). The *lin* 麟 (or *qilin*; J. *kirin* 麒麟) is a mythical chimeric beast considered auspicious. It is said that Confucius left off writing the *Chunqiu* with the account of the taking of such a beast in the western regions.

Ancestral Master (*soshi* 祖師): The words of Qingyuan Xingsi 青原行思 (d. 740), at *Jingde chuandeng lu* 景德傳燈錄, T.2076.51:240b10.

TREASURY OF THE TRUE DHARMA EYE

NUMBER 38

Tangled Vines
Kattō

葛藤

Tangled Vines

Kattō

INTRODUCTION

According to its colophon, this work was composed at Kōshōji in the seventh month of 1243. Since during this month Dōgen is thought to have left Kōshōji for his new residence in Echizen, "Kattō" may be the last chapter of the *Shōbōgenzō* he composed in the capital area. Number 38 in both the seventy-five- and sixty-chapter compilations, the work occurs as number 46 in the Honzan edition.

The term *kattō* 葛藤 ("arrowroot and wisteria") has the colloquial sense, often encountered in Zen texts, of an "entanglement," a "complexity," "complication," or "difficulty." Zen texts typically treat the term as referring to (especially intellectual and linguistic) obstacles to be cut through, but Dōgen prefers to see it here as the "entanglement," or "intertwining," of master and disciple.

Thus, while seemingly inspired by a saying about vines by the author's master, Tiantong Rujing 天童如淨, the bulk of this short text is taken up with the question of transmission of the dharma from master to disciple — especially the famous account of the dharma transmission by the first Chinese ancestor, Bodhidharma, to his disciple Huike 慧可. Here, Dōgen cites the famous story of Bodhidharma's four disciples, from which derives the Zen expression "skin, flesh, bones, and marrow" (*hi niku kotsu zui* 皮肉骨髓), and argues against the common notion that these four terms signify a hierarchy of understanding. Finally, the essay closes with a note dismissing the legend that Bodhidharma rose from his grave and returned to India.

正法眼藏第三十八
Treasury of the True Dharma Eye
Number 38

葛藤

Tangled Vines

[38:1] {1:416}

釋迦牟尼佛の正法眼藏無上菩提を證傳せること、靈山會には迦葉大士のみ
なり。嫡嫡正證二十八世、菩提達磨尊者にいたる。尊者みづから震旦國に
祖儀して、正法眼藏無上菩提を大祖正宗普覺大師に附囑し、二祖とせり。

In the community on Vulture Peak, only Kāśyapa the Great One verified and transmitted the unsurpassed bodhi of the treasury of the true dharma eye of Buddha Śākyamuni.[1] In successor after successor through twenty-eight generations of correct verification, it reached Venerable Bodhidharma. The Venerable, conducting the ancestral rites in Cīnasthāna, bequeathed the unsurpassed bodhi of the treasury of the true dharma eye to the Great Ancestor, Great Master Zhengzong Pujue, and made him the Second Ancestor.[2]

[38:2]

第二十八祖、はじめて震旦國に祖儀あるを初祖と稱す、第二十九祖を二祖
と稱するなり。すなはちこれ東土の俗なり。初祖、かつて般若多羅尊者の
みもとにして、佛訓道骨、まのあたり證傳しきたれり。根源をもて根源を
證取しきたれり、枝葉の本とせるところなり。

---

1 **Kāśyapa the Great One** (*Kashō daishi* 迦葉大士): I.e., Mahākāśyapa, to whom the Buddha is said to have transmitted the *shōbōgenzō* 正法眼藏 on Vulture Peak. The name "Mahākāśyapa" means "Great Kāśyapa"; the title *daishi* 大士 used here often translates Sanskrit *mahāsattva* ("great being").

verified and transmitted (*shōden* 證傳): I.e., personally experienced and passed down; a compound predicate appearing in the *Shōbōgenzō* only here and in section 2, immediately below.

2 **conducting the ancestral rites** (*sogi shite* 祖儀して): *Sogi* is usually interpreted as the deportment, or conduct, of the [buddhas and] ancestors.

Cīnasthāna (*Shintan* 震旦): Dōgen here and below uses the transliteration of a Sanskrit term for China, "Land of the Qin."

Great Ancestor, Great Master Zhengzong Pujue (*Taiso Shōshū Fukaku daishi* 大祖正宗普覺大師): I.e., the Second Ancestor, Huike 慧可 (487–593).

174 DŌGEN'S *SHŌBŌGENZŌ* VOLUME III

The Twenty-eighth Ancestor, being the first to conduct the ancestral rites in the Land of Cīnasthāna, is called the First Ancestor; the Twenty-ninth Ancestor is called the Second Ancestor. This is the custom in the Land of the East.[3] The First Ancestor, under Venerable Prajñātāra, directly verified and transmitted the instructions of the buddha and the bones of the way; he verified the root source with the root source; he made it the root of the branches and leaves.[4]

[38:3]
おほよそ諸聖ともに、葛藤の根源を截斷する參學に趣向すといへども、葛藤をもて葛藤をきるを截斷といふ、と參學せず、葛藤をもて葛藤をまつふ、としらず、いかにいはんや葛藤をもて葛藤に嗣續することをしらんや。嗣法これ葛藤としれるまれなり、きけるものなし。道著せる、いまだあらず。證著せる、おほからんや。

Although the sages all devise study that severs the root source of tangled vines, they do not study that "severing" means to cut tangled vines with tangled vines; they do not know that tangled vines are entwined by tangled vines.[5] How much less, then, could they know that tangled vines are succeeded by tangled vines. Few understand that inheritance of the dharma is tangled vines. No one has heard this. No one has ever uttered it. How could there be many who have verified it?

---

3 **Land of the East** (*Tōdo* 東土): I.e., China.

4 **Venerable Prajñātāra** (*Hannyatara sonja* 般若多羅尊者): I.e., Bodhidharma's master, the Twenty-seventh Ancestor according to the traditional legend of the Zen ancestors in India.

instructions of the buddha and the bones of the way (*bukkun dōkotsu* 佛訓道骨): "Bones of the way" (*dōkotsu* 道骨) is typically interpreted as the "bones and marrow" (i.e., essential message) of the buddhas and ancestors; hence, the fundamental truth of Zen.

root source (*kongen* 根源); **root of the branches and leaves** (*shiyō no moto* 枝葉の本): Dōgen is here playing with the vegetative imagery suggested by his title theme. The "branches and leaves" could be taken either metaphysically, as the multiplicity appearing in the world from the hidden root, or historically, as the proliferation of Chan lineages after Bodhidharma.

5 **sages** (*shoshō* 諸聖): The term can refer to holy men in general, to the sages of Chinese religions, or to advanced Buddhist adepts (S. ārya); here, probably a (somewhat ironic?) reference to the Chinese Chan monks.

tangled vines (*kattō* 葛藤): Our title theme, a loose translation of two terms denoting climbing plants — the former, sometimes translated "arrowroot," is regularly used for the kudzu vine; the latter is most often taken as "wisteria." As a compound term, *kattō* has the common colloquial sense, often encountered in Zen texts, of an "entanglement," a "complexity," "complication," or "difficulty"; see Supplementary Notes, s.v. "Tangled vines."

38. Tangled Vines *Kattō* 葛藤 175

[38:4] {1:417}

先師古佛云、葫蘆藤種纏葫蘆。

My former master, the Old Buddha, said, "The bottle gourd vine entwines the bottle gourd."[6]

[38:5]

この示衆、かつて古今の諸方に見聞せざるところなり、はじめて先師ひとり道示せり。葫蘆藤の葫蘆藤をまつふは、佛祖の佛祖を參究し、佛祖の佛祖を證契するなり。たとへば、これ以心傳心なり。

This presentation to the assembly is something never seen or heard in any other quarter past or present.[7] My former master alone first expressed it. The bottle gourd vine entwining the bottle gourd vine is the buddhas and ancestors investigating the buddhas and ancestors, the buddhas and ancestors verifying and according with the buddhas and ancestors. It is, for example, to *transmit the mind by the mind.*[8]

* * * * *

[38:6]

第二十八祖、謂門人曰、時將至矣、汝等盍言所得乎。時門人道副曰、如我今所見、不執文字、不離文字、而爲道用。祖云、汝得吾皮。尼総持曰、如我今所解、如慶喜見阿閦佛國、一見更不再見。祖云、汝得吾肉。道育曰、四大本空、五蘊非有、而我見處、無一法可得。祖曰、汝得吾骨。最後慧可、禮三拜後、位依而立。祖曰、汝得吾髓。果爲二祖、傳法傳衣。

The Twenty-eighth Ancestor addressed his followers, saying, "The time is coming. Why don't you say what you've attained?"[9]

---

6 **My former master, the Old Buddha** (*senshi kobutsu* 先師古佛): Honorific reference to Dōgen's Chinese teacher, Tiantong Rujing 天童如淨 (1162-1227).

"The bottle gourd vine entwines the bottle gourd" (*koro tōshu ten koro* 葫蘆藤種纏葫蘆): A saying found in the *Rujing heshang yulu* 如淨和尚語錄 (T.2002A.48:128b20). In its occurrence there, it seems to indicate a state of complete entanglement in words. See Supplementary Notes, s.v. "The bottle gourd vine entwines the bottle gourd."

7 **presentation to the assembly** (*jishu* 示衆): A standard expression for a Zen master's lecture to his followers.

8 **transmit the mind by the mind** (*i shin den shin* 以心傳心): A famous Zen expression for the transmission of awakening from master to disciple.

9 **Twenty-eighth Ancestor** (*dainijūhachi so* 第二十八祖): Opening the famous account of the occasion on which Bodhidharma is supposed to have designated the monk Huike 慧可 as his successor. (See *shinji Shōbōgenzō* 眞字正法眼藏, DZZ.5:230, case 201.) It is from this story that Dōgen gets the expression "skin, flesh, bones, and marrow" (*hi niku kotsu zui* 皮肉骨髓) occurring frequently throughout his writings to indicate the essential understanding of Buddhism handed down in the ancestral tradition. See Supplementary Notes, s.v. "Skin, flesh, bones, and marrow."

176　DŌGEN'S *SHŌBŌGENZŌ* VOLUME III

At that time, the follower Daofu said, "My present view is, without being attached to words and letters or being detached from words and letters, one still engages in the function of the way."[10]

The Ancestor said, "You've gotten my skin."

The Nun Zongchi said, "My present understanding is, it's like Ānanda's seeing the land of Buddha Akṣobhya: seen once, it isn't seen again."[11]

The Ancestor said, "You've gotten my flesh."

Daoyu said, "The four elements are originally empty; the five aggregates are nonexistent. My view is that there's not a single dharma to attain."[12]

The Ancestor said, "You've gotten my bones."

Finally, Huike, after making three bows, stood in his place.

The Ancestor said, "You've gotten my marrow."

Consequently, [Bodhidharma] made him the Second Ancestor, transmitting the dharma and transmitting the robe.

[38:7] {1:418}
いま參學すべし、初祖道の汝得吾皮・肉・骨・髓は祖道なり。門人四員、ともに得處あり、聞著あり。その聞著ならびに得處、ともに跳出身心の皮・肉・骨・髓なり、脱落身心の皮・肉・骨・髓なり。知見解會の一著子をもて、祖師を見聞すべきにあらざるなり。能所・彼此の十現成にあらず。しかあるを、正傳なきともがらおもはく、四子おのおのの所解に親疎あるによりて、祖道また皮・肉・骨・髓の淺深不同なり。皮・肉は骨・髓よりも疏なり、とおもひ、二祖の見解すぐれたるによりて、得髓の印をえたり、といふ。かくのごとくいふいひは、いまだかつて佛祖の參學なく、祖道の正傳あらざるなり。

10　**Daofu** (*Dōfuku* 道副): Sometimes identified with Sengfu 僧副 (464-524), said to have been a disciple of Bodhidharma.

11　**Nun Zongchi** (*Ni Sōji* 尼総持): Otherwise unknown.

Ānanda (*Keiki* 慶喜): Said to have been a relative of Gautama, he became a follower of the Buddha and, following the latter's nirvāṇa, a disciple of Mahākāśyapa.

land of Buddha Akṣobhya (*Ashuku butsu koku* 阿閦佛國): A realm usually located in the eastern direction from Śākyamuni's Sahā world. The reference to Ānanda's seeing this land only once likely derives from the story that Buddha Śākyamuni, before Ānanda and a multitude of followers, used his paranormal powers briefly to reveal Akṣobhya and his retinue and then, withdrawing his powers, caused the vision to vanish. (See the *Mahā-prajñā-pāramitā-sūtra* (*Mohe bore boluomi jing* 摩訶般若波羅蜜經, T.223.8:363b29-c9.)

12　**Daoyu** (*Dōiku* 道育): Otherwise unknown.

38. Tangled Vines *Kattō* 葛藤   177

We should study this. The saying of the First Ancestor, "*You've gotten my skin, flesh, bones, and marrow,*" is the saying of an ancestor.[13] His four followers have all gotten it, have all heard it. Both what they have heard and what they have gotten is the skin, flesh, bones, and marrow that springs forth from body and mind, the skin, flesh, bones, and marrow that sloughs off body and mind.[14]

The Ancestral Master is not to be perceived by one move of our knowledge and understanding; he is not ten realizations of subject and object or this and that.[15] Still, those without the correct transmission think that, since the understandings of the four disciples are familiar and remote, so the skin, flesh, bones, and marrow spoken of by the Ancestor differ from shallow to deep.[16] They think skin and flesh are more remote than bones and marrow and say that the Second Ancestor received the seal, "you've gotten my marrow," because his understanding was superior.[17] Those who talk like this have never studied the buddhas and ancestors, and lack the correct transmission of the words of the Ancestor.[18]

[38:8]

しるべし、祖道の皮・肉・骨・髓は、淺深にあらざるなり。たとひ見解に殊劣ありとも、祖道は得吾なるのみなり。その宗旨は、得吾髓の爲示、ならびに得吾骨の爲示、ともに爲人接人、拈草落草に足・不足あらず。たとへば拈華のごとし、たとへば傳衣のごとし。四員のために道著するところ、はじめより一等なり。祖道は一等なりといへども、四解かならずしも一等なるべきにあらず。四解たとひ片片なりとも、祖道はただ祖道なり。

---

13 **saying of an ancestor** (*sodō* 祖道): Perhaps intended in the sense, "saying worthy of an ancestor."

14 **springs forth from body and mind** (*chōshutsu shinjin* 跳出身心); **sloughs off body and mind** (*datsuraku shinjin* 脱落身心): The two expressions are virtually synonymous. The verb in the former phrase, which might also be rendered, "jumps out of body and mind," is often found in Zen texts in the sense, "to escape," as a fish escapes a net. The latter phrase, while not found in the Chinese literature, is quite common in Dōgen's writing, often attributed to his teacher, Rujing 如淨; see Supplementary Notes, s.v. "Body and mind sloughed off."

15 **one move** (*ichi jakusu* 一著子); **ten realizations** (*jū genjō* 十現成): "One move" is used in reference to moving a piece in a board game; in Zen texts, often a rhetorical "move" in a dialogue. The phrase "he is not ten appearances of" might be rendered "he is not fully manifest in"; the translation here seeks to preserve the parallel construction and play with numbers in the original.

16 **familiar and remote** (*shinso* 親疏): A term often used in reference to familial lines; here, probably meaning "closer to and farther from" Bodhidharma's understanding.

17 **seal** (*in* 印): I.e., the "seal of approval" from Bodhidharma. The term is regularly used to indicate the bestowing of transmission on a disciple.

18 **words of the Ancestor** (*sodō* 祖道): A term one might well be tempted to read "the way of the ancestors," but its sense here seems clear from its use in the following section.

178 DŌGEN'S *SHŌBŌGENZŌ* VOLUME III

We should understand that, in the words of the Ancestor, "skin, flesh, bones, and marrow," there is no shallow or deep. Even if there are superior and inferior in the understandings, the words of the Ancestor are just "*gotten my.*"[19] The essential point is that both the instruction "gotten my marrow" and the instruction "gotten my bones" are neither adequate nor inadequate in engaging the person for the sake of the person, in taking up the grass and falling into the grass.[20] They are, for example, like holding up a flower; they are like transmitting the robe.[21] What is said to the four is equal from the beginning. While the words of the Ancestor are equal, the four understandings are not necessarily equal. While the four understandings may be in pieces, the words of the Ancestor are just the words of the Ancestor.[22]

[38:9]

おほよそ道著と見解と、かならずしも相委なるべからず。たとへば、祖師の、四員の門人にしめすには、なんぢわが皮吾をえたり、と道取するなり。もし二祖よりのち、百千人の門人あらんにも、百千道の説著あるべきなり、窮盡あるべからず。門人ただ四員あるがゆえに、しばらく皮・肉・骨・髄の四道取ありとも、のこりていまだ道取せず、道取すべき道取おほし。

Generally speaking, sayings and understandings do not necessarily mandate each other.[23] For example, in the Ancestral Master's instruction

---

19 **"gotten my"** (*toku go* 得吾): Or "got me." I.e., Bodhidharma says in each case, "you've gotten my . . ." Here, as he will do below, Dōgen is playing with the terms in Bodhidharma's responses. The Chinese makes no distinction among the nominative ("I"), possessive ("my"), and accusative ("me") cases, and the translation struggles to interpret Dōgen's play with the pronouns here and below.

20 **engaging the person for the sake of the person** (*i nin setsu nin* 爲人接人); **taking up the grass and falling into the grass** (*nen sō raku sō* 拈草落草): Two phrases likely referring to the teaching activities of the masters — in this case, of Bodhidharma. The latter phrase seems unusual and may well represent Dōgen's play with Chan stories that "take up grass" as a topic and the Chan expression "to fall into the grass" (*rakusō* 落草) used in reference to discourse that descends to the level of the student's understanding.

21 **holding up a flower** (*nenge* 拈華); **transmitting the robe** (*denne* 傳衣): References to accounts of the transmission of the dharma; the former, to the famous story of the founding of the ancestral line on Vulture Peak, when Śākyamuni held up a flower, and Mahākāśyapa smiled (see Supplementary Notes, s.v. "Hold up a flower"); the latter, likely to accounts of the handing down of the robe of Bodhidharma through the generations to the Sixth Ancestor, Huineng 慧能 (though Dōgen may also have had in mind here Śākyamuni's bestowal of his robe to the next buddha, Maitreya).

22 **in pieces** (*henpen* 片片): I.e., are separate; the expression could also be interpreted as "are partial." Compare Supplementary Notes, s.v. "Bare mind in pieces."

23 **mandate each other** (*sōi* 相委): An unusual expression, not occurring elsewhere in the *Shōbōgenzō*; likely meaning here, "be in accord with each other."

38. Tangled Vines *Kattō* 葛藤

to his four followers, he says, "you've gotten my 'skin me.'"[24] If there were a hundred thousand followers after the Second Ancester, there would be a hundred thousand explanations; they would be inexhaustible. Since there are only four followers, we have just the four sayings, "skin, flesh, bones, and marrow"; but many sayings remain that were not said and could be said.

[38:10] {1:419}

しるべし、たとひ二祖に爲道せんにも、汝得吾皮、と道取すべきなり。たとひ汝得吾皮なりとも、二祖として正法眼藏を傳付すべきなり。得皮・得髓の殊劣によれるにあらず。

We should realize that, even in speaking to the Second Ancestor, he could say, "*You've gotten my skin.*" Even though [he were to say], "*You've gotten my skin,*" he would have transmitted the treasury of the true dharma eye [to Huike] as the Second Ancestor. "Gotten my skin" and "gotten my marrow" do not depend on superiority or inferiority.

[38:11]

また、道副・道育・総持等に爲道せんにも、汝得吾髓と道取すべきなり。吾皮なりとも、傳法すべきなり。祖師の身心、皮・肉・骨・髓ともに祖師なり。髓はしたしく、皮はうときにあらず。

Again, in speaking to Daofu, Daoyu, and Zongchi, he could have said, "*You've gotten my marrow.*" Although [he said,] "my skin," he could transmit the dharma [to them]. For the body and mind of the Ancestral Master, "skin, flesh, bones, and marrow" are all the Ancestral Master. It is not that "marrow" is intimate and "skin" is remote.

[38:12]

いま參學の眼目をそなへたらんに、汝得吾皮の印をうるは、祖師をうる參究なり。通身皮の祖師あり、通身肉の祖師あり、通身骨の祖師あり、通身髓の祖師あり。通身心の祖師あり、通身身の祖師あり、通心心の祖師あり、通祖師の祖師あり、通身得吾汝等の祖師あり。これらの祖師、ならびに現成して、百千の門人に爲道せんとき、いまのごとく汝得吾皮と説著するなり。百千の説著、たとひ皮肉骨髓なりとも、傍觀、いたづらに皮・肉・骨・髓の説著と活計すべきなり。もし祖師の會下に六・七の門人あらば、汝得吾心の道著すべし、汝得吾身の道著すべし。汝得吾佛の道著すべし、汝得吾眼睛の道著すべし、汝得吾證の道著すべし。いはゆる汝は、祖なる時節あり、慧可なる時節あり。得の道理を、審細に參究すべきなり。

Now, for one who would be equipped with the eye of study, getting the seal, "*You've gotten my skin,*" is the investigation of getting the Ancestral Master. There is an Ancestral Master whose body throughout

---

24 **"you've gotten my 'skin me'"** (*nanji waga higo o etari* なんぢわが皮吾をえたり): A literal rendering of an odd locution; presumably, meaning something like, "you've got me as my skin."

180   DŌGEN'S *SHŌBŌGENZŌ* VOLUME III

is skin; there is an Ancestral Master whose body throughout is flesh; there is an Ancestral Master whose body throughout is bones; there is an Ancestral Master whose body throughout is marrow.[25] There is an Ancestral Master whose body throughout is mind; there is an Ancestral Master whose body throughout is body; there is an Ancestral Master whose mind throughout is mind. There is an Ancestral Master who is the Ancestral Master throughout; there is an Ancestral Master whose *body throughout is "gotten my" and "you," and so forth.*[26]

When these Ancestral Masters appear together and speak to their hundred thousand followers, they explain, as here, "*You've gotten my skin.*"[27] While their explanations are of "skin, flesh, bones, and marrow," onlookers will vainly make their living on explanations of "skin, flesh, bones, and marrow."[28] If there had been six or seven followers in the Ancestral Master's community, he could have said, "*You've gotten my mind*"; he could have said, "*You've gotten my body.*" He could have said, "*You've gotten my buddha*"; he could have said, "*You've gotten my eyes*"; he could have said, "*You've gotten my verification.*" There are occasions when the "you" here is the Ancestor and occasions when it is Huike. We should investigate in detail the principle of "gotten."

[38:13]

しるべし、汝得吾あるべし、吾得汝あるべし、得吾汝あるべし、得汝吾あるべし。祖師の身心を參見するに、内外一如なるべからず、渾身は通身なるべからず、といはば、佛祖現成の國土にあらず。皮をえたらんは、骨・

---

25 **body throughout is skin** (*tsūshin hi* 通身皮): Here and in the following parallel sentences, Dōgen is likely inspired by the saying of Daowu Yuanzhi 道吾圓智 (769-835), discussed in the "Shōbōgenzō Kannon" 正法眼藏觀音, that Bodhisattva Avalokiteśvara's "body throughout is hands and eyes" (*tsūshin ze shugen* 通身是手眼). See Supplementary Notes, s.v. "His body throughout is hands and eyes."

26 **Ancestral Master throughout** (*tsū soshi* 通祖師): The English here loses the syntactical parallel with the preceding expressions (which, if it were maintained, could only produce the unlikely "Ancestor throughout is Master").

"gotten my" and "you" (*toku go nyo* 得吾汝): A tentative translation, assuming that Dōgen is again here playing with the words of Bodhidharma's saying (see Note 19, above). For other possible interpretations of this phrase, see Note 30, below.

27   **these Ancestral Masters** (*korera no soshi* これらの祖師): Dōgen here treats the various ways of thinking about Bodhidharma as a plurality of Bodhidharmas.

hundred thousand followers (*hyakusen no monjin* 百千の門人): I.e., the hundred thousand disciples of Bodhidharma that Dōgen imagines in section 9, above.

28 **make their living** (*kakkei su* 活計す): A common expression referring to one's "livelihood"; used in Zen texts more broadly for one's "way of life," "pursuits," etc. The point of this rather odd sentence would seem to be that, while Bodhidharma uses the terms "skin, flesh, bones, and marrow," those who do not understand his use occupy themselves with taking the terms as references simply to "skin, flesh, bones, and marrow."

38. Tangled Vines *Kattō* 葛藤　181

肉・髓をえたるなり。骨・肉・髓をえたるは、皮・肉面目をえたり。ただ
これを盡十方界の眞實體と曉了するのみならんや、さらに皮・肉・骨・髓
なり。このゆえに、得吾衣なり、汝得法なり。これによりて、道著も跳出
の條條なり、師資同參す、聞著も跳出の條條なり、師資同參す。師資の同
參究は、佛祖の葛藤なり、佛祖の葛藤は、皮肉骨髓の命脈なり。拈華瞬
目、すなはち葛藤なり、破顔微笑、すなはち皮肉骨髓なり。

We should realize that there should be, "*you've gotten me*"; there
should be, "*I've gotten you*"; there should be, "*gotten me and you*";
there should be, "*gotten you and me*."[29] In our examination of the body
and mind of the Ancestral Master, if we say that inner and outer are not
one, or that the whole body cannot be his body throughout, then we
are not in the land where the buddhas and ancestors appear.[30] To have
got the "skin" is to have got the bones, flesh, and marrow; to have got
the "bones, flesh, and marrow" is to have got the skin, flesh, and face.
How could this be clearly comprehended only as the true body of all the
worlds in the ten directions?[31] It is in addition the skin, flesh, bones, and
marrow.

Therefore, it is "*gotten my robe*"; it is "*you've gotten the dharma*."[32]
Hence, the sayings are instances of springing forth; master and disciple
study together.[33] The hearings are instances of springing forth; master
and disciple study together. Master and disciple studying together is the

29　**"gotten me and you"** (*toku go nyo* 得吾汝); **"gotten you and me"** (*toku nyo go* 得
汝吾): Tentative translations. In these and the two preceding phrases, Dōgen is playing
with the syntax of the same three terms. It is not clear how he wants us to parse these
phrases; they could well be read, "the you that got me," "the I that got you"; it is also
at least possible to read them as "got my you," "got your me" (or "got you as me," "got
me as you").

30　**the whole body cannot be his body throughout** (*konjin* [or *konshin*] *wa tsūshin
naru bekarazu* 渾身は通身なるべからず): The "whole body" is often used, as probably
here, in a metaphysical sense, to refer to the dharma body of a buddha; see following
note.

31　**true body of all the worlds in the ten directions** (*jin jippō kai no shinjitsu tai* 盡十
方界の眞實體): Presumably a reference to the dharma body of the buddha that pervades
the universe. The rhetorical question here and the surprising sentence that follows it
seem to suggest a common theme in Dōgen's writing — that we should not understand
the true nature of the awakened master simply in abstract metaphysical terms but must
see it in his concrete features, words, and deeds.

32　**"gotten my robe"** (*toku go e* 得吾衣); **"you've gotten the dharma"** (*nyo toku hō*
汝得法): From the tradition that Bodhidharma's robe was handed down to the early Chinese ancestors as a token of the fact that they had inherited his dharma.

33　**master and disciple study together** (*shishi dōsan su* 師資同參す): It is not clear
exactly how this clause, here and in the succeeding sentence, is related to the clause that
precedes it. Most likely, they are in apposition: i.e., "master and disciple studying together" are "instances of springing forth"; or, to put it more prosaically, in the interchange
between teacher and student, we transcend ourselves.

tangled vines of the buddhas and ancestors. The tangled vines of the buddhas and ancestors are the vital artery of the skin, flesh, bones, and marrow. *Holding up a flower and blinking the eyes* is tangled vines; *breaking into a smile* is the skin, flesh, bones, and marrow.[34]

[38:14] {1:420}

さらに参究すべし、葛藤種子すなはち脱體の力量あるによりて、葛藤を纒
遶する枝・葉・華・果ありて、回互・不回互なるがゆえに、佛祖現成し、
公案現成するなり。

We should investigate further. Since the seeds of tangled vines have the power of the body stripped, there are branches, leaves, flowers, and fruit that entwine tangled vines; and, because they are "interacting and not interacting," the buddhas and ancestors are realized, the kōan is realized.[35]

* * * * *

[38:15]

趙州眞際大師、示衆云、迦葉傳與阿難、且道、達磨傳與什麼人。因僧問、
且如二祖得髓、又作麼生。師云、莫謗二祖。師又云、達磨也有語、在外者
得皮、在裏者得骨。且道、更在裏者得什麼。僧問、如何是得髓底道理。師
云、但識取皮、老僧者裏、髓也不立。僧問、如何是髓。師云、與麼即皮也
摸未著。

Great Master Zhenji of Zhaozhou addressed the assembly, saying, "Kāśyapa transmitted to Ānanda. So, tell me, to whom did Dharma transmit?"[36]

---

34 **Holding up a flower and blinking the eyes** (*nenge shunmoku* 拈華瞬目); **breaking into a smile** (*hagan mishō* 破顔微笑): References to the story of Śākyamuni's transmission to Mahākaśyapa on Vulture Peak. See Note 21, above and Supplementary Notes, s.v. "Holding up a flower and blinking the eyes" and "Break into a smile."

35 **the body stripped** (*dattai* 脱體): A term that can also mean "to escape the body," in Chan texts, it often carries the sense, "to reveal all"; see Supplementary Notes, s.v. "Body stripped."

"interacting and not interacting" (*ego fuego* 回互不回互): Or "not interacting while interacting." From a line in the *Cantong qi* 參同契, of Shitou Xiqian 石頭希遷 (700-791) (*Jingde chuandeng lu* 景德傳燈錄, T.2076.51:459b10); usually interpreted to mean that two things (often subject and object) are both independent and interdependent.

buddhas and ancestors are realized, the kōan is realized (*busso genjō shi, kōan genjō suru* 佛祖現成し、公案現成する): "The kōan is realized" here translates one of Dōgen's favorite expressions, *kōan genjō* 公案現成 (also *genjō kōan* 現成公案), a phrase that, in ordinary Chinese, might simply be rendered, "the case is settled" (i.e., a legal judgment has been rendered), but in the *Shōbōgenzō* and subsequent Sōtō usage, takes on more metaphysical tones as something like "reality manifest." See Supplementary Notes, s.v. "Realized kōan."

36 **Great Master Zhenji of Zhaozhou** (*Jōshū Shinsai daishi* 趙州眞際大師). The posthumous title of Zhaozhou Congshen 趙州從諗 (778-897), famed disciple of Nanquan Puyuan 南泉普願. His saying here appears in the *Zhaozhou lu* 趙州錄, *Guzunxiu yulu* 古尊宿語錄 (ZZ.118:311a14-18).

38. Tangled Vines *Kattō* 葛藤　　　　　183

Thereupon, a monk asked, "Well, what about the Second Ancestor's *getting the marrow?*"

The Master said, "Don't slander the Second Ancestor."

The Master again said, "Dharma had a saying that those on the outside get his skin, those on the inside get his bones. So, tell me, what do those still further inside get?"

A monk asked, "What's the principle of getting the marrow?"

The Master said, "Just recognize the skin. Where this old monk is, he doesn't set up even the marrow."[37]

The monk asked, "What is the marrow?"

The Master said, "If you're like this, you don't touch even the skin."[38]

[38:16] {1:421}

しかあればしるべし、皮也摸未著のときは、髓也摸未著なり。皮を摸得するは、髓もうるなり。與麼即皮也摸未著の道理を功夫すべし。如何是得髓底道理と問取するに、但識取皮、老僧這裏、髓也不立、と道取現成せり。識取皮のところ、髓也不立なるを、眞箇の得髓底の道理とせり。かるがゆえに、二祖得髓、又作麼生の問取現成せり。迦葉傳與阿難の時節を當觀するに、阿難藏身於迦葉なり、迦葉藏身於阿難なり。しかあれども、傳與裏の相見時節には、換面目皮肉骨髓の行李をまぬかれざるなり。これによりて、且道、達磨傳與什麼人、としめすなり。達磨すでに傳與するときは達磨なり、二祖すでに得髓するには達磨なり。この道理の參究によりて、佛法なほ今日にいたるまで佛法なり。もしかくのごとくならざらんは、佛法の今日にいたるにあらず。この道理、しづかに功夫參究して、自道取すべし、教他道取すべし。在外者得皮、在裏者得骨、且道、更在裏者得什麼。いまいふ外、いまいふ裏、その宗趣、もとも端的なるべし。外を論ずるとき、皮・肉・骨・髓ともに外あり、裏を論ずるとき、皮・肉・骨・髓ともに裏あり。

Given this, we should realize that, when we "*don't touch even the skin,*" we *don't touch even the marrow.* To be able to touch the skin is to get the marrow. We should work away at the meaning of "*if you're*

"**Kāśyapa transmitted to Ānanda**" (*Kashō den yo Anan* 迦葉傳與阿難): A reference to the tradition that Mahākāśyapa transmitted the dharma he had received from the Buddha to his disciple Ānanda.

37　"**Where this old monk is**" (*rōsō shari* 老僧者裏): Zhaozhou uses a Chinese idiom for "here" (*zheli* 者裏) that contains the same term (*li* 裏) he has used for "inside"; hence, there may be the suggestion that, by being "here," he is, as it were, all the way "inside."

"**doesn't set up even the marrow**" (*zui ya furyū* 髓也不立): I.e., "doesn't set up" as a topic, "doesn't discuss."

38　"**you don't touch even the skin**" (*hi ya mo mijaku* 皮也摸未著): Literally, "you grope for but don't touch even the skin" (a sense Dōgen will play on below). The Chinese expression *mo michao* 摸未著 (or *mo buchao* 摸不著) has the idiomatic sense "can't understand," or, as we might say, "don't get it."

184 DŌGEN'S *SHŌBŌGENZŌ* VOLUME III

like this, you don't touch even the skin." When asked, "*What's the principle of getting the marrow?*" he expressed the words, "*Just recognize the skin. Where this old monk is, he doesn't set up even the marrow.*" With "*recognize the skin,*" he made "*doesn't set up even the marrow*" the true "principle of getting the marrow." For this reason, the question appeared, "*What about the Second Ancestor getting the marrow?*"

When we should observe the time when "*Kāśyapa transmitted to Ānanda,*" *Ānanda hides his body in Kāśyapa, Kāśyapa hides his body in Ānanda.*[39] Nevertheless, on the occasion when they encounter each other within the transmission, they do not escape the observances of *skin, flesh, bones, and marrow that change the face.*[40] Hence, [Zhaozhou] indicates, "*So tell me, to whom did Dharma transmit?*" Dharma was already Dharma when he "transmitted to"; the Second Ancestor was already Dharma when he "got the marrow."[41] Because of the investigation of this principle, the buddha dharma remains the buddha dharma down to today. If it were not like this, the buddha dharma would not have reached us today. Quietly working on and investigating the meaning of this, we should express it ourselves; we should have others express it. "*Those on*

---

39   **When we should observe the time** (*jisetsu o tōkan suru ni* 時節を當觀するに: The surprising deontic predicate *tōkan suru* 當觀す ("should observe") can probably be taken here simply as "observe" (or, perhaps, "observe now"); but the phrase "should observe the time" is likely intended to invoke a saying, based on the *Nirvāṇa Sūtra* (*Da banniepan jing* 大般涅槃經, T.374.12:532a18-19), that Dōgen discusses at length in his "Shōbōgenzō busshō" 正法眼藏佛性 (DZZ.1:17):

佛言、欲知佛性義、當觀時節因緣。

The Buddha said, "If you wish to know the meaning of 'buddha nature,' you should observe the conditions of the time."

For details of the widespread use of this saying in Zen texts and its possible origins in the *Nirvāṇa Sūtra* (*Da banniepan jing* 大般涅槃經), see Supplementary Notes, s.v. "If you wish to know the meaning of 'buddha nature,' you should observe the conditions of the time."

40   **they do not escape the observances of skin, flesh, bones, and marrow that change the face** (*kan menmoku hi niku kotsu zui no anri o manukarezaru nari* 換面目皮肉骨髓の行李をまぬかれざるなり): "Observances" (*anri* 行李) typically refers to the religious practices of the monastic. "To change (or exchange) one's face" (*kan menmoku* 換面目) is a multivalent idiom; here, perhaps, referring to awakening; see Supplementary Notes, s.v. "Turning the head and changing the face." This rather obscure passage might be paraphrased as follows:

Although in one sense, at the moment of dharma transmission, Kāśyapa and Ānanda are identified ("hide their bodies" in each other), their individual awakening must still be expressed in the actual give and take of the transmission (exemplified by the "skin, flesh, bones, and marrow" of the Bodhidharma story).

41   **"transmitted to"** (*den yo* 傳與): An odd locution; Dōgen here retains the preposition of Zhaozhou's question, "to whom did Dharma transmit?"

38. Tangled Vines *Kattō* 葛藤   185

the outside get his skin, those on the inside get his bones. So, tell me, what do those still further inside get?" The implication of this "outside" and "inside" should be quite obvious. When we discuss "outside," skin, flesh, bones, and marrow are all "outside"; when we discuss "inside," skin, flesh, bones, and marrow are all "inside."

[38:17]

しかあればすなはち、いま四員の達磨、ともに百千萬の皮・肉・骨・髓の向上を、條條に參究せり。髓よりも向上あるべからず、とおもふことなかれ、さらに三・五枚の向上あるなり。

This being the case, the four Dharmas here have all investigated what is beyond skin, flesh, bones, and marrow, in each of a hundred, thousand, myriad instances.[42] Do not think that there must be nothing beyond the "marrow"; there are still three or five beyond it.[43]

[38:18] {1:422}

趙州古佛のいまの示衆、これ佛道なり。自餘の臨濟・德山・大潙・雲門等のおよぶべからざるところ、いまだ夢見せざるところなり、いはんや道取あらんや。近來の杜撰の長老等、ありとだにもしらざるところなり。かれらに爲説せば、驚怖すべし。

This address to the assembly by the Old Buddha Zhaozhou is the saying of a buddha. It is something not reached by others like Linji, Deshan, Dawei, or Yunmen, something they have never dreamt of, much less spoken about.[44] It is something the recent illiterate elders do not even know exists, and they would be startled if we told them.[45]

---

42 **four Dharmas here** (*ima shiin no Daruma* いま四員の達磨): Dōgen seems here to be treating Bodhidharma's four followers as four versions of Bodhidharma.

43 **there are still three or five beyond it** (*sara ni san go mai no kōjō aru nari* さらに三・五枚の向上あるなり): Or, perhaps, "there are still three or five sheets of beyond." Here as elsewhere, Dōgen treats the adjective *kōjō* ("above," "beyond") as a noun, which he counts here with the classifier for thin, flat objects.

44 **Linji, Deshan, Dawei, or Yunmen** (*Rinzai Tokusan Daii Unmon* 臨濟・德山・大潙・雲門): I.e., the famous Tang-period Chan monks Linji Yixuan 臨濟義玄 (d. 866), Deshan Xuanjian 德山宣鑑 (780-865), Weishan Lingyou 潙山靈祐 (771-853), and Yunmen Wenyen 雲門文偃 (864-949).

something they have never dreamt of (*imada muken sezaru tokoro* いまだ夢見せざるところ): Japanese version of the Chinese insult *wei meng xian zai* 未夢見在 ("never seen even in one's dreams"); common in Dōgen's writing.

45 **illiterate** (*zusan* [or *zuzan*] 杜撰): Free translation of what is, more literally, "Du composition," used in pejorative reference to a literary work that, like those of Du, is ignorant of classical precedents. (Du is most often identified as the Song-dynasty poet Du Mo 杜默; for alternative theories, see M.14477.122.) Dōgen regularly uses the term to refer to those in the Chan tradition who are ignorant of the tradition.

186 DŌGEN'S *SHŌBŌGENZŌ* VOLUME III

[38:19]

雪竇明覺禪師云、趙・睦二州是古佛也。

Chan Master Xuedou Mingjue said, "The two Zhou, Zhao and Mu, are old buddhas."[46]

[38:20]

しかあれば、古佛の道は、佛法の證驗なり、自己の曾道取なり。

Therefore, the word of an old buddha is proof of the buddha dharma; it is something once said by the self.[47]

[38:21]

雪峰眞覺大師云、趙州古佛。

Great Master Zhenjue of Xuefeng said, "The Old Buddha Zhaozhou."[48]

[38:22]

さきの佛祖も、古佛、の讚歎をもて讚歎す、のちの佛祖も、古佛、の讚歎をもて讚歎す。しりぬ、古今の向上に超越の古佛なり、といふことを。

The prior buddha and ancestor praises him with the praise, "old buddha"; the latter buddha and ancestor praises him with the praise, "old buddha."[49] We know that he is an old buddha beyond past or present.

---

46 **Chan Master Xuedou Mingjue** (*Setchō Myōkaku zenji* 雪竇明覺禪師): I.e., Xuedou Zhongtou 雪竇重頭 (980-1052). His words here are probably not in fact a quotation; Dōgen's source is likely a comment on a story about Zhaozhou Congshen 趙州從諗 and Muzhou Daozong 睦州道蹤 (Venerable Chen 陳尊宿, dates unknown), in which Xuedou makes passing reference to them as "two old buddhas" (*niyuan gufo* 二員古佛). (*Mingjue chanshi yulu* 明覺禪師語錄, T.1996.47:672a5-6.). See Supplementary Notes, s.v. "Old buddha."

47 **the word of an old buddha is proof of the buddha dharma** (*kobutsu no dō wa buppō no shōken nari* 古佛の道は佛法の證驗なり): I.e., Zhaozhou's words reliably express the Buddhist teachings. The sentence could also be interpreted to mean, "the word, 'old buddha,' is evidence that [what Zhaozhou says] is the buddha dharma."

it is something once said by the self (*jiko no sō dōshu nari* 自己の曾道取なり): A tentative translation of a sentence the exact sense of which is uncertain. It could be interpreted to mean, "the self has said," or "Zhaozhou himself has said," or perhaps "the buddha dharma itself has said."

48 **Great Master Zhenjue of Xuefeng** (*Seppō Shinkaku daishi* 雪峰眞覺大師): I.e., Xuefeng Yicun 雪峰義存 (822-908). His saying is found in several sources; see, e.g., *Yuanwu Foguo chanshi yulu* 圜悟佛果禪師語錄, T.1997.47:799a19; *shinji Shōbōgenzo* 眞字正法眼藏, DZZ.5:268, case 283.

49 **The prior buddha and ancestor** (*saki no busso* さきの佛祖); **the latter buddha and ancestor** (*nochi no busso* のちの佛祖): I.e., both Xuedou 雪竇 and Xuefeng 雪峰 praise Zhaozhou.

38. Tangled Vines *Kattō* 葛藤

[38:23]

しかあれば、皮・肉・骨・髓の葛藤する道理は、古佛の示衆する汝得吾の標準なり。この標格を功夫參究すべきなり。

Thus, the principle that skin, flesh, bones, and marrow are entangling is the standard of "*you've gotten my*," presented to the assembly by the old buddha.[50] We should work at and investigate this norm.

[38:24]

また、初祖は西歸するといふ、これ非なりと參學するなり。宋雲が所見、かならずしも實なるべからず。宋雲、いかでか祖師の去就をみん。ただ、祖師歸寂ののち、熊耳山にをさめたてまつりぬるとならひしるを、正學とするなり。

Also, we study that saying the First Ancestor returned to the west is wrong.[51] What Song Yun saw is not necessarily the case. How could Song Yun see the conduct of the Ancestral Master? To know that, after the Ancestral Master returned to tranquility, he was interred at Mount Xiong'er is correct study.[52]

正法眼藏葛藤第三十八
Treasury of the True Dharma Eye
Tangled Vines
Number 38

[Ryūmonji MS:]

爾時寬元元年癸卯七月七日、在雍州宇治郡觀音導利興聖寶林寺示衆

Presented to the assembly at Kannon Dōri Kōshō Hōrin Monastery, Uji District, Yōshū; seventh day, seventh month of the junior water year of the rabbit, the first year of Kangen [25 July 1243][53]

---

50 **Thus** (*shika areba* しかあれば): The first sentence here might be somewhat more simply put, "Thus, the teaching of the old buddha [Zhaozhou] about "you've gotten my" gives us a standard for understanding what is meant by [Dōgen's saying that] "skin, flesh, bones, and marrow" are entangling.

51 **the First Ancestor returned to the west** (*Shoso wa saiki su* 初祖は西歸す): At issue here is the famous legend that, after Bodhidharma's death (sometimes said to be from poisoning by the monk Bodhiruci), the Chinese emissary Song Yun 宋雲 encountered an Indian monk in the Pamirs with one sandal. A subsequent investigation of Bodhidharma's grave revealed an empty tomb and one sandal. Recorded, e.g., at *Jingde chuandeng lu* 景德傳燈錄, T.2076.51:220b5-10.

52 **Mount Xiong'er** (*Yūjisan* 熊耳山): A mountain in Shanzhou 陝州 (present-day Henan). For this version of Bodhidharma's final resting place, see, e.g., *Jingde chuandeng lu* 景德傳燈錄, T.2076.51:220b4.

53 The Tōunji 洞雲寺 MS shares an identical colophon.

188 DŌGEN'S *SHŌBŌGENZŌ* VOLUME III

[Tōunji MS:]

寛元二年甲辰三月三日、在越州吉田郡吉峰寺侍司書寫。懷奘

Copied at the acolyte's office at Kippō Monastery, Yoshida District, Esshū; third day, third month of the senior wood year of the dragon, the second year of Kangen [11 April 1244]. Ejō

TREASURY OF THE TRUE DHARMA EYE

NUMBER 39

The Inheritance Certificate
Shisho

嗣書

The Inheritance Certificate

Shisho

INTRODUCTION

This chapter is dated in late spring of 1241 at Kōshōji. It occurs as number 39 in the seventy-five-chapter *Shōbōgenzō*, as number 16 in the ninety-five-chapter Honzan edition, and as number 8 in fascicle 2 of the twenty-eight-text collection; it is not found in the sixty-chapter *Shōbōgenzō*. The chapter is also extant in a 1243 holograph, typically referred to as the Satomi 里見 manuscript (after the family that once owned it), now in possession of Komazawa University. In addition, what is likely an earlier draft is preserved in a manuscript belonging to the Kōjakuji 香積寺, in Hiroshima Prefecture; this version is translated here below as Variant Text 2.

The title theme of the essay is the practice, common in the Zen tradition, of certifying a disciple's inheritance of the dharma from his master with a document of succession. In the first part of his essay, Dōgen is concerned with the issue of inheritance itself, especially with the Zen claim that its lineage of ancestors is directly descended from the seven buddhas of the past. He then turns to the subject of the documents of succession, including accounts of his own encounter with them in China and criticisms of those in China who covet and collect such documents. In addition to giving us information on Dōgen's experiences in China, these accounts provide rare detail on the nature and use of inheritance certificates in the Southern Song.

The essay concludes with the striking and controversial claim that, of the disciples of the Sixth Ancestor, Huineng 慧能, only Qingyuan Xingsi 青原行思, from whom Dōgen's own Sōtō lineage descends, received the direct transmission of the buddha dharma — a transmission witnessed in an inheritance certificate written in the mingled blood of Huineng and Qingyuan.

正法眼藏第三十九

Treasury of the True Dharma Eye
Number 39

嗣書

The Inheritance Certificate

[39:1] {1:423}

夫、佛佛必ず佛佛に嗣法し、祖祖かならず祖祖に嗣法する、これ證契なり、これ單傳なり。このゆえに、無上菩提なり。佛にあらざれば、佛を印證するにあたはず、佛の印證をえざれば、佛となることなし。佛にあらざるよりは、たれかこれを最尊なりとし、無上なりと印することあらん。

Buddha after buddha invariably inherits the dharma from buddha after buddha; ancestor after ancestor invariably inherits the dharma from ancestor after ancestor. This is the verification and accord; this is the unique transmission. Therefore, it is unsurpassed bodhi. If one is not a buddha, one cannot certify a buddha; if one does not receive the certification of a buddha, there is no becoming a buddha. Insofar as one is not a buddha, who would deem this as most honored or certify it as unsurpassed?[1]

[39:2]

佛の印證をうるとき、無師獨悟するなり、無自獨悟するなり。このゆえに、佛佛證嗣し、祖祖證契すといふなり。この道理の宗旨は、佛佛にあらざれば、あきらむべきにあらず、いはんや十地・等覺の所量ならんや、いかにいはんや經師・論師等の測度するところならんや。たとひ爲説とも、かれらきくべからず。

When one receives the certification of a buddha, one awakens alone without a teacher, one awakens alone without a self.[2] Therefore, it is said that buddha after buddha verifies and inherits, ancestor after ances-

---

1　**who would deem this as most honored or certify it as unsurpassed** (*tare ka kore o saison nari to shi, mujō nari to in suru koto aran* たれかこれを最尊なりとし、無上なりと印することあらん): "Most honored" (*saison* 最尊) is an epithet of a buddha; "unsurpassed" (*mujō* 無上) here is likely a reference to the "unsurpassed bodhi" (*mujō bodai* 無上菩提) of a buddha.

2　**one awakens alone without a teacher** (*mushi dokugo* 無師獨悟); **one awakens alone without a self** (*muji dokugo* 無自獨悟): The former phrase occurs fairly often in Buddhist texts, especially in reference to the *pratyeka-buddha*; the latter phrase represents Dōgen's play on the equally common phrase "awakens by oneself without a teacher" (*mushi jigo* 無師自悟). Since of course Dōgen emphasizes the importance of the teacher, both expressions are typically understood here as suggesting that, in the experience of

tor verifies and accords. The essential point of this principle cannot be clarified if one is not [one among] buddha after buddha; how could it be something measured by those on the ten stages or virtual awakening, not to mention something calculated by the sūtra masters or treatise masters, and the like.[3] Even if we were to explain it to them, they could not hear it.

[39:3] {1:424}

佛佛相嗣するがゆえに、佛道はただ佛佛の究盡にして、佛佛にあらざる時節あらず。たとへば、石は石に相嗣し、玉は玉に相嗣することあり、菊も相嗣し、松も印證するに、みな前菊後菊如如なり、前松後松如如なるがごとし。かくのごとくなるを明らめざるともがらは、佛佛正傳の道にあふといへども、いかにある道得ならん、とあやしむにもおよばず、佛佛相嗣の祖祖證契す、といふ領覽あることなし。あはれむべし、佛種族に相似なりといへども、佛子にあらざることを、子佛にあらざることを。

Because buddha after buddha inherits it, the way of the buddhas is just the exhaustive investigation of buddha after buddha, with no time that is not buddha after buddha. It is like, for example, stones inheriting from stones, and jewels inheriting from jewels; like, when chrysanthemums inherit from each other, and pines certify each other, *the prior chrysanthemums and later chrysanthemums are all such, and the prior pines and later pines are all such.*[4] Those who have not clarified that it is like this, though they may encounter the words "direct transmission of buddha after buddha," do not even wonder what this is saying and have no comprehension that the inheritance of buddha after buddha verifies and accords with ancestor after ancestor.[5] How pitiful that, though they may resemble the family of the buddha, they are not the children of the buddha, are not child buddhas.[6]

---

awakening, there is neither self nor other. A similar use occurs in the opening sentence of "Shōbōgenzō hosshō" 正法眼藏法性.

3 **the ten stages or virtual awakening** (*jitchi tōgaku* 十地・等覺): The final phases of the bodhisattva path according to the fifty-two stage system, the latter being the penultimate state, just preceding, but virtually equivalent to, buddhahood.

4 **the prior chrysanthemums and later chrysanthemums are all such, and the prior pines and later pines are all such** (*mina zen kiku go kiku nyonyo nari, zen shō go shō nyonyo naru* みな前菊後菊如如なり、前松後松如如なる): Dōgen here plays with the expression *nyonyo* 如如, a term used for the metaphysical notion of "suchness," or "thusness" (S. *tathatā*), used here in the sense that each is "like" the other.

5 **the inheritance of buddha after buddha verifies and accords with ancestor after ancestor** (*butsubutsu sōshi no soso shōkai su* 佛佛相嗣の祖祖證契す): An attempt to retain something of the awkward grammar of the original; likely meaning that what the buddhas inherit is what the ancestors verify. See Supplementary Notes, s.v. "Buddhas and ancestors."

6 **children of the buddha** (*busshi* 佛子); **child buddhas** (*shibutsu* 子佛): The former expression is a common reference to followers or descendants of the buddhas; the latter is Dōgen's novel reversal of the compound term.

39. The Inheritance Certificate *Shisho* 嗣書　　193

[39:4]

六祖、曹溪に、あるとき衆にしめしていはく、七佛より慧能にいたるまで
四十佛あり、慧能より七佛にいたるに四十祖あり。

The Sixth Ancestor, at Caoxi, once addressed the assembly saying,
"From the seven buddhas through Huineng, there are forty buddhas;
from Huineng through the seven buddhas, there are forty ancestors."[7]

[39:5]

この道理、あきらかに佛祖正嗣の宗旨なり。いはゆる七佛は、過去莊嚴劫
に出現せるもあり、現在賢劫に出現せるもあり。しかあるに、四十祖の面
授をつらぬるは、佛道なり、佛嗣なり。

This principle is clearly the essential point of the direct line of inheritance of the buddhas and ancestors. Of the seven buddhas, some
appeared in the past, Adornment Kalpa, some appeared in the present,
Worthy Kalpa.[8] Nevertheless, what links the face-to-face conferral of
the forty ancestors is the way of the buddhas, is the inheritance of the
buddhas.[9]

7　**The Sixth Ancestor** (*rokuso* 六祖): I.e., Caoxi Huineng 曹溪慧能. This saying, vari-
ations of which are also given in "Shōbōgenzō butsudō" 正法眼藏佛道 and "Kobutsushin" 古佛心, does not seem to occur in any other extant record of Huineng's teachings.
It may possibly reflect some tradition recorded in the Dunhuang manuscript of the *Liuzu
tan jing* 六祖壇經 (see T.2007.48:344c11), where Huineng identifies himself as the fortieth in a lineage beginning with the seven buddhas.

"From the seven buddhas through Huineng, there are forty buddhas" (*shichi butsu
yori enō ni itaru made shijū butsu ari* 七佛より慧能にいたるまで四十佛あり): I.e., the
Zen lineage, from the seven buddhas of the past, ending with Śākyamuni, through the
twenty-eight Indian ancestors, ending with Bodhidharma, to the six Chinese ancestors,
ending with Huineng. (The total of forty results from the fact that Bodhidharma is both
twenty-eighth Indian and first Chinese ancestor.) See Supplementary Notes, s.v. "Old
buddha," "Seven buddhas."

8　**the past, Adornment Kalpa** (*kako shōgon gō* 過去莊嚴劫); **the present, Worthy
Kalpa** (*genzai ken gō* 現在賢劫): It is commonly held that the first three of the seven
buddhas of the past belong to the previous æon, called "adornment" (*shōgon* 莊嚴; or
"array"; S. *vyūha*); while the last four are of our current æon, "worthy" (*ken* 賢; or "auspicious"; S. *bhadra*). See Supplementary Notes, s.v. "Seven buddhas." In section 41,
below, Dōgen will raise the issue of dharma transmission between buddhas of different
kalpas.

9　**what links the face-to-face conferral of the forty ancestors** (*shijisso no menju o
tsuranuru* 四十祖の面授をつらぬる): The claim would seem to be that there is something called "the way of the buddhas" or "the inheritance of the buddhas" that brings the
ancestors into "face-to-face" relationships even when they belong to different kalpas.

inheritance of the buddhas (*busshi* 佛嗣): Or "buddha inheritance"; an unusual term
appearing only in this chapter of the *Shōbōgenzō*, where it occurs often, in both nominal
and verbal senses ("to buddha inherit"). In section 8, below, it is used in the sense "buddha inheritor" (or "buddha heir") and is identified with the homophonous "buddha child"

[39:6]

しかあればすなはち、六祖より向上して七佛にいたれば、四十祖の佛嗣あり。七佛より向上して六祖にいたるに、四十佛の佛嗣なるべし。佛道祖道、かくのごとし。證契にあらず、佛祖にあらざれば、佛智慧にあらず、祖究盡にあらず。佛智慧にあらざれば、佛信受なし、祖究盡にあらざれば、祖證契せず。しばらく四十祖といふは、近をかつがつ擧するなり。

Thus, when we go beyond the Sixth Ancestor through the seven buddhas, there is the inheritance of the buddhas of forty ancestors; and when we go beyond the seven buddhas through the Sixth Ancestor, it should be the inheritance of the buddhas of forty buddhas.[10] The way of the buddhas, the way of the ancestors, is like this. If it is not verification and accord, not buddhas and ancestors, it is not the wisdom of the buddhas, not the exhaustive investigation of the ancestors. If it is not the wisdom of the buddhas, there is no trust in the buddhas; if it is not the exhaustive investigation of the ancestors, the ancestors do not verify and accord. That we talk for the moment of "forty ancestors" is just to bring up the ones that are close to us.[11]

[39:7]

これによりて、佛佛の相嗣すること、深遠にして、不退不轉なり、不斷不絶なり。その宗旨は、釋迦牟尼佛は七佛以前に成道すといへども、ひさしく迦葉佛に嗣法せるなり。降生より三十歳、十二月八日に成道すといへども、七佛以前の成道なり、諸佛齊肩同時の成道なり、諸佛以前の成道なり、一切諸佛より末上の成道なり。

According to this, the inheriting of buddha after buddha is profound and far-reaching; it does not regress, does not turn back; it is uninterrupted and unceasing. The essential point of this is that, although Buddha Śākyamuni may have attained the way before the seven buddhas, long after, he inherited the dharma of Buddha Kāśyapa; although he may have attained the way on the eighth day of the twelfth month, thirty years from his descent to birth, it was an attainment of the way preceding that of the seven buddhas, an attainment of the way equal to and simultaneous with

---

(or "follower of the Buddha"; *busshi* 佛子). In a note appended to the end of the chapter (section 43, below), Dōgen uses it in quoting his teacher, Tiantong Rujing 天童如淨 (1162-1227); but the passage, in Japanese, does not seem to have a source in Rujing's extant recorded sayings, nor does the term appear in those sayings.

10 **when we go beyond the Sixth Ancestor through the seven buddhas** (*rokuso yori kōjō shite shichi butsu ni itareba* 六祖より向上して七佛にいたれば): A similar passage, with the same notion of a transmission "back" from Huineng to the seven buddhas, occurs in "Shōbōgenzō kobutsushin" 正法眼藏古佛心.

11 **That we talk for the moment of "forty ancestors" is just to bring up the ones that are close** (*shibaraku shijisso to iu wa, chikaki o katsugatsu ko suru nari* しばらく四十祖といふは、近をかつがつ擧するなり): Presumably, meaning that we speak here of forty "ancestors," rather than forty "buddhas," simply because the ancestors are closer to us.

39. The Inheritance Certificate *Shisho* 嗣書

that of the other buddhas, an attainment of the way preceding that of the other buddhas, an attainment of the way first before all the buddhas.[12]

[39:8] {1:425}

さらに、迦葉佛は釋迦牟尼佛に嗣法する、と參究する道理あり。この道理をしらざるには、佛道をあきらめず、佛道をあきらめざれば、佛嗣にあらず。佛嗣といふことは、佛子といふことなり。

Futher, there is the principle to be investigated that Buddha Kāśyapa inherited the dharma from Buddha Śākyamuni. One who does not know this principle has not clarified the way of the buddhas; and, if one has not clarified the way of the buddhas, one is not an heir of the buddhas. To be an heir of the buddhas means to be a child of the buddhas.

[39:9]

釋迦牟尼佛、あるとき阿難にとはしむ、過去の諸佛は、これたれが弟子なるぞ。釋迦牟尼佛いはく、過去諸佛は、これ我釋迦牟尼佛の弟子なり。

Buddha Śākyamuni was once asked by Ānanda, "Whose disciples were the buddhas of the past?"[13]

Buddha Śākyamuni said, "The buddhas of the past were my, Buddha Śākyamuni's, disciples."

---

12 **long after, he inherited the dharma of Buddha Kāśyapa** (*hisashiku Kashō butsu ni shihō seru* ひさしく迦葉佛に嗣法せる): I.e., long after becoming a buddha, Śākyamuni succeeded the sixth buddha, Kāśyapa.

an attainment of the way first before all the buddhas (*issai no shobutsu yori matsujō no jōdō* 一切の諸佛より末上の成道): Taking *matsujō* 末上 in its normal meaning of "first of all"; many readers take it to mean "the last."

13 **Buddha Śākyamuni** (*Shakamuni butsu* 釋迦牟尼佛): Likely reflecting a tradition found in the *Zongmen tongyao ji* 宗門統要集 (ZTS.1:10c7-10):

世尊嘗與阿難行次、見一古佛塔。世尊便作禮。阿難云、此是什麼人塔。世尊云、此是過去諸佛塔。阿難云、過去諸佛是什麼人弟子。佛云、是吾弟子。阿難云、應當如是。

Once, when the World-Honored One was traveling with Ānanda, they saw an old Buddhist stūpa. The World-Honored One bowed to it. Ānanda said, "Whose stūpa is this?"

The World-Honored One said, "This is a stūpa of the buddhas of the past."

Ānanda said, "Whose disciples were the buddhas of the past?"

The Buddha said, "They were my disciples."

Ānanda said, "So it must be."

Dōgen refers to this tradition in his "Shōbōgenzō jinzū" 正法眼藏神通, and the story occurs as case number 245 in the Eishōin 永晶院 text of Dōgen's *shinji Shōbōgenzō* 眞字正法眼藏 (see DZZ.5:254, case 245n).

was once asked by Ānanda (*Anan ni towashimu* 阿難にとはしむ): The unexpected causative form of the verb here is thought to express an honorific.

196
DŌGEN'S *SHŌBŌGENZŌ* VOLUME III

[39:10]

諸佛の佛儀、かくのごとし。この諸佛に奉覲して、佛嗣し、成就せん、す
なはち佛佛の佛道にてあるべし。

The buddha deportment of the buddhas is like this. Attending these
buddhas, receiving the inheritance of the buddhas, and achieving [bud-
dhahood] — precisely this should be the way of the buddhas of buddha
after buddha.

* * * * *

[39:11]

この佛道、かならず嗣法するとき、さだめて嗣書あり。もし嗣法なきは、
天然外道なり。佛道もし嗣法を決定するにあらずば、いかでか今日にいた
らん。これによりて、佛佛なるには、さだめて佛嗣佛の嗣書あるなり、
佛嗣佛の嗣書をうるなり。その嗣書の爲體は、日月星辰をあきらめて嗣
法す、あるひは皮・肉・骨・髓を得せしめて嗣法す。あるひは袈裟を相嗣
し、あるひは拄杖を相嗣し、あるひは松枝を相嗣し、あるひは拂子を相嗣
し、あるひは優曇華を相嗣し、あるひは金襴衣を相嗣す。靸鞋の相嗣あ
り、竹篦の相嗣あり。

In this way of the buddhas, whenever someone inherits the dharma
there is definitely an inheritance certificate. Those who lack dharma inheritance belong to an other path of natural occurrence.[14] If there were
no determining dharma inheritance in the way of the buddhas, how could
it have reached us today? Accordingly, those who are [in the lineage of]
buddha after buddha, definitely have inheritance certificates of a buddha
inheriting from a buddha, definitely receive inheritance certificates of a
buddha inheriting from a buddha. As for the nature of those inheritance
certificates, some inherit the dharma by clarifying the sun, moon, and
stars; some inherit the dharma by getting the skin, flesh, bones, and marrow.[15] Some inherit a *kāṣāya*; some inherit a staff; some inherit a pine

---

14 **other path of natural occurrence** (*tennen gedō* 天然外道): I.e., non-Buddhist religion holding the view that things arise, not from causes and conditions, but from themselves of their own accord; synonymous with *jinen gedō* 自然外道. A criticism that will
be attributed below, section 42, to Tiantong Rujing 天童如淨.

15 **As for the nature of those inheritance certificates** (*sono shisho no teitaraku wa* そ
の嗣書の爲體は): The passage that follows here, listing examples of dharma inheritance
in the Chan tradition, has some similarities to examples of the prediction of buddhahood
given in "Shōbōgenzō juki" 正法眼藏授記.

clarifying the sun, moon, and stars (*nichigetsu seishin o akiramete* 日月星辰をあきら
めて); **getting the skin, flesh, bones, and marrow** (*hi niku kotsu zui o toku seshimete*
皮・肉・骨・髓を得せしめて): The former example may allude to the awakening of
Buddha Śākyamuni upon seeing the dawn star; the latter recalls Bodhidharma's test of
his four students, of whom he said in turn that they had gotten his skin, flesh, bones, and
marrow. See Supplementary Notes, s.v. "Skin, flesh, bones, and marrow."

39. The Inheritance Certificate *Shisho* 嗣書   197

branch; some inherit a whisk; some inherit an *udumbara* flower; some inherit a gold brocade robe.[16] There is an inheritance of shoes; there is an inheritance of bamboo sticks.[17]

[39:12] {1:426}

これらの嗣法を相嗣するとき、あるひは指血をして書嗣し、あるひは舌血をして書嗣す。あるひは油乳をもてかき、嗣法する、ともにこれ嗣書なり。嗣せるもの、得せるもの、ともにこれ佛嗣なり。まことにそれ佛祖として現成するとき、嗣法かならず現成す。現成するとき、期せざれどもきたり、もとめざれども嗣法せる佛祖おほし。嗣法あるは、かならず佛佛祖祖なり。

When these dharma inheritances are inherited, blood from a finger may be used to document the inheritance, or blood from the tongue may be used to document the inheritance; or the dharma inheritance may be written with oil or milk: all of these are inheritance certificates.[18] Both the one who has made the inheritance and the one who has received it are

16 *kāṣāya* (*kesa* 袈裟); **staff** (*shujō* 拄杖); **pine branch** (*shōshi* 松枝); **whisk** (*hossu* 拂子): Objects that regularly appear in the stories of interactions between Zen masters and their disciples. The pine branch figured in dharma succession ceremonies, while the staff and fly whisk were insignia of the Zen master's office often invoked in the master's teachings (see Supplementary Notes, s.v. "Staff," "Whisk."); the *kāṣāya*, or outer robe, was sometimes bestowed on the disciple as an emblem of succession, as most famously in the case of the robe of Bodhidharma handed down to the Sixth Ancestor. Apart, perhaps, from this last case, there is probably no need to imagine that Dōgen had specific historical cases in mind here.

udumbara **flower** (*udonge* 優曇華): Reference to the rare flower regularly appearing in Buddhist texts as an auspicious sign. Its mention here is likely an allusion to the famous legend of the founding of the Zen lineage, in which Buddha Śākyamuni held up a flower, the disciple Mahākāśyapa smiled, and the Buddha announced that he had transmitted "the treasury of the true dharma eye" to Mahākāśyapa; although the tradition does not typically identify the flower as the *udumbara*, Dōgen seems to have made this association (see, e.g., *Eihei kōroku* 永平廣錄, DZZ.4:12, no. 428). See Supplementary Notes, s.v. "Hold up a flower."

gold brocade robe (*kinran e* 金襴衣): Likely, reference to the legend that Buddha Śākyamuni bestowed a gold brocade robe on Mahākāśyapa, to be handed on to the next buddha, Maitreya (see, e.g., *Jingde chuandeng lu* 景德傳燈錄, T.2076.51:205c3-5).

17 **shoes** (*sōai* 靸鞋); **bamboo sticks** (*shippei* 竹箆): The "bamboo stick" refers to the short staff used as a symbol of authority (and teaching tool) by abbots. The inheritance of shoes may allude to the well-known tradition that, when Touzi Yiqing 投子義青 (1032–1083) was asked by Fushan Fayuan 浮山法遠 (991–1067) to inherit the dharma of the deceased Zen Master Ming'an 明安禪師 (942–1027), he was given Ming'an's portrait, robe, and shoes. (See, e.g., *Jianzhong Jingguo xudeng lu* 建中靖國續燈錄, ZZ.136:351b1-6.)

18 **the dharma inheritance may be written with oil or milk** (*arui wa yu'nyū o mote kaki, shihō suru* あるひは油乳をもてかき、嗣法する): A tentative translation; the sense of the term *yu'nyū* 油乳 ("oil milk") here is uncertain; possibly a reference to ghee (*soyu* 酥油; S. *ghṛta*) or ghee and curd (*nyūraku* 乳酪; S. *dadhi*).

198 DŌGEN'S *SHŌBŌGENZŌ* VOLUME III

heirs of the buddha. Truly, whenever they appear as buddhas and ancestors, dharma inheritance always occurs. When it occurs, it comes unanticipated, and there are many buddhas and ancestors who have inherited the dharma although they did not seek it. Those who have dharma inheritance are invariably buddha after buddha and ancestor after ancestor.

* * * * *

[39:13]

第二十八祖、西來よりこのかた、佛道に嗣法ある宗旨を、東土に正聞するなり。それよりさきは、かつていまだきかざりしなり。西天の論師・法師等、およばず、しらざるところなり。および十聖三賢の境界およばざるところ、三藏義學の呪術師等、あるらん、と疑著するにもおよばず。かなしむべし、かれら道器なる人身を受けながら、いたづらに教網にまつはれて、透脱の法をしらず、跳出の期を期せざることを。かるがゆえに、學道を審細にすべきなり、參究の志氣を、もはらすべきなり。

Ever since the Twenty-eighth Ancestor came from the west, the essential point that there is dharma inheritance in the way of the buddhas has been heard correctly in the Land of the East. Prior to that, it had never been heard. It is something unreached by, unknown to, the likes of the treatise masters and dharma masters of Sindh in the West; it is something unreached in the realm of the ten sages and three worthies, while the masters of spells among the doctrinal scholars of the tripiṭaka, and the like, do not even wonder whether it exists.[19] How sad that, while receiving the human body that is a vessel of the way, being futilely entangled in a web of doctrine, they do not know how to transcend it and have no expectation of a chance to spring forth from it. Therefore, we should study the way with the utmost care and should be single-minded in our resolve to investigate it.

---

19 **Sindh in the West** (*Saiten* 西天): A term denoting the Indian subcontinent, from the transliteration of *sindhu* as *tianzhu* 天竺; Dōgen sometimes, as in section 18, below, treats it as the "Western Heavens," in contrast to the "Eastern Earth" (*Tōchi* 東地; i.e., China).

ten sages and three worthies (*jisshō sanken* 十聖三賢): I.e., those on the ten "noble" (S. ārya) stages of the bodhisattva path and the three "worthy" (S. *bhadra*) stages just preceding them.

masters of spells among the doctrinal scholars of the tripiṭaka (*sanzō gigaku no jujusshi* 三藏義學の呪術師): The referent is unclear, the combination of "doctrinal scholar" (*gigaku* 義學) and "spell master" (*jujusshi* 呪術師) being unusual; perhaps learned masters of mantra, perhaps reciters of the canon.

39. The Inheritance Certificate *Shisho* 嗣書　　199

[39:14]

道元在宋のとき、嗣書を禮拜することをえしに、多般の嗣書ありき。その
なかに、惟一西堂とて、天童に掛錫せしは、越上の人事なり、前住廣福寺
の堂頭なり。先師と同郷人なり。先師つねにいはく、境風は一西堂に問取
すべし。

When Dōgen was in the Song and was able to pay obeisance to inheritance certificates, [I found that] there were many types of inheritance
certificates.[20] Among them was [one shown to me by] the West Hall Weiyi, a person of Yue enrolled at Tiantong, who had formerly served as
head of hall at Guangfu Monastery.[21] He was from the same birthplace
as my former master. My former master always said, "You should ask
West Hall Yi about the customs of the region."[22]

[39:15]

あるとき、西堂いはく、古蹟の可觀は人間の珍玩なり、いくばくか見來せ
る。道元いはく、見來すくなし。時に西堂いはく、吾那裏に一軸の古蹟あ
り、甚麼次第なり、與老兄看といひて、携來をみれば、嗣書なり。すなは
ち法眼下のにてありけるを、老宿の衣鉢のなかより得たりけり。惟一長老
のにはあらざりけり。かれに、かきたりし樣は、

On one occasion, the West Hall said, "To be able to inspect old cal-
ligraphy is one of the rare pleasures of a human. How many have you
seen?"

Dōgen said, "I've only seen a few."[23]

Whereupon, the West Hall said, "In my place, I have a scroll of old cal-
ligraphy, somewhat questionable.[24] *Let me show it to my elder brother.*"

When I saw what he brought, it was an inheritance certificate. It had

---

20　**When Dōgen was in the Song** (*Dōgen zaisō no toki* 道元在宋のとき): Here and
below, Dōgen refers to himself by name, which we treat here as a first person pronoun.
Dōgen was in Song-dynasty China 1223-1227.

21　**West Hall Weiyi** (*Iitsu seidō* 惟一西堂): Otherwise unknown. "West Hall" (*seidō*
西堂) is a title for the former abbot of another monastery. "Yue" 越 refers to a region
in present-day Zhejiang province; "Tiantong" 天童 is the mountain name of the Jingde
Monastery 景徳寺, in the same region, of which Tiantong Rujing 天童如淨 was abbot
during Dōgen's residence there; "head of hall" (*dōchō* 堂頭) refers to the abbot of a
monastery; there are several monasteries named "Guangfusi" 廣福寺, and the one in
question here is uncertain.

22　**"the customs of the region"** (*kyōfū* 境風): Probably, a reference to the ways of the
Yue region from which both Weiyi and Rujing hailed.

23　**"I've only seen a few"** (*kenrai sukunashi* 見來すくなし): The Kōjakuji 香積寺
manuscript reads here "I've never seen one" (*kenrai seru koto nashi* 見來せることなし).

24　**"somewhat questionable"** (*jinmo shidai nari* 甚麼次第なり): A tentative translation, perhaps meaning "of uncertain provenance" or "questionable authenticity."

200 DŌGEN'S *SHŌBŌGENZŌ* VOLUME III

been in the lineage of Fayan and had been obtained from among the robe and bowl of an elder.[25] It was not Elder Weiyi's own. On it was written the following:

[39:16] {1:427}

初祖摩訶迦葉悟於釋迦牟尼佛、釋迦牟尼佛悟於迦葉佛

かくのごとくかきたり。

"The First Ancestor Mahākāśyapa was awakened under Buddha Śākyamuni; Buddha Śākyamuni was awakened under Buddha Kāśyapa."

It was inscribed like this.

[39:17]

予道元、これらを見しに、正嫡の、正嫡に嗣法あることを決定信受す。未曾見の法なり。佛祖の、冥感して兒孫を護持する時節なり、感激不勝なり。

Upon seeing this, I, Dōgen, became firmly convinced that there is dharma inheritance by a direct descendant from a direct descendant. It was something I had never seen. This was an instance of the buddhas and ancestors using their hidden influence to protect one of their descendants. I was unbearably moved.

[39:18]

雲門下の嗣書とて、宗月長老の、天童の首座職に充せしとき、道元にみせしは、いま嗣書をうる人のつぎかみの師、および西天東地の佛祖をならべつらねて、その下頭に、嗣書をうる人の名字あり。諸佛諸祖より、直にいまの新祖師の名字につらぬるなり。しかあれば、如來より四十餘代、ともに新嗣の名字へきたれり。たとへば、おのおの新祖にさづけたるがごとし。摩訶迦葉・阿難陀等は、餘門のごとくにつらなれり。

When Elder Zongyue held the position of head seat at Tiantong, he showed Dōgen an inheritance certificate from the Yunmen lineage.[26] The [name of the] master just preceding the recipient of the inheritance certificate was lined up in a row with the buddhas and ancestors of Sindh in the West and the Land of the East, and below those was the name of the recipient of the inheritance certificate.[27] There was a direct connection from the buddhas and ancestors to the name of the new ancestral

---

25 **robe and bowl** (*ehatsu* 衣鉢): A term indicating the personal possessions of a monk, auctioned off to other monks of his community following the owner's death.

26 **Elder Zongyue** (*Shūgetsu chōrō* 宗月長老): Otherwise unknown. The "head seat" (*shuso* 首座) is the leader of the monks in the saṃgha hall.

27 **the buddhas and ancestors of Sindh in the West and the Land of the East** (*Saiten Tōchi no busso* 西天東地の佛祖): I.e., the names of the representatives of the Zen lineage in Indian and China.

39. The Inheritance Certificate *Shisho* 嗣書

master.[28] Thus, it extended from the Tathāgata, through more than forty generations, down to and including the name of the new heir. It was as if each had bestowed [the transmission] on the new ancestor. Mahākāśyapa, Ānanda, and the rest, were lined up as in other traditions.[29]

[39:19]

ときに道元、宗月首座に問ふ、和尚、いま五家宗派をつらぬるに、いささか同異あり、そのこころいかん。西天より嫡嫡相嗣せられば、なんぞ同異あらんや。宗月いはく、たとひ同異はるかなりといへども、ただまさに雲門山の佛はかくのごとくなる、と學すべし。釋迦老子、なにによりてか尊重他なる、悟道によりて尊重なり。雲門大師、なにによりてか尊重他なる、悟道によりて尊重なり。道元、この語をきくに、いささか領覽あり。

At the time, Dōgen asked Head Seat Zongyue, "Reverend, what is the meaning of the fact that there are slight discrepancies in the delineation of the lineages of the present five houses?[30] If they have been inherited from successor to successor from Sindh in the West, how could there be any discrepancies?"

Zongyue said, "Even were the discrepancies vast, you should just think that the buddhas of Mount Yunmen are like this. For what was old man Śākya honored? He was honored for his awakening to the way.[31] For what was Great Master Yunmen honored? He was honored for his awakening to the way."

Upon hearing these words, Dōgen had a slight understanding.

---

28 **the new ancestral master** (*shin soshi* 新祖師): As was the custom in Song China, the recipient of the certificate is treated here and below as having already become an ancestor of the fictive Zen family.

29 **Mahākāśyapa, Ānanda, and the rest** (*Makakashō Ananda tō* 摩訶迦葉・阿難陀等): I.e., the members of the lineage beginning with the first and second Indian ancestors — for Dōgen's list of which, see "Shōbōgenzō busso" 正法眼藏佛祖.

30 **"lineages of the present five houses"** (*ima goke shūha* いま五家宗派): I.e., the five lineages (Linji 臨濟, Weiyang 潙仰, Caodong 曹洞, Yunmen 雲門, and Fayan 法眼) recognized in the Chan literature of the Song, all of which originate after the Sixth Ancestor. Given the following sentence, Dōgen's question seems to concern differences in the names of the Indian ancestors supposed to be shared by all Chan factions.

31 **"For what was old man Śākya honored?"** (*Shaka rōshi, nani ni yorite ka sonjūta naru* 釋迦老子、なにによりてか尊重他なる): "Old man Śākya" (*Shaka rōshi* 釋迦老子) is a common Zen term of endearment for Buddha Śākyamuni. The glyph *ta* 他 in *sonjūta* 尊重他 may be read as a colloquial Chinese auxiliary attached to the verb.

[39:20] {1:428}

いま江浙に大刹の主とあるは、おほく臨済・雲門・洞山等の嗣法なり。しかあるに、臨済の遠孫と自称するやから、ままにくはだつる不是あり。いはく、善知識の會下に参じて、頂相一幅、法語一軸を懇請して、嗣法の標準にそなふ。しかあるに、一類の狗子あり、尊宿のほとりに法語・頂相等を懇請して、かくし、たくはふることあまたあるに、晩年におよむで、官家に陪錢し、一院を討得して、住持職に補するときは、法語・頂相の師に嗣法せず、當代の名譽のともがら、あるひは王臣に親附なる長老等に嗣法するときは、得法をとはず、名譽をむさぼるのみなり。かなしむべし、末法惡時、かくのごとくの邪風あることを。かくのごとくのやからのなかに、いまだかつて一人として、佛祖の道を夢にも見聞するあらず。

At present, in Jiangzhe, leaders of the great monasteries mostly have dharma inheritance from Linji, Yunmen, or Dongshan.[32] But a bunch calling themselves distant descendants of Linji occasionally engage in scheming improprieties: joining the community of a wise friend and beseeching him for a scroll with his portrait or a scroll with his dharma words, they provide themselves with a sign of their dharma inheritance.[33] And then there is one kind of dog that, begging in the vicinity of venerables for dharma words, a portrait, or the like, hides them away and builds up a large store of them. Then, in his later years, he bribes government officials and is granted a cloister; and, when the position of abbot is conferred on him, instead of inheriting the dharma from a master whose dharma words or portrait he has, he inherits the dharma from among the bunch that is currently famous or some elder intimately connected with the imperial court. At that time, there is no question of his having attained the dharma; it is just desire for fame. How lamentable that there are such corrupt customs in this evil age at the end of the dharma. Among this type, there has never been one who saw or heard the way of the buddhas and ancestors even in his dreams.

[39:21]

おほよそ法語・頂相等をゆるすことは、教家の講師、および在家の男女等にも授く、行者・商客等にもゆるすなり。その旨、諸家の録にあきらかなり。あるひはその人にあらざるが、みだりに嗣法の證據を望むによりて、一軸の書をもとむこと、有道のいたむところなりといへども、なまじいに援筆するなり。しかるごとき則は、古來の書式によらず、いささか師吾のよしをかく。近來の法は、ただその師の會にて得力すれば、すなはちかの師を師と嗣法するなり。かつてその師の印を得ざれども、ただ入室・上堂に咨参して、長連牀にあるともがら、住院のときは、その師承を擧するにいとまあらざれども、大事打開するとき、その師を師とせるのみおほし。

---

32 **Jiangzhe** (*Kōsetsu* 江浙): I.e., the provinces of Jiangsu and Zhejiang, the heartland of the Southern Song dynasty.

33 **the community of a wise friend** (*zen chishiki no eka* 善知識の會下): I.e., the congregation of a Zen teacher.

39. The Inheritance Certificate *Shisho* 嗣書

In general, in the granting of dharma words, portraits, and such, they are given even to lecturers in the teaching houses, as well as to male and female householders.[34] They are also granted to postulants, merchants, and the like.[35] This point is clear in the records of the various houses. Or, again, an unqualified person, shamelessly desiring proof of dharma inheritance, may seek a scroll of writing; though this may be painful for those who possess the way, they reluctantly take up the brush. In such cases, they do not follow the traditional form of composition, but just write a little something to the effect, "the teacher, I . . . ."[36] The practice in recent times is that, when one gains authority in the community of some master, one immediately inherits the dharma with that master as one's master. This bunch has never received the teacher's certification, but has merely sought instruction in his room-entering and convocations, while spending time on the long platforms; though, once they become abbots of cloisters, they have no time to bring up their inheritance from their master, there are many of them who simply regard as their master the master at the time that the great matter was opened.[37]

[39:22] {1:429}

また龍門の佛眼禪師清遠和尚の遠孫にて、傳藏主といふものありき。かの師傳藏主、また嗣書を帶せり。嘉定のはじめ、隆禪上座、日本國人なりといへども、かの傳藏主病しけるに、隆禪よく傳藏主を看病しけるに、勤勞しきりなるによりて、看病の勞を謝せんがために、嗣書をとりいだして、禮拜せしめけり。見がたきものなり、與儞禮拜といひけり。

---

34 **lecturers in the teaching houses** (*kyōke no kōshi* 教家の講師): I.e., teachers in the Buddhist traditions that emphasize scriptural study. In Song-dynasty China, some Buddhist monasteries were categorized as "Teachings" (*jiao* 教), "Chan" (*chan* 禪), and "Vinaya" (*lü* 律) facilities; in this classification, the abbots of the Teachings monasteries typically belonged to the Tiantai 天台 lineage.

35 **merchants** (*shōkaku* 商客): Although in ordinary parlance, this term typically refers to a traveling merchant, here it may indicate a merchant visitor to the monastery.

36 **write a little something to the effect, "the teacher, I . . . ."** (*isasaka shi go no yoshi o kaku* いささか師吾のよしをかく): A tentative translation; the unusual expression *shigo* 師吾 ("teacher I") may be shorthand for something like "being the teacher," or perhaps simply "teacher so-and-so."

37 **room-entering and convocations** (*nisshitsu jōdō* 入室・上堂): I.e., teaching sessions in the master's quarters and formal addresses in the dharma hall, respectively.

long platforms (*chōrenjō* 長連牀): The extended daises in the saṃgha hall (*sōdō* 僧堂) on which monks of the great assembly (*daishu* 大衆) sat in meditation, chanted sūtras in prayer services, took their meals, and slept at night.

they have no time to bring up their inheritance from their master (*sono shijō o ko suru ni itoma arazaredomo* その師承を舉するにいとまあらざれども): I.e., are too busy to raise the matter of their spiritual patrimony.

the great matter was opened (*daiji dakai* 大事打開): I.e., the meaning of the Buddha's teaching (or of life and death) was understood.

204 DŌGEN'S *SHŌBŌGENZŌ* VOLUME III

Again, there was a person named Canon Prefect Chuan, a distant descendant of Reverend Qingyuan, Chan Master Foyan of Longmen.[38] That Canon Prefect Chuan also had an inheritance certificate. At the beginning of Jiading, Senior Seat Ryūzen, though a person from the Land of Japan, carefully nursed Canon Prefect Chuan when the latter fell ill.[39] Because Ryūzen had been so diligent, in order to thank him for his help in nursing, Canon Prefect Chuan took out his inheritance certificate and allowed him to pay obeisance to it. "It's something one rarely gets to see," he had said, "but *I'll let you pay obeisance to it.*"

[39:23]
それよりこのかた、八年ののち、嘉定十六年癸未あきのころ、道元はじめて天童山に寓居するに、隆禪上座、ねんごろに傳藏主に請して、嗣書を道元にみせしは、その嗣書の樣は、七佛よりのち、臨濟にいたるまで、四十五祖をつらねてかきて、臨濟よりのちの師は、一圓相をつくりて、そのなかにめぐらして、法諱と華字とをうつしかけり。新嗣はをはりに、年月の下頭にかけり。臨濟の尊宿に、かくのごとくの不同あり、としるべし。

After that, eight years later, in the autumn of the junior water year of the sheep, the sixteenth year of Jiading, when Dōgen first lodged at Mount Tiantong, Senior Seat Ryūzen kindly made a request of Canon Prefect Chuan, who permitted Dōgen to see the inheritance certificate.[40] In the format of the inheritance certificate, it listed in a row the forty-five ancestors from the seven buddhas through Linji; for the masters after Linji, there was a circle with the dharma names and signatures copied around the interior. The new heir was last, written beneath the year and month. We should realize that there are such differences among [the inheritance certificates of] the venerables of Linji.

---

38 **Canon Prefect Chuan** (*Den zōsu* 傳藏主): Otherwise unknown. "Canon Prefect" (*zōsu* 藏主) is the title of the monk in charge of the monastic library.

Reverend Qingyuan, Chan Master Foyan of Longmen (*Ryūmon no Butsugen zenji Seion oshō* 龍門の佛眼禪師清遠和尚): I.e., Longmen Qingyuan 龍門清遠 (1067-1120).

39 **Jiading** (*Katei* 嘉定): The Jiading era of the Song Emperor Ningzong 寧宗, 1194-1225.

Senior Seat Ryūzen (*Ryūzen jōza* 隆禪上座): Presumably, the monk Butsugen Ryūzen 佛眼隆禪 of the Kongō Zanmai Cloister 金剛三昧院 on Mount Kōya 高野山. "Senior Seat" (*jōza* 上座) is an honorific for a senior monk, used variously for an abbot, a head monk, an elder, a monk of over twenty years standing, etc.

40 **the junior water year of the sheep, the sixteenth year of Jiading** (*Katei jūroku nen kimi* 嘉定十六年癸未): I.e., 1223, the tenth stem, eighth branch of the sexagenary calendar.

39. The Inheritance Certificate *Shisho* 嗣書　　205

[39:24]

先師天童堂頭、ふかく、人のみだりに嗣法を稱することを、いましむ。誠に先師の會は、これ古佛の會なり、叢林の中興なり。みづからもまだらなる袈裟をかけず。芙蓉山の道楷禪師の衲法衣つたはれりといへども、上堂・陞座にももちいず。おほよそ住持職として、まだらなる法衣、かつて一生のうちにかけず。心あるも、物しらざるも、ともにほめき、眞の善知識なりと尊重す。

My former master, Head of Hall of Tiantong, warned against people's improperly claiming dharma inheritance. My former master's community was truly the assembly of an old buddha, the revival of the monastery. He himself did not wear a patterned *kāṣāya*. Although the patchwork dharma robe of Chan Master Daokai of Mount Furong had come down to him, he did not use it even when ascending to the hall or mounting the seat.[41] In general, while serving as an abbot, he never once donned a patterned dharma robe throughout his entire life.[42] Both the thoughtful and the ignorant alike praised and respected him as a true wise friend.

[39:25] {429}

先師古佛、上堂するに、常に諸方をいましめていはく、近來多く祖道に名をかれるやから、みだりに法衣を搭し、長髮をこのみ、師號に署するを出世の舟航とせり。あはれむべし、誰かこれをすくはん。うらむらくは、諸方の長老、無道心にして、學道せざることを。嗣書・嗣法の因緣を見聞せるもの、なほまれなり、百千人中一箇也無。これ祖道陵遲なり。かくのごとく、よの常にいましむるに、天下の長老うらみず。

In his convocations, my former master, the Old Buddha, regularly admonished those of all quarters, saying,[43]

In recent times, many of those who borrow the name of the way of the ancestors improperly don dharma robes, like to grow out their hair, and regard signing with the title of master as a vessel for appearance in the world.[44] How pitiful. Who can save them? It is regrettable that the el-

---

41　**the patchwork dharma robe of Chan Master Daokai of Mount Furong** (*Fuyōzan no Dōkai zenji no nōhōe* 芙蓉山の道楷禪師の衲法衣): The *kāṣāya* of Furong Daokai 芙蓉道楷 (1043-1118), a leading figure in the Southern Song revival of the Caodong tradition. This robe was supposed to have been passed on to Dōgen by Rujing.

ascending to the hall or mounting the seat (*jōdō shinzo* 上堂・陞座): I.e, during the formal occasions of the dharma hall convocation or sermon from the altar.

42　**In general, while serving as an abbot** (*ōyoso jūjishoku toshite* おほよそ住持職として): Rujing served as abbot of several monasteries before assuming the position at Tiantong.

43　**those of all quarters** (*shohō* 諸方): I.e., assembled monks (or here, likely abbots) of various monasteries. Rujing's words here, given in Japanese, have no known source; perhaps, Dōgen's own recollection.

44　**vessel for appearance in the world** (*shusse no shūkō* 出世の舟航): I.e., a means to gaining promotion to a major abbacy.

206 DŌGEN'S *SHŌBŌGENZŌ* VOLUME III

ders of all quarters lack the mind of the way and do not study the way. Those who have seen or heard the circumstances of dharma certificates and dharma inheritance are even more rare, not one in a hundred thousand. This is the erosion of the way of the ancestors.

When he repeatedly remonstrated in this way, the elders from everywhere did not resent it.[45]

[39:26] {1:430}

しかあればずなはち、誠心に辨道することあらば、嗣書あることを見聞すべし。見聞することあるは、學道なるべし。

Thus, when there is sincere pursuit of the way, one will surely see and hear that there are inheritance certificates; seeing and hearing it is surely the study of the way.

* * * * *

[39:27]

臨濟の嗣書は、まづその名字をかきて、某甲子われに參ず、ともかき、わが會にきたれり、ともかき、入吾堂奥ともかき、嗣吾ともかきて、ついでのごとく前代をつらぬるなり。かれも、いささかいひきたれる法訓あり。いはゆる宗趣は、嗣はおはり・はじめにかかはれず、ただ眞の善知識に相見する、的的の宗旨なり。臨濟にはかくのごとくかけるもあり。まのあたりみしによりて、しるす。

In Linji inheritance certificates, [the master] first writes his name, then writes, "disciple so-and-so inquired of me," or writes, "joined my community," or writes, "entered the interior of my hall," or writes, "inherited from me," and then lines up the previous generations in order.[46] Those, too, have a few dharma instructions handed down by word of mouth. The import of what they say is the clear point that inheritance, whether in the end or the beginning, is only of meeting a true wise friend.[47] In

---

45 **the elders from everywhere did not resent it** (*tenka no chōrō uramizu* 天下の長老うらみず): Presumably, meaning that the abbots who heard these remarks recognized their truth, though it might also mean that they felt no remorse.

46 **"disciple so-and-so inquired of me"** (*bōkōshi ware ni sanzu* 某甲子われに參ず): The four alternative inscriptions given here represent four degrees of intimacy, in ascending order, that a student may have with the master. To "inquire of" (*sanzu* 參ず) a teacher means to visit them and ask about Buddhist teachings or practice. To "join the community" (*e ni kitaru* 會にきたる) means to train under the master as a monk in residence at a monastery where they are abbot. To "enter the interior of the hall" (*nyū dōō* 入堂奥) means to be accepted as a "room-entering disciple" (*nisshitsu deshi* 入室弟子) — i.e., a disciple who has individual access to the teacher in their private rooms in the abbot's quarters. Finally, to "inherit from" (*shi* 嗣) a master is to be recognized as a dharma heir.

47 **inheritance, whether in the end or the beginning** (*shi wa owari hajime ni kakawarezu* 嗣はおはり・はじめにかかはれず): The exact sense of "beginning" and

39. The Inheritance Certificate *Shisho* 嗣書　　　207

Linji, there are some written like this. Since I have seen one with my own eyes, I present it here.[48]

[39:28]

了派藏主 威武人也 今吾子也 德光參侍徑山杲和尚 徑山嗣夾山勤 勤嗣楊岐
演 演嗣海會白雲端 端嗣楊岐會 會嗣慈明圓 圓嗣汾陽昭 昭嗣首山念 念嗣
風穴昭 昭嗣南院顒 顒嗣興化裝 裝嗣是臨濟高祖之長嫡也

Canon Prefect Liaopai is a person of Weiwu.[49] He is now my offspring. Deguang trained under Reverend Gao of Mount Jing.[50] Jingshan inherited from Qin of Mount Jia.[51] Qin inherited from Yan of Yangqi.[52] Yan inherited from Paiyun Duan of Haihu.[53] Duan inherited from Hui of Yangqi.[54] Hui inherited from Yuan of Ciming.[55] Yuan inherited from Zhao of Fenyang.[56] Zhao inherited from Nian of Mount Shou.[57] Nian inherited from Zhao of Fengxue.[58] Zhao inherited from Yong of

"end" here is subject to interpretation. Perhaps the most plausible is that they refer to the beginning and end of the relationship between master and disciple; but they have also been taken as the disciple's first and last master, or as first and last in the order of disciples receiving inheritance from a given master.

48　**Since I have seen one with my own eyes, I present it here** (*mano atari mishi ni yorite, shirusu* まのあたりみしによりて、しるす): What follows (in section 28) is entirely in Chinese, presumably copied down by Dōgen from the inheritance certificate he saw.

49　**Canon Prefect Liaopai is a person of Weiwu** (*Ryōha zōsu Ibu nin ya* 了派藏主威武人也): I.e., Wuji Liaopai 無際了派 (1149-1224), abbot of Tiantong 天童 when Dōgen first arrived there. His title here of "Canon Prefect" (*zōsu* 藏主) presumably reflects his previous office at Mount Ayuwang 阿育山, when his master, Deguang 德光, was abbot there. Weiwu 威武 was in Jian'an (present Fujian).

50　**Deguang** (*Tokkō* 德光): I.e., Zhuoan Deguang 拙菴德光 (1121-1203), the author of the certificate, referring to himself in the third person.

Reverend Gao of Mount Jing (*Kinzan Kō oshō* 徑山杲和尚): I.e., Dahui Zonggao 大慧宗杲 (1089-1163), who twice served as abbot of the Xingsheng Wanshou Chansi on Mount Jing (*Jingshan xingsheng wanshou chansi* 徑山興聖萬壽禪寺) in Hangzhou 杭州, Lin'an Prefecture 臨安府. Perhaps the most famous Linji master of the Southern Song, sharply criticized by Dōgen.

51　**Qin of Mount Jia** (*Kassan Gon* 夾山勤): I.e., Yuanwu Keqin 圜悟克勤 (1063-1135).

52　**Yan of Yangqi** (*Yōgi En* 楊岐演): I.e., Wuzu Fayan 五祖法演 (d. 1104).

53　**Paiyun Duan of Haihu** (*Kaie Hakuun Tan* 海會白雲端): I.e., Paiyun Shouduan 白雲守端 (1025-1072).

54　**Hui of Yangqi** (*Yōgi E* 楊岐會): I.e., Yangqi Fanghui 楊岐方會 (992-1049).

55　**Yuan of Ciming** (*Jimyō En* 慈明圓): I.e., Shishuang Chuyuan 石霜楚圓 (986-1039).

56　**Zhao of Fenyang** (*Fun'yō Shō* 汾陽昭): I.e., Fenyang Shanzhao 汾陽善昭 (947-1024).

57　**Nian of Mount Shou** (*Shuzan Nen* 首山念): I.e., Shoushan Shengnian 首山省念 (926-993).

58　**Zhao of Fengxue** (*Fūketsu Shō* 風穴沼): I.e., Fengxue Yanzhao 風穴延沼 (896-973).

208 DŌGEN'S *SHŌBŌGENZŌ* VOLUME III

Nanyuan.[59] *Yong inherited from Jiang of Xinghua.*[60] *Jiang's inheritance was as the oldest legitimate heir of the Eminent Ancestor Linji.*[61]

[39:29] {1:431}

これは、阿育王山佛照禪師德光、かきて派無際にあたふるを、天童住持なりしとき、小師僧智庚、ひそかにもちきたりて、了然寮にて道元にみせし。ときに大宋嘉定十七年甲申正月二十一日、はじめてこれをみる、喜感いくそばくぞ。すなはち佛祖の冥感なり、燒香禮拜して披看す。

This was written by Deguang, Chan Master Fozhao, of Mount Ayuwang, who gave it to Pai Wuji.[62] When the latter was abbot of Tiantong, the young monk Zhigeng confidentially brought it and showed it to Dōgen in the Liaoran quarters.[63] I first saw this on the twenty-first day of the first month of the senior wood year of the monkey, the seventeenth year of Jiading in the Great Song.[64] How great was my joy! It was surely due to the hidden influence of the buddhas and ancestors. Burning incense and making bows, I unrolled and examined it.

[39:30]

この嗣書を請出することは、去年七月のころ、師廣都寺、ひそかに寂光堂にして道元にかたれり。道元ちなみに都寺にとふ、如今、たれ人かこれを帶持せる。都寺いはく、堂頭老漢那裏有相似。のちに請出ねんごろにせば、さだめて見することあらん。道元、このことばをききしより、もとむるこころざし日夜に休せず。このゆえに今年、ねんごろに小師の僧智庚を堀請し、一片心をなげて請得せりしなり。

---

59 **Yong of Nanyuan** (*Nan'in Gyō* 南院顒): Nanyuan Huiyong 南院慧顒 (d. 930).

60 **Jiang of Xinghua** (*Kōke Shō* 興化獎): I.e., Xinghua Cunjiang 興化存獎 (830-888).

61 **the Eminent Ancestor Linji** (*Rinzai kōso* 臨濟高祖): I.e., Linji Yixuan 臨濟義玄 (d. 866), founder of the Linji 臨濟 lineage.

62 **Deguang, Chan Master Fozhao, of Mount Ayuwang** (*Aikuōzan Busshō zenji Tokkō* 阿育王山佛照禪師德光): I.e., Zhuoan Deguang 拙菴德光, who had also served as abbot at Ayuwang 阿育王, an important monastery near Tiantong 天童, famous for its relic of the Buddha.

Pai Wuji (*Ha Musai* 派無際): I.e., Wuji Liaopai 無際了派.

63 **the young monk Zhigeng** (*shōshi sō Chikō* 小師僧智庚): Otherwise unknown. "Young monk" translates *shōshi sō* 小師僧, a term sometimes said to refer to monks with less than ten years since their bhikṣu ordination; in modern usage, a "disciple monk"; here, more likely simply a reference to a young monk in training.

the Liaoran quarters (*Ryōnen ryō* 了然寮): The residence at Tiantong 天童 of Dōgen's Japanese master, Myōzen 明全 (1184-1225), with whom the former traveled to China. Dōgen may have been serving as Myōzen's attendant at the residence.

64 **the twenty-first day of the first month of the senior wood year of the monkey, the seventeenth year of Jiading in the Great Song** (*Daisō Katei jūshichi nen kōshin shōgatsu nijūichi nichi* 大宋嘉定十七年甲申正月二十一日): I.e., 11 February 1224, the first stem, ninth branch of the sexagenary calendar.

39. The Inheritance Certificate *Shisho* 嗣書　　　209

I had asked that this inheritance certificate be taken out because, in the seventh month of the previous year, the Prior Shiguang had told Dōgen about it in private in the Jiguang Hall.[65] At the time, Dōgen asked the Prior, "Who has it now?"

The Prior said, "*It seems to be in the old man head of hall's place.*[66] Later, if you ask him politely to take it out, I'm sure you can see it."

After Dōgen heard these words, my desire to see it did not let up day or night. Therefore, in the following year, I politely begged the young monk Zhigeng and, with my single-mindedness, I got my request.

[39:31]
そのかける地は、白絹の表背せるにかく。表紙はあかき錦なり、軸は玉なり、長九寸ばかり、濶七尺餘なり。閑人にはみせず。道元すなはち智庚を謝す、さらに即時に堂頭に参じて燒香禮拜して無際和尚に謝す。ときに無際いわく、遮一段事、少得見知、如今老兄知得、便是學道之實歸也。ときに道元、喜感無勝。

The material on which it was written was mounted on white silk. The backing was red brocade; the spindle was jade.[67] The height was just nine inches; the length, more than seven feet.[68] It was not shown to outsiders.

Dōgen thanked Zhigeng; further, I immediately called upon the head of hall, burned incense, made bows, and thanked Reverend Wuji. Whereupon, Wuji said, "*This is something that few are able to see for themselves. Now, elder brother, you know of it, and it will be a true refuge in your study of the way.*"

At the time, Dōgen's joy was unbearable.

65　**Prior Shiguang** (*Shikō tsūsu* 師廣都寺): Otherwise unknown. The prior (*tsūsu* 都寺) was the monastic officer in charge of overall administration.

Jiguang Hall (*Jakkō dō* 寂光堂): "Tranquil Light Hall," name of the outer abbot's quarters at Tiantong 天童.

66　**"in the old man head of hall's place"** (*dōchō rōkan nari* 堂頭老漢那裏): I.e., in the abbot's quarters.

67　**The backing was red brocade** (*hyōshi wa akaki nishiki nari* 表紙はあかき錦なり): The "backing" (*hyōshi* 表紙; literally, "cover paper") refers to the sturdier material to which the silk is attached that serves as its cover when the scroll is rolled up.

68　**The height was just nine inches; the length, more than seven feet** (*take kyū sun bakari, hirosa shichi shaku amari nari* 長九寸ばかり、濶七尺餘なり): The certificate was a long, narrow scroll unrolled horizontally for reading. The length of the Chinese "foot" (*chi* 尺) varied somewhat over time but was roughly equal to the English foot; the "inch" (*cun* 寸) was one tenth of a *chi*.

210　DŌGEN'S *SHŌBŌGENZŌ* VOLUME III

[39:32] {1:432}

のちに寶慶のころ、道元、台山・雁山等に雲遊するついでに、平田の萬年
寺にいたる。ときの住持は、福州の元鼐和尚なり。宗鑑長老退院ののち、
元鼐和尚、補す、叢席を一興す。人事のついでに、むかしよりの佛祖の家
風を往來せしむるに、大爲・仰山の令嗣話を擧するに、長老いはく、曾看
我這裏嗣書也否。道元のいはく、いかでか看ることをえん。長老すなはち
みづからたちて、嗣書をささげていはく、這箇は縱ひ親しき人なりとも、
またたとひ侍僧のとしをへたるといへども、これを見せしめず。これすな
はち佛祖の法訓なり。しかあれども、元鼐ひごろ出城し、見知府のために
在城のとき、一夢を感ずるにいはく、大梅山法常禪師とおぼしき高僧あ
りて、梅華一枝をさしあげていはく、もし既に船舷をこゆる實人あらんに
は、華を惜しむことなかれ、といひて、梅華をわれにあたふ。元鼐おぼえ
ずして夢中に吟じていはく、未跨船舷、好與三十棒。しかあるに、不經五
日、與老兄相見す。いはんや老兄既に船舷跨來、この嗣書、また梅華の綾
にかけり。大梅のをしふるところならん、夢想と符合するゆえにとりいだ
すなり。老兄、もしわれに嗣法せんともとむや、縱いもとむとも、をしむ
べきにあらず。

Later, during the Baoqing era, while Dōgen was wandering to Mount
Tai, Mount Yan, and so on, I arrived at the Wannian Monastery of Ping-
tian.[69] At the time, the abbot was Reverend Yuanzi of Fuzhou.[70] After
the retirement of Elder Zongjian, Reverend Yuanzi filled the post and
greatly revived the monastic seat.[71] When I had an interview with him,
we conversed about the house styles of the buddhas and ancestors from
ancient times; and, when we raised the topic of Dawei and Yangshan's
talk on designating an heir, the Elder said, "*Have you ever seen the inheritance certificate I have here?*"[72]

69　**the Baoqing era** (*Hōkyō* 寶慶): The Baoqing era of the Emperor Lizong 理宗 corresponds to CE 1225-1228.

wandering to Mount Tai, Mount Yan, and so on (*Daisan Ganzan tō ni unyū suru* 台
山・雁山等に雲遊する): "Mount Tai" (*Daisan* 台山) here refers to Mount Tiantai 天台
山, home of several monasteries, including the Guoqing Monastery 國清寺, headquarters
of the Tiantai school, and the Wannian Monastery 萬年寺, referred to here; "Mount Yan"
(*Ganzan* 雁山) is the mountain name of the Neng'ren Monastery 能仁寺 in Wenzhou
溫州. During his stay in China, Dōgen never left the areas known at the time as the
Liangzhe West Circuit (*Liangzhe xilu* 兩浙西路) and the Liangzhe East Circuit (*Liangzhe tonglu* 兩浙東路), which together have been called Zhejiang Province 浙江省 from
the Ming dynasty down to the present.

70　**Reverend Yuanzi of Fuzhou** (*Fukushū no Genshi oshō* 福州の元鼐和尚): Also read
Gensu. Otherwise unknown.

71　**Elder Zongjian** (*Sōkan chōrō* 宗鑑長老): Identity uncertain.

72　**Dawei and Yangshan's talk on designating an heir** (*Daii Kyōzan no ryōshi wa* 大
爲・仰山の令嗣話): This conversation, between Weishan Lingyou 爲山靈祐 (771-853)
and his future dharma heir Yangshan Huiji 仰山慧寂 (803-887), is recorded in Dōgen's
shinji Shōbōgenzō 眞字正法眼藏 (DZZ.5:180, case 103):

　大爲山大圓禪師坐次、仰山侍立。師云、寂子、近日宗門中令嗣作麼生。仰曰、大

39. The Inheritance Certificate *Shisho* 嗣書　　211

Dōgen said, "How could I have seen it?"

The Elder immediately stood up himself, presented it to me, and said:

I would not show this even to people close to me, even to an acolyte monk after years of service. This is the rule of the buddhas and ancestors. However, recently, when Yuanzi went out to the city and stayed there to see the prefectural governor, I had a dream, in which an eminent monk I thought was Chan Master Fachang of Mount Damei held out a sprig of plum blossoms and said, "If there is a real person who has crossed the gunwales, do not begrudge him the flowers."[73]

So saying, he gave me the plum blossoms. Without thinking, in the dream, Yuanzi recited the lines, *"Even before you crossed the gunwales, I should have given you thirty blows."*[74]

有人疑著此事。師云、寂子又作麼生。仰云、某甲祇管困來合眼、健即坐禪。所以未曾說著。師云、到這田地也難得。仰曰、據某甲見處、著一句語亦不得。師云、子爲一人也不得。仰云、自古聖人盡皆如是。師云、大有人笑汝與麼祇對。仰云、解笑某甲是某甲同參。師云、出頭作麼生。仰遶禪牀一匝。師云、裂破古今。

> When Chan Master Dayuan of Mount Dawei was sitting, Yangshan stood by him in attendance. The Master asked, "Jizi, what do you make of the present-day issue of designating an heir in our lineage?"
> Yang replied, "There are many people with doubts about this matter."
> The Master said, "Jizi, again, what do you make of it?"
> Yang said, "When I get tired, I just close my eyes; when I'm healthy, I sit in meditation. So, I've never said anything."
> The Master said, "It's hard to reach such a field."
> Yang said, "As far as I can see, I can't say even a word."
> The Master said, "You can't do it even for someone."
> Yang said, "From ancient times all the sages have been like this."
> The Master said, "Many are the people who would laugh at you for such a reply."
> Yang said, "To laugh at me is to practice with me."
> The Master said, "What about putting yourself forward?"
> Yang circumambulated the [master's] meditation seat, once around.
> The Master said, "Ripping apart past and present."

73　**Chan Master Fachang of Mount Damei** (*Daibaizan Hōjō zenji* 大梅山法常禪師): I.e., Damei Fachang 大梅法常 (752-839), a follower of Mazu Daoyi 馬祖道一. He is said to have spent some forty years in isolation on Mount Damei 大梅山 (in modern Zhejiang). His biography can be found at *Jingde chuandeng lu* 景德傳燈錄, T.2076.51:254c2ff. His appearance in Yuanzi's dream of the plum branch likely represents an association with his sobriquet Damei 大梅 ("Great Plum").

"a real person who has crossed the gunwales" (*sengen o koyuru jitsunin* 船舷をこゆる實人): I.e., an authentic practitioner from across the sea.

74　**"Even before you crossed the gunwales, I should have given you thirty blows"** (*mika sengen, kō yo sanjū bō* 未跨船舷、好與三十棒): From a famous exchange between Chan Master Deshan Xuanjian 德山宣鑑 (780-865) and a monk from the Korean kingdom of Silla. The anecdote is recorded in Dōgen's *shinji Shōbōgenzō* 眞字正法眼藏 (DZZ.5:144, case 31):

And now, *not five days have passed, and I meet my elder brother.*[75] What's more, the elder brother has crossed the gunwales, and this inheritance certificate is written on plum blossom figured damask. It must be what Damei was teaching me. It is because it matches my dream vision, that I've brought this out. Do you seek to inherit the dharma from me? Should you seek it, I could not refuse.

[39:33]
道元、信感さしおくところなし。嗣書を請すべしといへども、ただ燒香禮拜して、恭敬供養するのみなり。ときに燒香侍者法寧といふ人あり、はじめて嗣書を見る、といひき。

Dōgen could not help but believe him. Although I was supposed to request an inheritance certificate, I only offered my respects, merely burning incense and bowing. At the time, there was an incense acolyte named Faning there, who said that it was the first time he had seen the inheritance certificate.[76]

[39:34] {1:433}
道元ひそかに思惟しき、この一段の事、まことに佛祖の冥資にあらざれば、見聞なほかたし。邊地の愚人として、なんのさいはひありてか數番、これをみる。感涙霑袖。

Dōgen thought to himself, truly without the unseen help of the buddhas and ancestors, it would be hard to experience this event. By what good fortune could an ignorant person from a peripheral land see these several times? Tears of joy wet my sleeves.

鼎州德山見性大師〈嗣龍潭、諱宣鑑〉小參示衆云、老僧今夜不答話、問話者三十棒。時有僧出禮拜。師便打。僧曰、某甲話也未問、因甚打某甲。師云、儞甚處人。僧曰、新羅人。師曰、未跨船舷、好與三十拄杖。

Great Master Jianxing of Deshan in Zhenzhou (succeeded Longtan, named Xuanjian) addressed the assembly at a small convocation saying, "This evening, I won't say any answers, and anyone who says a question will get thirty blows."
At that time, there was a monk who came forward and bowed. The Master hit him.
The monk said, "I haven't said a question yet. Why did you hit me?"
The Master said, "Where are you from?"
The monk said, "I'm from Silla."
The Master said, "Even before you crossed the gunwales, I should have given you thirty blows of my staff."

75 **my elder brother** (*rōhin* 老兄): I.e, "you (Dōgen)."

76 **incense acolyte named Faning** (*shōkō jisha Hōnei to iu hito* 燒香侍者法寧といふ人): Otherwise unknown. The "incense acolyte" (*shōkō jisha* 燒香侍者) is the attendant tasked with assisting the abbot in offering incense; one of the "five acolytes" (*go jisha* 五侍者) in a Zen monastery.

39. The Inheritance Certificate *Shisho* 嗣書　213

[39:35]

ときに維摩室・大舎堂等に、閑関無人なり。

At the time, the Weimo room, Dasheng hall, and the rest, were silent and empty.[77]

[39:36]

この嗣書の地は、梅の綾のしろきにかけり。長九寸餘、濶一尋餘なり。軸子は黄玉なり、表紙は錦なり。

The material on which this inheritance certificate was written was white damask silk with a plum pattern.[78] The height was over nine inches; the length was over eight feet.[79] The spindle was yellow jade; the backing was brocade.

[39:37]

道元、台山より天童にかへる路程に、大梅山護聖寺の旦過に宿するに、大梅祖師きたり、開華せる一枝の梅華をさづくる靈夢を感ず。祖鑑もとも仰憑するものなり。その一枝華の縦横は、一尺餘なり。梅華あに優曇華にあらざらんや。夢中と覺中と、おなじく眞實なるべし。道元在宋のあひだ、歸國よりのち、いまだ人にかたらず。

On my way back to Tiantong from Mount Tai, Dōgen stayed at the overnight quarters at Husheng Monastery on Mount Damei.[80] There, I experienced a numinous dream, in which the Ancestral Master Damei came and presented me with a sprig of plum blossoms in full bloom. The mirror of the ancestors is a most reliable thing. The diameter of the blossoms on the sprig was more than one foot. How could the plum blossoms be anything but *udumbara* blossoms? What happens in dreams and

---

77　**Weimo room, Dasheng hall, and the rest** (*Yuima shitsu Taisha dō tō* 維摩室・大舎堂等): I.e., rooms associated with the abbot's quarters at Wannian Monastery 萬年寺; the Dasheng hall 大舎堂 was the front abbot's quarters (*qian fangzhang* 前方丈), immediately behind the dharma hall. (See "Gozan jissatsu zu" 五山十刹圖, *Zengaku daijiten* 禅学大辞典, *Bekkan* 別巻, p. 13.) This arresting recollection and that of the preceding section do not occur in the Kōjakuji 香積寺 text.

78　**The material on which this inheritance certificate was written was white damask silk with a plum pattern** (*kono shisho no chi wa, ume no aya no shiroki ni kakeri* この嗣書の地は、梅の綾のしろきにかけり): Some MS witnesses have here, "This inheritance certificate was written on white damask patterned with fallen plum" (*kono shisho wa rakuchi mei rin no shiroki ni kakeri* この嗣書は落地梅綾のしろきにかけり).

79　**the length was over eight feet** (*hirosa hito hiro yo* 濶一尋餘): The term *hito hiro* is the Japanese rendering of the Chinese *yi xun* 一尋, a measure, like the English "fathom," based on the armspan; standardized as eight Chinese feet (*chi* 尺).

80　**overnight quarters at Husheng Monastery on Mount Damei** (*Daibaizan Goshōji no tanga* 大梅山護聖寺の旦過): The guest quarters of the monastery founded by Damei Fachang 大梅法常. The term *tanga* 旦過 refers to a monk's one-night stay at a monastery; here, short for *tangaryō* 旦過寮, the accommodations for such monks.

214 DŌGEN'S *SHŌBŌGENZŌ* VOLUME III

in waking must be equally real. While Dōgen was in the Song and after my return to this land, I have never spoken of this to anyone.

* * * * *

[39:38]
いまわが洞山門下に、嗣書をかけるは、臨濟等にかけるには、ことなり。佛祖の衣裡にかかれけるを、青原高祖したしく曹溪の几前にして、手の指より淨血をいだしてかき、正傳せられけるなり。この手の指血に、曹溪の指血を合して書傳せられける、と相傳せり。初祖・二祖のところにも、合血の儀おこなはれける、と相傳す。これ、吾子參吾などとはかかず、諸佛および七佛のかきつたへられける嗣書の儀なり。

The writing of inheritance certificates in our present Dongshan lineage differs from their writing in Linji and the rest.[81] What was affixed within the robes of the buddhas and ancestors, the Eminent Ancestor Qingyuan received in direct transmission, personally drawing pure blood from his finger and writing at the desk of Caoxi.[82] Tradition has it that it was written and transmitted by mingling the blood from his finger with the blood from Caoxi's finger. Tradition has it that the rite of mingling blood was carried out in the case of the First Ancestor and Second Ancestor as well. Without writing such things as "my offspring" or "made inquiries of me," this is the procedure for the inheritance certificate written and handed down among the buddhas as well as the seven buddhas.[83]

---

81 **our present Dongshan lineage** (*ima waga Tōzan monka* いまわが洞山門下): I.e., Dōgen's Caotong (Sōtō 曹洞) lineage, descended from Dongshan Liangjie 洞山良价 (807-869).

82 **What was affixed within the robes of the buddhas and ancestors** (*busso no eri ni kakarekeru* 佛祖の衣裏にかかれける): Likely an allusion to the famous parable in the *Lotus Sūtra*, in which a priceless gem (representing the spiritual wealth of the buddha nature) is sewn into the lining of a garment (*Miaofo lianhua jing* 妙法蓮華經, T.262.9:29a6-16).

Eminent Ancestor Qingyuan received in direct transmission, personally drawing pure blood from his finger and writing at the desk of Caoxi (*Seigen kōso shitashiku Sōkei no kizen ni shite, te no yubi yori jōketsu o idashite kaki, shōden serarekeru nari* 青原高祖したしく曹溪の几前にして、手の指より淨血をいだしてかき、正傳せられけるなり): "Eminent Ancestor Qingyuan" (*Seigen kōso* 青原高祖) refers to Qingyuan Xingsi 青原行思 (d. 740), founder of the lineage leading to Dongshan 洞山; "Caoxi" (Sōkei 曹溪) refers to Qingyuan's master, the Sixth Ancestor, Caoxi Huineng 曹溪慧能. The translation here follows the most likely reading of the Japanese grammar in making "Qingyuan" the subject of "writing," but it is highly unlikely that Dōgen wants us to think Qingyuan wrote out his own inheritance certificate. Dōgen's source for the tradition he describes here, as well as that, mentioned just below, of an inheritance certificate written in the mingled blood of Bodhidharma and Huike 慧可, is unknown.

83 **the buddhas as well as the seven buddhas** (*shobutsu oyobi shichi butsu* 諸佛および七佛): I.e., all the buddhas, including the seven buddhas of the past of which Śākyamuni is the last; see Supplementary Notes, s.v. "Seven buddhas."

39. The Inheritance Certificate *Shisho* 嗣書   215

[39:39] {1:434}

しかあればしるべし、曹溪の血氣は、かたじけなく青原の淨血に和合し、
青原の淨血、したしく曹溪の親血に和合して、まのあたり印證をうること
は、ひとり高祖青原和尚のみなり、餘祖のおよぶところにあらず。この事
子をしれるともがらは、佛法はただ青原のみに正傳せる、と道取するな
り。

Thus, we should realize that, the lifeblood of Caoxi being graciously mingled with the pure blood of Qingyuan, and the pure blood of Qingyuan intimately mingled with the parental blood of Caoxi, the personal reception of the seal of verification was only by the Eminent Ancestor Reverend Qingyan alone and was not something attained by any other ancestor. Those who know the facts of this matter say that the buddha dharma was directly transmitted only to Qingyuan.[84]

嗣書
The Inheritance Certificate[85]

[39:40]

先師古佛天童堂上大和尚、しめしていはく、諸佛かならず嗣法あり、いは
ゆる、釋迦牟尼佛者、迦葉佛に嗣法す、迦葉佛者、拘那含牟尼佛に嗣法
す、拘那含牟尼佛者、拘留孫佛に嗣法するなり。かくのごとく佛佛相嗣し
て、いまにいたると信受すべし。これ學佛道なり。

My former master, the Old Buddha, Most Reverend Chief of Hall of Tiantong, taught:[86]

The buddhas always have dharma inheritance. That is, Buddha Śākyamuni inherited the dharma from Buddha Kāśyapa; Buddha Kāśyapa inherited the dharma from Buddha Kanakamuni; Buddha Kanakamuni

---

84 **the buddha dharma was directly transmitted only to Qingyuan** (*buppō wa tada Seigen nomi ni shōden seru* 佛法はただ青原のみに正傳せる): I.e., Qingyuan 青原 represents the principal heir to the Sixth Ancestor. Dongshan 洞山, the founder of Dōgen's lineage, was, of course, descended from Qingyuan.

85 **The Inheritance Certificate** (*shisho* 嗣書): This title apparently represents the beginning of the original colophon, marking the end of the document as it was first composed. The remainder of the colophon, with time and place of composition, appears at this point in the Kōjakuji MS but in our text here is found below the following appended material. The Satomi 里見 MS holograph seems to treat these words as the title of what follows here.

86 **My former master, the Old Buddha, Most Reverend Chief of Hall of Tiantong** (*senshi kobutsu Tendō dōjō daioshō* 先師古佛天童堂上大和尚): I.e., Tiantong Rujing 天童如淨. Rujing's words, given here in Japanese, are not recorded elsewhere and apparently represent Dōgen's own report.

216 DŌGEN'S *SHŌBŌGENZŌ* VOLUME III

inherited the dharma from Buddha Krakucchanda.[87] We should have faith that buddha after buddha has inherited in this way down to the present. This is studying the way of the buddhas.[88]

[39:41]

ときに道元まうす、迦葉佛入涅槃ののち、釋迦牟尼佛は始めて出世成道せり。いはんやまた賢劫の諸佛、いかにしてか莊嚴劫の諸佛に嗣法せん、この道理いかん。

At the time, Dōgen said,

Buddha Śākyamuni appeared in the world and attained the way only after Buddha Kāśyapa had entered nirvāṇa. Not to mention, moreover, [the problem of] how the buddhas of the Worthy Kalpa could inherit the dharma from the buddhas of the Adornment Kalpa.[89] What is the reasoning here?

[39:42]

先師いはく、なんぢがいふところは、聽教の解なり、十聖三賢等の道なり、佛祖嫡嫡の道にあらず。わが佛佛相傳の道は、しかあらず。釋迦牟尼佛、まさしく迦葉佛に嗣法せり、とならひきたるなり。釋迦佛の、嗣法してのちに、迦葉佛は入涅槃すと參學するなり。釋迦佛、もし迦葉佛に嗣法せざらんには、天然外道とおなじかるべし、誰か釋迦佛を信ずるあらん。かくのごとく佛佛相嗣して、いまにおよびきたれるによりて、箇箇佛ともに正嗣なり。つらなれるにあらず、あつまれるにあらず。まさにかくのごとく佛佛相嗣すると學するなり。諸阿笈摩教のいふところの劫量・壽量等にかかはらざるべし。もしひとへに釋迦佛よりおこれりといはば、わづかに二千餘年なり、ふるきにあらず。相嗣もわづかに四十餘代なり、あらたなるといひぬべし。この佛嗣は、しかのごとく學するにあらず。釋迦佛は迦葉佛に嗣法すると學し、迦葉佛は釋迦佛に嗣法すると學するなり。かくのごとく學するとき、まさに諸佛諸祖の嗣法にてあるなり。

My former master said,

What you say is the understanding of the heard teachings, the way of the ten sages and three worthies, not the way of successor after successor of buddhas and ancestors.[90] Our way of the transmission of

---

87 **Śākyamuni** (*Shakamuni* 釋迦牟尼); **Kāśyapa** (*Kashō* 迦葉); **Kanakamuni** (*Kunagonmuni* 拘那含牟尼); **Krakucchanda** (*Kuruson* 拘留孫): I.e., the seventh, sixth, fifth, and fourth, respectively, of the seven buddhas of the past, those appearing in our Worthy Kalpa (*kengō* 賢劫; S. *bhadra-kalpa*); see Supplementary Notes, s.v. "Seven buddhas."

88 **This is studying the way of the buddhas** (*kore gaku butsudō nari* これ學佛道なり): Parsing the expression *gaku butsudō* 學佛道 according to its use elsewhere in the *Shōbōgenzō*. However, the variant text of this chapter, as well as some versions of our text, read here *gakubutsu no dō* 學佛の道 ("the way of studying the buddhas").

89 **Worthy Kalpa** (*kengō* 賢劫); **Adornment Kalpa** (*shōgongō* 莊嚴劫): See above, Note 8.

90 **the understanding of the heard teachings** (*chōkyō no ge* 聽教の解): I.e., the view of the early scriptural literature; akin to "the teachings of the *āgamas*" later in this section.

39. The Inheritance Certificate *Shisho* 嗣書　217

buddha after buddha is not like this. We study that Buddha Śākyamuni did indeed inherit the dharma from Buddha Kāśyapa. We study that Buddha Kāśyapa entered nirvāṇa only after Buddha Śākya inherited the dharma. If Buddha Śākyamuni had not inherited the dharma from Buddha Kāśyapa, it would be the same as an other path of natural occurrence; who would have faith in Buddha Śākya?[91] Because buddha after buddha has inherited in this way reaching down to the present, each and every buddha is a direct heir. They are not lined up; they are not bunched together.[92] We study that truly buddha after buddha inherits in this way. It has nothing to do with the numbers of kalpas or numbers of lifespans discussed in the teachings of the *āgamas*.[93] If we say it occurred only from Buddha Śākya, it is merely two thousand and some years, not very old. The inheritance, too, is a mere forty-some generations and would have to be called something new. This inheritance of the buddhas is not studied in this way. We study that Buddha Śākya inherited the dharma from Buddha Kāśyapa; we study that Buddha Kāśyapa inherited the dharma from Buddha Śākya.[94] When we study in this way, this is truly the dharma inheritance of the buddhas and the ancestors.

[39:43] {435}
この時道元、はじめて佛祖の嗣法あることを稟受するのみにあらず、從來の舊窠をも脱落するなり。

It was then that Dōgen not only first accepted that there was a dharma inheritance of the buddhas and ancestors but also sloughed off his past old nest.[95]

正法眼藏嗣書第三十九
Treasury of the True Dharma Eye
The Inheritance Certificate
Number 39[96]

---

the ten sages and three worthies (*jisshō sanken* 十聖三賢): See above, Note 19.

91　**other path of natural occurrence** (*tennen gedō* 天然外道): See above, section 11.

92　**They are not lined up; they are not bunched together** (*tsuranareru ni arazu, atsumareru ni arazu* つらなれるにあらず、あつまれるにあらず): Probably meaning, "they are neither arrayed across time nor simultaneous."

93　**the *āgamas*** (*agōma* 阿笈摩): I.e., the early, non-Mahāyāna Buddhist sūtras.

94　**Buddha Kāśyapa inherited the dharma from Buddha Śākya** (*Kashō butsu wa Shaka butsu ni shihō suru* 迦葉佛は釋迦佛に嗣法する): The claim that the transmission goes both forward and back through time is repeated several times in the *Shōbōgenzō*.

95　**sloughed off his past old nest** (*jūrai no kyūka o mo datsuraku suru* 從來の舊窠をも脱落する): A mixed metaphor for getting free from fixed ways of thinking. For the use of "slough off" (*datsuraku* 脱落), see Supplementary Notes, s.v. "Slough off."

96　This end title is supplied by Kawamura's edition; it does not occur in the manuscript.

218 DŌGEN'S *SHŌBŌGENZŌ* VOLUME III

[Ryūmonji MS:]

于時日本仁治二年歳次辛丑三月二七日、觀音導利興聖寶林寺、
宋傳法沙門道元記

Recorded at Kannon Dōri Kōshō Hōrin Monastery; twenty-seventh day, third month of the junior metal year of the ox, the second year of Ninji in Japan [9 May 1241], by the Śramaṇa Dōgen, who entered the Song and transmitted the dharma[97]

佛祖傳法語假名嗣書終、靈巖山興惠禪寺住持比丘喆卤賢拜

Copied the kana "Inheritance Certificate" of the dharma words transmitted by the buddhas and ancestors. Obeisance by Bhikṣu Tessō Ken, abbot of Reiganzan Kōtoku Zen Monastery[98]

入室的傳之外、不可披見、及他眼者徧身紅爛、可祕可祕、
佛祖之靈感勿生疑。
右太宋寶慶元季九月十八日、前住天童景德寺堂頭和尚如淨大和尚授
道元式如是。
祖日侍者于時燒香侍者也、宗端知客・廣平侍者等周旋行此戒儀、
太宋寶慶之中傳之。

Those without the transmission of entering the room are not permitted ever to see this, till their eyes are all red and rotten. Keep it secret; keep it secret. Do not doubt the spiritual response of the buddhas and ancestors.[99] *The ceremony in which, on the eighteenth day, ninth month, first year of Baoqing in the Great Song [21 October 1225], the Reverend Head of Hall, the Most Reverend Rujing, former abbot of Tiantong Jingde Monastery, bestowed [the bodhisattva precepts] on Dōgen was like the above. Acolyte Zuri was the incense acolyte at the time, and Guest Prefect Zongduan, Acolyte Guangping, and others assisted in the performance of this precept ritual. This was transmitted during the Baoqing of the Great Song.*[100]

---

97 The Tōunji 洞雲寺 MS shares an identical colophon; colophons almost identical to this are shared by the Satomi 里見 and Himitsu 秘密 MSS.

98 **Tessō Ken**: I.e., Tessō Hōken 喆卤芳賢 (d. 1551), copyist of the Ryūmonji 龍門寺 MS.

99 This warning and the material in the following paragraph are appended by the copyist, Tessō Hōken.

transmission of entering the room (*nisshitsu teki den* 入室的傳): I.e., dharma transmission as the disciple of a teacher.

100 This paragraph, appended by Tessō Hōken, is a quotation of a passage at the end of the *Busso shōden bosatsu kai sahō* 佛祖正傳菩薩戒作法 (DZZ.6:188), a precept ritual manual by Dōgen.

39. The Inheritance Certificate *Shisho* 嗣書 219

[Satomi MS:]

寛元癸卯九月二十四日、掛錫於越州吉田縣吉峯古寺草庵＜花押＞

Having hung up my staff at the thatched hermitage of the old monastery of Kippō, Yoshida District, Esshū; twenty-fourth day, ninth month of the junior water year of the rabbit, the first year of Kangen [7 November 1243]. Signed [by Dōgen's monogram (kaō 花押)][101]

[*Himitsu* MS:]

彼御本奧書曰ク、仁治癸卯二月廿五日、書寫之於侍者寮頭。侍者惠上
寛元々年十月廿三日、以越州御書御本交之。云云

The colophon of his autograph says:[102]

"Copied this in the acolyte's quarters, twenty-fifth day, second month, junior water year of the rabbit, Ninji [17 March 1243]. Acolyte Ejō[103] *Collated with his Esshū manuscript in his own hand, Twenty-third day, tenth month, first year of Kangen [6 December 1243]."*[104]

---

101 This second colophon, with its rare monogram (*kaō* 花押), is written separately on an extra sheet following the main text, perhaps intended simply to authenticate the holograph.

102 Colophon by an unknown copyist of the *Himitsu* manuscript, quoting the colophon of Ejō's own copy of the chapter.

103 **Ejō** 惠上: Written with homonymous glyphs for Ejō 懷奘.

104 **his Esshū manuscript in his own hand** (*Esshū gosho gohon* 越州御書御本): I.e., holograph by Dōgen done in Echizen; widely assumed to refer to the Satomi MS, completed just one month before the date of this notice.

TREASURY OF THE TRUE DHARMA EYE

NUMBER 40

The Cypress Tree
Hakujushi

柏樹子

The Cypress Tree

Hakujushi

INTRODUCTION

This text was composed at Kōshōji in 1242. It occurs as number 40 in both the seventy-five-chapter and sixty-chapter compilations of the *Shōbōgenzō* and as number 35 in the Honzan edition.

The text takes its title from a saying by the famous Tang-dynasty Chan master Zhaozhou Congshen 趙州從諗. Rather than launching directly into his comments on this saying, Dōgen devotes the first half of his essay to a treatment of the figure of Zhaozhou himself, as revealed in his biography and poetry. He tells here the story of Zhaozhou's encounter with his master, Nanquan Puyuan 南泉普願, and goes on to praise the strict austerity of his later life as abbot of the Guanyin Cloister 觀音院, where he served till his death at the remarkable age, it is said, of 120.

Dōgen then turns to the title theme of the essay, the meaning of Zhaozhou's mysterious remark, "the cypress tree at the front of the garden," in response to the question of why Bodhidharma came to China. He goes on to discuss a second saying of Zhaozhou, that the cypress tree has the buddha nature and will become a buddha "once space falls to the ground." Dōgen's comments in this section are sometimes quite difficult to interpret and may well leave some readers asking the question with which the essay closes: "what is it?"

正法眼藏第四十

Treasury of the True Dharma Eye
Number 40

柏樹子

The Cypress Tree

[40:1] {1:436}

趙州眞際大師は、釋迦如來より第三十七世なり。六十一歳にしてはじめて發心し、いへをいでて學道す。このときちかひていはく、たとひ百歳なりとも、われよりもおとれらんは、われ、かれを、をしふべし。たとひ七歳なりとも、われよりもすぐれば、われ、かれにとふべし。恁麼ちかひて、南方へ雲遊す。道をとぶらひゆくちなみに、南泉にいたりて、願和尚を禮拜す。ちなみに南泉、もとより方丈内にありて臥せるついでに、師、來參するに、すなはちとふ、近離什麼處。師いはく、瑞像院。南泉いはく、還見瑞像麼。師いはく、瑞像即不見、即見臥如來。ときに南泉、いましに起してとふ、儞はこれ有主沙彌、無主沙彌。師、對していはく、有主沙彌。南泉いはく、那箇是儞主。師いはく、孟春猶寒、伏惟和尚尊體、起居萬福。南泉すなはち維那をよんでいはく、此沙彌別處安排。

Zhaozhou, Great Master Zhenji, was the thirty-seventh generation from Tathāgata Śākya.[1] At the age of sixty-one, he first brought forth the mind [of bodhi] and, leaving home, studied the way.[2] At this time, he

---

1 **Cypress Tree** (*hakujushi* 柏樹子): Also written 栢樹子. An evergreen, native to China, used in decorative planting; traditionally thought of as a symbol of constancy and long life.

Zhaozhou, Great Master Zhenji (*Jōshū Shinsai daishi* 趙州眞際大師): I.e., Zhaozhou Congshen 趙州從諗 (778-897). Zhenji dashi 眞際大師 is a posthumous title. His biography appears at *Jingde chuandeng lu* 景德傳燈錄, T.2076.51:276c-278b; *Song Gaoseng zhuan* 宋高僧傳, T.2061.50:775c6ff; *Zhaozhou Zhenji chanshi yulu bing xingzhuang* 趙州眞際禪師語錄并行狀, *Guzunsu yulu* 古尊宿語錄, ZZ.118:304a13ff, etc.

thirty-seventh generation (*dai sanjūshichi sei* 第三十七世): Zhaozhou represents the fourth generation after the Sixth Ancestor of the Chinese Chan tradition, Huineng 慧能, in the lineage of Nanyue Huairang 南嶽懷讓 (677-744), Mazu Daoyi 馬祖道一 (709-788), and Nanquan Puyuan 南泉普願 (748-835).

2 **At the age of sixty-one, he first brought forth the mind [of bodhi] and, leaving home, studied the way** (*rokujūissai ni shite hajimete hosshin shi, ie o idete gakudō su* 六十一歳にしてはじめて發心し、いへをいでて學道す): The source for Dōgen's claim that Zhaozhou "left home" at the advanced age of sixty-one is unclear. The latter's biography in the *Jingde chuandeng lu* 景德傳燈錄 (T.2076.51:276c7-8) states that, as a youth he donned the robe and shaved his head (*piti* 披剃) at Hutong Cloister 扈通院, in present-day Shandong, but did not yet receive the precepts (*wei nai jie* 未納戒) — this would explain Nanquan's reference to him in our text as a *śrāmaṇera*, or "novice." His biography in the *Zhaozhou yulu* 趙州語錄 (*Guzunsu yulu* 古尊宿語錄,

224   DŌGEN'S *SHŌBŌGENZŌ* VOLUME III

made a vow, saying, "Even if they are one hundred years old, if they are inferior to me, I will teach them; even if they are seven years old, if they are superior to me, I will inquire of them." Vowing thus, he wandered south. As he went inquiring of the way, he reached Nanquan and paid obeisance to Reverend Yuan.[3]

At the time, Nanquan was in the abbot's quarters, where he had been lying down. When the Master approached, he [i.e., Nanquan] asked, *"Where are you coming from?"*

The Master said, *"Ruixiang Cloister ['Cloister of the Auspicious Image']."*[4]

Nanquan said, *"And have you seen the auspicious image?"*

The Master said, *"I haven't seen the auspicious image, but I have seen a recumbent tathāgata."*[5]

Thereupon Naquan promptly arose and said, "Are you a *śrāmaṇera* with a master, or a *śrāmaṇera* without a master?"[6]

The Master replied, saying, "A *śrāmaṇera* with a master."

ZZ.118:304a16-b10) says that he accompanied his "original master" (*benshi* 本師) — presumably the (unidentified) monk under whom he became a novice — to visit Nanquan (who died in 834, when Zhaozhou was 56); then, after he received the precepts (*shou jie* 受戒) — presumably from Nanquan — he returned to his home district in Caozhou 曹州 to visit "the master from whom he received the work" (*shou ye shi* 受業師) — again, no doubt, his "original master." When his family heard that he had returned and sought to visit him, he escaped in the night and set off on his travels (*bianli zhufang* 遍歷諸方), always saying to himself,

　　七歲童兒勝我者、我即問伊。百歲老翁不及我者、我即教他。

A seven-year-old child who surpasses me, I'll inquire of him; a hundred-year-old elder who doesn't reach me, I'll teach him.

3　**Nanquan** (*Nansen* 南泉): I.e., the mountain range in present-day Anhui Prefecture.

Reverend Yuan (*Gan oshō* 願和尚): I.e., the Chan master Nanquan Puyuan 南泉普願. The following dialogue occurs in several Chan sources; see, e.g., *Zhaozhou yulu* 趙州語錄, ZZ.118:304a17-b4; *Jingde chuandeng lu* 景德傳燈錄, T.2076.51:276c9-13. Dōgen tells the story here in a mixture of Japanese and Chinese.

4　**"Ruixiang Cloister"** (*Zuizō in* 瑞像院): The temple on Mount Nanquan 南泉山 founded by Nanquan Puyuan 南泉普願. Since the conversation would seem to be taking place in the abbot's quarters of this temple, Zhaozhou's answer might be understood as an assertion that he has been "right here." (Such is the interpretation, e.g., at *Shōbōgenzō monge* 正法眼藏聞解, SCZ.5:218.)

5　**"a recumbent tathāgata"** (*ga nyorai* 臥如來): A reference, of course, to the reclining abbot.

6　**"śrāmaṇera with a master"** (*ushu shami* 有主沙彌): A *śrāmaṇera* is a novice, who has not taken the full precepts of the monk. The term "master" here translates the Chinese *zhu* 主, a term meaning "chief" or "head," also "host" (as opposed to "guest"), "subject," etc.; as such, the question here may imply an issue of self-understanding.

40. The Cypress Tree *Hakujushi* 柏樹子   225

Nanquan said, "*Who is your master?*"

The Master said, "*It is the first of spring and still cold. I trust the Reverend's health is blessed.*"[7]

Nanquan called the rector and said, "*Assign this śrāmaṇera somewhere.*"[8]

[40:2] {1:437}

かくのごとくして南泉に寓直し、さらに餘方にゆかず、辦道功夫すること三十年なり。寸陰をむなしくせず、雜用あることなし。つひに傳道受業よりのち、趙州の觀音院に住することも又三十年なり。その住持の事形、つねの諸方にひとしからず。

Thus he lodged at Nanquan and, without traveling anywhere else, pursued the way with concentrated effort for thirty years.[9] Without wasting an inch of shadow, he had no extraneous activities.[10] Eventually, after transmission of the way and reception of the work, he resided at Guanyin Cloister in Zhaozhou for another thirty years.[11] The circumstances of his abbacy were not like those of the usual quarters.

---

7 **"It is the first of spring and still cold"** (*mō shun yū kan* 孟春猶寒): Zhaozhou's answer here is a formulaic polite salutation, of the sort that might be written by a monk to his senior; by implication, he assumes the posture of Nanquan's student.

8 **"Assign . . . somewhere"** (*bessho anbai* 別處安排): The Chinese expression *biechu* 別處 ("elsewhere"), tentatively translated here simply as "somewhere," may connote a "special place"; hence, the possible sense here "give . . . special treatment to" (as interpreted at *Shōbōgenzō monge* 正法眼藏聞解, SCZ.5:218). The version in the *Jingde chuandeng lu* 景德傳燈録 (T.2076.51: 276c14) has at this point simply,

南泉器之而許入室

Nanquan respected him and permitted him to "enter the room" [i.e., become a disciple].

9 **lodged** (*gūchoku shi* 寓直し): Probably a variant of the more common *gūshi* 寓止; the glyph *choku* 直 here may be a locative marker, cognate with *choku* 値.

for thirty years (*sanjū nen* 三十年): The source of Dōgen's claim here that Zhaozhou spent thirty years on Mount Nanquan 南泉山 before moving to Guanyin Cloister is not clear; it is usually said that he traveled widely, visiting other teachers. Dōgen's version may be a conflation with the biography of Zhaozhou's teacher, Nanquan 南泉, in which it is said that "he did not descend Nanquan for over thirty years" (*Jingde chuandeng lu* 景德傳燈録, T.2076.51:257b26).

10 **an inch of shadow** (*sun'in* 寸陰): A literary expression for "a minute of time," occurring often in Dōgen's writings.

11 **transmission of the way and reception of the work** (*dendō jugō* 傳道受業): "Transmission of the way" typically refers to the recognition of a student's spiritual qualifications by a teacher. The less common "reception of the work" often means "to accept the precepts," but it may also refer to receiving instruction or transmission from a teacher.

Guanyin Cloister in Zhaozhou (*Jōshū no Kannon in* 趙州の觀音院): In present-day Hebei. The temple was known as Yong'an Cloister 永安院 from the Southern Song; the current name, Bailin Monastery 栢林寺, dates from the Qing dynasty.

[40:3]

或時いはく、煙火徒勞望四隣、饅頭餡子前年別、今日思量空嚥津、持念少嗟歎頻、一百家中無善人、來者祇道覓茶喫、不得茶嘗去又嗔。

On one occasion, he said,[12]

> Smoking fires: I futilely gaze on the neighborhood.
> Parted from buns and dumplings last year.
> Thinking of them today, I swallow my spittle in vain;
> Rarely maintaining my thoughts; repeatedly sighing.
> There's no good person in a hundred households.[13]
> The ones that come say they're just looking for tea;
> If they don't get their tea, they go away angry.

[40:4]

あはれむべし、煙火まれなり、一味すくなし。雜味は前年よりあはず。一百家人きたれば茶をもとむ、茶をもとめざるはきたらず。將來茶人は、一百家人にあらざらん。これ見賢の雲水ありとも、思齊の龍象なからん。

What a pity. His smoking fires are few; he rarely has a single taste; he has not met a varied taste since last year.[14] When the people of the hundred households come, they are seeking tea; those not seeking tea do not come.[15] There is likely no one in the hundred households who brings him tea. There may be clouds and water that "meet someone good," but there are likely no dragons or elephants that "think to equal him."[16]

---

12 **On one occasion, he said** (*aru toki iwaku* 或時いはく): From the *Zhaozhou yulu* 趙州語錄, ZZ.118:333a11-13. The verse comes from Zhaozhou's *Shier shi ge* 十二時歌, a set of poems dedicated to the twelve times, or two-hour periods into which the day was traditionally divided. As its theme suggests, this poem is dedicated to the "meal time" (*shi shi* 食時), in the fifth, or "dragon," hour (*chen* 辰) — i.e., 7:00-9:00 a.m.

13 **Smoking fires** (*enka* 煙火): I.e., the smoke from the neighbors' cooking fires.

good person (*zennin* 善人): Usually refers to a morally good person; it may also carry the connotation of a "person of good family" — i.e., a worthy lay follower (or donor).

14 **single taste** (*ichimi* 一味); **varied taste** (*zōmi* 雜味): Perhaps something like "a simple meal" and "a full-course meal" respectively.

15 **people of the hundred households** (*ippyaku kajin* 一百家人): Presumably, the villagers in the neighborhood of Zhaozhou's temple, but it is possible to read this as a metaphor for the "monks" (*unsui* 雲水) in the following sentence — in which case, one might also want to give a metaphorical reading to the "tea" here.

16 **clouds and water** (*unsui* 雲水): A common term for Buddhist monks, conveying the sense that they drift through the world like clouds and water.

"meet someone good" (*kenken* 見賢); **"think to equal him"** (*shisai* 思齊): After the common saying, quoted elsewhere in the *Shōbōgenzō*, from the *Lunyu* 論語 4 (KR.1h0005.002.14b):

見賢思齊焉。見不賢而內自省也。

40. The Cypress Tree *Hakujushi* 柏樹子 227

[40:5]

あるときまたいはく、思量天下出家人、似我住持能有幾、土榻牀破蘆簟、
老楡木枕全無被、尊像不燒安息香、灰裏唯聞牛糞氣。

On another occasion, he said,[17]

> *Thinking of those who've left home in this realm,*
> *How many could there be with an abbacy like mine?*
> *An earthen bed with a tattered reed mat,*
> *An old elmwood headreast with no cover at all.*
> *At the icon, I don't burn the incense of Arsaces,*
> *In the ashes, I just smell the odor of cow dung.*[18]

[40:6] {1:438}

これらの道得をもて、院門の潔白しりぬべし、いまこの蹤跡を學習すべ
し。僧衆おほからず、不滿二十衆といふは、よくすることのかたきにより
てなり。僧堂おほきならず、前架・後架なし。夜間は燈光あらず、冬天に
は炭火なし。あはれむべき老後の生涯といひぬべし。古佛の操行、それか
くのごとし。

From these sayings, we can understand the purity of his cloister. We
should study these traces. That his monastic assembly was not many,
said to have been less than twenty, is because being able to do it is hard.[19]

When you meet someone good, think to equal him; when you meet someone not
good, then look within yourself.

dragons or elephants (*ryūzō* 龍象): A term for superior religious practitioners found
throughout Zen texts and often in Dōgen's writings. Although originally used in reference to great elephants (S. *hasti-nāga*), it is often interpreted as "dragons and elephants"
— as suggested here in its parallel with "clouds and water."

17　**On another occasion, he said** (*aru toki mata iwaku* あるときまたいはく): From
Zhaozhou yulu 趙州錄, ZZ.118:333b17-334a1. Another of the verses from Zhaozhou's
Shier shi ge 十二時歌, this one dedicated to "midnight" (*banye* 半夜), the first hour (*zi*
子), 11:00 p.m.-1:00 a.m. Dōgen has omitted the opening line of the poem:

心境何曾得暫止。

The mind and its objects, how can they ever be stopped?

18　**At the icon** (*sonzō* 尊像): I.e., the "venerated image" of a sacred Buddhist figure.

incense of Arsaces (*Ansoku kō* 安息香): Incense made from gum benzoin, the resin of a
tree (*styrax benzoin*) of Southeast Asia; identified with the Indian incense *guggulu*. The
Chinese *Anxi* 安息 transliterates "Arsaces," the name taken by the kings of the Arsacid
empire of Parthia.

odor of cow dung (*gofun ki* 牛糞氣): I.e., dried dung used for fuel.

19　**less than twenty** (*fuman nijū shu* 不滿二十衆): Dōgen here slips into Chinese syntax, as if quoting a text; no source has been identified.

being able to do it is hard (*yoku suru koto no kataki* よくすることのかたき): A Japanese idiom likely reflecting the Chinese saying, "Knowing it is not hard; it is being able
to do it that is hard" (*fei zhi zhi nan, neng zhi nan ye* 非知之難、能之難也).

The saṃgha hall was not large and lacked both front shelving and back shelving.[20] There was no lamplight at night and no charcoal fire in winter weather.[21] One could say it was a pitiful life for an aged one.[22] Such was the conduct of the Old Buddha.[23]

[40:7]

あるとき連牀のあしのおれたりけるに、燼木をなはにてゆひつけて、年月をふる。知事、つくりかへんと報ずるに、師、ゆるさざりけり。希代の勝躅なり。

Once, when the leg of the joined platform was broken, he spliced it by binding twine to a piece of burned wood [and continued to use it] for months and years.[24] When the stewards reported it to be replaced, the Master would not permit it.[25] [This incident] is an excellent vestige, rare throughout the generations.[26]

---

20 **front shelving and back shelving** (*zenka goka* 前架・後架): The former term refers to shelves located in the outer section of the saṃgha hall (*sōdō* 僧堂), used for food service; the latter refers to shelves in the lavatory behind the saṃgha hall, or by extension, to the lavatory itself. Dōgen is here drawing on the *Zhaozhou yulu* 趙州語錄, at ZZ.118:304b12:

僧堂無前後架。

The saṃgha hall lacked front and back shelving.

21 **no lamplight at night** (*yakan wa tōkō arazu* 夜間は燈光あらず): Dōgen is here perhaps drawing again on Zhaozhou's *Shier shi ge* 十二時歌 (ZZ.118:333b11-12): the verse for eventide (*huang hun* 黄昏), the hour of *xu* 戌 (7:00-9:00 p.m.), begins:

獨坐一間空暗室。陽焰燈光永不逢、眼前純是金州漆。

Sitting alone in a dark, empty room.
Long without greeting sunshine or lamplight;
Before me, it's all just the [black] lacquer of Jin.

22 **a pitiful life for an aged one** (*awaremu beki rōgo no shōgai* あはれむべき老後の生涯): Or, "the life of a pitiful aged one."

23 **conduct of the Old Buddha** (*kobutsu no sōgyō* 古佛の操行): "Conduct" here in the sense of proper behavior. The term *kobutsu* ("old buddha") could be plural; but, as Dōgen will point out below, Zhaozhou was known as "the old buddha." See Supplementary Notes, s.v. "Old buddha."

24 **joined platform** (*renjō* 連牀): Or "continuous bench"; the structure used communally by the monks in the saṃgha hall for sitting, eating, and sleeping. Dōgen is here recounting an incident recorded in the *Zhaozhou yulu* 趙州語錄 (ZZ.118:304b12-13), where the furniture in question is called a "cord bench" (*jōshō* 繩床), a standard term for an individual monk's meditation platform.

25 **stewards** (*chiji* 知事): The six major officers of a Zen monastery. The story in the *Zhaozhou yulu* 趙州語錄 makes no mention of them.

26 **an excellent vestige, rare throughout the generations** (*kidai no shōchoku* 希代の勝躅): A somewhat unusual expression also appearing in the *Eihei kōroku* 永平廣錄 (DZZ.3:72, no. 128). The glyph *choku* 躅 here is used in the sense "trace" (*seki* 跡).

40. The Cypress Tree *Hakujushi* 柏樹子   229

[40:8]

よのつねには、解齋粥米全無粒、空對閑窓與隙塵なり。あるひは、この
み、をひろひて、僧衆もわが身も、茶飯の日用に活計す。いまの晩進、こ
の操行を讚頌する、師の操行におよばざれども、慕古を心術とするなり。

Ordinarily,

In the breakfast gruel, there isn't any grain of rice;
I vacantly face the quiet window and the dust in the cracks.[27]

Or he would pick up nuts, and both he and the monks would live on
them as their daily fare.[28] Latecomers now eulogize this conduct, and,
though they do not reach the Master's conduct, they assume the attitude
of admiring the ancients.

[40:9]

あるとき、衆にしめしていはく、われ南方にありしこと三十年、ひとすぎ
に坐禪す。なんだち諸人、この一段の大事をえんとおもはば、究理坐禪し
てみるべし。三年、五年、二十年、三十年せんに、道をえずといはば、老
僧が頸をとりて、杓につくりて小便をくむべし。

On one occasion, he addressed the assembly, saying,[29]

27　**In the breakfast gruel, there isn't any grain of rice** (*gesai shuku bei zen mu ryū*
解齋粥米全無粒): A quotation again from the *Shier shi ge* 十二時歌, the verse for dawn
(*pingdan* 平旦), in the third period (*yin* 寅), 3:00 a.m.-5:00 a.m. (*Zhaozhou yulu* 趙州語
錄, ZZ.118:333a5-6). Interpreters disagree on how to parse the Chinese of the first sentence here, some taking *zhaizhou* 齋粥 as the common compound for a monastic meal
and the object of the initial *jie* 解 — a reading that might yield something like "dissecting
the gruel" (or possibly "in the dissolved gruel"). The translation here takes *jiezhai* 解齋
as a compound meaning "break the fast" (i.e., the monks' morning meal).

28　**pick up nuts** (*konomi o hiroite* このみをひろひて): The source for this information
is not clear. It is possible that Dōgen is asking us to take literally the notice on a stele,
recorded in the *Zhaozhou yulu* 趙州語錄 (ZZ.118:304a17), which says that, at the time of
the persecution of Buddhism in the Huichang era 會昌 (841-846), Zhaozhou withdrew to
Mount Julai 岨崍山 in Shandong and continued his practice as a monk, living with "tree
food and grass robes" (*mokujiki sōe* 木食草衣). Eating only gathered fruits and nuts is
one of the standard Buddhist ascetic practices (S. *dhūtāṅga*).

29　**On one occasion** (*aru toki* あるとき): Although presented here as a Japanese rendering of a Chinese text, there seems to be no closely equivalent extant source for this
passage. In his *Eihei kōroku* 永平廣錄 (DZZ.3:26, no. 33), Dōgen cites a somewhat
abbreviated version of Zhaozhou's remarks.

趙州云、兄弟但究理坐看。三二十年若不會道、取老僧頭去、作酌大小便杓。

Zhaozhou said, "Brothers, just try investigating the principle and sitting. If, in twenty
or thirty years, you haven't understood the way, take off this old monk's head and
make a ladle to scoop shit and piss."

Similar sayings (without the scatological flourish) appear in Zhaozhou's recorded sayings (*Zhaozhou yulu* 趙州語錄, ZZ.118:319a7-8) and in his notice in the *Jingde chuandeng lu* 景德傳燈錄 (T.2076.51:446b21-23), which has:

一心不生、萬法無咎。汝但究理坐看、三二十年。若不會道、截取老僧頭去。

In the thirty years I was in the south, I exclusively practiced seated meditation. If you all think to get this "prime great matter," you should try investigating the principle and practicing seated meditation.[30] If, in three years, or five years, or twenty years, or thirty years, you haven't attained the way, you can take off this old monk's head, make it into a ladle, and scoop piss with it.

[40:10]
かくのごとくちかひける。まことに坐禪辨道は、佛道の直路なり、究理坐看すべし。のちに人いはく、趙州古佛なり。

He made such a vow. Truly, pursuing the way in seated meditation is the direct path of the way of the buddhas. We should "*try investigating the principle and sitting.*"[31] Later, people said, "Zhaozhou is an old buddha."[32]

* * * * *

[40:11]
大師、因有僧問、如何是祖師西來意。師云、庭前柏樹子。僧曰、和尚莫以境示人。師云、吾不以境示人。僧云、如何是祖師西來意。師云、庭前柏樹子。

[As is said in the *Xin xin ming* 信心銘,] "When a single thought does not arise, there's nothing wrong with the myriad dharmas." Just try investigating the principle and sitting. If, in twenty or thirty years, you haven't understood the way, cut off this old monk's head.

30 **"prime great matter"** (*ichidan no daiji* 一段の大事): From the common Zen expression *ichidan daiji* 一段大事 or simply *ichidan ji* 一段事 ("prime matter"); i.e., the most important point. The translation "prime" takes the Chinese *duan* 段 here as "rank"; taken simply as a counter, the expression could be read "one great matter."

31 **"try investigating the principle and sitting"** (*kyūri zakan* 究理坐看): Dōgen has here picked up an expression from the version of Zhaozhou's saying found in the *Chuandeng lu* 傳燈錄. This is not a term of art in his vocabulary and here likely just conveys the sense "try sitting" — as seen in Dōgen's interpretation above: "try . . . practicing seated meditation" (*zazen shite miru* 坐禪してみる). The term *tsokan* 坐看 also occurs in Zen texts in the sense "sit and watch" — perhaps especially from the saying (attributed to Guanyin Cloister Zhaoxian 觀音院從顯, at *Jingde chuandeng lu* 景德傳燈錄, T.2076.51:417b20):

行到水窮處、坐看雲起時。

He walks and arrives where the waters end;
He sits and watches when the clouds arise.

32 **"Zhaozhou is an old buddha"** (*Jōshū kobutsu* 趙州古佛): The practice of calling Zhaozhou "an old buddha" is common in Zen texts. It is said to originate in a saying of Zhaozhou's younger contemporary Xuefeng Yicun 雪峰義存 (822-908) recorded in the *shinji Shōbōgenzō* 眞字正法眼藏 (DZZ.5:268, case 283); see Supplementary Notes, s.v. "Old buddha."

40. The Cypress Tree *Hakujushi* 柏樹子

231

The Great Master was once asked by a monk, "What is the intention of the Ancestral Master's coming from the west?"[33]

The Master said, "The cypress tree at the front of the garden."

The monk said, "Reverend, don't show a person with an object."[34]

The Master said, "I don't show a person with an object."

The monk said, "What is the intention of the Ancestral Master's coming from the west?"

The Master said, "The cypress tree at the front of the garden."

[40:12] {1:439}

この一則公案は、趙州より起首せりといへども、必竟じて諸佛の渾身に作家しきたれるところなり、たれかこれ主人公なり。いましるべき道理は、庭前柏樹子、これ境にあらざる宗旨なり、祖師西來意、これ境にあらざる宗旨なり、柏樹子、これ自己にあらざる宗旨なり、和尚莫以境示人なるがゆえに、吾不以境示人なるがゆえに。いづれの和尚か和尚にさへられん、さへられずば、吾なるべし。いづれの吾か吾にさへられん、たとひさへらるとも、人なるべし。いづれの境か西來意に罣礙せられざらん、境はかならず西來意なるべきがゆえに。しかあれども、西來意の、境をもちて相待せるにあらず、祖師西來意、かならずしも正法眼藏涅槃妙心にあらざるなり。不是心なり、不是佛なり、不是物なり。

This one kōan, though it is said to have originated from Zhaozhou, is in the end something authored by the whole body of the buddhas.[35]

33　**The Great Master** (*daishi* 大師): I.e., Zhaozhou 趙州. Versions of this famous dialogue can be found in a number of sources; see, e.g., *Zhaozhou yulu* 趙州語錄 (ZZ.118:307a15-b2); *Liandeng huiyao* 聯燈會要 (ZZ.136:666b12-14); *shinji Shōbōgenzō* 眞字正法眼藏 (DZZ.5:190, case 119). The question of Bodhidharma's intention in coming to China seems to have preoccupied the monks in Zhaozhou's community; it occurs with great frequency thoughout his recorded sayings. For Zhaozhou's answer here, See Supplementary Notes, s.v. "Cypress tree at the front of the garden."

34　**"show a person with an object"** (*i kyō shi nin* 以境示人): Or, more colloquially, "don't use things to teach people"; the somewhat awkward translation here tries to highlight the contrast between "person" and "object" with which Dōgen seems to be playing in his comments below. "Object" here translates the Chinese *jing* 境, used for the objects of the senses (S. *viṣaya*, *ālambana*). The English "show" here renders the Chinese *si* 示, which means both "to indicate" and "to instruct." The question of what a master uses "to teach people" (*shi ren* 示人) is a common topic of conversation in Zen texts and occurs several times in Zhaozhou's recorded sayings. One instance is particularly close to ours here and may have influenced Dōgen's commentary; see below, Note 47.

35　**originated** (*kishu seri* 起首せり): Literally, "raised its head"; the corporeal image is likely meant to work with the subsequent "whole body."

authored by the whole body of the buddhas (*shobutsu no konjin ni sakke shikitareru* 諸佛の渾身に作家しきたれる): The term *konjin* (or *konshin*) 渾身 ("whole body") appears very often in the *Shōbōgenzō* in the sense of the entirety of something; here, it can probably be understood either as the buddhas taken as a "body" or as the "body" that all buddhas share. The phrase *sakke shikitareru* 作家しきたれる, translated here as

232 DŌGEN'S *SHŌBŌGENZŌ* VOLUME III

Who is the one in charge?[36] The principle we should understand here is the essential point that "the cypress at the front of the garden" is not an "object," the essential point that "the intention of the Ancestral Master's coming from the west" is not an "object," the essential point that "the cypress tree" is not the self; for [it is said], "*Reverend, don't show a person with an object*"; for [it is said,] "*I don't show a person with an object.*" Which "Reverend" is impeded by "Reverend"? If he is not impeded, he must be "I." Which "I" is impeded by "I"? Even if it is impeded, it must be "a person." Which "object" is not obstructed by the "intention in coming from the west"?[37] For the "object" must inevitably be the "intention in coming from the west." Nevertheless, the "intention in coming from the west" is not dependent on the "object." "The intention of the Ancestral Master's coming from the west" is not necessarily "the treasury of the true dharma eye, the wondrous mind of nirvāṇa."[38] It is "*not the mind*"; it is "*not the buddha*"; it is "*not a thing.*"[39]

"authored," represents an unusual verbal form derived from the Chinese *zuojia* 作家, indicating an author or poet and, in Zen usage, an accomplished master.

36 **Who is the one in charge?** (*tare ka kore shujinkō nari* たれかこれ主人公なり): Taking *nari* なり as *naran* ならん. The Chinese term *zhurengong* 主人公, translated rather casually here as "the one in charge," is a colloquial expression for the "proprietor," the "head," the "host," the "subject," etc.; commonly used in Zen texts for the true self. Here, the question would seem to be asking about the true creater of "this one kōan," or, more broadly, the true nature of Zhaozhou. This is the only occurrence of the term in the *Shōbōgenzō*; its use here may reflect Nanquan's question, above, "Are you a *śrāmaṇera* with a master" (*shu* 主), as well as, more importantly, dialogues found in Zhaozhou's recorded sayings, in which he is himself asked about "who is in charge" of him. See, e.g., *Zhaozhou yulu* 趙州語錄 (ZZ.118:308b5):

問、如何是趙州主人公。師云、田厙奴。
Someone asked, "Who's in charge of Zhaozhou?"
The Master answered, "A field hand."

37 **impeded** (*saeraren* さへられん); **obstructed** (*keige sera[ru]* 罣礙せら[る]): Probably to be taken in the sense, "identified," "defined"; a common usage in Dōgen's writings.

38 **"the treasury of the true dharma eye, the wondrous mind of nirvāṇa"** (*shōbōgenzō nehan myōshin* 正法眼藏涅槃妙心): The essence of the Buddha's awakening, traditionally said to have first been transmitted from Śākyamuni to Mahākāśyapa on Vulture Peak; what Bodhidharma is said to have brought to China. See Supplementary Notes, s.v. "Treasury of the true dharma eye."

39 **"not the mind"** (*fu ze shin* 不是心); **"not the buddha"** (*fu ze butsu* 不是佛); **"not a thing"** (*fu ze motsu* 不是物): Words attributed both to Mazu Daoyi (e.g. at *Jingde chuandeng lu* 景德傳燈錄, T.2076.51:445ba7) and to Nanquan Puyuan 南泉普願. The latter attribution, since the context involves Zhaozhou, may be the more relevant here; it occurs in the following passage in Nanquan's notice in the *Jingde chuandeng lu* 景德傳燈錄 (T.2067:51.257c13-15; quoted by Dōgen in the *Eihei kōroku* 永平廣錄, DZZ.4:192):

40. The Cypress Tree *Hakujushi* 柏樹子 233

[40:13]

いま如何是祖師西來意と道取せるは、問取のみにあらず、兩人同得見のみにあらざるなり。正當恁麼問時は、一人也未可相見なり、自己也能得幾なり。さらに道取するに、渠無不是なり。このゆえに錯錯なり、錯錯なるがゆえに將錯就錯なり。承虛接響にあらざらんや。

[The monk's] saying here, "*What is the intention of the Ancestral Master's coming from the west?*" is not merely a question; it is not merely that "*both people can see the same.*"[40] *At the very time he asks*, it is, *he cannot see anyone*; it is, *how much of himself can he get?*[41] Going further, [we can say,] *he is without fault.* Therefore, it is "mistake, mistake."[42] Because it is mistake, mistake, it is *making a mistake of a mistake.*[43] Is this *not to accept the hollow and entertain the echo?*[44]

師有時云、江西馬祖説即心即佛。王老師不恁麼道。不是心、不是佛、不是物。恁麼道、還有過麼。趙州禮拜而出。

The Master on one occasion said, "Mazu of Jiangxi teaches, 'This mind itself is the buddha.' This old master Wang [i.e., Nanquan] doesn't talk like this. It isn't mind; it isn't buddha; it isn't a thing. Is there any mistake in talking like this?" Zhaozhou bowed and left.

40 **"both people can see the same"** (*ryōnin dō tokuken* 兩人同得見): Likely meaning that the monk and Zhaozhou share the same view. The Chinese phrase comes from a verse attributed to the eighteenth Zen ancestor, Gayaśata 伽耶舍多, on which Dōgen comments in his "Shōbōgenzō kokyō" 正法眼藏古鏡 (*Jingde chuandeng lu* 景德傳燈錄, T.2076.51:212b18-19):

諸佛大圓鑑、內外無瑕翳、兩人同得見、心眼皆相似。

The great round mirror of the buddhas,
Without flaw or blur inside or out.
Both people can see the same.
Mind and eye, all alike.

41 **he cannot see anyone** (*ichinin ya mi ka shōken* 一人也未可相見); **how much of himself can he get?** (*jiko ya nō toku ki* 自己也能得幾): Dōgen slips again into Chinese syntax for these somewhat mysterious remarks, which are generally interpreted to mean that, when the monk asks the question, there is no one to whom it is addressed and no one who is asking it. Though it is possible to read this passage as a criticism of the monk, most interpreters take it as an affirmation of his understanding.

42 **"mistake, mistake"** (*shaku shaku* 錯錯): A common retort of Zen masters, sometimes used in ironic praise —which, given the context, seems the most likely interpretation here. Some readers take the expression to mean that the monk makes one "mistake" after another; others suggest that both the monk and Zhaozhou make the "mistakes."

43 **making a mistake of a mistake** (*shōshaku jushaku* 將錯就錯): An idiom, found in Zen texts, meaning "to recognize one's mistake as such," "to turn a mistake to one's advantage," or "to make one mistake after another"; see Supplementary Notes, s.v. "Make a mistake of a mistake."

44 **to accept the hollow and entertain the echo** (*shōkyo* [or *shōko*] *sekkyō* 承虛接響): A Chinese idiomatic expression meaning something like "to take seriously what is vacuous." Though the connotation is negative, most interpreters take it in a positive sense here.

234 DŌGEN'S *SHŌBŌGENZŌ* VOLUME III

[40:14] {1:440}

谿達靈根無向背なるがゆえに、庭前柏樹子なり。境にあらざれば柏樹子にあるべからず。たとひ境なりとも、吾不以境示人なり、和尚莫以境示人なり。古祠にあらず。すでに古祠にあらざれば、埋没しもてゆくなり。すでに埋没しもてゆくことあれば、還吾功夫來なり。還吾功夫來なるがゆえに、吾不以境示人なり。さらになにをもてか示人する、吾亦如是なるべし。

Because "*the all-pervading spiritual root turns neither toward nor away*," it is "*the cypress tree at the front of the garden*": if it is not an "object," it cannot be a cypress tree; even if it is an object, it is [said,] "*I don't show a person with an object*," and "*Reverend Preceptor, don't show a person with an object*."[45] It is not an old ancestral shrine.[46] Since it is not an old ancestral shrine, he goes on burying.[47] Since he goes on

---

45 **"the all-pervading spiritual root turns neither toward nor away"** (*kattatsu reikon mu kōhai* 谿達靈根無向背): Or "the all-pervading spiritual root has neither front nor back." After a line from the *Caoan ge* 草庵歌, by the Tang-dynasty master Shitou Xiqian 石頭希遷 (700-790); see Supplementary Notes, s.v. "*Reverend Shitou's Song of the Thatched Hut*." The point here would seem to be that Zhaozhou's "cypress tree," like Shitou's "root," is neither affirmed nor denied in its identity as an "object."

46 **It is not an old ancestral shrine** (*koshi ni arazu* 古祠にあらず): The rationale for this seeming non sequitur is not clear. Some interpreters have speculated that it is an allusion to the cypress trees traditionally planted at ancestral shrines in symbolic expression of eternal life; hence, the point is presumably that Zhaozhou's cypress is not eternal.

47 **he goes on burying** (*maimotsu* [or *maibotsu*] *shimoteyuku* 埋没しもてゆく): Or perhaps "it goes on burying (or being buried)"; the grammatical subject is unexpressed. Some interpreters take this to mean that Zhaozhou's cypress tree is continually "dying" (and "being reborn") in each moment. More likely, the reference is to Zhaozhou's teaching. Chan masters sometimes use the Chinese compound *maimei* 埋没 as a transitive verb to deny or dismiss someone. The translation here is based on such use, as seen in Zhaozhou's recorded sayings: e.g., *Zhaozhou yulu* 趙州語錄, ZZ.118:315B12-15:

問、佛祖在日、佛祖相傳。佛祖滅後、什麼人傳。師云、古今總是老僧分上。學云、未審傳箇什麼。師云、箇箇總屬生死。云、不可埋沒却祖師也。師云、傳箇什麼。

[A monk] asked, "When the buddhas and ancestors were alive, the buddhas and ancestors transmitted [the dharma]. After the extinction of the buddhas and ancestors, who transmits it?"
The Master said, "All of past and present is this old monk's lot."
The student said, "So what do you transmit?"
The Master said, "Everyone is included in birth and death."
[The student] said, "You shouldn't bury the ancestral masters."
The Master said, "So what do they transmit?"

Or, again, at ZZ.118:323a2-5:

師有時屈指云, 老僧喚作拳, 儞諸人喚作什麼。僧云, 和尚何得將境示人。師云, 我不將境示人。若將境示闍黎, 即埋沒闍黎去也。云, 爭奈箇何。師便珍重。

The Master once clenched his fingers and said, "This old monk calls it a fist. What do you all call it?"

40. The Cypress Tree *Hakujushi* 柏樹子   235

burying, it is *return my concentrated effort*.[48] Since it is return my concentrated effort, it is *"I don't show a person with an object."* Then what else does he use to "show a person"? It must be *"I'm also like this."*[49]

* * * * *

[40:15]

大師有僧問、柏樹還有佛性也無。大師云、有。僧曰、柏樹幾時成佛。大師云、待虛空落地。僧曰、虛空幾時落地。大師云、待柏樹子成佛。

The Great Master was asked by a monk, "Does the cypress tree have the buddha nature or not?[50]

The Great Master said, "It does."

The monk said, "When does the cypress attain buddhahood?"

The Great Master said, "Wait till empty space falls on the ground."[51]

The monk said, "When does empty space fall on the ground?"

The Great Master said, "Wait till the cypress tree attains buddhahood."

[40:16]

いま大師の道取を聽取し、這僧の問取をすてざるべし。大師道の虛空落地時、および柏樹成佛時は、互相の相待なる道得にあらざるなり。柏樹を問取し、佛性を問取す、成佛を問取し、時節を問取す、虛空を問取し、落地を問取するなり。

A monk said, "Reverend, how can you use an object to teach people?"
The Master said, "I don't use an object to teach people. If I used an object to teach you, Acārya, it would bury the Acārya."
[The monk] said, "Then what about that?"
The Master bid them farewell [and left].

If these passages are influencing Dōgen's remarks here, his point might be, at least in part, that Zhaozhou's cypress tree is not a memorial to Chan ancestor Bodhidharma but what he is using to "bury" (i.e., teach) people.

48 **return my concentrated effort** (*gen go kufū rai* 還吾功夫來): Or "give me back my concentrated effort." The Chinese imperative construction here, *huan wu . . . lai* 還吾 . . . 來 ("give me back . . ."), is a fairly common challenge in Chan texts; Dōgen uses it (or the closely similar *gen ga . . . rai* 還我 . . . 來) several times in the *Shōbōgenzō*.

49 **"I'm also like this"** (*go yaku nyo ze* 吾亦如是): The words of the Sixth Ancestor, Huineng 慧能, from a dialogue, much quoted by Dōgen, with his disciple Nanyue Huairang 南嶽懷讓 (677-744). Recorded at *shinji Shōbōgenzō* 眞字正法眼藏 (DZZ.5:178, case 101); see Supplementary Notes, s.v. "You're also like this, I'm also like this."

50 **The Great Master** (*daishi* 大師): I.e., Zhaozhou 趙州. A dialogue found in the *Zhaozhou yulu* 趙州語錄 (ZZ.118:321b14-16) and elsewhere.

51 **"Wait till empty space falls on the ground"** (*tai kokū rakuchi* 待虛空落地): Or "once empty space falls to earth." Dōgen will play below on the predicate *tai* 待 ("to wait for," "to depend on").

236 DŌGEN'S *SHŌBŌGENZŌ* VOLUME III

We should not listen to the saying of the Great Master here and discard the question of this monk. The Great Master's words, "*Wait till empty space falls on the ground,*" or "*Wait till the cypress attains buddhahood,*" are not mutually dependent sayings.[52] They are questioning "the cypress," questioning "the buddha nature"; they are questioning "attaining buddhahood," questioning the time ["when"]; they are questioning "empty space," questioning "falling on the ground."

[40:17]

いま大師の向僧道するに、有と道取するは、柏樹佛性有なり。この道を通達して、佛祖の命脈を通暢すべきなり。いはゆる柏樹に佛性ありといふこと、尋常に道不得なり、未曾道なり。すでに有佛性なり、その爲體あきらむべし。有佛性なり、柏樹、いまその地位の高低いかん。壽命・身量の長短たづぬべし、種姓・類族きくべし。さらに百千の柏樹、みな同種姓なるか、別種胤なるか。成佛する柏樹あり、修行する柏樹あり、發心する柏樹あるべきか。柏樹は成佛あれども、修行・發心等を具足せざるか。柏樹と虚空と、有甚麼因縁なるぞ。柏樹の成佛、さだめて待儞落地時なるは、柏樹の樹功、かならず虚空なるか。柏樹の地位は、虚空それ初地か、果位か、審細に功夫參究すべし。我還問汝趙州老、儞亦一根枯柏樹なれば、恁麼の活計を消息せるか。

In the great master's speaking to the monk here, when he says, "It does," he means the "existence of the buddha nature of the cypress."[53] Penetrating these words, we should penetrate the vital artery of the buddhas and ancestors.[54] That the cypress tree has the buddha nature usually cannot be said, has never been said. It has the buddha nature; so we should clarify its state. It has the buddha nature; how about the level of its ground and stage?[55] We should inquire into its lifespan and physical dimensions; we should ask about its family and clan.[56] Further, in a hun-

---

52 **mutually dependent sayings** (*gosō no sōtai naru dōtoku* 互相の相待なる道得): The translation masks Dōgen's play with the term *tai* 待 ("to wait for") in *sōtai* 相待 ("dependent").

53 **"existence of the buddha nature of the cypress"** (*hakuju busshō u* 柏樹佛性有): A tentative translation of an ambiguous phrase. The English loses Dōgen's play here with the graph *u* 有 ("to have," "to be"), translated as "it does" in Zhaozhou's answer. Readers differ on how to parse this phrase; some would read it, "the buddha nature of the cypress is existence"; others suggest, "the cypress is the buddha nature, is existence."

54 **the vital artery of the buddhas and ancestors** (*busso no meimyaku* 佛祖の命脈): The term *meimyaku* 命脈 ("vital artery") occurs often in the *Shōbōgenzō*, in the senses both of the "lifeblood" and the "bloodline" (especially of the lineage of the buddhas and ancestors).

55 **ground and stage** (*chii* 地位): Also read *jii*. Or simply "position." The clumsy translation here seeks to preserve Dōgen's pun, to which he will return below, on the "grounds" (*ji* 地; S. *bhūmi*) and "stages" (*i* 位; S. *avasthā*, etc.) of the bodhisattva path leading to buddhahood.

56 **family and clan** (*shushō ruizoku* 種姓・類族): The compound *ruizoku*, translated here as "clan," may refer to a range of groupings, from familial "relatives" or larger so-

40. The Cypress Tree *Hakujushi* 柏樹子   237

dred thousand cypress trees, are they all of the same family, or are they of distinct familial lines? Should there be cypress trees that attain buddhahood? Cypress trees that practice? Cypress trees that bring forth the mind [of bodhi]? Does the cypress tree, although it attains buddhahood, not fulfill practice and bringing forth the mind? What are the causes and conditions between the cypress tree and empty space? Does the fact that the cypress tree's attaining buddhahood is definitely *wait till you fall on the ground* mean that the cypress tree's virtue as a tree is necessarily space?[57] Regarding the ground and stage of the cypress tree: is empty space the first ground? Is it the fruit stage?[58] We should make concentrated effort to study this in detail. *I ask you, old man Zhaozhou*, "Did you convey such business because *you are yourself one dead cypress tree?*"[59]

[40:18] {1:441}

おほよそ柏樹有佛性は、外道・二乗等の境界にあらず、經師・論師等の見聞にあらざるなり。いはんや枯木死灰の言華に開演せられんや。ただ趙州の種類のみ參學參究するなり。いま趙州道の柏樹有佛性は、柏樹被柏樹礙也無なり、佛性被佛性礙也無なり。この道取、いまだ一佛二佛の究盡するところにあらず。佛面あるもの、かならずしもこの道得を究盡することうべからず。たとひ諸佛のなかにも、道得する諸佛あるべし、道不得なる諸佛あるべし。

In sum, that the cypress tree has the buddha nature is not in the realm of the other paths or the two vehicles, is not seen or heard by the sūtra masters or treatise masters.[60] How much less is it proclaimed in the word

---

cial units (such as a "people") to more abstract "types." "Family" (*shushō* 種姓) may be intended to evoke the common notion that the bodhisattva aiming to become a buddha belongs to the "family" (*shō* 姓; S. *gotra*) of the buddha. Here and in the following sentences, Dōgen is raising the common Buddhist question of what it means to claim that insentient beings can become buddhas.

57 **wait till you fall on the ground** (*tai ni raku chi ji* 待儞落地時): Dōgen has here playfully substituted the pronoun "you" (*ni* 儞) for "space" in Zhaozhou's words.

58 **the first ground** (*shoji* 初地); **the fruit stage** (*kai* 果位): I.e., the first of the ten "grounds" (S. *bhūmi*) of the bodhisattva's practice, and the final effect of that practice, buddhahood, known as the "fruit" (S. *phala*) stage. Dōgen is playing here with the terms "space" and "ground," "tree" and "fruit."

59 **"convey such business"** (*inmo no kakkei o shōsoku seru* 恁麼の活計を消息せる): A loose translation. *Kakkei* 活計 typically refers to one's "livelihood," "way of life," etc.; often applied to the Zen master's activities. *Shōsoku* 消息 is a noun meaning "news," "circumstances," etc.; here put in a verbal form.

60 **other paths or the two vehicles** (*gedō nijō* 外道二乗): I.e., those of non-Buddhist religions (S. *tīrthika*) and those of non-Mahāyāna traditions of Buddhism; a common pejorative in Dōgen's writing.

sūtra masters or treatise masters (*kyōshi ronshi* 經師・論師): I.e., specialists in the interpretation of the sūtras and treatises; scholastics. Another pejorative term commonly found in Dōgen's works.

238 DŌGEN'S *SHŌBŌGENZŌ* VOLUME III

flowers of dried-up trees and dead ashes.[61] Only a type like Zhaozhou studies and investigates it. Zhaozhou's saying here that the cypress has the buddha nature is [asking], "*Is the cypress obstructed by the cypress or not?*"[62] "*Is the buddha nature obstructed by the buddha nature or not?*" This saying is something not yet exhaustively investigated by one buddha or two buddhas. Even those with the face of a buddha are not necessarily able exhaustively to investigate this saying. Even among the buddhas, there will be buddhas who can say it and buddhas who cannot say it.

[40:19]

いはゆる待虚空落地は、あるべからざることをいふにあらず、柏樹子の成佛する毎度に、虚空落地するなり。その落地響かくれざること、百千の雷よりもすぎたり。柏樹成佛の時は、しばらく十二時中なれども、さらに十三時中なり。その落地の虚空は、凡聖所見の虚空のみにはあらず、このほかに一片の虚空あり、餘人所不見なり、趙州一箇見なり。虚空のおつるところの地、また凡聖所領の地にあらず、さらに一片の地あり、陰陽所不到なり、趙州一箇到なり。虚空落地の時節、たとひ日月山河なりとも、待なるべし。たれか道取する、佛性かならず成佛すべし、と。佛性は成佛以後の莊嚴なり、さらに成佛と同生同參する佛性もあるべし。

[The phrase] "*Wait till empty space falls on the ground*" is not saying something that could not be the case: every time the cypress tree attains buddhahood, empty space falls on the ground. The sound of its falling on the ground is not hidden: it exceeds a hundred thousand claps of thunder. The time when "the cypress attains buddhahood," while for the time being is within the twelve times, is further within thirteen times.[63] The empty space that falls on the ground is not just the empty space seen by

---

61 **word flowers of dried-up trees and dead ashes** (*koboku shikai no gonka* 枯木死灰 の言華): "Dried-up trees and dead ashes" is a common Zen expression, used most often in a pejorative sense, for the mind in trance; here, no doubt, practitioners or advocates of contemplative trance. See Supplementary Notes, s.v. "Dried-up tree." "Word flowers" (*gonka* 言華) is an unusual term, perhaps coined after the common Buddhist expression "sky flowers" (*kūge* 空華), the illusory "spots" or "stars," as we might say, seen by defective eyes; see Supplementary Notes, s.v. "Clouded eyes and sky flowers." Dōgen is here no doubt playing with the wood and flowers of Zhaozhou's tree (ignoring the fact that the cypress does not flower).

62 **"Is the cypress obstructed by the cypress or not"** (*hakuju hi hakuju ge ya mu* 柏 樹被柏樹礙也無): This and the following clause are rendered in Chinese syntax. The idiosyncratic usage of "obstructed" here follows that seen above, Note 37.

63 **while for the time being is within the twelve times, is further within thirteen times** (*shibaraku jūni ji chū naredomo, sara ni jūsan ji chū nari* しばらく十二時中なれども、さらに十三時中なり): Generally taken to mean that the buddhahood of the cypress occurs both within and beyond time. For the twelve times, see above, Note 12. Some versions of the text give the second clause here as the puzzling *sara ni jūni ji chū nari* さらに十二時中なり: "is further within the twelve times."

40. The Cypress Tree *Hakujushi* 柏樹子   239

common people and sages: there is an additional piece of empty space; it is "*something not seen by others*"; it is, *Zhaozhou alone sees it.*[64] The ground where empty space falls is also not the ground occupied by commoners and sages: there is a further piece of ground; it is something *not reached by shade or sunlight*; it is, Zhaozhou alone reaches it.[65] At the time empty space falls on the ground, even the sun and moon, mountains and rivers, must be "waiting."[66] Who says that the buddha nature necessarily attains buddhahood? The buddha nature is an adornment after one attains buddhahood; further, there must be a buddha nature that is born together and studies together with attaining buddhahood.

[40:20] {1:442}

しかあればすなはち、柏樹と佛性と、異音同調にあらず。爲道すらくは、何必なるに、作麼生と參究すべし。

Therefore, the cypress and the buddha nature are *not different notes with the same tune.*[67] What we say is, since it is *why necessarily so?* we should investigate it [by asking,] "*what about it?*"[68]

---

64 **common people and sages** (*bonshō* 凡聖): A standard Buddhist expression for ordinary humans (S. *pṛthagjana*, "born apart") and advanced Buddhist adepts (S. ārya, "nobles"), respectively.

"something not seen by others" (*yonin shofuken* 餘人所不見): Likely from a verse in the *Lotus Sūtra* (*Miaofa lianhua jing* 妙法蓮華經, T.262.9:50a6-7):

菩薩於淨身、皆見世所有。唯獨自明了、餘人所不見。
The bodhisattva, in his pure body,
Sees all things in the world.
Only he alone comprehends this;
It is something not seen by others.

65 **a further piece of ground; it is something not reached by shade or sunlight** (*sara ni ippen no chi ari, onyō* [or *inyō*] *sho futō nari* さらに一片の地あり、陰陽所不到なり): Allusion to the well-known tale of the seven wise maidens (see, e.g., *Zongmen liandeng huiyao* 宗門聯燈會要, ZZ.136:444a8-16), who ask the god Śakra for "a piece of ground without shade or sunlight." Dōgen invokes this tale elsewhere: e.g., in his "Shōbōgenzō muchū setsu mu" 正法眼藏夢中説夢 (DZZ.1:297) and *Eihei kōroku* 永平廣錄 (DZZ.3:42-44, no. 64).

66 **even the sun and moon, mountains and rivers, must be "waiting"** (*tatoi jitsugetsu* [or *nichigatsu*] *senga nari tomo, tai naru beshi* たとひ日月山河なりとも、待なるべし): Generally taken to mean that everything in the world occurs at the time that space falls on the ground. Dōgen is here playing with the predicate *tai* 待 ("to wait") from Zhaozhou's statement, "wait till space falls on the ground."

67 **not different notes with the same tune** (*ion dōchō ni arazu* 異音同調にあらず): Usually interpreted to mean that the cypress and the buddha nature are neither different nor the same.

68 **since it is why necessarily so? we should investigate it [by asking,] "what about it?"** (*kahitsu naru ni, somosan to sankyū su beshi* 何必なるに、作麼生と參究すべし): A tentative translation of a rather odd sentence. The antecedent of "it" here is not clear;

240 DŌGEN'S *SHŌBŌGENZŌ* VOLUME III

正法眼藏柏樹子第四十
Treasury of the True Dharma Eye
The Cypress Tree
Number 40

[Ryūmonji MS:]

仁治三年壬寅五月菖節二十一日記

Recorded the twenty-first day, fifth month, sweet flag season of the senior water year of the tiger, the third year of Ninji [20 June 1242][69]

[Tōunji MS:]

爾時仁治三年壬寅五月菖節二十一日記、在雍州宇治郡觀音導利院示衆

Presented to the assembly at the Kannon Dōri Cloister, Uji District, Yōshū; recorded the twenty-first day, fifth month, sweet flag season of the senior water year of the tiger, the third year of Ninji [20 June 1242]

寛元元年癸卯七月三日丁未書寫于越州吉田郡志比莊吉峰寺院主房。
懷奘

Copied at the residence of the head of cloister, Kippō Monastery, Shihi Estate, Yoshida District, Etchū; on the junior fire day of the sheep, the third day of the [intercalary] seventh month of the junior water year of the rabbit, the first year of Kangen [19 August 1243]. Ejō

---

presumably the buddha nature of the cypress or the relationship between the two terms. The awkward "why necessarily so" is a loose rendering of the Chinese interrogative *hebi* 何必: "why must" something be the case, or be done (sometimes in the rhetorical sense, "not necessarily"). Some editions of the text read *nari* なり ("it is") here for *naru ni* なるに ("since it is" or "while it is").

69 **sweet flag season** (*shōsetsu* 菖節): The fifth month, on the fifth day of which was celebrated sweet flag day (*shōbu no hi* 菖蒲の日).

TREASURY OF THE TRUE DHARMA EYE

NUMBER 41

The Three Realms Are Only Mind
Sangai yui shin

三界唯心

The Three Realms Are Only Mind

Sangai yui shin

INTRODUCTION

This text was composed on 17 August 1243, soon after Dōgen's move from Kōshōji, his monastery near the capital, to the domain of his samurai patron Hatano Yoshishige 波多野義重 in Echizen (modern Fukui). The work occurs as number 41 in the seventy-five-chapter *Shōbōgenzō*, number 32 in the sixty-chapter compilation, and number 47 in the Honzan edition.

The "three realms" of the title is standard Buddhist nomenclature for the threefold world system of saṃsāra: the realm of desire (S. *kāma-dhātu*), the realm of form (S. *rūpa-dhātu*), and the realm of formlessness (S. *ārūpya-dhātu*). The identification of these realms with the mind is often associated especially with the Yogācāra and Chinese Huayan schools of Buddhist thought, but versions of the expression, "the three realms are only mind," are found throughout Buddhist literature, including the sayings of the Zen masters.

In his essay, Dōgen comments on three passages on the "three realms" attributed to Buddha Śākyamuni. The first identifies mind, buddha and living beings; the second claims the three realms as the property of the Buddha and living beings as his children; the third warns against the non-Buddhist view that there is a realm of living beings outside the three realms. The essay closes with comments on a conversation on the three realms between the ninth-century Chan master Xuansha Shibei 玄沙師備 and his disciple Lohan Guichen 羅漢桂琛.

正法眼藏第四十一

Treasury of the True Dharma Eye
Number 41

三界唯心

The Three Realms Are Only Mind

[41:1] {1:443}

釋迦大師道、三界唯一心、心外無別法。心・佛及衆生、是三無差別。

Great Master Śākya said,[1]

The three realms are only one mind;
Outside the mind, there's no other dharma.
The mind, the buddha, and living beings —
These three are without distinction.

[41:2]

一句の道著は、一代の擧力なり、一代の擧力は盡力の全擧なり。たとひ強
爲の爲なりとも、云爲の爲なるべし。このゆえに、いま如來道の三界唯心
は、全如來の全現成なり。全一代は全一句なり。三界は全界なり、三界は
すなはち心といふにあらず。そのゆえは、三界はいく玲瓏八面も、なほ三
界なり。三界にあらざらんと誤錯すといふとも、総不著なり。内外中間、
初中後際、みな三界なり。三界は、三界の所見のごとし。界にあらざるも
のの所見は、三界を見不正なり。三界には三界の所見を舊窠とし、三界の
所見を新條とす。舊窠也三界見、新條也三界見なり。このゆえに、

His single saying is all the efforts of a single lifetime; all the efforts
of a single lifetime are the whole of his exhaustive efforts. While it may

---

1 **Great Master Śākya** (*Shaka daishi* 釋迦大師): I.e., Buddha Śākyamuni, here given
the honorific title of a Zen master. The four-line saying attributed to him here, while quoted elsewhere in Chinese and Japanese texts, is not so common in the Chinese Buddhist
literature. Though traditionally held to be a passage from the *Avataṃsaka-sūtra* (*Huayan
jing* 華嚴經), it is in fact assembled from disparate sources. The first line reflects the
language of the Śikṣānanda translation of the *Huayan jing* 華嚴經 (T.279.10:194a14):

三界所有、唯是一心。

What exists in the three realms is only the one mind.

See Supplementary Notes, s.v. "The three realms are only mind." The second line is not
in a sūtra but occurs frequently in Chinese treatises and commentaries. The third and
fourth lines are taken verbatim from the Buddhabhadra translation of the *Huayan jing* 華
嚴經 (T.278.9:465c29). For "the three realms" (*sangai* 三界), see Supplementary Notes,
s.v. "Three realms."

244 DŌGEN'S *SHŌBŌGENZŌ* VOLUME III

be an act of deliberate action, it must be an act of speaking and acting.[2] Therefore, the "*three realms are only mind*" spoken of by the Tathāgata is the whole manifestation of the whole Tathāgata; the whole of his single lifetime is the whole of his single line.[3] "The three realms" are the whole realm; he is not saying "the three realms" are [merely] the mind. The reason is that, on any of their eight sides, crystal clear, "the three realms" are still the three realms.[4] While one might mistakenly hold that they are not the three realms, that is completely untenable. The *inside, outside, and in between, the beginning, middle, and end* — all are "the three realms." "The three realms" are as the three realms are seen.[5] Seen as not being the three realms is the three realms seen incorrectly. In the three realms, the three realms seen are taken as an old den, or the three realms seen are taken as a new item.[6] *"Old den" is a seeing of the three reams; "new item" is a seeing of the three realms.* Therefore,

[41:3] {1:444}

釋迦大師道、不如三界、見於三界。

Great Master Śākya said, "Not as the three realms do I see the three realms."[7]

---

2   **it must be an act of speaking and acting** (*un'i no i naru beshi* 云爲の爲なるべし): A usage, seen elsewhere in Dōgen's writing, that contrasts *gōi* 強爲 (translated here "deliberate action") and *un'i* 云爲 ("words and acts"); the former suggests intentional, premeditated action, while the latter seems to be used for behavior that comes naturally.

3   **the whole manifestation of the whole Tathāgata** (*zen nyorai no zengenjō* 全如來の全現成): Or "the whole manifestation of all tathāgatas." Similarly, the following "the three realms are the whole realm" could be read "the three realms are all the worlds." The translations here aim to preserve Dōgen's repeated use of the word *zen* 全 ("whole") throughout this passage.

4   **any of their eight sides, crystal clear** (*iku reirō hachimen mo* いく玲瓏八面も): From the saying, "all eight sides are crystal clear" (*hachimen reirō* 八面玲瓏); i.e., perfectly clear in all the eight cardinal and ordinal directions. See Supplementary Notes, s.v. "Crystal clear on all eight sides."

5   **"The three realms" are as the three realms are seen** (*sangai wa, sangai no shoken no gotoshi* 三界は、三界の所見のごとし): Likely an allusion to the sentence from the *Lotus Sūtra* that Dōgen quotes in the next section: "Not as the three realms do I see the three realms."

6   **old den** (*kyūka* 舊窠): A standard metaphor for old, habitual ways of thinking, "tired" concepts or clichés.

7   **Great Master Śākya** (*Shaka daishi* 釋迦大師): From the *Lotus Sūtra* (*Miaofa lianhua jing* 妙法蓮華經, T.262.9:42c13-15):

如來如實知見三界之相。無有生死若退若出。亦無在世及滅度者。非實非虛非如非異。不如三界見於三界。

The Tathāgata views the marks of the three realms as they really are. There is no birth or death, no withdrawal or emergence; again, there is no remaining in the world nor passing to extinction. It is neither real nor vacuous, neither similar nor different. Not as the three realms do I see the three realms.

41. The Three Realms Are Only Mind *Sangai yui shin* 三界唯心 245

[41:4]

この所見、すなはち三界なり、この三界は、所見のごとくなり。三界は、本有にあらず、三界は、今有にあらず、三界は、新成にあらず、三界は、因縁生にあらず、三界は、初・中・後にあらず。出離三界あり、今此三界あり。これ機關の、機關と相見するなり、葛藤の、葛藤を生長するなり。今此三界は、三界の所見なり。いはゆる所見は、見於三界なり、見於三界は、見成三界なり、三界見成なり、見成公案なり。よく三界をして發心・修行・菩提・涅槃ならしむ、これすなはち皆是我有なり。このゆえに、

What is seen here is precisely the three realms; these three realms are as they are seen. The three realms are not original being; the three realms are not present being; the three realms are not a new item; the three realms are not arisen from causes and conditions; the three realms are not in the beginning, middle, or end.[8] There is *"departing the three realms"*; there is *"now, these three realms."*[9] This is workings meeting workings; it is entanglements growing entanglements.[10] *"Now, these three realms"* are what is seen by the three realms. "What is seen" is

---

"Not as the three realms do I see the three realms" (*fu nyo sangai, ken o sangai* 不如三界、見於三界): I.e., I do not view the three realms in the way that [the foolish commoners (S. *bāla-pṛthagjana*)] in the three realms view them. Some have wanted to read this line "there is nothing like [i.e., so good as] the three realms seeing the three realms."

8 **original being** (*hon'u* 本有); **present being** (*kon'u* 今有): A common set, as in the verse of the *Nirvāṇa Sūtra* (*Da banniepan jing* 大般涅槃經, T.374.12:422c15-16):

本有今無、本無今有、三世有法、無有是處。

Originally existent, now nonexistent,
Originally nonexistent, now existent:
For the dharmas of the three times,
There is no such thing.

9 **"departing the three realms"** (*shutsuri sangai* 出離三界); **"now, these three realms"** (*kon shi sangai* 今此三界): The latter phrase is the first line of the verse from the *Lotus Sūtra* that Dōgen will quote in the next section; the former phrase (which might also be read "the three realms departed") is a common expression throughout Buddhist literature, no doubt inspired here by the lines of the *Lotus Sūtra* (*Miaofa lianhua jing* 妙法蓮華經, T.262.9:14c24-25) just preceding that first line of verse:

如來已離、三界火宅、寂然閑居、安處林野。

The Tathāgata has already departed
The burning house of the three realms
And dwells quietly at leisure,
Safely residing in forest and field.

For the parable that informs these lines, see Supplementary Notes, s.v. "Burning house."

10 **workings meeting workings** (*kikan no, kikan to shōken suru* 機關の、機關と相見する); **entanglements growing entanglements** (*kattō no, kattō o shōchō suru* 葛藤の、葛藤を生長する): The antecedent of the grammatical subject, "this" (*kore* これ) is perhaps best taken as the two phrases of the preceding sentence: "departing the three realms" and "now these three realms" — i.e., the two aspects or views (transcendent and immanent, respectively) of the three realms. For the term "entanglements" (*kattō* 葛藤), see Supplementary Notes, s.v. "Tangled vines."

246 DŌGEN'S *SHŌBŌGENZŌ* VOLUME III

"*seeing the three realms*"; "*seeing the three realms*" *is realizing the three realms, is the realization of the three realms, is the realized kōan.*[11] To turn the three realms into bringing forth the mind [of bodhi], practice, bodhi, and nirvāṇa — this is "all my property."[12] Therefore,

[41:5]

釋迦大師道、今此三界、皆是我有、其中衆生、悉是吾子。

Great Master Śākya said,[13]

Now, these three realms
Are all my property,
And the living beings within them
Are all my children.

[41:6]

いまこの三界は、如來の我有なるがゆえに、盡界みな三界なり、三界は盡界なるがゆえに。今此は、過・現・當來なり、過・現・當來の現成は、今此を罣礙せざるなり、今此の現成は、過・現・當來を罣礙するなり。

Since "now these three realms" are "my property" of the Tathāgata, all the worlds are "the three realms"; for "the three realms" are all the worlds.[14] "Now these" is past, present, and future. The realization of

---

11 **"What is seen" is "seeing the three realms"** (*iwayuru shoken wa, ken o sangai nari* いはゆる所見は、見於三界なり): I.e., what is seen as the three realms is what the Buddha refers to in the line, "Not as the three realms do I see the three realms" (*ken o sangai* 見於三界).

"seeing the three realms" is realizing the three realms (*ken o sangai wa, genjō sangai nari* 見於三界は、見成三界なり): The translation loses the play on the glyph *ken* 見 ("to see") in *genjō* 見成 ("to realize, or manifest," otherwise written *genjō* 現成).

realized kōan (*genjō kōan* 見成公案): Or "settled case." A Dōgen favorite, the title theme of one of the most celebrated chapters of his *Shōbōgenzō*; see Supplementary Notes.

12 **this is "all my property"** (*kai ze ga u* 皆是我有): Anticipating the words of the Buddha quoted in the immediately following section.

13 **Great Master Śākya** (*Shaku daishi* 釋迦大師): From the *Lotus Sūtra* (*Miaofa lianhua jing* 妙法蓮華經, T.262.9:14c26), in a passage in which the Buddha likens himself to a father who saves his children from their burning house. See Supplementary Notes, s.v. "Burning house."

14 **"now these three realms" are "my property" of the Tathāgata** (*ima kono sangai wa, nyorai no ga u naru* いまこの三界は、如來の我有なる): Dōgen here translates the first line of the Buddha's verse into Japanese. The awkward "'my property' of the Tathāgata" seeks to preserve something of Dōgen's use of the expression *ga u* 我有 ("belongs to me," "mine"), but the English loses the important additional meaning, "my being," "my existence," with which Dōgen is playing here.

for "the three realms" are all the worlds (*sangai wa jinkai naru ga yue ni* 三界は盡界なるがゆえに): The translation of this non sequitur follows Kawamura's punctuation. The clause could also be read with the following sentence, yielding, "Since 'now these

41. The Three Realms Are Only Mind *Sangai yui shin* 三界唯心 247

past, present, and future does not obstruct "now these"; the realization of "now these" obstructs past, present, and future.[15]

[41:7]

我有は、盡十方界眞實人體なり、盡十方界沙門一隻眼なり。衆生は、盡十方界眞實體なり、一一衆生の生衆なるゆえに衆生なり。

"My property" is *all the worlds in the ten directions are the true human body*; it is *all the worlds in the ten directions are the single eye of the śramaṇa.*"[16] "The living beings" are *the true body of all the worlds in the ten directions*. Because each of the living beings is multiple lives, they are "living beings."[17]

[41:8]

悉是吾子は、子也全機現の道理なり。しかあれども、吾子かならず身體髪膚を慈父にうけて、毀破せず、虧闕せざるを、子現成とす。而今は父前子後にあらず、子前父後にあらず、父・子あひならべるにあらざるを、吾子の道理といふなり。與授にあらざれども、これをうく、奪取にあらざれども、これをえたり。去來の相あらず、大小の量にあらず、老少の論にあらず、老少を、佛祖老少のごとく保任すべし。父少子老あり、父老子少あり、父老子老あり、父少子少あり。ちちの老を學するは子にあらず、子の少をへざらんは父にあらざらん。子の老少と、父の老少と、かならず審細に功夫參究すべし、倉卒なるべからず。父子同時に生現する父子あり、父子同時に現滅する父子あり、父子不同時に現生する父子あり、父子不同

---

three realms' are 'my property' of the Tathāgata, all the worlds are 'the three realms.' Since 'the three realms' are all the worlds, 'now these' is past, present, and future."

15 **the realization of "now these" obstructs past, present, and future** (*kon shi no genjō wa, ka gen tōrai o keige suru nari* 今此の現成は、過・現・當來を罣礙するなり): Probably meaning that past, present, and future are defined by, or delimited by, "now these" (rather than vice versa).

16 **"My property" is "all the worlds in the ten directions are the true human body"** (*ga u wa, jin jippō kai shinjitsu nintai nari* 我有は、盡十方界眞實人體なり): I.e., the term "my property" (or "my being") here is equivalent to "the true human body" in the saying, quoted several times by Dōgen, attributed to Xuansha Shibei 玄沙師備 (835-908). Found at *shinji Shōbōgenzō* 眞字正法眼藏, DZZ.5:196, case 131; see Supplementary Notes, s.v. "True human body."

"all the worlds in the ten directions are the single eye of the śramaṇa" (*jin jippō kai shamon isseki gen* 盡十方界沙門一隻眼): Also read *isseki gan*. From a saying, cited elsewhere in the *Shōbōgenzō*, of the ninth-century Chan figure Changsha Jingcen 長沙景岑 (dates unknown); see Supplementary Notes, s.v. "All the worlds in the ten directions are the single eye of the śramaṇa."

17 **Because each of the living beings is multiple lives, they are "living beings"** (*ichiichi shujō no shōshu naru yue ni shujō nari* 一一衆生の生衆なるゆえに衆生なり): A play with the term *shujō* 衆生 that is lost in translation. The term, usually translated "living beings" or "sentient beings," is composed of the plural marker *shu* 衆 plus *shō* 生, "living being," "life," "birth," etc. Dōgen reverses the two elements to create the neologism *shōshu* 生衆, suggesting "a group of lives," "a multitude of living beings," etc.

時に現滅する父子あり。慈父を罣礙せざれども、吾子を現成せり、吾子を罣礙せずして、慈父現成せり。有心衆生あり、無心衆生あり、有心吾子あり、無心吾子あり。かくのごとく吾子・子吾、ことごとく釋迦慈父の令嗣なり。十方盡界にあらゆる過・現・當來の諸衆は、十方盡界の過・現・當の諸佛なり。諸佛の吾子は衆生なり、衆生の慈父は諸佛なり。

"*Are all my children*" is the principle, *children*, "*the manifestation of the full function*."[18] Nevertheless, that "my children" do not damage or diminish "the bodies, hair, and skin" always received from their compassionate father is taken as the realization of "children."[19] In the present case, it is not that the father is before and the child after, nor that the child is before and the father after; it is not that father and child are lined up side by side — this is called the principle of "my children." It is not that they are given to them, but they "receive" them; it is not that they are snatched away from them, but they have "received" them.[20]

They have no mark of coming or going; they are not measured by large or small; they are not an issue of old or young; we should maintain old and young as the old and young of the buddhas and ancestors.[21] There

---

18 **children, "the manifestation of the full function"** (*shi ya zenki gen* 子也全機現): Variation on a verse comment by Yuanwu Keqin 圜悟克勤 (1063–1135) on a saying of Daowu Yuanzhi 道吾圓智 (769–835). When Daowu was asked at a funeral whether what was in the coffin was alive or dead, he said, "Alive, I don't say; dead, I don't say." On this Yuanwu commented,

生也全機現、死也全機現。

Alive, the manifestation of the full function;
Dead, the manifestation of the full function.

For the funeral story and Yuanwu's verse comment, see Supplementary Notes, s.v. "Manifestation of the full function."

19 **do not damage or diminish "the bodies, hair, and skin" always received from their compassionate father** (*shintai happu o jifu ni ukete, kiha sezu, kiketsu sezaru* 身體髮膚を慈父にうけて、毀破せず、虧闕せざる): Variation on the famous line from the opening of the Confucian *Classic of Filial Piety* (*Xiaojing* 孝經, Kaizong mingyi 開宗明義, KR.1f0001.001.1a):

身體髮膚，受之父母，不敢毀傷，孝之始也。

Our bodies, hair, and skin are received from our parents; we dare not damage or wound them. This is the beginning of filial piety.

20 **It is not that they are given to them, but they "receive" them** (*yoju ni arazaredomo, kore o uku* 與授にあらざれども、これをうく): I.e., "it is not that the 'bodies, hair, and skin' are given to 'my children,' but 'my children' do 'receive' them from their compassionate father."

21 **They have no mark of coming or going** (*korai no sō arazu* 去來の相あらず): The unexpressed grammatical subject throughout this sentence is taken as "the father and his children."

we should maintain old and young as the old and young of the buddhas and ancestors (*rōshō o, busso rōshō no gotoku hōnin su beshi* 老少を、佛祖老少のごとく保任す

41. The Three Realms Are Only Mind *Sangai yui shin* 三界唯心　　249

are cases where the father is young and the child old, cases where the father is old and the child young, cases where the father is old and the child old, cases where the father is young and the child young.[22] One who studies the father's old age is not a child; one who does not go through the child's youth is not a father.[23] Old and young in the children and old and young in the father, we should work at and investigate in detail, we should not treat hastily.

There are fathers and children in which father and child are born and appear at the same time; there are fathers and children in which father and child manifest extinction at the same time; there are fathers and children in which father and child do not appear at the same time; there are fathers and children in which father and child do not manifest extinction at the same time.[24] Although they do not obstruct the compassionate father, they have manifest "my children"; without obstructing "my children," the compassionate father manifests.[25] There are "living beings" with minds; there are "living beings" with no minds; there are "my children" with minds; there are "my children" with no minds. In this way, whether "my children" or "we children" — all are worthy successors of the compassionate father Śākya.[26] All beings of past, present, and future throughout all the worlds in the ten directions are the buddhas of past,

---

べし): This could be understood either as "we should take 'old and young' here as similar to their use in reference to the buddhas and ancestors," or as "we should treat 'old and young' as they are understood by the buddhas and ancestors."

22　**There are cases where the father is young and the child old** (*fu shō shi rō ari* 父少子老あり): Dōgen may have in mind here the passage in the *Lotus Sūtra* (*Miaofa lianhua jing* 妙法蓮華經, T.262.9:42a11-14) in which Śākyamuni's claim to have trained myriad bodhisattvas is likened to a young man claiming to have fathered a child of one hundred.

23　**One who studies the father's old age is not a child; one who does not go through the child's youth is not a father** (*chichi no rō o gaku suru wa ko ni arazu, ko no shō o hezaran wa chichi ni arazaran* ちちの老を學するは子にあらず、子の少をへざらんは父にあらざらん): Perhaps meaning that there are no children of a buddha who are not themselves already buddhas; there are no buddhas who are not themselves children of a buddha.

24　**father and child manifest extinction at the same time** (*fushi dōji ni genmetsu suru* 父子同時に現滅する): I.e., the two enter nirvāṇa simultaneously.

25　**Although they do not obstruct the compassionate father, they have manifest "my children"** (*jifu o keige sezaredomo, goshi o genjō seri* 慈父を罣礙せざれども、吾子を現成せり): Perhaps meaning that being the child of the buddha does not interfere with being the parent buddha. Some texts read here *goshi to genjō seri* 吾子と現成せり ("they have manifest as my children").

26　**whether "my children" or "we children"** (*goshi shigo* 吾子・子吾): "We children" is an attempt to capture Dōgen's playful reversal of the syntax of the expression "my children" (*goshi* 吾子); perhaps meaning, whether from the perspective of the father or of the child.

present, and future throughout all the worlds in the ten directions. "My children" of the buddhas are the living beings; the compassionate fathers of the living beings are the buddhas.

[41:9] {1:445}

しかあればすなはち、百草の華果は、諸佛の我有なり、巌石の大小は、諸佛の我有なり。安處は林野なり、林野は已離なり。

Such being the case, the flowers and fruits of the hundred grasses are "my property" of the buddhas; the large and small rocks and stones are "my property" of the buddhas. Their "safely residing" is "forest and field"; "forest and field" is their having "already departed."[27]

[41:10]

しかもかくのごとくなりといふとも、如來道の宗旨は、吾子の道のみなり、其父の道、いまだあらざるなり、參究すべし。

Although this may be so, the essential point of the Tathāgata's words are only the words, "my children"; we should investigate the fact that he never uses the words, "their father."

[41:11]

釋迦牟尼佛道、諸佛應化法身、亦不出三界。三界外無衆生、佛何所化。是故我言、三界外別有一衆生界藏者、外道大有經中説、非七佛之所説。

Buddha Śākyamuni said,[28]

The response, transformation, and dharma bodies of the buddhas do not go beyond the three realms.[29] *Outside the three realms, there are no living beings; so, what would be converted by the buddha? Therefore, I say, [the claim] that there is a store of a realm of living beings outside the three realms is a theory in the Scripture of Great Being of an other path, not something taught by the seven buddhas.*[30]

---

27 Their "safely residing" is "forest and field"; "forest and field" is their having "already departed" (*ansho wa rinya nari, rinya wa iri nari* 安處は林野なり、林野は已離なり): From the *Lotus Sūtra* verse noted above; see Note 9.

28 Buddha Śākyamuni (*Shakamuni butsu* 釋迦牟尼佛): From the *Renwang jing* 仁王經, T.245.8:827a1-4.

29 response, transformation, and dharma bodies of the buddhas (*shobutsu ōke hosshin* 諸佛應化法身): The exact sense of this expression is unclear, depending on whether the "response" body (*ōjin* 應身) is taken as (a) a more exalted form of the "transformation" body (*keshin* 化身; S. *nirmāṇa-kāya*), the body that appears as a human, or (b) another term for the reward body (*hōshin* 報身; S. *saṃbhoga-kāya*), the perfected body developed through practice on the bodhisattva path.

30 *Scripture of Great Being* of an other path (*gedō Daiu kyō* 外道大有經): Unidentified; often attributed to the Vaiśeṣika school of Hinduism but may be a generic term for scriptures asserting the concept of *brahman*.

41. The Three Realms Are Only Mind *Sangai yui shin* 三界唯心 251

[41:12] {1:446}

あきらかに参究すべし、諸佛應化法身は、みなこれ三界なり、無外なり。
たとへば、如來の無外なるがごとし、牆壁無外なるがごとし、三界の無外
なるがごとく、衆生無外なり。無衆生のところ、佛何所化なり、佛所化
は、かならず衆生なり。

We should clearly investigate that the response, transformation, and
dharma bodies of the buddhas are all "the three realms," are without
outside.[31] This is like the tathāgatas being without outside, like fences
and walls being without outside; just as the three realms are without outside, living beings are without outside. Where it is without living beings,
"*what would be converted by the buddha?*" "What is converted by the
buddha" is always living beings.

[41:13]

しるべし、三界外に一衆生界藏を有せしむるは、外道大有經なり、七佛經
にあらざるなり。唯心は一二にあらず、三界にあらず、出三界にあらず、
無有錯謬なり。有慮知念覺なり、無慮知念覺なり、牆壁瓦礫なり、山河大
地なり。心、これ皮肉骨髓なり、心、これ拈華破顔なり。有心あり、無心
あり、有身の心あり、無身の心あり、身先の心あり、身後の心あり。身を
生ずるに、胎・卵・湿・化の種品あり、心を生ずるに、胎・卵・湿・化の
種品あり。青黄赤白、これ心なり、長短方円、これ心なり、生死去來、こ
れ心なり、年月日時、これ心なり、夢幻空華、これ心なり、水沫泡焔、こ
れ心なり、春花秋月、これ心なり、造次顚沛、これ心なり。しかあれど
も、毀破すべからず。かるがゆえに、諸法實相心なり、唯佛與佛心なり。

We should realize that the granting of being to "a store of a realm of
living beings outside the three realms" is from "the *Scripture of Great
Being* of an other path," not a sūtra of the seven buddhas. "Only mind"
is not one or two, is not "the three realms," is not "beyond the three
realms," is "without error."[32] It is having thinking and perceiving; it is
lacking thinking and perceiving.[33] It is "fences, walls, tiles, and pebbles";

31　**are without outside** (*muge nari* 無外なり): Dōgen reverses the syntax of the predicate *ge mu* 外無 ("outside there are no") in the quotation.

32　**"without error"** (*mu u shakumyō* 無有錯謬): Reflecting the line in the *Lotus Sūtra* (*Miaofa lianhua jing* 妙法蓮華經, T.262.9:42c16) just following the quotation in section 3, above:

　　不如三界見於三界。如斯之事、如來明見無有錯謬。

　　Not as the three realms do I see the three realms. Such things, the Tathāgata sees
　　clearly, without error.

33　**thinking and perceiving** (*ryo chi nen kaku* 慮知念覺): A loose translation of terms
for cognitive functions not commonly found as a set in Buddhist literature but appearing
several times in the *Shōbōgenzō*, where they seem to stand collectively for the ordinary
operations of consciousness. The translation takes them as two compound expressions
(the first of which does occur elsewhere in the *Shōbōgenzō* in reference to the thinking
mind); as individual terms, they might be rendered "considering, knowing, thinking, and
perceiving." See Supplementary Notes.

252 DŌGEN'S *SHŌBŌGENZŌ* VOLUME III

it is mountains, rivers, and the whole earth.[34] Mind is skin, flesh, bones, and marrow; mind is holding up a flower and breaking into a smile.[35]

There is having mind; there is lacking mind. There is mind with a body; there is mind without a body. There is mind before the body; there is mind after the body.[36] When the body is born, there are the types: from womb, egg, moisture, and transformation; when the mind is born, there are the types: from womb, egg, moisture, and transformation.[37] Blue, yellow, red, and white — these are mind; long, short, square, and round — these are mind; birth and death, coming and going — these are mind; years, months, days, and hours — these are mind; dreams, phantasms, sky flowers — these are mind; water spray, foam, and flames — these are mind; the spring flowers and the autumn moon — these are mind; "in haste and at risk" — these are mind.[38] Nevertheless, we should not

---

34 **"fences, walls, tiles, and pebbles"** (*shō heki ga ryaku* 牆壁瓦礫): A well-known expression in Zen texts, often identified with the buddha mind; see Supplementary Notes, s.v. "Fences, walls, tiles, and pebbles."

mountains, rivers, and the whole earth (*senga daichi* 山河大地): A common expression for "the physical world," occurring very frequently throughout Dōgen's writings.

35 **skin, flesh, bones, and marrow** (*hi niku kotsu zui* 皮肉骨髓); **holding up a flower and breaking into a smile** (*nenge hagan* 拈華破顔): Two stock expressions for the transmission of Zen: the first is from the story of Bodhidharma's transmission to the second Chinese ancestor, Huike 慧可; the second is from the story of the first transmission, on Vulture Peak, from Buddha Śākyamuni to Mahākāśyapa. See Supplementary Notes, s.v. "Skin, flesh, bones, and marrow," "Hold up a flower," and "Break into a smile."

36 **mind before the body** (*shinsen no shin* 身先の心): "Before the body and after the body" (*shinsen shingo* 身先身後) are most often used in reference to lifetimes before and after this lifetime; see Supplementary Notes, s.v. "Body and mind."

37 **womb, egg, moisture, and transformation** (*tairanshikke* 胎・卵・湿・化): The four ways in which living beings are born in saṃsāra: "womb born" (S. *jarāyujā*) refers to mammals; "egg born" (S. *aṇḍaja*) refers to birds and reptiles; "moisture born" (S. *saṃsvedajā*) refers to lower forms of animal life, such as insects; "transformation born" (S. *upapāḍukā*) refers to those in the heavens and hells, as well as the incarnations of buddhas and advanced bodhisattvas.

38 **sky flowers** (*kūge* 空華): S. *khapuṣpa*; spots appearing to the diseased eye; a standard metaphor in Buddhist texts for what is mere appearance without objective reality; see Supplementary Notes, s.v. "Clouded eyes and sky flowers."

"in haste and at risk" (*zōji tenpai* 造次顛沛): A fixed idiom for fleeting experience, from a saying in the *Lunyu* 論語 4 (KR.1h0005.002.11b):

君子無終食之間違仁，造次必於是，顛沛必於是。

The gentleman does not violate humaneness even for the space of a meal: even when in haste, he keeps to it; even when at risk, he keeps to it.

41. The Three Realms Are Only Mind *Sangai yui shin* 三界唯心

damage them.³⁹ Therefore, "the real marks of the dharmas" are mind; "*only buddhas with buddhas*" are mind.⁴⁰

* * * * *

[41:14]

玄砂院宗一大師、問地藏院眞應大師云、三界唯心、汝作麼生會。眞應指椅子云、和尚喚遮箇作什麼。大師云、椅子。眞應曰、和尚不會三界唯心。大師云、我喚遮箇作竹木、汝喚作什麼。眞應曰、桂琛亦喚作竹木。大師云、盡大地覓一箇會佛法人不可得。

> *Great Master Zongyi of the Xuansha Cloister asked Great Master Zhenying of Dizang Cloister, "'The three realms are only mind.' How do you understand it?"⁴¹*
>
> *Zhenying pointed to a chair and said, "What does the Reverend call this?"*
>
> *The Great Master said, "A chair."*
>
> *Zhenying said, "The Reverend doesn't understand 'the three realms are only mind.'"*
>
> *The Great Master said, "I call it bamboo and wood. What do you call it?"*
>
> *Zhenying said, "Guichen also calls it bamboo and wood."*
>
> *The Great Master said, "I can't find a single person on all the whole earth who understands the buddha dharma."*

---

39 **we should not damage them** (*kiha su bekarazu* 毀破すべからず): Recalling the Confucian maxim noted above, Note 19.

40 **"the real marks of the dharmas" are mind; "only buddhas with buddhas" are mind** (*shohō jissō shin nari, yuibutsu yo butsu shin nari* 諸法實相心なり、唯佛與佛心なり): Or "it [i.e., mind] is the mind of 'the real marks of the dharmas'; it is the mind of 'only buddhas with buddhas.'" From a passage in the *Lotus Sūtra* often cited by Dōgen; see Supplementary Notes, s.v. "Only buddhas with buddhas can exhaustively investigate the real marks of the dharmas."

41 **Great Master Zongyi of Xuansha Cloister** (*Genshain Sōitsu daishi* 玄砂院宗一大師): I.e., Xuansha Shibei 玄沙師備. The interlocutor here, "Great Master Zhenying of Dizang Cloister" (*Jizōin Shinnō daishi* 地藏院眞應大師), is Xuansha's disciple Luohan Guichen 羅漢桂琛 (867-928). Their conversation can be found at *Jingde chuandeng lu* 景德傳燈錄, T.2076.51:371a9-13), as well as in Dōgen's *shinji Shōbōgenzō* 眞字正法眼藏 (DZZ.5:186, case 112).

254   DŌGEN'S *SHŌBŌGENZŌ* VOLUME III

[41:15] {1:447}

いま大師の問取する三界唯心汝作麼生會は、作麼生會・未作麼生會、おな
じく三界唯心なり。このゆえに、未三界唯心なるべし。眞應、このゆえに
椅子をさしていはく、和尚喚遮箇作什麼。しるべし、汝作麼生會は、喚遮
箇作什麼なり。

In the Great Master's question — "'*The three realms are only mind.*'
How do you understand it?" — "How do you understand it?" and "How
do you not understand it?" are equally "the three realms are only mind."
Therefore, it must be "not the three realms are only mind."[42] Zhenying,
therefore, points at the chair and says, "*What does the Reverend call
this?*" We should recognize that "How do you understand it?" is "What
do you call this?"

[41:16]

大師道の椅子は、且道すべし、これ會三界語なりや、不會三界語なりや、
三界語なりや、非三界語なりや、椅子道なりや、大師道なりや。かくのご
とく試道看の道究すべし。試會看の會取あり、試參看の究參あるべし。

The Great Master's saying "chair" — tell me, is this a word of understanding the three realms, or is it a word of not understanding the
three realms? Is it a word of the three realms, or is it a word not of the
three realms? Is it the saying of the chair, or is it the saying of the Great
Master? In this way, we should investigate the saying by trying to say it.
There should be an understanding that tries to understand it, a thorough
study that tries to study it.

[41:17]

眞應いはく、和尚不會三界唯心。この道、たとへば道趙州するなかの東
門・南門なりといへども、さらに西門・北門なり。さらに東趙州・南趙
州あり。たとひ會三界唯心ありとも、さらに不會三界唯心を參究すべきな
り。さらにまた會・不會にあらざる三界唯心あり。

Zhenying said, "*The Reverend doesn't understand 'the three realms
are only mind.'*" This saying may be, for example, the "East Gate" and
"South Gate" in speaking of Zhaozhou, but it is in addition the "West
Gate" and "North Gate."[43] There is in addition an East Zhaozhou and

---

42   **"How do you understand it?" and "How do you not understand it?"** (*somosan
e mi somosan e* 作麼生會・未作麼生會); **it must be "not the three realms are only
mind"** (*mi sangai yui shin naru beshi* 未三界唯心なるべし): Dōgen plays here with
Zhenying's, "The Reverend doesn't understand 'the three realms are only mind,'" creating two improbable negative versions of the original question. Presumably, "how do you
understand it?" is to "the three realms are only mind" as "how do you not understand it?"
is to "not the three realms are only mind."

43   **This saying may be, for example, the "East Gate" and "South Gate" in speaking
of Zhaozhou, but it is in addition the "West Gate" and "North Gate"** (*kono dō, tatoeba dō Jōshū suru naka no tōmon nanmon nari to iedomo sara ni seimon hokumon nari*

41. The Three Realms Are Only Mind *Sangai yui shin* 三界唯心　　255

a South Zhaozhou. We should investigate the fact that, even if there is understanding "the three realms are only mind," there is in addition "not understanding the three realms are only mind." In addition, there is also "the three realms are only mind" that is neither understood nor not understood.

[41:18]

大師道、我喚遮箇作竹木。この道取、かならず聲前句後に光前絶後の節目を参徹すべし。いはゆる我喚遮箇作竹木、いまの喚作よりさきは、いかなる喚作なりとかせん。從來の八面玲瓏に、初・中・後ともに竹木なりとやせん。いまの喚作竹木は、道三界唯心なりとやせん、不道三界唯心なりとやせん。しるべし、あしたに三界唯心を道取するには、たとひ椅子なりとも、たとひ唯心なりとも、たとひ三界なりとも、暮に三界唯心を道取するには、我喚遮箇作竹木、と道取せらるるなり。

The Great Master said, "I call it bamboo and wood." In this saying, before the speech and after the words, we should investigate and penetrate the item that is bright before and extinct after.[44] "*I call it bamboo and wood*" — before he called it that here, what was it called? When up till now the eight sides were crystal clear, were beginning, middle, and end all "bamboo and wood"?[45] Is "calling it bamboo and wood" here saying

---

この道、たとへば道趙州するなかの東門・南門なりといへども、さらに西門・北門なり): Allusion to a saying of Zhaozhou Congshen 趙州從諗 (778-897) appearing in the *Dahui Pujue chanshi yulu* 大慧普覺禪師語錄 (T.1998A.47:844b28-c1) and recorded in Dōgen's *shinji Shōbōgenzō* 眞字正法眼藏 (DZZ.5:150, case 46):

> 趙州因僧問、如何是趙州。師曰、東門南門西門北門。僧曰、不問這箇。師曰、儞問趙州覽。
>
> Zhaozhou was once asked by a monk, "What is Zhaozhou."
> The Master said, "East Gate, South Gate, West Gate, North Gate."
> The monk said, "I didn't ask about that."
> The Master said, "You asked about Zhaozhou."

Zhaozhou's answer plays on the fact that his sobriquet is that of the city of Zhaozhou 趙州 — hence, the four city gates. Dōgen's sentence seems to suggest that the Reverend's "not understanding the three realms are only mind" is not only two of the gates (half the story?) but all four; however, some texts give here "but there should be in addition the West Gate and North Gate" (*sara ni seimon hokumon aru beshi* さらに西門北門あるべし), which suggests, there may be more to Xuansha than "not understanding."

44　**before the speech and after the words** (*shōzen kugo* 聲前句後): A fairly common phrase in Zen literature, seemingly a development from the expression "words before speech" (*shōzen ku* 聲前句, or *shōzen ikku* 聲前一句): i.e., expressing what precedes language, or cannot be said.

bright before and extinct after (*kōzen zetsugo* 光前絶後): An idiom for something unique — better than anything preceding it and not to be replicated in the future; variant of "empty before and extinct after" (*kūzen zetsugo* 空前絶後).

45　**When up till now the eight sides were crystal clear, were beginning, middle, and end all "bamboo and wood"?** (*jūrai no hachimen reirō ni sho chū go tomo ni chikuboku nari to ya sen* 從來の八面玲瓏に、初・中・後ともに竹木なりとやせん):

256 DŌGEN'S *SHŌBŌGENZŌ* VOLUME III

it is "the three realms are only mind"? Or is it not saying it is "the three realms are only mind"? We should realize that, when we speak of "the three realms are only mind" in the morning, we may speak of a "chair," or of "only mind," or of "the three realms"; but when we speak of "the three realms are only mind" in the evening, it is spoken of as "*I call it bamboo and wood.*"

[41:19] {1:448}

眞應道の桂琛亦喚作竹木、しるべし、師資の對面道なりといふとも、同參の頭正尾正なるべし。しかありといへども、大師道の喚遮箇作竹木と、眞應道の亦喚作竹木と、同なりや、不同なりや、是なりや、不是なりや、と參究すべきなり。

Zhenying says, "*Guichen also calls it bamboo and wood.*" We should recognize that, while this may be words exchanged face-to-face between master and disciple, they must be [the words] correct from head to tail of a fellow student.[46] Although this may be so, we should thoroughly investigate whether the "*I call it bamboo and wood*" said by the Great Master and the "*I also call it bamboo and wood*" said by Zhengyin are the same, are not the same, are right, or are not right.

[41:20]

大師云盡大地覓一箇會佛法人不可得。この道取をも、審細に辨肯すべし。

The Great Master said, "I can't find a single person anywhere on all the whole earth who understands the buddha dharma." This saying, we should confirm in detail.

[41:21]

しるべし、大師もただ喚作竹木なり、眞應もただ喚作竹木なり。さらに、いまだ三界唯心を會取せず、三界唯心を不會取せず、三界唯心を道取せず、三界唯心を不道取せず。しかもかくのごとくなりといへども、宗一大師に問著すべし、覓一箇會佛法人不可得は、たとひ道著すとも、試道看、なにを喚作してか盡大地とする。

We should realize that the Great Master is only, "*I call it bamboo and wood,*" and Zhenying is also only, "*I call it bamboo and wood.*" Beyond that, they have not understood "the three realms are only mind"; they have not failed to understand "the three realms are only mind"; they have said that "the three realms are only mind"; they have not failed to say that "the three realms are only mind." Nevertheless, while this may

---

Likely meaning, "was it always everywhere obviously 'bamboo and wood'?" Cf. Supplementary Notes, s.v. "Chairs, bamboo, and wood."

46　**they must be [the words] correct from head to tail of a fellow student** (*dōsan no zushin bishin naru beshi* 同參の頭正尾正なるべし): I.e., Zhengying's words, though those of the disciple, are the correct statement of one who studies together with Xuansha.

41. The Three Realms Are Only Mind *Sangai yui shin* 三界唯心   257

be so, we should ask Great Master Zongyi, "You say that you '*can't find a single person who understands the buddha dharma,*' but try saying what you are calling 'all the whole earth.'"[47]

[41:22]

おほよそ恁麼、参究功夫すべきなり。

In sum, we should investigate and work on it like this.

正法眼藏三界唯心第四十一
Treasury of the True Dharma Eye
The Three Realms Are Only Mind
Number 41

[Ryūmonji MS:]

爾時寛元元年癸卯閏七月初一日、在越宇禪師峰頭示衆
Presented to the assembly on Yamashibu Peak, Etsuu; first day of the intercalary seventh month of the junior water year of the rabbit, the first year of Kangen [17 August 1243][48]

[Tōunji MS:]

同年月廿五日、書寫于院主坊。懷奘
Copied in the administrator's quarters; twenty-fifth day of the same month and year [10 September 1243]. Ejō

于時日本永正七年庚午七月七夕日、於阿陽之桂林丈室下。暮齡七十三
用兼謹寫之
Respectfully copied in the abbot's quarters of Keirin, Ayō, day of the Star Festival; seventh month, senior metal year of the horse, the seventh year of Eishō in Japan [11 August 1510]. Yōken, an elder of seventy-three[49]

47　**try saying what you are calling "all the whole earth"** (*shi dō kan, nani o kansa shite ka jin daichi to suru* 試道看、なにを喚作してか盡大地とする): From Xuansha's saying, "I can't find a single person on all the whole earth who understands the buddha dharma."

48　The Tōunji 洞雲寺 MS shares an identical colophon.

49　**Ayō** 阿陽: I.e., Awa 阿波, present-day Tokushima Prefecture.

Star Festival (*shichiseki* 七夕): The festival known in Japan as *Tanabata* 七夕, held on the seventh day of the seventh month.

Yōken 用兼: I.e., Kinkō Yōken 金岡用兼 (1437–1513?).

TREASURY OF THE TRUE DHARMA EYE

NUMBER 42

Talking of the Mind, Talking of the Nature
Sesshin Sesshō

説心説性

Talking of the Mind, Talking of the Nature

Sesshin Sesshō

INTRODUCTION

According to its colophon, this work was composed in 1243, at Kippō-ji, the monastery in Echizen (present-day Fukui) where Dōgen resided following his departure from the capital area in the summer of the same year. It occurs as number 42 in the seventy-five-chapter compilation of the *Shōbōgenzō* and as number 48 in the Honzan edition. It is also found as number 6 in fascicle 3 of the twenty-eight-text *Himitsu* collection; as is typical of texts in this collection, it does not occur in the sixty-chapter compilation.

The text represents a commentary on a conversation between the Tang-dynasty monks Shenshan Sengmi 神山僧密 and his dharma brother Dongshan Liangjie 洞山良价, famed founder of Dōgen's Caodong (Sōtō) lineage. The title derives from Dongshan's remark in the conversation that "there's someone inside who's talking of the mind and talking of the nature."

In the Chinese Chan literature (and perhaps even in Dongshan's use), to talk of the mind and the nature was sometimes seen as a waste of time. In a passing remark in the "Shōbōgenzō sansui kyō" 正法眼藏山水經, Dōgen seems to agree with this view; but here he takes the opposite position, arguing forcefully that talking of the mind and the nature is the very essence of the Zen tradition, what he calls in his final sentence "the essential functions of the seven buddhas and the ancestral masters." Talking of the nature, he says, is the nature "talking," the buddha nature expressing itself in the world; and it is participation in this activity that constitutes the teaching, practice, and awakening of the way of the buddhas.

From this position, Dōgen criticizes those who think that one must give up talking of the mind and the nature in order to attain the way. In particular, he singles out the Song-dynasty master Dahui Zonggao 大慧宗杲 as someone who does not understand the mind and the nature, someone who has not "tasted the tea and rice of the buddhas and an-

42. Talking of the Mind, Talking of the Nature *Sesshin Sesshō* 説心説性 261

cestors." This attack on a leading figure of the Linji house of Chan, as well as a passing jibe at the founder of the house, Linji Yixuan 臨濟義玄, himself, together with the praise of the Caodong founder, Dongshan, as "the most honored among the ancestors," has led some readers to see the present work as in part an argument for the superiority of Dōgen's Sōtō tradition.

262

正法眼藏第四十二
Treasury of the True Dharma Eye
Number 42

説心説性

Talking of the Mind, Talking of the Nature

[42:1] {1:449}
神山僧密禪師、與洞山悟本大師行次、悟本大師、指傍院曰、裏面有人説心
説性。僧密師伯曰、是誰。悟本大師曰、被師伯一問、直得去死十分。僧密
師伯曰、説心説性底誰。悟本大師曰、死中得活。

*Once, when Chan Master Shenshan Sengmi was traveling with Great
Master Dongshan Wuben, Great Master Wuben pointed out a cloister
beside [the road] and said, "Inside, there's someone talking of the mind
and talking of the nature."[1]*

Elder brother Sengmi said, "Who is it?"[2]

---

1 **Chan Master Shenshan Sengmi** (*Shinzan Sōmitsu zenji* 神山僧密禪師): Tang-dynasty figure (dates unknown); disciple of Yunyan Tansheng 雲巖曇晟. "Great Master
Dongshan Wuben" (*Tōzan Gohon daishi* 洞山悟本大師) is the title of Dongshan Liangjie 洞山良价 (807-869), founder of the Caodong 曹洞 tradition of Chan; also a disciple of
Yunyan Tansheng. Their story, quoted here in Chinese, appears in Dōgen's *shinji Shōbōgenzō* 眞字正法眼藏 (DZZ.5:158, case 62), probably taken from the *Zongmen tongyao
ji* 宗門統要集 (ZTS.1:159b); see also *Liandeng huiyao* 聯燈會要 (ZZ.136:768b14-16).

cloister beside [the road] (*bō in* 傍院): Supplying *ro* 路 from the Chinese versions of the
story, which give *lu bang yuan* 路傍院.

"Inside" (*rimen* 裏面): The element *men* 面, while here having little semantic function
in the Chinese, has the etymological sense, "face" or "surface" — a sense Dōgen will
take advantage of in his commentary below, section 18.

"there's someone" (*unin* 有人): Or simply "someone"; Dōgen will play with the predi-
cate-nominative syntax of the Chinese idiom in his commentary, section 18.

"talking of the mind and talking of the nature" (*sesshin sesshō* 説心説性): A famous
phrase that gets picked up in other Zen texts. "Mind" and "nature" can be understood either as two topics (the mind and its true nature) or as two elements of a single compound
expression, *shinshō* 心性, "the nature of the mind." The predicate, *setsu* 説, taken here
simply as "to talk about," also has the meanings, "to explain," "to expound," "to teach,"
"to preach." Hence, especially in the setting of the cloister here, Dongshan's remark
could be read, "There's someone preaching the mind and preaching the nature."

2 **Elder brother Sengmi** (*Sōmitsu shihaku* 僧密師伯): The term *shihaku* 師伯, translated here as "elder brother," reflects the fact that Shenshan 神山 and Dongshan 洞山 were
fellow disciples of Yunyan 雲巖 and, hence, are "dharma brothers." While the Chinese

42. Talking of the Mind, Talking of the Nature *Sesshin Sesshō* 説心説性 263

Great Master Wuben said, "Once he's questioned by my elder brother, he's definitely completely dead."[3]

Elder brother Sengmi said, "Who is it that's talking of the mind and talking of the nature?"

Great Master Wuben said, "In death, he lives."[4]

[42:2]

説心説性は、佛道の大本なり、これより佛佛祖祖を現成せしむるなり。説心説性にあらざれば、轉妙法輪することなし、發心・修行することなし、大地有情同時成道することなし、一切衆生無佛性することなし。拈華瞬目は、説心説性なり、破顔微笑は、説心説性なり、禮拜依位而立は、説心説性なり、祖師入梁は、説心説性なり、夜半傳衣は、説心説性なり、拈拄杖、これ説心説性なり、横拂子、これ説心説性なり。

"*Talking of the mind and talking of the nature*" is the great origin of the way of the buddhas; from it are caused to appear buddha after buddha and ancestor after ancestor. Without "*talking of the mind and talking of the nature*," there would be no turning the wheel of the wondrous dharma; there would be no bringing forth the mind [of bodhi] or practicing; there would be no "*whole earth and sentient beings simultaneously attaining the way*"; there would be no "*all living beings have no buddha nature*."[5] *Holding up a flower and blinking the eyes is "talking of the*

---

sources (and the *shinji Shōbōgenzō*) identify Shenshan simply as "the Master" (*shih* 師), Dōgen introduces here the honorific term that Dongshan will use in reference to Shenshan. Commentators often parse this term as "the Master's (i.e., Dongshan's) elder brother" and treat it as an honorific among Dongshan's followers; this interpretation may work for Dōgen's use in this line, but it hardly fits with Dongshan's own use in the next line.

3 **"he's definitely completely dead"** (*jiki toku kyoshi jūbun* 直得去死十分): The expression *kyoshi jūbun* 去死十分 ("totally dead") is an idiom occurring in Zen texts with a sense something like "is as good as dead"; in his commentary below, Dōgen will play with the element *jūbun* 十分 ("completely," "totally"), which has a literal sense, "ten parts" (or "a hundred percent"). The grammatical subject is unexpressed here; it is usually taken as the "someone" (*unin* 有人) who is "talking of the mind and talking of the nature," but it could be Dongshan himself.

4 **"In death, he lives"** (*shi chū toku katsu* 死中得活): Or "he revives," "he survives." Perhaps derived from the Chinese idiom, "to seek life in death" (*si chung qiu huo* 死中求活) — i.e., to hope to survive a desperate situation.

5 **Without "talking of the mind and talking of the nature"** (*sesshin sesshō ni arazareba* 説心説性にあらざれば): The hyperbolic praise of the expression, "talking of the mind and talking of the nature," here and throughout this chapter is in stark contrast to Dōgen's opinion in his "Shōbōgenzō sansui kyō" 正法眼藏山水經 (from 1240) (DZZ.1:318):

説心説性は佛祖の所不肯なり。

"Talking of the mind and talking of the nature" is something not condoned by the buddhas and ancestors.

"whole earth and sentient beings simultaneously attaining the way" (*daichi ujō dōji*

264 DŌGEN'S *SHŌBŌGENZŌ* VOLUME III

mind and talking of the nature"; breaking into a smile is "talking of the mind and talking of the nature"; "making a bow and standing in place" is "talking of the mind and talking of the nature"; "the Ancestral Master entering the Liang" is "talking of the mind and talking of the nature"; "transmitting the robe in the middle of the night" is "talking of the mind and talking of the nature."[6] Raising the staff is *"talking of the mind and talking of the nature"; lowering the whisk is "talking of the mind and talking of the nature."*[7]

---

jōdō 大地有情同時成道): A reference to the Buddha's awakening under the bodhi tree. The expression, which appears in several of Dōgen's texts, is from a line that he will quote in his "Shōbōgenzō hotsu bodai shin" 正法眼藏發菩提心 chapter (DZZ.2:164; also quoted at *Eihei kōroku* 永平廣錄, DZZ.3:28, no. 37):

> 釋迦牟尼佛言、明星出現時、我與大地有情、同時成道。
>
> Buddha Śākyamuni said, "When the dawn star appeared, I, together with the whole earth and sentient beings, simultaneously attained the way."

Although the passage appears in Chan texts from this period (see, e.g, *Jianzhong Jingguo xudeng lu* 建中靖國續燈錄, ZZ.136:36b17-18), it has not been located in any extant sūtra. The translation here follows the usual reading of *daichi ujō* 大地有情 as a compound subject; the phrase could also be read, "sentient beings of the whole earth."

"all living beings have no buddha nature" (*issai shujō mu busshō* 一切衆生無佛性): A saying attributed to Weishan Lingyu 潙山靈祐 (771-853); see, e.g., *shinji Shōbōgenzō* 眞字正法眼藏 (DZZ.5:188, case 115). Often interpreted to mean that the buddha nature is "empty" — i.e., not some thing that sentient beings have. Perhaps intended here as what we might call the reverse of the relationship between buddha and sentient beings given in the preceding clause.

6 **Holding up a flower and blinking the eyes** (*nenge shunmoku* 拈華瞬目); **breaking into a smile** (*hagan mishō* 破顏微笑): References to the famous founding story of Zen (found, e.g., at *shinji Shōbōgenzō* 眞字正法眼藏, DZZ.5:258, case 253), in which the Buddha held up a flower on Vulture Peak, his disciple Mahākāśyapa smiled, and the Buddha recognized him as the heir to his "treasury of the true dharma eye." See Supplementary Notes, s.v. "Break into a smile" and "Holding up a flower and blinking the eyes."

"making a bow and standing in place" (*raihai ei ni ryū* 禮拜依位而立): Reference to the account of Huike's 慧可 recognition as the Second Ancestor of Chinese Chan. Bodhidharma asked four of his disciples for expressions of their understanding of his teaching. Huike's response was simply to bow and stand in place, whereupon Bodhidharma declared, "You've gotten my marrow." See Supplementary Notes, s.v. "Skin, flesh, bones, and marrow."

"the Ancestral Master entering the Liang" (*soshi nyūryō* 祖師入梁): Reference to Bodhidharma's bringing the Zen tradition to China from India. The Liang dynasty ruled southern China during the period 502-557; Bodhidharma is said to have had an interview with the founder of the dynasty, Wudi 武帝 (r. 502-550).

"transmitting the robe in the middle of the night" (*yahan den'e* 夜半傳衣): Reference to the ascension of the Sixth Ancestor, Huineng 慧能, who is said to have received the robe of Bodhidharma from the Fifth Ancestor, Hungren 弘忍, in secret during the night.

7 **Raising the staff** (*nen shujō* 拈拄杖); **lowering the whisk** (*ō hossu* 橫拂子): Gestures

42. Talking of the Mind, Talking of the Nature *Sesshin Sesshō* 説心説性 265

[42:3] {1:450}

おほよそ佛佛祖祖のあらゆる功德は、ことごとくこれ説心説性なり。平常
の説心説性あり、牆壁瓦礫の説心説性あり。いはゆる、心生種種法生の道
理現成し、心滅種種法滅の道理現成する、しかしながら心の説なる時節な
り、性の説なる時節なり。

In sum, every virtue of buddha after buddha and ancestor after ancestor is "*talking of the mind and talking of the nature.*" There is the
"*talking of the mind and talking of the nature*" of "the ordinary"; there
is the "*talking of the mind and talking of the nature*" of "fences, walls,
tiles, and pebbles."[8] The realization of the principle, "*when the mind
arises, the various dharmas arise,*" and the realization of the principle,
"*when the mind ceases, the various dharmas cease,*" are in either case
occasions of "talking of the mind," occasions of "talking of the nature."[9]

[42:4]

しかあるに、心を通ぜず、性に達せざる庸流、くらくして説心説性をしら
ず、談玄談妙をしらず、佛祖の道にあるべからざるといふ、あるべからざ
るとをしふ。説心説性を説心説性としらざるによりて、説心説性を説心説
性とおもふなり。これ、ことに大道の通塞を批判せざるによりてなり。

Yet, mediocre types, who have not penetrated the mind, who have not
reached the nature, without knowing "*talking of the mind and talking of
the nature,*" without knowing "*discussing the dark, discussing the subtle,*" say that and teach that, these must not be the words of the buddhas

---

of Zen masters associated with their teaching. The staff (*shujō* 拄杖) is a walking stick,
often carried by the master when he "ascends to the hall" (*jōdō* 上堂; i.e., holds a formal
convocation); the whisk (*hossu* 拂子) is a ceremonial fly-whisk, often held by the master
during convocations and other rituals. See Supplementary Notes, s.v. "Staff," "Whisk."

8 **"the ordinary"** (*byōjō* 平常): Likely an allusion to the famous saying of Nanquan Puyuan 南泉普願 (748-835) (found, e.g., at *shinji Shōbōgenzō* 眞字正法眼藏,
DZZ.5:134, case 19); see Supplementary Notes, s.v. "Ordinary mind is the way."

"fences, walls, tiles, and pebbles" (*shō heki ga ryaku* 牆壁瓦礫): A fairly common
definition of the "old buddha mind" (*kobutsushin* 古佛心), first attributed to Nanyang
Huizhong 南陽慧忠 (d. 775); see Supplementary Notes, s.v. "Fences, walls, tiles, and
pebbles."

9 **The realization of the principle** (*dōri genjō* 道理現成): An unusual locution, found
occasionally in Dōgen's writings, probably meaning something like, "the expression (or
appearance) of the truth that . . ."

"when the mind arises, the various dharmas arise" (*shin shō shuju hō shō* 心生種
種法生); **"when the mind ceases, the various dharmas cease"** (*shin metsu shuju hō
metsu* 心滅種種法滅): A fixed combination, commonly found together in Zen texts;
usually said to derive from the *Dasheng qishin lun* 大乘起信論 (T.1666.32:577b22),
though a similar set can be found in the *Laṅkāvatāra-sūtra* (*Ru lengqie jing* 入楞伽經,
T.671.16:568c12).

266 DŌGEN'S *SHŌBŌGENZŌ* VOLUME III

and ancestors.[10] Because they do not know "*talking of the mind and talking of the nature*" as "*talking of the mind and talking of the nature*," they think of "*talking of the mind and talking of the nature*" as "*talking of the mind and talking of the nature*."[11] This is particularly because they have not judged the passage and blockage of the great way.[12]

* * * * *

[42:5]

後來、徑山大慧禪師宗杲といふありていはく、いまのともがら、説心説性をこのみ、談玄談妙をこのむによりて、得道おそし。ただまさに心・性ふたつながらなげすてきたり、玄・妙ともに忘じきたりて、二相不生のとき、證契するなり。

Of late, there was a certain Zonggao, Chan Master Dahui of Jingshan, who said,

> People today, because they like *talking of the mind and talking of the nature* or *discussing the dark and discussing the subtle*, are slow to gain the way.[13] When, you have thrown away both "mind" and

---

10   **mediocre types** (*yōru* 庸流): One of Dōgen's favorite terms for those with whose views of Zen he disagrees.

have not penetrated the mind (*shin o tsū zezu* 心を通ぜず); **have not reached the nature** (*shō ni tatsu sezaru* 性に達せざる): A play with the compound term *tsūdatsu* 通達 ("to penetrate," "to master").

"discussing the dark, discussing the subtle" (*dan gen dan myō* 談玄談妙): The compound expression *genmyō* ("dark and subtle" or "deep and marvelous") is a common one in Buddhist texts, and in Chinese writing more generally, for what is profound and mysterious. Here, a reference to the words of Dahui Zonggao 大慧宗杲 that Dōgen will quote in the next section.

11   **they think of "talking of the mind and talking of the nature" as "talking of the mind and talking of the nature"** (*sesshin sesshō o sesshin sesshō to omou* 説心説性を説心説性とおもふ): Usually interpreted to mean that they take "talking of the mind and talking of the nature" in some literal sense of "talking."

12   **they have not judged the passage and blockage of the great way** (*daidō no tsūsoku o hihan sezaru* 大道の通塞を批判せざる): Usually interpreted to mean that they have not thought critically about what is and is not integral to the great way. "Passage and blockage" here translates *tsūsoku* 通塞, meaning that a road or way is "open or blocked"; often carrying the idiomatic sense of "affairs going smoothly or not."

13   **Of late** (*kōrai* 後來): Ordinarily an adverb meaning "subsequently," "thereafter," etc., this term seems to appear in Dōgen's writings exclusively in dismissive reference to what is merely recent (cf. the more "classic" *korai* 古來).

Zonggao, Zen Master Dahui of Jingshan (*Kinzan Daie zenji Sōkō* 徑山大慧禪師宗杲): Dahui Zonggao 大慧宗杲 (1089-1163), a leading figure in the Linji 臨濟 lineage during the Southern Song. The *Shōbōgenzō* contains several criticisms of him (see especially "Shōbōgenzō jishō zanmai" 正法眼藏自證三昧). Mount Jing (*Kinzan* 徑山) was a major Chan monastery located in Hangzhou 杭州, Lin'an Prefecture 臨安府.

42. Talking of the Mind, Talking of the Nature *Sesshin Sesshō* 説心説性　267

"nature" and forgotten both "dark" and "subtle," so that the two do not arise, you will verify and accord.[14]

[42:6]

この道取、いまだ佛祖の繍繝　をしらず、佛祖の列辟をきかざるなり。これによりて、心はひとへに慮知念覺なりとしりて、慮知念覺も心なることを學せざるによりて、かくのごとくいふ。性は澄湛寂靜なるとのみ妄計して、佛性・法性の有無をしらず、如是性をゆめにもいまだみざるによりて、しかのごとく佛法を辟見せるなり。佛祖の道取する心は、皮肉骨髓なり、佛祖の保任せる性は、竹箆・拄杖なり。佛祖の證契する玄は、露柱・燈籠なり、佛祖の擧拈する妙は、知見・解會なり。

This saying does not know the pale yellow silk of the buddhas and ancestors, has not heard of the monarchal line of the buddhas and ancestors.[15] Consequently, he says this because he knows only that the mind is solely thinking and perceiving, and does not learn that thinking and perceiving are also the mind.[16] Mistakenly figuring only that the nature

---

Dahui's words here are given in Japanese and in fact do not seem to be a direct quotation from any extant text. The records of Dahui's teachings do contain several passages in which he is critical of the practices of "talking of the mind and talking of the nature" (*shuo xin shuo xing* 説心説性) and "talking of the dark and talking of the subtle" (*shuo xuan shuo miao* 説玄説妙). (See, e.g., *Dahui yulu* 大慧語錄, T.1998A.47:830c4-5; 47:927b26-7.)

14 **the two do not arise** (*nisō fushō* 二相不生): Literally, "the two characteristics do not arise." Could be understood as a reference either to the two pairs, "mind and nature" and "dark and subtle," or to the two members of each pair.

verify and accord (*shōkai* 證契): A tentative translation of a term occurring a number of times in Dōgen's writings but more rarely in the Chinese Chan texts. Both elements of the compound are common Zen terms, with legal connotations, for spiritual understanding: *shō* 證 ("verify") has the sense of "bearing witness" to something; *kai* 契 ("accord") has the sense of "agreeing" with someone or something (from the nominal usage as "tally," "contract," or "agreement"). The translation here treats both elements as verbs, but interpretations of Dōgen's use of *shōkai* regularly treat it as a subject-predicate compound, meaning one's "verification accords" (often, with that of one's master); the relationship could also be understood as a predicate-object, meaning that one "verifies the accord" (with the teachings or one's master). This term does not seem to occur in Dahui's writings, though he does use the two elements in reverse: *qisheng* 契證, perhaps to be understood, "to accord with the verification."

15 **the pale yellow silk of the buddhas and ancestors** (*busso no kenshō* 佛祖の繍繝); **the monarchal line of the buddhas and ancestors** (*busso no reppeki* 佛祖の列辟): "Pale yellow silk" (*kenshō* 繍繝) refers to the silk threads used to decorate books; hence, as a synecdoche, "texts." "Monarchal line" (*reppeki* 列辟, or *retsuheki*), not occurring elsewhere in the *Shōbōgenzō*, is usually taken as a reference to the Zen lineage; some interpret *heki* 辟 here as "law"; others take it as a substitute for the homonymous graph *heki* 璧 ("jade").

16 **the mind is solely thinking and perceiving** (*shin wa hitoe ni ryo chi nen kaku nari* 心はひとへに慮知念覺なり); **thinking and perceiving are also the mind** (*ryo chi nen kaku mo shin naru* 慮知念覺も心なる): "Thinking and perceiving" represents a loose

268 DŌGEN'S *SHŌBŌGENZŌ* VOLUME III

is pure, deep, quiescent, and still, he does not know about the existence or non-existence of the buddha nature or dharma nature. Because he has never seen "such a nature" even in his dreams, he has this biased view of the buddha dharma.[17]

The "mind" spoken of by the buddhas and ancestors is the skin, flesh, bones, and marrow; the "nature" maintained by the buddhas and ancestors is the bamboo stick and staff.[18] The "dark" that the buddhas and ancestors verify and accord with is pillars and lanterns; the "subtle" that the buddhas and ancestors take up is knowledge and understanding.[19]

[42:7] {1:451}
佛祖の、眞實に佛祖なるは、はじめよりこの心・性を聽取し、説取し、行取し、證取するなり。この玄・妙を保任取し、參學取するなり。かくのごとくなるを學佛祖の兒孫といふ。しかのごとくにあらざれば・學道にあらず。

---

translation of *ryo chi nen kaku* 慮知念覺, terms for cognitive functions not commonly found as a set in Buddhist literature but appearing several times in the *Shōbōgenzō*, where they seem to stand collectively for the ordinary operations of consciousness. The translation takes them as two compound expressions (the first of which does occur elsewhere in the *Shōbōgenzō* in reference to the thinking mind); as individual terms, they might be rendered "considering, knowing, thinking, and perceiving." See Supplementary Notes, s.v. "Thinking and perceiving." The point here appears to be that Dahui thinks that the mind has mental activities but does not understand that these activities are themselves the mind.

17 **"such a nature"** (*nyoze shō* 如是性): The adjective "such" (*nyoze* 如是) here could refer simply to the preceding "buddha nature" and "dharma nature," but it also suggests the famous list, often evoked in the *Shōbōgenzō*, of ten "suchnesses" (*jū nyoze* 十如是), appearing in Kumārajīva's translation of the *Lotus Sūtra*, one of which is "such a nature." (*Miaofa lianhua jing* 妙法蓮華經, T.262.9:5c12.)

biased view (*hekiken* 辟見): Reading *heki* 辟 here as *heki* 僻.

18 **skin, flesh, bones, and marrow** (*hi niku kotsu zui* 皮肉骨髓): An expression used throughout Dōgen's writings for the essence or entirety of what is transmitted in the Zen tradition; from the account, mentioned above, of Bodhidharma's interview with his four disciples (see Note 6). Here, Dōgen is no doubt playing with the contrast between these body parts and the mind.

the bamboo stick and staff (*shippei shujō* 竹篦・拄杖): Two insignia of the Zen master. The master's bamboo stick (*shippei* 竹篦) is a short rod often held during lectures; for his staff, see above, Note 7.

19 **pillars and lanterns** (*rochū tōrō* 露柱・燈籠): The free-standing pillars and the lanterns of monastic buildings; an expression, fairly common in Zen texts, for the ordinary, insentient things of the world around the monk; see Supplementary Notes, s.v. "Pillars and lanterns."

knowledge and understanding (*chiken ge'e* 知見・解會): I.e., our ordinary experience of the world; the subjective correlate, we might say, to "pillars and lanterns."

42. Talking of the Mind, Talking of the Nature *Sesshin Sesshō* 説心説性 269

The buddhas and ancestors who are truly buddhas and ancestors, from the beginning, hear this "mind and nature," teach it, practice it, and verify it. They maintain this "dark and subtle," and they study it. Those who are like this are called the children and grandchildren studying the buddhas and ancestors.[20] Those who are not like this are not students of the way.[21]

[42:8]

このゆえに、得道の得道せず、不得道のとき不得道ならざるなり。得不の時節、ともに蹉過するなり。たとひなんぢがいふがごとく、心・性ふたつながら亡ずといふは、心の説あらしむる分なり、百千萬億分の少分なり。玄・妙ともになげすてきたるといふ、談玄の談ならしむる分なり。この關棙子を學せず、おろかに、亡ず、といはば、手をはなれんずるとおもひ、身にのがれぬるとしれり。いまだ小乘の局量を解脱せざるなり、いかでか大乘の奥玄におよばん、いかにいはんや向上の關棙子をしらんや。佛祖の茶飯を喫しきたれる、といひがたし。

Therefore, [Dahui's] "gaining the way" does not gain the way; when it does not gain the way, it is not that it does not gain the way.[22] It misses the occasions of both gaining and not [gaining]. While, to say, as you say, "forget both mind and nature," is a part expressing the talk of the mind; it is a small part, a hundredth, thousandth, ten thousandth, a hundred thousandth part.[23] To say, "discard both dark and subtle," is a part forming the discussion of discussing the dark.[24]

---

20 **children and grandchildren** (*jison* 兒孫): Or simply "descendants." The expression "descendants of the buddhas and ancestors" is used repeatedly throughout the *Shōbōgenzō* for (authentic) members of the Zen tradition.

21 **Those who are not like this are not students of the way** (*shika no gotoku ni arazareba, gakudō ni arazu* しかのごとくにあらざれば、學道にあらず): Or "If it is not like this, it is not the study of the way."

22 **Therefore, [Dahui's] "gaining the way" does not gain the way; when it does not gain the way, it is not that it does not gain the way** (*tokudō no tokudō sezu, futokudō no toki futokudō narazaru* 得道の得道せず、不得道のとき不得道ならざる): The subject of the second clause is unexpressed here. The translation treats it as Dahui's words, "gain the way," but it may also be understood as Dahui himself or perhaps as "those who are not like this" from the preceding sentence. In any case, the passage is generally interpreted to mean that Dahui's sense of "attaining the way" is not really attaining the way; similarly, what he thinks of as not attaining the way is not in fact not attaining the way.

23 **as you say** (*nanji ga iu ga gotoku* なんぢがいふがごとく): I.e., as Dahui has said above. As is not uncommon in Zen comments, Dōgen is here directly addressing the person he is quoting. The translation continues the use of the second person throughout the passage, though the grammatical subject is unexpressed and could as well be read as "he" (i.e., Dahui).

24 **a part expressing the talking of the mind** (*shin no setsu arashimuru bun* 心の説あらしむる分); **a part forming the discussion of discussing the dark** (*dan gen no dan narashimuru bun* 談玄の談ならしむる分): The particle *no* in both these phrases is

270 DŌGEN'S *SHŌBŌGENZŌ* VOLUME III

Not having studied this pivot, if you stupidly say, "forgetting," you think [it is] leaving the hand, you know it as escaping the body.[25] You are not yet liberated from the confines of the Small Vehicle; how could you reach the innermost darkness of the Great Vehicle, let alone know the higher pivot?[26] It is difficult to say that you have tasted the tea and rice of the buddhas and ancestors.[27]

[42:9]
参師勤恪するは、ただ説心説性を身心の正當恁麼時に體究するなり、身先身後に参究するなり、さらに二三のことなることなし。

To study with a teacher and be diligent in your work is just personally to investigate "*talking of the mind and talking of the nature*" at the very moment of body and mind, to investigate it before the body and after the body.[28] There are not two or three other ways.

* * * * *

---

ambiguous. It is possible to interpret *shin no setsu* 心の説 either as "talking about the mind" or as "the mind's talking"; similarly, it is possible to interpret *dan gen no dan* 談玄の談 either as "the discussion that is discussing the dark" or as "discussing the dark's discussion."

25 **pivot** (*kanreisu* 關捩子): I.e. crucial point; see Supplementary Notes. The text repeats the term just below in the expression "higher pivot" (*kōjō no kanreisu* 向上の關捩子).

leaving the hand (*te o hanarenzuru* 手をはなれんずる); **escaping the body** (*mi ni nogarenuru* 身にのがれぬる): Both phrases express the abandonment of something.

26 **confines of the Small Vehicle** (*shōjō no kyokuryō* 小乗の局量): Like many Mahāyāna authors, Dōgen often associates the Hīnayāna with the negation of, or urge to escape from, the phenomenal world. Note the three-tiered hierarchy here, common in his writings, of Small Vehicle, Great Vehicle, and the tradition of the buddhas and ancestors; the progression seems to be expressed here through a metaphoric journey into the "household" of the buddhas and ancestors. See Supplementary Notes, s.v. "Three vehicles."

innermost darkness (*ōgen* 奥玄): A somewhat unusual term, no doubt introduced here to pick up the "darkness" (*gen* 玄) of the "dark and subtle" (*genmyō* 玄妙) above. *Ō* 奥 connotes the "interior" of a structure; hence, what is "hidden" from public view, what is "private" and "remote."

27 **tea and rice of the buddhas and ancestors** (*busso no sahan* 佛祖の茶飯): I.e., the spiritual "fare" provided by the tradition. The expression "everyday tea and rice" (*kajō sahan* 家常茶飯) is a fairly common one in Dōgen's writings and in Chinese Chan texts; see Supplementary Notes.

28 **personally to investigate** (*taikyū su* 體究す): The translation of *taikyū* 體究 as "personally investigate" masks the corporeal connotation of the glyph *tai* 體 ("body") with which Dōgen may be playing here in his subsequent "before the body and after the body" (*shinsen shingo* 身先身後) — an expression typically indicating "past lives and future lives."

42. Talking of the Mind, Talking of the Nature *Sesshin Sesshō* 説心説性 271

[42:10]

爾時初祖、謂二祖曰、汝但外息諸緣、内心無喘、心如牆壁、可以入道。二
祖種種説心説性、俱不證契。一日忽然省得。果白初祖曰、弟子此回始息諸
緣也。初祖知其已悟、更不窮詰。只曰、莫成斷滅否。　二祖曰、無。初祖
曰、子作麼生。二祖曰、了了常知、故言之不可及。初祖曰、此乃從上諸佛
諸祖所傳心體、汝今既得、善自護持。

At that time, the First Ancestor said to the Second Ancestor, "Externally, put a stop to conditions; internally, the mind will be without panting.[29] With the mind like fences and walls, you will enter the way."

The Second Ancestor talked of the mind and talked of the nature but did not verify and accord [with them].[30] One day, he suddenly understood. Subsequently, he addressed the First Ancestor, saying, "Your disciple has this time finally put a stop to conditions."

The First Ancestor recognized that he had awakened and did not further press him, saying only, "Haven't you achieved severance and extinction?"[31]

The Second Ancestor said, "No."

The First Ancestor said, "How is the Master?"[32]

The Second Ancestor said, "Clear, clear, ever knowing; therefore, words cannot reach it."

The First Ancestor said, "This is the substance of the mind transmitted down from the buddhas and ancestors. Now you've gotten it; protect it well."

29　**the First Ancestor said to the Second Ancestor** (*Shoso, i Niso* 初祖、謂二祖):
A story found in several texts; see, e.g., *Zongmen tongyao ji* 宗門統要集 (ZTS.1:21a).
Also quoted by Dahui, which may explain its presence here; see *Dahui yulu* 大慧語
錄 (T.1998A.47:925b17-24). The protagonists are, of course, Bodhidharma ("the First
Ancestor") and his disciple Huike 慧可 ("the Second Ancestor").

"conditions" (*shoen* 諸緣): I.e., involvements in worldly affairs.

"without panting" (*mutan* 無喘): Or "without busyness." The English loses what may
be a play in the Chinese with the graph *xi* 息, translated here as "put a stop to" but also
meaning "breath."

30　**verify and accord** (*shōkai* 證契): See above, Note 14. The Chinese versions of the
story use only the verb *qi* 契 ("accord").

31　**"severance and extinction"** (*danmetsu* 斷滅): A term typically understood as indicating a spiritually undesirable state; sometimes associated with the "annihilationist"
position (*danken* 斷見; S. *uccheda-vāda*) that denies karma and rebirth.

32　**"How is the Master?"** (*shi somosan* 子作麼生): "Master" here renders the diminutive *shi* 子, used here in direct address.

[42:11] {1:452}

この因緣、疑著するものあり、舉拈するあり。二祖の、初祖に參侍せし因緣のなかの一因緣、かくのごとし。二祖、しきりに説心説性するに、はじめは相契せず。やうやく積功累德して、つひに初祖の道を得道しき。庸愚おもふらくは、二祖、はじめに説心説性せしときは證契せず、そのとが、説心説性するにあり、のちには説心説性をすてて證契せり、とおもへり。心如牆壁可以入道の道を參徹せざるによりて、かくのごとくいふなり。これ、ことに學道の區別にくらし。

There are those who have doubts about this episode, those who take it up.[33] One episode among the episodes of the Second Ancestor's service under the First Ancestor is like this. When the Second Ancestor was persistently *talking of the mind and talking of the nature*, at first, he did not accord with it. Finally, "*accumulating merit and amassing virtue*," he gained the way of the words of the First Ancestor. The mediocre fools think that, [if] the Second Ancestor failed to verify and accord when he was first talking of the mind and talking of the nature, the fault lay in his *talking of the mind and talking of the nature*; subsequently, having discarded *talking of the mind and talking of the nature*, he verified and accorded. They say this because they have not penetrated the words, "*with the mind like fences and walls, you will enter the way*." This is particularly ignorant of distinctions in studying the way.

[42:12]

ゆえいかんとなれば、菩提心をおこし、佛道修行におもむくのちよりは、難行をねんごろにおこなふとき、おこなふといへども百行に一當なし。しかあれども、或從知識・或從經卷して、やうやくあたることをうるなり。いまの一當は、むかしの百不當のちからなり、百不當の一老なり。聞教・修道・得證、みなかくのごとし。きのふの説心説性は百不當なりといへども、きのふの説心説性の百不當、たちまちに今日の一當なり。行佛道の初心のとき、未練にして通達せざればとて、佛道をすてて餘道をへて佛道をうることなし。佛道修行の始終に達せざるともがら、この通塞の道理なることを、あきらめがたし。

Why is this? After we have brought forth the mind of bodhi and turned to the practice of the way of the buddhas, when we are wholeheartedly performing the difficult practices, though we may be performing them, we do not have one hit in a hundred practices.[34] Still, *whether from a wise friend, whether from a sūtra scroll*, eventually we hit it.[35] This one

---

33 **those who have doubts** (*gijaku suru mono* 疑著するもの); **those who take it up** (*konen suru* 舉拈する): To "doubt" may refer either to "being suspicious of" or to "wondering about." To "take it up" refers to "taking as a topic for study or comment."

34 **mind of bodhi** (*bodai shin* 菩提心): I.e., the bodhisattva's aspiration for unsurpassed, perfect awakening; see Supplementary Notes, s.v. "Bring forth the mind."

35 **whether from a wise friend, whether from a sūtra scroll** (*waku jū chishiki waku jū kyōkan* 或從知識・或從經卷): Dōgen here shifts to Chinese for this formulaic expres-

42. Talking of the Mind, Talking of the Nature *Sesshin Sesshō* 説心説性　273

hit in the present is [due to] the power of a hundred misses in the past, is the "one maturation" of a hundred misses.[36] Hearing the teachings, cultivating the way, attaining the verification are all like this. Yesterday's *"talking of the mind and talking of the nature"* may be a hundred misses, but yesterday's hundred misses of *"talking of the mind and talking of the nature"* are suddenly today's one hit.

When we have the beginner's mind in the practice of the way of the buddhas, if [we think that], since we are untrained and have not penetrated it, we might discard the way of the buddhas and take an other path, then we cannot attain the way of the buddhas. Those types who have not mastered the beginning and end of the practice of the way of the buddhas have difficulty clarifying the fact that this passage and blockage is reasonable.[37]

[42:13] {1:453}

佛道は、初發心のときも佛道なり、成正覺のときも佛道なり、初・中・後ともに佛道なり。たとへば、萬里をゆくものの、一歩も千里のうちなり、千歩も千里のうちなり。初一歩と千歩とことなれども、千里のおなじきがごとし。しかあるを、至愚のともがらはおもふらく、學佛道の時は佛道にいたらず、果上のときのみ佛道なり、と。舉道說道をしらず、舉道行道をしらず、舉道證道をしらざるによりて、かくのごとし。迷人のみ佛道修行して大悟すと學して、不迷の人も佛道修行して大悟すとしらず、きかざるともがら、かくのごとくいふなり。

The way of the buddhas is the way of the buddhas at the time of the initial bringing forth of the mind [of bodhi]; it is the way of the buddhas at the time of attaining right awakening.[38] It is the way of the buddhas throughout beginning, middle, and end. For example, for one walking ten thousand miles, one step is within a thousand miles; the thousandth step is within a thousand miles.[39] The first one step and the thousandth step may be different, but the thousand miles are the same.

---

sion found often in the *Shōbōgenzō*; see Supplementary Notes.

36　**"one maturation"** (*ichirō* 一老): *Rō* 老 is usually taken here as *rōren* 老練 ("mature," "veteran").

37　**that this passage and blockage is reasonable** (*kono tsūsoku no dōri naru koto* この通塞の道理なること): "Reasonable" here translates *dōri* 道理, elsewhere rendered as "principle," "truth." For the idiom, "passage and blockage" (*tsūsoku* 通塞), see above, Note 12.

38　**initial bringing forth of the mind** (*sho hosshin* 初發心); **right awakening** (*shōgaku* 正覺): I.e., the outset and the culmination of the bodhisattva path. At issue here is the interpretation of the term *butsudō* 佛道 ("way of the buddhas"), which, depending on context, can mean (a) buddhahood, (b) the path to buddhahood, or (c) the expression of buddhahood.

39　**a thousand miles** (*sen ri* 千里): The value of the Chinese "mile" (*li* 里) varies throughout history, generally around one-third of the English mile.

274 DŌGEN'S *SHŌBŌGENZŌ* VOLUME III

Yet, an extremely stupid bunch thinks that, when we are studying the way of the buddhas, we have not reached the way of the buddhas; only when we attain the fruit is it the way of the buddhas. They are like this because they do not know about *taking up the way and talking of the way*, they do not know about *taking up the way and practicing the way*, they do not know about *taking up the way and verifying the way*. Those who talk like this are the bunch who learn that only the deluded practice the way of the buddhas and have the great awakening; they do not know, and have not heard, that the non-deluded also practice the way of the buddhas and have the great awakening.

[42:14]
證契よりさきの説心説性は、佛道なりといへども、説心説性して證契するなり。證契は、迷者のはじめて大悟するをのみ證契といふ、と參學すべからず。迷者も大悟し、悟者も大悟し、不悟者も大悟し、不迷者も大悟し、證契者も證契するなり。

Though we say that "*talking of the mind and talking of the nature*" before verification and accord is the way of the buddhas, we verify and accord through "*talking of the mind and talking of the nature.*" We should not learn that "verification and accord" refers only to the deluded initially having the great awakening: the deluded have the great awakening; the awakened have the great awakening; the unawakened have the great awakening; the undeluded have the great awakening; those who have verified and accorded verify and accord.

[42:15]
しかあれば、説心説性は、佛道の正直なり。杲公、この道理に達せず、説心説性すべからず、といふ、佛法の道理にあらず。いまの大宋國には、杲公におよべるもなし。

Thus, "*talking of the mind and talking of the nature*" is the direct [approach] of the way of the buddhas.[40] Mister Gao's saying, without his having mastered this principle, that we should not engage in "*talking of the mind and talking of the nature*" is not a principle of the buddha dharma.[41] In the present Land of the great Song, there is no one who even reaches Mister Gao.

* * * * *

---

40 **direct [approach] of the way of the buddhas** (*butsudō no shōjiki* 佛道の正直): A loose translation of a somewhat odd locution; the term *shōjiki* 正直 would normally function as a modifier ("direct," "directly," "straightforward," etc.).

41 **Mister Gao** (*Kōkō* 杲公): "Mister" renders *kō* 公, a title not normally applied to a Zen master; here probably carries a certain ironic tone.

42. Talking of the Mind, Talking of the Nature *Sesshin Sesshō* 説心説性   275

[42:16]

高祖悟本大師、ひとり諸祖のなかの尊として、説心説性の、説心説性なる
道理に通達せり。いまだ通達せざる諸方の祖師、いまの因縁のごとくなる
道取なし。

The Eminent Ancestor, Great Master Wuben, the single most honored
among the ancestors, penetrated the principle that "*talking of the mind
and talking of the nature*" is "*talking of the mind and talking of the nature.*"[42] The ancestral masters of all quarters who have not penetrated it
have no sayings like this present episode.[43]

[42:17] {1:454}

いはゆる僧密師伯と大師と行次に、傍院をさしていはく、裏面有人、説心
説性。

When elder brother Sengmi and the Great Master were traveling,
[Dongshan] pointed out a cloister beside [the road] and said, "*Inside,
there's someone talking of the mind and talking of the nature.*"

[42:18]

この道取は、高祖出世よりこのかた、法孫かならず祖風を正傳せり、餘
門の、夢にも見聞せるところにあらず、いはんや夢にも領覧の方をしら
んや。ただ嫡嗣たるもの、正傳せり。この道理、もし正傳せざらんは、い
かでか佛道に達本ならん。いはゆるいまの道理は、或裏・或面、有人・人
有、説心説性なり。面裏心説、面裏性説なり。これを参究功夫すべし。性
にあらざる説、いまになし、説にあらざる心、いまだあらず。

Ever since the Eminent Ancestor appeared in the world, his dharma
descendants have always correctly transmitted this saying [as] the ancestral style. It is not something other traditions have seen even in their
dreams; still less have they known, even in their dreams, how to understand it.[44] Only those who are legitimate heirs have correctly transmitted
it. How can one who does not correctly transmit this truth reach the
origin on the way of the buddhas? The truth in question here is: *whether
"inside" or "surface," "there's someone" and "someone's there" "talking*

---

42   **The Eminent Ancestor, Great Master Wuben** (*Kōso Gohon Daishi* 高祖悟本大
師): I.e., Dongshan Liangjie 洞山良价.

43   **this present episode** (*ima no innen* いまの因縁): Literally, "causes and conditions,"
the term *innen* is regularly used in Zen texts to indicate a story, or "old case" (*kosoku* 古
則), or kōan. The reference is to the Dongshan story with which this piece began; Dōgen
now proceeds to a line-by-line Japanese translation and commentary on the story.

44   **not something other traditions have seen even in their dreams** (*yomon no, yume
ni mo kenmon seru tokoro ni arazu* 餘門の、夢にも見聞せるところにあらず): I.e.,
something others have never dreamt of; a Japanese rendering of a standard Zen insult
often used by Dōgen in its Chinese form, *mu ya mikenzai* 夢也未見在. "Other traditions"
(*yomon*) presumably refers to those outside the Caodong (Sōtō) lineage of Dongshan.

276 DŌGEN'S *SHŌBŌGENZŌ* VOLUME III

of the mind and talking of the nature."[45] It is *within the surface, the mind is talking; within the surface, the nature is talking.*[46] We should investigate and work at this. There has not yet been "talking" that is not "nature"; there is no "mind" that is not "talking."

[42:19]

佛性といふは、一切の説なり、無佛性といふは、一切の説なり。佛性の性なることを參學すといふとも、有佛性を參學せざらんは學道にあらず、無佛性を參學せざらんは參學にあらず。説の性なることを參學する、これ佛祖の嫡孫なり、性は説なることを信受する、これ嫡孫の佛祖なり。

"Buddha nature" means all "talking." "No buddha nature" means all "talking." Though one studies the nature of the buddha nature, those who do not study "having buddha nature" are not studying the way; those who do not study "no buddha nature" are not studying the way. Those who study that "talking" is "the nature" are the legitimate descendants of the buddhas and ancestors; those who believe and accept that "the nature" is "talking" are the buddhas and ancestors of the legitimate descendants.

[42:20]

心は疏動し、性は恬靜なり、と道取するは外道の見なり。性は澄湛にして、相は遷移する、と道取するは、外道の見なり。佛道の學心・學性、しかあらず、佛道の行心・行性は、外道にひとしからず、佛道の明心・明性は、外道その分あるべからず。

To say that the mind is disturbed and the nature is composed is the view of other paths; to say that the nature is clear and deep and the characteristics shift and move is the view of other paths.[47] The study of

---

45 **"inside" or "surface"** (*waku ri waku men* 或裏或面): Dōgen is here playing with the two elements of the binome *rimen* 裏面; see above, Note 1. Presumably, he is thereby calling into question any assumption that the "someone" is only "inside."

"there's someone" and "someone's there" (*unin nin'u* 有人人有): Dōgen is simply reversing the order of subject and predicate in Dongshan's phrase, "there's someone."

46 **within the surface, the mind is talking; within the surface, the nature is talking** (*menri shin setsu, menri shō setsu* 面裏心説、面裏性説): Here, Dōgen reverses the syntax of all three expressions: *rimen* 裏面 ("inside"), *sesshin* 説心 ("talking of the mind"), and *sesshō* 説性 ("talking of the nature").

47 **the mind is disturbed and the nature is composed** (*shin wa sodō shi, shō wa tenjō nari* 心は疏動し、性は恬靜なり): I.e., the common notion that, although our minds are active, the true nature of our minds is calm.

the nature is clear and deep and the characteristics shift and move (*shō wa chōtan ni shite, sō wa sen'i suru* 性は澄湛にして、相は遷移する): I.e., the standard distinction between the unchanging nature and the changing features of things.

other paths (*gedō* 外道): I.e., non-Buddhist, or heterodox, religious traditions; S. *tīrthika*.

42. Talking of the Mind, Talking of the Nature *Sesshin Sesshō* 説心説性 277

the mind and study of the nature on the way of the buddhas are not like this. The practice of the mind and practice of the nature on the way of the buddhas are not equivalent to the other paths. The clarification of the mind and the clarification of the nature on the way of the buddhas, the other paths have no share in.

[42:21]

佛道には、有人の説心説性あり、無人の説心説性あり、有人の不説心不説性あり、無人の不説心不説性あり、説心未説心、説性未説性あり。無人のときの説心を學せざれば、説心未到田地なり。有人のときの説心を學せざれば、説心未到田地なり。説心無人を學し、無人説心を學し、説心是人を學し、是人説心を學するなり。

On the way of the buddhas, there is the "*talking of the mind and talking of the nature*" of "someone"; there is the "*talking of the mind and talking of the nature*" of no one. There is the *not talking of the mind and not talking of the nature* of "someone"; there is the *not talking of the mind and not talking of the nature* of no one. There is *talking of the mind and not talking of the mind; talking of the nature and not talking of the nature.* When one has not studied "talking of the mind" at the time when there is no one, then "*talking of the mind*" *has not reached the field.*[48] When one has not studied "talking of the mind" at the time when there is "someone," then "*talking of the mind*" *has not reached the field.* We study *no one who* "*talks of the mind*"; we study *no one* "*talking of the mind*"; we study *this one who* "*talks of the mind*"; we study *this one* "*talking of the mind.*"[49]

[42:22] {1:455}

臨濟の道取する盡力は、わづかに無位眞人なりといへども、有位眞人をいまだ道取せず。のこれる參學、のこれる道取、いまだ現成せず、未到參徹地といふべし。説心説性は説佛説祖なるがゆえに、耳處に相見し、眼處に相見すべし。

Linji's total power to say something is just "the true person of no rank," but he still has not said, "the true person of rank."[50] He has not

---

48 **"talking of the mind" has not reached the field** (*sesshin mitō denchi* 説心未到田地): Usually interpreted to mean that [unless one understands "no one" "talking of the mind,"] one has not yet understood "talking of the mind." The agricultural term *denchi* 田地 ("paddy field") is often used in Zen texts for a realm of discourse or state of mind.

49 **no one who "talks of the mind"** (*sesshin munin* 説心無人); **no one "talking of the mind"** (*munin sesshin* 無人説心): Tentative translations of phrases that could be parsed in several other ways: e.g., "talking of the mind is without anyone," "there is no one who talks of the mind," etc.

50 **"true person of no rank"** (*mui shinnin* 無位眞人): A famous saying by Linji Yixuan 臨濟義玄 (d. 866), founder of the Linji 臨濟 house of Chan (of which Dahui was a member). See Supplementary Notes, s.v. "True person of no rank."

278 DŌGEN'S *SHŌBŌGENZŌ* VOLUME III

realized what remains to be studied, what remains to be said; we can say he *has not reached the ground of penetration*.[51] Because "*talking of the mind and talking of the nature*" are *talking of the buddhas and talking of the ancestors*, we meet them in the ear, we meet them in the eye.[52]

[42:23]

ちなみに僧密師伯いはく、是誰。

The elder brother Sengmi said, "*Who is it?*"

[42:24]

この道取を現成せしむるに、僧密師伯、さきにもこの道取に乗ずべし、のちにもこの道取に乗ずべし。是誰は、那裏の説心説性なり。しかあれば、是誰と道取せられんとき、是誰と思量取せられんときは、すなはち説心説性なり。この説心説性は、餘方のともがら、かつてしらざるところなり。子をわすれて賊とするゆえに、賊を認じて子とするなり。

When he expresses this saying, elder brother Sengmi should previously avail himself of this saying and should subsequently avail himself of this saying.[53] "*Who is it?*" is the "*talking of the mind and talking of the nature*" over there. [54] Therefore, when "*who is it?*" is said, when "*who is it?*" is thought, this is itself "*talking of the mind and talking of the nature.*" This "*talking of the mind and talking of the nature*" is something

---

51 **he has not reached the ground of penetration** (*mitō santetsu chi* 未到參徹地): A phrase that picks up the expression "has not reached the field" in the preceding paragraph. The English "ground" here tries to capture something of the semantic functions of the term *chi* 地, which reminds the reader both of the earlier "field" (*denchi* 田地) and of the "grounds," or "ranks" (*chi* 地; S. *bhūmi*), of the Buddhist path that Linji's saying is dismissing.

52 **we meet them in the ear, we meet them in the eye** (*nisho ni shōken shi, gensho ni shōken su* 耳處に相見し、眼處に相見す): Or "we see them in the visual sphere, we see them in the auditory sphere." The terms *nisho* 耳處 (S. *śrotāyatana*) and *gensho* 眼處 (S. *cakṣurāyatana*) are used in technical Buddhist vocabulary respectively for the sense fields of vision and hearing.

53 **When he expresses this saying** (*kono dōshu o genjō seshimuru ni* この道取を現成せしむるに): Or "when this saying is brought to realization." The verb in the original is a causative, the agent of which is unexpressed; it could be understood either as "we" or as "he."

previously avail himself (*saki ni mo . . . jōzu* さきにも. . . 乗ず); **subsequently avail himself** (*nochi ni mo . . . jōzu* のちにも. . . 乗ず): This could be interpreted to mean simply that, in the story, Sengmi asks the question twice; but commentators regularly take it to suggest that the question is a timeless one.

54 **over there** (*nari* 那裏): The translation masks what may be a play with this term, which includes the element *ri* 裏 of Dongshan's "inside" (*menri* 面裏); hence, the suggestion that Sengmi's question is itself what is being talked about there in the cloister. Some would interpret *nari* here to be an oblique reference to the "teaching of the mind and teaching of the nature" that is "over there," beyond a conventional meaning.

42. Talking of the Mind, Talking of the Nature *Sesshin Sesshō* 説心説性 279

that those of other quarters have never known.[55] They have forgotten their child and taken it for a thief; so "they see the thief as their child."[56]

[42:25]

大師いはく、被師伯一問、直得去死十分。

The Great Master said, "*Once he's questioned by my elder brother, he's definitely completely dead.*"

[42:26]

この道をきく參學の庸流おほくおもふ、説心説性する有人の、是誰といはれて、直得去死十分なるべし。そのゆえは、是誰のことば、對面不相識なり、全無所見なるがゆえに死句なるべし。かならずしもしかにはあらず。この説心説性は、徹者まれなりぬべし。十分の去死は、一二分の去死にあらず、このゆえに去死の十分なり。被問の正當恁麽時、たれかこれを遮天蓋地にあらずとせん。照古也際斷なるべし、照今也際斷なるべし、照來也際斷なるべし、照正當恁麽時也際斷なるべし。

When mediocre types of students hear these words, they think that the "someone" who is "*talking of the mind and talking of the nature,*" upon being asked, "*who is it?*" is "definitely completely dead." The reason is that they are facing the words, "*who is it?*" without recognizing them, without any view of them at all; hence, [the words] are "dead words."[57] This is not necessarily the case. Those who have penetrated this "*talking of the mind and talking of the nature*" are rare. To be "dead" a hundred percent is not to be "dead" ten or twenty percent; hence "dead" is a hundred percent.[58] At the very moment of being "questioned," who would hold that this is not shielding the heavens and covering the earth?[59] *Illumining the past is cut off; illumining the present is cut off; illumining the future is cut off. Illumining this very moment is cut off.*

---

55 **those of other quarters** (*yohō no tomogara* 餘方のともがら): A term of ambiguous reference; presumably, those (like Dahui and Linji) in other Chan traditions.

56 **"see the thief as their child"** (*zoku o ninjite ko to su* 賊を認じて子とす): Dōgen's vernacular rendering of a common Zen saying (*nin zoku i shi* 認賊爲子), used to describe an egregious error; usually traced to the *Śūraṅgama-sūtra* (*Shulengyan jing* 首楞嚴經, T.945.19:108c21).

57 **"dead words"** (*shiku* 死句): A standard expression for empty, ineffective language. Dōgen is, of course, playing with the term *shi* 死 ("dead") in Dongshan's remark. To retain something of this play, one might treat *shiku* 死句 here not only as "dead words" but as "deadly words."

58 **"dead" a hundred percent** (*jūbun no kyoshi* 十分の去死); **"dead" is a hundred percent** (*kyoshi no jūbun* 去死の十分): Dōgen is here playing with Dongshan's expression, *kyoshi jūbun* 去死十分 ("completely dead").

59 **shielding the heavens and covering the earth** (*shaten gaichi* 遮天蓋地): Generally interpreted to mean "all inclusive."

280 DŌGEN'S *SHŌBŌGENZŌ* VOLUME III

[42:27] {1:456}
僧密師伯いはく、説心説性底誰。

The elder brother Sengmi said, "*Then who is it that's talking of the mind and talking of the nature?*"

[42:28]
さきの是誰といまの是誰と、その名は張三なりとも、その人は李四なり。

The previous "*who is it?*" and this "*who is it?*" though the name is Zhang's third, the person is Li's fourth.[60]

[42:29]
大師いはく、死中得活。

The Great Master said, "*In death, he lives.*"

[42:30]
この死中は、直得去死を直指すとおもひ、説心説性底を直指して是誰とは、みだりに道取するにあらず。是誰は、説心説性の有人を差排す、かならず十分の去死を萬期せずといふと、參學することありぬべし。大師道の死中得活は、有人説心説性の聲色現前なり、またさらに、十分の去死のなかの一兩分なるべし。活は、たとひ全活なりとも、死の變じて活と現ずるにあらず、得活の頭正尾正に脱落なるのみなり。

In regard to this "in death," [we should not] think that it is directly pointing to the "definitely dead"; it is not directly pointing to [the one who is] "*talking of the mind and talking of the nature*" and arbitrarily saying, "*who is it?*"[61] "*Who is it?*" arranges the "someone" who is "*talking of the mind and talking of the nature.*"[62] There should be a study holding that he does not wait ten thousand times to be a hundred percent "dead."[63] The Great Master's words, "*In death, he lives,*" are the voices and forms of "*someone talking of the mind and talking of the nature*" right before us. Again, they are also one or two parts of a hundred

---

60 **Zhang's third** (*Chō san* 張三); **Li's fourth** (*Li shi* 李四): From the Chinese idiom *Zhang san Li si* 張三李四 ("Zhang's third son, Li's fourth son"), used (as we might use "Tom, Dick, and Harry") to indicate anyone at all. The sentence is usually interpreted to mean simply that Sengmi is asking twice about the same person.

61 **In regard to this "in death"** (*kono shichū wa* この死中は): A sentence difficult to parse, for which there are varied readings. The translation takes the final negative to govern both clauses. However the sentence is read, the point seems to be that we should not think that "in death" refers to the same state as "dead," or that "who is it?" refers to the one who is "talking of the mind and talking of the nature."

62 **arranges the "someone"** (*unin o sahai su* 有人を差排す): Taken to mean that the question "who is it?" refers to an array of "someones."

63 **he does not wait ten thousand times** (*banki sezu* 萬期せず): Or "does not have ten thousand expectations." Usually understood to mean, "is already always [a hundred percent dead]."

42. Talking of the Mind, Talking of the Nature *Sesshin Sesshō* 説心説性　281

percent "dead." Life may be fully alive, but it is not death changing to appear as life: it is just the sloughing off of "he lives" that is true from head to tail.[64]

[42:31]

おほよそ佛道・祖道には、かくのごとくの説心説性ありて、参究せらるるなり。又且のときは十分の死を死して、得活の活計を現成するなり。

In general, there is this kind of "*talking of the mind and talking of the nature*" that is investigated on the way of the buddhas and the way of the ancestors. When we go further, by dying a complete death, we realize the way of life of "he lives."

[42:32]

しるべし、唐代より今日にいたるまで、説心説性の、佛道なることをあきらめず、教・行・證の説心説性にくらくて、胡説乱道する可憐憫者おほし。身先身後にすくふべし。爲道すらくは、説心説性はこれ七佛祖師の要機なり。

We should realize that, from the Tang period till today, there have been many pitiable types who have not clarified the fact that "*talking of the mind and talking of the nature*" are the way of the buddhas, who are in the dark about the "*talking of the mind and talking of the nature*" in teaching, practice, and verification, and who talk rashly and speak wildly. We should save them before the body and after the body.[65] What I say to them is this: "*talking of the mind and talking of the nature*" are the essential functions of the seven buddhas and the ancestral masters.

正法眼藏説心説性第四十二
Treasury of the True Dharma Eye
Talking of the Mind, Talking of the Nature
Number 42

64　**true from head to tail** (*zushin bishin* 頭正尾正): A fairly common expression meaning "correct throughout," "entirely right."

This is perhaps the most difficult passage of the text. One possible paraphrase of its "argument" might look like this.

The "death" in Dongshan's statement, "in death," does not refer simply to the state he calls "dead," just as Sengmi's "who is it" does not refer simply to a person "talking of the mind and talking of the nature." Rather, the question "who is it?" refers to the array of phenomena that are all "talking of the mind and talking of the nature"; and these phenomena are always "dead," always alive in death. They are what is occurring right before us. They are all both "dead" and "alive"; they are all completely liberated even as they live and die.

65　**before the body and after the body** (*shinsen shingo* 身先身後): See above, Note 28.

[Ryūmonji MS:]

爾時寛元元年癸卯、在于日本國越州吉田縣吉峰寺示衆

Presented to the assembly at Kippō Monastery, Yoshida District, Esshū, Land of Japan; junior water year of the rabbit, the first year of Kangen [1243]

[*Himitsu* MS:]

彼本奧書云

尒時寛元々年癸卯、在于日本國越州吉田吉峯寺示衆

同二年甲辰正月十一日書寫之、在侍者寮下。懷奘

The colophon to that manuscript says:[66]
"Presented to the assembly at Kippō Monastery, Yoshida District, Esshū, Land of Japan; junior water year of the rabbit, the first year of Kangen [1243]
Copied this eleventh day, first month, senior wood year of the dragon, the second year of the same era [20 February 1244]. Ejō"

---

66 Copyist unknown. The identity of "that manuscript" (*tahon* 彼本) is likewise unknown.

Treasury of the True Dharma Eye

Number 43

The Real Marks of the Dharmas
Shohō jissō
諸法實相

The Real Marks of the Dharmas

Shohō jissō

INTRODUCTION

This essay was composed at Kippōji (also known as Yoshiminedera) in the autumn of 1243, some two months after its author had ended his mission in the capital and withdrawn to the rural province of Echizen. The text represents number 43 in the seventy-five-chapter *Shōbōgenzō* and number 50 in the Honzan edition; it does not appear in the sixty-chapter compilation but is listed as number 6 of fascicle 1 in the twenty-eight-text *Himitsu Shōbōgenzō*.

Like some other chapters from this period, "Shohō jissō" includes some sharp criticism of recent Chan masters in Song China, whom Dōgen takes to task for their association of Buddhism with Daoism and Confucianism, their ignorance of the wisdom of the Zen ancestors, and their failure to appreciate the significance of the title phrase of this essay, "the real marks (or mark) of the dharmas." The phrase occurs in a famous passage in Kumārajīva's translation of the *Lotus Sūtra* as the object of knowledge available only to the buddhas. While the translation here follows one likely reading of the phrase, taking it to mean something like "the true features of phenomena," the Japanese Tendai tradition in which Dōgen was trained tended to interpret the phrase as the metaphysical claim that "the dharmas are the real mark" — i.e., that "all phenomena are marked by reality (or are ultimately real)." While the *Lotus Sūtra* plays a central role in Dōgen's Buddhism, it is much less conspicuous in the sayings of the Song-dynasty Chan masters — hence, Dōgen's disappointment that they seemed largely to ignore this phrase.

Dōgen often quotes or alludes to the *Lotus Sūtra* throughout the *Shōbōgenzō*; here, however, he is not merely using the sūtra as a proof text in support of his comments on Zen but is commenting on passages of the sūtra itself, much as he comments on the sayings of the Zen masters. This practice of treating the sūtra as the recorded sayings of Śākyamuni has no real precedent in the Chinese Chan literature and makes the "Shohō jissō" chapter an interesting expression of the Buddhism of a Japanese Tendai convert to Zen. Equally interesting as the the expression of a young Japanese pilgrim in China is a passage near the end of the chapter, in which Dōgen relates his personal experience of a late-night talk by his teacher, Rujing.

285

正法眼藏第四十三
Treasury of the True Dharma Eye
Number 43

諸法實相

The Real Marks of the Dharmas

[43:1] {1:457}

佛祖の現成は、究盡の實相なり、實相は諸法なり、諸法は如是相なり、如是性なり、如是身なり、如是心なり、如是世界なり、如是雲雨なり、如是行住坐臥なり、如是憂喜動靜なり、如是拄杖拂子なり、如是拈華破顏なり、如是嗣法授記なり、如是參學辦道なり、如是松操竹節なり。

The realization of the buddhas and ancestors is the real marks exhaustively investigated.[1] The real marks are the dharmas; the dharmas are "such marks," are "such natures," are such bodies, are such minds, are such worlds, are such clouds and rain, are such walking, standing, sitting, and reclining, are such anger and joy, motion and rest; they are such staffs and whisks, are such holding up a flower and breaking into a smile; they are such inheriting the dharma and conferring a prediction, are such investigating and pursuing the way, are such constancy of pine and restraint of bamboo.[2]

* * * * *

---

1 **the real marks exhaustively investigated** (*gūjin no jissō* 究盡の實相): Or "the real marks of exhaustive investigation." From the line in the *Lotus Sūtra* quoted in the next section: "Only buddhas and buddhas can exhaustively investigate the real marks of the dharmas."

2 **"such marks"** (*nyoze sō* 如是相); **"such natures"** (*nyoze shō* 如是性): Dōgen begins here a list, initially derived from the *Lotus Sūtra* passage he will quote in the next section, but continuing on to members of his own invention. "Marks" (*sō* 相; S. *lakṣaṇa*) refers to the attributes, or distinctive features, by which a thing is recognized; "natures" (*shō* 性; S. *svabhāva*) refers to the essence of a thing.

holding up a flower and breaking into a smile (*nenge hagan* 拈華破顏): From the famous founding legend of Zen, in which Buddha Śākyamuni holds up a flower and his disciple Mahākāśyapa smiles. See Supplementary Notes, s.v. "Holding up a flower and breaking into a smile."

constancy of pine and restraint of bamboo (*shōsō chikusetsu* 松操竹節): A play with the term *sōsetsu* 操節, meaning to be well-disciplined and steadfast, combined with the image of the pine as evergreen and, thus, constant, and the bamboo, the nodes of which are designated by the term (*setsu* 節) used for "limit," or "restraint." An unusual expression, not occurring elsewhere in Dōgen's writing.

286 DŌGEN'S *SHŌBŌGENZŌ* VOLUME III

[43:2]

釋迦牟尼佛言、唯佛與佛、乃能究盡諸法實相。所謂諸法、如是相・如是
性・如是體・如是力・如是作・如是因・如是緣・如是果・如是報・如是本
末究竟等。

Buddha Śākyamuni said, "Only buddhas with buddhas can exhaustively investigate the real marks of the dharmas — i.e., that the dharmas are of such marks, such natures, such substance, such power, such actions, such causes, such conditions, such effects, such recompense, such ultimate equivalence from beginning to end."[3]

[43:3]

いはゆる如來道の本末究竟等は、諸法實相の自道取なり、闍梨自道取な
り、一等の參學なり、參學は一等なるがゆえに。

The "ultimate equivalence from beginning to end" said by the Tathāgata is what "the real marks of the dharmas" themselves say, is "*The Ācārya said it himself*"; it is the study of equivalence; for their study is equivalent.[4]

---

3 **Buddha Śākyamuni** (*Shakamuni butsu* 釋迦牟尼佛): From the *Lotus Sūtra* (*Miaofa lianhua jing* 妙法蓮華經, T.262.9:5c10-13); see Supplementary Notes, s.v. "Only buddhas with buddhas can exhaustively investigate the real marks of the dharmas." One of the most famous passages in the sūtra, the source of the so-called "ten suchnesses" (*jū nyoze* 十如是) of Tiantai exegesis (see, e.g., *Fahua xuanyi* 法華玄義, T.1716.33:693b9ff). The extant Sanskrit for this passage is somewhat different from Kumārajīva's version and lists only five aspects of the dharmas known by the tathāgata: which (*ya*) the dharmas are, how (*yathā*) they are, what they are like (*yādṛś*), what their marks (*lakṣaṇa*) are, what their natures (*svabhāva*) are.

Only buddhas with buddhas (*yui butsu yo butsu* 唯佛與佛): I.e., "only the buddhas" (no doubt rendering the Sanskrit *tathāgata eva*). The awkward English here tries to retain Kumārajīva's four-word expression with which Dōgen will play below.

4 **"The Ācārya said it himself"** (*jari ji dōshu* 闍梨自道取): I.e., "you said it yourself." The term "ācārya," originally meaning a Buddhist instructor, is regularly used by Zen teachers in direct address to their students. Perhaps reflecting the words of Dongshan Liangjie 洞山良价 (807-869) (*Jingde chuandeng lu* 景德傳燈錄, T.2076.51:323a26-27):

僧便問、如何是主中主。師曰、闍梨自道取。

The monk asked further, "What is the master within the master?"
The Master [Dongshan] said, "The Ācārya said it himself."

it is the study of equivalence; for their study is equivalent (*ittō no sangaku nari, sangaku wa ittō naru ga yue ni* 一等の參學なり、參學は一等なるがゆえに): The punctuation here follows Kawamura's edition; the last phrase could also be read with the sentence following: "Because their study is equivalent, 'only buddhas with buddhas' are 'the real marks of the dharmas'; 'the real marks of the dharmas' are 'only buddhas with buddhas.'" The translation assumes that the term *ittō* 一等 refers to the "equivalent" study by the three speakers: "the Tathāgata," "the real marks of the dharmas," and "the Ācārya"; and it can also of course refer to their study of the "equivalence" (*tō* 等) in the phrase "ultimate equivalence from beginning to end."

43. The Real Marks of the Dharmas *Shohō jissō* 諸法實相   287

[43:4] {1:458}

唯佛與佛は、諸法實相なり、諸法實相は、唯佛與佛なり。唯佛は、實相なり、與佛は、諸法なり。諸法の道を聞取して、一と參じ、多と參ずべからず。實相の道を聞取して、虚にあらずと學し、性にあらずと學すべからず。實は、唯佛なり、相は、與佛なり、乃能は、唯佛なり、究盡は、與佛なり、諸法は、唯佛なり、實相は、與佛なり。諸法のまさに諸法なるを、唯佛と稱す、諸法のいまし實相なるを、與佛と稱す。

"Only buddhas with buddhas" are "the real marks of the dharmas"; "the real marks of the dharmas" are *"only buddhas with buddhas."* "Only buddhas" are "the real marks"; "with buddhas" are "the dharmas." Hearing the words "the dharmas," we should not study them as one, nor study them as many; hearing the words "the real marks," we should not study that they are not vacuous, nor study that they are not the nature.[5] "Real" is "only buddhas"; "marks" are "with buddhas"; "can" is "only buddhas"; "exhaustively investigate" is "with buddhas"; "the dharmas" are "only buddhas"; "the real marks" are "with buddhas." That "the dharmas" are truly "the dharmas" is called "only buddhas"; that "the dharmas" at this moment are "the real marks" is called "with buddhas."

[43:5]

しかあれば、諸法のみづから諸法なる、如是相あり、如是性あり。實相のまさしく實相なる、如是相あり、如是性あり。唯佛與佛と出現於世するは、諸法實相の説取なり、行取なり、證取なり。その説取は、乃能究盡なり。究盡なりといへども、乃能なるべし。初・中・後にあらざるゆえに、如是相なり、如是性なり。このゆえに初・中・後善といふ。

Thus, there are "such marks," there are "such natures," in which "the dharmas" are themselves "the dharmas"; there are "such marks," there are "such natures," in which "the real marks" are truly "the real marks." "To appear in the world" as *"only buddhas with buddhas"* is the preaching, is the practice, is the verification, of "the real marks of the dharmas."[6] The preaching is "can exhaustively investigate." While it may be "exhaustively investigate," it should be "can."[7] Because it is not begin-

---

5 **we should not study them as one, nor study them as many** (*ichi to sanji, ta to sanzu bekarazu* 一と參じ、多と參ずべからず): I.e., though the term *shohō* 諸法 ("dharmas") is a plural form, we should not treat it as either singular or plural.

not vacuous (*ko ni arazu* 虚にあらず); **not the nature** (*shō ni arazu* 性にあらず): I.e., we should not think that "real" implies the opposite of empty of reality; we should not think that "marks" implies phenomenal characteristics as opposed to essential nature.

6 **"To appear in the world"** (*shutsugen o se* 出現於世): Allusion to the famous lines of the *Lotus Sūtra*, in which Śākyamuni announces that the purpose of Buddhism is to lead beings to buddhahood. See Supplementary Notes, s.v. "Buddhas, the world-honored ones, appear in the world for the reason of one great matter alone."

7 **While it may be "exhaustively investigate," it should be "can"** (*gūjin nari to iedomo, nai nō naru beshi* 究盡なりといへども、乃能なるべし): Perhaps meaning

288   DŌGEN'S *SHŌBŌGENZŌ* VOLUME III

ning, middle, and end, it is "such marks," it is "such natures"; therefore, it is said, "good in the beginning, middle, and end."[8]

[43:6]

乃能究盡といふは、諸法實相なり、諸法實相は、如是相なり、如是相は、乃能究盡如是性なり、如是性は、乃能究盡如是體なり、如是體は、乃能究盡如是力なり、如是力は、乃能究盡如是作なり、如是作は、乃能究盡如是因なり、如是因は、乃能究盡如是緣なり、如是緣は、乃能究盡如是果なり、如是果は、乃能究盡如是報なり、如是報は、乃能究盡本末究竟等なり。

"Can exhaustively investigate" means "the true marks of the dharmas." "The true marks of the dharmas" are "such marks"; "such marks" are "*such natures*" that "*can exhaustively investigate*"; "such natures" are "*such substance*" that "*can exhaustively investigate*"; "such substance" is "*such power*" that "*can exhaustively investigate*"; "such power" is "*such actions*" that "*can exhaustively investigate*"; "such actions" are "*such causes*" that "*can exhaustively investigate*"; "such causes" are "*such conditions*" that "*can exhaustively investigate*"; "such conditions" are "*such effects*" that "*can exhaustively investigate*"; "such effects" are "*such recompense*" that "*can exhaustively investigate*"; "such recompense" is "*such ultimate equivalence from beginning to end*" that "can exhaustively investigate."[9]

[43:7]

本末究竟等の道取、まさに現成の如是なり。かるがゆえに、果果の果は、因果の果にあらず、このゆえに、因果の果は、すなはち果果の果なるべし。この果、すなはち相・性・體・力をあひ罣礙するがゆえに、諸法の相・性・體・力等、いく無量無邊も實相なり。この果、すなはち相・性・體・力を罣礙せざるがゆえに、諸法の相・性・體・力等、ともに實相なり。この相・性・體・力等を、果・報・因・緣等のあひ罣礙するに一任するとき、八九成の道あり。この相・性・體・力等を、果・報・因・緣等のあひ罣礙せざるに一任するとき、十成の道あり。

The saying "ultimate equivalence from beginning to end" is truly "suchness" realized.[10] Hence, the "effects" of the effects of effects are

---

something like, "while the buddha's preaching expresses the ultimate meaning ('exhaustively investigate'), it must also include practical instruction ('can')."

8 **"good in the beginning, middle, and end"** (*sho chū go zen* 初・中・後善): Variation on a common description of the buddha dharma, as seen in the *Lotus Sūtra* and many other Buddhist texts; see Supplementary Notes, s.v. "Good in the beginning, middle, and end."

9 **"such natures" that "can exhaustively investigate"** (*nai nō gūjin nyoze shō* 乃能究盡如是性): Presumably, to be understood, "such natures that [only buddhas with buddhas] can exhaustively investigate"; and similarly, *mutatis mutandis*, throughout this sentence.

10 **"suchness" realized** (*genjō no nyoze* 現成の如是): Or "the suchness of realization." I.e., the ultimate truth manifest in the world.

43. The Real Marks of the Dharmas *Shohō jissō* 諸法實相　　289

not the "effects" of causes and effects; therefore, the "effects" of causes and effects must be the "effects" of the effects of effects.[11] Because these "effects" obstruct the "marks," "natures," "substance," and "power," the "marks," "natures," "substance," "power," and the rest, of "the dharmas," however incalculable and limitless, are "the real marks."[12] Because these "effects" do not obstruct the "marks," "natures," "substance," and "power," the "marks," "natures," "substance," "power," and the rest, of "the dharmas," are together "the real marks." When the "effects," "recompense," "causes," "conditions," and the rest, are left entirely to obstruct the "marks," "natures," "substance," "power," and the rest, we have a saying of eighty or ninety percent; when the "effects," "recompense," "causes," "conditions," and the rest, are left entirely not to obstruct the "marks," "natures," "substance," "power," and the rest, we have a saying of a hundred percent.

[43:8] {1:459}

いはゆるの如是相は、一相にあらず、如是相は、一如是にあらず、無量無邊、不可道、不可測の如是なり。百千の量を量とすべからず、諸法の量を量とすべし、實相の量を量とすべし。そのゆえは、唯佛與佛乃能究盡諸法實相なり、唯佛與佛乃能究盡諸法實性なり、唯佛與佛乃能究盡諸法實體なり、唯佛與佛乃能究盡諸法實力なり、唯佛與佛乃能究盡諸法實作なり、唯佛與佛乃能究盡諸法實因なり、唯佛與佛乃能究盡諸法實緣なり、唯佛與佛乃能究盡諸法實果なり、唯佛與佛乃能究盡諸法實報なり、唯佛與佛乃能究盡諸法實本末究竟等なり。

11　**the "effects" of the effects of effects** (*ka ka no ka* 果果の果): I.e., the effect that is the ultimate spiritual result. Reflecting a passage in the *Nirvāṇa Sūtra* (*Da banniepan jing* 大般涅槃經, T.374.12:524a5-8):

> 善男子、佛性者有因有因因、有果有果果。有因者即十二因緣。因因者即是智慧。有果者即是阿耨多羅三藐三菩提。果果者即是無上大般涅槃。

> Good man, in the buddha nature there are causes and there are causes of causes; there are effects and there are effects of effects. That there are "causes" refers to the twelvefold causes and conditions; "causes of causes" refers to wisdom. That there are "effects" refers to *anuttara-samyak-saṃbodhi;* "effects of effects" refers to unsurpassed great *parinirvāṇa.*

therefore, the "effects" of causes and effects must be the "effects" of the effects of effects (*kono yue ni, inga no ka wa, sunawachi ka ka no ka naru beshi* このゆえに、因果の果は、すなはち果果の果なるべし): The logic of this apparently contradictory conclusion may be something like this: since the ultimate effect, unlike ordinary effects, is universal, it must subsume ordinary effects.

12　**Because these "effects" obstruct the "marks," "natures," "substance," and "power"** (*kono ka, sunawachi sō shō tai riki o ai keige suru ga yue ni* この果、すなはち相・性・體・力をあひ罣礙するがゆえに): Here and below, the verb *keige* 罣礙 ("to obstruct") likely has the sense "to define," "to distinguish as" — a usage common in the *Shōbōgenzō*. Hence, the ten "suchnesses" may be "obstructed" (distinguished one from the other) or may be "unobstructed" (taken as a single "suchness").

290 DŌGEN'S *SHŌBŌGENZŌ* VOLUME III

"Such marks" are not a single mark; "such marks" are not a single suchness: they are incalculable, limitless, inexpressible, unfathomable suchness.[13] We should not take the measure of hundreds of thousands as their measure; we should take the measure of "the dharmas" as their measure; we should take the measure of "the real marks" as their measure. The reason is "*only buddhas with buddhas can exhaustively investigate the real marks of the dharmas*"; it is "*only buddhas with buddhas can exhaustively investigate*" the real natures of the dharmas; it is "*only buddhas with buddhas can exhaustively investigate*" the real substance of the dharmas; it is "*only buddhas with buddhas can exhaustively investigate*" the real power of the dharmas; it is "*only buddhas with buddhas can exhaustively investigate*" the real action of the dharmas; it is "*only buddhas with buddhas can exhaustively investigate*" the real causes of the dharmas; it is "*only buddhas with buddhas can exhaustively investigate*" the real conditions of the dharmas; it is "*only buddhas with buddhas can exhaustively investigate*" the real effects of the dharmas; it is "*only buddhas with buddhas can exhaustively investigate*" the real recompense of the dharmas; it is "*only buddhas with buddhas can exhaustively investigate*" the real ultimate unity from beginning to end of the dharmas.[14]

[43:9]
かくのごとくの道理あるがゆえに、十方佛土は唯佛與佛のみなり、さらに
一箇半箇の唯佛與佛にあらざるなし。唯と與とは、たとへば、體に體を具
し、相の相を證せるなり。また、性を體として、性を存せるがごとし。こ
のゆえにいはく、

Because there is a principle like this, the buddha lands of the ten directions are nothing but "*only buddhas with buddhas*"; there is not in addition one or a half that is not "*only buddhas with buddhas*." "Only" and "with" are like providing "substance" with "substance," like "marks"

---

13 **a single mark** (*issō* 一相): Or "the one mark," a term often used to express the ultimate sameness of all phenomena; the mark of suchness.

14 **The reason is "only buddhas with buddhas can exhaustively investigate the real marks of the dharmas"** (*sono yue wa, yui butsu yo butsu nai nō gūjin shohō jissō nari* そのゆえは、唯佛與佛乃能究盡諸法實相なり): Dōgen simply repeats here the line from the *Lotus Sūtra* quoted above, and then proceeds to use the same pattern with the other members of the list of ten "suchnesses." It may be, however, that here he would like us to take the pattern as modifying these members, a reading that would yield something like this:

The reason is that they are "the real marks of the dharmas" that "only buddhas with buddhas can exhaustively investigate"; they are the real natures of the dharmas that "only buddhas with buddhas can exhaustively investigate"; and so on, *mutatis mutandis*.

43. The Real Marks of the Dharmas Shohō jissō 諸法實相

verifying "marks."[15] Or, again, it is like maintaining "natures" by taking "natures" as "substance."[16] Therefore, it is said,

[43:10]
我及十方佛、乃能知是事。

"I and the buddhas of the ten directions can know these matters."[17]

[43:11] {1:460}
しかあれば、乃能究盡の正當恁麽時と、乃能知是の正當恁麽時と、おなじくこれ面面の有時なり。我もし十方佛に同異せば、いかでか及十方佛の道取を現成せしめん。這頭に十方なきがゆえに、十方は這頭なり。ここをもて、實相の、諸法に相見すといふは、春は華にいり、人は春にあふ、月は月をてらし、人はおのれにあふ、あるひは人の水をみる、おなじくこれ相見底の道理なり。

Thus, the very time of "can exhaustively investigate" and the very time of "can know these" are both equally instances of "sometimes."[18] If "I" were the same as or different from "the buddhas of the ten directions," why would he express the words "and the buddhas of the ten directions"?[19] Because right here there are no "ten directions," the "ten

---

15 **"Only" and "with" are like providing "substance" with "substance," like "marks" verifying "marks"** (*yui to yo to wa, tatoeba, tai ni tai o gu shi, sō no sō o shō seru nari* 唯と與とは、たとへば、體に體を具し、相の相を證せるなり): Probably meaning that "only" and "with," in the phrase "only buddhas with buddhas," are redundant — like substance added to substance or marks realizing themselves as marks.

16 **like maintaining "natures" by taking "natures" as "substance"** (*shō o tai toshite, shō o zon seru ga gotoshi* 性を體として、性を存せるがごとし): Though the exact sense is obscure, again, apparently indicating something superfluous, or unnecessary: among the ten "suchnesses," preserving the item "natures" by treating it as the following item, "substance."

17 **"I and the buddhas of the ten directions can know these matters"** (*ga gyū jippō butsu, nai nō chi ze ji* 我及十方佛、乃能知是事): From the *Lotus Sūtra* (*Miaofa lianhua jing* 妙法蓮華經, T.262.9:5c23-24):

如是大果報、種種性相義、我及十方佛、乃能知是事。

Such great effects and recompense,
The manifold meanings of natures and marks —
I and the buddhas of the ten directions
Can know these matters.

18 **are both equally instances of "sometimes"** (*onajiku kore menmen no uji nari* おなじくこれ面面の有時なり): "Sometimes" here translates *uji* 有時, a term that receives extended treatment in the famous *Shōbōgenzō* chapter of the same name; often translated "being-time."

19 **If "I" were the same as or different from "buddhas of the ten directions"** (*ga moshi jippō butsu ni dōi seba* 我もし十方佛に同異せば): Or simply, "if 'I' were different from 'buddhas of the ten directions.'" Generally understood to mean, "if Buddha Śākyamuni and the other buddhas were separate beings subject to comparisons." The oddity of the argument here suggests that, in the sūtra phrase *ga gyū jippō butsu* 我及十

292 DŌGEN'S *SHŌBŌGENZŌ* VOLUME III

directions" are right here.[20] Accordingly, "the real marks" meeting "the dharmas" is spring starting with the flowers, and people meeting the spring.[21] The moon illuminating the moon, people meeting themselves, or a person looking at water — these are similarly the principle of their meeting each other.[22]

[43:12]

このゆえに、實相の、實相に參學するを、佛祖の、佛祖に嗣法する、とす。これ、諸法の、諸法に授記するなり。唯佛の、唯佛のために傳法し、與佛の、與佛のために嗣法するなり。

Therefore, "the real marks" studying with "the real marks" represents the buddhas and ancestors inheriting the dharma of the buddhas and ancestors. This is "the dharmas" bestowing predictions on "the dharmas"; it is "only buddhas" transmitting the dharma for the sake of "only buddhas," "with buddhas" inheriting the dharma for the sake of "with buddhas."

[43:13]

このゆえに、生死去來あり、このゆえに發心・修行・菩提・涅槃あり。發心・修行・菩提・涅槃を擧して、生死去來眞實人體を參究し接取するに、把定し放行す。これを命脈として、華開・結果す、これを骨髓として、迦葉・阿難あり。

Therefore, there are birth and death, coming and going; therefore, there are bringing forth the mind [of bodhi], practice, bodhi, and nirvāṇa.[23] Taking up bringing forth the mind, practice, bodhi, and nirvāṇa, as we investigate and treat "*birth and death, coming and going, as the*

方佛 ("I and the buddhas of the ten directions"), Dōgen may want us to read the word *gyū* 及, not as the conjunction "and," but as the verb "to reach" — hence, "I extend to the buddhas of the ten directions."

20 **Because right here there are no "ten directions," the "ten directions" are right here** (*shatō ni jippō naki ga yue ni, jippō wa shatō nari* 這頭に十方なきがゆえに、十方は這頭なり): Perhaps meaning that "the ten directions" in the phrase "the buddhas of the ten directions" means "right here" where the "I" exists; for there are no ten directions other than this "right here."

21 **spring starting with the flowers, and people meeting the spring** (*haru wa hana ni iri, hito wa haru ni au* 春は華にいり、人は春にあふ): I.e., spring is experienced as flowers blooming. "The real marks" is to "the dharmas" as "spring" is to "flowers."

22 **a person looking at water** (*hito no mizu o miru* 人の水をみる): Some MS witnesses have "looking at fire" (*hi* 火) here, but clearly the metaphor is seeing one's reflection on the surface of water.

23 **bringing forth the mind [of bodhi], practice, bodhi, and nirvāṇa** (*hosshin shugyō bodai nehan* 發心・修行・菩提・涅槃): I.e., the bodhisattva path, beginning with the aspiration for bodhi and ending with buddhahood and final nirvāṇa. See Supplementary Notes, s.v. "Bring forth the mind."

43. The Real Marks of the Dharmas *Shohō jissō* 諸法實相 293

true human body," we hold fast, and we let go.[24] With this as their vital artery, the flower opens and the fruit forms; with this as their bones and marrow, there are Kāśyapa and Ānanda.[25]

[43:14]

風・雨・水・火の如是相、すなはち究盡なり、青・黄・赤・白の如是性、すなはち究盡なり。この體・力によりて轉凡入聖す、この果・報によりて超佛越祖す。この因・縁によりて握土成金あり、この果・報によりて傳法附衣あり。

"Such marks" of wind, rain, water, and fire, are "exhaustively investigate"; "such natures" of blue, yellow, red, and white, are "exhaustively investigate." By this "substance" and "power," we "turn the commoner into a sage"; by this "effects" and "recompense," we "transcend the buddhas and surpass the ancestors."[26] By this "causes" and "conditions,"

---

24 **"birth and death, coming and going, as the true human body"** (*shōji korai shinjitsu nintai* 生死去來眞實人體): After the words of Yuanwu Keqin 圓悟克勤 (1063-1135); see Supplementary Notes, s.v. "True human body."

we hold fast, and we let go (*hajō shi hōgyō su* 把定し放行す): An expression, often used by Dōgen, likely reflecting a line in a verse by Tiantong Rujing 天童如淨 (1162-1227) (*Rujing chanshi yulu* 如淨禪師語錄, T.2002A.48:122c18):

放行把住逞風流。

Letting go and holding on, full of style.

25 **with this as their vital artery, the flower opens and the fruit forms** (*kore o meimyaku toshite, kekai kekka su* これを命脈として、華開・結果す): The term *meimyaku* 命脈 ("vital artery") occurs often in the *Shōbōgenzō*, in the senses both of the "lifeblood" and the "bloodline" (especially of the lineage of the buddhas and ancestors). The vegetative image here no doubt recalls the transmission verse attributed to Bodhidharma (*Jingde chuandeng lu* 景德傳燈錄, T.2076.51:589b27-28):

吾本來玆土、傳法救迷情。一華開五葉、結果自然成。

I originally came to this land
To transmit the dharma and save deluded beings.
A single flower opens five petals;
The fruit forms, ripening naturally of itself.

See Supplementary Notes, s.v. "A single flower opens five petals."

with this as their bones and marrow, there are Kāśyapa and Ānanda (*kore o kotsuzui toshite, Kashō Anan ari* これを骨髓として、迦葉・阿難あり): Another allusion to the Zen lineage. "Bones and marrow" (*kotsuzui* 骨髓) recalls Bodhidharma's testing of four disciples, to whom he said of each in turn that he (or, in one case, she) had got his skin, flesh, bones, and marrow; the story is recorded at *shinji Shōbōgenzō* 眞字正法眼藏, DZZ.5:230, case 201; see Supplementary Notes, s.v. "Skin, flesh, bones, and marrow." "Kāśyapa" (*Kashō* 迦葉) is Mahākāśyapa, the disciple of Śākyamuni recognized as the first ancestor of Zen; "Ānanda" (*Anan* 阿難) is Śākyamuni's cousin and attendant, who became Mahākāśyapa's disciple and is reckoned as the second ancestor.

26 **"turn the commoner into a sage"** (*tenbon nisshō* 轉凡入聖): I.e., advance on the Buddhist path from the status of a "common person" (*bonbu* 凡夫; S. pṛthagjana) to the "noble" (*shō* 聖; S. ārya). An expression apparently first appearing in the *Si nianchu* 四

294 DŌGEN'S *SHŌBŌGENZŌ* VOLUME III

there is "grasping earth and making gold"; by this "effects" and "recompense," there is transmitting the dharma and bequeathing the robe.[27]

[43:15]

如來道、爲説實相印。

The Tathāgata said, "For them, I preach the seal of the real mark."[28]

[43:16]

いはゆるをいふべし、爲行實相印、爲聽實性印、爲證實體印。かくのごとく参究し、かくのごとく究盡すべきなり。その宗旨、たとへば珠の盤をはしるがごとく、盤の珠をはしるがごとし。

What is said here could be said, "*for them I practice the seal of the real mark*," "*for them I hear the seal of the real mark*," "*for them I verify the seal of the real mark*." We should investigate it like this, should exhaus-

---

念處, attributed to Zhiyi 智顗 (538–597) (T.1918.46:579a16).

"transcend the buddhas and surpass the ancestors" (*chōbutsu osso* 超佛越祖): A popular expression for the ultimate spiritual state, best known from a dialogue involving Yunmen Wenyan 雲門文偃 (864–949) found in several sources; see, e.g., *Yunmen Kuangzhen chanshi guanglu* 雲門匡眞禪師廣錄, T.1988.47:548b5-6:

> 時有僧問、如何是超佛越祖之談。師云、餬餅。
>
> At the time, a monk asked, "What is the talk that transcends the buddhas and surpasses the ancestors?"
> The Master [Yunmen] said, "Rice cakes."

27 **"grasping earth and making gold"** (*aku do jō gon* 握土成金): Or "the earth in one's hand turns to gold"; a metaphor for abrupt spiritual transformation, from the legend concerning Śākyamuni's follower Śākya Mahānāma (*Shaku Makanan* 釋摩訶男) that whatever he held turned into a treasure. The phrase here is found in a criticism of asceticism without understanding by the seventh-century monk Huiman 慧滿 (dates unknown) (*Jingde chuandeng lu* 景德傳燈錄, T.2076.51:221a28-29):

> 慧滿曰、祖師心印非專苦行。但助道耳。若契本心、發隨意眞光之用、則苦行如握土成金。
>
> Huiman said,
> The mind seal of the ancestral masters is not focused on the austere practices; they are only a subsidiary way. If you accord with your original mind, and produce the spontaneous functioning of the true radiance, then the austere practices will be like "grasping earth and making gold."

transmitting the dharma and bequeathing the robe (*denbō fue* 傳法附衣): I.e., the Zen lineage; from the tradition that the first ancestors of the lineage in China passed down the robe of Bodhidharma to their successors.

28 **The Tathāgata** (*nyorai* 如來): Quoting a verse by Śākyamuni in the *Lotus Sūtra* (*Miaofa lianhua jing* 妙法蓮華經, T.262.9:8b3-3):

> 我以相嚴身、光明照世間、無量衆所尊、爲説實相印。
>
> My body adorned with the [thirty-two] marks [of a buddha],
> My radiance illumining the world;
> Honored by incalculable multitudes,
> For them I preach the seal of the real mark.

43. The Real Marks of the Dharmas *Shohō jissō* 諸法實相   295

tively investigate it like this. The essential point of this is like "the pearl rolling round the bowl, like the bowl rolling round the pearl."[29]

* * * * *

[43:17] {1:461}

日月燈明佛言、諸法實相義、已爲汝等説。

Buddha Candrasūryapradīpa said,[30]
The doctrine of the real marks of the dharmas,
I have preached to you.

[43:18]

この道取を參學して、佛祖は、かならず説實相義を一大事とせり、と參究すべし。佛祖は、十八界ともに實相義を開説す。身心先、身心後、正當身心時、説實相・性・體・力等なり。實相を究盡せず、實相をとかず、實相を會せず、實相を不會せざらんは、佛祖にあらざるなり、魔黨畜生なり。

Studying these words, we should investigate [the fact] that the buddhas and ancestors have always taken preaching "the doctrine of the real marks" as the "one great matter."[31] The buddhas and ancestors preach that the eighteen constituents are all "the doctrine of the real marks."[32] Before their bodies and minds, after their bodies and minds, at the very moment of their bodies and minds, they preach the "real marks," "nature," "body," "power," and the rest.[33] Those who do not "exhaustively

---

29 like "the pearl rolling round the bowl, like the bowl rolling round the pearl" (*tama no ban o hashiru ga gotoku, ban no tama o hashiru ga gotoshi* 珠の盤をはしるがごとく、盤の珠をはしるがごとし): I.e., the multiple ways of saying this are like different ways of viewing the same event. A Japanese version of a line, quoted in "Shōbōgenzō shunjū" 正法眼藏春秋 (DZZ.1:412), by Yuanwu Keqin 圜悟克勤 (*Yuanwu Foguo chanshi yulu* 圜悟佛果禪師語錄; T.1997.47:780c24):

如珠走盤、如盤走珠。
Like a pearl rolling round a bowl; like the bowl rolling round the pearl.

30 **Buddha Candrasūryapradīpa** (*Nichigetsutōmyō butsu* 日月燈明佛; also read *Jitsugetsutōmyō* and *Nichigatsutōmyō*): From the final words of this buddha, said to have preached the *Lotus Sūtra* innumerable kalpas ago (*Miaofa lianhua jing* 妙法蓮華經, T.262.9:5a10).

31 **"one great matter"** (*ichi daiji* 一大事): I.e., the reason the buddhas appear in the world. From the *Lotus Sūtra* passage cited above, Note 6.

32 **the eighteen constituents are all "the doctrine of the real marks"** (*jūhachi kai tomo ni jissō gi* 十八界ともに實相義): Taking as *jissō gi naru o* 實相義なるを. The "eighteen constituents" (*kai* 界; S. *dhātu*) is an ancient list of dharmas comprised of the six sense organs (*kon* 根; S. *indriya*), the six sense objects (*kyō* 境; S. *viṣaya*), and the six types of consciousness (*shiki* 識; S. *vijñāna*) resulting from the contact between organ and object.

33 **Before their bodies and minds, after their bodies and minds** (*shinjin sen, shinjin*

296   DŌGEN'S *SHŌBŌGENZŌ* VOLUME III

investigate" the "real marks," do not explain the "real marks," do not understand the "real marks," do not not understand the "real marks," are not buddhas and ancestors; they are the minions of Māra or beasts.[34]

* * * * *

[43:19]

釋迦牟尼佛道、一切菩薩阿耨多羅三藐三菩提、皆屬此經。此經開方便門、示眞實相。

Buddha Śākyamuni said, "The anuttara-samyak-saṃbodhi of all bodhisattvas belongs wholly to this sūtra. This sūtra opens the gate of expedient means and reveals the true real marks."[35]

[43:20]

いはゆる一切菩薩は、一切諸佛なり。諸佛と菩薩と異類にあらず、老少なし、勝劣なし。此菩薩と彼菩薩と、二人にあらず、自・他にあらず、過・現・當來箇にあらざれども、作佛は行菩薩道の法儀なり。初發心に成佛し、妙覺地に成佛す。無量百千萬億度作佛せる菩薩あり。作佛よりのちは、行を廢してさらに所作あるべからず、といふは、いまだ佛祖の道をしらざる凡夫なり。

"All bodhisattvas" means "all buddhas." Buddhas and bodhisattvas are not different types, not senior and junior, not superior and inferior. This bodhisattva and that bodhisattva are not two people, not self and other; although not past, present, or future, becoming a buddha is their procedure for practicing on the bodhisattva path. They attain buddhahood at the initial bringing forth of the mind [of bodhi]; they attain buddhahood at the stage of marvelous awakening.[36] *There are bodhisattvas who have*

---

go 身心先、身心後): A variant of the more common "before the body, after the body" (*shinsen shingo* 身先身後), suggesting past and future lives. See Supplementary Notes, s.v. "Body and mind."

34 **minions of Māra** (*matō* 魔黨): Also written 魔儻. Followers of Māra, the Evil One (S. *pāpīyān*), lord of the sixth heaven of the realm of desire (*yokkai* 欲界; S. *kāma-loka*), who seeks to obstruct Buddhist awakening; a common pejorative in Dōgen's writings.

35 **Buddha Śākyamuni** (*Shakamuni butsu* 釋迦牟尼佛): From the *Lotus Sūtra* (*Miaofa lianhua jing* 妙法蓮華經, T.262.9:31c15-17).

The *anuttara-samyak-saṃbodhi* of all bodhisattvas (*issai bosatsu anokutara sanmyaku sanbodai* 一切菩薩阿耨多羅三藐三菩提): Dōgen's comments in the following section suggest that he wants us to read this phrase as stating that all bodhisattvas already have the unsurpassed perfect awakening of a buddha.

gate of expedient means (*hōben mon* 方便門): I.e., the teachings accommodated to the spiritual needs and understandings of the buddha's audience, in contrast to "the true real marks" (*shinjissō* 眞實相), or ultimately true teachings.

36 **the initial bringing forth of the mind** (*sho hosshin* 初發心); **the stage of marvelous awakening** (*myōkaku chi* 妙覺地): I.e., the first and last stages of the bodhisattva's

43. The Real Marks of the Dharmas *Shohō jissō* 諸法實相　　297

become buddhas incalculable *hundreds of thousands of myriads of koṭis of times.* Those who say that, after they have become a buddha, they abandon practice and have nothing more to do are common people who do not yet know the way of the buddhas and ancestors.

[43:21] {1:462}

いはゆる一切菩薩は、一切諸佛の本祖なり、一切諸佛は、一切菩薩の本師なり。この諸佛の無上菩提、たとひ過去に修證するも、現在に修證するも、未來に修證するも、身先に修證するも、心後に修證するも、初・中・後ともにこの經なり。能屬・所屬、おなじくこの經なり。この正當恁麼時、これ此經の、一切菩薩を證するなり。

"All bodhisattvas" are the original ancestors of all buddhas; all buddhas are the original teachers of all bodhisattvas. The unsurpassed bodhi of these buddhas — whether practiced and verified in the past, whether practiced and verified in the present, whether practiced and verified in the future, whether practiced and verified before this body, whether practiced and verified after this mind — is all, in beginning, middle, and end, "this sūtra." Both that which "belongs" and that to which it "belongs" are equally "this sūtra."[37] This very time is "this sūtra" verifying "all bodhisattvas."[38]

[43:22]

經は、有情にあらず、經は、無情にあらず、經は、有爲にあらず、經は無爲にあらず。しかあれども、菩薩を證し、人を證し、實相を證し、此經を證するとき、開方便門するなり。方便門は、佛果の無上功德なり、法住法位なり、世相常住なり。方便門は、暫時の伎倆にあらず、盡十方界の參學なり。諸法實相を拈じ、參學するなり。この方便門あらはれて、盡十方界に蓋十方界すといへども、一切菩薩にあらざれば、その境界にあらず。

The "sūtra" is not sentient; the "sūtra" is not insentient. The "sūtra" is not conditioned; the "sūtra" is not unconditioned.[39] Nevertheless, when it verifies the bodhisattva, verifies the person, verifies the "real marks,"

---

career: the initial aspiration to achieve the unsurpassed perfect awakening of a buddha, and the final attainment of that state.

37　**Both that which "belongs" and that to which it "belongs" are equally "this sūtra"** (*nōzoku shozoku, onajiku kono kyō nari* 能屬・所屬、おなじくこの經なり): I.e. both the "sūtra" and the "unsurpassed bodhi" are "this sūtra."

38　**This very time is "this sūtra" verifying "all bodhisattvas"** (*kono shōtō inmo ji, kore kono kyō no, issai bosatsu o shō suru nari* この正當恁麼時、これ此經の、一切菩薩を證するなり): Taking "this very time" (*kono shōtō inmo ji* この正當恁麼時) as the grammatical subject; it is also possible to read, "at this very time, this sūtra verifies all bodhisattvas."

39　**not conditioned** (*ui ni arazu* 有爲にあらず); **not unconditioned** (*mui ni arazu* 無爲にあらず): Following the standard interpretation of these terms as translations of Sanskrit *saṃskṛta* and *asaṃskṛta* respectively; but in this context, the sense may be that the sūtra neither has nor lacks intentional action.

298　　　DŌGEN'S *SHŌBŌGENZŌ* VOLUME III

verifies "this sūtra," it "opens the gate of expedient means."[40] "The gate of expedient means" is the unsurpassed virtue of the fruit of buddhahood; it is "*the dharmas abide in their dharma positions*"; it is "*the marks of the world constantly abide.*"[41] "The gate of expedient means" is not a temporary device; it is the study of the entire world in the ten directions; it is taking up "the real marks of the dharmas" and studying them. Although this "gate of expedient means" is appearing and, in the entire world in the ten directions, is covering the world in the ten directions, those who are not "all bodhisattvas" are not in its realm.

[43:23]

雪峰いはく、盡大地是解脱門、曳人不肯入。

Xuefeng said, "*All the whole earth is the gate of liberation, but even if you drag them, people don't consent to go in.*"[42]

[43:24]

しかあればしるべし、盡地・盡界たとひ門なりとも、出入たやすかるべきにあらず、出入箇のおほきにあらず。曳人するに、いらず、いでず。不曳に、いらず、いでず。進歩のもの、あやまりぬべし、退歩のもの、とどこほりぬべし。亦且いかん。人を擧して門に出入せしむれば、いよいよ門と、とほざかる。門を擧して人にいるるには、出入の分あり。

Therefore, we should realize that, while all the earth, all the worlds, may be a "gate," it is not easy to go in and out of it, and those who go in and out are few. Even if you "drag them," they do not go in or out; even if you do not "drag them," they do not go in or out. Those that step forward will make a mistake; those that step back will get stuck.[43] Now what? If we take up the people and try to get them in and out of the gate, they get further from the gate; when we take up the gate and put it in the people, there will be some who go in and out.

40　**it verifies the bodhisattva** (*bosatsu o shō shi* 菩薩を證し): The grammatical subject is unstated; presumably the "sūtra."

41　**"the dharmas abide in their dharma positions"** (*ze hō jū hōi* 是法住法位); "**the marks of the world constantly abide**" (*seken sō jō jū* 世間相常住): The traditional reading of a phrase in Kumārajīva's translation of the *Lotus Sūtra* that is often cited by Dōgen; see Supplementary Notes, s.v. "Dharmas abide in their dharma positions."

42　**Xuefeng** (*Seppō* 雪峰): I.e., Xuefeng Yicun 雪峰義存 (822–908). The quotation is a variant of a saying found in several sources; see, e.g., *Zongmen tongyao ji* 宗門統要集, ZTS.1:183c10; *Liandeng huiyao* 聯燈會要, ZZ.136:784a12.

43　**Those that step forward** (*shinpo no mono* 進歩のもの); **those that step back** (*taiho no mono* 退歩のもの): The expression "stepping forward and stepping back" (*shinpo taiho* 進歩退歩) occurs regularly in Dōgen's writings; it can refer simply to all the ordinary movements of the agent, or more specifically, to motion forward and back. See Supplementary Notes, s.v. "Stepping forward and stepping back." Here, no doubt, those who try to enter the "gate of liberation" and those who do not.

43. The Real Marks of the Dharmas *Shohō jissō* 諸法實相 299

[43:25] {1:463}

開方便門といふは、示眞實相なり。示眞實相は蓋時にして、初・中・後、際斷なり。その開方便門の正當開の道理は、盡十方界に開方便門するなり。この正當時、まさしく盡十方界を覰見すれば、未曾見の様子あり。いはゆる、盡十方界を一枚二枚、三箇四箇拈來して、開方便門ならしむるなり。これによりて、一等に開方便門とみゆといへども、如許多の盡十方界は、開方便門の少許を得分して、現成の面目とせり、とみゆるなり。かくのごとくの風流、しかしながら屬經のちからなり。

"Opening the gate of expedient means" is "revealing the true real marks." "Revealing the true real marks" covers all time, with beginning, middle, and end cut off.[44] The principle of that very opening of the "opening of the gate of expedient means" is the "opening of the gate of expedient means" throughout all the worlds in the ten directions.[45] At this very moment, if we truly look at all the worlds in the ten directions, they have a form never before seen: one or two sheets and three or four pieces of all the worlds in the ten directions have been taken up and made the "opening of the gate of expedient means." According to this, while it may appear that they are equally "opening the gate of expedient means," it appears rather that so many of all the worlds in the ten directions have taken their share of a small portion of "opening the gate of expedient means" and made it their realized face.[46] A style like this is entirely the power of "belonging to the sūtra."

---

44 **covers all time, with beginning, middle, and end cut off** (*gaiji ni shite, sho chū go saidan nari* 蓋時にして、初・中・後際斷なり): Probably meaning that the activity of "revealing the true real mark" is going on all the time, in each individual moment. For the expression "before and after cut off" (*zengo saidan* 前後際斷), see Supplementary Notes, s.v. "Before and after cut off."

45 **the "opening of the gate of expedient means" throughout all the worlds in the ten directions** (*jin jippō kai ni kai hōben mon suru* 盡十方界に開方便門する): Probably meaning that the "opening" is occurring everywhere around us. This entire section is quite difficult; one possible paraphrase of the argument might look something like this:

> The revelation of the ultimate truth is going on everywhere at all times. When we see the world in this light, we see the revelation in each experience of the world. This does not mean that all these experiences can be reduced to a single revelation of the ultimate truth; rather, each of our countless experiences of the world is a unique revelation. Such a way of seeing is the unsurpassed perfect bodhi that the sūtra offers the bodhisattvas.

46 **made it their realized face** (*genjō no menmoku to seri* 現成の面目とせり): Or "made it the face of their realization"; presumably, meaning that countless worlds are manifest when the gate of expedient means is opened.

300　　DŌGEN'S *SHŌBŌGENZŌ* VOLUME III

[43:26]

示眞實相といふは、諸法實相の言句を、盡界に風聞するなり、盡界に成道
するなり。實相諸法の道理を、盡人に領覽せしむるなり、盡法に現出せし
むるなり。

"Revealing the true real marks" means to spread talk of the words,
"the real marks of the dharmas," throughout all the worlds, to attain the
way throughout all the worlds. It is to make the truth, "the dharmas of
the real marks," discernable among all humans, to make it appear among
all dharmas.[47]

[43:27]

しかあればすなはち、四十佛・四十祖の無上菩提、みな此經に屬せり、屬
此經なり、此經屬なり。蒲團・禪版の阿耨菩提なる、みな此經に屬せり。
拈華破顏、禮拜得髓、ともに皆屬此經なり、此經之屬なり。開方便門、示
眞實相なり。

Therefore, the unsurpassed bodhi of the forty buddhas and forty ancestors "belongs wholly to this sūtra."[48] It "belongs to this sūtra," and
"this sūtra belongs" to it. That the rush cushion and meditation board
are *anuttara-bodhi* "belongs wholly to this sūtra.[49] *Holding up a flower
and breaking into a smile, making a bow and getting the marrow,* both
"belong wholly to this sūtra," are "the belongings of this sūtra."[50] They
are "*opening the gate of expedient means, revealing the true real marks.*"

* * * * *

47　**the words, "the real marks of the dharmas"** (*shohō jissō no gonku* 諸法實相の
言句); **the truth, "the dharmas of the real marks"** (*jissō shohō no dōri* 實相諸法の道
理): Or "the words, 'the dharmas are the real marks'; the truth, 'the real marks are the
dharmas.'"

48　**forty buddhas and forty ancestors** (*shijū butsu shijisso* 四十佛・四十祖): I.e.,
the seven buddhas, twenty-seven Indian ancestors of Zen from Mahākāśyapa through
Prajñātāra, and six ancestors in China from Bodhidharma through Huineng. Calculation
of the numbers in the lineage is complicated by the fact that traditional listings of the
members typically count Bodhidharma twice, as both the twenty-eighth Indian and first
Chinese ancestor. See Supplementary Notes, s.v. "Seven buddhas," and "Buddhas and
ancestors."

49　**rush cushion and meditation board** (*futon zenpan* 蒲團・禪版): I.e., the meditation cushion and the stick used to support the chin during meditation.

50　**Holding up a flower and breaking into a smile** (*nenge hagan* 拈華破顏): See
above, Note 2.

making a bow and getting the marrow (*raihai tokuzui* 禮拜得髓): Reference to
Bodhidharma's testing of his disciples (see above, Note 25), in which Huike 慧可 is recognized as having gotten his master's marrow when he simply bowed without speaking.

43. The Real Marks of the Dharmas *Shohō jissō* 諸法實相   301

[43:28]

しかあるを、近來大宋國杜撰のともがら、落處をしらず、寳所をみず、實
相の言を虚説のごとくし、さらに老子・莊子の言句を學す。これをもて、
佛祖の大道に一齊なり、といふ。また、三教は一致なるべし、といふ。あ
るひは三教は鼎の三脚のごとし、ひとつもなければくつがへるべし、とい
ふ。愚癡のはなはだしき、たとひをとるに物あらず。

Nevertheless, recently a type of illiterate in the Land of the Great
Song, not knowing the destination, not seeing the treasure trove, treats
the words "real marks" as empty talk and goes on to study the words of
Laozi and Zhuangzi.[51] These, they say, are the equal of the great way
of the buddhas and ancestors. Or they say the three teachings are one.
Or they say the three teachings are like the three legs of a tripodal pot,
which will fall over if it lacks one of them.[52] Idiocy to this extreme is
beyond compare.

[43:29]

かくのごとくのことばあるともがらも、佛法をきけり、とゆるすべから
ず。ゆえいかんとなれば、佛法は、西天を本とせり。在世八十年、説法五
十年、さかりに人天を化す。化一切衆生、皆令入佛道なり。それよりこの
かた、二十八祖正傳せり。これをさかりなるとし、微妙最尊なるとせり。
もろもろの外道・天魔、ことごとく降伏せられをはりぬ。成佛作祖する人
天、かずをしらず。しかあれども、いまだ儒教・道教を震旦國にとぶらは
ざれば、佛道の不足といはず。もし決定して三教一致ならば、佛法出現せ
んとき、西天に儒宗・道教等も、同時に出現すべし。しかあれども、佛法
は天上天下唯我獨尊なり。かのときの事、をおもひやるべし、わすれ、あ
やまるべからず。三教一致のことば、小兒子の言音におよばず、壊佛法の
ともがらなり。かくのごとくのともがらのみおほきなり。あるひは人天の
導師なるよしを現じ、あるひは帝王の師匠となれり。大宋佛法衰薄の時節
なり。先師古佛、ふかくこのことをいましめき。

We should not acknowledge that the type that has words like this has
heard the buddha dharma. Why is this? The buddha dharma had its origin in Sindh in the West. For the eighty years [the Buddha] was in the
world, for the fifty years he preached the dharma, he actively converted
humans and devas.[53] He *"converted all living beings, causing them all*

---

51   **not knowing the destination, not seeing the treasure trove** (*rakusho o shirazu,
hōsho o mizu* 落處をしらず、寳所をみず): I.e., not recognizing the ultimate significance of the words "real marks." The metaphor of the "treasure trove" (*hōsho* 寳所) as
the true goal of Buddhism comes from a famous parable in the *Lotus Sūtra*, in which the
buddha is depicted as a caravan leader taking people to a treasure (*Miaofa lianhua jing*
妙法蓮華經, T.262.9:25c26ff).

52   **the three teachings are like the three legs of a tripodal pot** (*sankyō wa kanae
no sankyaku no gotoshi* 三教は鼎の三脚のごとし): A standard simile often associated
especially with the Song-dynasty monk Gushan Zhiyuan 孤山智圓 (976-1022).

53   **For the eighty years [the Buddha] was in the world, for the fifty years he
preached the dharma** (*zaise hachijū nen, seppō gojū nen* 在世八十年、説法五十年):

302 DŌGEN'S *SHŌBŌGENZŌ* VOLUME III

to enter the way of the buddhas."[54] Thereafter, twenty-eight ancestors transmitted it directly.[55] This was considered the height, considered the most subtle and exalted: followers of other paths and the Deva Māra were all continually defeated; and countless humans and devas attained buddhahood and became ancestors.[56]

Yet no one said the way of the buddhas was insufficient because they had not inquired into Confucianism and Daoism in the Land of Cīnasthāna.[57] If it were definitely the case that the three teachings are one, then when the buddha dharma emerged, Confucianism and Daoism should also have emerged at the same time in Sindh in the West. Instead, the buddha dharma was "*I alone am honored in heaven and beneath heaven.*"[58] We should recall the events of this time; we should not forget it or be mistaken about it. The words, "the three teachings are one," do not amount to the sounds of little children; they are [the words of] a type that would destroy the buddha dharma. Types like this are very common. Some adopt the manner of guides of humans and devas; some have become the teachers of kings and emperors. It is a time of decline of the buddha dharma in the Great Song. My former master, the Old Buddha, warned strongly about this.[59]

[43:30] {1:464}

かくのごときのともがら、二乗・外道の種子なり。しかのごときの種類は、實相のあるべしとだにもしらずして、すでに二三百年をへたり。佛祖の正法を參學しては、流轉生死を出離すべし、とのみいふ。あるひは、佛祖の正法を參學するはいかなるべし、ともしらざるおほし、ただ住院の稽古と思へり。あはれむべし、祖師道、廢せることを。有道の尊宿、おほきになげくところなり。しかのごときともがら、所出の言句、きくべからず、あはれむべし。

I.e., the lifespan and teaching career of Buddha Śākyamuni. The latter figure is common despite the tradition that Siddhārtha achieved buddhahood at the age of 35.

54　**"converted all living beings, causing them all to enter the way of the buddhas"** (*ke issai shujō, kai ryō nyū butsudō* 化一切衆生、皆令入佛道): The words of Buddha Śākyamuni in the *Lotus Sūtra* (*Miaofa lianhua jing* 妙法蓮華經, T.262.9:8b7).

55　**twenty-eight ancestors** (*nijūhasso* 二十八祖): I.e., the lineage of Indian ancestral masters from Mahākāśyapa through Bodhidharma.

56　**followers of other paths and the Deva Māra** (*gedō tenma* 外道・天魔): I.e., followers of non-Buddhist religions and the god Māra, who seeks to obstruct Buddhism.

57　**Land of Cīnasthāna** (*Shintan koku* 震旦國): Dōgen uses here the transliteration of a Sanskrit name for China.

58　**"I alone am honored in heaven and beneath heaven"** (*tenjō tenge yui ga doku son* 天上天下唯我獨尊): Words attributed to Buddha Śākyamuni as a newborn baby; see Supplementary Notes, s.v. "I alone am honored."

59　**My former master, the Old Buddha** (*senshi kobutsu* 先師古佛): A reference to Dōgen's Chinese teacher, Tiantong Rujing 天童如淨.

43. The Real Marks of the Dharmas *Shohō jissō* 諸法實相   303

Types like this are seeds of the two vehicles and the other paths.[60] Such types have already spent two or three hundred years without even knowing of the existence of the "real marks."[61] They say only that, by studying the true dharma of the buddhas and ancestors, we will escape from transmigration through birth and death. Or there are many who do not even know what it would mean to study the true dharma of the buddhas and ancestors, and who think it is only imitating the ancients as abbot of a cloister. How sad that they have abandoned the way of the ancestral masters — something much lamented by venerables possessed of the way. Such types should be pitied, without listening to the words they produce.

[43:31]

圜悟禪師いはく、生死去來、眞實人體。

Chan Master Yuanwu said, "*Birth and death, coming and going, are the true human body.*"[62]

[43:32] {1:465}

この道取を拈擧して、みづからをしり、佛法を商量すべし。

Taking up this saying, we should know ourselves and should consider the buddha dharma.

[43:33]

長沙いはく、盡十方界、眞實人體。盡十方界、自己光明裏。

Changsha said, "*All the worlds in the ten directions are the true human body; all the worlds in the ten directions are within the radiance of the self.*"[63]

---

60   **seeds of the two vehicles and the other paths** (*nijō gedō no shūji* 二乘・外道の種子): I.e., have the karma of the *śrāvaka* (*shōmon* 聲聞) and *pratyeka-buddha* (*engaku* 緣覺) vehicles and of non-Buddhist religions.

61   **have already spent two or three hundred years** (*sude ni nisanbyaku nen o hetari* すでに二三百年をへたり): This could refer to the lifetimes of the individuals of this type, but it is more likely a reference to the recent history of the type in Song China.

62   **Chan Master Yuanwu** (*Engo zenji* 圜悟禪師): I.e., Yuanwu Keqin 圜悟克勤. For his saying, see above, Note 24.

63   **Changsha** (*Chōsa* 長沙): I.e., Changsha Jingcen 長沙景岑 (dates unknown), a disciple of Nanquan Puyuan 南泉普願 (748-835). The quotation here has no known extant source and appears to be a conflation of two different sayings. The second clause does indeed represent the words of Changsha, quoted elsewhere in the *Shōbōgenzō*; see Supplementary Notes, s.v. "All the worlds in the ten directions are the single eye of the śramaṇa." The first clause, however, also appearing elsewhere in the *Shōbōgenzō*, is a saying, not of Changsha, but of Xuansha Shibei 玄沙師備 (835-908), recorded, e.g., in *shinji Shōbōgenzō* 眞字正法眼藏 (DZZ.5:196, case 131); see Supplementary Notes, s.v. "True human body."

304 DŌGEN'S *SHŌBŌGENZŌ* VOLUME III

[43:34]

かくのごとくの道取、いまの大宋國の諸方長老等、おほよそ參學すべき道理と、なほしらず、いはんや參學せんや。もし擧しきたりしかば、ただ赤面、無言するのみなり。

A saying like this, the elders of all quarters in the Land of the Great Song do not even recognize as a truth to be studied, let alone would they study it. If someone were to bring it up to them, they would merely be red-faced and speechless.

[43:35]

先師古佛いはく、いま諸方長老は、照古なし、照今なし。佛法道理不曾有なり。盡十方界等恁麼擧、那得知、他那裏也未曾聽相似。

My former master, the Old Buddha, said,[64]

The elders of all quarters nowadays lack illumination of the past, lack illumination of the present.[65] *They have never had the truth of the buddha dharma. How could they know to bring up "all the worlds in the ten directions" like this? It seems they have never even heard of it over there.*[66]

[43:36]

これをききてのち、諸方長老に問著するに、眞箇聽來せるすくなし。あはれむべし、虛説にして職をけがせることを。

After hearing this, when I questioned the elders in all quarters, in fact few had heard [such sayings]. How sad that they sully their office with empty talk.

* * * * *

[43:37]

應庵曇華禪師、ちなみに德徽大德にしめしていはく、若要易會、祇向十二時中起心動念處、但即此動念、直下頓豁了不可得、如大虛空、亦無虛空形段、表裏一如、智境雙泯、玄解俱亡、三際平等、到此田地、謂之絕學無爲閑道人也。

---

64 **My former master, the Old Buddha** (*senshi kobutsu* 先師古佛): The source for these words of Dōgen's Chinese teacher, Rujing 如淨, is unknown. Judging from Dōgen's comment in the following section, perhaps a report of words he himself heard from Rujing. The passage is in a mix of Chinese and Japanese.

65 **elders of all quarters** (*shohō chōrō* 諸方長老): I.e., abbots of monasteries throughout the land.

illumination of the past (*shōko* 照古); **illumination of the present** (*shōkon* 照今): Fixed expressions often as a four-glyph phrase, or as *shōkokon* 照古今; knowledge of history, or of "past and present" (*kokon* 古今); when used in reference to a mirror of history, perhaps better rendered "reflection of past and present."

66 **over there** (*ta nari* 他那裏): I.e., in the elders' communities.

43. The Real Marks of the Dharmas *Shohō jissō* 諸法實相 305

Chan Master Tanhua of Ying'an once addressed the Most Virtuous Dehui, saying,[67]

If you want to understand easily, then in the twelve times, just face the mind that arises and the thoughts that move, and immediately clarify on the spot that they are ungraspable, like vast empty space, and without empty space or shape.[68] Exterior and interior are one; knowledge and objects are both obliterated; the dark mystery and its understanding are both annihilated; and the three junctures are equivalent.[69] One who reaches this field is known as "a person at ease in the way, finished learning, with nothing to do."[70]

[43:38] {1:466}

これは、應庵老人盡力道得底句なり。これただ影をおふて、休歇をしらざるがごとし。表裏一如ならんときは、佛法あるべからざるか、なにかこれ表裏。また虚空有形段を、佛祖の道取とす。なにをか虚空とする。おもひやるに、應庵いまだ虚空をしらざるなり、虚空をみざるなり、虚空をとらざるなり、虚空をうたざるなり。

This is a saying old Ying'an gave all his strength to make. It is as if he's just chasing shadows and knows no rest.[71] When exterior and interior are not one, will the buddha dharma no longer exist?[72] What are "exterior and interior"? Moreover, that "empty space" has "shape" is something the buddhas and ancestors say. What does he take as "empty space?" When we think about it, Ying'an does not yet know "empty

---

67 **Chan Master Tanhua of Ying'an** (*Ōan Donge zenji* 應庵曇華禪師): 1103-1163, disciple of Huqiu Shaolong 虎丘紹隆. His saying occurs in the *Ying'an heshang yulu* 應庵和尚語錄, ZZ.120:858a17-b2, as a teaching presented to Chan Person Hui 徽禪人.

68 **in the twelve times** (*jūni ji chū* 十二時中): I.e., throughout the twenty-four hours of the day, traditionally divided into twelve two-hour periods.

69 **the three junctures are equivalent** (*sansai byōdō* 三際平等): I.e., past, present, and future are equal.

70 **"a person at ease in the way, finished learning, with nothing to do"** (*zetsugaku mui kandōnin* 絕學無爲閑道人): A fixed expression for one who has completed the Buddhist path, from the opening line of the *Zhengdao ge* 證道歌, attributed to Yongjia Xuanjue 永嘉玄覺 (or Zenjue 眞覺, d. 713) (T.2014.48:395c9).

71 **It is as if he's just chasing shadows and knows no rest** (*kore tada kage o oute, kyūkatsu o shirazaru ga gotoshi* これただ影をおふて、休歇をしらざるがごとし): Though the image is slightly different, somewhat reminiscent of the man in the *Zhuangzi* 莊子 (Yufu 漁父, KR.5c0126.031.5a) who died by running from his shadow without ever stopping.

72 **When exterior and interior are not one** (*hyōri ichinyo narazaran toki* 表裏一如ならんとき): Some MSS read here *hyōri ichinyo naran toki* 表裏一如ならんとき ("when exterior and interior are one").

space," has not yet seen "empty space," has not caught hold of "empty space," has not hit "empty space."[73]

[43:39]

起心動念といふ、心はいまだ動ぜざる道理あり、いかでか十二時中に起心あらん。十二時中には、心、きたり、いるべからず、十二心中に十二時きたらず、いはんや起心あらんや。動念とはいかん。念は動・不動するか、動・不動ぜざるか。作麼生なるか動、また、作麼生なるか不動。なにをよんでか念とする、念は、十二時中にあるか、念裏に十二時あるか、兩頭にあらざらんとき、あるべきか。

He says, "the mind that arises and the thoughts that move." There is a principle that the mind has never moved. How could there be a "mind that arises" "in the twelve times"? The "mind" ought not come up and get inside "in the twelve times," and "the twelve times" have not come into "in the twelve minds"; so how could there be a "mind that arises"? What are "the thoughts that move"? Do "thoughts" "move" or not move? Do they neither move nor not move? What is "moving"? What is not "moving"? What does he mean by "thoughts"? Are "thoughts" "in the twelve times"? Are "the twelve times" inside "thoughts"? Are there times it is neither one?

[43:40]

十二時中に祇向ぜば易會ならん、といふ、なにごとを易會すべきぞ。易會といふ、もし佛祖の道をいふか。しかあらば、佛道は易會・難會にあらざるゆえに、南嶽・江西ひさしく師にしたがひて辨道するなり。

He says that, if we "just face" "in the twelve times," it will be "easy to understand." What exactly will be "easy to understand"? Does "easy to understand" mean the way of the buddhas and ancestors?[74] If so, the way of the buddhas is neither easy to understand nor difficult to understand. Therefore, Nanyue and Jiangxi long pursued the way under their masters.[75]

---

73 **has not caught hold of "empty space"** (*kokū o torazaru nari* 虚空をとらざるなり): Possibly reflecting a story recorded at *shinji Shōbōgenzō* 眞字正法眼藏, DZZ.5:256, case 248, and discussed in the "Shōbōgenzō kokū" 正法眼藏虚空; see Supplementary Notes, s.v. "Nose."

74 **the way of the buddhas and ancestors** (*busso no dō* 佛祖の道): Or "the words of the buddhas and ancestors."

75 **Nanyue and Jiangxi** (*Nangaku Kōzei* 南嶽・江西): I.e., Nanyue Huairang 南嶽懷讓 (677–744), who studied with the Sixth Ancestor, Huineng 慧能, and Mazu Daoyi 馬祖道一 (709–788), who studied with Nanyue.

43. The Real Marks of the Dharmas *Shohō jissō* 諸法實相　　307

[43:41]

頓豁了不可得といふ、佛祖道未夢見なり。恁麼の力量、いかでか要易會の
所堪ならん。はかりしりぬ、佛祖の大道をいまだ參究しきたらずといふこ
とを。佛法もしかくのごとくならば、いかでか今日にいたらん。

He says, "immediately clarify the ungraspable." He has never seen the
way of the buddhas and ancestors even in his dreams. How could one
with this kind of ability be worthy of "wanting to understand easily"? It
is obvious that he has never investigated the great way of the buddhas
and ancestors. If the buddha dharma were like this, how could it have
reached us today?

[43:42]

應庵、なほかくのごとし。いま現在せる諸山の長老のなかに、應庵のご
とくなるものをもとめんに、歷劫にもあふべからず。まなこは、うげな
んとすとも、應庵とひとしき長老をば、みるべからざるなり。ちかくの人
は、おほく應庵をゆるす、しかあれども、應庵に、佛法およべり、とゆる
しがたし。ただ叢席の晩進なり、尋常なりといふべし。ゆえはいかん。應
庵は、人をしりぬべき氣力あるゆえなり。いまあるともがらは、人をしる
べからず、みづからをしらざるゆえに。應庵は、未達なりといへども、學
道あり、いまの長老等は、學道あらず。應庵は、よきことばをきくといへ
ども、みみにいらず、みみにみず、まなこにいらず、まなこにきかざるの
みなり。應庵そのかみは恁麼なりと、いまは自悟在なるらん。いまの大宋
諸山の長老等は、應庵の内外をうかがはず、音容すべて境界にあらざるな
り。しかのごとくのともがら、佛祖の道取せる實相は、佛祖の道なり、佛
祖の道にあらず、ともしるべからず。このゆえに、二三百年來の長老杜撰
のともがら、すべて不見道來實相なり。

Even Ying'an was like this. When we look for someone like Ying'an
among the elders of the various mountains today, we would not encounter one for kalpas.[76] We could not find an elder equal to Ying'an if we
looked till our eyeballs collapsed. Recent people mostly accept Ying'an.
Nevertheless, it is difficult to accept that the buddha dharma reached
Ying'an. He was just a latecomer to his monastic seat; we can say he was
ordinary. Why? Because Ying'an did have the mettle to know people.
Those today do not know people, because they do not know themselves.
Ying'an may not have arrived, but he did have some study of the way;
the elders today lack any study of the way. Ying'an may have heard good
words, but they did not enter his ears, he did not see them with his ears;
they did not enter his eyes, he did not hear them with his eyes. Ying'an
was like this at the time; now, he may himself be awakened. The elders
of the various mountains of the Great Song today do not deduce the
inside and outside of Ying'an; his voice and form are not of their realm.

76　**elders of the various mountains** (*shozan no chōrō* 諸山の長老): I.e., abbots at the
major monasteries.

308 DŌGEN'S *SHŌBŌGENZŌ* VOLUME III

Types like this do not even know whether the "real marks" spoken of by the buddhas and ancestors are the words of the buddhas and ancestors or not the words of the buddhas and ancestors. Therefore, for the past two or three hundred years, we do not see any of the elder illiterate types speaking of the "real marks."

* * * * *

[43:43] {1:467}

先師天童古佛、ある夜間に方丈にして普説するにいはく、天童今夜有牛兒、黄面瞿曇拈實相、要買那堪無定價、一聲杜宇孤雲上。

My former master, the Old Buddha of Tiantong, while giving a public sermon in the abbot's quarters one evening, said,[77]

> *Tiantong this evening has a calf;*
> *The golden-faced Gautama takes up the real marks.*[78]
> *If you want to buy it, how could it have no price?*
> *The cry of a cuckoo above a single cloud.*

[43:44]

かくのごとくあれば、尊宿の、佛道に長ぜるは、實相をいふ。佛法をしらず、佛道の參學なきは、實相をいはざるなり。

In this way, venerables accomplished in the way of the buddhas speak of the "real marks"; those who do not know the buddha dharma, who lack study of the way of the buddhas, do not speak of the "real marks."

[43:45]

この道取は、大宋寶慶二年丙戌春三月のころ、夜間やや四更になりなんとするに、上方に鼓聲三下きこゆ。坐具をとり、搭袈裟して、雲堂の前門よりいづれば、入室牌かかれり。まづ衆にしたがうて法堂上にいたる。法堂の西壁をへて、寂光堂の西階をのぼる。寂光堂の西壁のまへをすぎて、大光明藏の西階をのぼる。大光明藏は方丈なり。西屛風のみなみより、香臺のほとりにいたりて、焼香禮拜す。入室このところに雁列すべしとおもふに、一僧もみえず、妙高臺は下簾せり。ほのかに堂頭大和尚の法音きこゆ。ときに西川の祖坤維那きたりて、おなじく焼香禮拜しをはりて、妙高臺をひそかにのぞめば、満衆たちかさなれり、東邉西邉をいはず。ときに普説あり、ひそかに衆のうしろにいり、たちて聽取す。

77　**My former master, the Old Buddha of Tiantong** (*senshi Tendō kobutsu* 先師天童古佛): This anecdote has no known written source and seems to represent Dōgen's personal experience at Tiantong.

public sermon (*fusetsu* 普説): I.e., a talk to the monastic community, as opposed to private consultations.

78　**a calf** (*gyūji* 牛兒): Likely a reference to Rujing himself, as offspring of the Buddha; perhaps reflecting a traditional derivation of Buddha Śākyamuni's surname, Gautama, from "most excellent of cattle."

43. The Real Marks of the Dharmas *Shohō jissō* 諸法實相   309

These words [are from] the third month, in the spring of the senior fire year of the dog, second year of Baoqing, of the Great Song.[79] At almost the fourth watch of the night, I heard three beats of the drum from above.[80] Taking my sitting cloth and donning my *kāṣāya*, I went out the front door of the cloud hall, where the room-entering placard had been hung up.[81] First, I followed the assembly above the dharma hall. Passing the west wall of the dharma hall, I climbed the western stairs of the Jiguang Hall.[82] Passing in front of the west wall of the Jiguan Hall, I climbed the western stairs of the Daguangming Treasury.[83] The Daguangming Treasury is the abbot's quarters. From south of the western screens, I went to the incense stand, offered incense, and bowed. At the room entrance, I expected a queue, but I did not see a single monk. The blinds were lowered at the Miaogao Terrace.[84] The voice of the dharma of the Most Reverend Head of Hall could be faintly heard.[85] Then, the rector, Zukun of Xichuan, came up and similarly offered incense and bowed; when he finished, we stealthily peeked into the Miaogao Terrace and found it was packed full both east and west.[86] At the time, there was a public sermon; I slipped stealthily into the back, stood and listened.

---

79 **the third month, in the spring of the senior fire year of the dog, second year of Baoqing, of the Great Song** (*Daisō Hōkyō ninen heijutsu haru sangatsu no koro* 大宋寶慶二年丙戌春三月のころ): I.e., March-April, 1226, the third stem, eleventh branch of the cyclical calendar, in the Song dynasty's Baoqing era (1225-1227). The location is the monastery on Mount Tiantong 天童山, of which Rujing was abbot at this time.

80 **fourth watch** (*shikō* 四更): I.e., 2:00-4:00 a.m.

81 **cloud hall** (*undō* 雲堂): I.e., the saṃgha hall, in which the monks of the "great assembly" (*daishu* 大衆) reside.

room-entering placard (*nisshitsu hai* 入室牌): I.e., the signboard announcing an audience in the abbot's quarters.

82 **Jiguang Hall** (*jakkōdō* 寂光堂): "Hall of Tranquil Light"; the abbot's outer quarters at Tiantong, a building located just north of the dharma hall.

83 **Daguangming Treasury** (*dai kōmyō zō* 大光明藏): "Treasury of great radiance"; the abbot's middle quarters at Tiantong, just north of the Jiguang Hall.

84 **Miaogao Terrace** (*myōkōdai* 妙高臺): "Terrace of Sumeru"; the inner chamber of the abbot's quarters at Tiantong.

85 **The voice of the dharma of the Most Reverend Head of Hall** (*dōchō daioshō no hōon* 堂頭大和尚の法音): I.e., the voice of the abbot, Rujing, teaching the dharma.

86 **the rector, Zukun of Xichuan** (*Seisen no Sokon ino* 西川の祖坤維那): Not otherwise known. The rector (*ino* 維那) is the monastic administrator in charge of maintaining discpline in the "great assembly" (*daishu* 大衆) of monks.

310 DŌGEN'S *SHŌBŌGENZŌ* VOLUME III

[43:46] {1:468}

大梅の法常禪師住山の因縁、擧せらる。衣荷食松のところに、衆家おほく
なみだをながす。靈山釋迦牟尼佛の安居の因縁、くはしく擧せらる。きく
もの、なみだをながすおほし。

The episode of the mountain residence of Chan Master Fachang of Damei was brought up.[87] At the point where his robes are from the lotus and
his food from the pine, many in the audience shed tears. The episode of
Buddha Śākyamuni's retreat on Vulture Peak was brought up in detail.[88]
Many of the listeners shed tears.

[43:47]

天童山安居ちかきにあり、如今春間、不寒不熱、好坐禪時節也、兄弟如何
不坐禪。

"The retreat at Mount Tiantong is about to begin.[89] *Now it is spring-
time, neither cold nor hot, a good time for seated meditation. Brothers,
why not practice seated meditation?*"

[43:48]

かくのごとく普説して、いまの頌あり。頌、をはりて、右手にて禪椅のみ
ぎのほとりをうつこと一下していはく、入室すべし。入室の話にいはく、
杜鵑啼山竹裂。かくのごとく入室語あり、別の話なし。衆家おほしといへ
ども下語せず。ただ惶恐せるのみなり。

After giving such a public sermon, he had the present verse. Upon
finishing the verse, he hit the right side of his meditation chair once with
his right hand and said, "Enter!" In his room-entering talk, he said, "*The
cuckoo cries, and the mountain bamboo splits.*" Such were his room-entering words; he had no other talk. Though the audience was large, they
made no comment. They were just intimidated.

---

87 **Chan Master Fachang of Damei** (*Daibai no Hōjō zenji* 大梅の法常禪師): I.e.,
Damei Fachang 大梅法常 (752-839), a follower of Mazu Daoyi 馬祖道一. He is said to
have spent some forty years in isolation on Mount Damei 大梅山 (in modern Zhejiang).
His biography can be found at *Jingde chuandeng lu* 景德傳燈錄, T.2076.51:254c2ff.
Dōgen discusses him in "Shōbōgenzō gyōji" 正法眼藏行持, part 1, where he includes
the familiar trope in ascetic hagiography that Fachang dressed in lotus leaves and ate
pine nuts.

88 **Buddha Śākyamuni's retreat on Vulture Peak** (*Ryōzen Shakamuni butsu no ango*
靈山釋迦牟尼佛の安居): A topic no doubt occasioned by the date of Rujing's talk, just
preceding the monastic summer retreat.

89 "The retreat at Mount Tiantong is about to begin" (*Tendōzan ango chikaki ni ari* 天
童山安居ちかきにあり): Though the first sentence is put in Japanese, presumably, the
words of Rujing on the occasion being described. Dates of the summer retreat vary; a
common practice was to start on the fifteenth or sixteenth of the fourth month.

43. The Real Marks of the Dharmas *Shohō jissō* 諸法實相 311

[43:49] {1:469}

この入室の儀は、諸方にいまだあらず、ただ先師天童古佛のみ、この儀を儀せり。普説の時節は、椅子・屏風を周匝して、大衆雲立せり。そのままにて、雲立しながら、便宜の僧家より入室すれば、入室、をはりぬる人は、例のごとく方丈門をいでぬ。のこれる人は、ただもとのごとくたてれば、入室する人の威儀・進止、ならびに堂頭和尚の容儀、および入室話、ともにみな見聞するなり。この儀、いまだ他那裏の諸方にあらず、他長老は儀不得なるべし。他時の入室には、人よりはさきに入室せんとす。この入室には、人よりものちに入室せんとす。この人心道別、わすれざるべし。

This ritual of room-entering does not exist in other quarters; only my former master, the Old Buddha of Tiantong, practiced it. During the public sermon, the assembly surrounded his chair and screens like clouds. Then, as they continued to stand like clouds, just as they were, from among the monks, one would enter the room at his convenience, while the person who had finished the room-entering left in the usual way from the door of the abbot's quarters. Those remaining, since they just remained standing as they were, could all observe the deportment and movements of the person entering the room, as well as the manner of the Reverend Head of Hall and his room-entering talk. This ritual is not that of other quarters; other elders must not be able to perform it. In room-entering on other occasions, [the monks] wanted to enter the room before other people; in this room-entering, they wanted to enter the room after others. We should not forget this distinction in people's thoughts and words.

[43:50]

それよりこのかた、日本寛元元年癸卯にいたるに、始終一十八年、すみやかに風光のなかにすぎぬ。天童よりこのやまにいたるに、いくそばくの山水とおぼえざれども、美言奇句の實相なる、身心骨髄に銘しきたれり。かのときの普説入室は、衆家おほくわすれがたしとおもへり。この夜は、微月、わづかに樓閣より、もりきたり、杜鵑、しきりになくといへども、靜間の夜なりき。

Since then, till the junior water year of the rabbit, the first year of Kangen in Japan, fully eighteen years have quickly passed amidst wind and light.[90] I know not how many mountains and waters separate this mountain from Tiantong, but [the fact that] his beautiful words and rare phrases are the "real mark" is incised in my body and mind, bones and

---

90 **the junior water year of the rabbit, the first year of Kangen in Japan** (*Nihon Kangen gannen mizunoto-u* 日本寛元元年癸卯): I.e., 1243, the year in which Dōgen is writing; the first year of the Japanese Kangen era (1243-1247), tenth stem, fourth branch of the cyclical calendar.

wind and light (*fūkō* 風光): An idiom for scenes of natural beauty, from the image of sunlight reflected off leaves moved by the wind.

312   DŌGEN'S *SHŌBŌGENZŌ* VOLUME III

marrow. The public sermon and room-entering on that occasion must
have been unforgettable for many in the audience. That evening, thin
light from a crescent moon filtered down from among the tall buildings;
despite the frequent cry of cuckoos, the night was still.

* * * * *

[43:51]

玄沙院宗一大師、參次聞燕子聲曰、深談實相、善説法要。下座。尋後有僧
請益曰、某甲不會。師云、去、無人信汝。

*Great Master Zongyi of Xuansha Cloister, during a convocation, heard
the singing of a swallow and said, "Deeply discussing the real marks,
skillfully talking on the essentials of the dharma."*[91]

*He came down from his seat. Afterwards, a monk begged instruction,
saying, "I don't understand."*

The Master said, "Go away! No one believes you."

[43:52] {1:470}

いはゆる深談實相といふは、燕子ひとり實相を深談すると、玄沙の道 きき
ぬべし。しかあれども、しかにはあらざるなり。參次に聞燕子聲あり、燕
子の、實相を深談するにあらず、玄沙の、實相を深談するにあらず。兩頭
にわたらざれども、正當恁麼、すなはち深談實相なり。

We might well hear Xuansha's words, "deeply discussing the real
marks," as saying that the swallow alone was "deeply discussing" "the
real marks." Nevertheless, this is not the case. "During a convocation,"
there is "hearing the singing of a swallow." It is not that the "swallow" is
"deeply discussing" the "real marks"; it is not that "Xuansha" is "deep-
ing discussing" the "real marks." It does not extend to both of them;
however, just as it is it is "deeply discussing the real marks."

---

91 **Great Master Zongyi of Xuansha Cloister** (*Genshain Sōitsu daishi* 玄沙院宗一
大師): I.e., Xuansha Shibei 玄沙師備. This saying is recorded in Dōgen's *shinji Shōbōgenzō* 眞字正法眼藏 (DZZ.5:252, case 241) and can be found, for example, at *Liandeng
huiyao* 聯燈會要, ZZ.136:823a16-17.

during a convocation (*san ji* 參次): Probably an informal talk (*shōsan* 小參), often held
in the abbot's quarters.

**"Deeply discussing the real marks, skillfully talking on the essentials of the dhar-
ma"** (*shindan jissō, zensetsu hōyō* 深談實相、善説法要): Variant of the words of
Bodhisattva Mañjuśrī describing Vimalakīrti (*Weimojie shoshuo jing* 維摩詰所説經,
T.475.14:544a28):

深達實相善説法要。

He has deeply mastered the real marks and is good at talking on the essentials of the
dharma.

43. The Real Marks of the Dharmas *Shohō jissō* 諸法實相　313

[43:53]

しばらくこの一段の因縁を参究すべし。參次あり、聞燕子聲あり、深談實
相、善説法要の道取あり、下座あり、尋後有僧請益曰某甲不會あり、師云
去無人信汝あり。某甲不會、かならずしも請益實相なるべからざれども、
これ佛祖の命脈なり、正法眼藏の骨髓なり。

We should investigate this episode for a bit. There is "during a convocation"; there is "hearing the singing of a swallow"; there are the words,
"*deeply discussing the real marks, skillfully talking on the essentials of
the dharma*"; there is "coming down from his seat"; there is "*afterwards,
a monk begged instruction, saying, 'I don't understand'*"; there is "*the
Master said, 'Go away! No one believes you.'*" "I don't understand" is
not necessarily "begging instruction" on "the real marks," but it is the
vital artery of the buddhas and ancestors, the bones and marrow of the
treasury of the true dharma eye.

[43:54]

しるべし、この僧、たとひ請益して某甲會得と道取すとも、某甲説得と道
取すとも、玄沙は、かならず去無人信汝と爲道すべきなり。會せるを不會
と請益するゆえに、去無人信汝といふにはあらざるなり。まことに、この
僧にあらざらん張三・李四なりとも、諸法實相なりとも、佛祖の命脈の正
直に通ずる時處には、實相の參學、かくのごとく現成するなり。青原の會
下に、これすでに現成せり。

We should realize that, even had this monk begged instruction by saying, "I understand it," or "I can explain it," Xuansha should still say to
him, "*Go away! No one believes you.*" It is not that he says, "*Go away!
No one believes you,*" because he begs instruction by saying he doesn't
understand what he has understood. Indeed, whether it is not this monk
but Zhang's third or Li's fourth, whether it is "the real marks of the dharmas," at the time and place where we directly pass through the vital artery of the buddhas and ancestors, the study of "the real marks" appears
like this.[92] It appeared among the followers of Qingyuan.[93]

[43:55]

しるべし、實相は嫡嫡相承の正脈なり、諸法は究盡參究の唯佛與佛なり、
唯佛與佛は如是相好なり。

We should realize that "the real marks" are the main bloodline inherited by successor after successor; "the dharmas" are "*only buddhas with

---

92　**Zhang's third or Li's fourth** (*Chō san Ri shi* 張三・李四): From the Chinese idiom
Zhang san Li si 張三李四 ("Zhang's third son, Li's fourth son"), used (as we might use
"Tom, Dick, and Harry") to indicate anyone at all.

93　**the followers of Qingyuan** (*Seigen no eka* 青原の會下): I.e., in the lineage of
Qingyuan Xingsi 青原行思 (d. 740), of which Xuansha was a member (and from which
Dōgen's Caotong 曹洞 lineage emerged).

314 DŌGEN'S *SHŌBŌGENZŌ* VOLUME III

buddhas" who "exhaustively investigate"; and "only budddhas with buddhas" are "such marks" and signs.[94]

正法眼藏諸法實相第四十三
Treasury of the True Dharma Eye
The Real Marks of the Dharmas
Number 43

[Ryūmonji MS:]

爾時寬元元年癸卯九月日、在于日本越州吉峰寺示衆
Presented to the assembly at Kippō Monastery, Esshū, Japan; on a day in the ninth month of the junior water year of the rabbit, the first year of Kangen [October-November 1243]

---

94 **"such marks" and signs** (*nyoze sōgō* 如是相好): I.e., the thirty-two "marks" (*sō* 相; S. *lakṣana*) and eighty auspicious "signs" (*kō* 好; S. *vyañjana*) that adorn the body of a buddha.

Treasury of the True Dharma Eye

Number 44

The Way of the Buddhas
Butsudō

佛道

The Way of the Buddhas

Butsudō

INTRODUCTION

This chapter was composed in 1243, soon after Dōgen moved from the capital to Echizen (modern Fukui). It represents number 44 in the seventy-five-chapter compilation of the *Shōbōgenzō* and number 49 in the Honzan edition but does not appear in the sixty-chapter compilation. The twenty-eight text *Himitsu* collection of *Shōbōgenzō* texts contains two works entitled "Butsudō," listed in fascicle 1 as numbers 7 and 9. The latter of these is rather similar to our text here; but the former is sufficiently different that it was included separately in the Honzan edition as number 93, under the new title "Dōshin" 道心 ("Mind of the Way"; translated here below in Volume 7 as Supplementary Text 9).

The central theme of "Butsudō" concerns what we might call the institutional character or identity of Dōgen's tradition. The title reflects the claim, made at the very outset of the text, that the lineage of the ancestral masters of the tradition is continuous with the ancient line of the seven buddhas, of which Śākyamuni was the last; it is thus a lineage of buddhas, not merely a Buddhist school. From this, Dōgen goes on to criticize sharply the common practice of referring to this lineage as the "Zen" (Sanskrit *dhyāna*, or "meditation") school.

The text then moves to the question of the five houses (*goke* 五家) into which the Chan historians in the Song dynasty often divided the tradition. Quoting the dismissal of distinctions among the houses by his teacher, Tiantong Rujing 天童如淨, Dōgen attributes the notion of distinct houses to the decline of the tradition in China. He then takes up each of the five houses in turn, arguing that none of the ostensible founders of these houses ever spoke of them as distinct schools. Near the end of this section, he singles out for criticism the twelfth-century work, *Rentian yanmu* 人天眼目 ("The Eye of Humans and Devas"), by Huiyan Zhizhao 晦巖智昭, which provides a summary account of Chan based on the history and teachings of the five schools.

Finally, the text returns to the broader issue of school identity, pointing out that the true transmission of the Buddha's wisdom is not a school, and that the establishment of a Buddhist school is a violation of the Buddha's own practice.

正法眼藏第四十三

Treasury of the True Dharma Eye
Number 44

佛道

The Way of the Buddhas

[44:1] {1:471}

曹溪古佛、あるとき衆にしめしていはく、慧能より七佛にいたるまで四十祖あり。

The Old Buddha of Caoxi once addressed the assembly saying, "There are forty ancestors from Huineng through the seven buddhas."[1]

---

1 **The Way of the Buddhas** (*butsudō* 佛道): Or "way of the Buddha." An extremely common expression in East Asian Buddhism, often meaning simply what we would call "Buddhism"; also used in reference variously to the "teachings" of a buddha (roughly equivalent to *buppō* 佛法; S. *buddha-dharma*); the "wisdom" attained by a buddha (*bodai* 菩提; S. *bodhi*); the state of "buddhahood" (*busshō* 佛性; S. *buddhatva*); the "vehicle" (*jō* 乘; S. *yāna*) or "path" (*dō* 道; S. *mārga*) leading to buddhahood; the practice that expresses buddhahood; etc. While these various connotations may sometimes be at play here, the predominant sense of *butsudō* in our text seems to be something like "the tradition" of the buddha(s) — i.e., the authentic teachings, practices, people, and institutions descended from the buddhas.

The Old Buddha of Caoxi (*Sōkei kobutsu* 曹溪古佛; also written 曹谿): An epithet, appearing often in Dōgen's writing, for the famous Sixth Ancestor, Huineng of Caoxi 曹溪慧能. Mount Caoxi (*Sōkeizan* 曹溪山), in present-day Guangdong, is the site of his temple, the Baolinsi 寶林寺. The expression *kobutsu* 古佛, literally "old (or 'ancient' or 'past') buddha," is regularly used in reference to "the buddhas of the past," especially the seven buddhas mentioned here; Zen texts also employ it as an honorific for past masters of the tradition — a use Dōgen will take quite literally below; see Supplementary Notes, s.v. "Old buddha."

Dōgen's Japanese rendering of Huineng's words here closely resembles a passage in the "Shōbōgenzō shisho" 正法眼藏嗣書, originally composed in 1241 and edited in 1243 (the date of our text). There is no known source for these words. The Dunhuang version of the *Liuzu tan jing* 六祖壇經 (T.2007.48:344c11) does contain a statement by Huineng that he represents the fortieth generation in a line beginning with the seven buddhas; but this manuscript was of course not known to Dōgen, and other extant versions of the work that he might have seen do not seem to contain this passage.

"forty ancestors" (*shijisso* 四十祖): The seven buddhas, twenty-seven Indian ancestors of Zen from Mahākāśyapa through Prajñātāra, and six ancestors in China from Bodhidharma to Huineng 慧能. Calculation of the numbers in the lineage is complicated by the fact that traditional listings of the members typically count Bodhidharma twice, as both the twenty-eighth Indian and first Chinese ancestor; see Supplementary Notes, s.v. "Buddhas and ancestors."

318　DŌGEN'S *SHŌBŌGENZŌ* VOLUME III

[44:2]

この道を參究するに、七佛より慧能にいたるまで四十佛なり。佛佛祖祖を
算數するには、かくのごとく算數するなり。かくのごとく算數すれば、七
佛は七祖なり、三十三祖は三十三佛なり。曹溪の宗旨、かくのごとし。こ
れ正嫡の佛訓なり。正傳の嫡嗣のみ、その算數の法を正傳す。

When we investigate these words, it is forty buddhas from the seven
buddhas to Huineng.[2] When we count buddha after buddha and ancestor after ancestor, this is the way to count. Counting in this way, the
seven buddhas are seven ancestors, and the thirty-three ancestors are
thirty-three buddhas. Such is Caoxi's essential point. This is the instruction of a buddha of direct descent: only a legitimate heir to the direct
transmission directly transmits this way of counting.

[44:3]

釋迦牟尼佛より曹溪にいたるまで、三十四祖あり。この佛祖相承、ともに
迦葉の、如來にあひたてまつれりしがごとく、如來の、迦葉をえましたます
がごとし。

From Buddha Śākyamuni to Caoxi, there are thirty-four ancestors.[3]
This inheritance of buddhas and ancestors is in each case like Kāśyapa
having encountered the Tathāgata, like the Tathāgata gaining Kāśyapa.[4]

[44:4]

釋迦牟尼佛の、迦葉佛に參學しましますがごとく、師資ともに于今有在な
り。このゆえに、正法眼藏まのあたり嫡嫡相承しきたれり。佛法の正命、
ただこの正傳のみなり。佛法は、かくのごとく正傳するがゆえに、附囑の
嫡嫡なり。

Just as Buddha Śākyamuni studied under Buddha Kāśyapa, so do all

---

"seven buddhas" (*shichi butsu* 七佛): I.e., Śākyamuni and six buddhas said to have preceded him; commonly referred to as "the seven buddhas of the past" (*kako shichi butsu*
過去七佛); see Supplementary Notes, s.v. "Seven buddhas."

2 **When we investigate these words** (*kono dō o sankyū suru ni* この道を參究するに):
Dōgen's comment on Huineng's saying here echoes passages elsewhere in the *Shōbōgenzō* — e.g., in "Shōbōgenzō shisho" 正法眼藏嗣書 and "Shōbōgenzō kobutsushin" 正
法眼藏古佛心.

3 **thirty-four ancestors** (*sanjūshi so* 三十四祖): Presumably, Dōgen here adds Śākyamuni to the traditional list of thirty-three Zen ancestors from Mahākāśyapa to Huineng.

4 **like Kāśyapa having encountered the Tathāgata, like the Tathāgata gaining
Kāśyapa** (*Kashō no, nyorai ni aitatematsurerishi ga gotoku, nyorai no, Kashō o emashi-
masu ga gotoshi* 迦葉の、如來にあひたてまつれりしがごとく、如來の、迦葉をえま
しますがごとし): Though somewhat ambiguous, given the predicates used here, the reference is likely to the relationship between Buddha Śākyamuni ("the Tathāgata") and his
disciple, the First Ancestor, Mahākāśyapa ("Kāśyapa"; not to be confused with Buddha
Kāśyapa, mentioned just below).

44. The Way of the Buddhas *Butsudō* 佛道

the masters and disciples even today.[5] Therefore, the treasury of the true dharma eye has actually been inherited by successor after successor. The correct life of the buddha dharma is nothing but this correct transmission. Because the buddha dharma is thus correctly transmitted, it is successor after successor to the bequest.

[44:5] {1:472}

しかあれば、佛道の功德・要機、もらさずそなはれり。西天より東地につたはれて十萬八千里なり、在世より今日につたはれて二千餘載。この道理を參學せざるともがら、みだりにあやまりていはく、佛祖正傳の正法眼藏涅槃妙心、みだりにこれを禪宗と稱す、祖師を禪祖と稱す、學者を禪子と號す、あるひは禪和子と稱し、あるひは禪家流の自稱あり。これみな僻見を根本とせる枝葉なり。西天東地、從古至今、いまだ禪宗の稱あらざるを、みだりに自稱するは、佛道をやぶる魔なり、佛祖のまねかざる怨家なり。

Thus, it has been wholly endowed with the virtues and the essential functions of the way of the buddhas. Transmitted from Sindh in the West to the Land of the East, it is one hundred eight thousand miles; transmitted from his lifetime to the present, more than two thousand years.[6] The type that has not studied this truth talks rashly and mistakenly. "The treasury of the true dharma eye, the wondrous mind of nirvāṇa," directly transmitted by the buddhas and ancestors, they rashly call the "Zen school." The ancestral masters, they call "Zen ancestors"; the students, they designate "Zen master" or call "Zen reverend"; or there are those

---

5 **Buddha Kāśyapa** (*Kashō butsu* 迦葉佛): I.e., the sixth of the seven buddhas of the past. Śākyamuni is traditionally held to have studied under countless buddhas in the past, including Kāśyapa. While Dōgen here treats Kāśyapa and Śākyamuni as master and disciple, the traditional understanding of the historical relationships among members of the list of seven buddhas is of course rather different from those in the Zen lineage. The lives of these buddhas do not overlap; rather, Kāśyapa's career as a buddha (said to have lasted twenty-thousand years) ended long before the advent of Buddha Śākyamuni, and legends that place the latter among Kāśyapa's followers refer to events in Śākayamuni's former lives as a bodhisattva, long before he was born as Siddhārtha and went on to attain awakening. In an addendum to the "Shōbōgenzō shisho" 正法眼藏嗣書, Dōgen recalls a conversation about this issue with his teacher, Tiantong Rujing 天童如淨 (1162-1227).

6 **one hundred eight thousand miles** (*jūman hassen ri* 十萬八千里): A fixed expression indicating a great distance. The Chinese unit *li* 里 varies throughout history but was generally around one-third mile. (At that length, the distance between Varanasi and Kyoto would be roughly 10,000 *li*.)

his lifetime (*zaise* 在世): I.e., when Buddha Śākyamuni walked the earth.

more than two thousand years (*nisen yo sai* 二千餘載): The number here reflects the traditional East Asian Buddhist reckoning of the date of Śākyamuni's *parinirvāṇa* as 949 BCE (the 52nd year of the reign of the Chou Emperor Mu Wang 穆王; see e.g., *Jingde chuandeng lu* 景德傳燈錄, T.2076.51:305c18-19).

DŌGEN'S *SHŌBŌGENZŌ* VOLUME III

that call themselves "followers of the Zen house."[7] These are all but branches and leaves that have taken a biased view as the root. When the name "Zen school" has not existed throughout Sindh in the West and the Land of the East, from ancient times till the present, rashly to call oneself this is to be a demon who would destroy the way of the buddhas, an unbidden enemy of the buddhas and ancestors.[8]

* * * * *

[44:6]

石門林間錄云、菩提達磨、初自梁之魏。經行於嵩山之下、倚杖於少林、面壁燕坐而已、非習禪也。久之人莫測其故。因以達磨爲習禪。夫禪那、諸行之一耳。何足以盡聖人。而當時之人、以之爲史者、又從而傳於習禪之列、使與枯木死灰之徒爲伍。雖然聖人非止於禪那、而亦不違禪那。如易出于陰陽、而亦不違陰陽。

In Shimen's Grove Record, it is said,[9]

When Bodhidharma first went from Liang to Wei, he proceeded to the foot of Mount Song, where he rested his staff at Shaolin.[10] There he just sat facing a wall. It was not the practice of dhyāna, but after a while, others, unable to fathom what he was doing, made Dharma a practitioner of dhyāna. Now, dhyāna is but one among various practices; how could it suffice to exhaust [the practice of] the sage?

---

7   **"Zen master"** (*zenji* 禪師); **"Zen reverend"** (*zennasu* 禪和子): The former term doubtless reflects its broad use for a practitioner of meditation; some MS witnesses give here *zensu* 禪子 ("Zennist"); others, *zensō* 禪僧 ("Zen monk"). The translation of *zennasu* 禪和子 reflects the fact that it is thought to incorporate the term *oshō* 和尚 (or *wajō*, "preceptor"), used in polite reference to a monk (hence, "reverend").

8   **the name "Zen school"** (*zenshū no shō* 禪宗の稱): The use of the term *Chanzong* 禪宗 ("Zen school" or "Zen lineage") in reference to the lineage of Bodhidharma seems to have begun in China during the ninth century. It is unclear what Dōgen might mean by his claim that the name did not exist in the "Land of the East" (*Tōchi* 東地), a term normally indicating China.

9   **Shimen's Grove Record** (*Sekimon Rinkan roku* 石門林間錄): "Shimen" 石門 is a sobriquet for the author Juefan Huihong 覺範慧洪 (1071-1128); this passage from his *Linjian lu* 林間錄 can be found at ZZ.148:590b7-12. Dōgen also cites the passage in his "Shōbōgenzō gyōji" 正法眼藏行持 and *Eihei kōroku* 永平廣錄.

10   **Liang** (*ryō* 梁); **Wei** (*gi* 魏): From the legend that, upon his arrival in China, Bodhidharma first visited the territory of the Liang dynasty (502-557) in the south and then went to the land of the Northern Wei dynasty (386-534).

Mount Song (*Sūzan* 嵩山): The mountain in the Dengfeng 登封 district of modern Henan Province.

rested his staff at Shaolin (*ijō o shōrin* 倚杖於少林): I.e., stopped at the Shaolinsi 少林寺 on Mount Song, traditionally identified as Bodhidharma's residence; see Supplementary Notes, s.v. "Staff."

44. The Way of the Buddhas *Butsudō* 佛道

321

Nevertheless, people of the time took it in this way; and those who wrote histories followed this and recorded him among practitioners of dhyāna, thus making him a confederate of the partisans of "dried-up trees and dead ashes."[11] Although the sage does not stop at dhyāna, he does not oppose dhyāna. It is like "change," which is beyond yin and yang and yet does not oppose yin and yang.

[44:7] {1:473}

第二十八祖と稱するは、迦葉大士を初祖として稱するなり。毗婆尸佛より
は第三十五祖なり。七佛および二十八代、かならずしも禪那をもて證道を
つくすべからず。このゆえに、古先いはく、禪那は諸行のひとつならくの
み、なんぞもて聖人をつくすにたらん。

To call him the "twenty-eighth ancestor" is to speak of Kāśyapa, the Great One, as the "first ancestor"; from Buddha Vipaśyin, he is the thirty-fifth ancestor.[12] The seven buddhas and twenty-eight generations have never taken dhyāna to exhaust the verification of the way. Therefore, our old forebear says here, "Dhyāna is but one among various practices; how could it suffice to exhaust [the practice of] the sage?"

[44:8]

この古先、いささか人をみきたれり、祖宗の堂奥にいれり、このゆえにこ
の道あり。近日は大宋國の天下に、難得なるべし、ありがたかるべし。た
とひ禪那なりとも、禪宗と稱すべからず、いはんや禪那いまだ佛法の總要
にあらず。

This old forebear has seen something of the person, has entered the interior of the hall of the ancestors; therefore, he has these words. Nowadays, throughout the entire Land of the Great Song, [his type] would be difficult to meet, would be welcome indeed. Even if it were dhyāna, we

---

11 **those who wrote histories** (*i shi sha* 爲史者): Likely a reference to Daoxuan 道宣 (596-667), whose *Xu gaoseng zhuan* 續高僧傳 includes Bodhidharma's biographical notice in the section of the work devoted to eminent monks who were "practitioners of dhyāna" (*shūzen* 習禪). See Supplementary Notes, s.v. "Practitioner of dhyāna."

"dried-up trees and dead ashes" (*koboku shikai* 枯木死灰): Or, as we might say, "dead wood and cold ashes"; a common expression in Zen texts, used in reference, often pejorative, to a state of mind free from thoughts. Occurs several times in this sense in Dōgen's corpus. See Supplementary Notes, s.v. "Dried-up tree."

12 **To call him the "twenty-eighth ancestor"** (*dainijūhachi so to shō suru wa* 第二十八祖と稱するは): The antecedent of "him" here is Bodhidharma.

Kāśyapa, the Great One (*Kashō daishi* 迦葉大士): I.e., Mahākāśyapa; Dōgen here provides a Chinese translation of *mahāsattva* ("great being") or *mahāpuruṣa* ("great person") for the element *mahā* in the First Ancestor's name, a convention reflecting the passage from the *Jingde chuandeng lu* 景德傳燈錄 he will quote below.

Buddha Vipaśyin (*Bibashi butsu* 毘婆尸佛): I.e., the first of the seven buddhas, said to have lived in the Adornment Kalpa (*shōgon kō* 莊嚴劫; S. *vyūha-kalpa*), preceding ours.

322   DŌGEN'S *SHŌBŌGENZŌ* VOLUME III

should not call it the "Dhyāna [i.e., Zen] school." Much less is dhyāna the essence of the entire buddha dharma.

[44:9]

しかあるを、佛佛正傳の大道を、ことさら禪宗と稱するともがら、佛道は未夢見在なり、未夢聞在なり、未夢傳在なり。禪宗を自號するともがらにも、佛法あるらんと聽許することなかれ。禪宗の稱、たれか稱しきたる、諸佛祖師の、禪宗と稱する、いまだあらず。しるべし、禪宗の稱は、魔波旬の稱するなり、魔波旬の稱を稱しきたらんは、魔儻なるべし、佛祖の兒孫にあらず。

Those who nevertheless intentionally speak of the great way directly transmitted by buddha after buddha as the "Zen school" *have never seen even in their dreams* the way of the buddhas, *have never heard of it in their dreams, have never transmitted it in their dreams.* Do not acknowledge that those who designate themselves the "Zen school" have the buddha dharma. Who has called themselves the "Zen school"? There have never been buddhas or ancestral masters who called themselves the "Zen school." We should realize that the name "Zen school" is used by Māra-pāpīyān; and those who would call themselves by Māra-pāpīyān's name must be the minions of Māra, not the descendants of the buddhas and ancestors.[13]

* * * * *

[44:10]

世尊靈山百萬衆前、拈優曇華瞬目、衆皆默然。唯迦葉尊者、破顔微笑。世尊云、吾有正法眼藏涅槃妙心、竝以僧伽梨衣、附囑摩訶迦葉。

The World-Honored One, before an assembly of a million on Vulture Peak, held up an udumbara flower and blinked his eyes.[14] *The assembly was silent; only Venerable Kāśyapa broke into a smile. The*

---

13   **Māra-pāpīyān** (*Mahajun* 魔波旬): Dōgen uses here the Sanskrit term for the demonic figure, Māra, the Evil One, lord of the sixth heaven of the realm of desire (*yokkai* 欲界; S. *kāma-loka*), who seeks to obstruct Buddhist awakening. Māra famously brought his legions (*matō* 魔儻; also written 魔黨) to prevent Siddhārtha from attaining buddhahood under the bodhi tree.

14   **The World-Honored One** (*seson* 世尊): A telling of the famous story of the transmission of Zen from Śākyamuni to the First Ancestor, of which there are several variants. Dōgen recorded the story in his *shinji Shōbōgenzō* 眞字正法眼藏 (DZZ.5: 258, case 253) and retells it in his *Eihei kōroku* 永平廣錄 (DZZ.4:182, no. 1).

held up an udumbara flower and blinked his eyes (*nen udon ge shunmoku* 拈優曇華瞬目): This expression, though repeated elsewhere in the *Shōbōgenzō*, does not seem to occur in any extant Chinese source. See Supplementary Notes, s.v. "Holding up a flower and blinking the eyes." The *udumbara* flower (*udon ge* 優曇華), often identified with the blossom of the tree *ficus glomerata*, is said to bloom only once every three thousand years; the raining down of this blossom appears regularly in Buddhist literature as a sign of an auspicious event or person.

44. The Way of the Buddhas *Butsudō* 佛道

World-Honored One said, "I have a treasury of the true dharma eye, the wondrous mind of nirvāṇa; together with my saṃghāṭī robe, I bequeath it to Mahākāśyapa."[15]

[44:11] {1:474}

世尊の、迦葉大士に附屬しましします、吾有正法眼藏涅槃妙心なり。このほかさらに吾有禪宗付囑摩訶迦葉にあらず。竝以僧伽梨衣といひて、竝付禪宗といはず。しかあればすなはち、世尊在世に禪宗の稱、またくきこえず。

The World-Honored One's bequest to Kāśyapa, the Great One, was, "*I have a treasury of the true dharma eye, the wondrous mind of nirvāṇa.*" He did not go on to add, "*I have a 'Zen school,' which I bequeath to Mahākāśyapa.*" He said, "*Together with my saṃghāti robe,*" not "*together with my 'Zen school.'*" Thus, we simply do not hear of the name "Zen school" during the lifetime of the World-Honored One.

* * * * *

[44:12]

初祖、そのとき、二祖にしめしていはく、諸佛無上妙道、曠劫精勤、難行苦行、難忍能忍。豈以小德小智輕心慢心、欲冀眞乘。またいはく、諸佛法印、匪從人得。またいはく、如來以正法眼藏、附囑迦葉大士。

At that time, the First Ancestor addressed the Second Ancestor saying, "*The unsurpassed wondrous way of the buddhas takes vast kalpas of spiritual fortitude, painfully practicing what is difficult to practice, enduring what is difficult to endure.*[16] *How could one of little virtue and little wisdom, of frivolous mind and vain mind, aspire to the true vehicle?*"

He also said, "*The dharma seal of the buddhas is not obtained from another.*"

And he said, "*The Tathāgata bequeathed the treasury of the true dharma eye to Kāśyapa, the Great One.*"

---

15 **"saṃghāṭī robe"** (*sōgyari e* 僧伽梨衣): The "assembly robe," most formal of the traditional three robes (*kesa* 袈裟; S. *kāṣāya* or *kaṣāya*) of the monk, sewn in nine to twenty-five sections. A famous legend has it that Mahākāśyapa retired to Mount Kukkuṭapāda (*Keisokusen* 鷄足山), where he awaits the advent of the future Buddha Maitreya, to whom he will transmit this robe. See Supplementary Notes, s.v. "Robe of the Tathāgata."

16 **At that time, the First Ancestor addressed the Second Ancestor** (*shoso, sono toki, niso ni shimeshite* 初祖、そのとき、二祖にしめして): I.e., Bodhidharma addressed the second Chinese ancestor of Chan, Huike 慧可. The phrase "at that time" (*sono toki*) has no intelligible antecedent here. The three quotations are slight variants on passages in the notice on Bodhidharma in the *Jingde chuandeng lu* 景德傳燈錄, T.2076.51:219b14-16; 219b20-21; 219c6 (the first quotation cuts off the text in mid-sentence).

324   DŌGEN'S *SHŌBŌGENZŌ* VOLUME III

[44:13]

いましめすところ、諸佛無上妙道、および正法眼藏、ならびに諸佛法印なり。當時すべて禪宗と稱することなし、禪宗と稱すべき因縁きこえず。いまこの正法眼藏は、揚眉瞬目して面授しきたる、身心骨髓をもてさづけきたる、身心骨髓に稟授しきたるなり。身先身後に傳授し稟受しきたり、心上心外に傳授し稟受するなり。

What is presented here is "the unsurpassed wondrous way of the buddhas," and the "treasury of the true dharma eye," together with the "dharma seal of the buddhas." At that time, they were never called the "Zen school," nor does one hear of any occasion to call them a "Zen school."[17] This "treasury of the true dharma eye" here has been personally bestowed by *raising the eyebrows and blinking the eyes*, has been handed down by the "bones and marrow of body and mind," has been conferred to the "bones and marrow of body and mind."[18] It has been transmitted and received "before the body and after the body," transmitted and received "upon the mind and beyond the mind."[19]

* * * * *

17 **occasion to call them a "Zen school"** (*zenshū to shō su beki innen* 禪宗と稱すべき因縁): Or "reason to call them the 'Zen school.'" The term *innen* 因縁 here may be taken in the sense either of "cause and condition" or of historical "instance" or "case."

18 **raising the eyebrows and blinking the eyes** (*yōbi shunmoku* 揚眉瞬目): Here, perhaps suggesting the Buddha's blink in Dōgen's version of the transmission to Mahākāśyapa. "Raising the eyebrows and blinking the eyes" is a set phrase used in Zen texts to represent the ordinary actions through which Buddhism is expressed; see Supplementary Notes, s.v. "Raise the eyebrows and blink the eyes."

"bones and marrow of body and mind" (*shinjin kotsuzui* 身心骨髓): Or "body and mind, bones and marrow"; a fairly common combination in Dōgen's writings. The term "bones and marrow" (*kotsuzui* 骨髓) evokes the set expression "skin, flesh, bones, and marrow" (*hi niku kotsu zui* 皮肉骨髓) derived from the story of the transmission from Bodhidharma to Huike 慧可. See Supplementary Notes, s.v. "Skin, flesh, bones, and marrow," and "Body and mind."

conferred (*bonju* 稟授): As in "impart a commission"; some texts give *bonju* 稟受 ("receive a commission").

19 **"before the body and after the body"** (*shin sen shin go* 身先身後): An expression suggesting either (a) what exists before and after one has a body, or (b) what precedes and follows a given lifetime. Occurs also in the "Shōbōgenzō sesshin sesshō" 正法眼藏 説心説性, in the lines "investigate before the body and after the body" (*shinsen shingo ni sankyū su* 身先身後に参究す) (DZZ.1:451), and "save them before the body and after the body" (*shinsen shingo ni sukuu* 身先身後にすくふ) (DZZ.1:456); here, likely akin to the following "upon the mind and beyond the mind" to indicate transcendence of the individual participants in the transmission.

"upon the mind and beyond the mind" (*shinjō shinge* 心上心外): Or "above the mind and outside the mind." An unusual expression not occurring elsewhere in Dōgen's writings; could be taken to refer to either (a) what is in the mind and what is beyond it, or (b) what is above and beyond the mind.

44. The Way of the Buddhas *Butsudō* 佛道 325

[44:14]

世尊・迦葉の會に、禪宗の稱きこえず、初祖・二祖の會に、禪宗の稱きこ
えず、五祖・六祖の會に、禪宗の稱きこえず、青原・南嶽の會に、禪宗の
稱きこえず。いづれのときより、たれ人の稱じきたるとなし。學者のなか
に、學者のかずにあらずして、ひそかに壞法・盜法のともがら、稱しきた
るならん。佛祖いまだ聽許せざるを、晩學みだりに稱するは、佛祖の家門
を損するならん。又、佛佛祖祖の法のほかに、さらに禪宗と稱する法のあ
るにたり。もし佛祖の道のほかにあらんは、外道の法なるべし。すでに
佛祖の兒孫としては、佛祖の骨髓面目を參學すべし。佛祖の道に投ぜるな
り、這裏を逃逝して、外道を參學すべからず。まれに人間の身心を保任せ
り、古來の辦道力なり。この恩力をうけて、あやまりて外道を資せん、佛
祖を報恩するにあらず。

One does not hear the name "Zen school" in the communities of the
World-Honored One and Kāśyapa; one does not hear the name "Zen
school" in the communities of the First and Second Ancestors; one does
not hear the name "Zen school" in the communities of the Fifth and Sixth
Ancestors; one does not hear the name "Zen school" in the communities
of Qingyuan and Nanyue.[20] One cannot tell when or by whom it was so
named. Probably it was named among students unworthy of reckoning
as students, a group who secretly sought to destroy the dharma or steal
the dharma. For later students rashly to use a name never acknowledged
by the buddhas and ancestors would be the ruin of the house of the buddhas and ancestors.

Moreover, [such use] suggests that there is some dharma called the
"Zen school" other than the dharma of buddha after buddha and ancestor
after ancestor. If there were [a dharma] other than the way of the buddhas
and ancestors, it would be a dharma of an other path.[21] As descendants
of the buddhas and ancestors, we should study the bones and marrow,
face and eyes of the buddhas and ancestors.[22] We have cast ourselves on
the way of the buddhas and ancestors and should not skulk off from here
to study an other path. We are entrusted with the rare body and mind of

---

20 **Fifth and Sixth Ancestors** (*goso rokuso* 五祖・六祖): I.e., Huineng 慧能 and his
teacher, the Fifth Ancestor of Chan in China, Daman Hongren 大滿弘忍 (602-675).

Qingyuan and Nanyue (*Seigan Nangaku* 青原・南嶽): I.e., the two most prominent
disciples of Huineng: Qingyuan Xingsi 青原行思 (d. 740) and Nanyue Huairang 南嶽
懷讓 (677-744).

21 **dharma of an other path** (*gedō no hō* 外道の法): I.e., the teaching of a non-Buddhist religion.

22 **bones and marrow, face and eyes** (*kotsuzui menmoku* 骨髓面目): Or "bones, marrow, and countenance." The term *menmoku* 面目 is a standard expression for the "face,"
often used in Zen texts as a synecdoche for the (real) person (as in the famous "original face" [*honrai menmoku* 本來面目]); the translation seeks to retain the parallel with
"bones and marrow." The only instance of this combination in the *Shōbōgenzō*.

326   DŌGEN'S *SHŌBŌGENZŌ* VOLUME III

a human, [through] the power of our past pursuit of the way.[23] Having received this beneficent power, mistakenly to serve an other path is no way to repay the beneficence of the buddhas and ancestors.[24]

[44:15] {1:475}

大宋の近代、天下の庸流、この妄稱禪宗の名をききて、俗徒おほく禪宗と稱し、達磨宗と稱し、佛心宗と稱する、妄稱きほひ風聞して、佛道をみだらんとす。これは、佛祖の大道、かつていまだしらず、正法眼藏、ありとだにも見聞せず、信受せざるともがらの亂道なり。正法眼藏をしらん、たれか佛道をあやまり稱することあらん。

Recently in the Great Song, mediocre types throughout the land hear the appellation of this falsely named "Zen school," and the lay followers compete to spread talk of such false names as the "Zen school," or the "Dharma school," or the "Buddha Mind school," till they would disrupt the way of the buddhas.[25] This is the disruptive talk of those who have never known the great way of the buddhas and ancestors, who have not seen or heard, believed or accepted even that there is a treasury of the true dharma eye.[26] Who that would know the treasury of the true dharma eye would use a false name for the way of the buddhas?

* * * * *

[44:16]

このゆえに、南嶽山石頭菴無際大師、上堂示大衆言、吾之法門、先佛傳受、不論禪定・精進、唯達佛之知見。

---

23   **[through] the power of our past pursuit of the way** (*korai no bendō riki* 古來の辨道力): A tentative translation, understanding the point to be that our present body and mind are the results of our past practice of Buddhism. The clause might also be read, "they [i.e., our body and mind] are the power to pursue the way [coming down to us] from the past."

24   **beneficent power** (*onriki* 恩力): Or "benevolent power"; a term usually indicating another's power, here (if the interpretation of the preceding sentence is correct), applied to the influence of karma. Does not occur elsewhere in the *Shōbōgenzō*.

25   **"Dharma school"** (*Daruma shū* 達磨宗); **"Buddha Mind school"** (*Busshin shū* 佛心宗): The term *Daruma shū* 達磨宗 (i.e., "Bodhidharma school"; also written 達摩宗), though seemingly not in fact particularly common in the Chinese Chan literature, was sometimes used in Japan during Dōgen's time to refer to the nascent Japanese Zen movement. The term *busshin shū* 佛心宗 had wider usage, both in China and Japan, and was a common designation for Zen in the Tendai 天台 school in which Dōgen was originally trained.

26   **disruptive talk** (*randō* 亂道): The translation loses what may be a play in the original on *daidō* 大道 ("great way") and *randō* 亂道 (suggestive of a "reckless or corrupt way").

44. The Way of the Buddhas *Butsudō* 佛道

Therefore,

Great Master Wuji of the Shitou Hermitage on Mount Nanyue, in a convocation, addressed the great assembly, saying, "My dharma gate has been transmitted from prior buddhas.[27] *It isn't concerned with meditation or vigor; it solely masters the knowledge and insight of a buddha."*[28]

[44:17]

しるべし、七佛諸佛より正傳ある佛祖、かくのごとく道取するなり。ただ吾之法門先佛傳受と道現成す。吾之禪宗先佛傳受と道現成なし。禪定・精進の條條をわかず、佛之知見を唯達せしむ。精進・禪定をきらはず、唯達せる佛之知見なり。これを吾有正法眼藏附囑とせり。吾之は吾有なり、法門は正法なり。吾之・吾有・吾髓は、汝得の附囑なり。

We should know that the buddhas and ancestors who have direct transmission from the seven buddhas, from all the buddhas, speak like this. He states only, "*My dharma gate has been transmitted from prior buddhas*"; he has no statement, "*My Zen school has been transmitted from prior buddhas.*" Without distinguishing the individual items "meditation or vigor," he makes [them] "solely master" "the knowledge and insight of a buddha."[29] He does not disdain vigor and meditation; [they are] "the knowledge and insight of a buddha" "solely mastered." This was treated as the bequest, "I have a treasury of the true dharma eye": "my" is "I

---

27 **Great Master Wuji of the Shitou Hermitage on Mount Nanyue** (*Nangakusan Sekitō an Musai daishi* 南嶽山石頭菴無際大師): I.e., the famous Tang-dynasty Chan figure Shitou Xiqian 石頭希遷 (700-790), disciple of Qingyuan Xingsi 青原行思. The words quoted here occur at several places in Zen literature; see, e.g., the *Jingde chuandeng lu* 景德傳燈錄 (T.2076.51:309b12-14).

28 **"meditation or vigor"** (*zenjō shōjin* 禪定・精進): Likely reference to the members of the list of the six perfections (*rokudo* 六度) practiced by the bodhisattva, of which vigor (S. *vīrya-pāramitā*) is the fourth, and meditation (S. *dhyāna-pāramitā*) is the fifth (the sixth being wisdom [S. *prajñā-pāramitā*]).

"solely masters the knowledge and insight of a buddha" (*yui tatsu butsu shi chiken* 唯達佛之知見): I.e., simply achieves the ultimate understanding of Buddhism. The expression "knowledge and insight of a buddha" (*butsu shi chiken* 佛之知見; also *butsu shi chiken* 佛知見; S. *tathagata-jñāna-darśana*) recalls Buddha Śākyamuni's revelation in the *Lotus Sūtra* (*Miaofa lianhua jing* 妙法蓮華經, T.262.9:7a23-27) that the buddhas appear in the world for the sole purpose of sharing their knowledge and insight with living beings.

29 **he makes [them] "solely master" "the knowledge and insight of a buddha"** (*butsu shi chiken o yui tatsu seshimu* 佛之知見を唯達せしむ): A tentative translation, taking the clause to mean that vigor and meditation are included in the mastery of the buddhas' knowledge and insight, as suggested in the following sentence. One might also take the accusative particle *o* を here as governing the causative verb: "he makes the knowledge and insight of a buddha solely master." An odd locution that begins a series of plays with Shitou's saying.

328 DŌGEN'S *SHŌBŌGENZŌ* VOLUME III

have"; "dharma gate" is the "true dharma."[30] "My," "I have," and "my marrow" are the bequest "you've gotten."[31]

[44:18] {1:476}

無際大師は、青原高祖の一子なり、ひとり堂奥にいれり。曹溪古佛の剃髮の法子なり。しかあれば、曹溪古佛は祖なり、父なり。青原高祖は兄なり、師なり。佛道祖席の英雄は、ひとり石頭菴無際大師のみなり。佛道の正傳、ただ無際のみ唯達なり。道現成の果果條條、みな古佛の不古なり、古佛の長今なり。これを正法眼藏の眼睛とすべし。自餘に比準すべからず、しらざるもの、江西大寂に比するは非なり。

Great Master Wuji was the only child of the Eminent Ancestor Qingyuan; he alone entered the interior of the hall. He was the dharma child through tonsure of the Old Buddha of Caoxi.[32] Thus, the Old Buddha of Caoxi was both his grandfather and his father; and the Eminent Ancestor Qingyuan was both his elder brother and his teacher. The only hero of the ancestral seat on the way of the buddhas was Great Master Wuji of the Shitou Hermitage; only Wuji "solely mastered" the direct transmission of the way of the buddhas.[33] Each point and each item in his statements is the agelessness of an old buddha, the everlasting presence of an old buddha; we should take them as the eye of the treasury of the true dharma eye.[34] We

---

30 **treated as the bequest** (*fuzoku to seri* 附囑とせり): I.e., Shitou's remark here is equivalent to what was expressed above, in the bequest to Mahākāśyapa, as "I have a treasury of the true dharma eye." The following clause explains the equivalence.

"my" is "I have"; "dharma gate" is the "true dharma" (*go shi wa go u nari, hōmon wa shōbō nari* 吾之は吾有なり、法門は正法なり): I.e., the word "my" in Shitou's saying, "my teaching," is equivalent to the words "I have" in the saying of Śākyamuni, "I have the treasury of the true dharma eye"; similarly, the words "dharma gate" in Shitou's saying is equivalent to the words "true dharma" in Śākyamuni's saying.

31 **"my marrow"** (*go zui* 吾髓); **"you've gotten"** (*nyo toku* 汝得): Dōgen is here playing with well-known language appearing in the bequest from Bodhidharma to Huike, "You've gotten my marrow" (*nyo toku go zui* 汝得吾髓); see above, Note 18.

32 **dharma child through tonsure of the Old Buddha of Caoxi** (*Sōkei kobutsu no teihatsu no hossu* 曹溪古佛の剃髮の法子): I.e., received the tonsure from the Sixth Ancestor, Huineng 慧能. Though he would have been only thirteen at the time of the Sixth Ancestor's death in 713, Shitou is said to have entered the order under Huineng before becoming a follower of Huineng's disciple Qingyuan 青原.

33 **hero of the ancestral seat on the way of the buddhas** (*butsudō soseki no eiyū* 佛道祖席の英雄): An expression of high praise for a past master, appearing several times in Dōgen's writings. The "ancestral seat" (*soseki* 祖席) is a common term for the Zen lineage.

34 **Each point and each item in his statements** (*dō genjō no kaka jōjō* 道現成の果果條條): A loose translation of the unusual expression *kaka jōjō* 果果條條 ("fruits and branches"), not occurring elsewhere in Dōgen's writing. It is unclear whether "his statements" (*dō genjō* 道現成) here refers only to the quoted saying or to everything that Shitou had to say.

the agelessness of an old buddha, the everlasting presence of an old buddha (*kobutsu*

44. The Way of the Buddhas *Butsudō* 佛道   329

should not compare him to others. Comparisons with Jiangxi Daji by those who do not know this are erroneous.[35]

[44:19]

しかあればしるべし、先佛傳受の佛道は、なほ禪定といはず、いはんや禪宗の稱論ならんや。あきらかにしるべし、禪宗と稱するは、あやまりのはなはだしきなり。つたなきともがら、有宗・空宗のごとくならんと思量して、宗の稱なからんは、所學なきがごとくなげくなり。佛道かくのごとくなるべからず、かつて禪宗と稱ぜず、と一定すべきなり。

Thus, we should know that the way of the buddhas transmitted and received by prior buddhas is not even called Zen meditation, much less described as the "Zen school." We should clearly understand that calling it the "Zen school" is an error in the extreme. Crude types, thinking that it must be like the school of being or school of emptiness, lament that, without a school name, there would seem to be nothing to study.[36] The way of the buddhas cannot be like this. We should be firmly convinced that it was never called the "Zen school."

[44:20]

しかあるに、近代の庸流、おろかにして古風をしらず。先佛の傳受なきやから、あやまりていはく、佛法のなかに五宗の門風あり、といふ。これ、自然の衰微なり。これを拯濟する一箇半箇、いまだあらず。先師天童古佛、はじめてこれをあはれまんとす。人の運なり、法の達なり。

---

no fuko nari, kobutsu no chōkon nari 古佛の不古なり、古佛の長今なり): The translation struggles to capture Dōgen's play with "old" here. "Agelessness" renders *fuko* 不古 ("not old," "not past"); "everlasting" translates *chōkon* 長今 ("long, or extended, present"); both expressions are generally taken to mean "timelessness." See Supplementary Notes, s.v. "Old buddha."

eye of the treasury of the true dharma eye (*shōbōgenzō no ganzei* 正法眼藏の眼睛): I.e., the eye that sees, or sees by means of, the *shōbōgenzō* 正法眼藏. The translation reads this as referring to Shitou's words, but it might also refer to Shitou himself. See Supplementary Notes, s.v. "Eye" and "Treasury of the true dharma eye."

35 **Jiangxi Daji** (*Kōzei Daijaku* 江西大寂): I.e., Shitou's famous contemporary Mazu Daoyi 馬祖道一 (709-788), disciple of Nanyue Huairang 南嶽懷讓; Shitou and Mazu are often considered together as the leading Chan figures of their generation and are said to have been personally close.

36 **school of being or school of emptiness** (*ushū kūshū* 有宗・空宗): Buddhist traditions emphasizing respectively the phenomenal world or the ultimate emptiness of the phenomenal world. Sometimes identified with the Sarvāstivāda (*Setsu issai u bu* 説一切有部) and Madhyamaka (*Sanron shū* 三論宗) traditions respectively; more likely reflecting the broader Tendai 天台 usage of *umon* 有門 ("gate [or 'teaching'] of being") and *kūmon* 空門 ("gate of emptiness"), in reference to a school's preference for assertion or denial of the reality of phenomena (dharmas). In the Japanese Tendai tradition of Dōgen's day, the Zen teaching was identified with the gate of emptiness in Tendai's perfect teaching (*engyō* 圓教) — in contrast to the Mantrayāna (*shingon* 眞言), which represented the gate of being.

330 DŌGEN'S *SHŌBŌGENZŌ* VOLUME III

Nevertheless, the mediocre types of recent generations are stupid and do not know the style of the ancients. Fellows without transmission from the prior buddhas erroneously say that within the buddha dharma there are the teaching styles of the five schools.[37] This is a natural decline and diminution. There has not been one or a half to rescue them. My former master, the Old Buddha of Tiantong, was the first to take pity on them.[38] It was the people's fortune and the dharma's fulfillment.[39]

[44:21] {1:477}

先師古佛、上堂示衆云、如今箇箇、祇管道雲門・法眼・潙仰・臨濟・曹洞等家風有別者、不是佛法也、不是祖師道也。

My former master, the Old Buddha, in a convocation, addressed the assembly, saying, "Nowadays everyone just says that the house styles of Yunmen, Fayan, Weiyang, Linji, and Caodong are distinct.[40] This is not the buddha dharma; it is not the way of the ancestral masters."

---

37 **teaching styles of the five schools** (*goshū no monpū* 五宗の門風): I.e., the five lineages into which Song-dynasty authors often divided the Chan tradition, to which Rujing will refer below: Yunmen 雲門, Fayan 法眼, Weiyang 潙仰, Linji 臨濟, and Caodong 曹洞.

38 **My former master, the Old Buddha of Tiantong** (*senshi Tendō kobutsu* 先師天童古佛): I.e., Tiantong Rujing 天童如淨, abbot of the Jingde Monastery 景德寺 on Mount Tiantong 天童山, in present-day Zhejiang province. Dōgen received transmission from Rujing in 1225.

39 **It was the people's fortune and the dharma's fulfillment** (*hito no un nari, hō no tatsu nari* 人の運なり、法の達なり): A tentative translation of an obscure remark, taking "people" here to refer to those on whom Rujing took pity. The juxtaposition of the "humans" by whom or to whom Buddhism is taught and the "dharma" that is taught is a common pattern.

40 **My former master, the Old Buddha** (*senshi kobutsu* 先師古佛): Though given here in Chinese as the quotation of a formal sermon by Rujing, Dōgen's source for this saying is unknown.

Yunmen, Fayan, Weiyang, Linji, and Caodong (*unmon hōgen igyō rinzai sōtō* 雲門・法眼・潙仰・臨濟・曹洞): I.e., the five houses (*goke* 五家), or schools, referred to in the preceding paragraph. They are said to have developed among the descendants of the two most prominent disciples of the Sixth Ancestor, Huineng 慧能: Qingyuan Xingsi 青原行思 and Nanyue Huairang 南嶽懷讓. In the lineage of the former, the Yunmen 雲門 house is named after Yunmen Wenyan 雲門文偃 (864-949); the Fayan 法眼 house, after Fayan Wenyi 法眼文益 (885-958); the Caodong house 曹洞, after Dongshan Liangjie 洞山良价 (807-869) and his disciple Caoshan Benji 曹山本寂 (840-901) (or, by other accounts, Dongshan and the Sixth Ancestor, Caoxi Huineng 曹溪慧能). In the lineage of Nanyue 南嶽, the Weiyang 潙仰 house is named after Weishan Lingyu 潙山靈祐 (771-853) and his disciple Yangshan Huiji 仰山慧寂 (807-883); the Linji 臨濟 house, after Linji Yixuan 臨濟義玄 (d. 866).

44. The Way of the Buddhas *Butsudō* 佛道　　331

[44:22]

この道現成は、千載にあひがたし、先師ひとり道取す。十方にききがた
し、圓席ひとり聞取す。しかあれば、一千の雲水のなかに、聞著する耳
垛なし、見取する眼睛なし。いはんや心を擧してきくあらんや、いはんや
身處に聞著するあらんや。たとひ自己の渾身心に聞著する億萬劫にありと
も、先師の通身心を擧拈して、聞著し、證著し、信著し、脱落著するなか
りき。あはれむべし、大宋一國の十方、ともに先師をもて諸方の長老等に
齊肩なりとおもへり。かくのごとくおもふともがらを、具眼なりとやせ
ん、未具眼なりとやせん。またあるひは、先師をもて臨濟・德山に齊肩な
りとおもへり。このともがらも、いまだ先師をみず、いまだ臨濟にあはず
といふべし。先師古佛を禮拜せざりしさきは、五宗の玄旨を參究せんと擬
す。先師古佛を禮拜せしよりのちは、あきらかに五宗の亂稱なるむねをし
りぬ。

This statement is hard to encounter in a thousand years; my former
master alone said it. It is hard to hear throughout the ten directions;
the perfect seat alone hears it.[41] This being the case, among one thousand monks, there is none with ears to hear it, none with eyes to see it.
How much less are there those who take up the mind and hear it, those
who hear it with the body?[42] Even though they heard it with their own
whole body and mind for one hundred million ten thousand kalpas, there
have not been those who, taking up my former master's body and mind
throughout, hear it, verify it, believe it, and slough it off.[43]

It is pitiful that, throughout the ten directions of the one Land of the
Great Song, all have thought that the elders of all quarters are of equal
stature to my former master.[44] Shall we take the group that thinks like
this as endowed with the eye, or as unendowed with the eye? Again,
some have thought that Linji and Deshan were of equal stature to my former master.[45] We have to say that this group also has never seen my former master, has never met Linji. Before I had paid obeisance to the Old

---

41　**the perfect seat** (*enseki* 圓席): I.e., the ideal Buddhist assembly.

42　**take up the mind and hear it** (*shin o koshite kiku* 心を擧してきく): I.e., hear it
with their minds.

43　**whole body and mind** (*kon shinjin* 渾身心); **body and mind throughout** (*tsū
shinjin* 通身心): Dōgen is here elaborating on two fairly common expressions for the
entire body: "whole body" (*konjin* 渾身) and "body throughout" (*tsūshin* 通身). See Supplementary Notes, s.v. "Body and mind" and "His body throughout is hands and eyes."

44　**elders of all quarters** (*shohō no chōrō tō* 諸方の長老等): I.e., the senior Chan
teachers or abbots throughout the land.

45　**Linji and Deshan** (*Rinzai Tokusan* 臨濟・德山): I.e., Linji Yixuan 臨濟義玄　and
Deshan Xuanjian 德山宣鑑 (780-865). These two prominent Tang-dynasty monks are
also dismissed elsewhere in the Shōbōgenzō: see "Shōbōgenzō kattō" 正法眼藏葛藤,
written two months before our text, and "Shōbōgenzō mitsugo" 正法眼藏密語, written
just four days after the "Butsudō" chapter.

332   DŌGEN'S *SHŌBŌGENZŌ* VOLUME III

Buddha, my former master, I thought to investigate the dark import of the five schools. After paying obeisance to the Old Buddha, my former master, I clearly knew the point that "five schools" is a corrupt name.

[44:23]

しかあればすなはち、大宋國の佛法さかりなりしときは、五宗の稱なし、また、五宗の稱を擧揚して家風をきこゆる古人、いまだあらず。佛法の澆薄よりこのかた、みだりに五宗の稱あるなり。これ、人の、參學おろかにして、辨道を親切にせざるによりて、かくのごとし。雲箇水箇、眞箇の參究を求覓せんは、切忌すらくは、五家の亂稱を記持することなかれ、五家の門風を記號することなかれ。いはんや三玄・三要、四料簡・四照用、九帶等あらんや。いはんや三句・五位・十同眞智あらんや。

Thus, when the buddha dharma flourished in the Land of the Great Song, there was no term "five schools," and there were no ancients who, taking up the term "five schools," tell us of "house styles." Ever since the buddha dharma became weak, we have this arbitrary term "five schools." It is like this because people are stupid in their study and are not keen about pursuing the way.

To each and every monk seeking authentic investigation, I offer this strict prohibition: do not note or retain the arbitrary term "five houses"; do not note or designate the "teaching styles" of the five houses.[46] Not to mention "the three mysteries and three essentials,"[47] "the four consider-

---

46   **each and every monk** (*unko suiko* 雲箇水箇): The loose translation loses the unusual play with the common term for monk, *unsui* 雲水 ("clouds and water"), used in the preceding section, here split into two terms by the classifier *ko* 箇 (repeated in the following "authentic" [*shinko no* 眞箇の]); more literally, suggesting something like "each cloud and each water." The only occurrence in the *Shōbōgenzō*.

47   **"the three mysteries and three essentials"** (*sangen sanyō* 三玄・三要): Dōgen begins here a list of catch phrases identified with various Chan teaching styles or techniques, especially as given in the *Rentian yanmu* 人天眼目, by Huiyan Zhizhao 晦巖智昭 (dates unknown), a twelfth-century work he will explicitly dismiss toward the end of our text. "The three mysteries and three essentials" is a teaching associated with Linji Yixuan 臨濟義玄, founder of the Linji school. See, e.g., *Linji lu* 臨濟錄 (T.1985.47:497a19-21):

師又云、一句語須具三玄門。一玄門須具三要。有權有用。汝等諸人、作麼生會。

The Master also said, "One line should contain the gates of the three mysteries. The gate of one mystery should contain the three essentials. There is the provisional; there is the functional. All of you, how do you understand it?"

The *Rentian yanmu* 人天眼目 (T.2006.48:301c24ff) quotes a variant of this saying and goes on to discuss various treatments of the topic. At a later point (T.2006.48:311b19-20), it summarizes the three by saying:

三玄者、玄中玄、體中玄、玄。三要者、一玄中具三要。

The three mysteries are the mystery within the mystery; the mystery within the body, the mystery within the phrase. The three essentials are the three essentials within one mystery.

44. The Way of the Buddhas *Butsudō* 佛道   333

ations,"[48] "the four illuminations and applications,"[49] "the nine spheres," and the like.[50] Not to mention "the three phrases" or "the five ranks" or

---

48 **"the four considerations"** (*shi ryōken* 四料簡): Also written 四料揀. A teaching method also associated with Linji 臨濟, based on a passage in the *Linji lu* 臨濟錄 (T.1985.47:497a22-23):

> 師晚參示眾云、有時奪人不奪境。有時奪境不奪人。有時人境俱奪。有時人境俱不奪。

> At the evening convocation, the Master addressed the assembly saying, "Sometimes, I snatch away the person but don't snatch away the object; sometimes, I snatch away the object but don't snatch away the person; sometimes, I snatch away both person and object; sometimes, I don't snatch away either person or object."

The saying is quoted and its interpretation by various masters recorded in the *Rentian yanmu* 人天眼目 (T.2006.48:300b6ff).

49 **"the four illuminations and applications"** (*shi shōyū* 四照用): Or "four understandings and applications." Again, attributed to Linji 臨濟, though apparently not occurring in early versions of the *Linji lu* 臨濟錄. The *Rentian yanmu* 人天眼目 discussion (T.2006.48:304a10ff) begins with a quotation of Linji 臨濟:

> 師一日示眾云、我有時先照後用。有時先用後照。有時照用同時。有時照用不同時。　先照後用有人在。先用後照有法在。照用同時。　驅耕夫之牛。奪饑人之食。敲骨取髓。痛下針錐。　照用不同時。有問有答。立主立賓。　合水和泥應機接物。

> One day, the Master addressed the assembly saying,
> Sometimes I illumine it first and apply it later; sometimes I apply it first and illumine it later; sometimes I illumine and apply it at the same time; sometimes I illumine and apply it not at the same time. When I illumine it first and apply it later, the person is there; when I apply it first and illumine it later, the dharma is there. When I illumine and apply it at the same time, I drive off the farmer's ox; I steal the food of the starving man; I pound the bones and get the marrow; I needle the pain. When I illumine and apply it not at the same time, I have questions, I have answers; I set up the host and set up the guest; I accord with the water and harmonize with the mud, dealing with things in response to the opportunity.

50 **"the nine spheres"** (*kutai* 九帶): An organization of Buddhist teachings attributed to Fushan Fayuan 浮山法遠 (991-1067), in the Linji 臨濟 lineage. The *Rentian yanmu* 人天眼目 discusses them at T.2006.48:308a26-310b8, opening with this explanation:

> 浮山每於示徒之際、遍舉宗門語句。而學者編集、乞師名之。師因其類聚、目之曰佛禪宗教義九帶集。蓋擬班固九流之作也。

> Whenever Fushan addressed his followers, he widely cited the words of the school. Then his students collected them and begged the Master to name them. The Master categorized them according to type and called them the *Fo chan zong jiaoyi jiudai ji* ("*Collection of the Nine Spheres of the Teachings of the Buddhist Zen School*"), perhaps in imitation of Bangu's *Jiuliu* ("*Nine Currents*") [of early Chinese philosophy].

Sources give somewhat variant versions of the nine; the *Rentian yanmu* 人天眼目 (T.2006.48:308b1ff *passim*) has: (1) *fo zhengfa yan zang dai* 佛正法眼藏帶 ("the sphere of the treasury of the true dharma eye of the buddha"), (2) *fofa zang dai* 佛法藏帶 ("the sphere of the treasury of the dharma of the buddha"), (3) *ri guan dai* 理貫帶 ("the sphere of principle throughout"), (4) *shi guan dai* 事貫帶 ("the sphere of phenomena throughout"), (5) *li shi zonghong dai* 理事縱橫帶 ("the sphere of principle and phenomena vertical and horizontal"), (6) *ququ chui dai* 屈曲垂帶 ("the sphere of letting down the

334　DŌGEN'S *SHŌBŌGENZŌ* VOLUME III

"the ten wisdoms of the truth of sameness."[51]

[44:24] {1:478}

釋迦老子の道、しかのごとくの小量ならず、しかのごとくを大量とせず、道現成せず、少林・曹溪にきこえず。あはれむべし、いま末代の不聞法の禿子等、その身心・眼睛くらくしていふところなり。佛祖の兒孫種子、かくのごとくの言語なかれ。佛祖の住持に、この狂言、かつてきこゆることなし。後來の阿師等、かつて佛法の全道をきかず、祖道の全靠なく、本分にくらきともがら、わづか一・兩の少分に矜高して、かくのごとく宗稱を立するなり。立宗稱よりこのかたの小兒子等は、本をたづぬべき道を學せざるによりて、いたづらに末にしたがふなり。慕古の志氣なく、混俗の操行あり。俗なほ世俗にしたがふことをいやしとして、いましむるなり。

The words of Old Master Śākya are not of such small measure as this and do not take something like this as of great measure; he does not state them, nor do we hear them at Shaolin or Caoxi.[52] It is pitiful, something said now by shavelings of the last age who have not heard the dharma

---

crooked and bent"), (7) *miao xie jian dai* 妙協兼帶 ("the sphere of wondrous accord and combination"), (8) *jin zhen shuang suo dai* 金鍼雙鎖帶 ("the sphere of double stitch with a golden thread"), (9) *ping huai chang shi dai* 平懷常實帶 ("the sphere of normal affections always true").

51　**"three phrases"** (*sanku* 三句): The expression "three phrases" (or "three statements") is applied to the teachings of various Chan masters, and it is impossible to say just which of these Dōgen may have had in mind here. The best-known case is that of the "three phrases" of Yunmen 雲門, cited elsewhere in the *Shōbōgenzō*; see Supplementary Notes, s.v. "Yunmen's three phrases."

"five ranks" (*goi* 五位): There are several versions of the "five ranks" formula, associated especially with the Caodong 曹洞 school and attributed originally to the school's founder, Dongshan Liangjie 洞山良价; see Supplementary Notes, s.v. "Five ranks."

"ten wisdoms of the truth of sameness" (*jū dōshin chi* 十同眞智): More commonly known as *jūchi dōshin* 十智同眞. A set of desiderata for teaching developed by Fenyang Shanzhao 汾陽善昭 (947-1024). They are given in the *Fenyang yulu* 汾陽語錄 (T.1992.47:596b22-25) as: (1) "sameness in quality" (*tong yi zhi* 同一質), (2) "sameness in the great matter" (*tong da shih* 同大事), (3) "sameness in all practicing" (*zong tong can* 總同參), (4) "sameness in true aspiration" (*tong zhen zhi* 同眞志), (5) "sameness in universality" (*tong pian pu* 同遍普), (6) "sameness in endowment" (*tong ju zu* 同具足), (7) "sameness in gain and loss" (*tong de shi* 同得失), (8) "sameness in birth and death" (*tong sheng sha* 同生殺), (9) "sameness in giving voice" (*tong yin hou* 同音吼), (10) "sameness in gaining entry" (*tong de ru* 同得入).

The *Rentian yanmu* 人天眼目 discusses the formula at T.2006.48:304c22ff. Its list (at T.2006.48:305a7-9) differs from the *Fenyang yulu* 汾陽語錄 version only in number 4, which it gives as "sameness in true wisdom" (*tong zhen zhi* 同眞智).

52　**The words of Old Master Śākya** (*Shaka rōshi no dō* 釋迦老子の道): Or "the way of Old Master Śākya."

Shaolin or Caoxi (*Shōrin Sōkei* 少林・曹溪): I.e., the residences of the First and Sixth Ancestors.

44. The Way of the Buddhas *Butsudō* 佛道

and whose bodies and minds and eyes are dark.[53] Descendants and seeds of the buddhas and ancestors, do not utter such words![54]

In what the buddhas and ancestors maintain, one never hears these mad words. Recent little teachers, types who have never heard the complete way of the buddha dharma, who lack complete reliance on the way of the ancestors, who are ignorant of their original lot, boasting of one or two little parts, set up such names of schools. Ever since they set up the names of schools, the little children, because they do not study the way that should seek out the root, vainly follow the branches. Lacking the aspiration that admires the ancients, they have the conduct that mixes with the secular. Even the secular warn that following along with the secular world is base.

* * * * *

[44:25]

文王問太公曰、君務舉賢、而不獲其功、世亂愈甚、以致危亡者何也。太公曰、舉賢而不用、是以有舉賢之名也、無得賢之實也。文王曰、其失安在。太公曰、其失在好用世俗之所譽、不得其眞賢。文王曰、好用世俗之所譽者何也。太公曰、好聽世俗之所譽者、或以非賢爲賢、或以非智爲智、或以非忠爲忠、或以非信爲信。君以世俗所譽者爲賢智、以世俗之所毀者爲不肖、則多黨者進、少黨者退。是以群邪比周而蔽賢、忠臣死於無罪、邪臣虛譽以求爵位。是以世亂愈甚、故其國不免於危亡。

King Wen asked the Grand Duke, "Why is it that the lord employs and promotes the worthy but does not garner the benefit, so that the disorder of the world increases to an extreme that becomes dangerous?" [55]

The Grand Duke said, "He elevates the worthy but does not use them. This is because he elevates the names of the worthy and does not get the reality of the worthy."

King Wen said, "Where is the fault?"

---

53 **the last age** (*matsudai* 末代): I.e., the final period in the historical decline of Buddha Śākyamuni's teachings, often thought in Dōgen's day to have begun in 1052 and to last for ten thousand years. A term occurring only infrequently in Dōgen's writing.

54 **Descendants and seeds of the buddhas and ancestors** (*busso no jison shūji* 佛祖の兒孫種子): An unusual expression, presumably meaning "those descended from the buddhas and ancestors and those with the karmic potential ('seeds') to become buddhas and ancestors."

55 **King Wen asked the Grand Duke** (*Bun ō mon Taikō* 文王問太公): Quoted (with some variation) from the Chinese military text *Liu tao* 六韜 (*Wen tao* 文韜, Ju xian 舉賢, KR.3b0002.001.8a-b). "King Wen" refers to the first emperor of the Zhou 周 dynasty (1046-256 BCE); "the Grand Duke" refers to his minister and military advisor Lü Shang 呂尚.

336 DŌGEN'S *SHŌBŌGENZŌ* VOLUME III

The Grand Duke said, "The fault is in using what the worldly praise and not getting the truly worthy."

King Wen said, "What is using what the worldly praise?"

The Grand Duke said, "To listen to the praise of the worldly is to take the unworthy as the worthy, to take the unintelligent as the intelligent, to take the disloyal as the loyal, to take the unfaithful as the faithful. If the lord takes as worthy and intelligent those praised by the worldly and takes as unworthy those reviled by the worldly, then the majority party will advance and the minority party will retreat. Thus, when the wicked band together, they obscure the worthy; the loyal ministers die without crime, and the wicked ministers seek court ranks with flattery. Thus, the disorder of the world increases to an extreme, and as a result, the country cannot avoid peril."

[44:26] {1:479}

俗なほ、その國、その道の危亡することをなげく、佛法・佛道の危亡せん、佛子、かならずなげくべし。危亡のもとゐは、みだりに世俗にしたがふなり。世俗にほむるところをきく時は、眞賢をうることなし。眞賢をえんとおもはば、照後觀前の智略あるべし。世俗のほむるところ、いまだかならずしも賢にあらず、聖にあらず。世俗のそしるところ、いまだかならずしも賢にあらず、聖にあらず。しかありといへども、賢にしてそしりをまねくと、僞にしてほまれあると、三察するところ、混ずべからず。賢をもちいざらんは、國の損なり、不肖をもちいん、國のうらみなり。

Even the secular lament when their country and its way are imperiled; when the dharma of the buddha and the way of the buddhas are imperiled, children of the buddha should naturally lament. The basis of the peril is the indiscriminate accord with the secular world. When one listens to what the worldly praise, one fails to get the "truly worthy." If one would get the truly worthy, one should have the wisdom to illumine behind and see ahead. Those the worldly praise are not always worthies, are not always sages; those the worldly disparage are not always worthies, are not always sages. While this is the case, where we thrice examine the worthy's inviting disparagement and the fraud's being praised, we should not confuse them. Not to use the worthy is a loss to the country; to use the unworthy is a regret for the country.

[44:27] {1:480}

いま五宗の稱を立するは、世俗の混亂なり。この世俗にしたがふものはおほしといへども、俗を俗としれる人すくなし。俗を化するを聖人とすべし、俗にしたがふは至愚なるべし。この俗にしたがはんともがら、いかでか佛正法をしらん、いかにしてか佛となり祖とならん。七佛嫡嫡相承しきたれり、いかでか西天にある依文解義のともがら、律の五部を立するがごとくならん。

44. The Way of the Buddhas *Butsudō* 佛道   337

To set up the name "five schools" is a confusion with the secular world. Though there are many who follow the secular world, there are few people who understand the secular as secular. The sage should convert the secular; to follow the secular is extremely stupid. Those that would follow the secular — how could they know the correct dharma of the buddha? How could they become buddhas or become ancestors? It has been inherited by successor after successor from the seven buddhas; how could it be like setting up the five denominations of the rules by the bunch in Sindh in the West who rely on the text to understand the meaning?[56]

[44:28]

しかあればしるべし、佛法の正命を正命とせる祖師は、五宗の家門ある、とかつていはざるなり。佛道に五宗あり、と學するは、七佛の正嗣にあらず。

Thus, we should realize that the ancestral masters who have taken the correct life of the buddha dharma as the correct life have never said that there are houses of the five schools. Those who learn that there are five houses in the way of the buddhas are not legitimate heirs of the seven buddhas.

[44:29]

先師示衆曰、近年祖師道廢、魔黨畜生多、頻頻擧五家門風。苦哉、苦哉。

My former master addressed the assembly, saying,[57]

In recent years, the way of the ancestral masters has declined. The beasts and minions of Māra are many. Again and again they bring up the teaching styles of the five houses. Painful. Painful.

[44:30]

しかあれば、はかりしりぬ、西天二十八代、東地二十二祖、いまだ五宗の家門を開演せざるなり。祖師とある祖師は、みなかくのごとし。五宗を立して各各の宗旨ありと稱するは、誑惑世間人のともがら、少聞薄解のたぐひなり。佛道におきて、各各の道を自立せば、佛道いかでか今日にいたらん。迦葉も自立すべし、阿難も自立すべし。もし自立する道理を正道とせば、佛法はやく西天に滅しなまし。各各自立せん宗旨、たれかこれ慕古せん。各各に自立せん宗旨、たれが正邪を決擇せん。正邪いまだ決擇せずば、たれかこれを佛法なりとし、佛法にあらずとせん。この道理あきら

---

56   **the five denominations of the rules** (*ritsu no gobu* 律の五部): Reference to the tradition that, some one hundred years after the time of Buddha Śākyamuni, there arose among the followers of Upagupta, separate vinaya collections in the five schools of Dharmaguptaka, Sarvāstivāda, Mahīśāsaka, Kāśyapīya, and Vātsīputrīya (sometimes replaced by Mahāsāṃghika).

57   **My former master** (*senshi* 先師): I.e., Tiantong Rujing 天童如淨. The source is unknown.

めずば、佛道と稱しがたし。五宗の稱は、各各祖師の現在に立せるにあら
ず。五宗の祖師と稱する祖師、すでに圓寂ののち、あるひは門下の庸流、
まなこ、いまだあきらかならず、あし、いまだあゆまざるもの、父にとは
ず、祖に違して、立稱しきたるなり。そのむねあきらかなり、たれ人もし
りぬべし。

Thus, we know clearly that the twenty-eight generations of Sindh in
the West and the twenty-two ancestors of the Land of the East never proclaimed the houses of the five schools.[58] The ancestral masters that are
ancestral masters are all like this. Those who set up the "five schools"
and claim that each has its own tenets are types who would deceive the
people of the world, the sort with little learning and slight understanding.
If, within the way the buddha, each sets up their own way, how could the
way of the buddhas have reached us today? Kāśyapa would have set up
his own; Ānanda would have set up his own.[59] If the principle of setting
up one's own [way] were the correct way, the buddha dharma would
have quickly disappeared in Sindh in the West. Who would "admire the
ancients" for the tenets set up by each [faction]? Who could judge the
truth or falsity of tenets set up by each? If we cannot judge its truth or
falsity, who could say this is the buddha dharma or this is not the buddha
dharma? If this principle is not clear, it is difficult to call it the buddha
dharma. The name "five schools" was not set up during the time of any
of the ancestral masters. After the perfect quiescence of the ancestral
masters who are called the ancestral masters of the five schools, perhaps
branches of their followers, those whose eyes were not yet clear, whose
feet had not yet walked, without asking their fathers, opposing their ancestors, set up this name. The point is clear. Anyone should recognize it.

* * * * *

[44:31] {1:481}
大潙山大圓禪師は、百丈大智子なり。百丈と同時に潙山に住す。いまだ、
佛法を潙仰宗と稱すべし、といはず。百丈も、なんぢがときより潙山に住
して潙仰宗と稱すべし、といはず。師と祖と稱せず、しるべし、妄稱とい
ふことを。たとひ宗號をほしきままにすといふとも、あながちに仰山をも
とむべからず。自稱すべくは自稱すべし、自稱すべからざるによりて、
前來も自稱せず、いまも自稱なし。曹溪宗といはず、南嶽宗といはず、
江西宗といはず、百丈宗といはず。潙山にいたりて曹溪にことなるべから
ず、曹溪よりもすぐるべからず、曹溪におよぶべからず。大潙の道取する

58　**the twenty-eight generations of Sindh in the West and the twenty-two ancestors
of the Land of the East** (*Saiten nijūhachi dai Tōchi nijūni so* 西天二十八代東地二十二
祖): I.e., the Indian lineage from Mahākāśyapa to Bodhidharma and the Chinese lineage
from Bodhidharma to Rujing 如淨.

59　**Kāśyapa** (*Kashō* 迦葉); **Ānanda** (*Anan* 阿難): I.e., the first and second ancestors in
the Zen lineage.

44. The Way of the Buddhas *Butsudō* 佛道　　　339

一言半句、かならずしも仰山と一條拄杖兩人昇せず。宗の稱を立せんとき
潙山宗といふべし、大潙宗といふべし、潙仰宗と稱すべき道理、いまだあ
らず。潙仰宗と稱すべくは、兩位の尊宿の在世に稱すべし。在世に稱すべ
からんを稱せざらんは、なにのさわりによりてか稱せざらん。すでに兩位
の在世に稱せざるを、父祖の道を違して潙仰宗と稱するは、不孝の兒孫な
り。これ大潙禪師の本懷にあらず、仰山老人の素意にあらず。正師の正傳
なし、邪黨の邪稱なることあきらけし。これを盡十方界に風聞することな
かれ。

Chan Master Dayuan of Mount Dawei was a child of Baizhang Dazhi.[60]
He lived on Mount Wei at the same time as Baizhang. He never said that
the buddha dharma should be called the "Weiyang school."[61] Nor did
Baizhang say, "From your time on, you should live on Mount Wei, and
be called the Weiyang school." The Master and Ancestor did not use the
name; we should realize it is a false name.[62] Even though it may be arbitrarily used as a school name, we should not necessarily trace it to Yangshan. Were personal names supposed to be used, they would have been
used; since personal names are not supposed to be used, personal names
were not used in the past, and we do not have personal names today. We
do not say "the Caoxi school"; we do not say "the Nanyue school"; we
do not say "the Jiangxi school"; we do not say "the Baizhang school."[63]

When it comes to Weishan, it cannot be that he is different from Caoxi;
he should not be superior to Caoxi; he should not be equal to Caoxi.
One word and half a line spoken by Dawei is not necessarily one staff
borne by two people with Yangshan.[64] If one were to set up the name of

---

60　**Chan Master Dayuan of Mount Dawei was a child of Baizhang Dazhi** (*Dai-
isan Daien zenji wa, Hyakujō Daichi shi nari* 大潙山大圓禪師は、百丈大智子なり):
I.e., Weishan Lingyu 潙山靈祐 was a disciple of Baizhang Huihai 百丈懷海 (749-814).
Mount Wei 潙山 is in present-day Hunan province. From this point, Dōgen takes up each
of the five houses in turn.

61　**"Weiyang school"** (*Igyō shū* 潙仰宗): I.e., the school named after Weishan Lingyu
潙山靈祐 and his disciple Yangshan Huiji 仰山慧寂.

62　**The Master and Ancestor did not use the name** (*shi to so to shō sezu* 師と祖と
稱せず): Probably meaning that the name "Weiyang" was never used by Baizhang, who
was teacher to Weishan and ancestor to Yangshan.

63　**"Caoxi school"** (*Sōkei shū* 曹溪宗): I.e., of the Sixth Ancestor, Huineng of Caoxi
曹溪慧能.

"Nanyue school" (*Nangaku shū* 南嶽宗): I.e., of the Sixth Ancestor's disciple Nanyue
Huairang 南嶽懷讓.

"Jiangxi school" (*Kōzei shū* 江西宗): I.e., of Mazu Daoyi 馬祖道一 of Jiangxi 江西.

"Baizhang school" (*Hyakujō shū* 百丈宗): I.e., of Baizhang Huihai 百丈懷海.

64　**one staff borne by two people** (*ichijō shujō ryōnin yo* 一條拄杖兩人昇): I.e., "they
are simply saying the same thing." An idiomatic expression in Chinese syntax indicating
"two statements with the same purport," or, as we might say, "a distinction without a

340 DŌGEN'S *SHŌBŌGENZŌ* VOLUME III

the school, one should call it the Weishan school, or one should call it
the Dawei school; there is no reason to call it the Weiyang school. Were
it supposed to be called the Weiyang school, it should have been called
that when both venerables were alive. Because of what obstacle was it
not called what it should have been called when they were alive? Those
who would go against the way of their father and grandfather and call it
what it was not called when the two were alive are unfilial children and
grandchildren. This is not the original desire of Chan Master Dawei; it is
not the genuine intention of the old man Yangshan. It has no direct transmission of a true master; it is clearly the false name of a false faction. Do
not spread this throughout the realms of the ten directions.

* * * * *

[44:32] {1:482}

慧照大師は、講經の家門をなげすてて、黄檗の門人となれり。黄檗の棒を
喫すること三番、あはせて六十拄杖なり。大愚のところに参じて省悟せ
り。ちなみに鎭州臨濟院に住せり。黄檗のこころを究盡せずといへども、
相承の佛法を、臨濟宗となづくべし、といふ一句の道取なし、半句の道取
なし、堅擧せず、拈拂せず。しかあるを、門人のなかの庸流、たちまちに
父業をまぼらず、佛法をまぼらず、あやまりて臨濟宗の稱を立す。慧照大
師の平生に結構せん、なほ曩祖の道に違せば、その稱を立せんこと予議あ
るべし。

Great Master Huizhao, abandoning a house that explicates scripture,
became a follower of Huangbo.[65] Three times he tasted Huangbo's stick,
altogether sixty staffs. Visiting Dayu, he had an awakening.[66] He subsequently resided at Linji Cloister in Zhenzhou.[67] While he may not have
exhaustively investigated Huangbo's mind, he has no saying of one line,
no saying of a half line, that the buddha dharma he inherited should be
called the Linji school; he does not raise his fist; he does not take up his
whisk.[68] Nevertheless, immediately, mediocre factions among his fol-

---

difference"; seemingly synonymous with the variant "two people leaning on one staff"
(*ichijō shujō ryōnin fu* 一條拄杖兩人扶). See Supplementary Notes, s.v. "Staff."

65 **Great Master Huizhao** (*Eshō daishi* 慧照大師): I.e., Linji Yixuan 臨濟義玄, after
whom the Linji 臨濟 school is named.

Huangbo (*Ōbaku* 黄檗): I.e., Huangbo Xiyun 黄檗希運 (dates unknown), disciple of
Baizhang Huaihai 百丈懷海.

66 **Visiting Dayu, he had an awakening** (*Daigu no tokoro ni sanjite seigo seri* 大愚
のところに参じで省悟せり): Recounting the famous story that, after being beaten three
times by Huangbo 黄檗, Linji consulted with Gaoan Dayu 高安大愚 (dates unknown)
and understood Huangbo's actions.

67 **Linji Cloister in Zhenzhou** (*Chinjū Rinzai in* 鎭州臨濟院): In present-day Hebei
province.

68 **he does not raise his fist; he does not take up his whisk** (*juken sezu, nenhotsu sezu*

44. The Way of the Buddhas *Butsudō* 佛道   341

lowers, without protecting the work of the father, without protecting the buddha dharma, mistakenly set up the name "Linji school." Were it constructed during the life of Great Master Huizhao, since it goes against the words of the Ancient Ancestor, there should have been prior discussion about setting up that name.

[44:33]

いはんや、臨濟將示滅、囑三聖慧然禪師曰、吾遷化後、不得滅却吾正法眼藏。慧然曰、爭敢滅却和尚正法眼藏。臨濟云、忽有人間汝、作麼生對。慧然便喝。臨濟云、誰知吾正法眼藏、向遮瞎驢邊滅却。かくのごとく、師資、道取するところなり。

Moreover,

When Linji was about to pass away, he entrusted Chan Master Sansheng Huiran, saying, "After my transformation, do not let my treasury of the true dharma eye be extinguished."[69]

Huiran said, "How could I let the Reverend's treasury of the true dharma eye be extinguished?"

Linji said, "If someone suddenly asks you, what will you answer?"

Huiran shouted.

Linji said, "Who could have known that my treasury of the true dharma would have been extinguished with this blind donkey?"[70]

Such is what master and disciple had to say.

[44:34]

臨濟いまだ、吾禪宗を滅却することえざれ、といはず、吾臨濟宗を滅却することえざれ、といはず、吾宗を滅却することえざれ、といはず、ただ、吾正法眼藏を滅却することえざれ、といふ。あきらかにしるべし、佛祖正傳の大道を、禪宗と稱すべからずといふこと、臨濟宗と稱すべからずといふことを。さらに禪宗と稱すること、ゆめゆめあるべからず。たとひ滅却は正法眼藏の理象なりとも、かくのごとく附囑するなり。向遮瞎驢邊の滅

堅擧せず、拈拂せず): "Raising the fist" and "taking up the whisk" are two common actions used in a Chan master's teachings; here, presumably, meaning that Linji did not use reference to a Linji school in his teaching.

69 **When Linji was about to pass away** (*Rinzai shō shimetsu* 臨濟將示滅): A famous passage supposed to record Linji's final words; it is found in many Zen sources and recorded in Dōgen's *shinji Shōbōgenzō* 眞字正法眼藏 (DZZ.5:210, case 167; probably taken from the *Hongzhi lu* 宏智錄, T.2001.48:19c8-12). Linji's disciple Sansheng Huiran 三聖慧然 (dates unknown) is traditionally credited with the compilation of his master's recorded sayings. A version of his exchange with Linji appears at the end of the text (*Linji lu* 臨濟錄, T.1985.47:506c3-7).

70 **"this blind donkey"** (*sha katsuro* 遮瞎驢): Scholarly opinion is divided on whether the glyph *katsu* 瞎 should be taken here as "blind" or "one-eyed" (i.e., "blind in one eye").

340 DŌGEN'S *SHŌBŌGENZŌ* VOLUME III

却、まことに附嘱の誰知なり。臨濟門下には、ただ三聖のみなり。法兄法
弟におよぼし、一列せしむべからず。まさに明窓下安排なり。臨濟・三聖
の因縁は佛祖なり。今日臨濟の附属は、昔日靈山の附屬なり。しかあれ
ば、臨濟宗と稱すべからざる道理、あきらけし。

Linji does not say, "Do not let my Zen school be extinguished." He
does not say, "Do not let my Linji school be extinguished." He does not
say, "Do not let my school be extinguished." He just says, "Do not let
my treasury of the true dharma eye be extinguished." Clearly, we should
realize that the great way correctly transmitted by the buddhas and ancestors should not be called "the Zen school," should not be called "the
Linji school." We should have no dreams of calling it "the Zen school."
Even though "extinguished" is the principle and form of the treasury of
the true dharma eye, this is how it is bequeathed.[71] The "extinguished"
"with this blind donkey" is truly the "who would have known" of the
bequeathal.[72] Among the followers of Linji, Sansheng is the only one;
he should not be compared with, or ranked with, his elder and younger
dharma brothers.[73] Truly, he is placed under the bright window.[74] The episode of Linji and Sansheng is the buddhas and ancestors. The bequeathal of Linji today is the bequeathal of Vulture Peak yesterday.[75] Therefore,
the reason we should not call it the Linji school is obvious.

---

71 **"extinguished" is the principle and form of the treasury of the true dharma eye**
(*mekkyaku wa shōbōgenzō no rishō nari* 滅却は正法眼藏の理象なり): I.e., the treasury
of the true dharma eye is by its nature and characteristics "extinguished." The term *rishō*
理象 ("principle and form") does not occur elsewhere in the *Shōbōgenzō*; it is generally
understood as equivalent to the common *riji* 理事 ("principle and phenomena").

72 **The "extinguished" "with this blind donkey" is truly the "who would have
known" of the bequeathal** (*kō sha katsuro hen no mekkyaku, makoto ni fuzoku no sui
chi nari* 向遮瞎驢邊の滅却、まことに附嘱の誰知なり): I.e., the extinction of Linji's
teaching that takes place with Sansheng is precisely the "who would have known" that
Linji transmits to Sansheng. The translation labors to preserve something of Dōgen's
play with the terms of Linji's statement.

73 **Among the followers of Linji, Sansheng is the only one** (*Rinzai monka ni wa,
tada Sanshō nomi nari* 臨濟門下には、ただ三聖のみなり): It is unclear why and in
what sense Dōgen singles out Sansheng among Linji's followers. Perhaps because his
version of the exchange (unlike most other versions) has Linji "entrusting" (*shoku* 嘱)
Sansheng, Dōgen takes Sansheng as the chief inheritor of Linji's teachings; the Linji
lineage, however, is traditionally held to descend, not from Sansheng, but from Linji's
disciple Xinghua Cunjiang 興化存獎 (830-888).

74 **placed under the bright window** (*meisō ka anbai* 明窓下安排): A fixed idiom for
one at home in the study of sūtras and Chan discourse records (*goroku* 語録); see Supplementary Notes, s.v. "Bright windows."

75 **The bequeathal of Linji today is the bequeathal of Vulture Peak yesterday** (*kon-
nichi Rinzai no fuzoku wa, sekijitsu Ryōzen no fuzoku nari* 今日臨濟の附属は、昔日靈
山の附屬なり): I.e., Linji's bequest to Sansheng is the same as Buddha Śākyamuni's
bequest to Mahākāśyapa on Gṛdhrakūṭa.

44. The Way of the Buddhas *Butsudō* 佛道   343

* * * * *

[44:35] {1:483}

雲門山匡眞大師、そのかみは陳尊宿に學す、黄檗の兒孫なりぬべし、のち
に雪峰に嗣す。この師、また正法眼藏を雲門宗と稱すべしといはず。門人
また潙仰・臨濟の妄稱を妄稱としらず、雲門宗の稱を新立せり。匡眞大師
の宗旨、もし立宗の稱をこころざさば、佛法の身心なりとゆるしがたから
ん。いま宗の稱を稱するときは、たとへば、帝者を匹夫と稱ぜんがごと
し。

Great Master Kuangzhen of Mount Yunmen in the past studied with
Venerable Chen; he would have been the grandson of Huangbo.[76] Later,
he succeeded Xuefeng.[77] This master did not say that the treasury of the
true dharma eye should be called the Yunmen school. His followers,
not realizing that the false names Weiyang and Linji were false names,
newly established the name Yunmen school. If the tenets of Great Master
Kuangzhen had aspired to a name that established a school, it would be
difficult to acknowledge him as the body and mind of the buddha dharma. When it is now called by the name of a school, it is like calling the
emperor a commoner.

* * * * *

[44:36]

清涼院大法眼禪師は、地藏院の嫡嗣なり。玄沙院の法孫なり。宗旨あり、
あやまりなし。大法眼は、署する師號なり。これを正法眼藏の號として、
法眼宗の稱を立すべし、といへることを、千言のなかに一言なし、萬句の
うちに一句なし。しかあるを、門人、また法眼宗の稱を立す。法眼もしい
まを化せば、いまの妄稱法眼宗の道をけづるべし。法眼禪師すでにゆき
て、この患をすくふ人なし。たとひ千萬年ののちなりとも、法眼禪師に孝
せん人は、この法眼宗の稱を稱とすることなかれ。これ本孝大法眼禪師な
り。おほよそ雲門・法眼等は、青原高祖の遠孫なり、道骨つたはれ、法髓
つたはれり。

Chan Master Da Fayan of Qingliang Cloister was the legitimate successor of Dizang Cloister; he was a dharma grandchild of Xuansha Cloister.[78] He had an essential point and no mistakes. "Da Fayan" is his offi-

---

76 **Great Master Kuangzhen of Mount Yunmen** (*Unmonzan Kyōshin daishi* 雲門山
匡眞大師): I.e., Yunmen Wenyan 雲門文偃, from whom the Yunmen 雲門 school takes
its name.

Venerable Chen (*Chin sonshuku* 陳尊宿): I.e., Muzhou Daozong 睦州道蹤 (also known
as Daoming 道明; dates unknown), a disciple of Huangbo 黄檗.

77 **Xuefeng** (*Seppō* 雪峰): I.e., Xuefeng Yicun 雪峰義存 (822-908).

78 **Chan Master Da Fayan of Qingliang Cloister** (*Seiryō in Dai Hōgen zenji* 清涼院
大法眼禪師): I.e., Fayan Wenyi 法眼文益, from whom the Fayan 法眼 school takes its
name.

344   DŌGEN'S *SHŌBŌGENZŌ* VOLUME III

cially recorded teacher's title. In his thousand words he had not a single word, in his ten thousand lines he had not a single line, in which he said that the name "Fayan school" should be established as the name of the treasury of the true dharma eye. Nevertheless, his followers established the name "Fayan school." If Fayan were converting people today, he would erase the term for the current falsely named Fayan school. With Chan Master Fayan already departed, there is no one to save us from this calamity. Even a thousand or ten thousand years later, people who would be filial to Chan Master Fayan must not take the name "Fayan school" as a name. This is basic filiality toward Chan Master Great Fayan. In sum, Yunmen and Fayan are the distant descendants of the Eminent Ancestor Qingyuan.[79] They transmitted the bones of the way; they transmitted the marrow of the dharma.

* * * * *

[44:37] {1:484}

高祖悟本大師は、雲巖に嗣法す。雲巖は藥山大師の正嫡なり、藥山は石頭大師の正嫡なり、石頭大師は青原高祖の一子なり。齊肩の二三あらず、道業ひとり正傳せり。佛道の正命なほ東地にのこれるは、石頭大師もらさず正傳せしちからなり。

    The Eminent Ancestor Great Master Wuben inherited the dharma from Yunyan.[80] Yunyan was the legitimate heir of Great Master Yaoshan; Yaoshan was the legitimate heir of Great Master Shitou.[81] Great Master Shitou was the only child of Eminent Ancestor Qingyuan. There are not two or three of equal stature; he correctly transmitted the work of the way. It is on the strength of Great Master Shitou's transmission without loss that the correct life of the way of the buddhas still remains in the Eastern Earth.

Dizang Cloister (*Jizō in* 地藏院): I.e., Luohan Guichen 羅漢桂琛 (867-928).

Xuansha Cloister (*Gensha in* 玄沙院): I.e., Xuansha Shibei 玄沙師備 (835-908).

79 **Eminent Ancestor Qingyuan** (*Seigen kōso* 青原高祖): I.e., Qingyuan Xingsi 青原行思, one of the two disciples of the Sixth Ancestor, Huineng 慧能, from whom the five houses traced their lineages.

80 **Eminent Ancestor Great Master Wuben** (*kōso Gohon daishi* 高祖悟本大師): I.e., Dongshan Liangjie 洞山良价, from whom the Caodong 曹洞 school takes its name. Dōgen here begins a discussion of his own tradition.

Yunyan (*Ungan* 雲巖): I.e., Yunyan Tansheng 雲巖曇晟 (782-841).

81 **Great Master Yaoshan** (*Yakusan daishi* 藥山大師): I.e., Yaoshan Weiyan 藥山惟儼 (751-834).

Great Master Shitou (*Sekito daishi* 石頭大師): I.e., Shitou Xiqian 石頭希遷.

44. The Way of the Buddhas *Butsudō* 佛道   345

[44:38]

青原高祖は、曹溪古佛の同時に、曹溪の化儀を青原に化儀せり。在世に出
世せしめて、出世を一世に見聞するは、正嫡のうへの正嫡なるべし、高祖
のなかの高祖なるべし。雄參學、雌出世にあらず。そのときの齊肩、いま
拔群なり。學者、ことにしるべきところなり。

At the same time as the Old Buddha of Caoxi, Eminent Ancestor
Qingyuan practiced Caoxi's teaching methods at Qingyuan. That he was
made to appear in the world during his lifetime and he saw his appearance in the world in the same generation means he must have been the
legitimate heir among legitimate heirs, must have been the eminent ancestor among eminent ancestors.[82] It is not a case of strong study and
weak appearance in the world.[83] Those of his stature at his time would be
outstanding today. This is something students should realize.

[44:39]

曹溪古佛、ちなみに現般涅槃をもて人天を化せし席末に、石頭すすみて所
依の師を請す。古佛ちなみに尋思去としめして、尋讓去といはず。しかあ
ればすなはち、古佛の正法眼藏、ひとり青原高祖の正傳なり。たとひ同得
道の神足をゆるすとも、高祖はなほ正神足の獨歩なり。曹溪古佛、すでに
青原を、わが子を子ならしむ。子の父の、父の父とある、得髓あきらかな
り、祖宗の正嗣なることあきらかなり。

On the occasion when the Old Buddha of Caoxi was converting humans and devas by manifesting his complete nirvāṇa, from the last seats
Shitou came forward and requested a master on whom to rely. On that
occasion, the Old Buddha indicated that he "go inquire of Si"; he did
not say that he "go inquire of Rang."[84] Therefore, the treasury of the
true dharma of the Old Buddha was correctly transmitted to the Eminent
Ancestor Qingyuan alone. Though we may grant that they were spir-

---

82   **That he was made to appear in the world during his lifetime** (*zaise ni shusse
seshimete* 在世に出世せしめて): I.e., was put forward as a teacher while his master,
Huineng 慧能, was still active. The following "same generation" (*isse* 一世) similarly
refers to the same generation as his teacher.

83   **It is not a case of strong study and weak appearance in the world** (*yū sangaku,
shi shusse ni arazu* 雄參學、雌出世にあらず): An unusual expression, the exact meaning of which is subject to interpretation. It is often taken to mean that Qingyuan was the
equal of Caoxi, but it could also be understood to mean that Qingyuan was as strong a
teacher as he was a student.

84   **"go inquire of Si"** (*jin Shi ko* 尋思去): I.e., go visit Qingyuan Xingsi 青原行思.
This advice is recorded in an amusing story in the *Jingde chuandeng lu* 景德傳燈錄
(T.2076.51:240a27-b5), in which Shitou initially takes Huineng's words, *xunsi qu* 尋思
去, to mean "go ponder it" and goes off to meditate.

"go inquire of Rang" (*jin Jō ko* 尋讓去): Reference to Nanyue Huairang 南嶽懷讓, the
disciple of Huineng from whom the lineages of the Weiyang 潙仰 and Linji 臨濟 schools
descend.

346 DŌGEN'S *SHŌBŌGENZŌ* VOLUME III

itual feet who gained the way together, the Eminent Ancestor was the sole pace of the real spiritual foot.[85] Since the Old Buddha of Caoxi had Qingyuan make a child of his child, the father of the child would be the father of the father; that he attained the marrow is obvious; that he was the legitimate heir of the ancestors is obvious.[86]

[44:40]

洞山大師、まさに青原四世の嫡嗣として、正法眼藏を正傳し、涅槃妙心開眼す。このほか、さらに別傳なし、別宗なし。大師かつて、曹洞宗と稱すべし、と示衆する拳頭なし、瞬目なし。また門人のなかに、庸流まじはらざれば、洞山宗と稱する門人なし、いはんや曹洞宗といはんや。

Great Master Dongshan, as the legitimate heir in the fourth generation of Qingyuan, correctly transmitted the treasury of the true dharma eye and opened the eye of the wondrous mind of nirvāṇa. Beside this, there is no separate transmission, there is no separate school. The Great Master never had a fist or a blink of the eye in which he instructs the assembly that they should be called the Caodong school. Among his followers as well, because they were not corrupted by mediocre types, there was no follower who called them the Dongshan school, much less said they were the Caodong school.

[44:41] {1:485}

曹洞宗の稱は、曹山を稱しくわふるならん。もししかあらば、雲居・同安をもくわへのすべきなり。雲居は人中天上の導師なり、曹山よりも尊崇なり。はかりしりぬ、この曹洞の稱は、傍輩の臭袋、おのれに齊肩ならんとて、曹洞宗の稱を稱するなり。まことに、白日あきらかなれども、浮雲、しもをおほふがごとし。

The name "Caodong school" may include the name "Caoshan."[87] If

---

85 **Though we may grant that they were spiritual feet who gained the way together, the Eminent Ancestor was the sole pace of the real spiritual foot** (*tatoi dō tokudō no jinsoku o yurusutomo, kōso wa nao shō jinsoku no doppo nari* たとひ同得道の神足をゆるすとも、高祖はなほ正神足の獨歩なり): I.e., although both Qingyuan 青原 and Nanyue 南嶽 may have been top disciples of Huineng, it was the former alone who was the authentic inheritor of the Sixth Ancestor's teachings. Dōgen puns here on the term *jinsoku* 神足 ("spiritual foot"), which is used both for paranormal physical powers (from the Sanskrit *ṛddhi-pāda*) and for a superior disciple.

86 **Since the Old Buddha of Caoxi had Qingyuan make a child of his child, the father of the child would be the father of the father** (*Sōkei kobutsu, sude ni Seigen o, waga shi o shi narashimu. shi no fu no, fu no fu to aru* 曹溪古佛、すでに青原を、わが子を子ならしむ。子の父の、父の父とある): I.e., Huineng 慧能 had his disciple Qingyuan 青原 take his disciple Shitou 石頭 as a disciple; Huineng was thus both the master of Shitou and the master of Shitou's master, Qingyuan.

87 **"Caoshan"** (*Sōzan* 曹山): I.e., Dongshan's disciple Caoshan Benji 曹山本寂. An alternative etymology of the name "Caodong" 曹洞 derives the element *cao* 曹 from the Sixth Ancestor's mountain name Caoxi 曹溪.

44. The Way of the Buddhas *Butsudō* 佛道   347

this is the case, Yunju and Tong'an ought also to be included.[88] Yunju was a guide among humans and the heavens above, more revered than Caoshan. So it is obvious regarding this name "Caodong" that the stinking skin bags of a marginal faction, seeking to be of equal stature, called themselves by this name "Caodong." Truly this is a case where, "though the noon sun is bright, the floating clouds cover it below."[89]

* * * * *

[44:42]

先師いはく、いま諸方、獅子の座にのぼるものおほし、人天の師とあるものおほしといへども、知得佛法道理箇渾無。

My former master said,[90]

Nowadays, in all quarters, while there may be many who ascend the lion seat, many who would be the teachers of humans and devas, *there are none at all who understand the principle of the buddha dharma*.[91]

[44:43]

このゆえに、きほうて五宗の宗を立し、あやまりて言句の句にとどこほれるは、眞箇に佛祖の怨家なり。あるひは、黄龍の南禪師の一派を稱して黄龍宗と稱しきたれりといへども、その派、とほからずあやまりをしるべし。おほよそ世尊現在、かつて佛宗と稱しましまさず、靈山宗と稱せず、祇園宗といはず、我心宗といはず、佛心宗といはず、いづれの佛語にか佛心宗と稱する。いまの人、なにをもてか佛心宗と稱する。世尊、なにのゆえにか、あながちに心を宗と稱せん、宗、なににによりてか、かならずしも心ならん。もし佛心宗あらば、佛身宗あるべし、佛眼宗あるべし、佛耳宗あるべし、佛鼻舌等宗あるべし、佛髓宗・佛骨宗・佛脚宗・佛國宗等あるべし、いまこれなし。しるべし、佛心宗の稱は僞稱なり、といふこと。

Therefore, those competing to establish the schools of the five schools, those mistakenly stuck on the lines of words and lines, are truly the enemies of the buddhas and ancestors. Again, the faction of Chan Master

---

88 **Yunju** (*Ungo* 雲居); **Tong'an** (*Dōan* 同安): I.e., Dongshan's disciple Yunju Daoying 雲居道膺 (d. 902) and Yunju's disciple Tong'an Daopi 同安道丕 (dates unknown), whose lineage (unlike that of Caoshan 曹山) continued into the Song dynasty and was inherited by Dōgen.

89 **"though the noon sun is bright, the floating clouds cover it below"** (*hakujitsu akiraka naredomo, fuun, shimo o ōfu* 白日あきらかなれども、浮雲、しもをおほふ): Paraphrasing the proverb from the *Huainanzi* 淮南子 (Qisu xun 齊俗訓, KR.3j0010.017-006a):

日月欲明、浮雲蓋之。

The sun and moon would be bright, but the floating clouds cover them.

90 **My former master** (*senshi* 先師): I.e., Tiantong Rujing 天童如淨. The source is unknown.

91 **lion seat** (*shishi no za* 獅子の座): The position of abbot; from the seat of a buddha, after the "lion throne" of Indian royalty.

348   DŌGEN'S *SHŌBŌGENZŌ* VOLUME III

Nan of Huanglong has been called the "Huanglung school," but it will not be long before this faction is known to be mistaken.[92]

In sum, when the Buddha was present, he never called [his teachings] "the Buddha school," or called them "the Vulture Peak school," or spoke of "the Jetavana school," or spoke of the "My Mind school," or spoke of the "Buddha Mind school."[93] Where in the words of the Buddha does he use the name "Buddha Mind school"? Why do people today use the name "Buddha Mind school"? Why would the World-Honored One necessarily call the mind a school? Why would a school necessarily be the mind? If there is a Buddha Mind school, there should be a Buddha Body school, should be a Buddha Eye school, should be a Buddha Ear school, should be a Buddha Nose or Tongue school, should be a Buddha Marrow school, Buddha Bones school, Buddha Feet school, Buddha Land school, and so on. Now, there are none of these. We should realize the fact that the name "Buddha Mind school" is a false name.

[44:44] {1:486}

釋迦牟尼佛、ひろく十方佛土中の諸法實相を擧拈し、十方佛土中をとくとき、十方佛土のなかに、いづれの宗を建立せりととかず。宗の稱、もし佛祖の法ならば、佛國にあるべし、佛國にあらば、佛説すべし。佛不説なり、しりぬ、佛國の調度にあらず。祖道せず、しりぬ、祖域の家具にあらずといふことを。ただ、人にわらはるるのみにあらざらん、諸佛のために制禁せられん、また自己のためにわらはれん。つつしんで宗稱することなかれ、佛法に五家あり、といふことなかれ。

When Buddha Śākyamuni takes up the real marks of the dharmas throughout the buddha lands of the ten directions and preaches of the buddha lands of the ten directions, he does not preach that he has constructed some school in the buddha lands of the ten directions. If the designation "school" is the dharma of the buddhas and ancestors, it should be in the land of the buddha; if it is in the land of the buddha, the buddha should preach it. The buddha does not preach it; we know it is not an implement in the land of the buddha. The ancestors do not talk of it; we know it is not a furnishing in the region of the ancestors. Not only will you be laughed at by people; you will be prohibited by the buddhas and

92   **Chan Master Nan of Huanglong** (*Ōryū no Nan zenji* 黃龍の南禪師): I.e., Huanglung Huinan 黃龍慧南 (1002-1069), considered the founder of the Huanglong (J. Ōryū 黃龍) school, one of the two lineages of the Linji 臨濟 house current in the Song. Dōgen's Japanese teacher, Myōzen 明全, belonged to this lineage; but most of Dōgen's contemporaries in the Linji (or Japanese Rinzai) school belonged to the more prominent Yangqi (J. Yōgi 楊岐) school, founded by Yangqi Fanghui 楊岐方會 (995-1049).

93   **"Vulture Peak school"** (*Ryōzen shū* 靈山宗); **"Jetavana school"** (*Gion shū* 祇園宗): Two places with which Buddha Śākyamuni's ministry was associated: Vulture Peak (*Ryōjusen* 靈鷲山; S. *Gṛdhrakūṭa*) and the Jetavana Vihāra (*Gion Shōja* 祇園精舍) at Anāthapiṇḍada.

44. The Way of the Buddhas *Butsudō* 佛道 349

laughed at by yourself. I beg of you, do not call it a school. There is no such thing as the five houses in the buddha dharma.

* * * * *

[44:45]

後來、智聰といふ小兒子ありて、祖師の一道・兩道をひろひあつめて、五家の宗派といひ、人天眼目となづく。人、これをわきまへず、初心・晩學のやから、まこととおもひて、衣領にかくしもてるもあり。人天眼目にあらず、人天の眼目をくらますなり。いかでか瞎却正法眼藏の功德あらん。

Lately, there was a little child named Zhicong, who collected one word or two words of the ancestral masters, said they were the denominations of the five houses, and called it *The Eye of Humans and Devas*.[94] People not knowing how to assess it, beginners and latecomers think it true, and some even keep it hidden in their robes. It is not "the eye of humans and devas"; it blinds the eye of human and devas. How could it have the virtue of blinding the treasury of the true dharma eye?

[44:46]

かの人天眼目は、智聰上座、淳熙戊申十二月のころ、天台山萬年寺にして編集せり。後來の所作なりとも、道是あらば聽許すべし。これは、狂亂なり、愚暗なり、參學眼なし、行脚眼なし、いはんや見佛祖眼あらんや、もちふるべからず。智聰といふべからず、愚蒙といふべし。その人をしらず、人にあはざるが、言句をあつめて、その人とある人の言句をひろはず。しりぬ、人をしらずといふことを。

This *Eye of Humans and Devas* was collected by Senior Seat Zhicong, in the twelfth month of the senior earth year of the monkey, in Chunxi, at the Wannian Monastery on Mount Tiantai.[95] Though it is a late production, if its words were right, we should attend to it. It is craziness; it is foolishness. It lacks the eye of study; it lacks the eye of pilgrimage. How much less could it have the eye that sees the buddhas and ancestors? We should not use it. He should not be called "Zhicong" ["wise and bright"]; he should be called "Yumeng" ["stupid and dull"]. He who does not know that person, who does not encounter the person, in collecting words and lines, does not pick words and lines of the person who would be that person.[96] We know that he does not know the person.

94 **Zhicong** (*Chisō* 智聰): I.e., Huiyan Zhizhao 晦巖智昭, author of the *Rentian yanmu* 人天眼目 (T.2006); see above, Note 48.

95 **the twelfth month of the senior earth year of the monkey, in Chunxi** (*Junki boshin jūni gatsu* 淳熙戊申十二月): I.e., the twelfth lunar month of the fifth stem ninth branch of the cyclical year of the Chunxi 淳熙 era [December 1188-January 1189]. This information occurs in the preface to the work, at T.2006.48:300a12, a19.

96 **that person** (*sono hito* その人): An expression occurring several times in the *Shōbōgenzō* in the sense "a real person," "a person with real understanding."

350 DŌGEN'S *SHŌBŌGENZŌ* VOLUME III

[44:47]

震旦國の教學のともがら宗稱するは、齊肩の彼彼あるによりてなり。いま
佛祖正法眼藏の附屬嫡嫡せり。齊肩あるべからず、混ずべき彼彼なし。

That those who study the teachings in the Land of Cīnasthāna called
themselves schools was because there were others of equal stature.[97]
Now, the treasury of the true dharma eye of the buddhas and ancestors
has been bequeathed from heir to heir; there are none of equal stature,
there are no others that could be confused with it.

[44:48] {1:487}

かくのごとくなるに、いまの杜撰長老等、みだりに宗の稱をもはらする、
自專のくはだて、佛道をおそれず。佛道は、なんぢが佛道にあらず、諸佛
祖の佛道なり、佛道の佛道なり。

Despite this, the illiterate elders nowadays always rashly call themselves a school; scheming on their own, they are not in awe of the way
of the buddhas. The way of the buddhas is not your way of the buddhas:
it is the buddhas' and ancestors' way of the buddhas; it is the way of the
buddhas' way of the buddhas.

[44:49]

太公謂文王曰、天下者、非一人之天下、天下之天下也。

The Grand Duke said to King Wen, "The realm is not one person's
realm: it is the realm's realm."[98]

[44:50]

しかあれば、俗士なほこれ智あり、この道あり。佛祖屋裏兒、みだりに佛
祖の大道をほしきままに愚蒙にしたがへて、立宗の自稱することなかれ、
おほきなるをかしなり、佛道人にあらず。宗稱すべくば、世尊みづから稱
しましますべし。世尊、すでに自稱しましまさず、兒孫として、なにゆえ
にか滅後に稱することあらん。たれ人か世尊よりも善巧ならん、善巧あら
ずば、その益なからん。もしまた、佛祖古來の道に違背して自宗を自立せ
ば、たれかなんぢが宗を宗とする佛兒孫あらん。照古觀今の參學すべし、
みだりなることなかれ。世尊在世に一毫もたがはざらんとする、なほ百千
萬分の一分におよばざることをうれへ、およべるをよろこび、違せざら
んとねがふを、遺弟の畜念とせるのみなり。これをもて多生の値遇奉覲を
ちぎるべし、これをもて多生の見佛聞法をねがふべし。ことさら世尊在世

---

97 **That those who study the teachings in the Land of Cīnasthāna called themselves
schools was because there were others of equal stature** (*Shintan koku no kyōgaku no
tomogara shūshō suru wa, seiken no hihi aru ni yorite nari* 震旦國の教學のともがら
宗稱するは、齊肩の彼彼あるによりてなり): I.e., the custom of designating schools in
Chinese Buddhism reflects the fact that there were various factions with more or less
equal claim to represent the religion.

98 **The Grand Duke** (*taikō* 太公): After a passage in the *Liu tao* 六韜 (*Wen tao* 文韜,
Wenshi 文師, KR.3b0002.001-2a); an almost identical passage also occurs at *Wu tao* 武
韜, Faqi 發啓, KR.3b0002.002-1a).

44. The Way of the Buddhas *Butsudō* 佛道   351

の化儀にそむきて、宗の稱を立せん、如來の弟子にあらず、祖師の兒孫に
あらず、重逆よりもおもし。たちまちに如來の無上菩提をおもくせず、自
宗を自專する、前來を輕忽し、前來をそむくなり。前來もしらずといふべ
し、世尊在日の功德を信ぜざるなり、かれらが屋裏に佛法あるべからず。

Thus, even the secular gentleman has this wisdom, has these words. Children within the house of the buddhas and ancestors must not arbitrarily follow "Stupid and Dull" in calling the great way of the buddhas and ancestors by the names of schools they establish. This is a major violation; not [worthy of] people of the way of the buddhas. If we should use the term "school," the World-Honored One would himself have used it. When the World-Honored One did not himself use it, how as his descendants can we use it after his extinction? Who is more skilled than the World-Honored One? Were he not skilled, we would not benefit. Again, when you turn against the traditional way of the buddhas and ancestors and independently establish your own school, which of the descendants of the buddha would take your school as a school? We should study by illuminating the past and observing the present. Do not be reckless. Trying not to differ one hair from the time when the World-Honored One was in the world, to lament our failure to reach even one part in a billion, to rejoice in reaching it, to aspire not to differ from it — only this is what the disciples left behind make their repeated thought. So we should vow to meet and serve him for many lives; so we should aspire to see the Buddha and hear the dharma for many lives. Those who, violating the teaching method when the World-Honored One was in the world, would intentionally set up the name of a school are not the disciples of the Tathāgata, are not the descendants of the ancestral masters; it is heavier than the grave offenses.[99] Taking lightly the unsurpassed bodhi of the Tathāgata, impulsively to devote oneself exclusively to one's own school is to neglect antecedents, to depart from antecedents. We must say they do not know the antecedents. They do not believe in the virtues of the days of the World-Honored One. Within their house, there can be no buddha dharma.

[44:51] {1:488}
しかあればすなはち、學佛の道業を正傳せんには、宗の稱を見聞すべから
ず。佛佛祖祖、附屬し正傳するは、正法眼藏無上菩提なり。佛祖所有の法
は、みな佛附屬しきたれり、さらに剩法のあらたなるあらず。この道理、
すなはち法骨道髓なり。

Thus, in correctly transmitting the work of the way of studying Buddhism, we should not see or hear the term "school." What buddha after buddha and ancestor after ancestor bequeath and correctly transmit is

---

99   **grave offenses** (*jūgyaku* 重逆): The serious violations of the monastic code: e.g., the ten grave violations (*jū jūzai* 十重罪) and the five heinous offenses (*gogyaku* 五逆).

352 DŌGEN'S *SHŌBŌGENZŌ* VOLUME III

the unsurpassed bodhi of the treasury of the true dharma eye. The dharma possessed by the buddhas and ancestors has all been bequeathed by the Buddha; there is no further additional dharma. This principle is the bones of the dharma, the marrow of the way.

正法眼藏佛道第四十四
Treasury of the True Dharma Eye
The Way of the Buddhas
Number 44

[Ryūmonji MS:]
爾時寬元元年癸卯九月十六日、在越州吉田縣吉峰寺示衆
Presented to the assembly at Kippō Monastery, Yoshida District, Esshū;
sixteenth day, ninth month of the junior water year of the rabbit, the
first year of Kangen [30 October 1243]

[*Himitsu* MS:]
尒時寬元々年癸卯九月十六日、在越州吉田縣吉峯寺。道
At Kippō Monastery, Yoshida District, Esshū; sixteenth day, ninth
month of the junior water year of the rabbit, the first year of Kangen
[30 October 1243]. Dō[100]

同癸卯十月廿三日夜三更書寫之。懷奘
Copied this, the third watch of the night, twenty-third day, tenth month,
junior water year of the rabbit, the same era [24 November 1243]. Ejō

同乙巳六月廿六日又交合、奧書云處也
Collated the twenty-sixth day, sixth month, junior wood year of the
snake, the same era [21 July 1245]. Stated in a colophon.[101]

---

100 This and the following two colophons are from the "Butsudō" text listed as volume 1, number 9, in the *Himitsu* collection. The odd final glyph *dō* 道 here would appear to be a copyist's error for Dōgen 道元.

101 Copyist unknown.

Treasury of the True Dharma Eye

Number 45

Secret Words

Mitsugo

密語

Secret Words

Mitsugo

INTRODUCTION

This essay was composed at Kippōji in the autumn of 1243. It represents number 45 in the seventy-five-chapter *Shōbōgenzō* and number 51 in the Honzan version; it is not found in the sixty-chapter compilation but is preserved in the twenty-eight-text *Himitsu Shōbōgenzō*, where it is listed as number 4 of fascicle 2.

The essay focuses on a single kōan, featuring the ninth-century monk Yunju Daoying 雲居道膺, a disciple of Dongshan Liangjie 洞山良价, on the claim that Buddha Śākyamuni had "secret words" (*mitsugo* 密語; also sometimes written as 蜜語) understood only by his disciple Mahākāśyapa. The claim reflects the tradition that Zen was first transmitted on Vulture Peak, when the Buddha held up a flower, and Mahākāśyapa smiled. Dōgen strongly rejects the notion that the Buddha's "secret words" refers to a truth beyond language conveyed through his act of holding up the flower. Rather, he says, "secret words" refers to what is most intimately true — a secret possessed by everyone and expressed wherever authentic Buddhism is taught and practiced.

The relatively short essay ends with an elegant verse by the twelfth-century figure Xuedou Zhijian 雪竇智鑑, which likens "secret words" to blossoms falling in the night, their fragrance perfuming the streams of the city.

355

正法眼藏第四十五
Treasury of the True Dharma Eye
Number 45

密語

Secret Words

[45:1] {1:489}
諸佛之所護念の大道を見成公案するに、汝亦如是、吾亦如是、善自護持、いまに證契せり。

When they express the great way that "*the buddhas bear in mind*" as "the realized kōan," [the words] "*you're also like this, I'm also like this*," "*protect it well*" have verified the accord in the present.[1]

[45:2]
雲居山弘覺大師、因官人送供問曰、世尊有密語、迦葉不覆藏。如何是世尊密語。大師召曰、尚書。其人應諾。大師云、會麼。尚書曰、不會。大師云、汝若不會、世尊密語、汝若會、迦葉不覆藏。

---

1 **When they express the great way that "the buddhas bear in mind" as "the realized kōan"** (*shobutsu shi shogonen no daidō o genjō kōan suru ni* 諸佛之所護念の大道を見成公案するに): "What the buddhas bear in mind" (*shobutsu shi shogonen* 諸佛之所護念) is a fixed phrase found widely in the canon; here, it alludes to the saying of the Sixth Ancestor, Huineng 慧能, in the famous exchange with his student Nanyue Huairang 南嶽懷讓 (677-744) (e.g., at *shinji Shōbōgenzō* 眞字正法眼藏, DZZ.5:178, case 101; see Supplementary Notes, s.v. "What thing is it that comes like this?"), which Dōgen goes on to quote in this sentence. When Nanyue says he is not defiled by practice and verification, Huineng says:

祇此不染污、是諸佛之所護念。汝亦如是、吾亦如是、乃至西天諸祖亦如是。

"Just this 'not defiled' is what the buddhas bear in mind. You're also like this, I'm also like this, and all the ancestors of Sindh in the West [i. e., India] are also like this."

The English "express . . . as the realized kōan" strives to render Dōgen's use here of the expression *genjō kōan* 見成公案 ("realized case") as a transitive verb, the agent of which is unexpressed; the translation takes it as Huineng's words, but one might also assume an unstated "one" or "we." See Supplementary Notes, s.v. "Realized kōan."

"protect it well" (*zen ji go ji* 善自護持): A common admonition to the student; while not in most versions of the Sixth Ancestor's saying, its presence here may reflect its occurrence in the version recorded in the *Rentian yanmu* 人天眼目 (T.2006.48:322b3-4).

have verified the accord in the present (*ima ni shōkai seri* いまに證契せり): Probably meaning that the truth of Huineng's words are verified here and now.

356 DŌGEN'S *SHŌBŌGENZŌ* VOLUME III

Great Master Hongjue of Mount Yunju, was once asked by an official presenting offerings, "The World-Honored One has secret words; for Kāśyapa, they are not concealed.[2] What are the secret words of the World-Honored One?"

The Great Master called him, saying, "Minister."

The man responded. The Great Master said, "Do you understand?"

The minister said, "I don't understand."

The Great Master said, "If you don't understand, it's the secret words of the World-Honored One; if you do understand, it's not concealed for Kāśyapa."

[45:3]

大師者、青原五世の嫡孫と現成して、天人師なり、盡十方界の大善知識なり。有情を化し、無情を化す。　四十六佛の佛嫡として、佛祖のために説法す。三峰庵主の住裏には、天厨送供す。傳法得道のときより、送供の境界を超越せり。

The Great Master appeared as the legitimate successor in the fifth generation from Qingyuan; he was the teacher to devas and men, a great wise friend to all throughout the ten directions.[3] He converted the sentient; he converted the insentient. As the buddha successor of forty-six buddhas, he preached the dharma for the buddhas and ancestors.[4] Where he was residing as master of the Sanfeng Hermitage, he was presented with offerings from the kitchens of the devas; after he received transmission of the dharma and gained the way, he transcended the realm of the offerings.[5]

2　**Great Master Hongjue of Mount Yunju** (*Ungozan Gukaku daishi* 雲居山弘覺大師): I.e., Yunju Daoying 雲居道膺 (d. 902), disciple of Dongshan Liangjie 洞山良价 (807-869). This conversation (which can be found at *Jingde chuandeng lu* 景德傳燈錄, T.2076.51:335c1-5; *shinji Shōbōgenzō* 眞字正法眼藏, DZZ.5:146, case 34; etc.) reflects the famous founding legend of Zen, in which Buddha Śākyamuni wordlessly transmitted the dharma to the First Ancestor, Mahākāśyapa, on Vulture Peak; see below, Note 11.

3　**the fifth generation from Qingyuan** (*Seigen gose* 青原五世): I.e., fifth in the line of masters descended from Qingyuan Xingsi 青原行思 (d. 740), one of the two leading disciples of the Sixth Ancestor.

4　**the buddha successor of forty-six buddhas** (*shijūroku butsu no butteki* 四十六佛の佛嫡): I.e., forty-sixth in the lineage of the seven buddhas, the thirty-four ancestors in India and China to Qingyuan, and the five generations from Qingyuan to Yunju; see Supplementary Notes, s.v. "Buddhas and ancestors" and "Seven buddhas."

5　**the Sanfeng Hermitage** (*Sanpōan* 三峰庵): The exact location is uncertain; perhaps near Dongshan 洞山, in present-day Jiangxi province. Yunju is said to have stayed here before studying with Dongshan.

he was presented with offerings from the kitchens of the devas (*tenchū sōku su* 天厨送供す): Dōgen's source for this legend that Yunju was fed by the gods is unknown;

45. Secret Words *Mitsugo* 密語　　357

[45:4] {1:490}

いまの道取する世尊有密語、迦葉不覆藏は、四十六佛の相承といへども、四十六代の本來面目として、　匪從人得なり、不從外來なり、不是本得なり、未嘗新條なり。この一段事の密語の現成なる、ただ釋迦牟尼世尊のみ密語あるにあらず、諸佛祖みな密語あり。すでに世尊なるは、かならず密語あり、密語あれば、さだめて迦葉不覆藏あり。百千の世尊あれば、百千の迦葉ある道理を、わすれず參學すべきなり。參學すといふは、一時に會取せんとおもはず、百廻・千廻も審細功夫して、かたきものをきらんと經營するがごとくすべし。かたる人あらば、たちどころに會取すべし、とおもふべからず。

The words said here, "*The World-Honored One has secret words; for Kāśyapa, they are not concealed,*" while they may be the inheritance of forty-six buddhas, as the original face of forty-six generations, they are not got from another, do not come from outside, were not originally possessed, have never been a new item.[6] That this incident is the expression of "secret words" does not mean that only the World-Honored One Śākyamuni has "secret words": the buddhas and ancestors all have "secret words." Since they are "World-Honored Ones," invariably they have "secret words"; when they have "secret words," definitely there is "*for Kāśyapa, they are not concealed.*" We should study this without forgetting the principle that, when there are a hundred thousand World-Honored Ones, there are a hundred thousand Kāśyapas. To study this means, without thinking to understand it all at once, we should work on it carefully, as if planning to cut through a hard object. If there is someone telling us something, we should not think we can understand it on the spot.

[45:5]

いま雲居山すでに世尊ならんに、密語そなはり、不覆藏の迦葉あり。喚尚書、書應諾は、すなはち密語なりと參學することなかれ。

Since Yunjushan here is a "World-Honored One," he possesses "secret words," he has "Kāśyapa," for whom "they are not concealed." Do not study that his calling the minister and the minister responding are themselves "secret words."

---

the account also occurs in "Shōbōgenzō gyōji" 正法眼藏行持 (DZZ.1:152), where it is said that, following his study with Dongshan, the gods were no longer able to see him — something of a familiar trope in Zen hagiography.

6　**they are not got from another** (*hi jū nin toku* 匪從人得): Perhaps reflecting the common expression, "the dharma seal of the buddhas is not got from another" (*shobutsu hōin hi jū nin toku* 諸佛法印匪從人得). The other three members of this list have no obvious sources.

358
DŌGEN'S *SHŌBŌGENZŌ* VOLUME III

[45:6]

大師ちなみに尚書にしめすにいはく、汝若不會世尊密語、汝若會迦葉不覆
藏。いまの道取、かならず多劫の辨道功夫を立志すべし。なんぢもし不
會なるは世尊の密語なり、といふ、いまの茫然とあるを不會といふにあら
ず、不知を不會といふにあらず。なんぢもし不會、といふ道理、しづかに
參學すべき處分を聽許するなり。功夫辨道すべし。さらにまた、なんぢも
し會ならんは、と道取する、いますでに會なるとにはあらず。

At that time, the Great Master instructed the minister, saying, "*If you
don't understand, it's the secret words of the World-Honored One; if
you do understand, it's not concealed for Kāśyapa*." We should definitely resolve to pursue the way and work for many kalpas on this saying. In his saying, "If you don't understand, it's the secret words of the
World-Honored One," it is not that he is calling [the minister's] present
bewilderment "not understanding"; it is not that he is calling ignorance
"not understanding." The principle of "if you don't understand" allows
for a way of dealing with it that should be quietly studied; we should
work on it and pursue the way. Furthermore, his saying, "if you understand," does not mean, "now you've already understood."

[45:7] {1:491}

佛法を參學するに多途あり。そのなかに、佛法を會し、佛法を不會する關
棖子あり。正師をみざれば、ありとだにもしらず、いたづらに絶見聞の眼
處・耳處におほせて、密語あり、と亂會せり。なんぢもし會なる、ゆえに
迦葉不覆藏なる、といふにあらず、不會の不覆藏もあるなり。不覆藏は、
たれ人も見聞すべし、と學すべからず。すでにこれ不覆藏なり、無處不覆
藏ならん正恁麼時、こころみに參究すべし。

There are many paths for studying the buddha dharma. Within them,
there is a pivot of understanding the buddha dharma and not understanding the buddha dharma.[7] When we have not seen a true master, we do not
know even that it exists; we mistakenly understand that there are secret
words we meaninglessly associate with a visual sphere or an auditory
sphere beyond seeing or hearing.[8] He is not saying that it is because of
"if you understand" that "*it's not concealed for Kāśyapa*": there is also
"not concealed" with not understanding. We should not study that what

---

7   **Within them, there is a pivot of understanding the buddha dharma and not
understanding the buddha dharma** (*sono naka ni, buppō o e shi, buppō o fue suru
kanreisu ari* そのなかに、佛法を會し、佛法を不會する關棖子あり): Probably mean-
ing that the issue of understanding and not understanding is a pivotal point in any study
of the buddha dharma. See Supplementary Notes, s.v., "Pivot."

8   **we mistakenly understand that there are secret words we meaninglessly associate with a visual sphere or an auditory sphere beyond seeing or hearing** (*itazura ni
zetsu kenmon no gensho nisho ni ōsete, mitsugo ari, to ran'e seri* いたづらに絶見聞の
眼處・耳處におほせて、密語あり、と亂會せり): I.e., we wrongly think that there are
secret words beyond what can be seen or heard by our eyes and ears.

45. Secret Words *Mitsugo* 密語

359

is "not concealed" anyone should be able to see and hear. We should try to investigate precisely the time when this is already "not concealed," when there is already *nowhere in which it is "not concealed."*

[45:8]

しかあれば、みづからしらざらん境界を、密語と參學しきたるにあらず、佛法を不會する正當恁麼時、これ、一分の密語なり。これ、かならず世尊有なり、有世尊なり。

Therefore, it is not that we have been studying as "secret words" some realm that we ourselves do not know: the very moment when we do not understand the buddha dharma — this is "secret words" in one part.[9] This is certainly what "the World-Honored One has," what has the World-Honored One.[10]

[45:9]

しかあるを、正師の訓教をきかざるともがら、たとひ師子座上にあれども、夢也未見這箇道理なり。かれらみだりにいはく、世尊有密語とは、靈山百萬衆前に拈華瞬目せしなり。そのゆえは、有言の佛説は淺薄なり、名相にわたれるがごとし。無言説にして拈華瞬目する、これ密語施設の時節なり。百萬衆は不得領覽なり、このゆえに、百萬衆のために密語なり。迦葉不覆藏といふは、世尊の拈華瞬目を、迦葉、さきよりしれるがごとく破顔微笑するゆえに、迦葉におほせて不覆藏といふなり。これ眞訣なり、箇箇相傳しきたれるなり。これをききてまこととおもふともがら、稻麻竹葦のごとく、九州に叢林をなせり。あはれむべし、佛祖の道の破廢せること、もととしてこれよりおこる。明眼漢まさに一一に勘破すべし。

Nevertheless, those who have never heard the instructions of a true master, though they may be in the lion seat, *have never seen this truth even in their dreams.* They irrationally say,

"The World-Honored One has secret words" refers to his having *held up a flower and blinked his eyes* before the assembly of a million on Vulture Peak.[11] The reason is that the Buddha's preaching with words is shallow and seems concerned with names and forms. *Holding up*

---

9 **"secret words" in one part** (*ichibun no mitsu go* 一分の密語): The exact sense is uncertain: often taken here to mean that the moment of not understanding is "wholly secret words;" could be read as "one part of secret words."

10 **This is certainly what "the World-Honored One has," what has the World-Honored One** (*kore, kanarazu seson u nari, u seson nari* これ、かならず世尊有なり、有世尊なり): Dōgen plays here with the phrase in the minister's question to Yunju, "The World-Honored One has secret words."

11 **held up a flower and blinked his eyes before the assembly of a million on Vulture Peak** (*Ryōzen hyakuman shu zen ni nenge shunmoku seshi* 靈山百萬衆前に拈華瞬目せし): Reference to (one version of) the famous story of the first transmission of Zen from Buddha Śākyamuni to Mahākāśyapa, recorded at *shinji Shōbōgenzō* 眞字正法眼藏, DZZ.5:258, case 253); see Supplementary Notes, s.v. "Holding up a flower and blinking the eyes."

360   DŌGEN'S *SHŌBŌGENZŌ* VOLUME III

the flower and blinking the eyes, being preaching without words, is an occasion of propounding with secret words. The assembly of a million was unable to comprehend it; hence, for the assembly of a million, it was secret words. "*For Kāśyapa, they are not concealed*" refers to Kāśyapa's *breaking into a smile*, as if he already knew that the World-Honored One would *hold up a flower and blink the eyes*; therefore, applied to Kāśyapa, it was not concealed. This is the true arcanum, handed down one to one.

Those that hear this and believe it to be true are like "rice, hemp, bamboo, and reeds" and form the monasteries throughout the Nine Provinces.[12] Pitiful. The abandoning of the way of the buddhas and ancestors arises from this source. A clear-eyed person should see through them one by one.

[45:10] {1:402}

もし、世尊の有言、淺薄なりとせば、拈華瞬目も淺薄なるべし。世尊の有言、もし名相なりとせば、學佛法の漢にあらず。有言は名相なることをしれりといへども、世尊に名相なきことをいまだしらず、凡情の未脱なるなり。佛祖は、身心の所通みな脱落なり、説法なり、有言説なり、轉法輪す。これを見聞して得益するものおほし。信行・法行のともがら、有佛祖處に化をかうぶり、無佛祖處に化にあづかるなり。百萬衆、かならずしも拈華瞬目を拈華瞬目と見聞せざらんや。迦葉と齊肩なるべし、世尊と同生なるべし。百萬衆と百萬衆と同參なるべし、同時發心なるべし、同道なり、同國土なり。有知の智をもて見佛聞法し、無知の智をもて見佛聞法す。はじめて一佛をみるより、すすみて恆沙佛をみる。一一の佛會上、ともに百萬億衆なるべし。各各の諸佛、ともに拈華瞬目の開演、おなじときなるを見聞すべし。眼處くらからず、耳處聡利なり。心眼あり、身眼あり。心耳あり、身耳あり。

If we take the World-Honored One's *having words* as shallow, his *holding up a flower and blinking his eyes* must also be shallow. If we take the World-Honored One's *having words* as names and forms, we are not a person who studies the buddha dharma. Although we may know that *having words* is names and forms, we do not yet know that the World-Honored One has no names and forms; we have yet to slough off common sentiment. The buddhas and ancestors slough off all throughout body and mind; they preach the dharma; they preach with words; they turn the wheel of dharma. Many are those who have benefited from seeing and hearing this. Those who practice by faith and those who practice

---

12 **are like "rice, hemp, bamboo, and reeds" and form the monasteries throughout the Nine Provinces** (*tō ma chiku i no gotoku, Kushū ni sōrin o naseri* 稻麻竹葦のごとく、九州に叢林をなせり): "Rice, hemp, bamboo, and reeds" (*tō ma chiku i* 稻麻竹葦), occurring several times in the *Shōbōgenzō*, is a fixed expression for "profuse," taken from the *Lotus Sūtra*; see Supplementary Notes. The "Nine Provinces" (*Kushū* 九州) is a term for China.

45. Secret Words *Mitsugo* 密語   361

by dharma receive the teaching where there are buddhas and ancestors and share in the teaching where there are no buddhas and ancestors.[13]

How could the assembly of a million not have perceived his *holding up the flower and blinking his eyes* as *holding up a flower and blinking his eyes*? They should be of equal stature to Kāśyapa; they should be born together with the World-Honored One. The assembly of a million and the assembly of a million should study together, should bring forth the mind [of bodhi] at the same time; they are on the same way; they are of the same land. They see the Buddha and hear the dharma by the wisdom with knowledge; they see the Buddha and hear the dharma by the wisdom without knowledge. After first seeing one buddha, they proceed to see buddhas numerous as the sands of the Ganges. Each of the buddha convocations is an assembly of hundreds of myriads of *koṭis*. They must perceive that the exposition of holding up a flower and blinking the eyes of each of the buddhas is at the same time. Their eyes are not dark; their ears are sharp. They have eyes of the mind; they have eyes of the body. They have ears of the mind; they have ears of the body.

[45:11]

迦葉の破顔微笑、儞作麼生會、試道看。なんぢたちがいふがごとくならば、これも密語といひぬべし。しかあれども、これを不覆藏といふ、　至愚のかさなれるなり。

Kāśyapa's *breaking into a smile, how do you understand it? Say something!* If it were as you people say, this too should be called "secret words." But you call it "not concealed," which is extreme stupidity compounded.

[45:12]

のちに世尊いはく、吾有正法眼藏涅槃妙心、附嘱摩訶迦葉。

Subsequently, the World-Honored One said, "*I have a treasury of the true dharma eye, the wondrous mind of nirvāṇa; I bequeath it to Mahākāśyapa.*"

---

13 **Those who practice by faith and those who practice by dharma** (*shingyō hōgyō no tomogara* 信行・法行のともがら): A traditional distinction between two types of Buddhists: "those who advance by faith" (*zuishingyō* 隨信行; S. *śraddhānusārin*) and "those who advance by [study of] dharma" (*zuihōgyō* 隨法行; S. *dharmānusārin*).

362 DŌGEN'S *SHŌBŌGENZŌ* VOLUME III

[45:13] {1:493}

かくのごとくの道取、これ有言なりや、無言なりや。世尊もし有言をきら
ひ、拈華を愛せば、のちにも拈華すべし。迦葉、なんぞ會取せざらん、衆
會、なんぞ聽取せざらん。かくのごとくともがらの説話、もちいるべから
ず。

A statement like this — is it with words or is it without words? If the
World-Honored One disliked having words and loved holding up the
flower, he should have held up the flower afterwards as well. How could
Kāśyapa have failed to understand it? How could the assembly have
failed to hear it? We should not use the talk of people like this.

[45:14]

おほよそ世尊に密語あり、密行あり、密證あり。しかあるを、愚人おも
はく、密は他人のしらず、みづからはしり、しれる人あり、しらざる人
ありと、西天東地、古往今來、おもひいふは、いまだ佛道の參學あらざる
なり。もしかくのごとくいはば、世間・出世間の學業なきもののうへには
密はおほく、遍學のものは密はすくなかりぬべし。廣聞のともがらは密あ
るべからざるか。いはんや天眼・天耳、法眼・法耳、佛眼・佛耳等を具せ
んときは、すべて密語・密意あるべからず、といふべし。佛法の密語・密
意・密行等は、この道理にあらず。人にあふ時節、まさに密語をきき、密
語をとく。おのれをしるとき、密行をしるなり。いはんや佛祖よく上來の
密意・密語を究辨す。しるべし、佛祖なる時節、まさに密語・密行、きほ
ひ現成するなり。

In sum, the World-Honored One has secret words, has secret practice,
has secret verification.[14] However, ignoramuses think the "secret" means
others do not know but we ourselves know, that there are people who
know and people who do not know; from Sindh in the West to the Land
of the East, from ancient time to the present, those who think and say
this have not studied the way of the buddhas. If they say this, for the
ones without mundane or transmundane learning there would be many
secrets, while those with extensive learning would have few secrets. Are
those of wide experience supposed to be without secrets? Not to mention
when one possesses the deva eye, the deva ear, the dharma eye, the dharma ear, the buddha eye, the buddha ear, and the like, they should say that
one would have no secret words or secret intentions at all.[15] The secret

---

14 **has secret words, has secret practice, has secret verification** (*mitsugo ari,
mitsugyō ari, misshō ari* 密語あり、密行あり、密證あり): The consistent rendering of
mitsu 密 as "secret" misrepresents the semantic range of the term here; a more natural
version might read "has secret words, has strict practice, has intimate verification"; see
Supplementary Notes, s.v. "Practice and verification."

15 **the deva eye, the deva ear** (*tengen tenni* 天眼・天耳): I.e., paranormal seeing and
hearing, two of the five (or six) spiritual powers (*jinzū* 神通; S. *abhijñā*) of the advanced
adept; see Supplementary Notes, s.v. "Spiritual powers." The deva eye is the second of
the "five eyes" (*gogen* 五眼) partially listed here: the physical eye (*nikugen* 肉眼), deva

45. Secret Words *Mitsugo* 密語 363

words, secret intentions, secret practice, and such, in the buddha dharma do not follow this logic. It is precisely when we meet a person that we hear secret words and speak secret words. When we know ourselves, we know secret practice. How much more do the buddhas and ancestors thoroughly examine the above "secret intentions" and "secret words." We should realize that, precisely when one is a buddha and ancestor, secret words and secret practice vie to appear.

[45:15]

いはゆる密は、親密の道理なり。無間斷なり、蓋佛祖なり、蓋汝なり、蓋自なり、蓋行なり、蓋代なり、蓋功なり、蓋密なり。密語の、密人に相逢する、佛眼也覻不見なり。密行は自他の所知にあらず、密我ひとり能知す、密他おのおの不會す、密却在汝邊のゆえに、全靠密なり、一半靠密なり。

"Secret" means the principle of intimacy. It is without interruption. It covers the buddhas and ancestors; it covers you; it covers me; it covers practice; it covers the generations; it covers our effort; it covers the secret.[16] The meeting of the secret words with the secret person, *even the buddha eye cannot see.* Secret practice is not something known by self or other: the secret self alone knows it; the secret others are each "I don't understand." Because "*the secret is rather with you,*" it wholly relies on the secret, it half relies on the secret.[17]

---

eye (*tengen* 天眼), wisdom eye (*egen* 慧眼) (that sees emptiness), dharma eye (*hōgen* 法眼) (of the advanced bodhisattva that clearly distinguishes all phenomena), and buddha eye (*butsugen* 佛眼) (of omniscience). Dōgen plays with the list here by adding "dharma ear" and "buddha ear."

16　**it covers the generations; it covers our effort** (*gai dai nari, gai kū nari* 蓋代なり、蓋功なり): "Generations" (*dai* 代) may refer to the generations of buddhas and ancestors. The translation takes *kū* 功 here as *kufū* 功夫 ("concentrated effort"); it could also be understood as *kudoku* 功德 ("virtue"; "merit").

17　**Because "the secret is rather with you," it wholly relies on the secret, it half relies on the secret** (*mitsu kyaku zai nyo hen no yue ni, zen kō mitsu nari, ippan kō mitsu nari* 密却在汝邊のゆえに、全靠密なり、一半靠密なり): "The secret is rather with you" comes from the words of the Fifth Ancestor, when asked about "secret words and secret intentions" (see, e.g., *Jingde chuandeng lu* 景德傳燈錄, T.2076.51:232a12-14):

祖曰、我今與汝説者、即非密也。汝若返照自己面目、密却在汝邊。

The Ancestor said, "What I'm telling you here is not the secret. If you reflect on your own face, the secret is rather with you."

The implied grammatical subject of the predicates "wholly relies" (*zen kō* 全靠) and "half relies" (*ippan kō* 一半靠) is unclear, and some read *zen* 全 and *ippan* 一半 as themselves the subjects — i.e., "the whole relies," "one half relies." The use here may reflect the words of Shitou Xiqian 石頭希遷 (700-791) when asked by his teacher to explain himself (e.g., at *Jingde chuandeng lu* 景德傳燈錄, T.2076.51:240b17-18):

曰、和尚也須道取一半。莫全靠學人。

[Shitou] said, "The Reverend should say half; don't rely wholly on your student."

364 DŌGEN'S *SHŌBŌGENZŌ* VOLUME III

[45:16] {1:494}

かくのごとくの道理、あきらかに功夫參學すべし。おほよそ爲人の處所、辨肯の時節、かならず擧似密なる、それ佛佛祖祖の正嫡なり。而今是甚麼時節のゆえに、自己にも密なり、他己にも密なり、佛祖にも密なり、異類にも密なり。このゆえに、密頭上あらたに密なり。かくのごとくの教・行・證、すなはち佛祖なるがゆえに、透過佛祖密なり。しかあれば、透過密なり。

We should clearly make concentrated effort and study such truth. In general, that the places where people are taught and the times when the teaching is confirmed are invariably the secret presented — this is the correct succession of buddha after buddha and ancestor after ancestor.[18] Because it is "what time is this?" it is secret to self, it is secret to others, it is secret to the buddhas and ancestors, it is secret to other beings.[19] Therefore, there are further secrets on top of secrets. Because such teaching, practice, and verification are precisely the buddhas and ancestors, they are secrets that pass beyond the buddhas and ancestors. Hence, they pass beyond secrets.

* * * * *

[45:17]

雪竇師翁、示衆曰、世尊有密語、迦葉不覆藏、一夜落華雨、滿城流水香。

Xuedou, my teacher's master, addressed the assembly saying,[20]
The World-Honored One has secret words;
For Kāśyapa, they are not concealed.
Throughout the night, a rain of falling blossoms;
In the whole city, the streams are fragrant.

---

18 **that the places where people are taught and the times when the teaching is confirmed are invariably the secret presented** (*inin no shosho, benkō no jisetsu, kanarazu kōji mitsu naru* 爲人の處所、辨肯の時節、かならず擧似密なる): A phrase that could also be parsed, "in the places where people are taught and the times when the teaching is affirmed, that the presentation is secret."

19 **"what time is this?"** (*nikon ze jinmo jisetsu* 而今是甚麼時節): Variation on the common Zen rhetorical question, "what place is this?" (*shari ze jinmo sho zai* 這裏是甚麼處在; i.e., "where are we here"?).

20 **Xuedou, my teacher's master** (*Setchō shiō* 雪竇師翁): I.e., Xuedou Zhijian 雪竇智鑑 (1105-1192), teacher of Dōgen's teacher, Tiantong Rujing 天童如淨 (1162-1227). His verse appears at *Jiatai pudeng lu* 嘉泰普燈錄, ZZ.137:258a2-3.

45. Secret Words *Mitsugo* 密語   365

[45:18]

而今雪竇道の一夜落華雨、満城流水香、それ親密なり。これを擧似して、佛祖の眼睛・鼻孔を檢點すべし。臨濟・德山のおよぶべきところにあらず。眼睛裏の鼻孔を參開すべし、耳處の鼻頭を尖聡ならしむるなり。いはんや耳鼻眼睛裏ふるきにあらず、あらたなるにあらざる渾身心ならしむ。これを華雨世界起の道理とす。

Xuedou's words here, "*Throughout the night, a rain of falling blossoms; in the whole city, the streams are fragrant*" — these are intimate.[21] Taking them up, we should examine the eye and the nose of the buddhas and ancestors. They are not a place Linji or Deshan could reach.[22] We should study and open the nose within our eye; we should sharpen the nose of the ear. Not to mention make our ear, nose, and eye our whole body, neither old nor new. This we take as the truth of "*a flower rains, and the world arises*."[23]

[45:19]

師翁道の満城流水香、それ藏身影彌露なり。かくのごとくあるがゆえに、佛祖家裏の家常には、世尊有密語、迦葉不覆藏を參究透過するなり。七佛・世尊、ほとけごとに、而今のごとく參學す。迦葉・釋迦、おなじく而今のごとく究辨しきたれり。

The words of my master's father, "*In the whole city, the streams are fragrant*" — this is *the body concealed, its shadow more exposed.*[24] Thus, in the daily fare within the house of the buddhas and ancestors, we investigate and pass beyond "the World-Honored One has secret words; for Kāśyapa, they are not concealed." The seven buddhas, the World-Honored ones, each of the buddhas, studies like this; Kāśyapa and Śākya, similarly have been thoroughly investigating like this.[25]

---

21   **these are intimate** (*sore shinmitsu nari* それ親密なり): The English "intimate" masks the play on the glyph *mitsu* 密 ("secret").

22   **They are not a place Linji or Deshan could reach** (*Rinzai Tokusan no oyobu beki tokoro ni arazu* 臨濟・德山のおよぶべきところにあらず): I.e., Linji Yixuan 臨濟義玄 (d. 866) and his contemporary Deshan Xuanjian 德山宣鑑 (780-865); one of several dismissive remarks in the *Shōbōgenzō* on these two famous Chan masters.

23   **"a flower rains and the world arises"** (*ke u sekai ki* 華雨世界起): Playing on the final line of a dharma transmission verse attributed to Bodhidharma's master, Prajñātāra. See Supplementary Notes, s.v. "A flower opens, and the world arises."

24   **the body concealed, its shadow more exposed** (*zō shin yo mi ro* 藏身影彌露): Variation on the idiom, "to conceal the body and expose the shadow" (*zō shin ro yo* 藏身露影): to speak with hidden meaning, to hint at something.

25   **Kāśyapa and Śākya** (*Kashō Shaka* 迦葉・釋迦): In the context here, perhaps better taken as Buddha Śākyamuni and the First Ancestor, Mahākāśyapa, rather than the more usual Śākyamuni and his predecessor, Buddha Kāśyapa.

366   DŌGEN'S *SHŌBŌGENZŌ* VOLUME III

正法眼藏密語第四十五
Treasury of the True Dharma Eye
Secret Words
Number 45

[Ryūmonji MS:]

爾時寛元元年癸卯九月二十日、在越州吉田県吉峰古精舍示衆

Presented to the assembly, at the old vihāra of Kippō, Yoshida District, Esshū; twentieth day, ninth month of the junior water year of the rabbit, the first year of Kangen [3 November 1243][26]

[*Himitsu* MS:]

同十月十六日、在同精舍侍司。慧上

In the acolyte's office of the same vihara; sixteenth day, tenth month of the same [year] [29 November 1243]. Ejō[27]

---

26 The *Himitsu* 秘密 MS shares an almost identical colophon.

27 **Ejō** 慧上: Written with a homonym for Ejō 懷奘, a practice also found in the *Himitsu* MS of the "Sansui kyō" 山水經 chapter.

The Sōtō Zen Text Project *Shōbōgenzō*

Volume I
The Seventy-five-Chapter Compilation, Part 1

1. The Realized Kōan *Genjō kōan* 現成公案
2. Mahā-prajñā-pāramitā *Maka hannya haramitsu* 摩訶般若波羅蜜
3. Buddha Nature *Busshō* 佛性
4. Studying the Way with Body and Mind *Shinjin gakudō* 身心學道
5. This Mind Itself Is the Buddha *Soku shin ze butsu* 即心是佛
6. Deportment of the Practicing Buddha *Gyōbutsu iigi* 行佛威儀
7. One Bright Pearl *Ikka myōju* 一顆明珠
8. The Mind Cannot Be Got *Shin fukatoku* 心不可得
9. The Old Buddha Mind *Kobutsushin* 古佛心
10. Great Awakening *Daigo* 大悟
11. Principles of Seated Meditation *Zazen gi* 坐禪儀
12. Needle of Seated Meditation *Zazen shin* 坐禪箴
13. Ocean Seal Samādhi *Kaiin zanmai* 海印三昧
14. Sky Flowers *Kūge* 空華
15. Radiance *Kōmyō* 光明

Volume II
The Seventy-five-Chapter Compilation, Part 2

16A. Sustained Practice, Part 1 *Gyōji jō* 行持上
16B. Sustained Practice, Part 2 *Gyōji ge* 行持下
17. Such *Inmo* 恁麼
18. Avalokiteśvara *Kannon* 觀音
19. The Old Mirror *Kokyō* 古鏡
20. Sometimes *Uji* 有時
21. Prediction *Juki* 授記
22. Full Function *Zenki* 全機
23. The Moon *Tsuki* 都機
24. Painted Cake *Gabyō* 畫餅
25. Sound of the Stream, Form of the Mountain *Keisei sanshoku* 谿聲山色
26. Beyond the Buddha *Butsu kōjō ji* 佛向上事
27. Talking of a Dream within a Dream *Muchū setsumu* 夢中説夢
28. Making a Bow and Getting the Marrow *Raihai tokuzui* 禮拜得髓
29. The Mountains and Waters Sūtra *Sansui kyō* 山水經
30. Sūtra Reading *Kankin* 看經

Volume III
The Seventy-five-Chapter Compilation, Part 3

31. Do No Evil *Shoaku makusa* 諸惡莫作
32. Transmitting the Robe *Den'e* 傳衣
33. Sayings *Dōtoku* 道得
34. The Teachings of the Buddhas *Bukkyō* 佛教
35. Spiritual Powers *Jinzū* 神通
36. The Arhat *Arakan* 阿羅漢

37. Spring and Autumn *Shunjū* 春秋
38. Tangled Vines *Kattō* 葛藤
39. The Inheritance Certificate *Shisho* 嗣書
40. The Cypress Tree *Hakujushi* 柏樹子
41. The Three Realms Are Only Mind *Sangai yui shin* 三界唯心
42. Talking of the Mind, Talking of the Nature *Sesshin sesshō* 説心説性
43. The Real Marks of the Dharmas *Shohō jissō* 諸法實相
44. The Way of the Buddhas *Butsudō* 佛道
45. Secret Words *Mitsugo* 密語

Volume IV
The Seventy-five-Chapter Compilation, Part 4

46. The Insentient Preach the Dharma *Mujō seppō* 無情説法
47. Sūtras of the Buddhas *Bukkyō* 佛經
48. Dharma Nature *Hosshō* 法性
49. Dhāraṇī *Darani* 陀羅尼
50. Washing the Face *Senmen* 洗面
51. Face-to-Face Conferral *Menju* 面授
52. Buddhas and Ancestors *Busso* 佛祖
53. Plum Blossoms *Baika* 梅華
54. Washing and Purifying *Senjō* 洗淨
55. The Ten Directions *Jippō* 十方
56. Seeing Buddha *Kenbutsu* 見佛
57. Extensive Study *Henzan* 遍參
58. The Eye *Ganzei* 眼睛
59. Everyday Matters *Kajō* 家常
60. The Thirty-seven Factors of Bodhi *Sanjūshichi hon bodai bunpō* 三十七品菩提分法

Volume V
The Seventy-five-Chapter Compilation, Part 5

61. Song of the Dragon *Ryūgin* 龍吟
62. The Intention of the Ancestral Master's Coming from the West
    Soshi seirai i 祖師西來意
63. Bringing Forth the Mind of Bodhi *Hotsu bodai shin* 發菩提心
64. The Udumbara Blossom *Udonge* 優曇華
65. The Entire Body of the Tathāgata *Nyorai zenshin* 如來全身
66. The King of Samādhis Samādhi *Zanmai ō zanmai* 三昧王三昧
67. Turning the Dharma Wheel *Ten hōrin* 轉法輪
68. Great Practice *Dai shugyō* 大修行
69. The Samādhi of Self Verification *Jishō zanmai* 自證三昧
70. Empty Space *Kokū* 虚空
71. The Pātra Bowl *Hou* 鉢盂
72. The Retreat *Ango* 安居
73. Reading Other Minds *Tashin tsū* 他心通
74. The King Requests Saindhava *Ō saku sendaba* 王索仙陀婆
75. Leaving Home *Shukke* 出家

Volume VI
The Twelve-Chapter Compilation

T1. The Merit of Leaving Home *Shukke kudoku* 出家功德
T2. Receiving the Precepts *Jukai* 受戒
T3. The Merit of the Kāṣāya *Kesa kudoku* 袈裟功德
T4. Bringing Forth the Mind of Bodhi *Hotsu bodai shin* 發菩提心
T5. Offerings to the Buddhas *Kuyō shobutsu* 供養諸佛
T6. Refuge in the Treasures of Buddha, Dharma, and Saṃgha
    Kie buppōsōbō 歸依佛法僧寶
T7. Deep Faith in Cause and Effect *Jinshin inga* 深信因果
T8. Karma of the Three Times *Sanjigō* 三時業
T9. Four Horses *Shime* 四馬
T10. The Bhikṣu of the Fourth Dhyāna *Shizen biku* 四禪比丘
T11. One Hundred Eight Gateways to the Illumination of the Dharma
    Ippyakuhachi hōmyōmon 一百八法明門
T12. The Eight Understandings of the Great Person *Hachi dainin gaku* 八大人覺

Volume VII
Supplementary Chapters, Variant Texts
Supplementary Chapters

S1. Talk on Pursuing the Way *Bendōwa* 辦道話
S2. Procedures for the Hall of Gathered Clouds *Jūundō shiki* 重雲堂式
S3. The *Lotus* Turns the *Lotus* *Hokke ten Hokke* 法華轉法華
S4. The Mind Cannot Be Got *Shin fukatoku* 心不可得
S5. The Four Attractions of the Bodhisattva *Bodaisatta shishōbō* 菩提薩埵四攝法
S6. Instructions to the Administration Cloister *Ji kuin mon* 示庫院文
S7. Only Buddhas with Buddhas *Yui butsu yo butsu* 唯佛與佛
S8. Birth and Death *Shōji* 生死
S9. The Way of the Buddhas *Butsudō* 佛道 (*Dōshin* 道心)

Variant Texts

V1. Talk on Pursuing the Way *Bendōwa* 辦道話
V2. The Inheritance Certificate *Shisho* 嗣書
V3. Beyond the Buddha *Butsu kōjō ji* 佛向上事
V4. Washing the Face *Senmen* 洗面
V5. Extensive Study *Henzan* 遍參
V6. Great Awakening *Daigo* 大悟
V7. Karma of the Three Times *Sanji gō* 三時業

Volume VIII

Introduction
Appendices
Supplementary Notes
Works Cited